Mathematics *for* JEE

Main and Advanced

Co-ordinate Geometry

Author

Rejaul Makshud

M.Sc. Calcutta University

UNICORN BOOKS

Publisher
UNICORN BOOKS

F-2/16, Ansari Road, Daryaganj, New Delhi-110002
E-mail: info@unicornbooks.in • Website: www.unicornbooks.in
☎ 011-23275434, 23262683

Branch : Mumbai
23-25, Zaoba Wadi Thakurdwar, Mumbai-401002
☎ 022-22010941, 022-22053387
E-mail: rapidex@bom5.vsnl.net.in

Showroom :

➤ **PM Publications, New Delhi**

- 10-B, Netaji Subhash Marg, Daryaganj, New Delhi-110002
- 6686, Khari Baoli, Delhi-110006

ISBN 978-81-7806-336-2

Edition: 2013

Printed at : *Param Offsetters, Okhla, New Delhi-110020*

Preface

It's give me a great pleasure and satisfaction to express myself before the student through a comprehensive text book on algebra after teaching so many years at national level institute .

Co-ordinate is a vital topic of mathematics and nearly 20 to 22% of questions asked in the IIT-JEE exam and also other engineering examinations. After so many years of teaching I have realized that it was necessary to design a book, which was made in a systematic way, where the reader can build their base, improve their level and enjoy about the subject.

This book is designed keeping in view of the new pattern of questions asked in JEE MAIN and Advanced Exams. This book contains seven chapters and each chapter is dealt thoroughly followed by a large number of worked out problems and exercise based problems, namely

- Level – I : Questions based on Fundamentals.
- Level – II : Objective type questions
- Level – III : Subjective type questions for JEE Advanced Exam

and then given some Linked Comprehension type questions, Match Matrix type questions, Assertion and Reason type questions and finally it was given, questions asked in past Roorkee as well as IIT-JEE Exams.

Remember friends, no problem in mathematics is difficult. Once you understand, each problem will become easy. So don't jump to exercise problems before you have gone through the theory, the worked out problems and the objective. Once you feel confident in theory, do the exercise problems. The exercise problems are so arranged that they gradually require more thinking.

I hope it will help them to enjoy the subject and improve their confidence to solve any type of problem easily.

My special thanks go to Mr. Rakesh Singh (IISc ,Bangalore), Mr. M P Singh (IISc ,Bangalore), Mr Ravi Bhushan (IIT , Delhi) , Mr Manoj Kumar (IIT, Delhi) , Mr. Vivek Bhatt (B I E T) , who has helped, inspired and motivated me to accomplish this very task and finally my sincere thanks to the publisher Dr. Ashok Gupta of Unicorn books for publishing this book.

I owe a special debt of gratitude to my early teachers Mr Swapan Halder, Mr. Mahadev Roy and Mr Dilip Bhattacharya for showing me what clear and engaging Mathematics teaching is all about.

I have tried my best to keep errors out of this book. I shall be grateful to the readers who point out any errors and / or make other constructive suggestions.

Rejaul Makshud

Contents

1 The Straight Line

1.1 INTRODUCTION

A french Mathematician and great philosopher Rane Descartes (1596 - 1665) introduced an idea to study geometry with the help of Algebra . This geometry is called Co-ordinate geometry or Analytical Geometry . Here we use points, lines and curves by the different forms of algebraic equations.

1.2 CO-ORDINATE AXES

The position of a point in a plane with referrence to two intersecting lines called the coordinate axes and their point of intersection called the origin. If these two axes cut at right angles, then they are called rectangular axes , else they are called obliques axes.

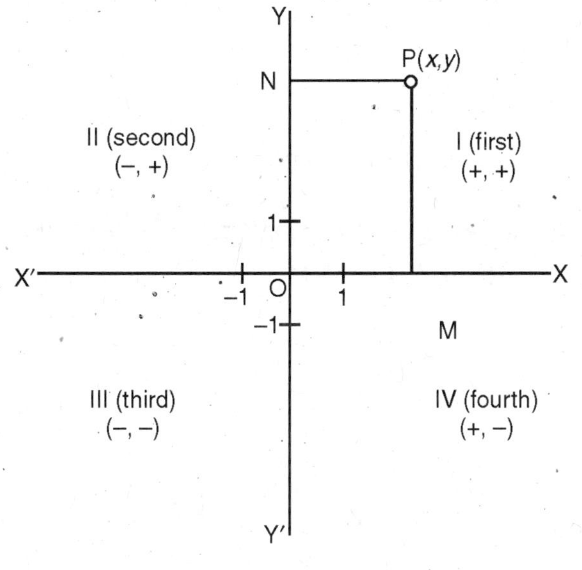

Let P be any point in the plane . Draw perpendiculars from P parallel to reference lines X'OX and YOY' respectively. Then the lengths PN and PM are called the co-ordinates of the point P.

The above system of representing a point in 2-dimensions is called Cartesian system. We normally denote PN by x and PM by y . Thus an ordered pair of two real numbers describes the cartesian co-ordinates of P.

The referrence lines XOX' and YOY' are respectively called x and y-axis respectively. These lines divide the plane into four equal parts and each part is called quadrant.

1.3 POLAR CO-ORDINATE OF A POINT

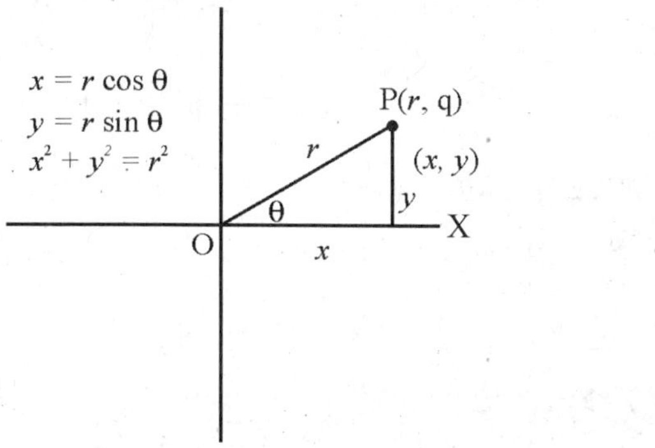

The position of a point in a plane can also be described by other co-ordinate syatem, called Polar co-ordinate system. In this case, we consider OX as initial line, O is origin.

If P be any point on the plane such that OP = r and $\angle POX = ?$, then (r, θ) is called the polar co-ordinate of the point P., where $r > 0$ and $0 \le \theta < 2\pi$.

1.4 RELATION BETWEEN THE CARTESIAN AND POLAR CO-ORDINATES

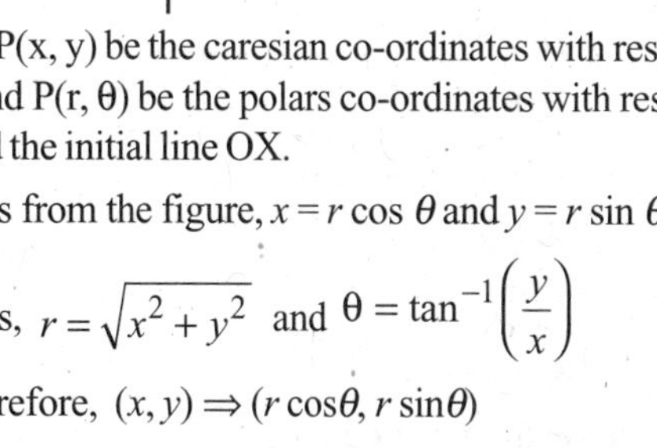

Let P(x, y) be the caresian co-ordinates with respect to OX and OY and P(r, θ) be the polars co-ordinates with respect to the pole O and the initial line OX.

Thus from the figure, $x = r\cos\theta$ and $y = r\sin\theta$

Thus, $r = \sqrt{x^2 + y^2}$ and $\theta = \tan^{-1}\left(\frac{y}{x}\right)$

Therefore, $(x, y) \Rightarrow (r\cos\theta, r\sin\theta)$

and $(r,\ \theta) \Rightarrow \left(\sqrt{x^2 + y^2},\ \tan^{-1}\left(\frac{y}{x}\right)\right)$.

Ex-1. Find the polar co-ordinates of the points whose cartesian co-ordinates are (3, -4) and (-3, 4).

Sol. We have

$$(3,-4) \Rightarrow \left(\sqrt{3^2+(-4)^2}, \tan^{-1}\left(-\frac{4}{3}\right)\right)$$

$$\Rightarrow \left(5, -\tan^{-1}\left(\frac{4}{3}\right)\right)$$

and $(-3,4) \Rightarrow \left(\sqrt{(-3)^2+(4)^2}, \tan^{-1}\left(-\frac{3}{4}\right)\right)$

$$\Rightarrow \left(5, p-\tan^{-1}\left(\frac{4}{3}\right)\right)$$

Ex-2. Transform the equation $r^2 = a^2 \cos 2\theta$ into cartesian form.

Son. We have $r^2 = a^2 \cos 2\theta$

$$\Rightarrow r^2 = a^2\left(\cos^2\theta - \sin^2\theta\right)$$

$$\Rightarrow r^2 = a^2\left(\frac{x^2}{r^2} - \frac{y^2}{r^2}\right)$$

$$\Rightarrow r^4 = a^2\left(x^2 - y^2\right)$$

$$\Rightarrow \left(x^2+y^2\right)^2 = a^2\left(x^2-y^2\right)$$

Ex-3. Transform the equation $r = 2a\cos\theta$ into cartesian form.

Sol. We have $r = 2a\cos\theta$

$$\Rightarrow r = 2a\left(\frac{x}{r}\right)$$

$\Rightarrow$ $r^2 = 2ax$

$\Rightarrow$ $(x^2+y^2) = 2ax$

Ex-4. Transform the equation $\frac{x^2}{a^2}+\frac{y^2}{b^2}=1$ into polar form.

Sol. We have $\frac{x^2}{a^2}+\frac{y^2}{b^2}=1$

$\Rightarrow$ $b^2x^2 + a^2y^2 = a^2b^2$

$\Rightarrow$ $b^2r^2\cos^2? + a^2r^2\sin^2? = a^2b^2$

$$\Rightarrow \frac{r^2\cos^2\theta}{a^2}+\frac{r^2\sin^2\theta}{b^2}=1$$

$$\Rightarrow \frac{\cos^2\theta}{a^2}+\frac{\sin^2\theta}{b^2}=\frac{1}{r^2}$$

Ex-5. Transform the equation $2x^2+3xy+2y^2=1$ into polar form.

Sol. We have $2x^2+3xy+2y^2=1$

$$\Rightarrow 2r^2\cos^2\theta+3r^2\sin\theta\cos\theta+2r^2\sin^2\theta=1$$

$$\Rightarrow r^2\left(2\cos^2?+3\sin?\cos?+2\sin^2?\right)=1$$

$$\Rightarrow r^2\left(2+\frac{3}{2}\sin 2?\right)=1$$

$$\Rightarrow r^2=\frac{2}{(4+3\sin 2?)}$$

1.5 DISTANCE BETWEEN TWO POINTS (CARTESIAN FORM) :

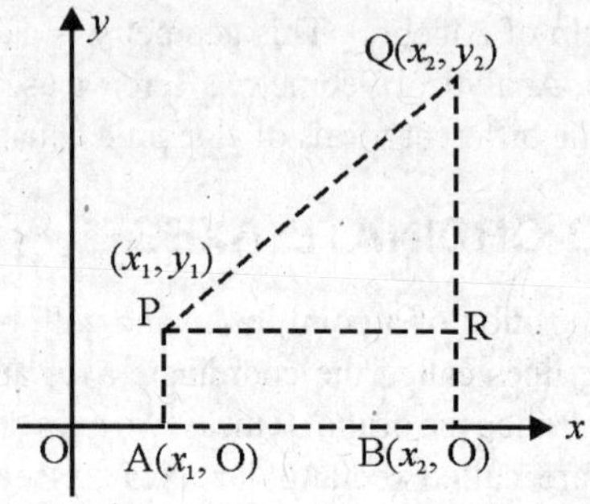

The distance between the points $P(x_1, y_1)$ and $Q(x_2, y_2)$ is $|PQ| = \sqrt{(x_2-x_1)^2+(y_2-y_1)^2}$.

Note : If the three points P, Q, R are collinear , then $|PQ| \pm |QR| = |PR|$

1.6 DISTANCE BETWEEN TWO POINTS (POLAR FORM)

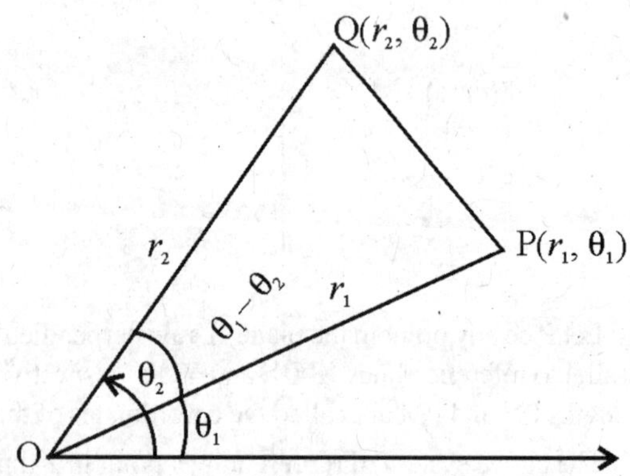

Let $P(r_1, \theta_1)$ and $Q(r_2, \theta_2)$ be two points in polar form and θ be the angle between them.

Then $\cos\theta = \frac{r_1^2 + r_2^2 - PQ^2}{2r_1r_2}$

$\Rightarrow \quad PQ^2 = r_1^{\,2} + r_2^{\,2} - 2 r_1 r_2 \cos ?$

$\Rightarrow \quad PQ = \sqrt{r_1^{\,2} + r_2^{\,2} - 2 r_1 r_2 \cos ?}$.

Note:

1. When 3 points are given and in order to prove

(i) an isosceles triangle , then show that any two sides are equal

(ii) an equilateral triangle , then show that all sides are equal

(iii) a scalene triangle , then show that all sides are unequal.

(iv) a right angled triangle, say, ? ABC , then show that $AB^2 + BC^2 = AC^2$

2. When 4 points are given and in order to prove

(i) a square, then show that, all sides and diagonals are equal.

(ii) a rhombus, then show that all sides are equal but diagonals are not equal.

(iii) a rectangle, then show that opposite sides are equal and diagonals are also equal.

(iv) a parallelogram, then show that opposite sides are equal and diagonals are not equal.

Ex-1. Find the distance between the points $(a\cos\alpha, a\sin\alpha)$ and $(a\cos\beta, a\sin\beta)$, where $a > 0$

Soln. Hence the required distance

$$= \sqrt{a^2 (\cos a - \cos ß)^2 + a^2 (\sin a - \sin ß)^2}$$

$$= a\sqrt{(\cos a - \cos ß)^2 + (\sin a - \sin ß)^2}$$

$$= a\sqrt{(\cos^2\alpha + \sin^2\alpha) + (\cos^2\beta + \sin^2\beta) - 2(\cos\alpha \cos\beta + \sin\alpha \sin\beta)}$$

$$= a \times \sqrt{2 - 2\cos(a\text{-}ß)}$$

$$= a \times \sqrt{2\,(1 - \cos(a\text{-}ß))}$$

$$= 2a\left|\sin\left(\frac{a - ß}{2}\right)\right|.$$

Ex.2 Find the distance between the points $\left(3, \frac{\pi}{4}\right)$ and $\left(7, \frac{5\pi}{4}\right)$

Soln. Hence the required distance

$$= \sqrt{3^2 + 7^2 - 2.3.7.\cos\left(\frac{5\pi}{4} - \frac{\pi}{4}\right)}$$

$$= \sqrt{3^2 + 7^2 - 2.3.7.\cos(p)}$$

$$= \sqrt{9 + 49 + 42} = \sqrt{100} = 10$$

Ex-3. If the point (x,y) be equidistant from the points (6, –1) and (2, 3) such that $Ax + By + C = 0$ then find the value of $A + B + C + 10$.

Soln. Let $P = (x, y)$, $A = (6, -1)$ and $B = (2, 3)$

We have PA = PB

$\Rightarrow \quad (x-6)^2 + (y+1)^2 = (x-2)^2 + (y-3)^2$

$\Rightarrow \quad x^2 - 12x + 36 + y^2 + 2y + 1 = x^2 - 4x + 4 + y^2 - 6y + 9$

$\Rightarrow \quad -12x + 36 + 2y + 1 = -4x + 4 - 6y + 9$

$\Rightarrow \quad -8x + 8y + 37 - 13 = 0$

$\Rightarrow \quad -8x + 8y + 24 = 0$

$\Rightarrow \quad A = -8,\ B = 8,\ C = 24$

Hence, the value of $A + B + C + 10 = -8 + 8 + 24 + 10 = 34$

Ex-4. The vertices of a triangle ABC are A(–2, 3), B(2, –1) and C (4, 0). Find cos A.

Soln. We have $AB = \sqrt{(2+2)^2 + (-1-3)^2} = 4\sqrt{2}$

$BC = \sqrt{(2-4)^2 + (-1)^2} = \sqrt{5}$ and

$CA = \sqrt{(4+2)^2 + (3)^2} = \sqrt{45} = 3\sqrt{5}$

Thus, $\cos A = \dfrac{(4\sqrt{2})^2 + (3\sqrt{5})^2 - (\sqrt{5})^2}{2.4\sqrt{2}.3\sqrt{5}}$

$\Rightarrow \quad \cos A = \dfrac{32 + 45 - 5}{24\sqrt{10}} = \dfrac{72}{24\sqrt{10}} = \dfrac{3}{\sqrt{10}}$

EXERCISE - 1

1. Prove that the points (-4, -1), (-2, -4), (4, 0) and (2, 3) are the vertices of a rectangle.

2. Two vertices of an equilateral triangle are (3, 4) and (-2, 3). Find the co-ordinates of the third vertex.

Ans. $\left(\dfrac{1 \pm \sqrt{3}}{2}, \dfrac{7 \pm 5\sqrt{3}}{2}\right)$.

1.7 SECTION FORMULAE

i. *Internal Section formula*: If a point R(x,y) divides the line segment joing the points $P(x_1, y_1)$ and $Q(x_2, y_2)$ internally in the ratio m:n, then

$$x=\frac{mx_2+nx_1}{m+n}, y=\frac{my_2+ny_1}{m+n}.$$

ii. ***External section formula:*** If a point R(x,y) divides the line segment joing the points $P(x_1, y_1)$ and $Q(x_2, y_2)$ externally in the ratio m:n , then

$$x=\frac{mx_2-nx_1}{m-n}, y=\frac{my_2-ny_1}{m-n}.$$

iii ***Mid-point formula:*** If a point R(x, y) divides the line segment joining the points $P(x_1, y_1)$ and $Q(x_2, y_2)$ internally in the same ratio, then

$$x=\frac{x_1+x_2}{2},\ y=\frac{y_1+y_2}{2}.$$

iv. If the line joining the points $(x_1, y_1)\&(x_2, y_2)$ is divided by the x-axis,then its ratio is $-\frac{y_1}{y_2}$ and by the y-axis, then its ratio is $-\frac{x_1}{x_2}$.

v. If the line $ax+by+c=0$ divides the line joining the points $P(x_1, y_1)$ and $Q(x_2, y_2)$ at R, then the ratio $\frac{PR}{RQ}$ is $-\frac{ax_1+by_1+c}{ax_2+by_2+c}$.

Ex-1. Find the point, which divides the join of (2,3) and (5,–3) in the ratio 1 : 2.

Soln. Let the point be (x, y)

Thus, $x=\frac{4+5}{2+1}=3,\ y=\frac{6-3}{2+1}=1$

Hence, the point is (3,1).

Ex-2. In what ratio does y-axis divide the line segment joining A(-3, 5) and B(7, 2)

Soln. Let the ratio be m : n.

Since the point lies on y-axis , so x co-ordinate will be zero.

Thus, $\frac{7m-3n}{m+n}=0$

$\Rightarrow\quad 7m-3n=0$

$\Rightarrow\quad \frac{m}{n}=\frac{3}{7}$

Ex-3. Find the ratio in which the join of the points (1, 2) and (-2, 3) is divided by the line $3x+4y=7$.

Soln. Let the ratio be $\lambda:1$

Thus, the point is $\left(\frac{1-2\lambda}{\lambda+1}, \frac{3\lambda-2}{\lambda+1}\right)$

Since, the point $\left(\frac{1-2\lambda}{\lambda+1}, \frac{3\lambda-2}{\lambda+1}\right)$ lies on the line

$3x+4y=7$, we get, $3\left(\frac{1-2\lambda}{\lambda+1}\right)+4\left(\frac{3\lambda-2}{\lambda+1}\right)=7$

$\Rightarrow\quad 3(1-2\lambda)+4(3\lambda-2)=7\lambda+7$

$\Rightarrow\quad 12\lambda-6\lambda-7\lambda=8+7-3$

$\Rightarrow\quad \lambda=-12$

Hence, the ratio is 12 : 1, externally.

Ex-4. Find the co-ordinates of the points which trisect the line segment joining (1, -2) and (-3, 4).

Soln. Let A = (1, -2) and B = (-3, 4) Consider the line AB is trisected at P and Q respectively.

Therefore P divides A and B internally in the ratio 1 : 2 and Q divides A and B in the ratio 2 :1

Thus , the co-ordinates of P and Q are

$\left(-\frac{2}{3}, 0\right)$ and $\left(-\frac{5}{3}, 2\right)$.

Ex-5. The co-ordinates of the mid-points of the sides of a triangle are (1, 1) ; (3, 2) and (4, 1) . Then find the co-ordinates of its vertices.

Soln. Let the co-ordinates of the vertices are (x_1, y_1), (x_2, y_2), (x_3, y_3)

Therefore, $x_1+x_2=1,\ x_2+x_3=4,\ x_1+x_3=3$

$\Rightarrow\quad x_1+x_2+x_3=4$

Thus, $x_1=0,\ x_2=1,\ x_3=3$

Also, $y_1+y_2=1,\ y_2+y_3=1,\ y_3+y_1=2$

$\Rightarrow\quad y_1+y_2+y_3=2$

Thus, $y_1=1,\ y_2=0,\ y_3=1$

Hence, the vertices are (0, 1) , (1, 0) and (3, 1) .

Ex-6. The co-ordinates of three consecutive vertices of a paral lelogram are (1, 3), (-1, 2) and (2, 5). Then find its fourth vertex.

Soln. Let the co-ordinates of the fourth vertex be (x,y)

As we know that, the diagonals of a parallelogram bisect each other.

Thus, $\frac{x-1}{2}=\frac{1+2}{2}$ & $\frac{y+2}{2}=\frac{5+3}{2}$

$\Rightarrow \quad x=4,\ y=6$

Hence, the third vertex be (4, 6)

1.8 IMPORTANT POINTS OF A TRIANGLE

(i) **Centroid**: The point of intersection of the medians of a triangle is called centroid.

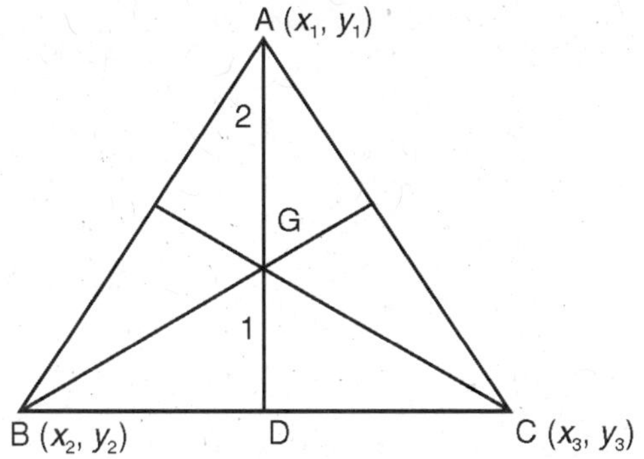

If the vertices of a triangle ABC are A x_1,y_1 , $B(x_2,y_2)$ & $C(x_3,y_3)$, then the co-ordinates of its centroid is $\left(\frac{x_1+x_2+x_3}{3}, \frac{y_1+y_2+y_3}{3}\right)$

(ii) If $(a_1,b_1),(a_2,b_2)\&(a_3,b_3)$ are the mid-points of the sides of a triangle, then its centrod is also given as $\left(\frac{a_1+a_2+a_3}{3}, \frac{b_1+b_2+b_3}{3}\right)$.

(iii) **Incenter** : The point of intersection of the angle bisectors of a triangle is called its incenter.

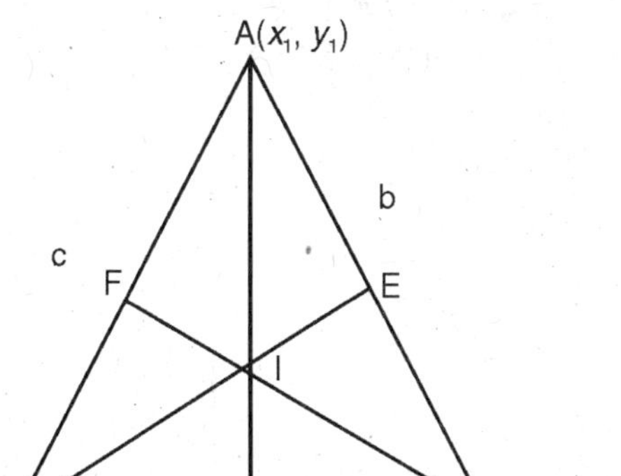

If the vertices of a triangle ABC are $A(x_1,y_1), B(x_2,y_2)$ & $C(x_3,y_3)$, then the co-ordinates of its in-center is

$$\left(\frac{ax_1+bx_2+cx_3}{a+b+c}, \frac{ay_1+by_2+cy_3}{a+b+c}\right)$$, where $a=BC$, $b=CA$, $c=AB$.

(iv) If ΔABC is an equilateral triangle, then in-center = centroid.

(v) **Ex-centre**: The point of intersection of the external bisectors of the angles of a triangle is called its ex-center.

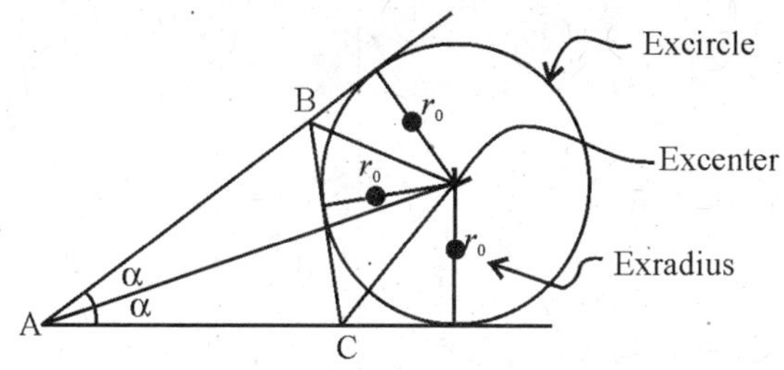

The circle opposite to the vertex A is called the escribed circle opposite A or the circle excribed to the side BC. If I_1 is the point of intersection of internal bisector of $\angle BAC$ and external bisector of $\angle ABC$ and $\angle ACB$,

then $I_1=\left(\frac{-ax_1+bx_2+cx_3}{-a+b+c}, \frac{-ay_1+by_2+cy_3}{-a+b+c}\right)$

$I_2=\left(\frac{ax_1-bx_2+cx_3}{a-b+c}, \frac{ay_1-by_2+cy_3}{a-b+c}\right)$ and

$I_3=\left(\frac{ax_1+bx_2-cx_3}{a+b-c}, \frac{ay_1+by_2-cy_3}{a+b-c}\right)$ respectively.

(vi) **Circum-center**: The point of intersection of perpendicular bisectors of a triangle is called its circum-center.

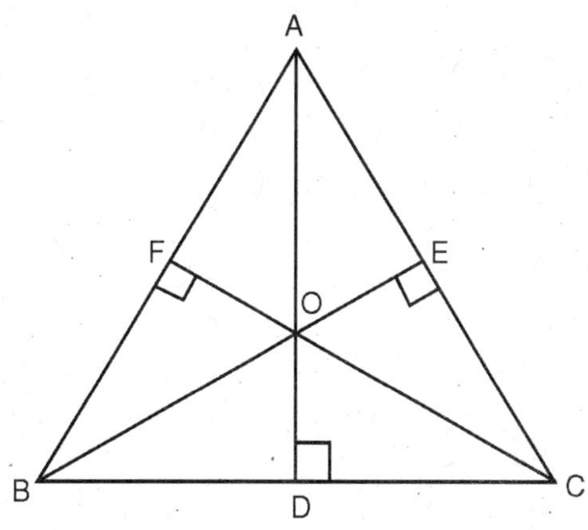

If the vertices of a triangle ABC are $A(x_1,y_1), B(x_2,y_2)$ & $C(x_3,y_3)$, then the co-ordinates of its circum-center is

$$\left(\frac{x_1\tan A+x_2\tan B+x_3\tan C}{\tan A+\tan B+\tan C}, \frac{y_1\tan A+y_2\tan B+y_3\tan C}{\tan A+\tan B+\tan C}\right)$$

Note: 1. If O(x, y) be the circum-centre of a triangle ABC, then its co-ordinates is determinedby the relation OA=OB=OC.

2. In case of a right angled triangle, mid-point of the hypotenuse is the circum-center.

(vii) **Ortho-center** : The point of intersection of the altitudes of a triangle is called its orthocenter.

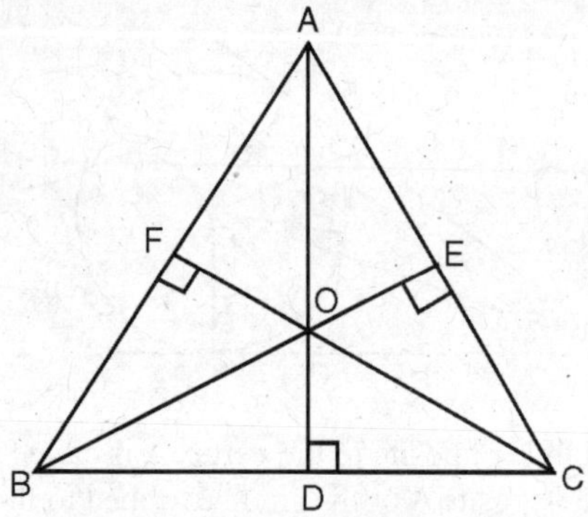

If the vertices of a triangle ABC are $A(x_1, y_1)$, $B(x_2, y_2)$ & $C(x_3, y_3)$, then the co-ordinates of its ortho-center is

$$\left(\frac{x_1\tan A + x_2\tan B + x_3\tan C}{\tan A + \tan B + \tan C}, \frac{y_1\tan A + y_2\tan B + y_3\tan C}{\tan A + \tan B + \tan C}\right)$$

Note:

1. In case of a right angled triangle, ortho-center is the right angled vertex.
2. In an isosceles triangle G, O, I and C lie on the same line and in an equilateral triangle, all these four points concide.
3. The ortho-center of a triangle with vertices (a, b), (b, a) and (a, a) is (a, a).
4. Orthocenter, Centroid and Circum-center are always collinear and Centroid divides the line joining Ortho-center and Circum-center in the ratio 2:1.

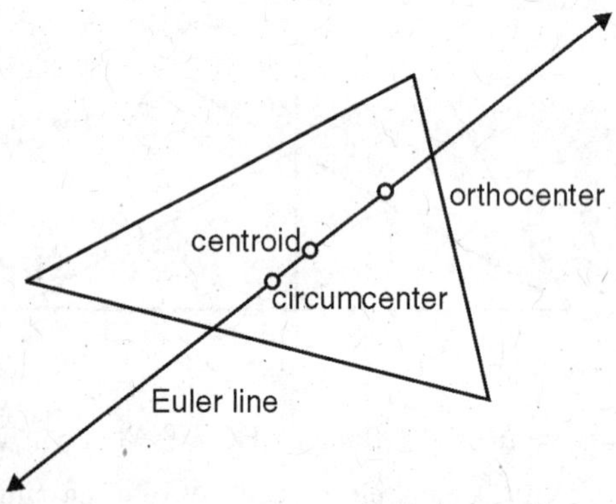

5. In case of an obtuse angled triangle, Circum-center and Ortho-center both are lie out side of the triangle.

Ex-1. Find the centroid of a triangle ABC, whose vertices are A(2, 4), B(6, 4), C(2, 0)

Soln. Hence, the co-ordinates of the centroid of the triangle ABC are $\left(\frac{2+6+2}{3}, \frac{4+4+0}{3}\right) = \left(\frac{10}{3}, \frac{8}{3}\right)$

Ex-2. Two vertices of a triangle are (-1, 4) and (5, 2). If its centroid is (0, -3), then find its third vertex.

Soln. Let the co-ordinates of the third vertex be (x, y)

Therefore, $\frac{x-1+5}{3} = 0 \Rightarrow x = -4$ and

$\frac{y+4+2}{3} = -3 \Rightarrow y = -15$

Hence, the co-ordinates of the third vertex be (- 4, - 15)

Ex-3. Find the in-center of a triangle ABC, whose vertices are A(1, 2), B(2, 3) and C(3, 4).

Soln. Let a = BC, b = CA, c = AB be the lengths of the side of the given triangle ABC.

Therefore, $a = \sqrt{(3-2)^2 + (4-3)^2} = \sqrt{2}$,

$b = \sqrt{(3-1)^2 + (4-2)^2} = 2\sqrt{2}$

and $c = \sqrt{(2-1)^2 + (3-2)^2} = \sqrt{2}$

Thus, the in-centre are

$$\left(\frac{a x_1 + b x_2 + c x_3}{a+b+c}, \frac{a y_1 + b y_2 + c y_3}{a+b+c}\right)$$

$$= \left(\frac{1.\sqrt{2} + 2.2\sqrt{2} + 3.\sqrt{2}}{\sqrt{2} + 2\sqrt{2} + \sqrt{2}}, \frac{2.\sqrt{2} + 3.2\sqrt{2} + 4.\sqrt{2}}{\sqrt{2} + 2\sqrt{2} + \sqrt{2}}\right)$$

$$= \left(\frac{8\sqrt{2}}{4\sqrt{2}}, \frac{12\sqrt{2}}{4\sqrt{2}}\right) = (2, 3)$$

Ex -4. If a triangle has its ortho-center at (1,1) and circum-centre at (3/2, 3/4), then find its centroid.

Soln. As we know that, the centroid divides the ortho-center and circum-center in the ratio 2 : 1.

Thus, the centroid are

$$\left(\frac{2.\frac{3}{2} + 1.1}{2+1}, \frac{2.\frac{3}{4} + 1.1}{2+1}\right) = \left(\frac{4}{3}, \frac{5}{6}\right)$$

Ex-5. The vertices of a triangle ABC are A(0, 0), B(0, 2) and C(2, 0). Then find the distance between the Circum-center and Ortho-center.

Soln. Clearly, it is a right angled triangle. As we know that, in case of a right angled triangle, Circum-centre is the mid-point of the hypotenuse and ortho-centre is at right angled.

Thus, Circum-centre $=\left(\frac{0+2}{2}, \frac{2+0}{2}\right)=(1, 1)$ and

Orthicentre $=(0,0)$

Hence, the required distance $=\sqrt{(1-0)^2+(1-0)^2}=\sqrt{2}$

1.9 AREA OF A TRIANGLE

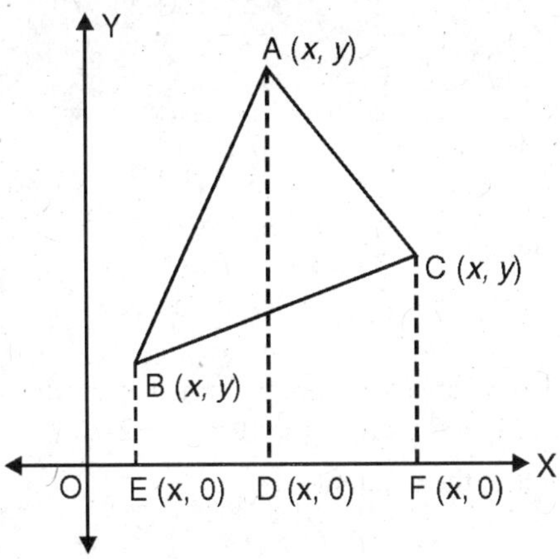

If $A(x_1, y_1), B(x_2, y_2)$ and $C(x_3, y_3)$ are the vertices of a triangle ABC, then its area is

$$=\frac{1}{2}\left[x_1\left(y_2-y_3\right)+x_2\left(y_3-y_1\right)+x_3\left(y_1-y_2\right)\right]$$

or $\quad \frac{1}{2}\left\|\begin{matrix} x_1 & y_1 & 1 \\ x_2 & y_2 & 1 \\ x_3 & y_3 & 1 \end{matrix}\right\|.$

or $\quad \frac{1}{2}\begin{vmatrix} x_1 & y_1 \\ x_2 & y_2 \end{vmatrix}+\frac{1}{2}\begin{vmatrix} x_2 & y_2 \\ x_3 & y_3 \end{vmatrix}+\frac{1}{2}\begin{vmatrix} x_3 & y_3 \\ x_1 & y_1 \end{vmatrix}$

Note:

1. The area of a polygon whose vertices are $\left(x_1, y_1\right),\left(x_2, y_2\right)$ $\left(x_3, y_3\right), \ldots\ldots\ldots,\left(x_n, y_n\right)$ is $\frac{1}{2}\begin{vmatrix} x_1 & y_1 \\ x_2 & y_2 \end{vmatrix}+\frac{1}{2}\begin{vmatrix} x_2 & y_2 \\ x_3 & y_3 \end{vmatrix}+\ldots$ $\ldots\ldots+\frac{1}{2}\begin{vmatrix} x_n & y_n \\ x_1 & y_1 \end{vmatrix}$

2. If the vertices of a triangle be $A\left(r_1, ?_1\right), B\left(r_2, ?_2\right)$ and $C\left(r_3, ?_3\right)$, then its area is $\frac{1}{2}\left[r_1 r_2 \sin\left(?_1-?_2\right)+r_2 r_3 \sin\left(?_2-?_3\right)+r_3 r_1 \sin\left(?_3-?_1\right)\right]$.

3. If $a_i x+b_i y+c_i=0, i=1,2,3$ are the sides of a triangle, then its area is $\frac{1}{2C_1C_2C_3}\begin{vmatrix} a_1 & b_1 & c_1 \\ a_2 & b_2 & c_2 \\ a_3 & b_3 & c_3 \end{vmatrix}^2$, where C_1, C_2 & C_3 are the cofactors of c_1, c_2 & c_3 in the determinant $\begin{vmatrix} a_1 & b_1 & c_1 \\ a_2 & b_2 & c_2 \\ a_3 & b_3 & c_3 \end{vmatrix}$.

4. If $A(x_1, y_1)$, $B(x_2, y_2)$ and $C(x_3, y_3)$ are the vertices of a triangle, then its area is $=\frac{1}{2}\begin{vmatrix} x_1-x_3 & x_2-x_3 \\ y_1-y_3 & y_2-y_3 \end{vmatrix}$.

5. If $A(x_1, y_1), B(x_2, y_2)$ and $C(x_3, y_3)$ three points are collinear, then $\begin{vmatrix} x_1-x_3 & x_2-x_3 \\ y_1-y_3 & y_2-y_3 \end{vmatrix}=0$

or

$$x_1\left(y_2-y_3\right)+x_2\left(y_3-y_1\right)+x_3\left(y_1-y_2\right)=0.$$

Ex-1. Find the area of a triangle whose vertices are (3, -4), (7, 5) (-1, 10).

Soln. Hence, the required area $=\frac{1}{2}\begin{vmatrix} x_1-x_3 & x_2-x_3 \\ y_1-y_3 & y_2-y_3 \end{vmatrix}$

$$=\frac{1}{2}\begin{vmatrix} 3-7 & 7+1 \\ -4-5 & 5-10 \end{vmatrix}=\frac{1}{2}\begin{vmatrix} -4 & 8 \\ -9 & -5 \end{vmatrix}$$

$$=\frac{1}{2}(20+72)=46 \text{ sq.u.}$$

Ex-2. Find the area of a triangle whose vertices are $(t, t+2)$, $(t+3, t)$ and $(t+2, t+2)$

Soln. Hence, the required area $=\frac{1}{2}\begin{vmatrix} x_1-x_3 & x_2-x_3 \\ y_1-y_3 & y_2-y_3 \end{vmatrix}$

$$=\frac{1}{2}\begin{vmatrix} t-t-3 & t+3-t-2 \\ t+2-t & t-t-2 \end{vmatrix}=\frac{1}{2}\begin{vmatrix} -3 & 1 \\ 2 & -2 \end{vmatrix}=\frac{1}{2}(6-2)=2 \text{ sq. u}$$

Ex-3. If A(x, y), B(1, 2) and C(2, 1) are the vertices of a triangle of area 6 sq.u prove that $x+y+9=0$.

Soln. Given area of a triangle is 9

$$\Rightarrow \frac{1}{2}\begin{vmatrix} x-1 & 1-2 \\ y-2 & 2-1 \end{vmatrix}=\pm 6$$

$$\Rightarrow \begin{vmatrix} x-1 & -1 \\ y-2 & 1 \end{vmatrix}=\pm 12$$

$$\Rightarrow (x-1)+(y-2)=\pm 12$$

$$\Rightarrow x+y-3+12=0, \; x+y-3-12=0$$

$$\Rightarrow x+y+9=0, \; x+y-15=0$$

Hence, the result.

Ex-4. Find the area of a quadrilateral whose vertices are $(1,1),(7,-3),(12,2)$ and $(7,21)$.

Soln. Hence, the required area of a quadrilateral

$$=\frac{1}{2}\begin{vmatrix}1 & 1\\ 7 & -3\\ 12 & 2\\ 7 & 21\\ 1 & 1\end{vmatrix}=\frac{1}{2}\{(-3+14+262+7)-(21+14-36-7)\}$$

$$=\frac{1}{2}(290+8)=149 \text{ sq. u.}$$

Ex-5. Find the area of a pentagon whose vertices are (4, 3), (-5, 6) (0, 7) (3, -6) and (-7, -2)

Soln. Hence, the required area of a pentagon

$$=\frac{1}{2}\begin{vmatrix}4 & 3\\ -5 & 6\\ 0 & 7\\ 3 & -6\\ -7 & -2\\ 4 & 3\end{vmatrix}$$

$$=\left|\frac{1}{2}\{(24-35+0-6-21)-(-8+42+21+0+15)\}\right|$$

$$=\frac{1}{2}(38+70)=54 \text{ sq. u.}$$

Ex-6. Prove that the points (a, b + c), (b, c + a) and (c, a + b) are collinear.

Soln. We have $\frac{1}{2}\begin{vmatrix}x_1-x_2 & x_2-x_3\\ y_1-y_2 & y_2-y_3\end{vmatrix}$

$$=\frac{1}{2}\begin{vmatrix}a-b & b-c\\ b+c-c-a & c+a-a-b\end{vmatrix}$$

$$=\frac{1}{2}\begin{vmatrix}a-b & b-c\\ b-a & c-b\end{vmatrix}$$

$$=\frac{1}{2}(a-b)(b-c)\begin{vmatrix}1 & 1\\ -1 & -1\end{vmatrix}=0.$$

Ex-7. Let the co-ordinates of A, B, C, D are (6, 3), (-3, 5), (4, -2) and (x, 3x) respectively. $\frac{\Delta DBC}{\Delta ABC}=\frac{1}{2}$, then find x.

Soln. Now, $\text{ar}(\Delta DBC)=\left|\frac{1}{2}\begin{vmatrix}x+3 & -3-4\\ 3x-3 & 5+2\end{vmatrix}\right|$

$$=\left|\frac{1}{2}(7x+21-21x-21)\right|=\left|\frac{1}{2}(-14x)\right|=7x$$

and $\text{ar}(\Delta ABC)=\frac{1}{2}\begin{vmatrix}6+3 & -3-4\\ 3\text{-}5 & 5+2\end{vmatrix}$

$$=\frac{1}{2}\begin{vmatrix}9 & -7\\ -2 & 7\end{vmatrix}=\frac{1}{2}(63-14)=\frac{49}{2}$$

Thus, $\frac{7x}{\frac{49}{2}}=\frac{1}{2} \Rightarrow x=\frac{7}{4}$

Ex-8. Find the area of a triangle formed by the lines $7x-2y+10=0$, $7x+2y-10=0$ and $9x+y+2=0$.

Soln. Hence, the required area

$$=\frac{1}{2\times|C_1C_2C_3|}\begin{vmatrix}7 & -2 & 10\\ 7 & 2 & -10\\ 9 & 1 & 2\end{vmatrix}^2$$

where $C_1=\begin{vmatrix}7 & 2\\ 9 & 1\end{vmatrix}=-11$, $C_2=-\begin{vmatrix}7 & -2\\ 9 & 1\end{vmatrix}=-25$

$$C_3=-\begin{vmatrix}7 & -2\\ 7 & 2\end{vmatrix}=-28$$

$$=\frac{1}{2\times 11\times 25\times 28}(96)^2=\frac{9216}{2\times 11\times 25\times 28}$$

$$=\frac{9216}{15400}=\frac{2304}{3850} \text{ sq. u}$$

1.10 LOCUS AND ITS EQUATION

The locus of a moving point is the path of a point which satisfies some geometrical condition or conditions.

If a point moves in a plane in such a way that its distance from a fixed point is always same. Then the locus of the movable point is called a circle.

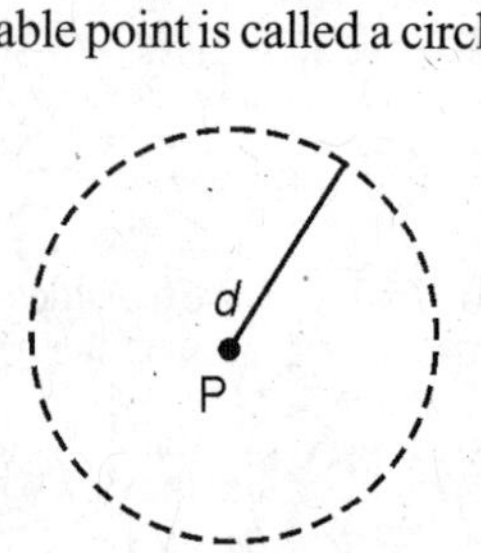

If a points moves in a plane in such a way that its distances from two fixed points are always same, then the locus of the point is a perpendicular bisector

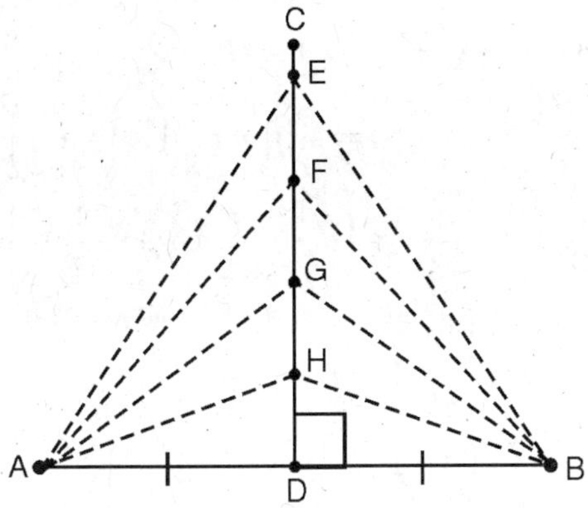

1.11 EQUATION OF A LOCUS

If the co-ordinates of every point on the locus satisfy the equation as well as if the co-ordinates of any point satisfy the equation , then that point must lie on the locus.

Rule to find out the locus of a moving point

(i) If x and y co-ordinates of the moving point are given in terms of a third variable , say , t .Eliminating t between x and y and then get the required locus

(ii) Some-times the co-ordinates of the moving point is taken as (x, y) . In this case the relation in x and y can be directly obtained by eliminating the variable.

(iii) If some geometrical conditions are given and we have to find the locus, then we take a variable point (α, β) and write the given condition in terms of α & β . Eliminate the variable and we get the relation between α & β . Finally replace α by x and β by y and then we get a required locus.

Ex-1. If the co-ordinates of a variable point P be $(a\cos\theta,\ a\sin\theta)$ where θ is a parameter , then find the locus of P.

Soln. Let $x = a\cos\theta,\ y = a\ \sin\ \theta$

Then $x^2 + y^2 = a^2\cos^2\theta + a^2\sin^2\theta = a^2$.

Which is the required locus of the given point P.

Ex-2. If the co-ordinates of a vaiable point P be $(at^2, 2at)$, then find the locus of P.

Soln. Let $x = at^2,\ y = 2at$.

Then, $y^2 = 4a^2t^2 = 4a(at^2) = 4ax$

Which is the required locus of P .

Ex-3. Find the locus of a movable point P, where its distance from the origin is 3 time its distance from y-axis

Soln. Let the movable point P be (x, y) and the point on y-axis be (0, y)

Given condition is $\sqrt{x^2 + y^2} = 3x$

$\Rightarrow\ x^2 + y^2 = 9x^2$

$\Rightarrow\ y^2 = 8x^2$

Which is the required locus of P.

Ex-4. If a point moves in a plane in such a way that its distance from the pont (a, 0) to its distance is equal to its distance from y-axis.

Soln. Let the movable point be (x, y)

Given condition is $\sqrt{(x-a)^2 + y^2} = x$

$\Rightarrow\ (x-a)^2 + y^2 = x^2$

$\Rightarrow\ y^2 = x^2 - (x-a)^2 = 2ax - a^2$

Which is the required locus of the given movable point.

Ex-5. If the co-ordinates of a variable point P be $\left(t+\frac{1}{t}, t-\frac{1}{t}\right)$, where t is a parameter., then find the locus of P.

Soln. Let the co-ordinates of the variable point P be (x, y)..

Thsn $x = t + \frac{1}{t},\ y = t - \frac{1}{t}$

$\Rightarrow\ x^2 - y^2 = \left(t+\frac{1}{t}\right)^2 - \left(t-\frac{1}{t}\right)^2 = 4$

Which is the required locus of P. Which represnts a rect angular hyperbola.

Ex-6. Find the locus of a movable point P, for which the sum of its distance from (0, 3) and (0, -3) is 8.

Soln. Let P be (x, y)

Given condition is $\sqrt{(x)^2+(y+3)^2} + \sqrt{(x)^2+(y-3)^2} = 8$

$\Rightarrow\ \sqrt{(x)^2+(y+3)^2} = 8 - \sqrt{(x)^2+(y-3)^2}$

$\Rightarrow\ (x)^2+(y+3)^2 = 64 + \left((x)^2+(y-3)^2\right) - 16\sqrt{(x)^2+(y-3)^2}$

$\Rightarrow\ 6y = 64 - 6y - 16\sqrt{(x)^2+(y-3)^2}$

$\Rightarrow\ 12y - 64 = 16\sqrt{(x)^2+(y-3)^2}$

$\Rightarrow\ 3y - 16 = 4\sqrt{(x)^2+(y-3)^2}$

$\Rightarrow\ (3y-16)^2 = 16\left((x)^2+(y-3)^2\right)$

$\Rightarrow\ 9y^2 - 96y + 256 = 16\left(x^2 + y^2 - 6y + 9\right)$

$$\Rightarrow \quad 16x^2 + 7y^2 = 256 - 144 = 112$$

$$\Rightarrow \quad \frac{x^2}{7} + \frac{y^2}{16} = 1$$

Which is the required locus of the given point . Which represents an ellipse.

Ex-7. A stick of length l slides with its ends on two mutually per pendicular lines. Find the locus of the mid point of the stick.

Soln. Let AB $= l$

Consider the point A on x-axis and B on y-axis. such that $A = (a, 0)$ and $B = (0, b)$

Therefore, $AB = l \Rightarrow \sqrt{a^2 + b^2} = l \Rightarrow a^2 + b^2 = l^2$ ....(i)

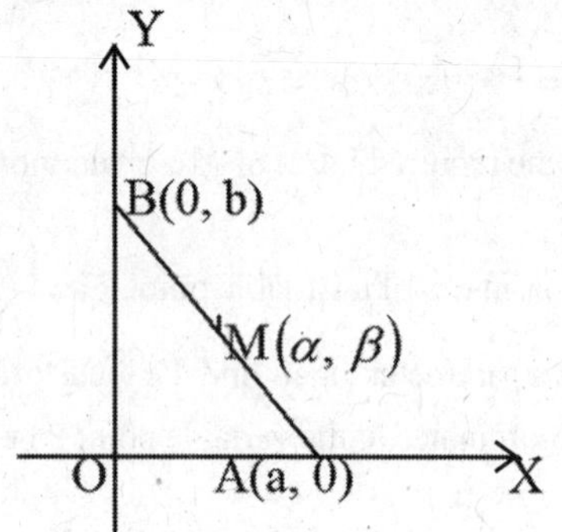

Let the mid point of A and B be (α, β)

Thus, $\alpha = \frac{a}{2}, \beta = \frac{b}{2} \quad \Rightarrow \quad a = 2\alpha, \; b = 2\beta$

From (i), we get, $\alpha^2 + \beta^2 = \frac{l^2}{4}$

Hence, the locus of (α, β) is $x^2 + y^2 = \frac{l^2}{4}$.

Ex-8: If O be the origin and A be a point on the line $y^2 = 8x$. Find the locus of the mid - point of OA

Soln. Let the point A be (α, β) and $M\left(\frac{\alpha}{2}, \frac{\beta}{2}\right)$ is the mid-point of OA.

Since A lies on the curve $y^2 = 8x$, so $\beta^2 = 8\alpha$

$$\Rightarrow \quad \left(\frac{\beta}{2}\right)^2 = 4\left(\frac{\alpha}{2}\right)$$

Hence, the required locus of M is $y^2 = 4x$.

Ex-9. If P is the mid point of the straight line joining the points A(1, 2) and Q where Q is a variable point on the curve $x^2 + y^2 + x + y = 0$. Find the locus of P.

Soln. We have $x^2 + y^2 + x + y = 0$

$$\Rightarrow \quad \left(x + \frac{1}{2}\right)^2 + \left(y + \frac{1}{2}\right)^2 = \left(\frac{1}{\sqrt{2}}\right)^2$$

Let the point Q be $\left(-\frac{1}{2} + \frac{1}{\sqrt{2}}\cos\theta, \; -\frac{1}{2} + \frac{1}{\sqrt{2}}\sin\theta\right)$

and P be (α, β)

Then $\alpha = \frac{1}{4} + \frac{1}{2\sqrt{2}}\cos\theta, \; \beta = \frac{3}{4} + \frac{1}{2\sqrt{2}}\sin\theta$.

Now, $8\left(\alpha - \frac{1}{4}\right)^2 + 8\left(\beta - \frac{3}{4}\right)^2 = \cos^2\theta + \sin^2\theta = 1$

$$\Rightarrow \quad 8\left(\alpha^2 + \beta^2 - \frac{\alpha}{2} - \frac{3\beta}{2}\right) + \frac{1}{2} + \frac{9}{2} - 1 = 0$$

$$\Rightarrow \quad 8\left(\alpha^2 + \beta^2 - \frac{\alpha}{2} - \frac{3\beta}{2}\right) + 4 = 0$$

$$\Rightarrow \quad 2\left(\alpha^2 + \beta^2\right) - \alpha - 3\beta + 1 = 0$$

Hence, the locus of (α, β) is $2\left(x^2 + y^2\right) - x - y + 1 = 0$

Ex-10 A circle has center (2, 2) and always touches x and y axes. If it always touches a line AB (where A and B lie on +ve x and y axes), then find the locus of the circum-center of the triangle ? OAB ,where O is the origin..

Soln. Let OA = a and OB = b. Since the circle touches both the axes and the line AB, so the in-radius of triangle OAB be 2.

From trigonometry, we can write $r = \frac{\Delta}{s}$,.......(i)

where Δ = area of a triangle ,

s = semi - perimeter of a triangle.

Let (x, y) be the circum-center of the triangle OAB , then

$x = \frac{a}{2}, \; y = \frac{b}{2}$ Thus, a = 2 x and b = 2y .

Putting the values of a and b in (i) we get ,

$$2 = \frac{\frac{1}{2}.(2x).(2y)}{\left(\frac{2x + 2y + \sqrt{4x^2 + 4y^2}}{2}\right)}$$

$\Rightarrow \quad xy = x + y + \sqrt{x^2 + y^2}$ is the required locus.

EXERCISE - 2

Q.1 Find the locus of a movable point P, for which the difference of its distances from (2, 0) and (-2, 0) is 6.

Q.2. If A(1,1) and B(-2, 3) are two fixed points, find the locus of a point P so that area of ΔPAB is 9 sq.u

Q.3 Find the locus of a point whose co-ordinates are given by $x = t^2 + t$, $y = 2t + 1$, where t is parameter.

Ans. Parabola

Q.4 If a variable line $\frac{x}{a} + \frac{y}{b} = 1$ intersects the axes at A and B respectively such that $a^2 + b^2 = 4$ and O be the origin. Find the locus of the circum-center of the triangle Δ OAB.

Ans. $x^2 + y^2 = 4$.

Q.5. A variable line cuts the x and y axes at A and B where OA = a, OB = b (O is the origin) such that $a^2 + b^2 = 9$, then find the locus of the centroid of the triangle OAB.

Ans. $x^2 + y^2 = 9$.

1.12 GEOMETRIC TRANSFORMATIONS

When talking about geometric transformations, we have to be very careful about the object being transformed. We have two alternatives, either the geometric objects are trans formed or the co-ordinate system is transformed. These two are very closely related; but, the formulae that carry out the job are different. We only cover transforming geometric objects here.

We shall start with the traditional Euclidean transformations that do not change lengths and angle measures,

1.13 EUCLIDEAN TRANSFORMATIONS

The Euclidean transformations are the most commonly used transformations. An Euclidean transformation is either a translation, a rotation, or a reflection. We shall discuss translations and rotations only.

(i) If the origin be shifted to a new point, say, (h, k), the new axes remains parallel to the original axes, then this transformation is called Translation of Axes.

(ii) If the axes are rotated through an angle θ, the orgin remains fixed, then this method is called Rotation of Axes.

(iii) If the origin be shifted to a new point, say, (h,k), and also the axes be rotated through an angle θ, then this transformation is termed as Translation and Rotation of Axes.

The co-ordinates of a point in a plane when the origin is shifted from origin to a new point (h,k), then the new axes remains parallel to the original axes.

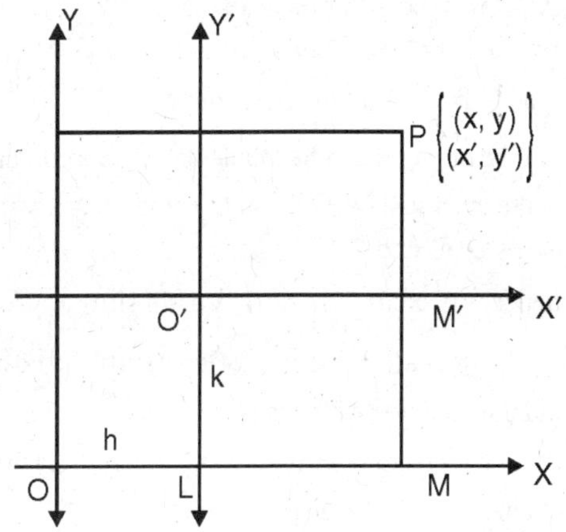

Let O be the origin and OX, OY the original axes. Let the origin O be shifted to a new point O, whose co-ordinates are (h, k).

Through O' draw O'X' and O'Y' parallel to OX and OY respectively. O' is the new origin and O'X', O'Y' are new axes.

Let P be any point in this plane, whose co-ordinates according to the original and new axes be (x, y) and (x, y)

Now we have to establish the relation between the new and the original co-ordinates.

From P drawn PM perpendicular to OX which intersects O X' at M'.

Again from O' draw O'L perpendicular to OX.

Then OL = h, O'L = k; OM = x, PM = y; O'M' = x', PM' = y'

Thus, x = OM = OL + LM = OL + O'M = h + x' = x' + h

and y = PM = P M' + M'M = P M' + M'M = y' + k

Hence, we obtained the following relations between new and original co-ordinates

$$\begin{cases} x = x' + h \\ y = y' + k \end{cases} \quad \text{and} \quad \begin{cases} x' = x - h \\ y' = y - k \end{cases}$$

1.14 ROTATION OF CO-ORDINATE AXES

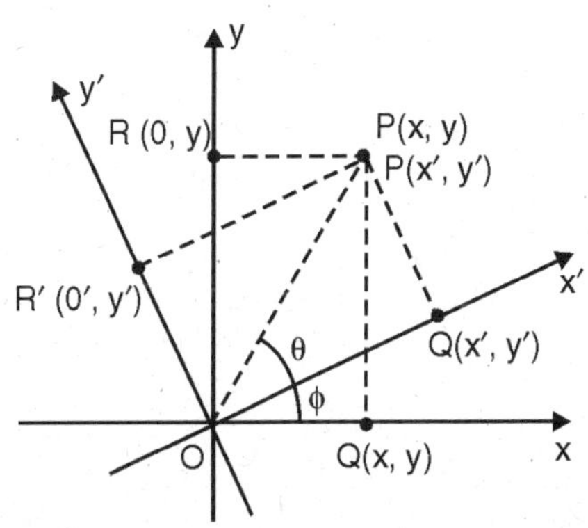

Let OX, OY be the original axes and O X' and O Y' be the new axes obtained after rotating OX and OY through an angle ? in the anticlockwise direction.

Let P be any point in the plane having coordinates (x, y) with respect to axes OX and OY and (x', y') with respect to axes O X' and O Y'.

Then $x = x'\cos\theta - y'\sin\theta$, $y = x'\sin\theta + y'\cos\theta$ ... (1)

and $x' = x\cos\theta + y\sin\theta$, $y' = -x\sin\theta + y\cos\theta$ .... (2)

Ex-1. Find the equation of the curve $2x^2 + y^2 - 3x + 5y - 8 = 0$, when the origin is shifted to the point (-1, 2) without changing the direction of axes.

Soln. Given curve is $2x^2 + y^2 - 3x + 5y - 8 = 0$ ....(i).

Replacing x by $x-1$ and y by $y+2$ in (i), we get,

$$2(x-1)^2 + (y+2)^2 - 3(x-1) + 5(y+2) - 8 = 0$$

$$\Rightarrow 2(x^2 - 2x + 1) + (y^2 + 4y + 4) - 3(x-1) + 5(y+2) - 8 = 0$$

$$\Rightarrow \quad 2x^2 + y^2 - 7x + 9y + 11 = 0.$$

Ex-2. The equation of a curve referred to the new axes retaining their direction and origin is (4, 5) is $x^2 + y^2 = 36$. Find the equation referred to the original axes.

Soln. Given curve is $x^2 + y^2 = 36$ ....(i)

Replacing x by x - 4 and y by y - 5 in (i), we get,

$$(x-4)^2 + (y-5)^2 = 36$$

$$\Rightarrow \quad x^2 + y^2 - 8x - 10y + 16 + 25 - 36 = 0$$

$$\Rightarrow \quad x^2 + y^2 - 8x - 10y + 5 = 0 .$$

Which is the required equation of the original axes.

Ex-3. At what point, the origin be shifted if co-ordinates of a point (-1, 8) become (-7, 3)?

Soln. Let the point be (x, y)

Thus $x - 1 = -7,\ y + 8 = 3$

$\Rightarrow \quad x = -6,\ y = -5$

Hence, the point be (-6, -5).

Ex-4. If the axes are turned through $45°$, find the transformed form of the equation $3x^2 + 3y^2 + 2xy = 2$.

Soln. Given equation is $3x^2 + 2xy + 3y^2 = 2$ Replacing x by $(x\cos 45° - y\sin 45°)$ and y by $(x\cos 45° + y\sin 45°)$ in (i), we get,

$$3\left(\frac{x-y}{\sqrt{2}}\right)^2 + 3\left(\frac{x+y}{\sqrt{2}}\right)^2 + 2\left(\frac{x-y}{\sqrt{2}}\right)\left(\frac{x+y}{\sqrt{2}}\right) = 2$$

$$\Rightarrow 3(x^2 + y^2) + (x^2 - y^2) = 2$$

$$\Rightarrow \quad 4x^2 + 2y^2 = 2$$

$$\Rightarrow 2x^2 + y^2 = 1$$

Ex-5. Transform to parallel axes through the point (1, -2) the equation $y^2 - 4x + 4y + 8 = 0$.

Soln. Given equation is $y^2 - 4x + 4y + 8 = 0$ ....(i)

Replacing x by x + 1 and y by y - 2 in (i), we get,

$$(y-2)^2 - 4(x+1) + 4(y-2) + 8 = 0$$

$$\Rightarrow \quad y^2 - 4y + 4 - 4x - 4 + 4y - 8 + 8 = 0$$

$$\Rightarrow \quad y^2 = 4x .$$

Which is the required trnsformed equation.

Ex-6. If a point P(1, 2) is translated itself 2 units along the +ve direction of x-axis and then it is rotated about the origin in anticlock-wise sense through an angle of $90°$, then find the new position of P.

Soln. If the point P (1, 2) is translated itself 2 units along the +ve direction of x a-xis, then P becomes (3, 2)

Let $Z = (3, 2) = 3 + 2i$.

Thus, the new position of $P = iZ = i(3 + 2i)$

$= -2 + 3i = (-2, 3)$

EXERCISE - 3

Q.1 If the axes are rotated through $\pi/4$, equation $x^2 - y^2 = a^2$ is transformed to $\lambda xy + a^2 = 0$, then find value of $\lambda + 10$.
Ans. 12.

Q.2 Transform to axes inclined at $\pi/3$ to the original axes the equation $x^2 + 2\sqrt{3}\,y - y^2 = 2a^2$. **Ans.** $x^2 - y^2 = a^2$

Q.3. What does the equation $3x^2 + 2xy + 3y^2 - 18x - 22y + 50 = 0$ become when referred to new rectangular axes through the point (2,3), the new set making $\pi/4$ with the old? **Ans.** $4x^2 + 2y^2 = 1$.

Q.4 If a point P(2, 3) is rotated through an angle of $90°$ about the origin in anti-clock wise sense, say, at Q, then find the co-ordinates of Q. **Ans.** (–3, 2)

Q.5 If a point P(3, 4) is rotated through an angle of 60° about the point Q(2, 0) in anti-clock wise sense, say, at R, then find the co-ordinates of R. **Ans.** $\left(-\frac{3}{2} - 2\sqrt{3},\ 2 + \frac{\sqrt{3}}{2}\right)$

THE STRAIGHT LINE

1.15 INTRODUCTION

The notion of line or straight line was introduced by ancient mathematicians to represent straight objects with negligible width and depth. Lines are an idealization of such objects. Thus, until seventeenth century, lines were defined like this: "The line is the first species of quantity, which has only one dimension, namely length, without any width nor depth, and is nothing else than the flow or run of the point which [...] will leave from its imaginary moving some vestige in length, exempt of any width. [...] The straight line is that which is equally extended between its points".

Euclid described a line as "breadthless length", and introduced several postulates as basic unprovable properties from which he constructed the geometry, which is now called Euclidean geometry to avoid confusion with other geometries which have been introduced since the end of nineteenth century (such as non-Euclidean geometry, projective geometry, and affine geometry).

When a geometry is described by a set of axioms, the notion of a line is usually left unde fined (a so-called primitive object). The properties of lines are then determined by the axioms which refer to them. One advantage to this approach is the flexibility it gives to users of the geometry. Thus in differential geometry a line may be interpreted as a geodesic (shortest path between points), while in some projective geometries a line is a 2-dimensional vector space (all linear combinations of two independent vectors). This flexibility also extends beyond mathematics and, for example, permits physicists to think of the path of a light ray as being a line.

A line segment is a part of a line that is bounded by two distinct end points and contains every point on the line between its end points. Depending on how the line segment is defined, either of the two end points may or may not be part of the line segment. Two or more line segments may have some of the same relationships as lines, such as being parallel, intersecting, or skew.

1.16 MATHEMATICAL DEFINITIONS

Definition-1:

A line is traced by a point travelling in a constant diterction.

Definition-2:

A line is a breadthless length.

Definition-3:

A straight line is a line which lies evenly with the points on itself

Definition-4:

A length without breadth or thickness, the trace of a mov ing point is a straight line.

Definiton-5:

A line in the plane is defined as the set of points whose coordinates satisfy a given linear equation.

Definition-6:

A line may be an independent object, distinct from the set of points which lie on it.

Definition-7:

A straight line is the shortest distance between any two points on a plane.

Definition-8:

A line is a set of points extending in both directions containing the shortest path between any two points on it.

Definition-9:

A line is straight if it has a constant gradient.

Definition-10:

If the gradients between any two points on the locus are equal, then the locus is a straight line

Definition-11:

In 3D geometry , the point of intersection of two planes be a line.

Definition-12:

Every first degree equation in x and y represents a striaght line.

Definition-13:

It is the locus of a point which moves in a plane in a con stant direction.

Definition-14:

A striaght line is also defined as the curve is such that the line segment joining any two points on it lies wholly on it.

Note:

The equation of a straight line is the relation between x and y , which is satisfied by the co-ordi nates of each and every point on the line.

A straight line consists of only two arbitrary constants

1.17 ANGLE OF INCLINATION OF A LINE

Angle of inclination of a line is the measure of the angle between the x-axis and the line measured in the anti-clock wise direction.

The angle of inclination of the line between $0°$ and $180°$.

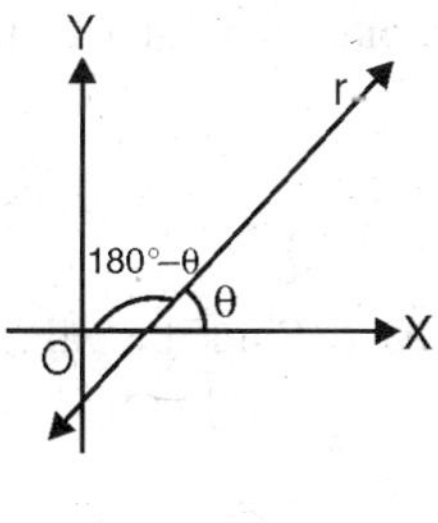

1.18 SLOPE OR GRADIENT OF A LINE :

If the inclination of a line be θ , then $\tan\theta$ is called the slope or gradient of the line. It is usually denoted as m. where

$0<\theta<180°$ and $\theta \neq \frac{\pi}{2}$.

(i) If a line is parallel to x-axis , then slope is zero.

(ii) If a line is perpendicular to x-axis , then slope is not defined.

(iii) If a line is equally inclined with the axes, then slope is ± 1.

(iv) If $P(x_1, y_1)$ and $Q(x_2, y_2)$ are two points on a line L, then slope of the line L is m and is equal to $m=\frac{y_2-y_1}{x_2-x_1}$.

(v) If three points A,B,C are collinear, then $m(AB)=m(BC)$ $=m(CA)$.

(vi) If two lines having slopes m_1 & m_2 and the angle between them be θ , then $\tan\theta=\left|\frac{m_1-m_2}{1+m_1m_2}\right|$.

(vii) If two lines having slopes m_1 & m_2 are parallel,then $m_1=m_2$

(viii) If two lines having slopes m_1 & m_2 are perpendicular, then $m_1.m_2=-1$

(ix) If m is a slope of a line, then the slope of a line perpendicular to it is $\frac{-1}{m}$.

(x) Equation of x-axis is $y=0$

(xi) Equation of y-axis is $x=0$.

(xii) Equation of a line parallel to x-axis is y=constant = b (say)

(xiii) Equation of a line parallel to y-axis is x=constant = a (say).

Ex-1. Find the slope of line PQ , where P(2, 4) and Q(3, 10)

Soln. Hence, the required slope of

$$PQ=\frac{y_2-y_1}{x_2-x_1}=\frac{10-4}{3-2}=6$$

Ex-2. Find the value of λ, if 2 is slope of the line through (2, 5) and (λ, 7)

Soln. Given slope = 2

$$\Rightarrow \quad \frac{7-5}{?-2}=2 \quad \Rightarrow \quad \lambda-2=1 \quad \Rightarrow \quad \lambda=3$$

Ex-3 Prove that the line joining the points (2,-3) and (-5, 1) is parallel to the line joining (7,-1) and (0,3).

Soln. Let m_1 be the line joining the points (2, -3) and (- 5, 1) and m_2 be the line joining the points (7, -1) and (0, 3)

Thus $m_1=\frac{1+3}{-5-2}=-\frac{4}{7}$ and $m_2=\frac{3+1}{0-7}=-\frac{4}{7}$.

Since, $m_1=m_2$, so the slopes are parallel.

Ex-4. Prove that the points (a, b + c) , (b, c + a) and (c, a + b) are collinear .

Soln. Consider the points P = (a, b + c) , Q = (b, c + a), R = (c, a + b)

Therefore, $m(PQ)=\frac{c+a-b-c}{b-a}=\frac{a-b}{b-a}=-1$

and $m(QR)=\frac{a+b-c\text{-}a}{c\text{-}b}=\frac{b\text{-}c}{c\text{-}b}=-1$

Since, $m(PQ)=m(QR) \Rightarrow$ Thus, the points P, Q and R are collinear .

Ex-5. Find the angle between the lines joining the points (0, 0), (2, 2) and (2, -2) (3, 5).

Soln. Let m_1 & m_2 be the slopes of the line joining the points (0, 0) , (2, 2) and (2, - 2) , (3, 5).

Therefore, $m_1=\frac{2-0}{2-0}=1$ & $m_2=\frac{5+2}{3-2}=7$

Let θ be the angle between them

Then $\tan\theta=\left|\left(\frac{7-1}{1+7.1}\right)\right| \Rightarrow \tan\theta=\frac{3}{4}$

$$\Rightarrow \quad \theta=\tan^{-1}\left(\frac{3}{4}\right).$$

Ex-6. If the angle between two lines is 45° and slope of one of them is 1/2, then find the slope of the other line.

Soln. Let m be the slope of the other line.

Given $\tan 45°=\left|\frac{m-\frac{1}{2}}{1+\frac{m}{2}}\right| \Rightarrow \tan 45°=\left|\frac{2m-1}{2+m}\right|$

$$\Rightarrow \quad (2m-1)=\pm\ (2+m)$$

$$\Rightarrow (2m-1) = (2+m) \ \& \ (2m-1) = -(2+m)$$

$$\Rightarrow m = 3 \ \& \ m = -\frac{1}{3}.$$

Hence, the slopes of the other line area 3 or - 1/ 3.

Ex-7. Find the equation of a line passing through the point (2, -3) and is parallel to x-axis.

Soln. Equation of a line parallel to x-axis is $y = k$.

Which is passing through (2, -3), we have, k = - 3.

Hence, the required equation of the line is $y + 3 = 0$.

Ex-8. Find the equation of a line passing through the point (3, 4) and is perpendicular to y-axis.

Soln. Equation of a line perpendicular to y - axis is $y = k$.

Which is passing through the point (3, 4), we have, $k = 4$.

Hence, the required equation of the line is $y = 4$.

Ex-9. Find the equation of a line which is equidistant from the lines $x = 6$ and $x = 10$.

Soln. Hence, the required equation of a line, which is equidistant from the lines $x = 6$ and $x = 10$ is $x = \frac{6+10}{2} = 8$

1.19 VARIOUS FORMS OF A STRAIGHT LINE

(i) **Slope-intercept form:** The equation of a straight line whose slope is m and which cuts an intercept c on the y-axis is $y = mx + c$.

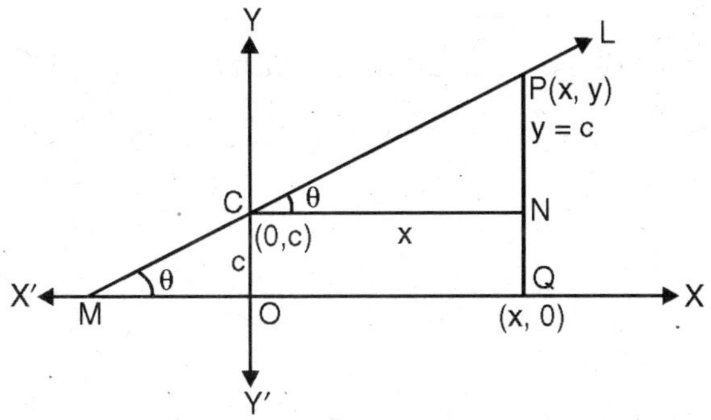

Note:

1. The genral equation of any straight line is $y = mx + c$.
2. Equation of any non-vertical lines in a plane is $y = mx + c$
3. The general equation of any line passing through the origin is $y = mx$.

Ex-1. Find the equation of a straight line which cuts off an inter cept of 7 units on y-axis and has slope 3.

Soln. Given $m = 3$ and $c = 7$.

Hence, the required equation of the line is $y = mx + c$
$= 3x + 7$.

Ex-2. Find the equation of a straight line which makes an angle of 135° with the +ve direction of x-axis and cuts an intercep of 5 units on the +ve direction of y-axis.

Soln. Here, $m = \tan(135°) = -1$ and $c = 5$.

Hence, required equation of the given line is

$y = mx + c = -x + 5$.

Ex-3. Find the equation of a straight line which makes an angle of $\tan^{-}\left(\frac{3}{5}\right)$ with the +ve direction of x-axis and cuts an intercept of 6 units in the negative direction of y-axis.

Soln. Given $? = \tan^{-1}\left(\frac{3}{5}\right) \Rightarrow \tan ? = \frac{3}{5} \Rightarrow m = \frac{3}{5}$

and $c = -6$.

Hence, the required equation of the given straight line is

$y = mx + c = \frac{3}{5}x - 6$.

Ex-4 Find the equation of a straight line which cuts off an inter cept of 4 units from y-axis and are equally inclined with the axes.

Soln. Given $m = \pm 1$ and $c = 4$.

Hence, the required equation of the line is

$y = mx + c = \pm x + 4$

Ex-5. Find the equations of bisectors of the angle between the co-ordinate axes.

Soln. Here, $m = \tan(45°) = 1$ & $m = \tan(135°) = -1$

and c = 0. Hence, the required equation of the bisectors is

$y = mx + c = \pm x$.

ii. **The point-slope form of a line**: The equation of a line passing through the point (x_1, y_1) and having slope m is $y - y_1 = m(x - x_1)$

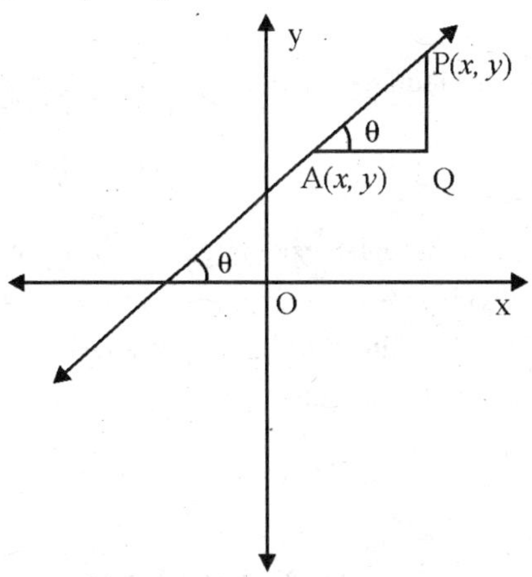

Note: The equation $y - y_1 = m(x - x_1)$ is also known as one point form of a line.

Ex-1. Find the equation of a line passing though the point (2, 3) and making an angle of 120° with the +ve direction of x-axis.

Soln. Here, $m = \tan(120°) = -\sqrt{3}$ and the point (x_1, y_1)

$= (2,3)$

Hence, the required equation of a striaght line is

$$y - y_1 = m(x - x_1)$$

$$\Rightarrow \quad y - 3 = -\sqrt{3}(x - 2)$$

$$\Rightarrow \quad \sqrt{3}\,x + y = 2\sqrt{3} + 3$$

Ex-2. Find the equation of the right bisectors of the line joining the points (1, 2) and (5, 7).

Soln. Let the points A and B are (1, 2) and (5,7) respectively.

Therefore, $m(AB) = \frac{7-2}{5-1} = \frac{5}{4}$ and the mid point of A and B are $\left(\frac{1+5}{2}, \frac{2+7}{2}\right) = \left(3, \frac{9}{2}\right)$

Hence, the required equation of the right (perpendicular) bisectors is $y - \frac{9}{2} = -\frac{4}{5}(x-3)$

$$\Rightarrow \quad 8x + 10y = 69.$$

Ex-3. Find the equation of a line which pass through the point (1, 2) and makes an angle θ with the +ve direction of x-axis , where $\cos\theta = -\frac{3}{5}$.

Soln. Given $\cos\theta = -\frac{3}{5} \Rightarrow \quad \tan\theta = -\frac{4}{5}$

$$\Rightarrow \quad m = -\frac{4}{5}$$

Hence, the required equation of the given line is

$$y - 2 = -\frac{4}{5}(x-1) \Rightarrow \quad 4x + 5y = 14$$

Ex-4. A line pass through the point A(2, 0) which makes an angle of 30° with the +ve direction of x-axis and is rotated about A in clockwise direction through an angle of $15°$. Find the equation of the straight line in the new position.

Soln. We have, $m = \tan(15°) = (2-\sqrt{3})$

Hence, required equation of line is $y - 0 = (2-\sqrt{3})(x-2)$

$$\Rightarrow \quad (2-\sqrt{3})x - y - 2(2-\sqrt{3}) = 0$$

iii. **The two point form of a line** : The equation of a line passing through two given points (x_1, y_1) and (x_2, y_2) is

$$y - y_1 = \left(\frac{y_2 - y_2}{x_2 - x_1}\right) \times (x - x_1) \quad \text{or}$$

$$y - y_2 = \left(\frac{y_2 - y_2}{x_2 - x_1}\right) \times (x - x_2) \quad \text{or}$$

$$\begin{vmatrix} x & y & 1 \\ x_1 & y_1 & 1 \\ x_2 & y_2 & 1 \end{vmatrix} = 0 \quad \text{or} \quad \begin{vmatrix} x - x_1 & y - y_1 \\ x_1 - x_2 & y_1 - y_2 \end{vmatrix} = 0$$

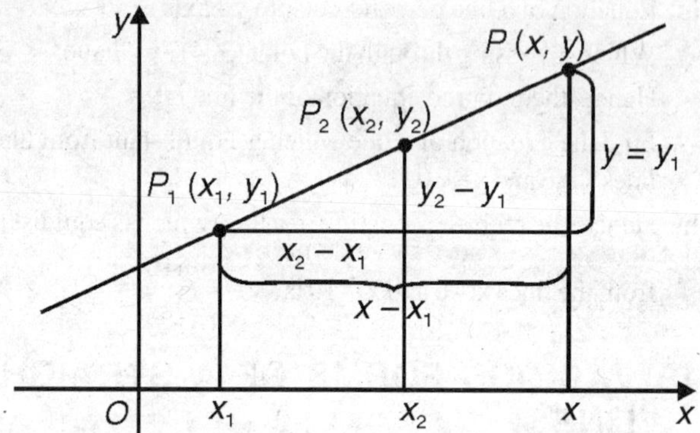

Ex-1. Find the equation of a line , passing through the points (1, 2) and (3, 4).

Soln. Hence, the required equation of a line is

$$\begin{vmatrix} x - x_1 & y - y_1 \\ x_1 - x_2 & y_1 - y_2 \end{vmatrix} = 0$$

$$\Rightarrow \quad \begin{vmatrix} x-1 & y-2 \\ 3\text{-}1 & 4\text{-}2 \end{vmatrix} = 0$$

$$\Rightarrow \quad 2(x-1) - 2(y-2) = 0$$

$$\Rightarrow \quad x - y + 1 = 0.$$

Ex-2. The vertices of a triangle are A(10, 4) , B(-4, 9) and C (–2, –1). Find the equation of its altitude through A.

Soln. Here slope of BC = $\frac{-1-9}{-2+4} = -\frac{10}{2} = -5$

Hence, the required equation of the altitude through *A* is

$$y - 4 = \frac{1}{5}(x - 10) \Rightarrow \quad x\text{-}5y + 10 = 0$$

Ex-3. The vertices of a triangle are A(1, 2) , B(2, 3) and C(5, 4) . Find the equation of its median through A.

Soln. The co-ordinates of the mid points of B and C are

$$\left(\frac{2+5}{2}, \frac{3+4}{3}\right)=\left(\frac{7}{2}, \frac{7}{2}\right)$$

Hence, the required equation of the median through A is

$$\begin{vmatrix} x-1 & y-2 \\ \frac{7}{2}-1 & \frac{7}{2}-2 \end{vmatrix}=0$$

$\Rightarrow \quad 3(x-1)-5(y-2)=0$

$\Rightarrow \quad 3x-5y+7=0$

Ex-4. Find the equation of the internal bisector of $\angle BAC$ of the ΔABC, whose vertices are A(5, 2), B (2, 3) and C(6, 5).

Soln. Here, $AB=\sqrt{10},\ AC=\sqrt{10},\ BC=2\sqrt{10}$

Let AD is the internal bisector of the angle $\angle BAC$ If AD is the internal bisector of the angle $\angle BAC$, then

$$\frac{BD}{DC}=\frac{AB}{AC}=\frac{\sqrt{10}}{\sqrt{10}}=\frac{1}{1} \qquad \Rightarrow \ BD:DC=1:1$$

Thus D is the mid - point of B and C . i.e. $D=(4,4)$

Hence, the required equation of the internal bisector is

$$y-2=\frac{4-2}{4-5}(x-5)=-2(x-5)$$

$\Rightarrow \quad 2x+y=12$

Ex-5. A square is inscribed in a triangle ABC , whose co-ordinates are A(0, 0) , B(2, 1) and C(3, 0) .
If two of its vertices lie on the side AC , then find the vertices of the given square.

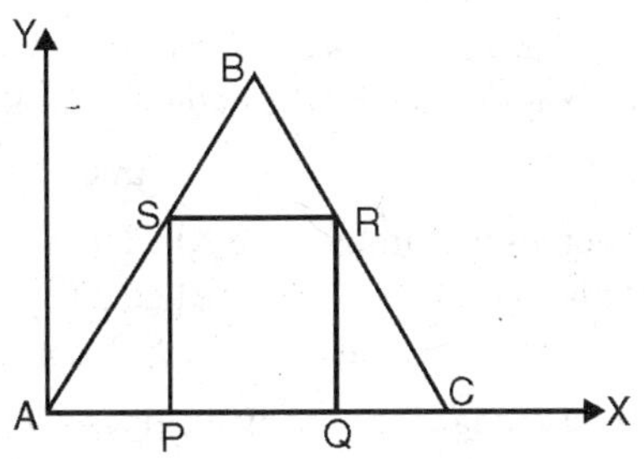

Let the square be PQRS, whose length of the side is k

Consider the point of P be (a, 0) . Then Q = (a + k, 0) , R = (a + k, k) and S = (a, k).

The equation of the line AB is $y-0=\frac{1-0}{2-0}(x-0)$

$\Rightarrow \quad x-2y=0$ ....(i)

and the equation of the line BC is $y-1=\frac{0-1}{3-2}(x-2)$

$\Rightarrow \quad x+y=3$ ....(ii)

Since, the point S (a,k) on (i) , we get , $a=2k$ and the point R (a + k , k) on (ii) , we get,

$a+2k=3$. Thus, $k=3/4$ and $a=3/2$.

Hence, the co-ordinates of P , Q, R and S are (3/2 , 0), (9/4, 0) , (9/4, 3/4) and (3/2 , 3/4).

Ex-6. The line joining the points A(2, 0) and B(3,1) is rotated about A in the anticlock wise direction through an angle of 15° . Find the equation of a line in the new posi tion .

Soln.

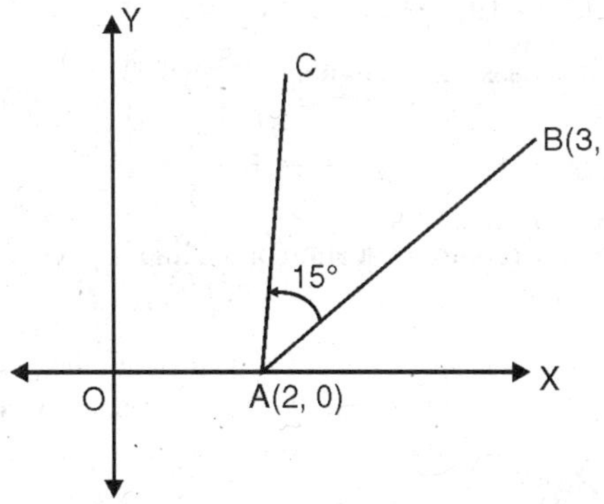

Let slope of AC is m. The slope of AB is 1.

We have $\tan(15°)=\left|\frac{m-1}{1+m}\right|$

$\Rightarrow \quad (2-\sqrt{3})m+(2-\sqrt{3})=m-1$

$\Rightarrow \quad (1-\sqrt{3})m=(-3+\sqrt{3})$

$\Rightarrow \quad (1-\sqrt{3})m=(-3+\sqrt{3})=\sqrt{3}(1-\sqrt{3})$

$\Rightarrow \quad m=\sqrt{3}$

Hence, required equation of line AC is $y-0=\sqrt{3}(x-2)$

$\Rightarrow \quad x\sqrt{3}-y-2\sqrt{3}=0$

iv. **Intercept form of a line** : The equation of a straight line which cuts off intercepts of a and b on x and y - axes respectively is

$$\frac{x}{a}+\frac{y}{b}=1.$$

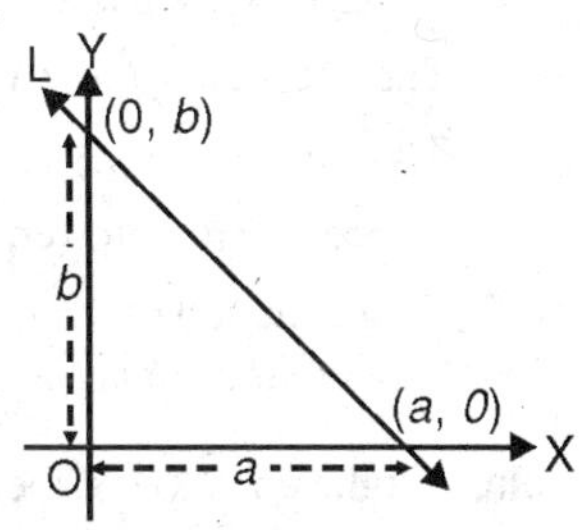

Note :

1. Here a and b may be +ve or -ve
2. Intercept cut on negative side of x and y axes are taken as -ve.

Ex-1. Find the equation of a line which passes through the point (3, 4) and makes equal intercept on the axes.

Soln. Let the equation of the line is $\frac{x}{a}+\frac{y}{b}=1$.

Since, the line make equal intercept with the axes, so a = b.

Thus $x+y=a$.

Which is passing through (3, 4) . Thefore a = 7.

Hence, the equation of the required line is $x+y=7$.

Ex-2. Find the equation of a line which passes through the point (2, 3) and whose x-intercept is twice of y-intercept.

Soln. Let the equation of the line is $\frac{x}{a}+\frac{y}{b}=1$ ....(i)

Given condition is $a=2b$ ....(ii)

From (i) and (ii) , we get, $2x+y=2b$

Which is passing through the point (2, 3)

Therefore, $2b=4+3=7 \Rightarrow b=\frac{7}{2}$

Hence, the required equation of the line is $2x+y=7$.

Ex-3. Find the equation of a line passes through the point (2, 3) so that the segment of the line intercepted between the axes is bisected at this point.

Soln. Let the equation of the line be $\frac{x}{a}+\frac{y}{b}=1$, where $A=(a,0)$ and $B=(0,b)$

Consider the given line is bisected at the point $M(2, 3)$

Thus, $2=\frac{a}{2} \Rightarrow a=4$ and $3=\frac{b}{2} \Rightarrow b=6$.

Hence, the required equation of the line is

$\frac{x}{4}+\frac{y}{6}=1 \Rightarrow 3x+2y=12$.

Ex-4. Find the equation of a line passing though the point (3, –4) and cutting off intercepts equal but of opposite signs from the two axes.

Soln. Let the equation of the line be $\frac{x}{a}+\frac{y}{b}=1$, where $A=(a,0)$ and $B=(0,b)$

Given condition is $a=-b$

Therefore , $x-y=a$. Which is passing through (3, - 4)

Thus, a = 7.

Hence, the required equation of the line is $x-y=7$.

Ex-5. Find equation of a line passing through point (3, 2) and cutts of intercepts a and b on x, y-axes such that a -b = 2.

Soln. Let the equation of the line is $\frac{x}{a}+\frac{y}{b}=1$.

Which is passing through (3,2) , so $\frac{3}{a}+\frac{2}{b}=1$ ....(i)

Also given condition is $a-b=2$ ....(ii)

From (i) and (ii) , we get, $3b+2a=ab=b(b+2)$

$\Rightarrow \quad 3b+2b+4=b^2+2b$

$\Rightarrow \quad b^2-3b-4=0$

$\Rightarrow \quad (b-4)(b+1)=0$

$\Rightarrow \quad b=-1, 4$

Thus, $a=1, 6$.

Hence, the required equation of the line are $x-y=1$, $2x-3y=12$.

Ex-6. Find the area of a triangle formed by lines $xy=0$ and $2x+3y=6$.

Soln.

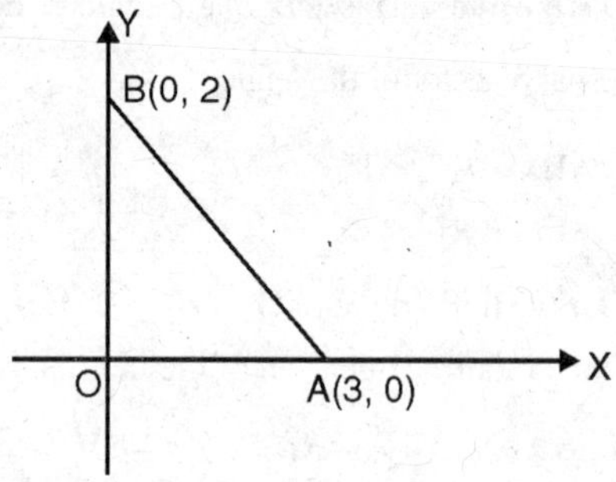

Let equation of line AB is $2x+3y=6 \Rightarrow \frac{x}{3}+\frac{y}{2}=1$

Given lines are $xy=0 \Rightarrow x=0,\ y=0$

Hence, the required area of a triangle = $\frac{1}{2}.3.2=3$ sq. u.

EXERCISE - 4

Q.1. Find the equation of a straight line passing through the point (3, 4) so that the segment of the ine intercepted between the axes is divided by the point in the ratio 2:3.

Ans. $2x+y=10$.

Q.2. Find the equation of the straight line which pass through the origin and trisect the intercept of the line $3x+4y=12$.

Ans. $3x-8y=0$, $3x-2y=0$.

Q.3. Find the area of a triangle formed by the lines $xy-x-y+1=0$ and $3x+4y=12$. **Ans.** 25/24 sq.U.

Q.4 A straight line cuts off intercepts from the axes of co-ordinates the sum of the reciprocals of which is a constant. Show that it always passes through a fixed point.

v. **Normal form of a line:**

The equation of the straight line upon which the length of perpendicular from the origin is p and this normal makes an angle α with the +ve direction of x-axis is $x\cos\alpha + y\sin\alpha = p$.

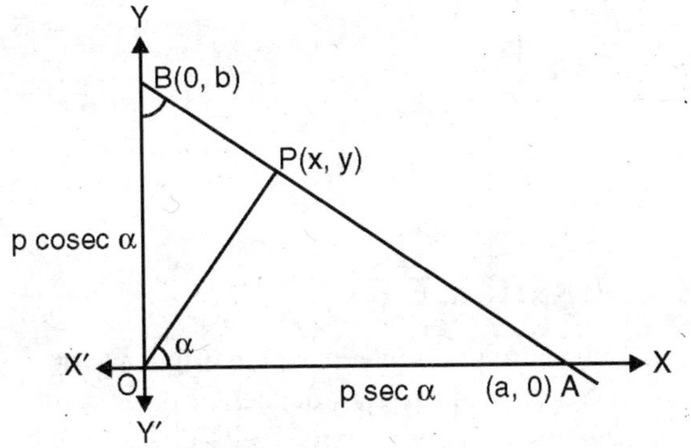

Note:

1. Here, p is always taken is +ve and α is measured from +ve direction of x-axis in anti-clockwise direction such that $0 \le \alpha < 2\pi$.

Ex-1. The length of perpendicular from the origin to a line is 5 and the line makes angle of 60° with the +ve direction of y-axis. Find the equation of the line.

Soln. Here , $p=5$ and $a = 60^o$

Hence, required equation of line is $x \cos a + y \sin a = p$

$\Rightarrow \quad x \cos(60^o) + y \sin(60^o) = 5$

$\Rightarrow \quad x + \sqrt{3}\, y = 10$.

Ex-2. Find the equation of the straight line upon which the length of the perpendicular from the origin is 2 and slope of the perpendicular is 5/12.

Soln. Here, $p=2$ and $\tan\theta = \frac{5}{12}$

$\Rightarrow \quad \sin\theta = \frac{5}{13}$ & $\cos\theta = \frac{12}{13}$

Hence, required equation of line is $x \cos? + y\sin? = p$

$\Rightarrow 12x + 5y = 26$

vi. **Distance form or parametric form or symmetric form of a line :**

The equation of a line passing through the point (x_1, y_1) and making angle θ with the +ve direction of x-axis is $\frac{x - x_1}{\cos\theta} = \frac{y - y_1}{\sin\theta} = r$, where r is the distance of the point (x, y) from the point (x_1, y_1).

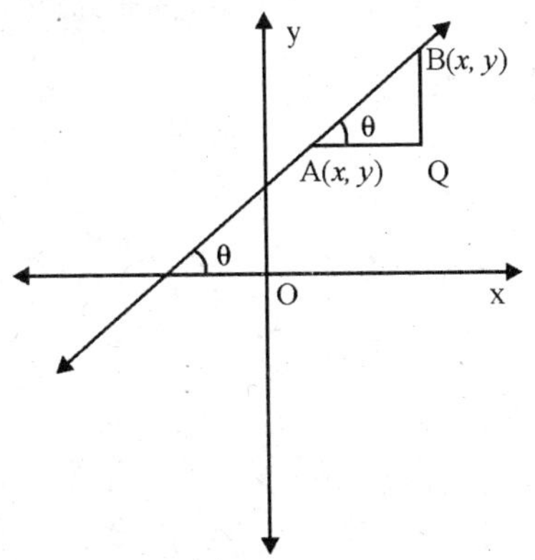

Note:

1. If $Q(x_1, y_1)$ be a point on a line AB which makes an angle θ with the +ve direction of x-axis , then there will be two points on the line AB at distance r from $Q(x_1, y_1)$ and their co-ordinates will be $(x_1 \pm r\cos?,\ y_1 \pm r\sin?)$

2. If a point , say, P lies above $Q(x_1, y_1)$ on the line AB , then we consider r is +ve . Thus, the co-ordinates of P will be $(x_1 + r\cos\theta,\ y_1 + r\sin\theta)$.

3. If a point , say, R lies below $Q(x_1, y_1)$ on the line AB , then we consider r is -ve.Thus , the co-ordinates of R will be $(x_1 - r\cos\theta,\ y_1 - r\sin\theta)$

Ex-1. A line passing through the point (3, 2) and making an angle θ with the +ve direction of x-axis such that $\tan\theta = \frac{3}{4}$. Find the co-ordinates of the points on the line that are 5 units away from the given point.

Soln.: Hence, the co-ordinates of the required points are $(x_1 \pm r\cos\theta,\ y_1 \pm r\sin\theta)$. Here $r=5$,

$(x_1, y_1) = (3, 2)$ and $\tan\theta = \frac{3}{4} \Rightarrow \cos\theta = \frac{4}{5},\ \sin\theta = \frac{3}{5}$

Thus, the required points are $(x_1 \pm r\cos\theta,\ y_1 \pm r\sin\theta)$ =

$$\left(3 \pm 5.\frac{4}{5},\ 2 \pm 5.\frac{3}{5}\right) = (3 \pm 4,\ 2 \pm 3) = (7, 5), (-1, -1)$$

Ex-2. Find the co-ordinates of the points at a distance $4\sqrt{2}$ units from the point (-2,3) in the direction making an angle of $45°$ with the +ve direction of x-axis.

Soln. Here, $r = 4\sqrt{2}$, $(x_1, y_1) = (-2, 3)$ and $? = 45°$.

Hence, co-ordinates of required points are $(x_1 \pm r\cos\theta,\ y_1 \pm r\sin\theta)$

$$= \left(-2 \pm 4\sqrt{2}.\frac{1}{\sqrt{2}}, 3 \pm 4\sqrt{2}.\frac{1}{\sqrt{2}}\right) = (-2 \pm 4, 3 \pm 4) = (2, 7)\ \&(-6, -1)$$

Ex-3. A point P(3, 4) moves in a plane in the direction of $\hat{i} + \hat{j}$. Then find the new position of P

Soln. Given point P is (3, 4)

Here , $r = \sqrt{2}$ & $\theta = 45°$

Let Q be the new position of P.

Hence, the required co-ordinates of Q are

$$\left(3 + \sqrt{2}.\frac{1}{\sqrt{2}},\ 4 + \sqrt{2}.\frac{1}{\sqrt{2}}\right) = (4, 5)$$

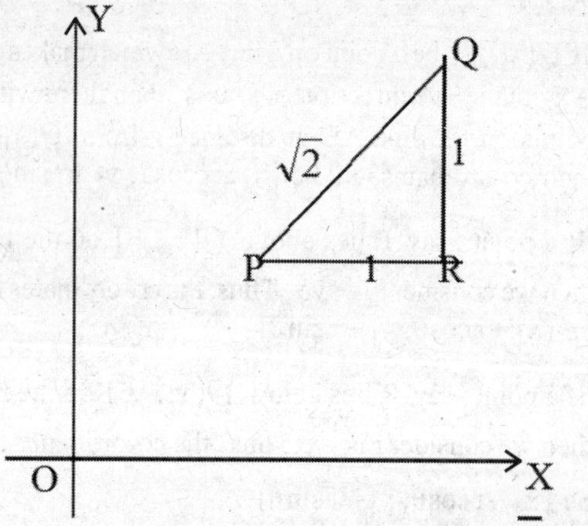

Ex-4. A line joining two points A(2, 0) and B(3, 1) is rotated about A in anti-clockwise direction through an angle of $15°$. Find the new position of B.

Soln.: Let the new position of B is C.

Here, $r = AB = AC = \sqrt{(3-2)^2 + (1-0)^2} = \sqrt{2}$ and

$? = 45° + 15° = 60°$

Thus, the co-ordinates of C are

$$\left(2+\sqrt{2}\cos(60°),\ 0+\sqrt{2}\sin(60°)\right)$$

$$= \left(2+\sqrt{2}.\frac{1}{2},\ \sqrt{2}.\frac{\sqrt{3}}{2}\right) = \left(2+\frac{1}{\sqrt{2}},\ \sqrt{\frac{3}{2}}\right).$$

Ex-5. Find the direction in which a straight line must be drawn through the point (1, 2) so that its point of intersection with the line x + y = 4 may be at a distance $\sqrt{\frac{2}{3}}$ from the point (1,2).

Soln. Let the point P be (1, 2) and the line PQ makes an angle θ with the +ve direction of x - axis.

Here, $r = \sqrt{\frac{2}{3}}$ and $(x_1, y_1) = (1, 2)$

Thus, co-ordinates of Q are $\left(1+\sqrt{\frac{2}{3}}\cos\theta,\ 2+\sqrt{\frac{2}{3}}\sin\theta\right)$

Since, the point Q lies on $x + y = 4$,

so $1+\sqrt{\frac{2}{3}}\cos\theta + 2 + \sqrt{\frac{2}{3}}\sin\theta = 4$

$\Rightarrow \quad \sqrt{\frac{2}{3}}\cos\theta + \sqrt{\frac{2}{3}}\sin\theta = 1$

$\Rightarrow \quad \cos\theta + \sin\theta = \sqrt{\frac{3}{2}}$

$\Rightarrow \quad \frac{1}{\sqrt{2}}\cos\theta + \frac{1}{\sqrt{2}}\sin\theta = \frac{\sqrt{3}}{2}$

$\Rightarrow \quad \left(\theta - \frac{\pi}{4}\right) = \pm\left(\frac{\pi}{6}\right)$

$\Rightarrow \quad \theta = \frac{\pi}{4} \pm \frac{\pi}{6} = 75°,\ 15°$

EXERCISE - 5

Q.1. The centre of a square is at the origin and one vertex is P(2, 1). Find the co-ordinates of other vertices of the square. **Ans.** R(-2, -1), Q(-1, 2) & S(1, -2)

Q.2. The extremities of a diagonal of a square are (1, 1) and (-2, -1). Find the other two vertices.

Ans. $\left(-\frac{3}{2}, \frac{3}{2}\right)$ & $\left(\frac{1}{2}, -\frac{3}{2}\right)$.

Q.3. A line through (2,3) makes an angle $\frac{3\pi}{4}$ with the -ve direction of x-axis. Find the length of the line segment cut off between (2, 3) and the line x + y = 7. **Ans.** $\sqrt{2}$

Q.4. If the straight line drawn through the point $P(\sqrt{3}, 2)$ and making an angle of $\frac{\pi}{6}$ with the x-axis meets the line $\sqrt{3}x - 4y + 8 = 0$ at Q. Find the length of PQ. **Ans.** 6.

Q.5. Find the distance of the point (2, 3) from the line 2 x - 3 y + 9 = 0 measured along line 2 x - 2 y + 5 = 0. **Ans.** $4\sqrt{2}$

Q.6 Find the distance of the point (3, 5) from the line 2x + 3y = 14 measured parallel to the line x - 2 y = 1 **Ans.** $\sqrt{5}$

Q.7. Find the distance of the point (2, 5) from the line 3x + y + 4 = 0 measured parallel to the line 3 x - 4 y + 8 = 0. **Ans.** 5.

Q.8 A line is drawn through A(4, -1) parallel to the line 3 x - 4 y + 1 = 0. Find the co-ordinates of the two points on this line which area at a distance of 5 units from A.

Ans. (8, 2) & (0, -4).

1.21 REDUCTION OF GENERAL EQUATION INTO STANDARD FORM

Let $Ax + By + C = 0$ be the genral equation of a straight line, where $A^2 + B^2 \neq 0$.

i. Reduction into slope intercept form : Given equation is

$Ax + By + C = 0$

$\Rightarrow By = -Ax - C \Rightarrow y = -\left(\frac{A}{B}\right)x - \left(\frac{C}{B}\right)$

which is in the form of $y = mx + c$

ii. Reduction into intercept form : Given equation is

$Ax + By + C = 0$.

$\Rightarrow Ax + By = -C \Rightarrow \frac{Ax}{-C} + \frac{By}{-C} = 1$

$$\Rightarrow \frac{x}{\left(-\frac{C}{A}\right)}+\frac{y}{\left(-\frac{C}{B}\right)}=1$$, which is in the form of

$$\frac{x}{a}+\frac{y}{b}=1$$

iii. Reduction into normal form : Given equation is

$$A x+B y+C=0 . \Rightarrow -Ax-By=C$$

$$\Rightarrow \left(\frac{-A}{\sqrt{A^2+B^2}}\right)x-\left(\frac{-B}{\sqrt{A^2+B^2}}\right)y=\frac{C}{\left(\sqrt{A^2+B^2}\right)}$$

which is the normal form of the line $Ax+By+C=0$.

Ex-1. Reduce $x+\sqrt{3}\,y+4=0$ into the

i. Slope intercept form and also find its slope and y-intercept.

ii. Intercept form and also find the !enthgs of x and y intercepts.

iii. Normal form and also find the values of p and α.

Soln. Given line is $x+\sqrt{3}\,y+4=0$

i. Slope intercept form is $\Rightarrow$ $y=\left(-\frac{1}{\sqrt{3}}\right)x+\left(-\frac{4}{\sqrt{3}}\right)$

Thus, slope $=-\frac{1}{\sqrt{3}}$ and y - intercept $=-\frac{4}{\sqrt{3}}$

ii. Intercept form of $x+\sqrt{3}\,y+4=0$ is $\frac{x}{(-4)}+\frac{y}{\left(-\frac{4}{\sqrt{3}}\right)}=1$

where x - intercept = 4 and y - intercept = $4/\sqrt{3}$.

iii. Normal form of $x+\sqrt{3}y+4=0$ is $-x-\sqrt{3}y=4$

$$\Rightarrow \left(-\frac{1}{4}\right)x+\left(\frac{-\sqrt{3}}{4}\right)y=1$$

$$\Rightarrow x\cos a+y\sin a=1, \text{where } a=p+\tan^{-1}\left(\sqrt{3}\right)=240°$$

6. Position of two points with respect to a given line :

The points $P(x_1, y_1)$ and $Q(x_2, y_2)$ lie on the same or

opposite sides of the line $ax+by+c=0$ according as

$$\frac{ax_1+by_1+c}{ax_2+by_2+c}>0 \text{ or } <0 .$$

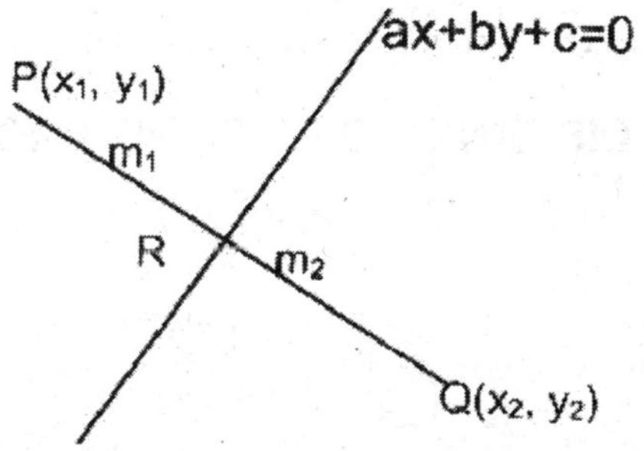

Note:

1. The side of line, where origin lies, is known as origin side.
2. A point (α, β) will lie on origin side of the line $ax+by+c=0$, if $a\alpha+b\beta+c$ and c have same sign.
3. A point (α, β) will lie on non-origin side of the line $ax+by+c=0$, if $a\alpha+b\beta+c$ and c have opposite signs.

Ex-1. Find the location of the points (2, 2) & (3, 5) with respect to the line

i. $2x+3y+4=0$

ii. $3x-2y+2=0$

iii. $x+y-7=0$.

Soln. i. Let $(x_1, y_1)=(2, 2)$ & $(x_2, y_2)=(3, 5)$ and a = 2 b = 3, c = 4.

Now, $\frac{ax_1+by_1+c}{ax_2+by_2+c}=\frac{2.2+3.2+4}{2.3+3.5+4}=\frac{14}{25}>0$

Thus, the points (2, 2) and (3, 5) lie on the same side of the line $2x+3y+4=0$.

ii. Do yourself

iii. Do yourself.

Ex-2. Determine whether the point (2, -7) lies on the origin side of the line $2x+y+2=0$ or not.

Soln. As we know that, if ax_1+by_1+c and c have the same sign, then the point (x_1, y_1) lies on the origin side of the line ax_1+by_1+c

Here, $2>0$ and $ax_1+by_1+c=2.2-7+2=6-7=-1<0$

Thus, the point (2, -7) does not lie on the origin side of the line $2x+y+2=0$.

1.21 EQUATION OF A LINE PARALLEL TO A GIVEN LINE

The equation of any line parallel to a given line $ax+by+c=0$ is $ax+by+k=0$

Note:

1. The equation of a line parallel to $ax+by+c=0$ and passing through (x_1, y_1) is $a(x-x_1)+b(y-y_1)=0$

Ex-1. Write the parallel line to each of the following lines.

i. $3x-4y+10=0$ ii. $2x+5y+10=0$

iii. $-x+y-2012=0$ iv. $y=x$

v. $x=5$ vi. $y=2013$

Soln. Do yourself.

Ex-2. Find the equation of a line parallel to $3x+4y+5=0$ and passes through (2,3).

Soln. Equation of a line parallel to $3x+4y+5=0$

is $3x+4y+k=0$

Which is passing through (2, 3) .

Therefore, $6+12+k=0 \Rightarrow \quad k=-18$

Hence, the required equation of line is $3x+4y-18=0$.

Ex-3. Find the equation of a line parallel to $3x-4y+6=0$ and passing through mid point of line joining points (2, 3) and (4,-1)

Soln. The co-ordinates of the mid-point of the line joining the points (2, 3) and (4, -1) is (3, 1).

Equation of any line parallel to $3x-4y+6=0$

`is $3x-4y+k=0$.

Which is passing through (3, 1) .

Therefore, $9-4+k=0 \Rightarrow \quad k=-5$.

Hence, the required equation of the line is $3x-4y-5=0$.

Ex-4. Find the equation of a line passing through (2, 1) and paral lel to the line joining the points (2, 3) and (3, -1).

Soln. The slope of the line joining the points (2, 3) and (3, - 1) is

$=\frac{-1-3}{3-2}=-4$

Equation of the line parallel to the given line and passing thorugh (2,1) is $y-y_1=m(x-x_1)$

$\Rightarrow \quad y-1=-4(x-2)$

$\Rightarrow \quad 4x+y=9$.

1.22 EQUATION OF A LINE PERPENDICULAR TO A GIVEN LINE

The equation of any line perpendicular to a given line $ax+by+c=0$ is $bx-ay+k=0$.

Note :. The equation of any line perpendicular to $ax+by+c=0$ and passing through (x_1, y_1) is $b(x-x_1)-a(y-y_1)=0$.

Ex-1. Write the perpendicular line to each of the following lines.

i. $5x-3y+2010=0$ ii. $3x+5y+2011=0$

iii. $-x+y-2012=0$ iv. $y=2011x$

v. $x=2014$ vi. $y=2013$.

Soln. Do yourself.

Ex-2. Find the equation of a line perpendicular to $2x+3y-2012=0$ and passing through (3, 4).

Soln. Equation of any line perpendicular to $2x+3y-2012=0$ is $3x-2y+k=0$.

Which is passing through (3, 4) .

Therefore, $9-8+k=0 \Rightarrow \quad k=-1$

Hence, the required equation of the line is $3x-2y-1=0$.

Ex-3. Find the equation of a line perpendicular to $2x-3y-5=0$ and cutting an intercept 1 on the x-axis.

Soln. Equation of any line perpendicular to $2x-3y-5=0$

is $3x+2y-k=0$

Which is passing through (1, 0)

Therefore, $3+0+k=0 \Rightarrow \quad k=-3$

Hence, the required equation of the line is $3x+2y+3=0$.

Ex-4. Find the equation of the right bisectors of the line joining the points (1, 2) and (3, 5).

Soln. The slope of the line joining the points (1, 2) and (3, 5) is $\frac{5-2}{3-1}=\frac{3}{2}$

The mid-point of the line joining the points (1, 2) and (3, 5)

is $\left(\frac{1+3}{2}, \frac{2+5}{2}\right)=\left(2, \frac{7}{2}\right)$

Hence, the required equation of line is $y-\frac{7}{2}=-\frac{2}{3}(x-2)$

$\Rightarrow \quad 4x+6y=29$

Ex-5. Find the equation of the altitude through A of a triangle ABC, whose vertices are A(1, 2), B(4, 5) and C(3, 8).

Soln. Solpe of BC $=\frac{8-5}{3-4}=-3$

Let the altitude through A is AD .

Therefore, the slope of AD is $\frac{1}{3}$.

Hence, the required equation of the altitude through A is

$y-2=\frac{1}{3}(x-1) \Rightarrow \quad x-3y+5=0$.

Ex-6. Find the equation of a line passing through the point of intersection of the lines $2x+y=8$ and $x-y=10$ and perpendicular to $3x+4y+2012=0$.

Soln. The point of intersection of $2x+y=8$ and $x-y=10$ is (6, - 4).

Equation of any line perpendicular to $3x+4y+2012=0$ is $4x-3y+k=0$.

Which is passing through (6, - 4) .

Therefore, $24+12+k=0 \Rightarrow \quad k=-36$

Hence, the required equation of the line is $4x-3y-36=0$

1.23 DISTANCE OF A POINT FROM A LINE

The length of perpendicular from a point (x_1, y_1) to the line $ax+by+c=0$ is $\left|\frac{ax_1+by_1+c}{\sqrt{a^2+b^2}}\right|$

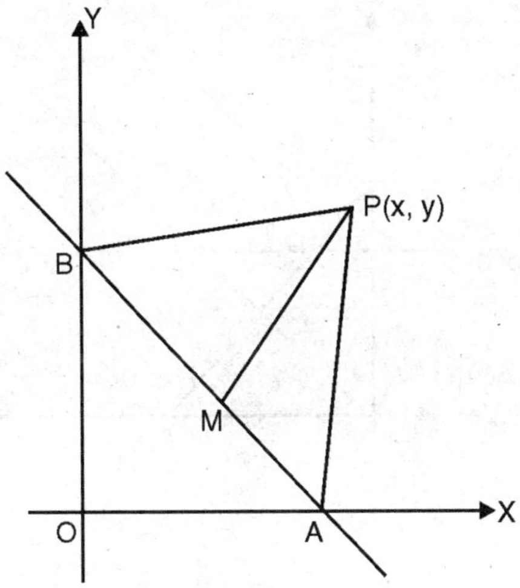

R-1. The length of perpendicular from the origin to the line

$ax+by+c=0$ is $\left|\dfrac{c}{\sqrt{a^2+b^2}}\right|$

R-2. The distance between two parallel lines are

$ax+by+c_1=0$ and $ax+by+c_2=0$ is $\left|\dfrac{c_1-c_2}{\sqrt{a^2+b^2}}\right|$

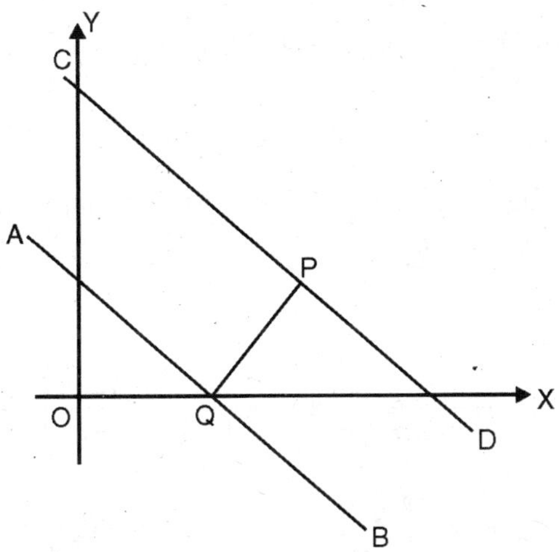

R-3. Area of a parallelogram whose sides are $a_1x+b_1y+c_1=0$, $a_1x+b_1y+d_1=0$,

$a_2x+b_2y+c_2=0$ and $a_2x+b_2y+d_2=0$ is

$$=\frac{p_1\times p_2}{\sin\theta}=\left|\frac{(c_1-d_1)(c_2-d_2)}{(a_1b_2-a_2b_1)}\right|\text{., where}$$

p_1 = distance between two parallel sides

$a_1x+b_1y+c_1=0$, $a_1x+b_1y+d_1=0$

is $=\left|\dfrac{(c_1-d_1)}{\sqrt{a_1^2+b_1^2}}\right|$

p_2 = distance between two parallel sides

$a_2x+b_2y+c_2=0, a_2x+b_2y+d_2=0$

is $=\left|\dfrac{(c_2-d_2)}{\sqrt{a_2^2+b_2^2}}\right|$.

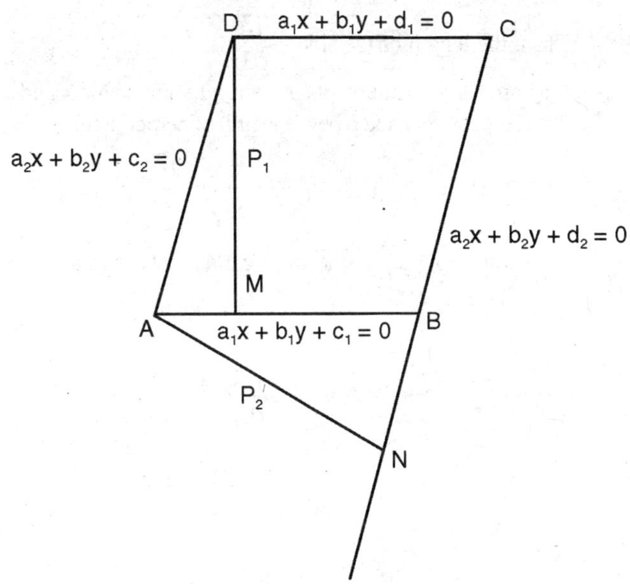

R-4. If $p_1=p_2$, then the parallelogram becomes a rhombus and its area is

$$\frac{(c_1-d_1)^2}{|(a_1b_2-a_2b_1)|\sqrt{\left(\dfrac{a_1^2+b_1^2}{a_2^2+b_2^2}\right)}}.$$

R-5. Area of a parallelogram whose sides are $y=mx+a$, $y=mx+b$, $y=nx+c$ and $y=nx+d$

is $\left|\dfrac{(a-b)(c-d)}{(m-n)}\right|$.

Ex-1. Find the distance of the point (4, 5) from the straight line $3x-5y+7=0$.

Soln. Hence, the required distance of the point (4, 5) from the straight line $3x-5y+7=0$ is

$$=\left|\frac{3\times4-5\times5+7}{\sqrt{3^2+5^2}}\right|=\left|\frac{12-25+7}{\sqrt{34}}\right|=\frac{6}{\sqrt{34}}.$$

Ex-2. The equation of the base of an equilateral traingle be $x+y=2$ and the vertex is $(2,-1)$. Find the length of the sides of the traingle.

Soln. Let ABC be an equilateral triangle, where A is (2, -1) and BC is $x+y=2$.

Let AD be the length of perpendicular from A on BC.

Thus, $AD = \left|\dfrac{2-1-2}{\sqrt{1^2+1^2}}\right| = \dfrac{1}{\sqrt{2}}$

Therefore, $\sin(60°) = \dfrac{AD}{AB}$

$\Rightarrow \quad AB = \dfrac{2}{\sqrt{3}} \times \dfrac{1}{\sqrt{2}} = \sqrt{\dfrac{2}{3}}$

Thus, the length of the side $= \sqrt{\dfrac{2}{3}}$

Ex-3. If a and b are the intercepts of a straight line on the x and y axes respectively and p be the length of perpendicular from the origin, then prove that $\dfrac{1}{a^2} + \dfrac{1}{b^2} = \dfrac{1}{p^2}$

Soln. Equation of a straight line, whose intercepts are a and b is

$\dfrac{x}{a} + \dfrac{y}{b} = 1$.

Given, the length of the perpendicular from the origin = p

$$\Rightarrow \quad \left|\dfrac{0+0-1}{\sqrt{\dfrac{1}{a^2}+\dfrac{1}{b^2}}}\right| = p$$

$$\Rightarrow \quad \dfrac{1}{a^2} + \dfrac{1}{b^2} = \dfrac{1}{p^2}$$

Ex-4. Find the distance between the lines $3x - 4y = 5$ and $6x - 8y + 11 = 0$

Soln. Clearly, both the lines are parallel.

Hence, the required distance =

$$\left|\dfrac{\dfrac{11}{2}+5}{\sqrt{3^2+4^2}}\right| = \left|\dfrac{11+10}{2.5}\right| = \dfrac{21}{10} = 2\dfrac{1}{10} \text{ units.}$$

Ex-5. Let L has intercepts a and b on the co-ordinate axes. When the axes are rotated through an angle, keeping the origin fixed, the same line L has intercepts p and q, then prove that $\dfrac{1}{a^2} + \dfrac{1}{b^2} = \dfrac{1}{p^2} + \dfrac{1}{q^2}$

Soln. Equation of the line L is $\dfrac{x}{a} + \dfrac{y}{b} = 1$

After rotation, the line L becomes, $\dfrac{x}{p} + \dfrac{y}{q} = 1$

Therefore, the lengths of perpendicular from the origin to both the lines are same.

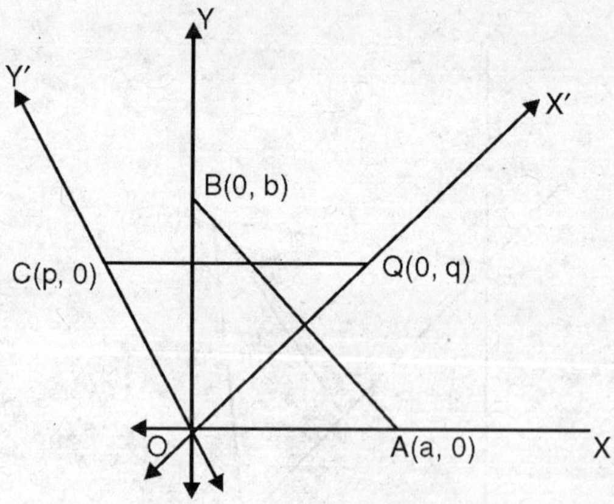

Thus, $\left|\dfrac{0+0-1}{\sqrt{\dfrac{1}{a^2}+\dfrac{1}{b^2}}}\right| = \left|\dfrac{0+0-1}{\sqrt{\dfrac{1}{p^2}+\dfrac{1}{q^2}}}\right|$

$$\Rightarrow \quad \dfrac{1}{a^2} + \dfrac{1}{b^2} = \dfrac{1}{p^2} + \dfrac{1}{q^2}$$

Hence, the result.

Ex-6. If the area of a parallelogram formed by the lines $x + 3y = a$, $3x - 2y + 3a = 0$, $x + 3y + 4a = 0$ and $3x - 2y + 7a = 0$ is $m\,a^2$, then find the value of $11m + 30$.

Soln. As we know that, area of a parallelogram whose sides are $a_1x + b_1y + c_1 = 0$, $a_1x + b_1y + d_1 = 0$, $a_2x + b_2y + c_2 = 0$ and $a_2x + b_2y + d_2 = 0$ is =

$$\left|\dfrac{(c_1-d_1)(c_2-d_2)}{(a_1b_2-a_2b_1)}\right| \therefore = \left|\dfrac{(4a+a)\times(7a-3a)}{(1\times(-2)-3\times3)}\right| = \dfrac{20a^2}{11}$$

Thus, $m = \dfrac{20}{11}$.

Now $11m + 30 = 20 + 30 = 50$.

Ex-7. Prove that the four lines $ax \pm by \pm c = 0$ enclose a rhombus, whose area is $\dfrac{2c^2}{|ab|}$.

Soln. Given four lines are $ax + by + c = 0$, $ax + by - c = 0$, $ax - by + c = 0$ and $ax - by - c = 0$.

Hence, the required area $= \left|\dfrac{(c+c)(-c-c)}{(a.(-b)-b.a)}\right| = \left|\dfrac{4c^2}{2ab}\right| = \left|\dfrac{2c^2}{ab}\right|$

1.24 POINT OF INTERSECTION OF TWO LINES

Let $a_1x+b_1y+c_1=0$ and $a_2x+b_2y+c_2=0$ be two lines.

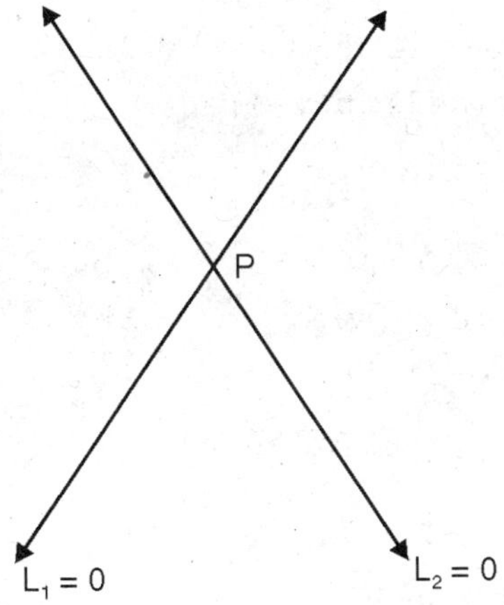

i. Simply solve the given equations and get the point of intersection P.

ii. Concurrent lines: If three or more than three lines meet at a point, then we say that these lines are concurent lines and the meeting point is known as point of concurrency.

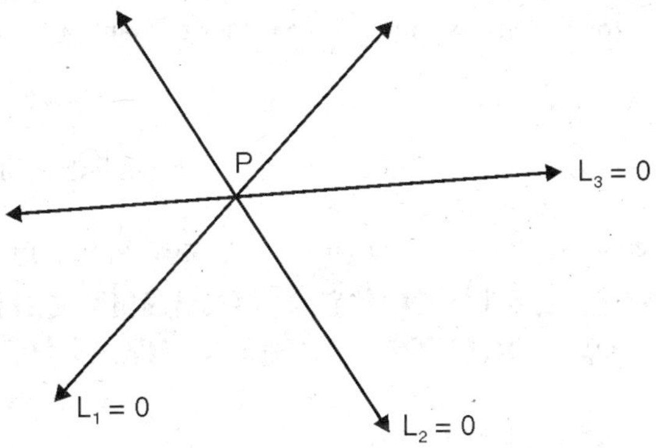

The three lines $a_ix+b_iy+c_i=0$, i = 1, 2, 3 are concurrent if

$$\begin{vmatrix} a_1 & b_1 & c_1 \\ a_2 & b_2 & c_2 \\ a_3 & b_3 & c_3 \end{vmatrix}=0$$

iii. **Family of lines:**

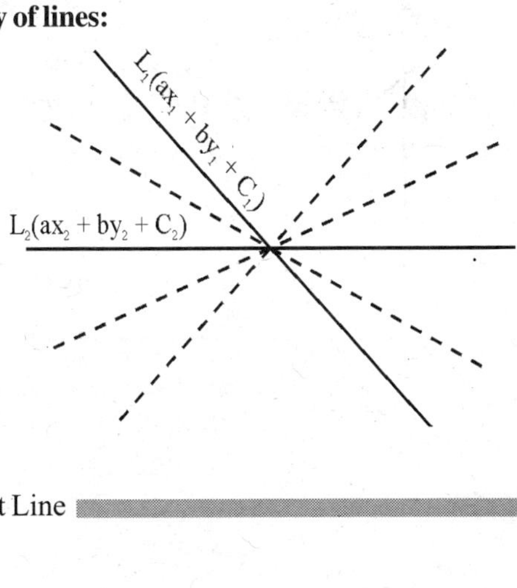

Any line passing through the point of intersection of the lines $a_1x+b_1y+c_1=0$ and $a_2x+b_2y+c_2=0$ can be defined as $(a_1x+b_1y+c_1)+\lambda(a_2x+b_2y+c_2)=0$, where $\lambda \in R$

Ex-1 Find the point of intersection of the lines $x - y + 4 = 0$ and $2x + y = 10$.

Soln. Hence, the required points of intersection of the given lines is (2, 6).

Ex-2. Prove that the three lines $2x - 3y + 5 = 0$, $3x + 4y = 7$ and $9x - 5y + 8 = 0$ are concurrent.

Soln. As we know that, the three lines $a_i x + b_i y + c_i = 0$, $i = 1$, 2, 3 are concurrent, if

Thus, we have $\begin{vmatrix} a_1 & b_1 & c_1 \\ a_2 & b_2 & c_2 \\ a_3 & b_3 & c_3 \end{vmatrix} = \begin{vmatrix} 2 & -3 & 5 \\ 3 & 4 & -7 \\ 9 & -5 & 8 \end{vmatrix} =$

$2(32-35)+3(24+63)+5(-15-36)$

$= -6+261-255$

$= 0$.

Hence, the three lines are concurrent.

Ex-3. Find the equation of line which is passing through the point of intersection of the lines $x + 3y - 8 = 0$ and $2x + 3y + 5 = 0$ and (1, 2)

Soln. Equation of any line passing through the point of intersection of the lines $x + 3y - 8 = 0$ and $2x + 3y + 5 = 0$ is

$(x-3y+8)+\lambda(2x+3y+5)=0$ ....(i)

Which is passing through (1, 2).

Therefore, $(1-6+8)+\lambda(2+6+5)=0 \Rightarrow \lambda=-\frac{3}{13}$

From (i), we get, $(x-3y+8)-\frac{3}{13}(2x+3y+5)=0$

$\Rightarrow \quad 13(x-3y+8)-3(2x+3y+5)=0$

$\Rightarrow \quad 7x-48y+89=0$.

Ex-4. Find the value of m so that the lines $y = x + 1$, $2x + y = 16$ and $y = mx - 4$ may be concurrent.

Soln. On solving $y = x + 1$ and $2x + y = 16$, we get, $x = 5$ and $y = 6$

Thus, the point of concurrency is (5, 6)

Since, the given lines are concurrent, so $6 = 5m - 4$

$\Rightarrow \quad 5m = 10 \Rightarrow \quad 5m = 10 \Rightarrow \quad m = 2$.

Hence, the value of m is 2.

Ex-5. If the lines $ax + y + 1 = 0$, $x + by + 1 = 0$ and $x + y + c = 0$ (where a , b , c are distinct and different from 1) are concurrent , then find the value of $\frac{1}{1-a}+\frac{1}{1-b}+\frac{1}{1-c}$.

Soln. Since the given lines $ax+y+1=0, x+by+1=0$ and $x+y+c=0$ are concurrent,

so $\begin{vmatrix} a & 1 & 1 \\ 1 & b & 1 \\ 1 & 1 & c \end{vmatrix}=0 \Rightarrow \begin{vmatrix} a-1 & 0 & 1 \\ 0 & b-1 & 1 \\ 1-c & 1-c & c \end{vmatrix}=0$

$\Rightarrow (a-1)(c(b-1)-(1-c))-(1-c)(b-1)=0$

$\Rightarrow c(a-1)(b-1)-(a-1)(1-c)-(1-c)(b-1)=0$

$\Rightarrow c(1-a)(1-b)+(1-a)(1-c)+(1-c)(1-b)=0$

$\Rightarrow \frac{c}{1-c}+\frac{1}{1-b}+\frac{1}{1-a}=0$

$\Rightarrow 1+\frac{c}{1-c}+\frac{1}{1-b}+\frac{1}{1-a}=1$

$\Rightarrow \frac{1}{1-a}+\frac{1}{1-b}+\frac{1}{1-c}=1$

Ex-6. If $2a+3b+6c=0$, the family of straight lines $ax+by+c=0$ passes through a fixed point. Find the co-ordinates of the fixed point.

Soln. Given family of lines are $ax+by+c=0$..................(i)

and also given condition is $2a+3b+6c=0$ ....(ii)

From (i) and (ii), we get, $ax+by-\frac{a}{3}-\frac{b}{2}=0$

$\Rightarrow a\left(x-\frac{1}{3}\right)+b\left(y-\frac{1}{2}\right)=0$

$\Rightarrow \left(x-\frac{1}{3}\right)+\frac{b}{a}\left(y-\frac{1}{2}\right)=0$

$\Rightarrow \left(x-\frac{1}{3}\right)=0 \ \& \ \left(y-\frac{1}{2}\right)=0$

$\Rightarrow x=\frac{1}{3} \ \& \ y=\frac{1}{2}$

Ex-7. If $4a^2+9b^2-c^2+12ab=0$, then the family of the straight lines $ax+by+c=0$ is either concurrent at (m, n) or (p, q). Find the value of $m+n+p+q+10$.

Soln. We have $4a^2+9b^2-c^2+12ab=0$

$\Rightarrow (4a^2+9b^2+12ab)-c^2=0$

$\Rightarrow (2a+3b)^2-c^2=0$

$\Rightarrow (2a+3b+c)(2a+3b-c)=0$

$\Rightarrow (2a+3b+c)=0 \ \& \ (2a+3b-c)=0$

Given family of lines are $ax+by+c=0$ ....(i) and also the given conditions are $(2a+3b+c)=0$ ....(ii)

and $(2a+3b-c)=0$ ....(iii)

From (i) and (ii), we get $ax+by-2a-3b=0$.

$\Rightarrow a(x-2)+b(y-3)=0$

$\Rightarrow (x-2)+\frac{b}{a}(y-3)=0$

$\Rightarrow x=2, y=3 \quad \Rightarrow m=2, n=3$

From (i) and (iii), we get, $ax+by+2a+3b=0$

$\Rightarrow a(x+2)+b(y+3)=0$

$\Rightarrow (x+2)+\frac{b}{a}(y+3)=0$

$\Rightarrow x=-2, \ y=-3$

$\Rightarrow p=-2, q=-3.$

Thus, the value of $m+n+p+q+10$

$=2+3-2-3+10=10.$

EXERCISE - 6

Q.1. The family of lines $x(a+2b)+y(a-3b)=a-b$ passes through a fixed point for all values of a and b. Find the co-ordinates of the fixed point. **Ans.** $\left(\frac{2}{5},\frac{3}{5}\right)$

Q.2 Find the equation of a line passing through the point of intersection of $2x+3y+1=0$ and $3x-5y-5=0$ and equally inclined to the axes. **Ans.** $19(x+y)+3=0$

1.25 EQUATION OF STRAIGHT LINES PASSING THROUGH A GIVEN POINT AND MAKING A GIVEN ANGLE WITH A GIVEN LINE.

The equation of the straight lines which pass through a given point (x_1, y_1) and make a given angle α with the given straight line $y=mx+c$ are $y-y_1=\tan(\theta\pm\alpha)(x-x_1)$, where $m=\tan\theta$.

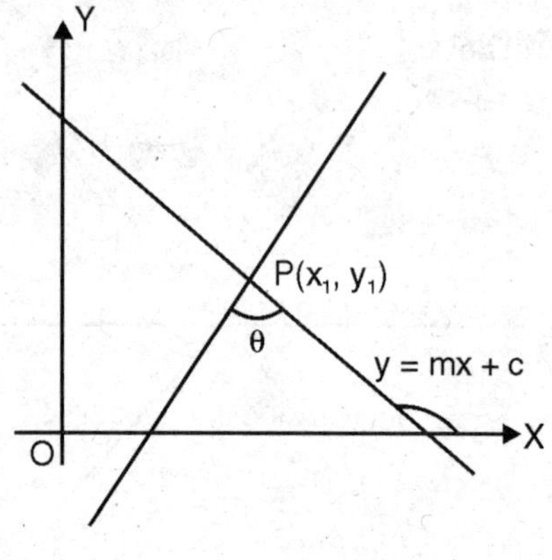

Ex-1. Find the slope of the lines which make an angle of $45°$ with the line $3x - y + 5 = 0$.

Soln. Let m be the slope of the given line and the slope of $3x - y + 5 = 0$ is 3.

Therefore, $\tan 45° = \left|\frac{m-3}{1+3m}\right|$

$$\Rightarrow \quad \frac{m-3}{1+3m} = \pm 1$$

$$\Rightarrow \quad \frac{m-3}{1+3m} = 1 \ \& \ \frac{m-3}{1+3m} = -1$$

$$\Rightarrow \quad 2m = -4 \ \& \ 4m = 2$$

$$\Rightarrow \quad m = -2 \ \& \ m = \frac{1}{2}.$$

Ex-2 Find the equations of the lines through the point (3, 2) which make an angle of $45°$ with the line $x - 2y = 3$.

Soln. Equation of any line passing through (3,2) is

$y - 2 = m(x - 3)$ ....(i)

The line makes an angle $45°$ with the line $x - 2y = 3$.

Therefore, $\tan(45°) = \left|\frac{m - \frac{1}{2}}{1 + \frac{m}{2}}\right|$

$$\Rightarrow \quad \left|\frac{2m-1}{2+m}\right| = 1$$

$$\Rightarrow \quad \frac{2m-1}{2+m} = 1 \quad \& \quad \frac{2m-1}{2+m} = -1$$

$$\Rightarrow \quad m = 3 \quad \& \quad m = -\frac{1}{3}$$

Hence, the required equation of the lines are

$$y - 2 = 3(x-3) \ \& \ y - 2 = -\frac{1}{3}(x-3)$$

$$\Rightarrow \quad 3x - y - 7 = 0 \ \& \ x + 3y - 9 = 0.$$

Ex-3. A vertex of an equilateral triangle is (2, 3) and the equation of the opposite side $x + y = 2$. Find the equation of the other sides of the triangle .

Soln. Let ABC be an equilateral triangle , where A is (2, 3) and BC is $x + y = 2$

Equation of any line passing through (2,3) is

$y - 3 = m(x - 2)$

The slope of the line $x + y = 2$ is (- 1).

Therefore, $\tan(60°) = \left|\frac{m+1}{1-m}\right|$

$$\Rightarrow \quad \frac{m+1}{1-m} = \pm\sqrt{3}$$

$$\Rightarrow \quad \frac{m+1}{1-m} = \sqrt{3} \ \& \ \frac{m+1}{1-m} = -\sqrt{3}$$

$$\Rightarrow \quad m\left(\sqrt{3}+1\right) = \left(\sqrt{3}-1\right) \ \& \ m\left(\sqrt{3}+1\right) = \left(\sqrt{3}-1\right)$$

$$\Rightarrow \quad m = \left(\frac{\sqrt{3}-1}{\sqrt{3}+1}\right) \ \& \ m = \left(\frac{\sqrt{3}+1}{\sqrt{3}-1}\right)$$

$$\Rightarrow \quad m = 2 - \sqrt{3} \ \& \ m = 2 + \sqrt{3}$$

Hence, the required equation of the line are

$$\Rightarrow \quad y - 3 = \left(2 - \sqrt{3}\right)(x-2) \ \& \ y - 3 = \left(2 + \sqrt{3}\right)(x-2)$$

$$\Rightarrow \quad \left(2+\sqrt{3}\right)x - y - \left(2\sqrt{3}+1\right) = 0 \ \&$$

$$\left(2-\sqrt{3}\right)x - y + \left(2\sqrt{3}-1\right) = 0.$$

Ex-4 A line $4x + y = 1$ through the point A(2, -7) meets the line BC, whose equation is $3x - 4y + 1 = 0$ at the point B. Find the equation of the line AC, so that AB = AC.

Soln. Let AB : $4x + y = 1$, AC : $3x - 4y + 1 = 0$ and slope of AC is m

The slope of AB = - 4 and the slope of AC = 3/4 .

Let $\angle ABC = ? = \angle ACB$.

Thus, $\left(\frac{\frac{3}{4} - m}{1 + \frac{3}{4}m}\right) = \left(\frac{-4 - \frac{3}{4}}{1 - 4.\frac{3}{4}}\right)$

$$\Rightarrow \quad \left(\frac{3-4m}{4+3m}\right) = \left(\frac{-16-3}{4-12}\right)$$

$$\Rightarrow \quad \left(\frac{3-4m}{4+3m}\right) = \frac{19}{8}$$

$$\Rightarrow \quad 57m + 76 = 24 - 32m$$

$$\Rightarrow \quad 89m = 24 - 76 = -52$$

$$\Rightarrow \quad m = -\frac{52}{89}.$$

Hence, the equation of AC is $y + 7 = -\frac{52}{89}(x-2)$

$$\Rightarrow \quad 52x + 89y + 519 = 0$$

Ex-5 Find the equations of straight lines passing through (-2,–7) and having an intercept of length 3 between the straight lines $4x+3y=12$ and $4x+3y=3$. Ans. $x+2=0$ & $7x+24y+182=0$.

Soln. Let PQ line intersects the line $4x+3y=12$ at A and $4x+3y=3$ at B respectively.

Equation of any line PQ passing through (-2,-7) is

$y+7=m(x+2)$ ....(i)

Thus, $A=\left(\frac{33-6m}{4+3m}, \frac{20m-28}{4+3m}\right)$ and

$B=\left(\frac{24-6m}{4+3m}, \frac{11m-28}{4+3m}\right)$

Given, $AB=3 \Rightarrow \quad AB^2=9$

$\Rightarrow \quad \frac{81}{(4+3m)^2}+\frac{81m^2}{(4+3m)^2}=9$

$\Rightarrow \quad 9+9m^2=16+24m+9m^2$

$\Rightarrow \quad 24m=-7$

$\Rightarrow \quad m=-7/24$ and $m=\infty$

Hence, the line PQ can be $x+2=0$ and $y+7=-\frac{7}{24}(x+2)$

$\Rightarrow \quad x+2=0$ & $7x+24y+182=0$

1.26 A LINE IS EQUALLY INCLINED WITH TWO LINES

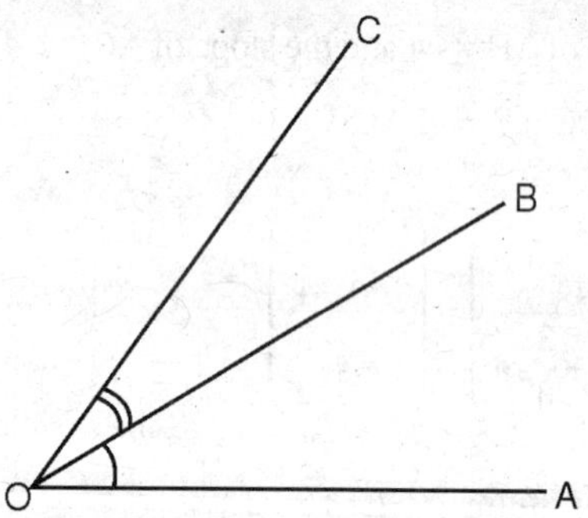

If two lines $y=m_1x+c_1$ & $y=m_2x+c_2$ be equally in clined to a line $y=mx+c$, then

$$\left(\frac{m_1-m}{1+m\,m_1}\right)=-\left(\frac{m_2-m}{1+m\,m_2}\right).$$

Ex-1 Find the equations of the lines passing through the point (2, 3) and equally inclined to the lines $3x-4y=7$ and $12x-5y+6=0$.

Soln. Equation of any line passing through (2, 3) is

$y-3=m(x-2)$ .... (i)

Equation (i) is equally inclined with the lines

$3x-4y=7$ ....(ii) and $12x-5y+6=0$ .... (ii)

Therefore, $\left(\frac{m-\frac{3}{4}}{1+\frac{3}{4}m}\right)=-\left(\frac{m-\frac{12}{5}}{1+\frac{12}{5}m}\right)$

$\Rightarrow \quad \left(\frac{m-\frac{3}{4}}{1+\frac{3}{4}m}\right)=-\left(\frac{m-\frac{12}{5}}{1+\frac{12}{5}m}\right)$

$\Rightarrow \quad \left(\frac{4m-3}{4+3m}\right)=\left(\frac{12-5m}{5+12m}\right)$

$\Rightarrow \quad 63m^2-32m-63=0$

$\Rightarrow \quad 63m^2-81m+49m-63=0$

$\Rightarrow \quad 9m(7m-9)+7(7m-9)=0$

$\Rightarrow \quad (7m-9)(9m+7)=0$

$\Rightarrow \quad m=\frac{9}{7}, -\frac{7}{9}$

From (i), we get,

$y-3=\frac{9}{7}(x-2)$ & $y-3=-\frac{7}{9}(x-2)$

$\Rightarrow \quad 9x-7y+3=0$ & $7x+9y=41$

Which is the required equations of the lines.

Ex-2 Two straight lines $3x+4y=5$ and $4x-3y=15$ intersect at A. Points B and C are chosen on these lines such that AB = AC. Determine the possible equations of the line BC passing through the point (1, 2).

Soln.

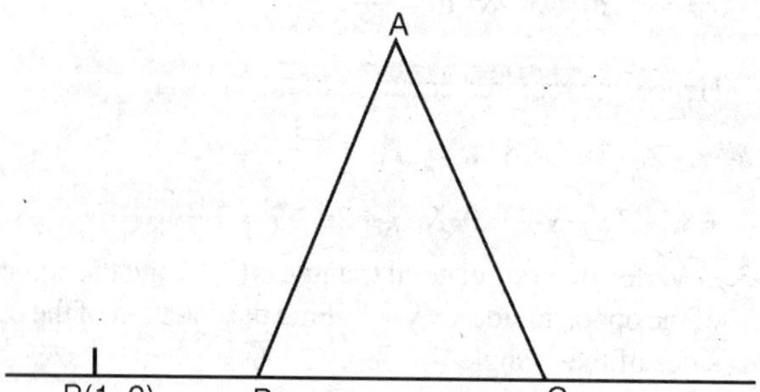

Let AB: $3x+4y=5$.........(i) and $4x-3y=15$ ....(ii)

On solving (i) and (ii), we get, $x=3$ and $y=1$.

Thus, the co-ordinates of the point A be (3, 1).

Equation of any line BC which pass through the point (1,2) is $y-2=m(x-1)$ ....(iii)

On solving (i) and (iii), we get, the co-ordinate B. ie.

$$B=\left(\frac{4m-3}{4m+3},\frac{2m+6}{4m+3}\right).$$

On solving (ii) and (iii), we get, the co-ordinate C i.e.

$$C=\left(\frac{21\text{-}3m}{4-3m},\frac{11m+8}{4-3m}\right).$$

Given condition is AB = AC

$$\Rightarrow \quad AB^2 = AC^2$$

$$\Rightarrow \quad \left(\frac{21\text{-}3m}{4\text{-}3m}-3\right)^2+\left(\frac{8+11m}{4-3m}+1\right)^2$$

$$\left(\frac{4m-3}{4m+3}-3\right)^2+\left(\frac{6+2m}{4m+3}+1\right)^2$$

$$\Rightarrow \quad \frac{(9+6m)^2+(12+8m)^2}{(4-3m)^2}=\frac{(-8m-12)^2+(6m+9)^2}{(4m+3)^2}$$

$$\Rightarrow \quad (4m+3)^2\left(100m^2+300m+225\right)$$
$$=(4-3m)^2\left(100m^2+300m+225\right)$$

$$\Rightarrow \quad \left(100m^2+300m+225\right)\left((4m+3)^2-(4-3m)^2\right)=0$$

$$\Rightarrow \quad \left(4m^2+12m+9\right)\left((4m+3)^2-(4-3m)^2\right)=0.$$

$$\Rightarrow \quad (2m+3)^2(m+7)(7m-1)=0$$

$$\Rightarrow \quad m=-\frac{3}{2},-7,\frac{1}{7}$$

Put $m=-\frac{3}{2}$ in (iii), we get, $y-2=-\frac{3}{2}(x-1)$

$$\Rightarrow \quad 3x+2y\text{-}7=0$$

Clearly, it is pass through A(3, -1). Thus, it can not be the equation of BC.

Put $m=-7$ in (iii), we get, $y=-7(x-1)=-7x+7$

Thus, the equation of BC is $7x+y=7$.

Also, put $m=1/7$ in (iii), we get,

$$y-2=\frac{1}{7}(x-1) \Rightarrow \quad x\text{-}7y+13=0$$

Hence, the equations of BC can be $x-7y+13=0$ and $7x+7=7$.

Ex-3. Two equal sides of an isosceles traingle have the equa tions $7x-y+3=0$ and $x+y=3$ and its third side passes through the point (1, -10). Find the equation of the third side.

Ans. $3x+y+7=0$ & $x-3y=31$.

Soln. Do yourself.

1.27 EQUATION OF THE BISECTORS

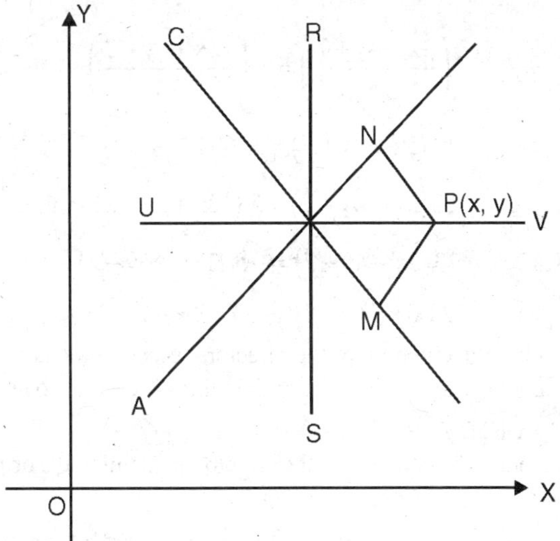

The equation of the bisectors of the angles between the lines $a_1x+b_1y+c_1=0$ and $a_2x+b_2y+c_2=0$ are given by $\left(\frac{a_1x+b_1y+c_1}{\sqrt{a_1^2+b_1^2}}\right)=\pm\left(\frac{a_2x+b_2y+c_2}{\sqrt{a_2^2+b_2^2}}\right)$.

Note:

1. When we shall find the equation of bisectors, first we make c_1 & c_2 are +ve.
2. Two bisectors are perpendicular to each other.
3. +ve one, the equation of the bisector containing the origin.
4. -ve one, the equation of the bisector does not containing the origin.
5. If $a_1a_2+b_1b_2>0$, then -ve one is the acute angle bisector and +ve one is the obtuse angle bisector.
6. If $a_1a_2+b_1b_2<0$, then +ve one is the acute angle bisector and -ve one is the obtuse angle bisector.
7. If $a_1a_2+b_1b_2>0$, then origin lies in obtuse angle and if $a_1a_2+b_1b_2<0$, then origin lies in acute angle.
8. The equation of the bisector of the angle between the two lines containing the point (α,β) will be +ve one according as $(a_1\alpha+b_1\beta+c_1)$ & $(a_2\alpha+b_2\beta+c_2)$ are

of same sign and will be -ve one if $(a_1\alpha+b_1\beta+c_1)$ and $(a_2\alpha+b_2\beta+c_2)$ are of opposite sign.

Ex-1 Find the equations of the bisectors of the angle between the straight lines $3x-4y+7=0$ and $12x+5y-2=0$.

Soln. Hence, the equiations of the bisectors are

$$\left|\frac{3x-4y+7}{\sqrt{3^2+4^2}}\right|=\left|\frac{12x+5y-2}{\sqrt{12^2+5^2}}\right|$$

$$\Rightarrow \quad \left(\frac{3x-4y+7}{5}\right)=\pm\left(\frac{12x+5y-2}{13}\right)$$

$$\Rightarrow \quad 13(3x-4y+7)=\pm 5(12x+5y-2)$$

$$\Rightarrow \quad 13(3x-4y+7)=5(12x+5y-2) \text{ and }$$

$$13(3x-4y+7)=-5(12x+5y-2)$$

$$\Rightarrow \quad 21x+77y=101 \quad \& \quad 3x-y+3=0$$

Ex-2 Find the equation of the bisectors bisecting the angle containing the origin of the straight lines $4x+3y=6$ and $5x+12y+9=0$.

Soln. Hence, the equation of the bisector, containing the origin is

$$\left(\frac{-4x-3y+6}{\sqrt{4^2+3^2}}\right)=\left(\frac{5x+12y+9}{\sqrt{5^2+12^2}}\right)$$

$$\Rightarrow \quad \left(\frac{-4x-3y+6}{5}\right)=\left(\frac{5x+12y+9}{13}\right)$$

$$\Rightarrow \quad 13(-4x-3y+6)=5(5x+12y+9)$$

$$\Rightarrow \quad 7x+9y=3$$

Ex-3. Find the bisector of the angle between the lines $2x+y=6$ and $2x-4y+7=0$, which contains the point (1, 2).

Soln. The given lines are $-2x-y+6=0$ and $2x-4y+7=0$.

Therefore, $-2.1-2+6=-4+6=2$ and

$2.1-4.2+7=9-8=1$

Thus, +ve one is the equation of the bisector.

Hence, the required equation of bisector is

$$\left(\frac{-2x-y+6}{\sqrt{2^2+1^2}}\right)=\left(\frac{2x-4y+7}{\sqrt{2^2+4^2}}\right)$$

$$\Rightarrow \quad \left(\frac{-2x-y+6}{\sqrt{5}}\right)=\left(\frac{2x-4y+7}{2\sqrt{5}}\right)$$

$$\Rightarrow \quad 2(-2x-y+6)=(2x-4y+7)$$

$$\Rightarrow \quad 6x-2y=5.$$

Ex-4. Find the equation of the bisector of the obtuse angle between the lines $3x-4y+7=0$ and $12x+5y=2$.

Soln. The given lines are $3x-4y+7=0$ and $-12x-5y+2=0$.

Now, $a_1a_2+b_1b_2=-36+20=-16<0$.

Therefore, negative one is the obtuse angle bisector.

Hence, the equation of the bisector of the obtuse angle is

$$\left(\frac{3x-4y+7}{\sqrt{3^2+4^2}}\right)=-\left(\frac{-12x-5y+2}{\sqrt{12^2+5^2}}\right)$$

$$\Rightarrow \quad \left(\frac{3x-4y+7}{5}\right)=-\left(\frac{-12x-5y+2}{13}\right)$$

$$\Rightarrow \quad 21x+77y=101.$$

Ex-5. Find the bisector of the acute angle between the lines $x+y=3$ and $7x-y+5=0$.

Soln. The given lines are $-x-y+3=0$ and $7x-y+5=0$.

Now, $a_1a_2+b_1b_2=-7+1=-6<0$.

Therefore, positive one is the acite angle bisector.

Hence, the equation of the acute angle bisector is

$$\left(\frac{-x-y+3}{\sqrt{1^2+1^2}}\right)=\left(\frac{7x-y+5}{\sqrt{7^2+1^2}}\right)$$

$$\Rightarrow \quad \left(\frac{-x-y+3}{\sqrt{2}}\right)=\left(\frac{7x-y+5}{5\sqrt{2}}\right)$$

$$\Rightarrow \quad 5(-x-y+3)=(7x-y+5)$$

$$\Rightarrow \quad 6x+2y=5.$$

Ex-6. Prove that the length of the perpendiculars drawn from any point of the line $7x-9y+10=0$ to the lines $3x+4y=5$ and $12x+5y=7$ are same.

Soln. The lengths of perpendicular from any point on the line $7x-9y+10=0$ to the lines $3x+4y=5$ and $12x+5y=7$ are same if $7x-9y+10=0$ is the bisector of $3x+4y=5$ and $12x+5y=7$. Hence, the equation of bisectors is

$$\left(\frac{-3x-4y+5}{\sqrt{3^2+4^2}}\right)=\left(\frac{-12x-5y+7}{\sqrt{12^2+5^2}}\right)$$

$$\Rightarrow \quad 13(-3x-4y+5)=5(-12x-5y+7)$$

$$\Rightarrow \quad 21x-27y+30=0$$

$$\Rightarrow \quad 7x-9y+10=0.$$

Hence, the result.

Ex-7. Find the co-ordinates of the incentre of the triangle whose sides are $x+1=0$, $3x-4y=5$, $5x+12y=27$.

Soln. Let ABC be a triangle, where AB : $x+1=0$, BC : $3x-4y=5$ and CA : $5x+12y=27$.

Case - I : Acute angle bisector between AB and AC

The given lines are $x+1=0$ and $-3x+4y+5=0$.

Now, $a_1 a_2 + b_1 b_2 = 1.(-3)+0=-3<0$.

Thus, positive one is the acute angle bisector.

Hence, the required acute angle bisector is

$$\left(\frac{x+1}{\sqrt{1^2}}\right)=\left(\frac{-3x+4y+5}{\sqrt{3^2+4^2}}\right)$$

$$\Rightarrow \quad \left(\frac{x+1}{1}\right)=\left(\frac{-3x+4y+5}{5}\right)$$

$$\Rightarrow \quad 5(x+1)=(-3x+4y+5)$$

$$\Rightarrow \quad 2x-y=0 \text{ ....(i)}$$

Case - II : the acute angle bisector between BC and AC.

The given lines are $-3x+4y+5=0$ and $-5x-12y+27=0$.

Now, $a_1 a_2 + b_1 b_2 = 15-48=-23<0$

Thus, the positive one is the acute angle bisector .

Hence, the required acute angle bisector is

$$\left(\frac{-3x+4y+5}{\sqrt{3^2+4^2}}\right)=\left(\frac{-5x-12y+27}{\sqrt{5^2+12^2}}\right)$$

$$\Rightarrow \quad \left(\frac{-3x+4y+5}{5}\right)=\left(\frac{-5x-12y+27}{13}\right)$$

$$\Rightarrow \quad x-8y=-5 \text{ ....(ii)}$$

On solving (i) and (ii), we get, $x=\frac{1}{3},\ y=\frac{2}{3}$.

Hence, the required in-centre is $\left(\frac{1}{3},\frac{2}{3}\right)$.

Ex-8. The bisectors of the angle between the lines $y=\sqrt{3}\,x+3$ and $\sqrt{3}\,y=x+3\sqrt{3}$ meet the x-axis at P and Q . Find the length of PQ.

Soln.

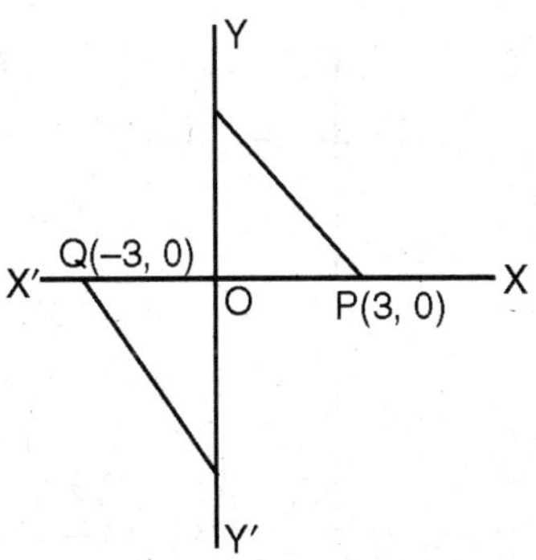

The given lines are $\sqrt{3}\,x-y+3=0$ and

$x-\sqrt{3}y+3\sqrt{3}=0$

Hence, the equation of bisectors are

$$\left|\left(\frac{\sqrt{3}x-y+3}{\sqrt{3+1}}\right)\right|=\left|\left(\frac{x-\sqrt{3}y+3\sqrt{3}}{\sqrt{1+3}}\right)\right|$$

and $\left(\sqrt{3}x-y+3\right)=-\left(x-\sqrt{3}y+3\sqrt{3}\right)$

$$\Rightarrow \quad \left(\sqrt{3}-1\right)x+\left(\sqrt{3}-1\right)y=3\left(\sqrt{3}-1\right)$$

$$\& \quad \left(\sqrt{3}+1\right)x+\left(\sqrt{3}+1\right)y=-3\left(\sqrt{3}+1\right)$$

$$\Rightarrow \quad x+y=3 \ \ \& \ \ x+y=-3$$

Thus, the point P is (3, 0) and the point Q is (-3, 0)

Hence, the length of PQ = 6.

Ex-9. Two opposite sides of a rhombus are $x+y=1$ and $x+y=5$. If one vertex is (2, -1) and the angle at that vertex be $45°$. Find the vertex opposite to the given vertex.

Soln.

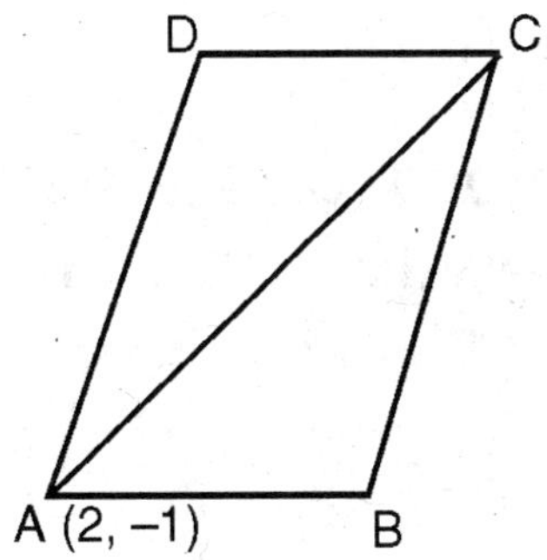

Give lines are AB: $x+y=1$ ....(i)

and CD: $x+y=5$................(ii)

Slope of AB = $-1=\tan(135°)$.

Since, AB makes an angle of $45°$ with AC , therefore it will make an angle of $(135°-45°)$ or $(135°+45°)$ i.e. $90°$ or $180°$ with the +ve direction of x - axis.

Thus, AB is parallel to x -axis or y-axis

Hence, $x-2=0$ and $y+1=0$.

Case - I : Consider the lines are $-x-y+1=0$ and $-x+2=0$

Now, $a_1a_2+b_1b_2=1+0=1>0$

Thus negative one is the acute angle bisector .

Hence , the equation of the acute angle bisector of

$\angle BAC$ is $\left(\frac{-x-y+1}{\sqrt{1^2+1^2}}\right)=-\left(\frac{-x+2}{\sqrt{1^2}}\right)$

$\Rightarrow \quad (\sqrt{2}+1)x+y=(2\sqrt{2}+1)$ ....(iii)

Case - II : Consider the lines are $-x-y+1=0$ and $y+1=0$

Now, $a_1 a_2 + b_1 b_2 = 0-1=-1<0$

Thus, positive one is the acute angle bisector

Hence, the equation of the acute angle bisector of

$\angle BAC$ is $\left(\frac{-x-y+1}{\sqrt{1^2+1^2}}\right)=\left(\frac{y+1}{\sqrt{1^2}}\right)$

$\Rightarrow \quad x+(\sqrt{2}+1)y=(1-\sqrt{2})$ ....(iv)

On solving (i) and (iii), we get,

$x=6+2\sqrt{2},\ y=-1-2\sqrt{2}$.

Thus, co-ordinates of C can be $(6+2\sqrt{2}, 1-2\sqrt{2})$

Again, solving (i) and (iv), we get,

$x=2-2\sqrt{2},\ y=3+2\sqrt{2}$

Thus, The co-ordinates of C may be

$(2-2\sqrt{2},\ 3+2\sqrt{2})$.

1.28 THE FOOT OF PERPENDICULAR DRAWN FROM THE POINT (x_1, y_1) TO THE LINE ax + by + c = 0.

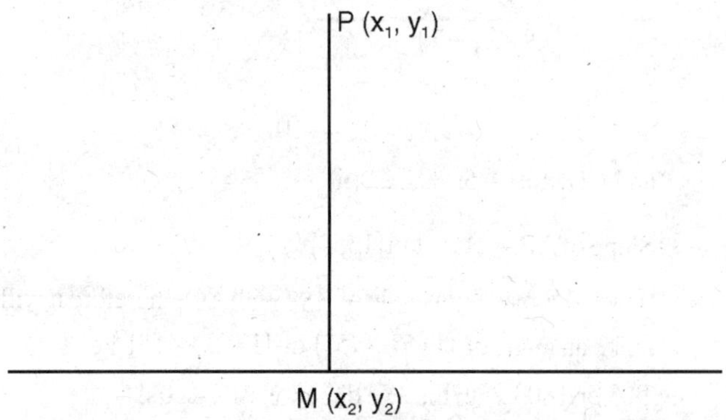

The foot of perpendicular from the point (x_1, y_1) to the line $ax+by+c=0$ is given by

$$\frac{x_2-x_1}{a}=\frac{y_2-y_1}{b}=-\frac{(ax_1+by_1+c)}{(a^2+b^2)}.$$

Q.1 Find the foot of perpendicular drawn from the point (2,3) to the line $y=3x+4$.

1.29 IMAGE OF A POINT (x_1,y_1) WITH RESPECT TO A LINE MIRROR ax + by + c = 0.

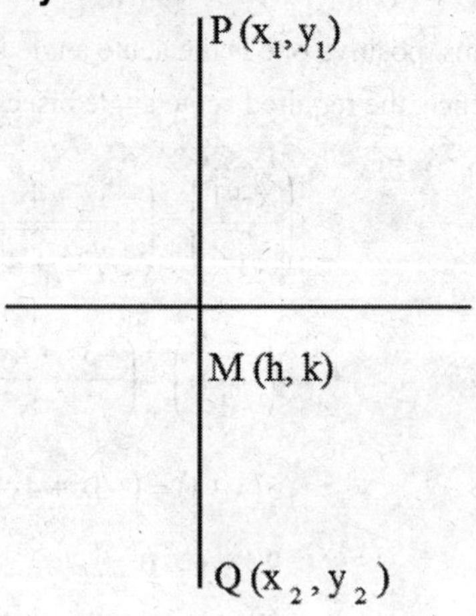

The image of a point (x_1, y_1) with respect to a line mirror $ax+by+c=0$ is given by $\frac{x_2-x_1}{a}=\frac{y_2-y_1}{b}=-2\left(\frac{ax_1+by_1+c}{a^2+b^2}\right)$

R-1 The image of a point $P(\alpha, \beta)$ with respect to x-axis is $Q(\alpha, -\beta)$

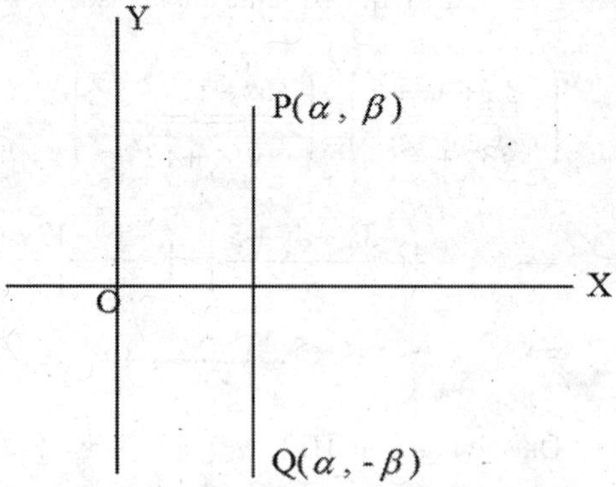

Note: The image of the line $ax+by+c=0$ about x-axis is $ax-by+c=0$.

R-2. The image of a point $P(\alpha, \beta)$ with respect to y-axis is $Q(-\alpha, \beta)$.

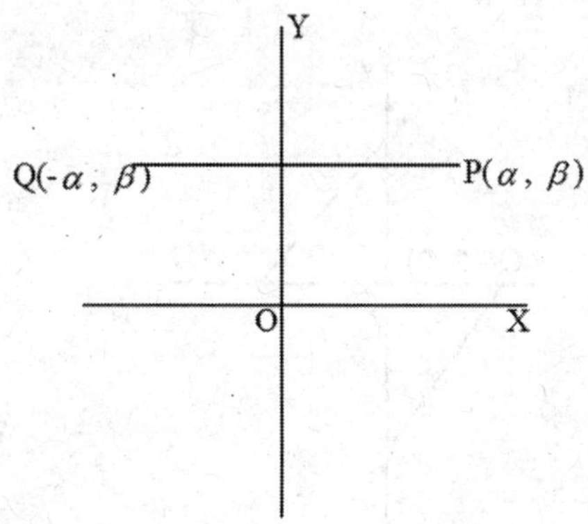

Note : The image of the line $a x+b y+c=0$ about y-axis is $-a x+b y+c=0$.

R-3. The image of a point $P(\alpha, \beta)$ with respect to the origin is $Q(-\alpha,-\beta)$.

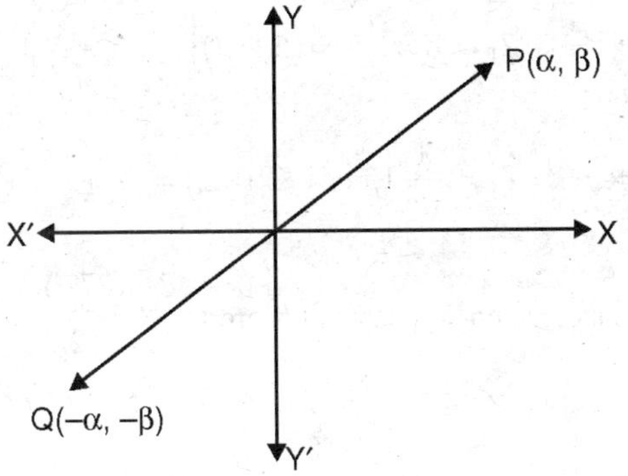

Note:. The image of the line $a x+b y+c=0$ is $-a x-b y+c=0$.

R-4 The image of a point $P(\alpha, \beta)$ with respect to the line $x=a$ is $Q(2a-\alpha, \beta)$.

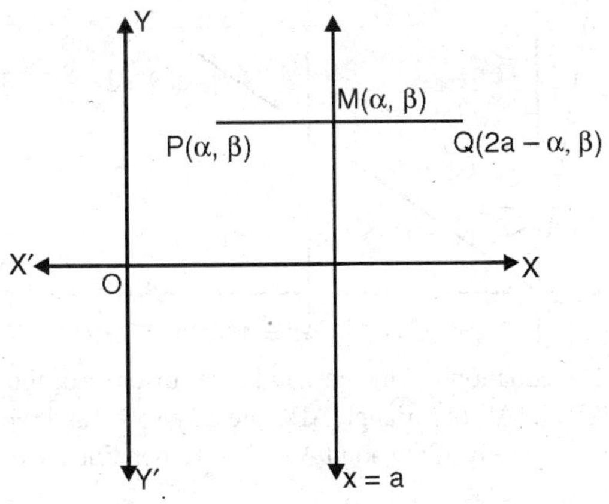

Note: The image of the line $a x+b y+c=0$ with respect to the line $x=\lambda$ is $a(2\lambda-x)+by+c=0$.

R-5. The image of a point $P(\alpha, \beta)$ with respect to the line $y=b$ is $Q(\alpha, 2b-\beta)$.

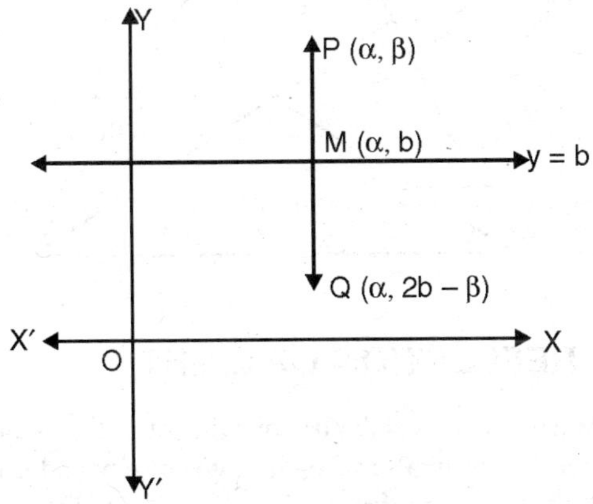

Note: The image of the line $a x+b y+c=0$ about the line $y=\mu$ is $ax+b(2\mu-y)+c=0$.

R-6. The image of a point $P(\alpha, \beta)$ with respect to the line $y=x$ is $Q(\beta, \alpha)$.

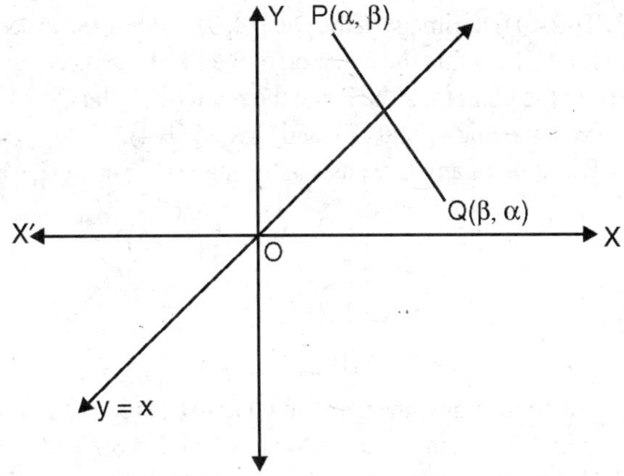

Note: The image of a line $a x+b y+c=0$ about the line $y=x$ is $a y+b x+c=0$.

R-7. The image of a point $P(\alpha,\beta)$ with respect to the line $y=m x$, where $m=\tan\theta$, is

$Q(\alpha\cos2\theta+\beta\sin2\theta,\ \alpha\sin2\theta-\beta\cos2\theta)$.

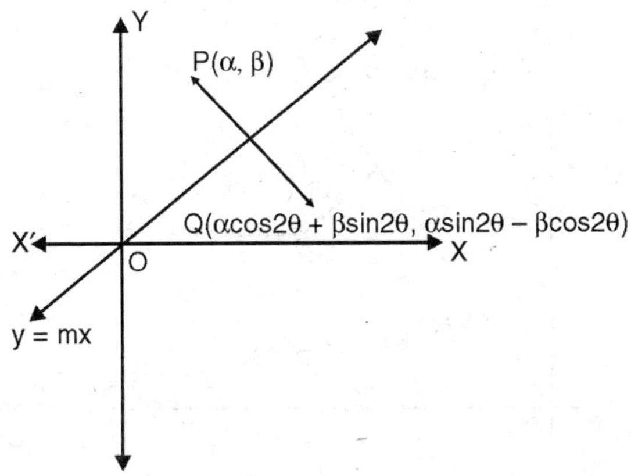

Note: The image of a line $ax+by+c=0$ with respect to the line $y=mx$, where $m=\tan\theta$ is

$$a(\alpha\ \cos 2\theta+\beta\sin 2\theta)+b(\alpha\ \sin 2\theta-\beta\cos 2\theta)+c=0.$$

Ex-1. Find the image of the point (-8, 12) with respect to the line mirror $4x+7y+13=0$.

Soln. Let the image of the point (-8, 12) be (x_2, y_2).

Then $\dfrac{x_2+8}{4}=\dfrac{y_2-12}{7}=-\dfrac{2(4.-8+7.12+13)}{(4^2+7^2)}$

$$=\frac{2(-32+84+13)}{65}=\frac{2\times65}{65}=2$$

$$\Rightarrow \frac{x_2+8}{4}=2 \quad \& \quad \frac{y_2-12}{7}=2$$

$$\Rightarrow x_2=0 \quad \& \quad y_2=28$$

Hence, the image of the point (-8, 12) is (0, 28).

Ex-2. Find the image of the point (3, 4) with respect to the line y = x.

Soln. Hence, the mage of the point (3, 4) with respect to the line y = x is (4, 3).

Ex-3. If (-2, 6) is the image of the point (4, 2) with respect to the line L = 0, then find the equation of the line L.

Soln. Let the point (4, 2) be P and the point (-2, 6) be Q.
Now the mid - point of P and Q is M (1, 4).
Equation of any line passing through (4, 2) and (-2, 6) is

$$y-2=\frac{6-2}{-2-4}(x-4)=-\frac{2}{3}(x-2).$$

$$\Rightarrow \quad 3y-6=-2x+4$$

$$\Rightarrow \quad 2x+3y=10 \text{ ....(i)}$$

Equation of any line perpendicular to (i) is 3 x - 2 y + k = 0.
Which is passing through M (1, 4). So k = 8 - 3 = 5.
Hence, the required equation of the line is 3 x - 2 y + 5 = 0.

Ex-4. The image of the point (4, 1) with respect to the line y = x is P. If the point P translate about the line x = 2, then the new position of P is Q. Find the co-ordinates of Q.

Soln.

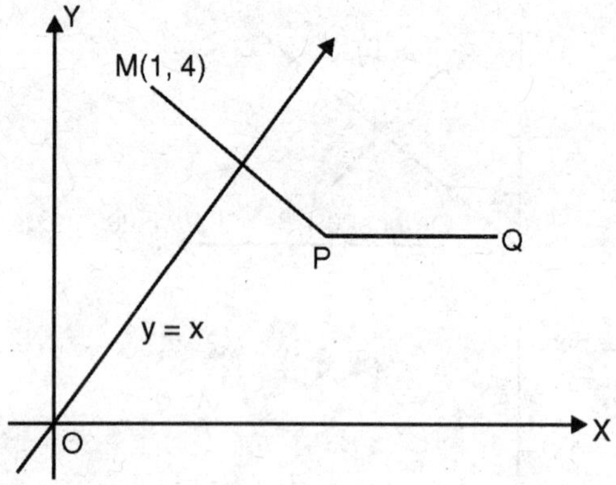

Let the point M be (4, 1).
The image of the point M (1, 4) with respect to the line y = x be P (4, 1).
Now, if the point P be translate about the line x = 2, then the new [position of P is (4+2, 1).
Hence, the Co-ordinates of Q is (6, 1).

Ex-5. The image of the point (3, 2) with respect to the line x = 4 is P. If P is rotated through an angle $\frac{\pi}{4}$ about the origin in anti-clockwise direction. Find the new position of P.

Soln. Let the point P be (3, 2).
The image of the point P with respect to the line x = 4 is Q (2..4- 3, 2) i.e. Q (5, 2).
Let Z = 5 +2 i and R be Z1
Now, by rotation theorem of complex number,

$$\Rightarrow \quad \frac{Z_1-0}{Z-0}=\frac{|Z-0|}{|Z_1-0|}e^{i\frac{\pi}{4}}$$

$$\Rightarrow \quad \frac{Z_1}{Z}=\frac{|Z_1-0|}{|Z-0|}e^{i\frac{\pi}{4}}=e^{i\frac{\pi}{4}}$$

$$\Rightarrow \quad Z_1=Z\times e^{i\frac{\pi}{4}}=(5+2i)\left(\frac{1}{\sqrt{2}}+\frac{i}{\sqrt{2}}\right)$$

$$\Rightarrow \quad Z_1=\frac{1}{\sqrt{2}}(5+5i+2i-2)=\frac{1}{\sqrt{2}}(3+7i)$$

Hence, the co-ordinates of R are $\left(\frac{3}{\sqrt{2}},\frac{7}{\sqrt{2}}\right)$.

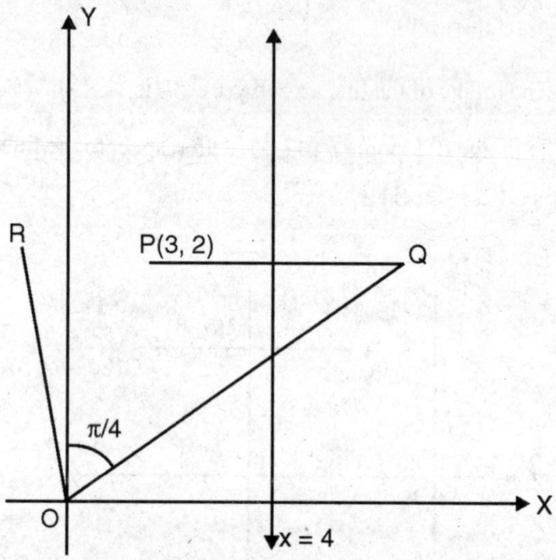

Ex-6. The equations of the perpendicular bisector of the sides AB and AC of a triangle ABC are x -y +5 = 0 and x + 2 y = 0 respectively. If the point A is (1, -2), then find the equation of the ine BC.

Soln.

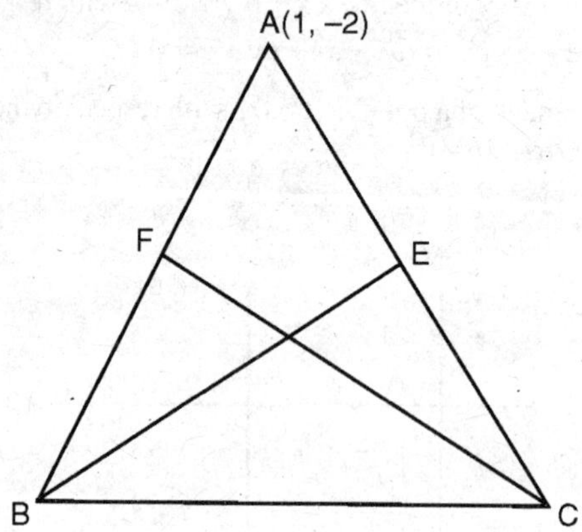

1.30 REFLECTION OF LIGHT

When you play billiards you will notice that when a ball bounces from a surface, the angle of rebound is equal to the angle of incidence. This observation is also true with light. When an inci dent light ray strikes a smooth surface (like a plane mirror) at an angle. The angle formed by the incident ray measured from the normal is equal to the angle formed by the reflected ray.

1.31 Law of Reflection

The angle of incidence is equal to the angle of reflection. The reflected and incident rays lie in a plane that is normal to the reflecting surface.

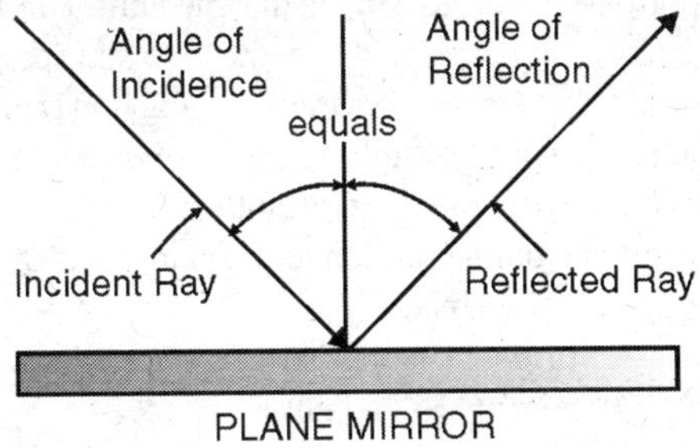

Note: The red line represents the normal line. The normal line is always perpendicular to the reflecting surface.

Ex-1 A ray of light is sent along the line x - 2 y = 3 . Upon reaching the line 3 x - 2 y = 5 , the ray is reflected from it. Find the equation of the line containing the reflected ray.

Soln. Let PM : x - 2 y + 3 = 0 be the incident ray and MR be the reflected ray.
Produced MQ in such a way that PM = MQ .
Now we shall find the image of Q w. r. t AB is R.
Co-ordinates of M are (1, - 1).
Let co-ordinates of Q be (3, 0). and R be (h, k).
Thus, R is the mage of Q with respect to 3 x - 2 y = 5.

Now $\dfrac{h-3}{3}=\dfrac{k-0}{-2}=-\dfrac{2(3.3+2.0-5)}{(3^2+2^2)}=-\dfrac{8}{13}$

$\Rightarrow \quad h=\dfrac{15}{13}$ and $k=\dfrac{16}{13}$

Thus, the co-ordinates of R be $\left(\dfrac{15}{13}, \dfrac{16}{13}\right)$

Slope of MR $=\dfrac{29}{2}$

Therefore, the equation of MR is $y+1=\dfrac{29}{2}(x-1)$

$\Rightarrow \quad 29x-2y=31$

Hence, the equation of the reflected ray is $29x-2y=31$

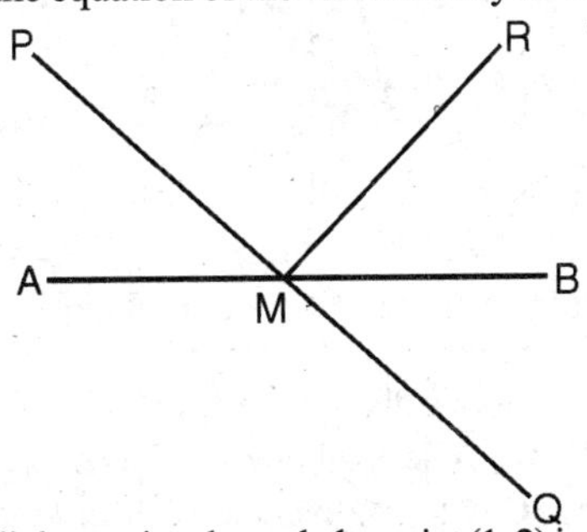

Ex-2 A ray of light passing through the point (1, 2) is reflected on the x-axis at a point P and passes through the point (5, 3) . Find the abscissa of the point P.

Soln. Let N be the image of M with respect to x-axis
Thus N is (5, -3)

Slope of NQ $=\dfrac{-3-2}{5-1}=-\dfrac{5}{4}$

Therefore, the equation QN is $y-2=-\dfrac{5}{4}(x-1)$

$\Rightarrow \quad 5x+4y=13$

Thus, the eco-ordinates of P be $\left(\dfrac{13}{5}, 0\right)$

Hence, the abscissa of the point P is $\dfrac{13}{5}$.

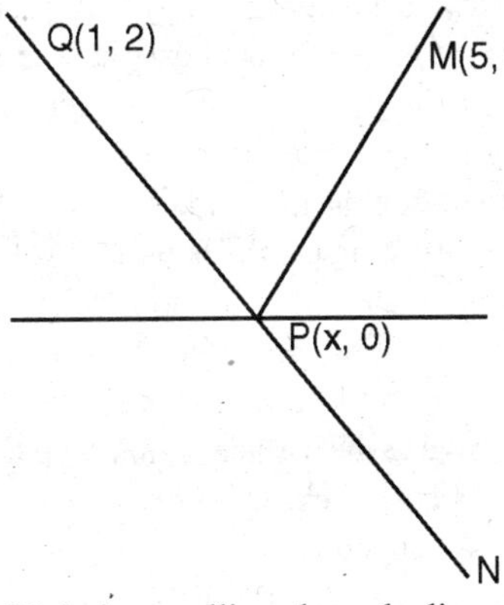

Ex-3. A ray of light is travelling along the line x = 1 and gets reflected from the line x + y = 1 , then find the equation of the line, which the reflected ray travel.

Soln. Let PM be the incident ray and
QM be the reflected ray
Let P (1, 5) be any point on the line x = 1
Produce Pm in such a way that PM = RM ., where M = (1, 0)
Clearly , R = (1, -5) , since Incident ray is parallel to y-axis.
Now , image of R with respect to the line
x + y = 1 is Q.
Let the co-ordinate of Q be (h, k)

Now, $\dfrac{h-1}{1}=\dfrac{k+5}{1}=\dfrac{-2(1-5-1)}{(1+1)}=5$

$\Rightarrow \quad h=6,\ k=0$

Thus, the co-ordinates of Q is (6, 0)
Since, the co-ordinates of M is (1, 0) and the co-ordinates of Q is (6, 0), so the equation of the reflected ray is y = 0 .

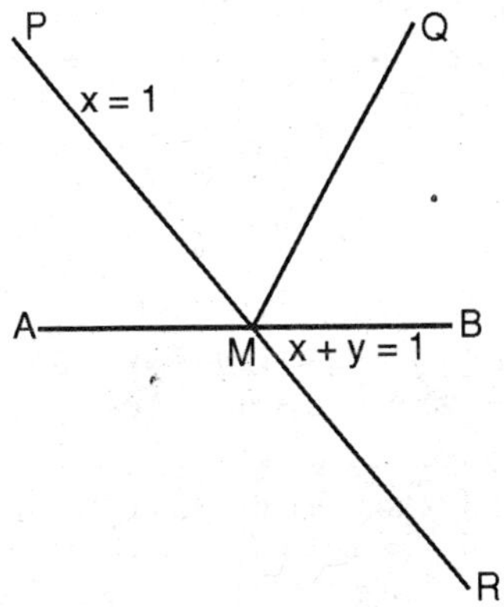

1.32 REFRACTION OF LIGHT

All electromagnetic transmissions including light are wave motions only. Since the wave length and the amplitudes are infinitely small, we indicate such wave motions as straight lines in our study.

Since light rays also indicate a wave motion, concept involved in refraction of light and in wave refraction are exactly the same.

When a light ray passes from one medium to another medium, the light ray may be totally absorbed by the boundary if it is an opaque surface. In such a case, no light is seen on the other medium. In some cases the light ray may be sent back, following a rule, to the same medium if the boundary has the ability to do so. This phenomenon of light ray 'being sent back' is called '*Reflection*' of light ray and the 'ability' of the boundary is called as 'reflective property' of the medium.

However, in most cases, the boundary is transparent and the light ray is able to enter the second medium. However, the path of the light ray will no longer be the same. Depending on many fac tors, it may bend towards the normal to the surface, away from the normal to the surface or, in excep tional cases, the ray be even be reflected back. In any case the phenomenon of any of such things happening is called the *'Refraction'* of the light ray. The refraction of light ray also follows a certain rule.

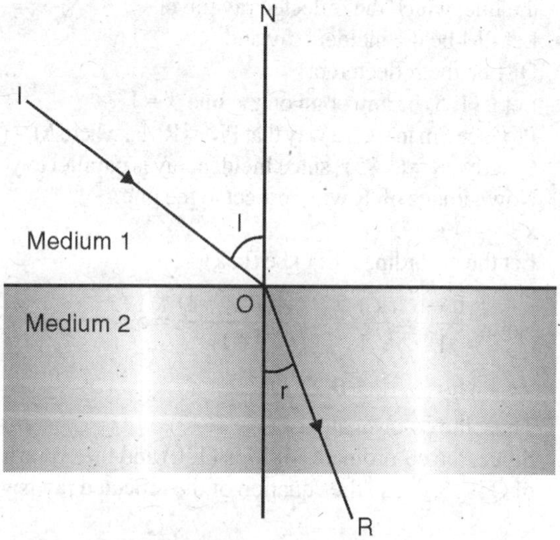

Refraction of Light

Index of Refraction

We will define a ratio of velocity of a light ray in vacuum to the velocity of the light ray in a given medium as a constant 'n'. This constant 'n' is called as the 'refractive index' of the medium or the
'index of refraction' of the medium.

n = cv

This concept will be of great use later when we discuss the law of refraction. That is, the rule which is followed by the refraction of a wave.

Law of Refraction

As mentioned earlier, a light ray travels in different veloci ties in different mediums. In the process the direction of ray changes when it enters the second medium. As per Snell's law, the sin of the angle made by the ray with the normal to the surface of interface between the mediums is directly proportional to the velocity in that medium. This law can be mathematically explained with the follow ing diagram.
We know that the phenomenon of refraction is taking place because the speed of light changes when it is travelling from one optical medium to another.
Thus we can define refractive index in terms of the speed of light in the two media.

As per Snell's law, $\dfrac{\sin i}{\sin r} = \dfrac{v_I}{v_R}$.

Where, v_I - The velocity of the incident light,

v_R - The velocity of the refracted light

i - The angle of incidence,

r - The angle of refraction

Thus $v = \dfrac{c}{n}$ and $\dfrac{\sin i}{\sin r} = \dfrac{n_2}{n_1}$

Negative Refraction

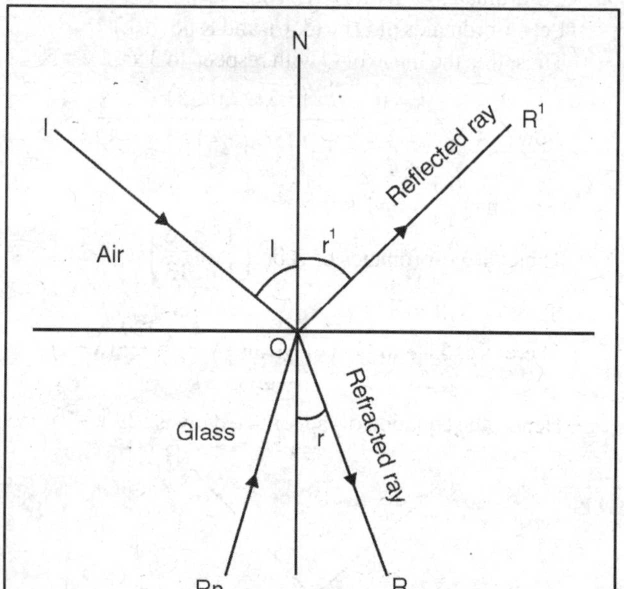

Refraction and Reflection of Light

Look at the above diagram. A ray IO crosses from medium 1 (Air) to medium 2 (Glass) at point O. Normally the ray undergoes refraction at O. It bends away from the normal as OR1 if the medium 2 is lighter than 1 or bends towards the normal as OR if the medium 2 is heavier than 1. In rare cases, if the medium has a negative permittivity and negative permeability, the ray gets bent as ORn, on the opposite side of normal. In a way it looks like as if the ray is reflected back, but to the second medium. This type of refraction is called *Negative Refraction.*

Ex-1 A ray of light is sent along the line x - 6 y = 8 . After refracting across the line x + y = 1, it enters the opposite side after turning by 15° away from the line x + y = 1 . Find the equation of the line along with the reflecetd ray travels.

Soln. Let PM : x - 6 y = 8 be the incident ray

AB : x + y = 1 is the mirror,

MQ is the reflected ray .

and MS is the refracted ray.

Clearly , M is (2, -1)

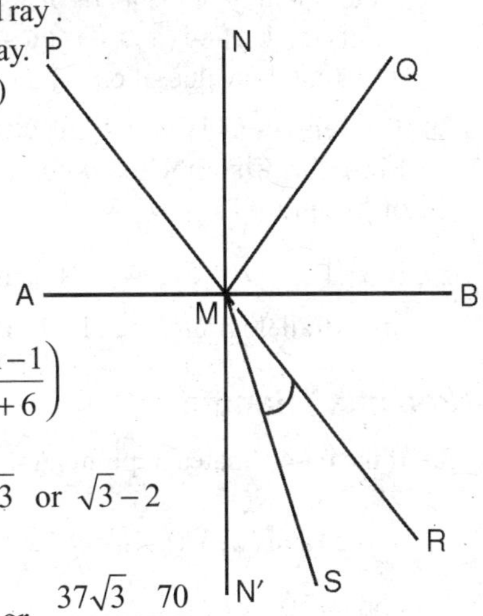

$$\text{Now, } \tan 15° = \left|\frac{m-\frac{1}{6}}{1+\frac{m}{6}}\right|$$

$$\Rightarrow \quad \left(2-\sqrt{3}\right) = \pm\left(\frac{6m-1}{m+6}\right)$$

$$\Rightarrow \quad \left(\frac{6m-1}{m+6}\right) = 2-\sqrt{3} \text{ or } \sqrt{3}-2$$

$$\Rightarrow \quad m = \frac{70 \quad 37\sqrt{3}}{13} \text{ or } \frac{37\sqrt{3} \quad 70}{13}$$

Let the angle between x + y = 1 and the line through M (2, -1) with the slope $m = \frac{70-37\sqrt{3}}{13}$ be α

$$\text{Then } \tan(\alpha) = \left|\frac{\frac{70-37\sqrt{3}}{13}+1}{1-\frac{70-37\sqrt{3}}{13}}\right| = \left|\frac{83-37\sqrt{3}}{37\sqrt{3}-57}\right| = \frac{83-37\sqrt{3}}{37\sqrt{3}-57}.$$

and the angle between x + y = 1 and the line through M (2, -1) with slope $m = \frac{37\sqrt{3}-70}{13}$ be β

$$\text{Then } \tan(\beta) = \left|\frac{\frac{37\sqrt{3}-70}{13}+1}{1-\frac{37\sqrt{3}-70}{13}}\right| = \left|\frac{37\sqrt{3}-9}{131-37\sqrt{3}}\right| = \frac{37\sqrt{3}-9}{131-37\sqrt{3}}$$

Here, $\tan(\alpha) > \tan(\beta) \Rightarrow$ a > ß

Therefore, the slope of the refracted ray is $\frac{70-37\sqrt{3}}{13}$.

Hence, the equation of the refracted ray is

$$y+1 = \frac{70-37\sqrt{3}}{13}(x-2)$$

$$\Rightarrow \quad 13y+13 = \left(70-37\sqrt{3}\right)x - 140 + 74\sqrt{3}$$

$$\Rightarrow \quad \left(70-37\sqrt{3}\right)x - 13y - 153 + 74\sqrt{3} = 0.$$

Level–I QUESTIONS BASED ON FUNDAMENTALS

DISTANCE BETWEEN TWO POINTS

1. If the distance between the points (a,2) and (3, 4) be 8, then find the value of 'a'.
2. Prove that the points
   (i) $(2a, 4a)$, $(2a, 6a)$ and $\left(2a+a\sqrt{3}, 5a\right)$ are vertices of an equilateral triangle.
   (ii) $(12,8)$, $(-2, 6)$ and $(6, 0)$ are the vertices of a right angled triangle.
   (iii) $(0,-1)$, $(2, 1)$, $(0, 3)$ and $(-2, 1)$ are the vertices of a square.
   (iv) $(-4, -1)$, $(-2, -4)$, $(4, 0)$ and $(2,3)$ are the vertices of a rectangle.
   (v) $(1, 1)$, $(2, -2)$ and $(-2, 2)$ are the vertices of a isosceles triangle.
   (vi) $(1, -2)$, $(3, 6)$, $(5, 10)$ and $(3, 2)$ are the vertices of a parallelogram.
3. If the point is equidistant from the points $(6, -1)$ and $(2, 3)$, then prove that $x - y = 3$.
4. If the point (x, y) is equidistant from points (a + b, b – a) and (a – b, a + b), prove that bx = ay.
5. Find the distance between the points $\left(3, \frac{\pi}{4}\right)$ and $\left(7, \frac{5\pi}{4}\right)$.
6. Prove that the points $(0, 0)$, $\left(3, \frac{\pi}{2}\right)$ and $\left(3, \frac{\pi}{6}\right)$ are the vertices of an equilateral triangle.
7. Find the point on the axis of y which is equidistant from (–1, 2) and (3, 4).
8. If the line segment joining the points (x_1, y_1) and

$$\cos? = \frac{x_1x_2 + y_1y_2}{\sqrt{x_1^2+y_1^2}\sqrt{x_2^2+y_2^2}}.$$

9. Let the vertices of a triangle are $A(1, 1)$, $B(4, 5)$ and $C(6, 13)$. Then find cos A .

10. If P(at^2, 2at), $Q\left(\frac{a}{t^2}, -\frac{2a}{t}\right)$ and S(a, 0) be any three points, show that $\frac{1}{SP}+\frac{1}{SQ}$ is independent of t.

11. An equilateral traingle has two vertices are $(3,\ 4)$ and $(-2,\ 3)$. Find the third vertex.

12. Let opposite vertices of a square are $(3,\ 4)$ and $(1,\ -1)$. Find the other vertices .

13. Find the circum-center of the triangle whose vertices are $(-2,-3),(-1,\ 0)$ and $(7,\ -6)$. And also find the circum - radius.

14. If a and b are real numbers between 0 and 1 such that the points (a, 1), (1, b) and (0, 0) form an equilateral triangle, then find a and b.

SECTION FORMULAE:

15. Find the co-ordinates of the point which divides the line segment joining the points (5, –2) and (9, 6) in ratio 3 : 1.

16. Determine the ratio in which y – x + 2 = 0 divides the joining (3, –1) and (8, 9).

17. In which ratio does x-axis divide the line segment joining (2, –3) and (5, 6) ?

18. Find the ratio in which the point $(2,\ y)$ divides the line segment joining $(4,3)$ and $(6,3)$. And also find the value of y.

19. Find the length of median through A of a triangle whose vertices are A(–1, 3), B (1, –1) and C (5, 1)

20. The co-ordinates of three consecutive vertices of a parallelogram are (1, 3), (–1, 2) and (2, 5). Then find the co-ordinates of the fourth vertex.

21. The vertices of a triangle are (–1,4) and (5, 2). If its centroid is (0, –3), find the third vertex.

22. Find the co-ordinates of incentre of the triangle whose vertices are (4, – 2), (–2, 4) and (5, 5).

23. Find the co-ordinates of the incenter and centroid of the traingle whose vertices are $(-36,\ 7)$, $(20,\ 7)$ and $(0,\ -8)$.

24. If $\left(\frac{3}{2},0\right),\left(\frac{3}{2},6\right)$ and (–1, 6) are the mid points of the sides of a triangle, then find the

(i) Centroid of the triangle

(ii) Incentre of the triangle

25. If a vertex of a triangle be (1, 1) and the middle points of two sides through it be (–2, 3) and (5, 2) then find the centroid and the incentre of the given triangle.

26. If α, β, γ are the real roots of the equation $x^3 - 3px^2 + 3qx - 1 = 0$ then find the centroid of the triangle whose vertices are $\left(\alpha,\frac{1}{\alpha}\right)$, $\left(\beta,\frac{1}{\beta}\right)$ and $\left(\gamma,\frac{1}{\gamma}\right)$.

27. If the equation of the locus of a point equidistant from the points (a_1, b_1) and (a_2, b_2) is $(a_1 - a_2)x + (b_1 - b_2)y + c = 0$, then find the value of c.

28. The vertices of a triangle are A (0, 0), B (0, 2) and C (2, 0). Find the distance between the circumcentre and orthocentre.

29. If $P(1,2)$, $Q(4,6)$, $R(5,\ 7)$ and $S(a,\ b)$ are the vertices of a parallelogram , then find a and b.

Area of a Triangle

30. If the co-ordinates of points A, B, C, D are (6, 3) , (-3, 5) , (4, -2) and (x, 3 x) respectively and if $\frac{\Delta DBC}{\Delta ABC}=\frac{1}{2}$, then find the value of x .

31. The co-ordinates of A, B, C are (6, 3), (–3, 5) and (4, –2) respectively and P is any point (x, y). Prove that $\frac{\Delta PBC}{\Delta ABC}=\frac{|x+y-2|}{7}$.

32. The co-ordinates of two points A and B are (3, 4) and (5, -2) resp. Find the co-ordinates of any point P if PA = PB and $\Delta PAB = 10$.

33. The area of a triangle is 5 sq. units . Two of its vertices are (2, 1) and (3, -2) resp. The third vertex lies on y = x + 3 . Find the third vertex.

34. Triangle is formed by the co-ordinates (0, 0) , (21, 0) and (0, 21) . Find the number of integral co-ordinates strictly inside the triangle. (integral co-ordinates both x and y) . .

35. Find the area of the pentagon whose vertices are A (1, 1), B(7, 21), C (7–3), D(12, 2) and E(0, –3).

36. A line passes through P(h, k) and is parallel to x-axis such that the area enclosed by the lines $y = x$ and $x + y = 4h^2$., then find the locus of the point P . ? PAB = 10

37. Let A (a, b), B (x_1, y_1) and C(x_2, y_2) are the vertices of a triangle. If a, x_1, x_2 are in GP with common ratio r and b, y_1, y_2 are in GP with common ratio s, then prove that area of ΔABC is $\frac{1}{2}ab(r-1)(s-1)(s-r)$ s.u.

38. Find the set of real numbers x such that x^2+2x, $2x+3$ and x^2+3x+8 are the sides

39. Let O (0, 0) , P(3, 4) and Q (6, 0) be the vertices of a triangle OPQ. The point R inside of the triangle OPQ is such that the triangles OPR, PQR , OQR are of equal area . Find the co-ordinates of R.

40. Prove that the points (a, b + c), (b, c + a) and (c, a + b) are collinear.

41. Are the points (- a , - b) , (0, 0) , (a, b) and (a^2 , b^2) vertices of a rectangle or collinear ?

Locus

42. Find the locus of a point whose co-ordinates are given by
   (i) $x = a\cos\theta$, $y = a\sin\theta$
   (ii) $x = a\cos\theta$, $y = b\sin\theta$
   (iii) $x = a\sec\theta$, $y = b\tan\theta$
   (iv) $x = at^2$, $y = 2at$.
   (v) $x = t^2 + t$, $y = 2t + 1$, where t is a parameter.

43. Find the locus of a point which moves such that its distance from the point (0, 0) is twice its distance from the y-axis.

44. Find the locus of the moving point P such that 2 PA = 3 PB, where A is (0, 0), and B is (4, – 3).

45. A point moves so that the sum of the squares of its distances from two fixed points A(a, 0) and B(–1, 0) is constant and equal to 2 c^2, find the locus of the point.

46. Find the locus of a point which moves in a plane in such a way that the sum of its distances from two points (-3, 0) and (3 , 0) is 10 units.

47. Find the equation of the locus of a point which moves so that the difference of its distances from the points (3, 0) and (–3, 0) is 4 units.

48. A rod of length l rest against the floor and a wall of a room. If the rod slides on the floor , then find the locus of its mid point.

49. If the co-ordinates of a variable point P be $\left(t+\frac{1}{t}, t-\frac{1}{t}\right)$, where t is the parameter. Find the locus of P.

50. A variable straight line passes through the points of intersections of the lines x + 2 y = 1 and 2 x - y = 1 and meets the co-ordinates axes in A and B . Find the locus of the mid. point of AB.of a triangle .

51. Find the area of a quadrilateral whose vertices are (-3, 2), (7, -6) , (-5, -4) and (5, 4).

52. The area of triangle is 5 s. u. Two of its vertices are (2, 1) and (3, -2) . The third vertex is (x, y) such that y = x + 3 . Find the co-ordinates of the third vertex..

53. If two vertices of an equilateral triangle is (0, 0) and $(3, \sqrt{3})$. Find the third vertex.

54. Find the ratio in which the join of the points (1, 2) and (-2, 3) is divided by the line 3 x + 4 y = 7.

55. Find the area of the pentagon whose vertices are $(4,3), (-5,6), (0,-7), (3,-6)$ and $(-7,-2)$.

56. Find the area of the hexagon whose vertices are $(5, 0), (4,2), (1,3), (-2,2), (-3,-1)$ and $(0,-4)$

57. Two vertices of a triangle are A (2, 1) and B (3, -2) . The third vertex C lies on the line y = x + 9. If the centroid of the triangle ABC lies on y-axis , find the co-ordinates of C and the centroid.

58. Prove that the co-ordinates of the vertices of an equilateral triangle cannot all be rational.

ANSWER

1. $(3 \pm 2\sqrt{15})$.	**5.** 10	**9.** (0, 5)	10. $\cos^{-1}\left(\frac{63}{65}\right)$
11. $\left(\frac{1+\sqrt{3}}{2}, \frac{7-5\sqrt{3}}{2}\right)$	**12.** (6, -3), (10, 2)	**14.** $a = 2-\sqrt{3} = b$	**15.** (8, 4)
16. 2:3 externally	**17.** 1:2	**18.** 1:2, y = 3	**19.** 5
20. (4. 6)		**21.** (-4, -15)	**22.** $\left(\frac{5}{2}, \frac{5}{2}\right)$
23. $\left(\frac{20}{3}, 2\right)$	**24.** (i) $\left(\frac{2}{3}, 4\right)$ (ii) (1, 2) 25. centroid : $\left(\frac{5}{3}, 3\right)$, incentre:		**26.** (p, q)
27. $\frac{1}{2}\left\{\left(a_2^2 - a_1^2\right) + \left(b_2^2 - b_1^2\right)\right\}$		**28.** $\sqrt{2}$	**29.** a = 0 , b = 1
30. x = 11/8	**32.** (7, 2) or (1, 0)	**33.** (7/2, 13/2) &(-3/2, 3/2)	**34.** 190
35. 215/2 sq. u.	**36.** $4x^2 = (1-y)^2$.	**37.**	**38.** $x \geq 5$.
39. R = (3, 4/3)	**41.** No.	**42.** (i) $x^2 + y^2 = a^2$ (ii) $\frac{x^2}{a^2} + \frac{y^2}{b^2} = 1$ (iii) $\frac{x^2}{a^2} - \frac{y^2}{b^2} = 1$	

(iv) $y^2 = 4ax$ (v) $y^2 = 4x+1$

43. $y^2 - 3x^2 = 0$

44. $5x^2 + 5y^2 - 72x + 54y + 225 = 0$

45. $2x^2 + 2y^2 + 2(1-a)x + (a^2 - 2c^2 + 1) = 0$

46. $\frac{x^2}{25} + \frac{y^2}{16} = 1$ **47.** $\frac{x^2}{4} - \frac{y^2}{5} = 1$ **48.** $4(x^2+y^2) = l^2$. **49.** Rectangular Hyperbola.

50. $10xy = x + 3y$. **51.** 80 s.u. **52.** (7/2, 13/2), (-3/2, 3/2). **53.** $(0, 2\sqrt{3})$ or $(3, -\sqrt{3})$.

54. 4 : 1 internally. **55.** 97 s. u. **56.** 34 s.u **57.** (-5, 4); (0, 1).

THE STRAIGHT LINE

Slope

1. Find the slope of the line through points (4, –6), (–2, –5).
2. Determine λ, so that 2 is the slope of the line through (2, 5) and (λ, 3).
3. Show that the line joining the points (2, –3) and (–5, 1) is parallel to the line joining (7, –1) and (0, 3).
4. For what value of k the points (k, 2–2k), (–k + 1, 2k) and (–4 – k, 6 – 2k) are collinear ?

Angle between two lines

5. Find the angle between the lines joining the points (0, 0), (2, 3) and (2, –2), (3, 5).
6. The angle between two lines is $\frac{\pi}{4}$ and the slope of one of them is $\frac{1}{2}$. Find the slope of the other line.
7. Without using Pythagoras theorem, show that the points A(–1, 3), B (0, 5) and C (3, 1) are the vertices of a right angled triangle ?
8. A line passes through the points A(2, –3) and B(6, 3). Find the slopes of the lines which are

   (i) parallel to AB (ii) perpendicular to AB

Intercept of a line on axes

9. If the straight line y = mx + c passes through the points (2, 4) and (–3, 6), find the values of m and c.
10. What are the inclination to the x-axis and intercept on y-axis of the line $3y = \sqrt{3}x + 6$?
11. Find the equation of the straight line cutting off an intercept of 3 units on negative direction of y-axis and inclined at an angle $\tan^{-1}\left(\frac{3}{5}\right)$ to the axis of x.
12. Find the equations of the bisectors of the angle between the co-ordinate axes.

Various form of a line

13. Find the equation of a line which makes an angle of 135° with the positive direction of x-axis and passes through the point (3, 5).
14. Find the equation of the right bisector of the line joining (1, 1) and (3, 5).
15. The vertices of a triangle are A(10, 4), B(–4, 9) and C(–2, –1). Find the equation of the altitude through A.
16. Find the equations of the medians of a triangle, the co-ordinates of whose vertices are (–1, 6),(–3, –9) and (5,–8).
17. Find the ratio in which the line segment joining the points (2, 3) and (4, 5) is divided by the line joining (6, 8) and (–3,–2).
18. Find the equation of the line through (2, 3) so that the segment of the line intercepted between the axes is bisected at this point.
19. Find the equation of the straight line through the point P(a,b) parallel to the line $\frac{x}{a} + \frac{y}{b} = 1$. Also find the intercepts made by it on the axes.
20. The slope of a straight line through A(3, 2) is $\frac{3}{4}$. Find the co-ordinates of the points on the line that are 5 units away from A.
21. Find the direction in which a straight line must be drawn through the point (1, 2) so that its point of intersection with the line x + y = 4 may be at a distance $\frac{1}{3}\sqrt{6}$ from this point.
22. A line through (2, 3) makes an angle $\frac{3\pi}{4}$ with the negative direction of x-axis. Find the length of the line segment cut off between (2, 3) and the line x + y – 7 = 0.
23. Find the distance of the point (2, 3) from the line 2x – 3y + 9 = 0 measured along the line 2x – 2y + 5 = 0.
24. The line AB whose equation is x - y = 2 cuts the x-axis at A and B is (4, 2). The line segment AB is rotated about A through an angle 45° in the anticlockwise sense. Find the new position of B and the equation of AB in the new position.

Position of two points w.r.t. a line

25. (i) Are the points (2, 1) and (–3, 5) on the same or opposite side of the line 3x –2y + 1 = 0 ?

(ii) Is the point (2, –7) lies on origin side of the line 2x + y + 2 = 0?

Perpendicular and Parallel forms of a line L

26. Find the general equation of the line which is parallel to 3x – 4y + 5 = 0.
    Also find such line through the point (–1, 2).
27. Find the general equation of the line which is perpendicular to x + y + 4 = 0.
    Also find such line through the point (1, 2).

Distance from a point w.r.t a line

28. Find the sum of the abscissas of all the points on the line x + y = 4 that lie at a unit distance from the line 4x + 3y – 10 = 0.
29. If p is the length of the perpendicular from the origin to the line $\frac{x}{a} + \frac{y}{b} = 1$, then prove that $\frac{1}{a^2} + \frac{1}{b^2} = \frac{1}{p^2}$.
30. Let the algebraic sum of the perpendicular distances from the points (2, 0), (0, 2) and (1, 1) to a variable straight line be zero , then the line passing through a pixed point, say $P(\alpha, \beta)$. Find the value of $\alpha + \beta + 10$.
31. Find the distance between the lines 5x – 12y + 2 = 0 and 5x – 12y – 3 = 0.
32. Find the equations of the line parallel to 5x – 12y + 26 = 0 and at a distance of 4 units from it.
33. Show that the area of the parallelogram formed by the lines x + 3y – a = 0, 3x – 2y + 3a = 0, x + 3y + 4a = 0 and 3x – 2y + 7a = 0 is $\frac{20}{11}a^2$ sq. units.
34. Find the area of the parallelogram formed by the lines $y = mx,\ y = mx + 1,\ y = nx,\ y = nx + 1$.
35. Show that the four lines $ax \pm by \pm c = 0$ enclose a rhombus whose area is $\frac{2c^2}{|ab|}$.

Point of Intersection of two Lines:

36. Show that the three straight lines 2x – 3y + 5 = 0, 3x + 4y – 7 = 0 and 9x – 5y + 8 = 0 meet in a point.
37. If the lines ax + y + 1 = 0, x + by + 1 = 0 and x + y + c = 0 (a, b and c being distinct and different from 1) are concurrent, then find the value of $\frac{1}{1-a} + \frac{1}{1-b} + \frac{1}{1-c}$.
38. Find the equation of the straight line passing through the point (2, 1) and through the point of intersection of the lines x + 2y = 3 and 2x – 3y = 4.
39. A variable straight line passes through the point of intersection of the lines x + 2 y = 1 and 2 x - y = 1 and meets the co-ordinate axes in A and B . Find the locus of the mid point of AB.
40. The family of lines x(a + 2b) + y (a + 3b) = a + b passes through the point for all values of a and b. Find the point.
41. If 3a + 2b + 6c = 0 the family of straight lines ax + by + c = 0 passes through a fixed point. Find the co-ordinates of fixed point.
42. If $4a^2 + 9b^2 - c^2 + 12ab = 0$, then find the points where the family of straight lines ax + by + c = 0 is concurrent .
43. Find the equation of straight line which passes through the intersection of the straight lines 3x – 4y + 1 = 0 and 5x + y – 1 = 0 and cuts off equal intercepts from the axes.

Circumcentre / Orthocentre of a Δ :

44. Find the co-ordinates of the circumcentre of the triangle whose vertices are A(5, –1), B(–1, 5) and C(6, 6). Find its radius also.
45. Find the orthocentre of the triangle ABC whose angular points are A(1, 2), B(2, 3) and C(4, 3).
46. If the orthocentre of the triangle formed by the lines 2x + 3y – 1 = 0, x + 2y – 1 = 0, ax + by – 1 = 0 is at origin, then find a + b + 10.

Equation of Bisectors:

47. Find the equations of the bisectors of the angles between the straight lines 3x – 4y + 7 = 0 and 12x + 5y – 2 = 0.
48. Find the equations of angular bisector bisecting the angle containing the origin and not containing the origin of the lines 4x + 3y – 6 = 0 and 5x + 12y + 9 = 0.
49. Find the equation of the bisector of the obtuse angle between the lines 3x – 4y + 7 = 0 and 12x + 5y – 2 = 0
50. Find the bisector of acute angle between the lines x + y – 3 = 0 and 7x – y + 5 = 0.
51. Find the equations of the straight lines passing through the point $(2,3)$ and inclined at $\pi/4$ radians to the line $2x + 3y = 5$.
52. A vertex of an equilateral triangle is $(2,3)$ and the opposite side is x + y = 2 . Find the equations of the other sides
53. Find the equation of the straight lines passing through the point $(2,3)$ and equally inclined to the lines 3 x - 4 y - 7 = 0 and 12 x - 5 y + 6 = 0 .
54. Two equal sides of an isosceles triangle are given by the equations 7 x - y + 3 = 0 and x + y - 3 = 0 and its third side passes through the point $(1, -10)$. Determine the equation of the third side.

Image of a Point w.r.t a Line Mirror

55. Find the image of the point (4, –13) with respect to the line mirror 5x + y + 6 = 0.
56. Find the image of the point (–2, –7) under the transformations (x, y) → (x – 2y, –3x + y).

57. The point (4, 1) undergoes the following three transfor mations successively:

(i) Reflection about the line y = x.

(ii) Translation through a distance 2 units along the positive direction of x-axis.

(iii) Rotation through an angle $\frac{\pi}{4}$ about the origin in the anticlockwise direction. Then find the co-ordinates of the final position.

58. Find the image of the point (3, 8) with respect to the line $x+3y=7$.

59. A ray of light is sent along the line $x-2y-3=0$. Upon reaching the line $3x-2y-5=0$, the ray is reflected from it. Find the equation of the line containing the reflected ray.

60. A ray of light is sent along the line $x-2y+5=0$, upon reaching the line $3x-2y+7=0$, the ray is reflected from it. Find the equation of the line containing the reflected ray.

61. A light beam, emanating from the point (3, 10) reflects from the straight line $2x+y-6=0$ and, then passes through the point (7, 2). Find the equations of the incident and reflected beams.

62. The image of a point P (2, 3) in the line mirror y = x is the point Q and the image of Q in the line mirror y = 0 is the point R (x, y). Then find the value of $x+y+10$.

63. Determine all the values of α for which the point (α, α^2) lies inside the triangle formed by the lines $2x+3y-1=0$, $x+2y-3=0$ and $5x-6y-1=0$.

64. A variable straight line passes through the point of intersection of the lines $x+2y=1$ and $2x-y=1$ and meets the co-ordinate axes in A and B. Find the locus of the middle point of AB.

65. The equation of the perpendicular bisectors of the sides AB and AC of a triangle ABC are $x-y+5=0$ and $x+2y=0$ respectively. If the point A is (1, –2). Find the equation of the line BC.

66. Two sides of a rhombus ABCD are parallel to the lines $y=x+2$ and $y=7x+3$. If the diagonals of the rhombus intersect at the point (1, 2) and the vertex A is on y-axis, find the possible co-ordinates of A.

ANSWERS

1. –1/8
2. $\lambda=1$
3. k=-1, 1/2
4.
5. $\theta=\tan^{-1}\left(\frac{11}{23}\right)$
6. m=3, - 1/3
8. (i) 3/2 (ii) - 2.3
9. m=-2/5
10. $\theta=\frac{\pi}{6}$; 2
11. $y=\frac{3}{5}x-3$
12. $y=\pm x$
13. x+y=8
14. x+2y=8
15. x-5y+10=0
16. 13x+4y=11, 16x-5y+3=0, 9x-14y+17=0.
17. externally, 5:7
18. 3x+2y=12
19. $\frac{x}{a}+\frac{y}{b}=2$
20. (7,5), (-1,-1)
21. ? = 15°, 75°
22. $\sqrt{2}$
23. $4\sqrt{2}$
24. $(2, 2\sqrt{2})$, x=2
25.
25. (i) opposite (ii) No.
26. 3x-4y+11=0
27. x-y+1=0
28. -4
30. 12
31. 5/13
32. 5x-12y-26=0; 5x-12y+78=0
34. $\frac{1}{|m-n|}$
37. 1
38. 5x+3y=13.
39.
40. (2,-1)
41. (1/2, 1/3)
42. (-2,-3), (2, 3)
43. 23x+23y=11.
44. $\left(\frac{23}{8}, \frac{23}{8}\right)$
45. (1,6)
46. 10
47. 21x+77y=101; 99x-77y+81=0
48. 7x+9y=3, 9x-7y=41
49. 21x+77y=101.
51. x-5y+13=0, 5x+y-13=0.
52. $(2\pm\sqrt{3})x-y=1\pm2\sqrt{3}$.
53. 9x-7y+3=0, x+9y-41=0.
54. x-3y-31=0 and 3x+y+7=0.
55. (-1,-14)
56. (12,-1)
57. (i) (1,4) (ii) (3,4) (iii) $\left(-\frac{1}{\sqrt{2}}, \frac{7}{\sqrt{2}}\right)$
58. (-1,-4)
59. 29x-2y-31=0.
60. 29x-2y+33=0
61. 3x-y+1=0, x+3y-13=0.
62. 11
63. $\alpha\in\left(-\frac{3}{2},-1\right)\cup\left(\frac{1}{2},1\right)$.
64. 10xy=x+3y
65. 14x+23y=40
66. (0,0) or (0, 5/2)

Level– II FOR JEE-MAIN AND ADVANCED EXAM ONLY

1. If P(1,2), Q(4,6), R(5,7) and S(a, b) are the vertices of a parallelogram PQRS, then
   (a) a=2, b=4 (b) a=3, b=4
   (c) a=2, b=3 (d) a=3, b=5
2. The extremities of the diagonal of a parallelogram are the points (3, -4) and (-6, 5). Third vertex is the point (-2, 1), then the fourth vertex is
   (a) (1, 1) (b) (1,0)
   (c) (0, 1) (d) (-1,0)
3. The centroid of a triangle is (2, 3) and two of its vertices are (5, 6) and (-1, 4). Then the third vertex of the triangle is
   (a) (2, 1) (b) (2,-1)
   (c) (1,2) (d) (1,-2)
4. If a and b are real numbers between 0 and 1 such that the points (a, 1), (1, b) and (0, 0) form an equilateral triangle, then a, b are
   (a) $2-\sqrt{3}$, $2-\sqrt{3}$ (b) $\sqrt{3}-1$, $\sqrt{3}-1$
   (c) $\sqrt{2}-1$, $\sqrt{2}-1$ (d) None.
5. If O be the origin and $Q_1(x_1, y_1)$ and $Q_2(x_2, y_2)$ be two points, then $OQ_1.OQ_2.\cos(\angle Q_1OQ_2)$ is
   (a) $x_1y_2+x_2y_1$ (b) $(x_1^2+y_1^2)(x_2^2+y_2^2)$
   (c) $(x_1-x_2)^2+(y_1-y_2)^2$ (d) $x_1x_2+y_1y_2$
6. The sides of a triangle are 3x+4y, 4x+3y and 5x+5y units, where x>0, y>0. The triangle is
   (a) rt angled (b) acute angled
   (c) obtuse angled (d) sosceles.
7. Triangle is formed by the co-ordinates (0, 0), (0, 21) and (21, 0). Find the number of integral co-ordinate strictly inside the triangle (integral co-ordinates of both x and y)
   (a) 190 (b) 105
   (c) 231 (d) 205
8. The set of all real numbers x such that $x^2+2x, 2x+3$ and x^2+3x+8 are the sides of a triangle is
   (a) $x\geq 4$ (b) $x\geq 5$
   (c) $x\leq 5$ (d) $x\leq 4$
9. The area of a triangle with vertices at the points $(a,b+c)$, $(b,c+a)$ and $(c,a+b)$ is
   (a) 0 (b) a+b+c
   (c) ab + bc + ca (d) None.
10. The vertices of a triangle ABC are $(\lambda,2-2\lambda)$, $(-\lambda+1,2\lambda)$ and $(-4-\lambda,6-2\lambda)$. If its are be 70 units, then the number of integral values of λ is
    (a) 1 (b) 2
    (c) 3 (d) 4
11. If the co-ordinates of points A, B, C, D are (6, 3), (-3, 5), (4, -2) and (x, 3x) respectively and if $\frac{\Delta DBC}{\Delta ABC}=\frac{1}{2}$, then x is
    (a) 8/11 (b) 11/8
    (c) 7/9 (d) 0
12. The area of a triangle is 5 and two of its vertices are A(2, 1), B(3, -2). The third vertex which lies On line y=x+3 is
    (a) $\left(\frac{7}{2},\frac{13}{2}\right)$ (b) $\left(\frac{5}{2},\frac{5}{2}\right)$
    (c) $\left(-\frac{3}{2},\frac{3}{2}\right)$ (d) (0,0)
13. If the points (2k, k), (k, 2k) and (k, k) with k>0 encloses a triangle of area 18 sq units then the centroid of triangle is equal to
    (a) (8,8) (b) (4,4)
    (c) (-4,-4) (d) $(4\sqrt{2},4\sqrt{2})$
14. If r is the geometric mean of p and q, then the line px+qy+r=0
    (a) has a fixed direction
    (b) passes through a fixed point
    (c) forms with the axes of a triangle of Constant area.
    (d) sum of its intercepts on the axes Is constant.
15. A line passing through the point (2, 2) cuts the axes of co-ordinates at A and B such that area OAB = k (k>0). The intercepts on the axes are the roots of the equation
    (a) $x^2-kx+2k=0$ (b) $x^2-2kx+k=0$
    (c) $x^2+kx+2k=0$ (d) $x^2+kx+k=0$.
16. If A and B are two points on the line 3x+4y+15=0 such that OA = OB = 9 units, the area of the triangle OAB is
    (a) $9\sqrt{2}$ (b) $18\sqrt{2}$
    (c) $12\sqrt{2}$ (d) None.
17. The line segment joining the points (1, 2) and (-2, 1) is divided by the line 3x+4y=7 in the ratio
    (a) 3:4 (b) 4:3
    (c) 9:4 (d) 4:9
18. If a straight line passes through (x_1, y_1) and its segment between the axes is bisected at this point, then its equation is given by
    (a) $\frac{x}{x_1}+\frac{y}{y_1}=2$ (b) $2(xy_1+x_1y)=x_1y_1$
    (c) $xy_1+x_1y=x_1y_1$ (d) None.
19. A straight line through the point P(3, 4) is such that its intercept between the axes is bisected at P. Its equation is
    (a) 3x−4y+7=0 (b) 4x+3y=24
    (c) 3x+4y=25 (d) x+y=7.
20. If the lines 4x+3y=1, y=x+5 and bx+5y=3 are concurrent, then b is
    (a) 1 (b) 3
    (c) 6 (d) 0
21. The lines ax+by+c=0, bx+cy+a=0 and cx+ay+b=0 are concurrent if
    (a) $\sum a^3=3abc$ (b) $\sum a=0$
    (c) $\sum a^2=\sum ab$ (d) None.
22. The lines ax+2y+1=0, bx+3y+1=0 and cx+4y+1=0 are concurrent if a,b,c are in
    (a) A.P (b) GP
    (c) H.P (d) None.

23. If the lines $ax+y+1=0$, $x+by+1=0$ and $x+y+c=0$ (a,b,c are distinct and $a,b,c \neq 1$) are concurrent, then the value of $\frac{1}{1-a}+\frac{1}{1-b}+\frac{1}{1-c}$ is
(a) 0 (b) 1
(c) 2 (d) None.

24. The points (-a, - b), (0, 0), (a, b) and (a^2, ab) are
(a) collinear
(b) vertices of a rectangle
(c) vertices of a parallelogram
(d) None.

25. If $25p^2+9q^2-r^2-30pq=0$, then a point on the line $px+qy+r=0$ is
(a) (-5,3) (b) (1,2)
(c) (0,0) (d)* (5,3)

26. The set of lines $ax+by+c=0$ where $3a+2b+4c=0$ are concurrent at the point
(a) (3,2) (b) (2,4)
(c) (3/4, ½) (d) None.

27. If a, b, c are in A.P then the straight lines $ax+by+c=0$ will always pass through the point
(a) (1, 1) (b) (2,2)
(c) (-2, 1) (d) (1,-2)

28. The equation of the line which passes through the point (-3, 8) and cuts off +ve intercepts on axes whose sum is 7, is
(a) $3x-4y=12$ (b) $4x+3y=12$
(c) $3x+4y=12$ (d) $4x-3y=12$

29. If a pair of opposite vertices of parallelogram are (1, 3) and (-2, 4) and the sides are parallel to $5x-y=0$ and $7x+y=0$, then the equation of a side through (1, 3) is
(a)* $5x-y=2$ (b) $7x+y=10$
(c) $5x-y+14=0$ (d) $7x+y+10=0$

30. The point P(a, b) and Q(b,a) lie on the lines $3x+2y-13=0$ and $4x-y-5=0$. The equation of the line PQ is
(a) $x-y=5$ (b) $x+y=5$
(c) $x-y=-5$ (d) $x+y=-5$.

31. The sides AB, BC, CD and DA of a quadrilateral are $x+2y=3$, $x=1$, $x-3y=4$, $5x+y+12=0$ respectively. The angle between diagonals AC and BD is
(a) 45° (b) 60°
(c) 90° (d) 30°

32. Let PS be the median of the triangle with vertices P(2, 2), Q(6, -1) and R (7,3). The equation of the line passing through (1, -1) and parallel to PS is
(a) $2x-9y-7=0$ (b) $2x-9y-11=0$
(c) $2x+9y-11=0$ (d) $2x+9y+7=0$

33. The equation of the base of an equilateral triangle is $x+y=2$ and the vertex is (2, -1). Then the length of its side is
(a) $\sqrt{\frac{1}{2}}$ (b) $\sqrt{\frac{3}{2}}$
(c) $\sqrt{\frac{2}{3}}$ (d) $\sqrt{2}$

34. The distance between the lines $4x+3y=11$ and $8x+6y=15$ is
(a) 7/2 (b) 7/3
(c) 7/5 (d) 7/10

35. A variable point $\left(1+\frac{\lambda}{\sqrt{2}}, 2+\frac{\lambda}{\sqrt{2}}\right)$ lies in between two parallel lines $x+2y=1$ and $2x+4y=15$, then the range of λ is given by
(a) $0<\lambda<\frac{5\sqrt{2}}{6}$ (b) $-\frac{4\sqrt{2}}{5}<\lambda<\frac{5\sqrt{2}}{6}$
(c) $-\frac{4\sqrt{2}}{5}<\lambda<0$ (d) None.

36. The sum of the abcissae of all the points on the line $x+y=4$ that lie at a unit distance from line $4x+3y-10=0$ is
(a) -4 (b) -3
(c) 3 (d) 4

37. Let the algebraic sum of the perpendicular distances from the points (2, 0), (0, 2), (1,1) to a variable straight line be zero, then the line passes through a fixed point whose co-ordinate are
(a) (1, 1) (b) (2,2)
(c) (0,0) (d) None.

38. If a ,b, c are related by $4a^2+9b^2+9c^2+12ab=0$, then the greatest distance between any two lines of the family of lines $ax+by+c=0$ is
(a) 4/3 (b) $\frac{2}{3}\times\sqrt{13}$
(c) $3\sqrt{3}$ (d) 0

39. If the axes are turned through an angle $\tan^{-1} 2$, then the equation $4xy-3x^2=a^2$ becomes
(a) $x^2-4y^2=2a^2$ (b) $x^2-4y^2=a^2$
(c) $x^2+4y^2=a^2$ (d) $x^2-2xy=a^2$

40. The number of integral values of m for which the x co-ordinate of the point of intersection of the lines $3x+4y=9$ and $y=mx+1$ is also an integer, is
(a) 2 (b) 0
(c) 4 (d) 1

41. Given family of lines $a(2x+y+4)+b(x-2y-3)=0$. The number of lines belonging to the family at a distance $\sqrt{10}$ from any point (2, -3) is
(a) 0 (b) 1
(c) 2 (d) 4

42. If $\frac{x}{c}+\frac{y}{d}=1$ be any line through the intersection of $\frac{x}{a}+\frac{y}{b}=1$ and $\frac{x}{b}+\frac{y}{a}=1$, then
(a) $\frac{1}{c}+\frac{1}{d}=\frac{1}{a}+\frac{1}{b}$ (b) $\frac{1}{a}+\frac{1}{d}=\frac{1}{c}+\frac{1}{b}$
(c) $\frac{1}{b}+\frac{1}{d}=\frac{1}{c}+\frac{1}{a}$ (d) None.

43. The point of intersection of the lines $\frac{x}{a}+\frac{y}{b}=1$ and $\frac{x}{b}+\frac{y}{a}=1$ lies on the line

(a) $x-y=0$

(b) $(x+y)(a+b)=2ab$

(c) $(px+qy)(a+b)=(p+q)ab$

(d) $(px-qy)(a-b)=(p-q)ab$

44. The equation of the right bisector of the line segment joining the points (7, 4) and (-1, -2) is

(a) $4x+3y=10$ (b) $3x-4y+7=0$

(c) $4x+3y=15$ (d) None.

45. The points (1, 3) and (5, 1) are two opposite vertices of a rectangle. The other two vertices lie on the line $y=2x+c$, then the other vertices and c are

(a) (1, 1), (2, 3), c=4 (b) (4, 4), (2, 0), c=-4

(c) (0, 0), (5, 4), c=3 (d) None.

46. The four lines $ax \pm by \pm c = 0$ enclose a

(a) square (b) parallelogram

(c) rectangle

(d) rhombus, whose area is $\frac{2c^2}{ab}$.

47. The area bounded by curves $y=|x|-1$ and $y=-|x|+1$ is

(a) 1 (b) 2

(c) $2\sqrt{2}$ (d) 4

48. Area of the parallelogram formed by the lines $y=mx$, $y=mx+1$, $y=nx$ and $y=nx+1$ is

(a) $\frac{|m+n|}{(m-n)^2}$ (b) $\frac{2}{|m+n|}$

(c) $\frac{1}{|m+n|}$ (d) $\frac{1}{|m-n|}$

49. The line which is parallel to x–axis and crosses the curve $y=\sqrt{x}$ at an angle of 45° is

(a) $x=\frac{1}{4}$ (b) $y=\frac{1}{4}$

(c) $y=\frac{1}{2}$ (d) $y=1$

50. The reflection of the point (4, -13) in line $5x+y+6=0$ is

(a) (-1, -14) (b) (3, 4)

(c) (1, 2) (d) (-4, 13)

51. The area enclosed within the curve $|x|+|y|=1$ is

(a) 4 (b) 2

(c) 1 (d) 3

52. The incenter of the triangle formed by the lines x = 0, y = 0 and $3x+4y=12$ is

(a) $\left(\frac{1}{2},\frac{1}{2}\right)$ (b) (1, 1)

(c) $\left(1,\frac{1}{2}\right)$ (d) $\left(\frac{1}{2},1\right)$

53. The incenter of the triangle formed by the axes and the line $\frac{x}{a}+\frac{y}{b}=1$ is

(a) $\left(\frac{a}{2},\frac{b}{2}\right)$ (b) $\left(\frac{a}{3},\frac{b}{3}\right)$

(c) $\left(\frac{ab}{a+b+\sqrt{a^2+b^2}},\frac{ab}{a+b+\sqrt{a^2+b^2}}\right)$

(d) $\left(\frac{ab}{a+b+\sqrt{ab}},\frac{ab}{a+b+\sqrt{ab}}\right)$

54. Orthocenter of triangle whose vertices are (0, 0), (3, 4), (4, 0) is

(a) $\left(3,\frac{7}{3}\right)$ (b) $\left(3,\frac{5}{4}\right)$

(c) $(5-2)$ (d) $\left(3,\frac{3}{4}\right)$

55. The orthocenter of the triangle formed by the lines xy = 0 and x + y = 1 is

(a) $\left(\frac{1}{2},\frac{1}{2}\right)$ (b) $\left(\frac{1}{3},\frac{1}{3}\right)$

(c) (0,0) (d) $\left(\frac{1}{4},\frac{1}{4}\right)$

56. The midpoints of the sides of a triangle are (5, 0), (5, 12) and (0, 12). The orthocenter of this triangle is

(a)* (0,0) (b) (10,0)

(c) (0,24) (d) $\left(\frac{13}{3},8\right)$

57. One side of an equilateral triangle is line $3x+4y+8=0$ and its centroid is at O(1, 1). The length of its side is

(a) 2 (b) $\sqrt{5}$

(c) $6\sqrt{3}$ (d) $\sqrt{7}$

58. The incenter of the triangle with vertices $\left(1,\sqrt{3}\right)$, (0, 0) and (2, 0) is

(a) $\left(1,\frac{\sqrt{3}}{2}\right)$ (b) $\left(\frac{2}{3},\frac{1}{\sqrt{3}}\right)$

(c) $\left(\frac{2}{3},\frac{\sqrt{3}}{2}\right)$ (d) $\left(1,\frac{1}{\sqrt{3}}\right)$

59. Let P(-1, 0), Q(0, 0) and R $\left(3,3\sqrt{3}\right)$ be three points. Then the equation of the bisector of the angle PQR is

(a) $\frac{\sqrt{3}}{2}x+y=0$ (b) $x+\sqrt{3}y=0$

(c) $y+x\sqrt{3}=0$ (d) $x+\frac{\sqrt{3}}{2}y=0$

60. The vertices of a triangle ABC are (1, 1), (4, -2) and (5, 5) respectively. Then the equation of perpendicular dropped from C to the internal bisector of angle A is

(a) y=5 (b) x=5

(c) $2x+3y=7$ (d) None.

61. The vertices of a triangle are A(-1, -7), B(5, 1) and C(1, 4). The equation of the internal bisector of the angle ABC is

(a) $3x-7y=8$ (b) $x-7y+2=0$
(c) $3x-3y-7=0$ (d) None.

62. The bisector of the acute angle formed between the lines $4x-3y+7=0$ and $4x-4y+14=0$ has the equation

(a) $x+y=7$ (b) $x-y+3=0$
(c) $2x+y=11$ (d) $x+2y=12$

63. The opposite angular points of a square are (3,4) and (1, -1), then the other two vertices are

(a) $\left(-\frac{1}{2},\frac{5}{2}\right),\left(\frac{9}{2},\frac{1}{2}\right)$ (b) $\left(\frac{9}{2},\frac{1}{2}\right),\left(\frac{7}{2},\frac{1}{2}\right)$

(c) $\left(\frac{7}{2},\frac{1}{2}\right),\left(-\frac{7}{2},\frac{1}{2}\right)$ (d) $\left(-\frac{7}{2},\frac{1}{2}\right),\left(-\frac{7}{2},\frac{9}{2}\right)$

64. A line through A(-5, -4) meets the lines $x+3y+2=0$, $2x+y+4=0$ and $x-y-5=0$ at B,C and D resp. If $\left(\frac{15}{AB}\right)^2+\left(\frac{10}{AC}\right)^2=\left(\frac{6}{AD}\right)^2$, then the equation of the line is

(a) $2x+3y+22=0$ (b) $5x-4y+7=0$
(c) $3x-2y+3=0$ (d) None.

65. The equation of the lines through the point (2, 3) and making an intercept of length 2 units between the lines $2x+y=3$ and $2x+y=5$ are

(a) $x+3=0, 3x+4y=12$ (b) $y-2=0, 4x-3y=6$
(c) $x-2=0, 3x+4y=18$ (d) None.

66. A line is such that its segment between the straight lines $5x-y=4$ and $3x+4y=4$ is bisected at the point (1, 5). Its equation is

(a) $23x-7y+6=0$ (b) $7x+4y+3=0$
(c) $83x-35y+92=0$ (d) None.

67. A straight line through the origin O meets the parallel lines $4x+2y=9$ and $2x+y+6=0$ at points P and Q respectively. Then the point O divides the segment PQ in the ratio

(a) 1:2 (b) 3:4
(c) 2:1 (d) 4:3

ANSWER

1. (c)	2. (d)	3. (b)	4. (a)	5. (a)	6. (c)	7. (a)	8. (b)	9. (a)	10. (a)
11. (b)	12. (a), (c)	13. (d)	14. (c)	15. (a)	16. (b)	17. (d)	18. (a)	19. (b)	20. (c)
21. (a)	22. (a)	23. (b)	24. (a)	25. (a), (d)	26. (c)	27. (d)	28. (b)	29. (a), (b)	30. (b)
31. (c)	32. (d)	33. (c)	34. (d)	35. (b)	36. (a)	37. (a)	38. (b)	39. (b)	40. (a)
41. (b)	42. (a)	43. (a), (b), (c)		44. (c)	45. (b)	46. (d)	47. (b)	48. (d)	49. (c)
50. (a)	51. (b)	52. (b)	53. (c)	54. (d)	55. (c)	56. (a)	57. (c)	58. (d)	59. (c)
60. (b)	61. (b)	62. (b)	63. (a)	64. (a)	65.(c)	66. (c)	67. (b)		

Level – III FOR JEE ADVANCED EXAM ONLY

1. Derive the conditions to be imposed on β so that $(0, \beta)$ should lie on or inside the triangle having sides $y+3x+2=0$, $3y-2x-5=0$ and $4y+x-14=0$

2. Find the number of integral values of m, for which the x-co-ordinate of the point of intersection of the lines $3x+4y=9$ and $y=mx+1$ is also an integer.

3. Let $P=(-1,0)$, $Q=(0,0)$ and $R=(3,3\sqrt{3})$ be three points. Then find the equation of the bisector of the angle PQR.

4. A straight line through the point (2, 2) intersects the lines $\sqrt{3}x+y=0$ and $\sqrt{3}x-y=0$ at the points A and B. Then find the equation to the line AB so that the triangle OAB is equilateral.

5. The area of the triangle formed by the intersection of a line parallel to x-axis and passing through P(h,k) with the lines $y=x$ and $x+y=2$ is $4h^2$. Find the locus of the point P

6. Two rays in the first quadrant $x+y=|a|$ and $ax-y=1$ intersects each other in the interval $a \in (a_0, \infty)$. Find the value of a_0.

7. A variable line is at constant distance p from the origin and meets the co-ordinate axes in A, B. Show that the locus of the centroid of the traingle OAB is $\frac{1}{x^2}+\frac{1}{y^2}=\frac{9}{p^2}$.

8. The line segment joining A(3, 0) and B(5, 2) is rotated about A in the anticlockwise direction through an angle of 45° so that B goes to C. If D(x, y) is the image of C with respect to y-axis, then find the value of $x+y+7$.

9.* Find the equation of the line passing through the point (4, 5) and equally inclined to the lines $3x-4y=7$ and $5y-12x=6$.

10. If A(0, 3), C(-2, 5) be the opposite vertices of a square, then find the co-ordinates of remaining two vertices.

11. For what values of the parameter m does the point P (m, m+1) lies with in the triangle ABC the vertices of which are A (0, 3), B(-2, 0) and C(6,1)?

12. A straight line passes through the point (h, k) and this point bisects the part of the intercepted between the axes. Show that equation of straight line is $x/2h+y/2k=1$.

13. Find the values of the parameter m for which the points (0, 0) and (m, 3) lie on the opposite lines $3x+2y-6=0$, $x-4y+16=0$.

14. If A (0, 3) , B (-2, 5) be the adjacent vertices of a square . Find the possible co-ordinates of remaining two vertices

15. Find the co-ordinates of two points on the line x + y = 3 which are situated at distances Ö8 from the point (2, 1) on the line.

16. If a and b are variable show that lines (a+b) x + (2a -b) y = 7b pass through a fixed point.

17. Determine all values of α for which the point $\left(\alpha,\alpha^2\right)$ lies inside the triangle formed by the lines 2x + 3y -1 = 0 , x + 2 y - 3 = 0, 5x - 6 y - 1 = 0.

18. The points (1, 3) and (5, 1) are two opposite vertices of a rectangle. The other two vertices lie on the line y = 2 x + c . Find c and the remaining two vertices.

19. A vertex of an equilateral triangle is (2, 3) and the equation of the opposite side is x + y = 2 . Find the equation of the other two sides .

20. Two consecutive sides of a parallelogram are 4 x + 5 y = 0 and 7x + 2 y = 0 . If the equation to one diagonal is 11 x + 7 y = 9 , then find the equation of the other diagonal.

21. A ray of light coming from the point (1, 2) is reflected at a point A on the x-axis and then passes through the point (5, 3) . Find the point A.

22. A man starts from the point P(-3, 4) and reaches the point Q(0, 1) after touching the line 2 x + y = 7 at R . Find R on the line so that he travels along the shortest path.

23. A ray of light is sent along the straight line $y=\frac{2}{3}x-4$. On reaching the x-axis. It is reflected. Find the point of incidence and the equation of the reflected ray.

24. The point (1, 1) is translated parallel to y = 2 x in the first quadrant through a unit distance. Find the new position of the point.

25. The equations of two sides of a triangle are 3 x - 2 y + 6 = 0 and 4 x + 5 y = 20 and the orthocentre is (1, 1) . Find the equation of the third side.

26. Two vertices of a triangle are (4, -3) and (-2, 5) . If the orthocentre of the triangle is (1, 2) . Prove that the third vertex is (33, 26).

27. The equations of the perpendicular bisectors of the sides AB and AC of triangle ABC are x - y +2 = 0 and x + 2 y = 0 respectively. If the point A is (1, -2) , find the equation of the line BC.

28. A line 4x + y = 1 through the point A(2, -7) meets the line BC whose equation is 3 x - 4 y + 1 = 0 at the point B. Find the equation of the line AC, so that AB = AC.

29. Find the equations of the straight lines passing through (-2, -7) and having an intercept of length 3 between the straight lines 4 x + 3 y = 12 and 8 x + 6 y = 6.

30. Two consecutive sides are 4x + 5 y = 0 and 7 x + 2 y = 0 . If the equation to one diagonal is 11x + 7 y = 9 , find the equation of the other diagonal.

31. The straight lines 3 x + 4 y = 5 and 4x - 3 y = 15 intersect at A. Points B and C are chosen on these lines , such that AB = AC . Determine the possible equations of the line BC passing through the point (1, 2).

32. Aman starts from the point P(-3, 4) and will reach the point Q (0, 1) touching the line 2 x + y = 7 at R. Find R on the line so that he will travel in the shortest distance.

33. Two equal sides of an isosceles triangle are 7 x - y + 3 = 0 and x + y - 3 = 0 and its third side passes through the point (1, -10). Find the equation of the third side.

34. Two opposite sides of a rhombus are x + y = 1 and x + y = 5 . If one vertex is (2, -1) and the angle at the vertex is $45°$. Find the vertex opposite to the given vector.

35. Two sides of a rhombus ABCD are parallel to the lines y = x + 2 and y = 7 x + 3 . If the diagonals of the rhombus intersect at the point (1, 2) and the vertex A is on y-axis . Find the possible co-ordinates of A.

36. The equation of two sides of a parallelogram are 3x - 2 y + 12 = 0 and x - 3 y + 11 = 0 and the point of intersection of its diagonals is (2, 2) . Find theequations of other two sides and its diago

37. Let the point B is symmetric to A (4, -1) with respect to the bisector of the first quadrant. Find AB.

38 A line segment AB through the point A(2, 0) which makes an angle of $30°$ with the positive direction of x-axis is rotated about A in anti-clock-wise direction through an angle of $15°$. If C be the new position of the point $B\left(2+\sqrt{3},1\right)$, Find the co-ordinates of C.

39. The point (1, -2) is reflected in the x-axis and then translated parallel to the +ve direction of x-axis through a distance of 3 units, then find the co-ordinates of the point in the new position.

40. A line through the point A (2, 0) which makes an angle of $30°$ with the +ve direction of x-axis is rotated about A in anti-clockwise direction through an angle $15°$. Find the equation of the straight line in the new position.

41. A line x - y + 1 = 0 cuts the y-axis at A . This line is rotated about A in the clock-wise direction through $75°$. Find the equation of the line in the new position.

42. The point (1, 1) is translated parallel to the line y = 2 x in the first quadrant through a unit distance. Find the new position of the point.

43. Two particles start from the same point (2, -1) , one moving 2 units along the line x + y = 1 and the other 5 units along the line x - 2 y = 4 . If the particle move towards increasing y, find their new positions and the distance between them.

44. If a line AB of length $2l$ moves with the end A always on the x-axis and the end B always on the line y = 6 x . Find the equation of the locus of the mid-point of AB.

ANSWERS

1. $\frac{5}{3} \le \beta \le \frac{7}{2}$ 2. 2 3. $\sqrt{3}x + y = 0$ 4. $y = 2$

5. $2x - y + 1 = 0, 2x + y - 1 = 0$. 6. $a_0 = 1$ 8. $5 + 2\sqrt{2}$

9

10. (-2, 3) and (0,5) 11. (-6/7, 3/2). 12. 13. R - (-4, 0).

14. (0, 7) and (-4, 3). 15. $-2\sqrt{2}$. 16. (0, 3), (4, -1) 17. $\alpha \in \left(-\frac{3}{2}, -1\right) \cup \left(\frac{1}{2}, 1\right)$

18. c = -1 ; (4, 4), (2, 0). 19. $y = (2 \pm \sqrt{3})x - 1 \pm 2\sqrt{3}$. 20. y = x. 21. (13/5, 0)

22. (42/25, 91/25) 23. (6, 0) ; $2x + 3y = 12$. 24. $\left(1 \pm \frac{1}{\sqrt{5}}, 1 \pm \frac{2}{\sqrt{5}}\right)$. 25. $26x - 122y = 1675$.

26. 27. B(-7, 6) ; C(11/5, 2/5) 28. $52x + 89y + 519 = 0$.

29. $x + 2 = 0$ and $7x + 24y + 182 = 0$. 30. x = y 31. $x - 7y + 13 = 0$ and $7x + y = 9$.

32. R(42/25, 91/25). 33. $3x + y + 7 = 0$ and $x - 3y - 31 = 0$.

34. $D(6 + 2\sqrt{2}, -1 - 2\sqrt{2})$ or $D(2 - 2\sqrt{2}, 3 + 2\sqrt{2})$ 35. (0, 0) or (0, 5/2).

36. sides are : $x - 3y = 3$, $3x - 2y = 16$, Diagonals are $x + 4y = 10$, $5x - 8y + 6 = 0$. 37. $5\sqrt{2}$.

38. $(2 + \sqrt{2}, \sqrt{2})$ 39. (4, 2). 40. $x - y = 2$ 41. $x + y\sqrt{3} - \sqrt{3} = 0$.

42. $\left(1 \pm \frac{1}{\sqrt{5}}, 1 \pm \frac{2}{\sqrt{5}}\right)$. 43. $(2 - \sqrt{2}, \sqrt{2} - 1), (2\sqrt{5} + 2, \sqrt{5} - 1), \sqrt{29 + 2\sqrt{10}}$ 44. $9x^2 + 10y^2 - 6xy - 9l^2 = 0$.

COMPREHENSIVE LINK PASSAGE

PASSAGE - I

Some-times we do not take x-axis and y-axis at $90°$ and assume that they are inclined at an angle ω.

Let 0X and OY be x-axis and y-axis is inclined at an angle ω. Let P be a point on the plane.

Drae parallel lines from P parallel to y and x-axis. We will write PN = x and PM = y and will say that the co-ordinates of P are (x, y), where such axes are called Oblique axes.

1. The distance of P(x, y) from origin must be

(a) $\sqrt{x^2 + y^2}$ (b) $\sqrt{x^2 + y^2 - 2xy\sin\omega}$

(c)* $\sqrt{x^2 + y^2 - 2xy\cos\omega}$ (d) None.

2. If $M(x_1, y_1), N(x_2, y_2)$ be two points in oblique system then the co-ordinates of the mid points of A and B are

(a)* $\left(\frac{x_1 + x_2}{2}, \frac{y_1 + y_2}{2}\right)$

(b) $\left(\frac{x_1 + x_2}{2}\sin\omega, \frac{y_1 + y_2}{2}\sin\omega\right)$

(c) $\left(\frac{x_1 + x_2}{2}\cos\omega, \frac{y_1 + y_2}{2}\cos\omega\right)$

(d) None.

3. If a line makes intercepts a and b on x and y axes (obviously oblique axes), then its equaion be

(a) $\frac{x}{a\cos\omega} + \frac{y}{b\cos\omega} = 1$ (b)* $\frac{x}{a} + \frac{y}{b} = 1$

(c) $\frac{x}{b\cos\omega} + \frac{y}{a\cos\omega} = 1$ (d) None.

4. If axes are inclined at $60°$ then the radius of the circle $x^2 + xy + y^2 - 4x - 5y - 2 = 0$

(a) 2 (b) 4

(c)* 3 (d) $\sqrt{5}$

PASSAGE - II

Let us a rectangular co-ordinate system OX and OY be rotated through an angle θ in the anti-clockwise direction. Then we get a new co-ordinate system OX' and OY'. If we consider a point

P(x, y) in the old co-ordinate system and P(X, Y) in the new co-ordinate system, then we can write $x = X\cos\theta - Y\sin\theta, y = X\sin\theta + Y\cos\theta$. Then

1. The value of X is

(a)* $X\cos\theta + Y\sin\theta$ (b) $X\sin\theta + Y\cos\theta$
(c) $X\cos\theta - Y\sin\theta$ (d) $X\sin\theta - Y\cos\theta$.

2. The equation of a curve in a plane $17x^2 - 16xy + 17y^2 = 225$. Through what angle must the axes be rotated, so that the equation becomes $9X^2 + 25Y^2 = 225$ θ

(a) 30° (b)* 45°
(c) 60° (d) 75°

3. If axes be rotated at 45°, then equation 17x2–16xy + 17y² = 225 reduces to $AX^2 + BY^2 = C^2$, then the value of A+ B+C is

(a)* 59 (b) 50
(c) 58 (d) 57.

4. If the axes are rotated through 45°, then the equation $3x^2 + 2xy + 3y^2 = 2$ reduces to

(a) $X^2 + 2Y^2 = 1$ (b)* $2X^2 + Y^2 = 1$
(c) $2X^2 + 3Y^2 = 1$ (d) $5X^2 + 3Y^2 = 1$.

5. The equation $4xy - 3x^2 = a^2$ become when the axes are turned through an angle $\tan^{-1} 2$ is

(a) $x^2 + 4y^2 = a^2$ (b)* $x^2 - 4y^2 = a^2$
(c) $4x^2 + y^2 = a^2$ (d) $4x^2 - y^2 = a^2$.

PASSAGE - III

The equations of adjacent sides of a parallelogram are $x + y + 1 = 0$ and $2x - y + 2 = 0$. If the equation of one of its diagonal is $13x - 2y - 32 = 0$. Then

1. Equation of the diagonal must be

(a) $7x - 8y + 1 = 0$ (b)* $2x - y = 0$
(c) $2x - y = 7$ (d) $3x + 4y = 5$.

2. Area of the given parallelogram must be

(a)* 45 (b) 45/2
(c) $3\sqrt{5}$ (d) $4\sqrt{2}$

3. Equation of the side of the parallelogram opposite to the given side $2x - y + 2 = 0$ must be

(a) $2x - y + 5 = 0$ (b) $2x - y = 0$
(c)* $2x - y = 7$ (d) $x + 3y = 4$

PASSAGE - IV

The vertex C of a right angled isosceles triangle ABC is (2, 2) and the equation of the hypotenuse AB is $3x + 4y = 4$. Then

1. The equations of the sides AC and AB must be

(a)* $7y - x = 12, 7x + y = 16$
(b) $3x - 4y + 2 = 0, 4x + 3y = 14$
(c) $x + y = 4, 2x - 3y = 10$
(d) $x - y = 2, 3x + 2y = 5$.

2. The area of the triangle ABC must be

(a) 1 s.u (b)* 2 s. u.
(c) $2\sqrt{2}$ s. u (d) 4 s.u

3. The in-radius of the triangle ABC must be

(a) $\frac{2}{2+\sqrt{2}}$ (b)* $\frac{4}{2+\sqrt{2}}$
(c) $\frac{2-\sqrt{2}}{2+\sqrt{2}}$ (d) $\frac{1}{\sqrt{2}}$

PASSAGE - V

The vertex A of a triangle ABC is (3, -1). The equations of median BE and angular bisector CF are $x - 4y + 10 = 0$ and $6x + 10y - 59 = 0$. Then

1. The equation of AB must be

(a) $x + y = 2$ (b)* $18x + 13y = 41$
(c) $23x + y = 70$ (d) $x + 4y = 0$.

2. Slope of the side BC must be

(a) 1/7 (b) 1/9
(c)* 2/9 (d) 3/4

3. The length of the side AC must be

(a) $\sqrt{83}$ (b)* $\sqrt{85}$
(c) $\sqrt{89}$ (d) $\sqrt{88}$

PASSAGE - VI

In triangle ABC equation of altitudes AM and BN and the side AB are given by equations $x + 5y = 3$, $x + y = 1$. Then

1. The equation of the third altitude CL must be

(a) $3x - y = 2$ (b)* $3x - y = 1$
(c) $3x + y + 1 = 0$ (d) $x + 3y + 1 = 0$.

2. The equation of BC must be

(a)* $5x - y = 5$ (b) $5x + y + 5 = 0$
(c) $x - 2y = 3$ (d) $x + 2y + 3 = 0$

3. If R is the circum-radius of the triangle, then 2R cos B must be equal to

(a) $\frac{1}{\sqrt{3}}$ (b)* $\frac{1}{\sqrt{2}}$
(c) $\frac{1}{3}$ (d) $\frac{1}{2}$

PASSAGE-VII

Let the curve be S: f(x, y) = 0 and line mirror L: ax + by + c = 0. We take a point P on the given curve in parametric form. Suppose Q be the image or reflection of point P about the line mirror L= 0, which again contains the same parameter. Let $Q = (\phi(t), \psi(t))$, where t is a parameter. Now, let $x = \phi(t)$ and $y = \psi(t)$. Eliminating t, we get the equation of the reflected curve S'. Then

1. The image of the line 3 x - y = 2 in the line y = x - 1 is

(a) x + 3 y = 2 (b) 3 x + y = 2
(c)* x - 3 y = 2 (d) x + y = 2.

2. The image of the circle $x^2 + y^2 = 4$ in the line x + y = 2 is

(a) $x^2 + y^2 - 2x - 2y = 0$
(b) $x^2 + y^2 - 4x - 4y + 6 = 0$
(c) $x^2 + y^2 - 2x - 2y + 2 = 0$
(d)* $x^2 + y^2 - 4x - 4y + 4 = 0$.

3. The image of the parabola $x^2 = 4y$ in the line x + y = a is

(a) $(x-a)^2 = -4(y-a)$ (b)* $(y-a)^2 = -4(x-a)$
(c) $(x-a)^2 = 4(y+a)$ (d) $(y-a)^2 = 4(x+a)$

4. The image of an ellipse $9x^2 + 16y^2 = 144$ in the line y = x is

(a)* $16x^2 + 9y^2 = 144$ (b) $9x^2 + 16y^2 = 144$
(c) $16x^2 + 25y^2 = 400$ (d) $25x^2 + 16y^2 = 400$.

5. The image of the rectangular hyperbola x y = 9 in the line y = 3 is

(a) x y + 9 = 0 (b)* x y - 6 x + 9 = 0
(c) xy + 6y - 9 = 0 (d) xy + 6x + 9 = 0.

MATCH MATRIX

1. Match the following columns: In ? ABC, AB : x + 2y = 3, BC : 2 x - y + 5 = 0 , AC : x - 2 = 0 be the sides, then

Column - I	Column - II
(A) circum-center of ? ABC is	(P) $\left(\frac{-7}{5}, \frac{11}{5}\right)$
(B) Centroid of ? ABC is	(Q) $\left(\frac{13}{15}, \frac{131}{30}\right)$
(C) Orthocenter of ? ABC is	(R) $\left(2, \frac{19}{4}\right)$

2. Match the following columns : A line cuts x-axis at A and y-axis at B such that $AB = l$, then the loci of the

Column - I	Column - II
(A) circum-center of ? ABC is	(P) $x^2 + y^2 = \frac{l^2}{9}$
(B) Orthocenter of ? ABC is	(Q) $x^2 + y^2 = \frac{l^2}{4}$
(C) In-center of ? ABC is	(R) $x^2 + y^2 = 0$
(D) centroid of ? ABC is	(S) $y = x$

3. Match the following columns: The vertex C of a triangle ABC is (4, -1) . The equation of altitude AD and median AE are 2 x - 3y + 12 = 0 and 2 x + 3 y = 0 , then

Column - I	Column - II
(A) Slope of side AB	(P) - 3 / 7
(B) Slope of side BC	(Q) - 3 / 2
(C) Slope of side AC	(R) - 9 / 11.

4. Match the following columns: The genral equation of 2nd degree is $\lambda x^2 + 2y^2 + 4xy + 2x + 4y + \lambda = 0$. Then it represents

Column - I	Column - II
(A) distinct lines if	(P) k = 1
(B) parallel lines if	(Q) k = 3
(C) imaginary lines if	(R) $k = \phi$.

5. Match the following columns :

Column - I	Column - II
(A) If 3a + 2b + 6c = 0, then the family of lines ax + by + c = 0 passes through a fixed point. Then the fixed point is	(P) (- 2, - 3)
(B) The family of lines x(a+2b)+y (a+3b) = a+b passes through a fixed point. Then the point is	(Q) $\left(\frac{1}{2}, \frac{1}{3}\right)$
(C) If $4a^2 + 9b^2 - c^2 + 12ab = 0$, then the family of straight lines a x + by + c = 0 passes through fixed point. Then the fixed point is	(R) (2, -1)

Ans. (A) $\rightarrow$ (Q), (B) $\rightarrow$ (R), (C) $\rightarrow$ (P),

6. Match the following columns :

Column - I	Column - II
The area of a parallelogram formed by the lines	
(A) 3x - 4 y + 1 = 0, 3x-4y+3 = 0 , 4x - 3y - 1 = 0 and 4x - 3 y - 2 = 0 is	(P) 20 / 11 units.
(B) x + 3 y = 1 , 3x - 2y + 3 = 0 , x + 3 y + 4 = 0 and 3 x - 2 y + 7 = 0 is	(Q) 2 / 7 Units
(C) y = 2 x + 3 , y = 2 x + 5 . y = 7 x + 4 and y = 7 x + 5 is	(R) 2/ 5 Units.

Ans. (A) $\rightarrow$ (P), (B) $\rightarrow$ (Q), (C) $\rightarrow$ (R),

7. Match the following columns:

Column - I	Column - II
(A) The equation of the obtuse angle bisector of the lines	(P) 6 x + 2 y - 5 = 0

$3x - 4y + 7 = 0$ and $12x + 5y - 2 = 0$ is

(B) The equation of the acute angle bisector of the lines $x + y = 3$ and $7x - y + 5 = 0$ is | (Q) $21x + 77y - 101 = 0$

(C) The bisector of the angle between the lines $2x + y = 6$ and $2x - 4y + 7 = 0$ which contains the point (1, 2) is | (R) $6x - 2y = 5$.

(D) The bisector of the angle between the lines $4x + 3y = 6$ and $5x + 12y + 9 = 0$ which containing the origin is | (S) $7x + 9y = 3$.

(E) The bisector of the angle between the lines $4x + 3y = 6$ and $5x + 12y + 9 = 0$ which does not containing the origin is | (T) $9x - 7y = 41$.

8. Match the following columns :

Column - I	Column - II
(A) The image of a line $2x + 3y + 4 = 0$ with respect to x - axis is	(P) $2x - y - 11 = 0$
(B) The image of a line $7x - 3y - 10 = 0$ with respect to y - axis is	(Q) $5x + 3y + 7 = 0$
(C) The image of a line $3x + 5y + 7 = 0$ with respect to the line $y = x$ is	(R) $x - 4y + 29 = 0$.
(D) The image of a line $2x + y + 3 = 0$ with respect to the line $x = 2$ is	(S) $7x + 3y + 10 = 0$
(E) The image of a line $x + 4y + 5 = 0$ with respect to the line $y = 3$ is	(T) $2x - 3y + 4 = 0$

9. Match the following Columns :

Column - I	Column - II
(A) The image of a point (2, 3) w.r.t x - axis is	(P) (4, 5)
(B) The image of a point (3, 4) w.r.t y-axis is	(Q) (1, -1)
(C) The image of a point (5, 4) w.r.t the line $y = x$ is	(R) (2, -3)
(D) The image of a point (2, 5) w.r.t the line $x = 3$ is	(S) (-3, 4)
(E) The image of a point (1, 5) w.r.t the line $y = 2$ is	(T) (4, 5)
(F) The image of a point (2, 4) w.r.t the line $y = \sqrt{3}x$ is	(U) $\left(2\sqrt{3} - 1, 2 + \sqrt{3}\right)$

10. Match the following columns:

Column - I	Column - II
(A) The ortho-center of triangle formed by lines $xy = 0$ and $x + y = 4$ is	(P) (3, 1)
(B) The ortho-center of triangle formed by the lines $x + y = 4$, $x - y = 2$ and $2x + 3y = 6$ is	(Q) $\left(-\frac{1}{4}, -\frac{1}{6}\right)$
(C) The ortho-center of triangle formed the lines $6x^2 + 5xy - 6y^2 + 3x - 2y = 0$ and $x + 4y = 5$ is	(R) (0, 0)

11. Match the following Columns

Column - I	Column - II
(A) A light beam emanating from the point (3, 10) reflects from the straight line $2x + y = 6$ and the passes through the point B(7, 2). Then the equation of the relected ray is	(P) $2x + 3y = 12$
(B) A ray of light is sent along the line $y = \frac{2}{3}x - 4$. On reaching the x-axis it is reflected. Then the equation of the reflected ray is	(Q) $x + 3y = 13$
(C) A ray of light is sent along the line $x - 2y + 5 = 0$. Upon reaching the line $3x + 2y + 7 = 0$, the ray is reflected from it. Then the equation of the line containing the reflected ray is	(R) $19x - 22y = -79$

ANSWER

1. **(A) → (R), (B) → (Q), (C) → (P)**
2. **(A) → (Q), (B) → (R), (S) → (R), (D) → (P)**
3. **(A) → (R), (B) → (Q), (C) → (P)**

4. (A) $\rightarrow$ (P), (B) $\rightarrow$ (R), (C) $\rightarrow$ (P)

5. (A) $\rightarrow$ (Q), (B) $\rightarrow$ (R), (C) $\rightarrow$ (P),

6. (A) $\rightarrow$ (P), (B) $\rightarrow$ (Q), (C) $\rightarrow$ (R),

8. (A) $\rightarrow$ (T), (B) $\rightarrow$ (S), (C) $\rightarrow$ (Q), (D) $\rightarrow$ (P), (E) $\rightarrow$ (R).

9. (A) $\rightarrow$ (R), (B) $\rightarrow$ (S), (C) $\rightarrow$ (T), (D) $\rightarrow$ (P), (E) $\rightarrow$ (Q), (F) $\rightarrow$ (U).

10. (A) $\rightarrow$ (R), (B) $\rightarrow$ (P), (C) $\rightarrow$ (Q).

11. (A) $\rightarrow$ (Q), (B) $\rightarrow$ (P), (C) $\rightarrow$ (R)

QUESTIONS ASKED IN ROORKEE EXAM.

1. The opposite angular points of a square are (3,4) and (1, -1). Find the co-ordinates of the other two vertices. **[Roorkee–1985]**

2. Two vertices of a triangle are (4, -3) and (-2, 5). If the ortho-center of the triangle is at (1, 2). Find the co-ordinates of the third vertex. **[Roorkee – 1987]**

3. A line is such that its segment between the straight lines $5x - y - 4 = 0$ and $3x + 4y - 4 = 0$ is bisected at the point (1, 5). Obtain its equation. **[Roorkee – 1988]**

4. The extremities of the diagonal of a square are (1, 1) and (-2,-1). Obtain the other two vertices and the equation of the other diagonal. **[Roorkee–1989]**

5. A variable straight line passes through the point of intersection of the lines x + 2y=1 and 2x-y=1 and meets the co-ordinate axes in A and B. Find the locus of the middle point of AB. **[Roorkee– 1989]**

6. A variable line, drawn through the point of intersection of the straight lines $\frac{x}{a}+\frac{y}{b}=1$ and $\frac{x}{b}+\frac{y}{a}=1$, meets the co-ordinates axes in A and B. Then the locus of AB is the curve. **[Roorkee – 1989]**

7. A line joining A(2, 0), B(3, 1) is rotated about A in anti-clockwise direction through $15°$. If B goes to C in the new position, what will be the co-ordinates of C? **[Roorkee – 1989]**

8. Which pair of points lie on ame side of $3x - 8y - 7 = 0$?
   (a) (0, -1) & (0, 0) (b) (4,-3) & (0,1)
   (c) (-3, -4) & (1, 2) (d) (-1, -1) & (3, 7)
   [Roorkee – 1990]

9. The angle between two straight line is $30°$. At a distance 5 m along one line, a line is drawn which is perpendicular to the other one at A. From A, similarly another perpendicular is drawn to the Ist line, and so on. The total length of all such lines is **[Roorkee – 1990]**
   (a) $15-3\sqrt{3}$ (b) $10-5\sqrt{3}$
   (c) $15+5\sqrt{3}$ (d) $10+5\sqrt{3}$

10. Determine conditions to be imposed on β so that $(0,\beta)$ should lie on or inside the triangle having sides $y + 3x + 2 = 0$, $3y - 2x - 5 = 0$ and $4y + x - 14 = 0$. **[Roorkee Main – 1990]**

11. A ray of light is sent along the line $x - 2y - 3 = 0$. Upon reaching the line $3x - 2y - 5 = 0$, the ray is reflected from it. Find the equation of line containing the reflected ray. **[Roorkee Main – 1990]**

12. A line parallel to the straight line $3x - 4y - 2 = 0$ and at a distance 4 units from it is
   (a) 3x - 4y + 30=0 (b) 4x - 3y + 12=0
   (c) 3x - 4y + 18=0 (d) 3x - 4y + 22=0
   [Roorkee – 1991]

13. The equation of a straight line passing through (-5, 4) which cuts an intercept of $\sqrt{2}$ between the lines x+y+1=0 and x + y-1= 0 is
   (a) x - 2y + 13 = 0 (b) 2x - y + 14 = 0
   (c) x-y+9=0 (d) x - y + 10 = 0
   [Roorkee – 1991]

14. The two adjacent sides of a cyclic quadrilateral are 2 and 3 and the angle between them is $60°$. If the area of the quadrilateral is $4\sqrt{3}$, then find the remaining two sides. **[Roorkee Main – 1991]**

15. P(3, 1), Q(6, 5) and R(x,y) are three points such that the angles PRQ is a right angle and the area of $\Delta RPQ = 7$, then the number of such points R is
   (a) 0 (b) 1
   (c) 2 (d) infinite.
   [Roorkee– 1992]

16. P is a point on either of the two lines $y-\sqrt{3}|x|=2$ at a distance of 5 units from their point of intersection, then the co-ordinates of the foot of the perpendicular from P on the bisector of the angle between them are **[Roorkee – 1992]**
   (a) $\left(0,\frac{4+5\sqrt{3}}{2}\right)$ or $\left(0,\frac{4-5\sqrt{3}}{2}\right)$ depending on which line P is taken
   (b) $\left(0,\frac{4+5\sqrt{3}}{2}\right)$ (c) $\left(0,\frac{4-5\sqrt{3}}{2}\right)$
   (d) $\left(\frac{5}{2},\frac{5\sqrt{3}}{2}\right)$

17. The extremities of a rectangle are (-4, 4) and (6, -1). A circle circumscribe the rectangle and cuts an intercept AB on the y-axis. Find the area of the triangle formed by AB and the tangents to the circle at A and B.

[Roorkee Main – 1992]

18. If one of the diagonals of the square is along the line x = 2y and one of its vertices is A(3, 0), then its sides through the vertex A are given by

    (a) $y+3x+9=0; 3y+x-3=0$
    (b) $y-3x+9=0; 3y+x-3=0$
    (c) $y-3x+9=0; 3y-x+3=0$
    (d) $y-3x+3=0; 3y+x+9=0$

[Roorkee – 1993]

19. The sides AB, BC, CD, DA of a quadrilateral have the equations $x+2y=3$, $x = 1$, $x - 3y = 4$, $5x + y + 12 = 0$ respectively. Find angle between diagonals AC and BD.

[Roorkee Main – 1993]

20. Given vertices A(1, 1), B(4, -2) and C(5, 5) of a triangle, Find the equation of the perpendicular dropped from C to the interior bisector of the angle A.

[Roorkee Main – 1994]

21. The co-ordinates of the foot of the perpendicular from the point (2, 4) on the line $x + y = 1$ are

    (a) (1/2, 3/2) (b) (-1/2, 3/2)
    (c) (4/3, ½) (d) (3/4, -1/2)

[Roorkee – 1995]

22. All points lying outside the triangle formed by the points (1, 3), (5, 0) and (-1, 2) satisfy

    (a) $3x+y\geq 0$ (b) $2x+y-13\geq 0$
    (c) $2x+y-12\leq 0$ (d) $-2x+y\geq 0$

[Roorkee – 1995]

23. In a triangle ABC, the equation of the perpendicular bisector of AC is $3x-2y+8=0$. If the co-ordinates of the points A and B are (1, -1) and (3, 1) respectively, find the equation of the line BC and the center of the circum-circle of the triangle ABC.

[Roorkee Main – 1995]

24. Two sides of a rhombus, lying in the first quadrant are given by $3x-4y=0$ and $12x-5y=0$. If the length of the longer diagonal is 12, find the equations of the other two sides of the rhombus. **[Roorkee Main – 1996]**

25. What is the equation of straight line equally inclined to the axes and equi-distant from the points (1, -2) and (3, 4)?

    (a) $x-y-2=0$ (b) $x+y-2=0$
    (c) $x-y-1=0$ (d) $x+y-1=0$

[Roorkee – 1997]

26. If the points (2a, a), (a, 2a) and (a, a) enclose a triangle of area 8, then find the value of a. **[Roorkee – 1997]**

27. One diagonal of a square $7x + 5y = 35$ intercepted by the axes. Obtain the extremities of the other diagonal.

[Roorkee Main -1998]

28. The equations of two equal sides AB and AC of an isosceles triangle ABC are $x+y=5$ and $7x-y=3$ respectively. Find the equations of the side BC if the area of the triangle ABC is 5 sq. units. **[Roorkee – 1999]**

29. Find the position of the point (4, 1) after it undergoes the following transformations successively

    (i) Reflection about the line $y = x - 1$
    (ii) Translation by one unit along x-axis in the positive direction.
    (iii) Rotation through an angle $\pi/4$ about the origin in the anti-clockwise direction.

[Roorkee Main – 2000]

30. Two vertices of a triangle are at (-1, 3) and (2, 5) and its orthocenter is at (1, 2). Find the co-ordinate of the third vertex. **[Roorkee Main – 2001]**

ANSWER

1. $\left(-\frac{1}{2},\frac{5}{2}\right);\left(\frac{9}{2},\frac{1}{2}\right)$ **2.** (17, 14) **3.** $83x-35y+92=0$ **4.** $\left(\frac{3}{2},-\frac{3}{2}\right),\left(-\frac{3}{2},\frac{3}{2}\right); x+y=0$

5. $(10x-3)(10y-1)=0$ **6.** $xy(a+b)=ab(x+y)$ **7.** $\left(\frac{4+\sqrt{2}}{2},\frac{\sqrt{6}}{2}\right)$ **8.** (d)

9. (d) **10.** $\frac{5}{2}<\beta<\frac{7}{2}$ **11.** $29x-2y-33=0$ **12.** (c) **13.** (c)

14. $x=3, y=2$ **15.** (b) **16.** (d) **17.** $\frac{1}{8}\times(105)^{3/2}$ **18.** (b)

19. $\tan^{-1}5$ **20.** $x=5$ **21.** (b) **22.** (a), (b), (c)

23. $x+4y=7$; (-4/5, 14/5) **24.** $4y-3x=\frac{108}{\sqrt{130}}; 5y-12x+\frac{480}{\sqrt{130}}=0$ **25.** (c)

26. $a=\pm 4$ **27.** $(6,5),(-1,0)$

28. $y-\frac{15}{2}=-3\left(x-\frac{3}{2}\right); y-\frac{15}{2}=2\left(x-\frac{3}{2}\right); y-\frac{1}{2}=\frac{1}{3}\left(x-\frac{1}{2}\right); y-\frac{1}{2}=-\frac{3}{2}\left(x-\frac{13}{2}\right)$

29. (i) $(2,3)$ (ii) $(3,3)$ (iii) $\left(0,3\sqrt{2}\right)$ **30.** $(5/7, 17/7)$

QUESTIONS ASKED IN IIT-JEE EXAMS

1. Three lines $px+qy+r=0$, $qx+ry+p=0$ and $rx+py+q=0$ are concurrent if : **[IIT 1985]**
   (a) $p+q+r=0$ (b) $p^2+q^2+r^2=pq+qr+rp$
   (c) $p^3+q^3+r^3=3pqr$ (d) none of these

2. The orthocentre of the triangle formed by the lines $x+y=1$, $2x+3y=6$ and $4x-y+4=0$ lies in quadrant number...... **[IIT 1985]**

3. All points inside the triangle formed by the points (1, 3), (5, 0) and (–1, 2) satisfy :
   (a) $3x+2y\geq 0$ *(b) $2x+y-13\geq 0$
   (c) $2x-3y-12\leq 0$ (d) none of these
   [IIT 1986]

4. The equation of the perpendicular bisectors of the sides AB and AC of a triangle ABC are $x-y+5=0$ and $x+2y=0$ respectively. If the point A is (1, –2). Find the equation of the line BC. **[IIT 1986]**

5. The lines $2x+3y+19=0$ and $9x+6y-17=0$ cut the co-ordinate axes in concylic points. (T/F) **[IIT 1988]**

6. Line L has intercepts a and b on the co-ordinate axes. When the axes are rotated through a given angle, keeping the origin fixed, the same line L has intercepts p and q, then: **[IIT 1990]**
   (a) $a^2+b^2=p^2+q^2$ (b) $\frac{1}{a^2}+\frac{1}{b^2}=\frac{1}{p^2}+\frac{1}{q^2}$
   (c) $a^2+p^2=b^2+q^2$ (d) $\frac{1}{q^2}+\frac{1}{p^2}=\frac{1}{b^2}+\frac{1}{q^2}$

7. A line cuts the x-axis at A(7, 0) and the y-axis at B(0, –5). A variable line PQ is drawn perpendicular to AB cutting the x-axis in P and the y-axis in Q. If AQ and BP intersect in R, find the locus of R. **[IIT 1990]**

8. Determine all values of α for which the point (α, α^2) lies inside the triangle formed by the lines $2x+3y-1=0$, $x+2y-3=0$, $5x-6y-1=0$. **[IIT 1992]**

9. The vertices of a triangle A(–1, –7), B(5, 1) and C(1, 4). The equation of the bisector of the angle $\angle ABC$ is .....
   [IIT 1993]

10. A line through A(–5, –4) meets the lines $x+3y+2=0$, $2x+y+4=0$ and $x-y-5=0$ at the points B, C and D respectively. **[IIT 1993]**
    If $\left(\frac{15}{AB}\right)^2+\left(\frac{10}{AC}\right)^2=\left(\frac{6}{AD}\right)^2$, find equation of the line.

11. A rectangle PQRS has its sides PQ parallel to the line $y=mx$ and vertices P, Q and S on the lines $y=a$, $x=b$ and $x=-b$ respectively. Find the locus of the vertex R. **[IIT 1996]**

12. The diagonals of a parallelogram PQRS are along the lines $x+3y=4$ and $6x-2y=7$. Then PQRS must be a :
    (a) rectangle (b) square
    (c) cyclic quadrilateral (d) rhombus **[IIT 1998]**

13. Let PS be the median of the triangle with vertices P(2, 2), Q(6, –1) and R(7, 3). The equation of the line passing through (1, –1) and parallel to PS is : **[IIT 2000]**
    (a) $2x-9y-7=0$ (b) $2x-9y-11=0$
    (c) $2x+9y-11=0$ *(d) $2x+9y+7=0$

14. Area of the parallelogram formed by the lines $y=mx$, $y=mx+1$, $y=nx$ and $y=nx+1$ equals :
    (a) $\frac{|m+n|}{(m-n)^2}$ (b) $\frac{2}{|m+n|}$
    (c) $\frac{1}{|m+n|}$ (d) $\frac{1}{|m-n|}$ **[IIT 2001]**

15. The number of integral values of m, for which the x-co-ordinate of the point of intersection of the lines $3x+4y=9$ and $y=mx+1$ is also an integer, is: **[IIT 2001]**
    (a) 2 (b) 0
    (c) 4 (d) 1

16. Let $P=(-1,0)$, $Q=(0,0)$ and $R=(3,3\sqrt{3})$ be three points. Then the equation of the bisector of the angle PQR is : **[IIT 2002]**
    (a) $\frac{\sqrt{3}}{2}x+y=0$ (b) $x+\sqrt{3}y=0$
    (c) $\sqrt{3}x+y=0$ (d) $x+\frac{\sqrt{3}}{2}y=0$

17. A straight line through the origin O meets the parallel lines $4x+2y=9$ and $2x+y+6=0$ at points P and Q respectively. Then the point O divides the segment PQ in the ratio :

(a) 1:2 (b) 3:4
(c) 2:1 (d) 4:3

[IIT 2002]

18. A straight line through the point (2, 2) intersects the lines $\sqrt{3}x + y = 0$ and $\sqrt{3}x - y = 0$ at the points A and B. The equation to the line AB so that the triangle OAB is equilateral, is :
(a) $x - y = 0$ (b) $y - 2 = 0$
(c) $x + y - 4 = 0$ (d) none of these

[IIT 2002]

19. If the equation of the locus of a point equidistant from the points (a_1, b_1) and (a_2, b_2) is $(a_1 - a_2)x + (b_1 - b_2)y + c = 0$, then the vlaues of 'c' is : **[IIT 2003]**
(a) $\frac{1}{2}(a_2^2 + b_2^2 - a_1^2 - b_1^2)$
(b) $a_1^2 - a_2^2 + b_1^2 - b_2^2$
(c) $\frac{1}{2}(a_1^2 + a_2^2 + b_1^2 + b_2^2)$
(d) $\sqrt{a_1^2 + b_1^2 \quad a_2^2 \quad b_2^2}$

20. No questions asked in **2004.**

21. The area of the triangle formed by the intersection of a line parallel to x-axis and passing through P(h, k) with the lines y = x and x + y = 2 is $4h^2$. Find the locus of point P.

[IIT 2005]

21. Two rays in the first quadrant x + y = | a | and ax – y = 1 intersects each other in the interval $a \in (a_0, \infty)$. Find the value of a_0. Ans $a_0 = 1$ **[IIT 2006]**

22. Lines $L_1 : y - x = 0$, $L_2 : 2x + y = 0$ intersect the line $L_3 : y + 2 = 0$ at P and Q respectively. The bisector of the acute angle between L_1 and L_2 intersect L_3 at R .
Statement 1 : The ratio PR: RQ equals $2\sqrt{2} : \sqrt{5}$
Statement 2 : In any triangle bisector of an angle divides the triangle into two similiar triangles.

[IIT-2007]

23. Consider the lines given by
$L_1 : x + 3y - 5 = 0$, $L_2 : 3x - ky - 1 = 0$, $L_3 : 5x + 2y - 12 = 0$

Column - I	Column - II
(a) L_1, L_2, L_3 are concurrent if	(p) k = - 9
(b) One of L_1, L_2, L_3 is parallel to at least of the other two , if	(q) k = - 6 / 5
(c) L_1, L_2, L_3 form a triangle , if	(s) k = 5 /6
(d) L_1, L_2, L_3 do not form a triangle, if	(t) k = 5.

[IIT-2008]

24. The locus of orthocenter of triangle formed by the lines $(1+p)x - py + p(1+p) = 0$, $(1+q)x - qy + q(1+q) = 0$ and y = 0 , where $p \neq q$ is
(a) a hyperbola (b) a parabola
(c) an ellipse (d) a straight line **[IIT-2009]**

25. A straight line L through the point (3, -2) is inclined at an angle 60° to the line $\sqrt{3}x + y = 1$. If L also intrersects the x-axis, then the equation of L is
(a) $y + \sqrt{3}x + (2 - 3\sqrt{3}) = 0$
(b) $y - \sqrt{3}x + (2 + 3\sqrt{3}) = 0$
(c) $-x + \sqrt{3}y + (3 + 2\sqrt{3}) = 0$
(d) $x + \sqrt{3}y + (-3 + 2\sqrt{3}) = 0$ **[IIT-2011]**

ANSWER

1. (a), (c)
3. (a), (c)
6. (b)
13. (d)
14. (d)
15. (a)
16. (c)
17. (b)
18. (b)
19. (d)
21. 2 x - y + 1 = 0 , 2 x + y - 1 = 0.
22. (c)
23. $(a) \to (s), (b) \to (p, q), (c) \to (r), (d) \to (p, q, s)$
24. (d)
25. (b)

SELF ASSESEMENT TEST

Time : 3 Hrs. **Ch: Straight Line** **M.M. : 100**

Give answers of the following questions:

1. The extremities of diagonal of a square are (1, 1), (-2, -1) . Find the other two vertices and the equation of the other diagonal.
2. The center of a square is at the origin and one vertex is A(2, 1) . Find the co-ordinates of the other vertices of the square.
3. Find the distance of the point (2, 3) from the line 2x - 3 y + 9 = 0 measured along the line x - y + 1 = 0.
4. If the algebraic sum of the perpendicular distances from the points (2, 0), (0, 2) and (1, 1) to a variable straight line is zero, then the line passes through the point............
5. The set of the lines ax + by + c = 0 , where 3a + 2 b + 4 c =

0 is concurrent at the point..........

6. A ray of light passing through the point (1, 2) is reflected on the x-axis at a point P and passes through the point (5, 3) . Find the abscissa of the point P.
7. A ray of light is sent along the line x - 2y + 5 = 0 , upon reaching the line 3x-2y+7=0 , the ray is reflected from it. Find the equation of the line containing the reflected ray.
8. If the distance of any point (x, y) from the origin is defined as $d(x,y) = \max\{|x|, |y|\}$, where d (x,y) = a non zero constant, then find its locus.
9. Find the area of the parallelogram formed by the lines $y = mx$, $y = mx + 1$, $y = nx$ and $y = nx + 1$.
10. Two rays in the first quadrant $x + y = |a|$ and $ax - y = 1$ intersects each other in the interval $a \in (a_0, \infty)$. Find the value of a_0

ANSWERS

1. (-3/2, 3/2), (1/2, -3/2), $6x + 4y + 3 = 0$.
2. (-1, 2) ; (-2, -1) ; (1, -2)
3. $4\sqrt{2}$
6. 3
7. $29x - 2y + 33 = 0$
8. Square.
9. $\frac{1}{|m-n|}$
10. $a_0 = 1$

2 The Pair of Straight Lines

CONCEPT BOOSTER

2.1 ABC OF PSL

Let the two equations be $a_1x+b_1y+c_1=0$ and

$$a_2x+b_2y+c_2=0$$

The joint equation of the given equation is

$$(a_1x+b_1y+c_1)(a_2x+b_2y+c_2)=0$$

and conversely if joint equation of two lines be

$$(a_1x+b_1y+c_1)(a_2x+b_2y+c_2)=0,$$

then their separate equations will be

$$a_1x+b_1y+c_1=0 \text{ and } a_2x+b_2y+c_2=0.$$

Note

1. In order to find the joint equation of two lines make R.H.S of equation of the straight lines is equal to zero and then multiply the equation.
2. In order to find the separate equations of two lines, when their joint equation is given. Simply fatorize the joint equation and reduces into two linear factors.

Ex-1. Find the joint equation of the lines $x - y + 2 = 0$ and $2z + y + 4 = 0$.

Sol. Hence, the joint equation of the given lines is

$$(x-y+2)(2x+y+4)=0.$$

$$\Rightarrow \quad 2x^2-y^2-xy+8x-2y+8=0$$

Ex-2. Find the joint equation of the lines $x = y$ and $x + y = 1$.

Sol. Hence, the joint equation of the lines is

$$(x-y)(x+y-1)=0.$$

$$\Rightarrow \quad x^2-y^2-x+y=0$$

Ex-3. Find the separate equations of the lines represented by $x^2-3xy+2y^2=0$

Sol. The given equation is $x^2-3xy+2y^2=0$

$$\Rightarrow \quad x^2-xy-2xy+2y^2=0$$

$$\Rightarrow \quad x(x-y)-2y(x-y)=0$$

$$\Rightarrow \quad (x-y)(x-2y)=0$$

Hence, the separate equations of the given lines are $x - y = 0$ and $x - 2y = 0$.

Ex-4. Find the separate equations of the lines represented by $x^2-y^2+2y-1=0$.

Sol. The given equation is $x^2-y^2+2y-1=0$

$$\Rightarrow \quad x^2-(y^2-2y+1)=0$$

$$\Rightarrow \quad x^2-(y-1)^2=0$$

$$\Rightarrow \quad (x+y-1)(x-y+1)=0.$$

Hence, the separate equations of the given lines are $x + y - 1 = 0$ and $x - y + 1 = 0$.

2.2 HOMOGENEOUS EQUATION

In an equation, if the degree of each term throughout the equation is same, then it is known as homogeneous equation.

Thus $ax^2+2hxy+by^2=0$ is a homogeneous equation of 2nd degree and $ax^3+2hx^2y+by^3=0$ is a homoge neous equation of degree 3.

2.3 A PAIR OF STRAIGHT LINES THROUGH THE ORIGIN

Theorem: Any homogeneous equation of 2nd degree in x and y represents two straight lines which are pass ing through the origin.

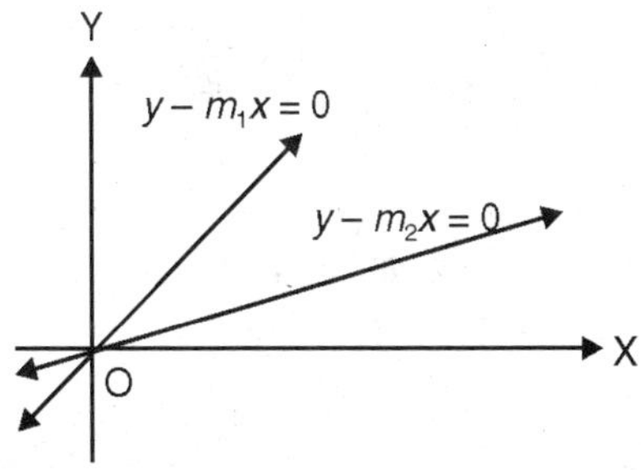

A homogeneous equation of 2nd degree in x and y is

$$ax^2+2hxy+by^2=0$$

$$\Rightarrow \quad y^2+\left(-\frac{2h}{b}\right)x+\frac{a}{b}x^2=0$$

$$\Rightarrow \quad (y-m_1x)(y-m_2x)=0,$$

where $m_1 + m_2 = -\frac{2h}{b}$ and $m_1.m_2 = \frac{a}{b}$

$\Rightarrow$ $y - m_1 x = 0,\ y - m_2 x = 0$, both of which are pass through the origin.

Ex-1. Find the straight lines which are represented by $x^2 + 5xy + 6y^2 = 0$.

Sol. The given equation $x^2 + 5xy + 6y^2 = 0$ can be written as $(x+2y)(x+3y) = 0$

$\Rightarrow$ $(x+2y) = 0$ & $(x+3y) = 0$

Hence, the required lines are

$(x+2y) = 0$ & $(x+3y) = 0$.

Ex-2. Find the area of the triangle formed by the lines $y^2 - 5xy + 6y^2 = 0$ and $y = 6$

Sol. The given equation of the lines $y^2 - 5xy + 6y^2 = 0$ can be reduces to $y = 2x$ and $y = 3x$.

Then , A = (2, 6) and B = (3, 6)

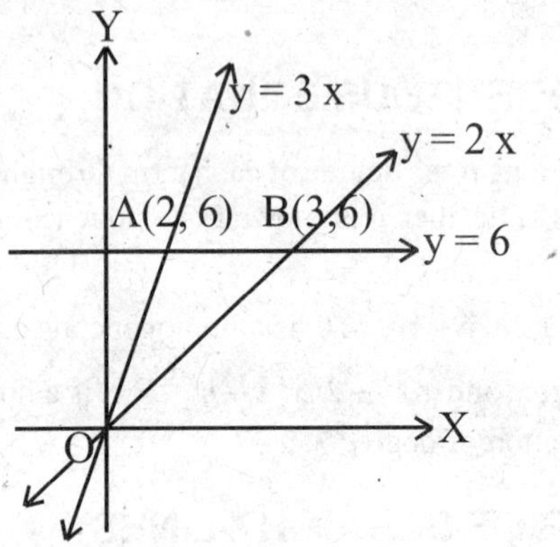

Hence, the area of the triangle OAB is

$$= \frac{1}{2}\begin{vmatrix} 0 & 0 \\ 3 & 6 \\ 2 & 6 \\ 0 & 0 \end{vmatrix} = \frac{1}{2}(18-12) = 3 \text{ sq. u.}$$

Ex-3. Find the orthocentre of the triangle formed by the lines $xy = 0$ and $x + y = 2$.

Sol. The equation $xy = 0$ gives to $x = 0$ and $y = 0$.

Clearly, OAB is a right angled triangle and right angle at O.

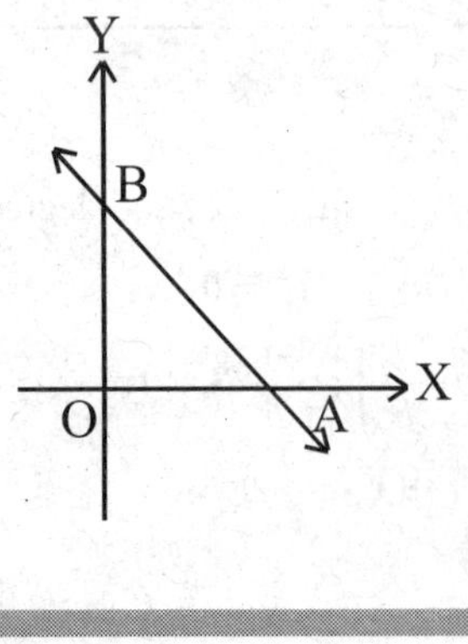

As we know that the point of intersection of two perpendicular sides of a triangle is known as othrocentre of the triangle.

Hence, the orthocentre is (0, 0) .

Ex-4. Find the circum-centre of the triangle formed by the lines $xy - x - y + 1 = 0$ and $x + y = 4$.

Sol. The given equation $xy - x - y + 1 = 0$ can be reduces to

$(x-1)(y-1) = 0$

$\Rightarrow$ $x - 1 = 0$ and $y - 1 = 0$

$\Rightarrow$ $x = 1$ and $y = 1$.

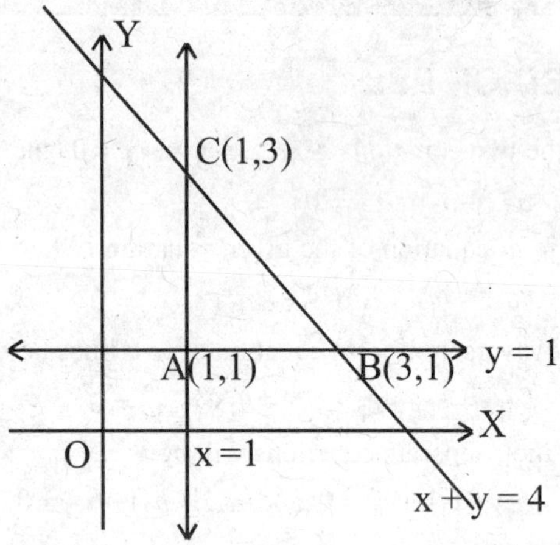

Here, ABC be a right angled triangle and right angle at A.

As we know that , the mid-point of the hypotenuse is the circum-centre of the right angle triangle.

Now, the mid-point of BC is (2, 2) .

Hence, the circum-centre is (2, 2) .

2.4 ANGLE BETWEEN THE LINES REPRESENTED BY $ax^2 + 2hxy + by^2 = 0$.

Let the lines represented by $ax^2 + 2hxy + by^2 = 0$ be $y - m_1 x = 0$ and $y - m_2 x = 0$

where $m_1 + m_2 = -\frac{2h}{b}$ and $m_1.m_2 = \frac{2a}{b}$

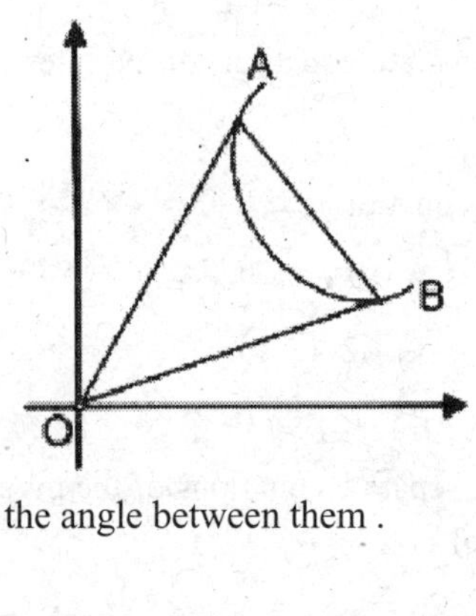

Let θ be the angle between them .

Then $\tan\theta = \left|\frac{m_1 - m_2}{1 + m_1 m_2}\right| = \left|\frac{\sqrt{(m_1 + m_2)^2 - 4m_1 m_2}}{1 + m_1 m_2}\right|$

$$= \left|\frac{\sqrt{\frac{4h^2}{b^2} - 4\frac{a}{b}}}{1 + \frac{a}{b}}\right| = \left|\frac{2\sqrt{h^2 - ab}}{a + b}\right|$$

Thus $\theta = \tan^{-1}\left(\left|\frac{2\sqrt{h^2 - ab}}{a + b}\right|\right)$.

(i) **Condition of parallelism :**

In this case, $\theta = 0 \Rightarrow h^2 = ab$

(ii) **Condition of perpendicularity** :

In this case, $\theta = \frac{\pi}{2} \Rightarrow a + b = 0$

(iii) **Condition of coincidency** :

In this case also, $\theta = 0 \Rightarrow h^2 = ab$

Ex-1. Find the angle between the lines represented by

$2013\,x^2 - 2014\,x\,y - 2013y^2 = 0$

Sol. Here, a = 2013, b = - 2013 and h = - 1007.

Since, a + b = 2013 - 2013 = 0 , so the angle between the lines is 90°.

Ex-2. Find the angles between the lines represented by

$2x^2 - 4\sqrt{3}\,x\,y + 6\,y^2 = 0$

Sol. Here , $a = 2$, $b = 6$ and $h = -2\sqrt{3}$.

Now, $h^2 - ab = 12 - 12 = 0$.

Hence, the angle between them is 0°.

Ex-3. Find the angle between the lines represented by

$x^2 + 4\,x\,y + y^2 = 0$

Sol. Here, a = 1 , b = 1 and h = 2 .

Let θ be the angle between them.

Then $\tan(?) = \left(\frac{2\sqrt{h^2 - ab}}{a + b}\right) = \left(\frac{2\sqrt{4 - 1}}{1 + 1}\right) = \sqrt{3}$

$\Rightarrow \quad \theta = \frac{\pi}{3}$

Hence, the angle between them is 60°.

2.5 BIECTORS OF ANGLES BETWEEN THE LINES REPRESENTED BY $ax^2 + 2hxy + by^2 = 0$

Let the given equation represent the straight lines $y - m_1 x = 0$ and $y - m_2 x = 0$

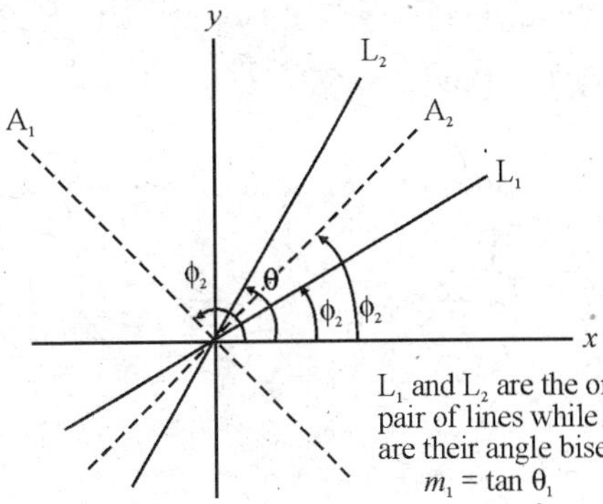

L_1 and L_2 are the original pair of lines while A_1 and A_2 are their angle bisectors
$m_1 = \tan\theta_1$
$m_2 = \tan\theta_2$

Then $m_1 + m_2 = -\frac{2h}{b}$, $m_1 m_2 = \frac{a}{b}$.

The equation of the bisectors of the angles between the given straight lines are

$$\frac{y - m_1 x}{\sqrt{1 + m_1^2}} = \frac{y - m_2 x}{\sqrt{1 + m_2^2}} \text{ and } \frac{y - m_1 x}{\sqrt{1 + m_1^2}} = -\frac{y - m_2 x}{\sqrt{1 + m_2^2}}$$

The joint equation of the bisectors is

$$\left(\frac{y - m_1 x}{\sqrt{1 + m_1^2}} - \frac{y - m_2 x}{\sqrt{1 + m_2^2}}\right)\left(\frac{y - m_1 x}{\sqrt{1 + m_1^2}} + \frac{y - m_2 x}{\sqrt{1 + m_2^2}}\right) = 0$$

$$\Rightarrow \left(\frac{y - m_1 x}{\sqrt{1 + m_1^2}}\right)^2 = \left(\frac{y - m_2 x}{\sqrt{1 + m_2^2}}\right)^2$$

$$\Rightarrow (y - m_1 x)^2 (1 + m_2^2) = (y - m_2 x)^2 (1 + m_2^2)$$

$$\Rightarrow (1 + m_2^2)(y^2 - 2m_1 xy + m_1^2 x^2)$$

$$= (1 + m_1^2)(y^2 - 2m_2 xy + m_2^2 x^2)$$

$$\Rightarrow (m_1^2 - m_2^2)(x^2 - y^2) + 2(m_1 m_2 - 1)(m_1 - m_2)xy = 0$$

$$\Rightarrow (m_1 + m_2)(x^2 - y^2) + 2(m_1 m_2 - 1)xy = 0$$

$$\Rightarrow \left(-\frac{2h}{b}\right)(x^2 - y^2) + 2\left(\frac{a}{b} - 1\right)xy = 0$$

$$\Rightarrow \left(-\frac{2h}{b}\right)(x^2 - y^2) = -2\left(\frac{a}{b} - 1\right)xy$$

$$\Rightarrow \frac{x^2 - y^2}{a - b} = \frac{xy}{h}$$

Which is the required equation of bisectors of the lines represented by

$ax^2 + 2hxy + by^2 = 0$.

Ex-1. Find the equation of the bisectors of the angle between the lines represented by $3x^2 - 5\,x\,y + 4y^2 = 0$.

Sol. The given equation is $3x^2-5xy+4y^2=0$

Here, a = 3, b = 4 and h = - 5/2

Hence, the equation of the bisector is $\frac{x^2-y^2}{a-b}=\frac{xy}{h}$

$$\Rightarrow \quad \frac{x^2-y^2}{3-4}=\frac{xy}{-(5/2)}$$

$$\Rightarrow \quad -\left(x^2-y^2\right)=-\frac{2}{5}xy$$

$$\Rightarrow \quad 5x^2-2xy-5y^2=0$$

Ex-2. If y = m x is one of the bisector of the lines $x^2+4xy+y^2=0$, then find the value of m.

Sol. Since y = m x is one of the bisector of the given lines $x^2+4xy+y^2=0$, then y = m x will satisfy the given lines.

Therefore, $x^2+4mx^2+m^2x^2=0$

$$\Rightarrow \quad 1+4m+m^2=0$$

$$\Rightarrow \quad m^2+4m+1=0$$

$$\Rightarrow \quad (m+2)^2=\left(\sqrt{3}\right)^2$$

$$\Rightarrow \quad m=\pm\sqrt{3}-2$$

Hence, the values of m are $\left(\sqrt{3}-2\right)$ & $\left(-\sqrt{3}-2\right)$

Ex-3. Prove that the lines $9x^2+14xy+16y^2=0$ are equally inclined to the lines $3x^2+2xy+4y^2=0$.

Sol. The given pair of lines are

$$9x^2+14xy+16y^2=0 \quad \text{...(i)}$$

and $3x^2+2xy+4y^2=0$ ...(ii)

The two pairs will be equally inclined if the two pairs of the straight lines have the same bisectors.

The equation of the bisectors of the angle between the lines represented by

$$9x^2+14xy+16y^2=0 \text{ is } \frac{x^2-y^2}{9-16}=\frac{xy}{7}$$

$$\Rightarrow \quad x^2+xy-y^2=0$$

The equation of the bisectors of the angle between the lines represented by

$$3x^2+2xy+4y^2=0 \text{ is } \frac{x^2-y^2}{3-4}=\frac{xy}{1}$$

$$\Rightarrow \quad x^2+xy-y^2=0$$

Hence, the pair of lines of (i) are equally inclined to the pair of lines of (ii).

Ex-3. Prove that the bisectors of the angle between the lines

$$ax^2+acxy+cy^2=0$$

and $\left(2013+\frac{1}{c}\right)x^2+xy+\left(2013+\frac{1}{a}\right)y^2=0$

are always same.

Sol. The given equations are

$$ax^2+acxy+cy^2=0 \quad \text{...(i)}$$

and $\left(2013+\frac{1}{c}\right)x^2+xy+\left(2013+\frac{1}{a}\right)y^2=0$ ...(ii)

The equation of bisectors of (i) is $\frac{x^2-y^2}{a-c}=\frac{xy}{ac/2}$

$$\Rightarrow \quad ac\left(x^2-y^2\right)=2(a-c)xy$$

$$\Rightarrow \quad ac\left(x^2-y^2\right)-2(a-c)xy=0$$

Also, the equation of bisectors of (ii) is

$$\frac{x^2-y^2}{\left(2013+\frac{1}{c}\right)-\left(2013+\frac{1}{a}\right)}=\frac{xy}{1/2}$$

$$\Rightarrow \quad \frac{ac\left(x^2-y^2\right)}{(a-c)}=2xy$$

$$\Rightarrow \quad ac\left(x^2-y^2\right)=2(a-c)xy$$

$$\Rightarrow \quad ac\left(x^2-y^2\right)-2(a-c)xy=0$$

Hence, the result.

Ex-4. If pairs of straight lines $x^2-2pxy-y^2=0$ and $x^2-2qxy-y^2=0$ be such that each pair bisects the angle between the other pair, then prove that pq = - 1.

Sol. From the problem, it is clear that, the bisectors of the angles between the lines given by

$$x^2-2pxy-y^2=0 \quad \text{...(i)}$$

is $x^2-2qxy-y^2=0$ ...(ii)

The equation of the bisectors of (i) is $\frac{x^2-y^2}{1-(-1)}=\frac{xy}{-q}$

$$\Rightarrow \quad -qx^2+2xy+qy^2=0 \quad \text{...(iii)}$$

Here, equations (ii) and (iii) are identical.

Thus, comparing the co-efficients,

we get, $\frac{1}{-q}=\frac{-2p}{-2}=\frac{-1}{q}$

$$\Rightarrow \quad pq=-1$$

Hence, the result.

2.6 A GENERAL EQUATION OF SECOND DEGREE IS

$ax^2+2hxy+by^2+2gx+2fy+c=0$

Theorem : The genral equation of 2nd degree $ax^2+2hxy+by^2+2gx+2fy+c=0$ represents a pair of straight lines if $abc+2fgh-af^2-bg^2-ch^2=0$.

Proof: The genral equation of 2nd degree is

$$ax^2+2hxy+by^2+2gx+2fy+c=0 \quad ...(i)$$

$$\Rightarrow by^2+2(hx+f)y+\left(ax^2+2gx+c\right)=0$$

$$\Rightarrow y=\frac{-2(hx+f)\pm\sqrt{4(hx+f)^2-4b\left(ax^2+2gx+c\right)}}{2b}$$

$$\Rightarrow y=\frac{-(hx+f)\pm\sqrt{\left(h^2-ab\right)x^2+2(gh-af)x+\left(g^2-ac\right)}}{b}$$

Equation (i) represent two straight line if left hand side of (i) can be resolved into two liear factors, therefore the expression under the square rppt shold be a perfect square..

Hence, $4(gh-af)^2-4\left(h^2-ab\right)\left(g^2-ac\right)=0$

$$\Rightarrow g^2h^2+a^2f^2-2afgh-h^2g^2+abg^2+ach^2-a^2bc=0$$

$$\Rightarrow a\left(af^2+bg^2+ch^2-2fgh-abc\right)=0$$

$$\Rightarrow abc+2fgh-af^2-bg^2-ch^2=0.$$

which is the required condition.

Ex-1. For what values of m, does the equation $mx^2-5xy-6y^2+14x+5y+4=0$ represents two straight lines.

Sol. The given equation is

$$mx^2-5xy-6y^2+14x+5y+4=0 \quad ...(i)$$

Here, $a=m, h=-5/2, b=-6, g=7, f=5/2$ and $c=4$.

The equation (i) represents a pair of straight lines if

$$abc+2fgh-af^2-bg^2-ch^2=0$$

$$\Rightarrow \quad -24m-\frac{175}{2}-\frac{25}{4}m+294-25=0$$

$$\Rightarrow \quad -\left(24m+\frac{25}{4}m\right)=\frac{175}{2}-269$$

$$\Rightarrow \quad -\frac{121}{4}m=-\frac{363}{2}$$

$$\Rightarrow \quad m=6$$

Hence, the value of m is 6.

Result - 2: The lines represented by

$$ax^2+2hxy+by^2+2gx+2fy+c=0$$

are parallel if

$$\Delta=abc+2fgh-af^2-bg^2-ch^2=0$$

and $h^2-ab=0$

Ex-1. Prove that the equation

$$x^2-2\sqrt{3}xy+3y^2-3x+3\sqrt{3}y-4=0$$

represents two parallel straight lines and also find the distance between them.

Sol. The given equation is

$$x^2-2\sqrt{3}xy+3y^2-3x+3\sqrt{3}y-4=0 \quad ...(i)$$

Here, $a=1, b=3$ and $h=-\sqrt{3}$

Now, $h^2-ab=3-3=0$

Thus, the given equation represents two parallel striaght lines.

Equation (i) can be reduces to

$$\left(x-\sqrt{3}y\right)^2-3\left(x-\sqrt{3}y\right)-4=0$$

$$\Rightarrow \quad m^2-3m-4=0, \text{ where } m=\left(x-\sqrt{3}y\right)$$

$$\Rightarrow \quad (m-4)(m+1)=0$$

$$\Rightarrow \quad m=4 \ \& \ m=-1$$

$$\Rightarrow \quad x-\sqrt{3}y-4=0 \ \& \ x-\sqrt{3}y+1=0$$

Hence, the required distance $=\left|\frac{1+4}{\sqrt{1+3}}\right|=\frac{5}{2}$.

Ex-2. Find the equation of the straight lines passing through the point (1, 1) and parallel to the lines represented by the equation $x^2-5xy+4y^2+x+2y-2=0$.

Sol. The given equation is

$$x^2-5xy+4y^2+x+2y-2=0$$

$$\Rightarrow \quad (x-y)(x-4y)+x+2y-2=0 \quad ...(i)$$

Thus, the equation (i) represents two parallel striaght lines, whose joint equation is

$$(x-y+\lambda)(x-4y+\mu)=0$$

Which is passing through (1, 1).

Therefore, $\lambda=0$ & $\mu=3$

Hence, the parallel lines are $x-y=0$ and $x-4y+3=0$.

Result - 3 : The lines represented by

$$ax^2+2hxy+by^2+2gx+2fy+c=0$$

are perpendicular if

$$\Delta=abc+2fgh-af^2-bg^2-ch^2=0$$

and $a+b=0$.

Ex-1. If the equation $3x^2+5xy-py^2+2x+3y=0$ represents two perpendicular straight lines, then find the value of $p+2010$.

Sol. The given equation is

$$3x^2+5xy-py^2+2x+3y=0 \quad ...(i).$$

Since, the equation (i) represents two perpendicular straight lines,

So, $a+b=0$

$\Rightarrow$ co-effi of x^2 + co – effi of $y^2 = 0$

$\Rightarrow$ $3-p=0 \Rightarrow p=3$

Hence, the value of $p+2010=2013$.

Result - 4: The point of intersection of the lines represented by $ax^2+2hxy+by^2+2gx+2fy+c=0$ is obtained by

$$\frac{df}{dx}=0 \text{ and } \frac{df}{dy}=0.$$

i.e $2ax+2hy+2g=0$ and $2hx+2by+2f=0$

$\Rightarrow$ $ax+hy+g=0$ and $hx+by+f=0$.

Ex-1. Find the point of intersection of the lines represented by $x^2-5xy+4y^2+x+2y-2=0$.

Sol. The given equation is

$$x^2-5xy+4y^2+x+2y-2=0.$$

Now, $\frac{df}{dx}=0 \Rightarrow 2x-5y+1=0$

and $\frac{df}{dy}=0 \Rightarrow 8y-5x+2=0$

On solving, we get, $x=2$ and $y=1$

Hence. the required point of intersection is (2, 1).

Result - 5: The point of intersection of the lines represented by $ax^2+2hxy+by^2+2gx+2fy+c=0$

is $\left(\sqrt{\frac{f^2-bc}{h^2-ab}}, \sqrt{\frac{g^2-ac}{h^2-ab}}\right)$ or $\left(\frac{bg-hf}{h^2-ab}, \frac{af-gh}{h^2-ab}\right)$.

Ex-1. Find the point of intersection of the straight lines represented by the equation

$$3x^2-2xy-8y^2-4x+18y-7=0$$

Sol. The given equation is

$$3x^2-2xy-8y^2-4x+18y-7=0$$

Here, $a=3, h=-1, b=-8, g=-2, f=9$ and $c=-7$.

Therefore, $h^2-ab=1+24=25$,

$bg-hf=16+9=25$, $af-gh=27-2=25$

Hence, the point of intersection is

$$=\left(\frac{bg-hf}{h^2-ab}, \frac{af-gh}{h^2-ab}\right)=\left(\frac{25}{25}, \frac{25}{25}\right)=(1, 1).$$

Result - 6 : The angle between the lines represented by $ax^2+2hxy+by^2+2gx+2fy+c=0$ is

$$\theta=\tan^{-1}\left|\frac{2\sqrt{h^2-ab}}{(a+b}\right|.$$

Ex-1. Find the angle between the lines represented by

$$x^2-5xy+4y^2+x+2y-2=0$$

Sol. The given equation is

$$x^2-5xy+4y^2+x+2y-2=0$$

Here, $a=1, h=-5/2, b=4, g=1/2, f=1, c=-2$.

Let θ be the angle between them.

Then, $\tan ?=\left(\frac{2\sqrt{h^2-ab}}{a+b}\right)=\left(\frac{2\sqrt{\frac{25}{4}-4}}{1+4}\right)=\frac{3}{5}$

$\Rightarrow$ $?=\tan^{-1}\left(\frac{3}{5}\right)$

Hence, the angle between them is $\tan^{-1}\left(\frac{3}{5}\right)$.

Result - 7: The lines represented by $ax^2+2hxy+by^2+2gx+2fy+c=0$ will be coincident

if $h^2-ab=0$, $g^2-ac=0$ and $f^2-bc=0$.

Ex-1. Prove that the lines represented by

$x^2-8xy+16y^2+2x-8y+1=0$ is coincident

Sol. The given equation is

$$x^2-8xy+16y^2+2x-8y+1=0 \quad ...(i)$$

Here, $a=1, h=-4, b=16, g=1, f=-4$ and $c=1$.

Now, $h^2-ab=16-16=0$, $g^2-ac=1-1=0$ and $f^2-bc=16-16=0$.

Hence, the equation (i) represents two coincident straight lines.

Result - 8 : The pair of bisectors of the lines represented by

$$ax^2+2hxy+by^2+2gx+2fy+c=0 \quad ...(i)$$

is $\frac{(x-a)^2-(y-ß)^2}{(a-b)}=\frac{(x-a)(x-ß)}{h}$,

where (α, β) be the point of intersection of the pair of straight lines represented by (i).

Ex-1. Find the equation of bisectors of the lines represented by $x^2-5xy+2y^2+x+2y-2=0$.

Sol. The given equation is

$$x^2-5xy+2y^2+x+2y-2=0 \quad ...(i)$$

Now, $\frac{df}{dx}=0 \Rightarrow 2x-5y+1=0$

and $\frac{df}{dy}=0 \Rightarrow -5x+4y+2=0$

On solving, we get, $x = 2$ and $y = 1$.
Therefore, the point of intersection is (2, 1).
Hence, the equation of bisector is

$$\frac{(x-a)^2-(y-ß)^2}{(a-b)} = \frac{(x-a)(x-ß)}{h}$$

$$\Rightarrow \quad \frac{(x-2)^2-(y-1)^2}{(1-2)} = \frac{(x-2)(y-1)}{(-5/2)}$$

$$\Rightarrow \quad 5x^2-2xy-5y^2-18x+24y+11=0$$

Result - 9: The combined equation of the straight lines joining the origin to the points of intersection of a second degreecurve $ax^2+2hxy+by^2+2gx+2fy+c=0$ and a straight line $lx+my+n=0$ is

$$ax^2+2hxy+by^2+2gx\left(\frac{lx+my}{-n}\right)$$
$$+2fy\left(\frac{lx+my}{-n}\right)+c\left(\frac{lx+my}{-n}\right)^2=0$$

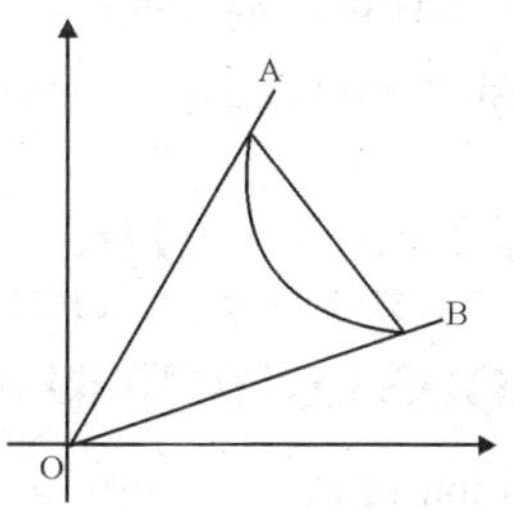

Which is a homegeneous equation of 2nd degree. After simplification, the above equation will be reduces to $Ax^2+2Hxy+By^2=0$ and it will represents two striaght lines, which are passing through the origin. Let θ be the angle between them.

Then $? = \tan^{-1}\left|\frac{2\sqrt{H^2-AB}}{A+B}\right|$.

Ex-1. Find the angle between the lines joining the origin to the points of intersection of the straight line y = 3 x + 2 with the curve $x^2+2xy+3y^2+4x+8y-11=0$.

Sol. The equation of the striaght line is $y = 3x + 2$

$$\Rightarrow \quad \frac{y-3x}{2}=1 \qquad ...(i)$$

The equation of the given curve is

$$x^2+2xy+3y^2+4x+8y-11=0 \qquad ...(ii)$$

Making the equation (ii) homogeneous in the second degree in x and y by means of (i),

we get, $x^2+2xy+3y^2+4\left(\frac{y-3x}{2}\right)x+8$

$$\left(\frac{y-3x}{2}\right)y-11\left(\frac{y-3x}{2}\right)^2=0$$

On simplification, we get, $7x^2-2xy-y^2=0$

Which is the required equation of the line joining the origin to the points of intersection of (i) and (ii).

Here, a = 7, h = - 1 and b = - 1

Let θ be the angle between them.

Then, $\tan ? = \left(\frac{2\sqrt{h^2-ab}}{a+b}\right)$

$$\Rightarrow \quad \tan ? = \left(\frac{2\sqrt{1+7}}{7-1}\right) = \frac{2\sqrt{8}}{6} = \frac{2\sqrt{2}}{3}$$

$$\Rightarrow \quad ? = \tan^{-1}\left(\frac{2\sqrt{2}}{3}\right)$$

Ex-2. Find the equation of the straight lines joining the origin to the points of intersection of the line $y = mx + c$ and the curve $x^2+y^2=b^2$.

Sol. The equation of the striaght line is $y = mx + c$

$$\Rightarrow \quad \left(\frac{y-mx}{c}\right)=1 \qquad ...(i)$$

The equation of the given curve is

$$x^2+y^2=b^2 \qquad ...(ii)$$

Making the equation (ii) homogeneous of the second degree in x and y by means of (i),

we get, $x^2+y^2=b^2\left(\frac{y-mx}{c}\right)^2$

$$\Rightarrow \quad c^2\left(x^2+y^2\right)=b^2(y-mx)^2$$

$$\Rightarrow \quad \left(c^2-b^2m^2\right)x^2+2b^2mxy+\left(c^2-b^2\right)y^2=0$$

Which is the required equation of the striaght lines joining the origin to the point of intersection of (i) and (ii).

Ex-3. Find the equation of the striaght lines joining the origin to the points of intersection of the line $lx+my=1$ and the curve $y^2=4bx$.

Sol. The given line is $lx+my=1$

$$\Rightarrow \quad \left(\frac{lx+my}{1}\right)=1 \qquad ...(i)$$

The given curve is $y^2=4bx$ ...(ii).

Making the equation (ii) homogeneous of the second degree in x and y by means of (i),

we get, $y^2=4bx(lx+my)$

$$\Rightarrow \quad 4blx^2+4bmxy-y^2=0$$

ABC OF PSL

1. Find the joint equation of the lines
   (i) $y=x, y=-x$
   (ii) $2x-3y+1=0, x=y+4$
2. Find the joint equation of the lines through (1, 2) and parallel to the lines $x-2y=5$ and $x=3y-4$.
3. Find the separate equation of the lines from the joint equation of
   (i) $x^2-5xy+6y^2=0$
   (ii) $x^2-y^2+6y-9=0$
   (iii) $x^2-4x-y^2+4=0$

HOMOGENEOUS EQUATION OF 2ND DEGREE

4. Prove that the homogeneous equation of 2nd degree $x^2-3xy+2y^2=0$ reprsents two straight lines which are passing through the origin.
5. Find the equations of the pair of lines passing through the origin and perpendicular to the lines represented by $2x^2-5xy+2y^2=0$
6. Find the area of the triangle formed by the lines $y^2-9xy+18x^2=0$ and $y=9$.
7. Find the condition that the slope of one of the lines represented by $ax^2+2hxy+by^2=0$ should be n-times to the slope of the other.
8. Prove that the product of the perpendiculars drawn from the point (α, β) on the lines

   $ax^2+2hxy+by^2=0$ is $\dfrac{|a\alpha^2+2h\alpha\beta+b\beta^2|}{\sqrt{(a-b)^2+4h^2}}$.
9. Prove that the triangle formed by the lines
   $$\left(2x^2-3xy-2y^2\right)(x+y-1)=0$$
   is an equilateral.
10. Find the co-ordinates of the centroid of the triangle formed by the lines
    $$\left(12x^2-20xy+7y^2\right)(2x-3y+4)=0.$$
11. The equations to a pair of opposite sides of a rectangle are $x^2-7x+6=0$ and $y^2-14y+40=0$. Find the equation to its diagonals.
12. Find the area of the triangle formed by the lines $ax^2+2hxy+by^2=0$ and $lx+my=1$

ANGLE BETWEEN THE PAIR OF LINES BY $ax^2+2hxy+by^2=0$

13. Find the angle between the pair of lines
    $$y^2\sin^2\theta-xy\sin^2\theta+x^2\left(\cos^2\theta-1\right)=0.$$
14. Find the angle the lines whose joint equation is $2x^2-3xy+y^2=0$.
15. Show that the lines $x^2-4xy+y^2=0$ and $x+y=1$ form an equilateral triangle and find its area.
16. Which of the following pair of lines intersect at right angles?
    (a) $2x^2=y(x+2y)$
    (b) $(x+y)^2=x(y+3x)$
    (c) $2y(x+y)=xy$
    (d) $y=\pm 2x$
17. Find the angle between the lines given by
    $$x^2+2xy\cot 2\alpha-y^2=0$$
18. Find the angle between the lines represented by
    $$\left(x^2+y^2\right)\sin^2\alpha=(x\cos\alpha-y\sin\alpha)^2.$$

BISECTORS OF THE ANGLE BETWEEN THE LINES GIVEN BY A HOMOGENOUS EQUATION

19. Find the equation of the bisectors of the angle between the lines represented by $3x^2-5xy+4y^2=0$.
20. If pair of lines $x^2-2pxy-y^2=0$ and
    $$x^2-2qxy-y^2=0$$
    be such that each pair bisects the angle between the other pair, then prove that $pq=-1$.
21. If the line $y = mx$ is one of the bisector of the lines $x^2+4xy-y^2=0$, then find the value of m.
22. If one of the lines of $my^2+\left(1-m^2\right)xy-mx^2=0$ is a bisector of the angle between the lines $xy=0$, then find m.
23. Prove that the lines $2x^2+6xy+y^2=0$ are equally inclined to the lines $4x^2+18xy+y^2=0$
24. Prove that the bisectors of the angle between the lines $ax^2+acxy+cy^2=0$ and
    $\left(3+\dfrac{1}{c}\right)x^2+xy+\left(3+\dfrac{1}{a}\right)y^2=0$ are always the same.
25. If one of the lines $ax^2+2hxy+by^2=0$ be the bisector of the angle between the co-ordinate axes, prove that $(a+b)^2=4h^2$
26. Find the equation of the pair of lines both of which pass through $(1, 2)$ and are parallel to the bisectors of the angle between the lines given by
    $$x^2+xy-2y^2+4x-y+3=0.$$

GENERAL EQUATION OF 2ND DEGREE

27. Find the separate equation of lines represented by
$x^2 - 5xy + 4y^2 + x + 2y - 2 = 0$
28. Prove that the equation
$16x^2 + 24xy + 9y^2 + 40x + 30y - 75 = 0$ represents two parallel straight lines
29. Prove that the four lines given by $3x^2 + 8xy - 3y^2 = 0$ and $3x^2 + 8xy - 3y^2 + 2x - 4y - 1 = 0$ form a square.
30. Find the angle between the lines represented by $3x^2 - 2xy - 8y^2 - 4x + 18y - 7 = 0$
31. Find the equation of bisectors of the angles represented by the lines $3x^2 - 7xy + 2y^2 + 9x + 2y - 12 = 0$.
32. For what value of λ does the equation
$12x^2 - 10xy + 2y^2 + 11x - 5y + \lambda = 0$ represents a pair of straight lines ?
33. If $\lambda x^2 + 10xy + 3y^2 - 15x - 21y + 18 = 0$ represents a pair of straight lines , then find the value of λ.
34. Find the point of intersection of the straight lines is given by the equation $3y^2 - 8xy - 3x^2 - 29x + 3y - 18 = 0$.
35. If the equation $12x^2 + 7xy - py^2 - 18x + qy + 6 = 0$ represents two perpendicular lines, then find the values of p and q.
36. If the angle between the lines represented by $2x^2 + 5xy + 3y^2 + 7y + 4 = 0$ is $\tan^{-1}(m)$, then find m.
37. Find the equation of a straight line passing through the point (1, 1) and parallel to the lines represented by the equation $x^2 - 5xy + 4y^2 + x + 2y - 2 = 0$.
38. Prove that the lines joining the origin to the points of intersection of the line 3x - 2 y = 1 and the curve $3x^2 + 5xy - 3y^2 + 2x + 3y = 0$ are perpendicular to each other.
39. If the equation $ax^2 + 2hxy + by^2 + 2gx + 2fy + c = 0$ represents two straight lines , then prove that the product of the perpendiculars drawn from the origin to the lines is
$$\frac{c}{\sqrt{(a-b)^2 + 4h^2}}$$
40. Find the value of m , if the lines joining the origin and the points of intersection of y = m x + 1 and $x^2 + y^2 = 1$ perpendicular to one another.

ANSWER

1. (i) $x^2 + y^2 = 0$
(ii) $2x^2 + 3y^2 - 5xy - 7x + 11y - 4 = 0 = 0$
2. $x^2 - 5xy + 6y^2 + 8x - 19y + 15 = 0$
3. (i) $x = 3y, x = 2y$
(ii) $x + y - 3 = 0, x - y + 3 = 0$
(iii) $x + y - 2 = 0, x - y - 2 = 0$.
5. $x + 2y = 0, 2x + y = 0$.
6. 27 / 4 sq. u
7. $4nh^2 = ab(1+n)^2$.
10. 4 sq. u.
11. 2x-y+2=0, $6x + 5y = 56$.
12. $\frac{\sqrt{h^2 - ab}}{(am^2 - 2hlm + bl^2)}$
14. $\tan^{-1}\left(\frac{1}{3}\right)$ 13. $\frac{\pi}{2}$ 16. (a)
17. $\frac{\pi}{2}$ 18. $\theta = 2\alpha$
19. $5x^2 - 2xy - 5y^2 = 0$
21. $m = \pm\sqrt{5}$ 22. $m = \pm 1$
26. $x^2 - 5xy + 4y^2 + 3x - 3y = 0$
27. $y = x - 1, 4y = x + 2$.
30. $\tan^{-1}(2)$ 32. λ=2 33. λ=3
34. $\left(-\frac{3}{2}, -\frac{5}{2}\right)$ 35. p = 12, q = 1, - 23/2
36. m = 1/5 37. $x^2 - 5xy + 4y^2 + 3x - 3y = 0$
40. $2c^2 = a^2(1 + m^2)$

Level – II OBJECTIVE QUESTIONS FOR JEE-MAIN AND ADVANCED EXAMS ONLY

1. The orthocentre of the triangle formed by the lines x y = 0 and 2 x + 3 y = 6 is
(a) (1, 1) (b) (0, 0) (c) (1, 2) (d) (2, 1)

2. The orthocentre of the triangle formed by the lines x y - x - y + 1 = 0 and 3x + 4y = 12 is
(a) (1,1) (b) (0, 0) (c) (2,2) (d) (3,3)

3. The image of the pair of lines represented by $ax^2 + 2hxy + by^2 = 0$ by the line mirror y = 0 is
(a) $ax^2 + 2hxy + by^2 = 0$ (b) $ax^2 + 2hxy - by^2 = 0$

(c) $ax^2-2hxy+by^2=0$ (d) $ax^2-2hxy-by^2=0$

4. The image of the pair of lines represented by $ax^2+2hxy+by^2=0$ by the line mirror x = 0 is

(a) $ax^2+2hxy+by^2=0$ (b) $ax^2+2hxy-by^2=0$

(c) $ax^2-2hxy+by^2=0$ (d) $ax^2-2hxy-by^2=0$

5. The point of intersection of the two lines given by $2x^2-5xy+2y^2-3x+3y+1=0$ is

(a) $\left(-\frac{1}{2},\frac{1}{2}\right)$ (b) $\left(\frac{1}{2},-\frac{1}{2}\right)$

(c) $\left(-\frac{1}{3},\frac{1}{3}\right)$ (d) $\left(\frac{1}{3},-\frac{1}{3}\right)$

6. If the equation $12x^2+7xy-py^2-18x+qy+6=0$ represents two perpendicular lines, then the value of p + q + 7 is

(a) 15 (b) 20 (c) 25 (d) 30

7. The angle between the lines $x^2+4xy+y^2=0$ is

(a) π/2 (b) π/6 (c) π/3 (d) π/4

8. The angle between the lines given by

$x^2+2013\,xy-y^2=0$ is

(a) π/2 (b) π/6 (c) π/3 (d) π/4

9. Area of the triangle formed by the lines

$y^2-9xy+18x^2=0$ and y = 9 is

(a) 27/4 (b) 31/4 (c) 18/5 (d) 27

10. If $x^2-3xy+\lambda y^2+3x-5y+2=0$ represents a pair of straight lines, then the value of λ is

(a) 1 (b) 4 (c) 3 (d) 2

11. If the equation $2x^2-3xy-ay^2+x+by-1=0$ represents two perpendicular lines, then a + b + 2 is

(a) 2 (b) 5 (c) 6 (d) 3

12. If x y + x + y + 1 = 0 and x + a y - 3 = 0 are concurrent, then the value of a + 10 is

(a) 5 (b) 7 (c) 6 (d) 4

13. The circum-center of the triangle formed by the lines x y + 2 x + 2 y + 4 = 0 and x + y + 2 = 0 is

(a) (0,0) (b) (-1,-1) (c) (-1,-2) (d) (-2,-2)

14. The distance between the pair of parallel lines $9x^2-24xy+16y^2-12x+16y-12=0$ is

(a) 5 (b) 8 (c) 8/5 (d) 5/8

15. If one of the lines given by $6x^2-xy+4cy^2=0$ is 3 x + 4 y = 0, then the value of c is

(a) 1 (b) -1 (c) -3 (d) 5

ANSWER

1 (b)	2. (a)	3. (a)	4.(c)	5.(d)	6 (b)	7. (a)	8. (a)	9.(a)	10.(d)
11 (b)	12. (c)	13. (b)	14.(c)	15.(c)					

Level – III FOR JEE ADVANCED EXAMS ONLY

1. Find the area of the triangle by the pair of lines $ax^2+2hxy+by^2=0$ and the lines lx + my = 1.

2. If (α,β) be the centroid of the triangle whose sides are the lines $ax^2+2hxy+by^2=0$ and lx + my = 1, then prove that $\frac{\alpha}{bl-hm}=\frac{\beta}{am-hl}=\frac{2}{3}\cdot\frac{1}{bl^2-2hlm+am^2}$.

3. A triangle has the lines $ax^2+2hxy+by^2=0$ for two of its sides and the point (l, m) for its orthocenter. Prove that the third side has the equation

$(a+b)(lx+my)=am^2-2hlm+bl^2$.

4. If the equation $ax^2+2hxy+by^2+2gx+2fy+c=0$ represents a pair of straight lines, then prove that the distance between the lines = $2\sqrt{\frac{g^2-ac}{a(a+b)}}$.

5. Prove that two of the four lines represented by the joint equation $ax^4+bx^3y+cx^2y^2+dxy^3+ay^4=0$ will bisects the angles between the other two if c + 6a = 0 and b + d = 0.

6. Find the new equation of the curve

$4(x-2y+1)^2+9(2x+y+2)^2=25$, if the lines 2 x + y + 2 = 0 and x – 2y + 1 = 0 are taken as the new x and y axes respectively.

7. The lines $x^2-3xy+2y^2=0$ are shifted parallel to themselves so that their point of intersection comes to (1, 1). Find the combined equation of the lines in the new position.

8. If the straight lines represented by

$ax^2+2hxy+by^2+2gx+2fy+c=0$

are equidistant from the origin, then prove that

$f^4-g^4=c(bf^2-ag^2)$.

9. If the lines joining the origin and point of intersection of the curves $a_1x^2+2h_1xy+b_1y^2+2g_1x=0$

and $a_2x^2+2h_2xy+b_2y^2+2g_2x=0$ are mutually perpendicular, then prove that $g_1(a_2+b_2)=g_2(a_1+b_1)$.

10. If one of the lines denoted by the line pair $ax^2+2hxy+by^2=0$ bisects the angle between the co-ordinate axes, then prove that $(a+b)^2=4h^2$

ANSWER

1. $\frac{\sqrt{h^2-ab}}{(bl^2-2hlm+am^2)}$.

6. $4x^2+9y^2=5$.

7. $x^2-3xy+2y^2+x-y=0$

COMPREHENSION LINK PASSAGE(FOR JEE MAIN AND ADVANCED EXAMS ONLY)

PASSAGE - I

Let the lines represented by $2x^2-5xy+2y^2=0$ be the two sides of a parallelogram and the line $5x+2y=1$ be one of its diagonals. Then

1. The one of the sides of the parallelogram passing through the origin is
   (a) $x-2y=0$ (b) $x+2y=0$
   (c) $x-3y=0$ (d) $x+3y=0$
2. The equation of the other diagonal is
   (a) $x-2y=0$ (b) $11x-10y=0$
   (c) $10x-11y=0$ (d) $10x+11y=0$
3. The area of the parallelogram is
   (a) $\frac{1}{36}$ sq. u (b) $\frac{1}{54}$ sq. u
   (c) $\frac{1}{72}$ sq. u (d) $\frac{1}{96}$ sq. u.

PASSAGE - II

A general equation of 2nd degree is

$$8x^2+8xy+2y^2+26x+13y+15=0 \quad ...(i).$$

Then

1. The given equation (i) represents two straight lines, which are
   (a) $2x+y+5=0, 4x+2y+3=0$
   (b) $x+2y+5=0, 2x+4y+3=0$.
   (c) $2x-y+5=0, 4x-2y+3=0$
   (d) $x-2y+5=0, 2x-4y+3=0$.
2. The given equation (i) represents
   (a) two perpendicular lines
   (b) two parallel lines
   (c) two intersecting lines
   (d) None of these.
3. The distance between the lines is
   (a) $\frac{7}{2\sqrt{5}}$ (b) $\frac{5}{2\sqrt{7}}$ (c) $\frac{2}{5\sqrt{7}}$ (d) $\frac{5}{7\sqrt{2}}$

MATCH MATRIX (FOR JEE ADVANCED EXAM ONLY)

1. Match the following columns :

Column - I	Column - II
(A) The separate equations of $x^2-y^2+2y-1=0$ are	(P) $x-2=0, y-2=0$
(B) The separate equations of $x^2-y^2+4x+4=0$ are	(Q) $x-y=0, x+y+1=0$
(C) The separate equations of $.x^2-x-y^2-y=0$ are	(R) $x-y+1=0, x+y-1=0$
(D) The separate equations of $xy-2x-2y+4=0$ are	(S) $x+y+2=0, x-y+2=0$.

2. Match the following columns :

Column - I	Column - II
(A) The joint equation of the lines $x=y$ and $x=-y$ is	(P) $xy-3y-2x+6=0$
(B) The joint equation of the lines $x=2$ and $y=3$ is	(Q) $x^2+y^2=0$
(C) The joint equation of the lines $x=y$ and $x=1-y$ is	(R) $x^2-y^2+4y-4=0$
(D) The joint equation of the lines $x+y-2=0$ and $x-y+2=0$.	(S) $x^2-y^2-x+y=0$

3. Match the following columns :

Column - I	Column - II
(A) The orthocentre of the triangle is formed by the lines $xy=0$ and $x+y=2013$ is	(P) (11/2, 9/2)
(B) The orthocentre of the triangle is formed by the lines	(Q) (-2, -2)

$x^2-y^2+4y-4=0$ and $y+2014=0$ is

(C) The circum0centre of the triangle is formed by the lines x y - y = 0 and x + y = 10 is — (R) (0, 2)

(D) The circum-centre of the triangle is formed by the lines x y - x - y + 1 = 0 and x + y + 4 = 0 is — (S) (0, 0)

4. Match the following columns :

Column - I	Column - II
(A) The image of the pair of lines represented by $2x^2+3xy+3y^2=0$ with respect to the line mirror $y=0$ is	(P) $24x^2+10xy+y^2=0$
(B) The image of the pair of lines represented by $x^2+5xy+6y^2=0$ with respect to the line mirror $x=0$ is	(Q) $2x^2-3xy+3y^2=0$
(C) The image of the pair of lines reprsented by $x^2+10xy+24y^2=0$ with respect to the line $y=x$ is	(R) $x^2-5xy+6y^2=0$

ANSWER

1. (A) → (R); (B) → (S); (C) → (Q); (D) → (P)

2. (A) → (Q); (B) → (P); (C) → (S); (D) → (R).

3. (A) → (S; (B) → (R); (C) → (P); (D) → (Q);

4. (A) → (Q; (B) → (R); (C) → (P);

QUESTIONS ASKED IN ROORKEE EXAM

1. Find the internal angles of the triangle formed by the pair of the straight lines $x^2-4xy+y^2=0$ and the straight line $x+y+4\sqrt{6}=0$. Give the co-ordinates of the vertices of the triangle so formed and also the area of the triangle.

[Roorkee – 1983]

2. From a point A(1, 1) straight lines AL and AM are drawn at right angles to the pair of straight lines

$3x^2+7xy+2y^2=0$.

Find the equations of the pair of straight lines AL and AM. Also find the area of the quadrilateral ALOM, where O is the origin of co-ordinates.

[Roorkee-1984]

3. The base of a triangle passes through a fixed point (f, g) and its sides are respectively bisected at right angles by the lines $y^2-8xy-9x^2=0$. Determine the locus of its vertex.

[Roorkee – 1985]

4. Show that the four straight lines given by

$12x^2+7xt-12y^2=0$ and

$12x^2+7xt-12y^2-x+7y-1=0$ lie along the sides of a square.

[Roorkee – 1986]

5. The distance between the two parallel lines given by the equation $x^2+2\sqrt{3}xy+3y^2-3x-3\sqrt{3}y-4=0$ is

[Roorkee – 1989]

(a) 3/2 units (b) 2 units

(c) 5/2 units (d) 3 units.

6. Pair of straight lines perpendicular to each other are represented by

(a) $2x^2=2y(2x+y)$ (b) $x^2+y^2+3=0$

(c) $2x^2=y(2x+y)$ (d) $x^2=2(x-y)$

[Roorkee – 1990]

7. If one of the lines represented by $ax^2+2hxy+by^2=0$ bisects the angle between positive directions of the axes, then a, b, h satisfy the relation

(a) $a+b=2|h|$ (b) $(a+b)^2=4h^2$

(c) $a-b=2|h|$ (d) $(a-b)^2=4h^2$

[Roorkee – 1992]

8. Show that all the chords of the curve

$3x^2-y^2-2x+4y=0$ which subtend a right angle at the origin are concurrent. Does this result also hold for the curve $3x^2+3y^2-2x+4y=0$

[Roorkee Main -1992]

9. A pair of straight lines drawn through the origin form with the line 2x + 3 y = 6 an isosceles triangle right angled at the origin. Find the equation of the pair of straight lines and the area of the triangle correct to two places of decimals.

[Roorkee Main – 1993]

10. The distance between the two parallel lines given by the equation is

(a) 3/2 units (b) 2 units

(c) 5/2 units (d) 3 units.

[Roorkee – 1994]

11. Mixed term x y is to be removed from the general equation of the second degree

$ax^2+2hxy+by^2+2gx+2fy+c=0$.

One should rotate the axes through an angle given by $\tan 2\theta$ equal to

[Roorkee – 1996]

(a) $\frac{a-b}{2h}$ (b) $\frac{2h}{a+b}$ (c) $\frac{a+b}{2h}$ (d) $\frac{2h}{a-b}$.

12. What is the conditions for the second degree polynomials in x and y to represent a pair of straight lines

$ax^2+2hxy+by^2+2gx+2fy+c=0$?

[Roorkee – 1997]

13. A variable line L passing through the point B(2, 5) intersects the lines $2x^2-5xy+2y^2=0$ at P and Q. Find the locus of the point R on L such that distances BP, BR and BQ are in harmonic progression.

[Roorkee Main -1998]

ANSWER

1. $16\sqrt{3}$ sq. units.; triangle is equilateral

2. $\frac{7}{10}$

8. 2nd part: Not Concurrent.

9. $5(x^2-y^2)-24xy=0$; 2.77

12. $abc+2fgh-af^2-bg^2-ch^2=0$.

13. $17x-10y=0$.

QUESTIONS ASKED IN IIT-JEE EXAMS

1. Show that all chords of the curve $3x^2-y^2-2x+4y=0$, which subtend a right angle at the origin, passes through a fixed point. Find the co-ordinates of the fixed point.

[IIT-JEE - 1991]

2. The equations to a pair of of opposite side of a parallelogram are $x^2-5x+6=0$ and $y^2-6y+5=0$. The equations to its diagonals are

(a) $x+4y=12$ and $y=4x-7$

(b) $4x+y=13$ and $4y=x-7$.

(c) $4x+y=13$ and $y=4x-7$

(d) $y-4x=13$ and $y+4x=7$.

[IIT-JEE - 1994]

3. Let PQR be a right angled isosceles triangle, right angled at P(2, 1). If the equation of the line QR is $2x+y=3$, then the equations representing the pair of lines PQ and PR is

(a) $3x^2-3y^2+8xy+20x+10y+25=0$

(b) $3x^2-3y^2+8xy-20x-10y+25=0$

(c) $3x^2-3y^2+8xy+10x+15y+20=0$

(d) $3x^2-3y^2-8xy-10x-15y-20=0$

[IIT-JEE - 1999]

4. Let $2x^2+y^2-3xy=0$ be the equations of a pair of tangents drawn from the origin O to a circle of radius 3 with centre in the first quadrant. If A is one of the points of contact, then find the length of OA.

[IIT-JEE - 2001]

5. Area of the triangle formed by the angle bisectors of the pair of lines $x^2-y^2+2y-1=0$ and the line $x+y=3$ (in sq units) is

(a) 1 (b) 2 (c) 3 (d) 4

[IIT-JEE-2004]

6. Let a and b be non zero real numbers . Then the equation

$\left(ax^2+by^2+c\right)\left(x^2-5xy+6y^2\right)=0$ represents

(a) four striaght lines , when c = 0 and a, b are of the same signs.

(b) two straight lines and a circle , when a = b , and c is of sign opposite to a.

(c) two straight lines and a hyperbola , when a and b are of the same sign and c is of sign opposite to a.

(d) a circle and an ellipse, when a and b are of the same sign and c is of sign opposite to that of a.

[IIT-JEE-2008]

ANSWER

1. (1,-2)

4. $\left(9+3\sqrt{10}\right)$ units.

SELF ASSESSMENT TEST

Time : 3 Hrs. Ch: The pair of straight lines M.M. : 100

Give answers the following questions :

1. If the distance of a given point (α, β) from each of two straight lines through the origin is d, such that $(a x-\beta y)^m = d^n(x^2+y^2)$, where m, $n \in N$, then find the value of $m+n+2009$.
2. Find the length of the straight line joining the feet of the perpendiculars let fall from the point (p, q) on the pair of lines $ax^2+2hxy+by^2=0$.
3. A point moves so that the distance between the feet of the perpendiculars drawn from it to the lines $ax^2+2hxy+by^2=0$ is a constant 2k. Then find its locus.
4. Find the orthocentre of the triangle formed by the lines $ax^2+2hxy+by^2=0$ and $lx+my=1$.
5. If the lines $ax^2+2hxy+by^2=0$ be two sides of a parallelogram and the line $lx+my=1$ be one of its diagonals. Find the equation of its other doagonal.
6. If the equation $ax^2+2hxy+by^2+2gx+2fy+c=0$ represents a pair of straight lines, which are equidistant from the origin, such that $f^m-g^n=c(bf^p-ag^q)$, then find the value of $m+n+p+q+8$.
7. Find the centroid of the triangle formed by the lines $ax^2+2hxy+by^2=0$ and $lx+my=1$
8. Let P be the point of intersection of the lines represented by $x^2-y^2+4y-4=0$. If P is translated 2 units parallel to the line $x+y=4$, where x increses, say at Q. Then find the image of Q with respect to the line $y=x$.

ANSWER

1. 2013.

2. $2\times\sqrt{\dfrac{(h^2-ab)(p^2+q^2)}{(a-b)^2+4h^2}}$

3. $(x^2+y^2)(h^2-ab)=k^2\{(a-b)^2+4h^2\}$

4. $\dfrac{x}{l}=\dfrac{y}{m}=\dfrac{a+b}{am^2-2hlm+bl^2}$

5. $(bl-hm)y=(am-hl)x$

6. 20

7. $\dfrac{x}{bl-hm}=\dfrac{y}{am-hl}=\dfrac{2}{3(am^2-2hlm+bl^2)}$

8. $(2-\sqrt{2}, \sqrt{2})$

3 The Circle

CONCEPT BOOSTER

3.1 INTRODUCTION

The word "circle" derives from the Greek, kirkos "a circle," from the base ker- which means to turn or bend. The origins of the words "circus" and "circuit" are closely related.

The circle has been known since before the beginning of recorded history. Natural circles would have been observed, such as the Moon, Sun, and a short plant stalk blowing in the wind on sand, which forms a circle shape in the sand. The circle is the basis for the wheel, which, with related inventions such as gears, makes much of modern civilisation possible. In mathematics, the study of the circle has helped inspire the development of geometry, astronomy, and calculus.

Early science, particularly geometry and astrology and astronomy, was connected to the divine for most medieval scholars, and many believed that there was something intrinsically "divine" or "per fect" that could be found in circles.

1700 BCE – The Rhind papyrus gives a method to find the area of a circular field. The result corresponds to 256 / 81 (3.16049...) as an approximate value of pie.

300 BCE – Book 3 of Euclid's Elements deals with the properties of circles.

In Plato's Seventh Letter there is a detailed definition and explanation of the circle. Plato explains the perfect circle, and how it is different from any drawing, words, definition or explanation.

1880 CE– Lindemann proves that pie is transcendental, effectively settling the millennia-old problem of squaring the circle.

3.2 MATHEMATICAL DEFINITIONS

Definition-1:

A circle is a simple shape of Euclidean geometry that is the set of all points in a plane that are a given distance from a given point, the centre. The distance between any of the points and the centre is called the radius.

Definition-2:

A circle is a simple closed curve which divides the plane into two regions: an interior and an exterior.

Definiton-3:

A circle can be defined as the curve traced out by a point that moves so that its distance from a given point is constant.

Definition-4:

A circle may also be defined as a special ellipse in which the two foci are coincident and the eccentricity is zero.

Definition - 5:

The intersection of a right circular cone and a plane is a circle, in which the plane is perpendicular to the axis of the cone.

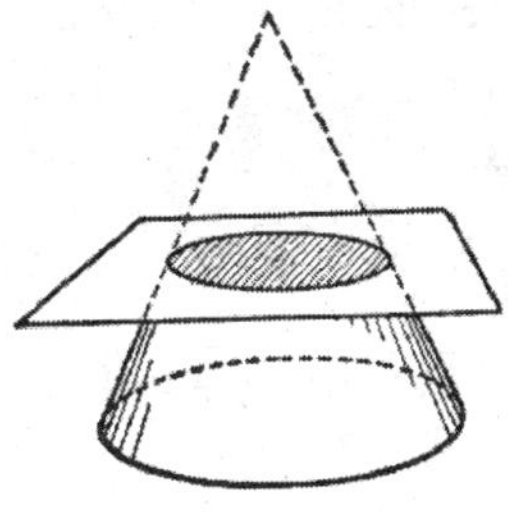

Definition - 6:

It is the locus of a point which moves in a plane in such a way that its distance from a fixed point is always same. The fixed point is called centre and the distance between the point and centre is known as radius of the circle.

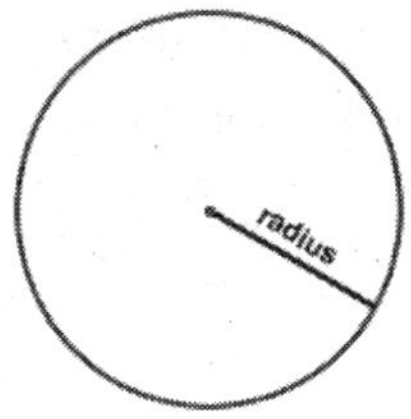

Definition - 7:

Circle is a conic section whose eccentricity is zero.

Definition-8:

A conic $ax^2 + 2hxy + by^2 + 2gx + 2fy + c = 0$ represents a circle if

(i) a = b (ii) h = 0 and (iii) $\Delta \neq 0$, where

$$\Delta = abc + 2fgh - af^2 - bg^2 - ch^2.$$

Definition-9: A super ellipse has an equation of the form

$$\left(\frac{x}{a}\right)^n + \left(\frac{y}{b}\right)^n = 1$$ for positive a, b, and n.

A supercircle has b = a. A circle is the special case of a super ellipse in which n = 2.

Definition-10:

A Cassini oval is a set of points such that the product of the distances from any of its points to two fixed points is a constant. When the two fixed points coincide, a circle results.

Definition-11:

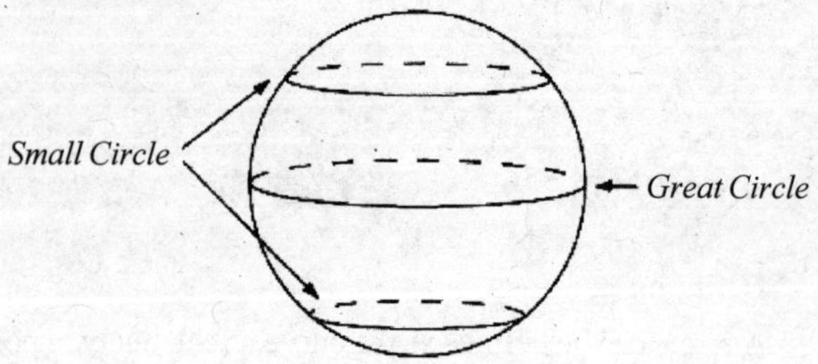

In 3D-geometry, section of a sphere by a plane is a circle.

Definition-12:

Let z be a complex number and 'a' be a +ve real number. If $|z| = a$, then the locus of z is a circle.

Definition - 13:

Let z be a complex number and $a \in R^+$, $b \in R$. If $|z - b| = a$, then the locus of z be a circle, with centre at 'b' and radius 'a'.

Definition-14:

Let z, z_1, z_2 be three non zero complex numbers such that $\left|\frac{z-z_1}{z-z_2}\right| = k$, where $k \neq 1$. Then the locus of z is a circle.

Definition-15:

Let z, z_1, z_2 be three non zero complex numbers such that $|z-z_1|^2 + |z-z_2|^2 = |z_1 - z_2|^2$. Then the locus of z is a circle with centre at $\left(\frac{z_1+z_2}{2}\right)$ and radius $\frac{1}{2}|z_1 - z_2|$.

Definition-16:

Let z, z_1, z_2 be three non zero complex numbers such that $\arg\left(\frac{z-z_2}{z-z_1}\right) = \frac{\pi}{2}$, then the locus of z is a circle.

Definition - 17:

Let z, z_1, z_2 be three non zero complex numbers such that $\arg\left(\frac{z-z_2}{z-z_1}\right) = \alpha$, where $\alpha \neq 0, \pi$.

Then the locus of z is a circle.

Definition-18:

Let C is the midpoint of the segment AB. If A, B, and C are given distinct points in the plane, then the locus of points P satisfying $\frac{|AP|}{|BP|} = \frac{|AC|}{|BC|}$ is called a "generalised circle." It may either be a true circle or a line. In this sense a line is a generalised circle of infinite radius.

3.3 STANDARD EQUATION OF A CIRCLE

(i) $x^2 + y^2 = a^2$, where centre is (0, 0) and radius is 'a'.

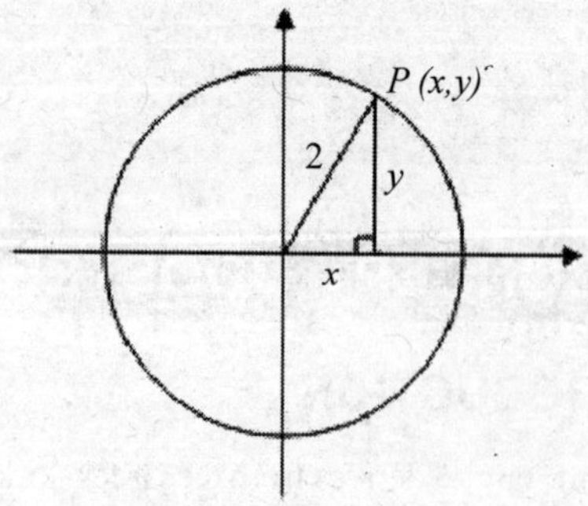

(ii) $(x-h)^2 + (y-k)^2 = a^2$, where centre is (h, k) and radius is 'a'.

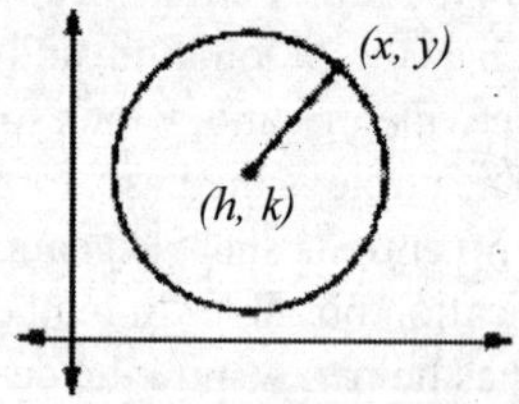

3.4 GENERAL EQUATION OF A CIRCLE :

The genral equation of a circle is $x^2 + y^2 + 2gx + 2fy + c = 0$, where centre is (-g, -f) and radius is $\sqrt{g^2 + f^2 - c}$.

As we know that, the equation any of circle, when centre of a circle is not origin, is $(x-h)^2 + (y-k)^2 = a^2$

$\Rightarrow \quad x^2 - 2hx + h^2 + y^2 - 2ky + k^2 = a^2$

$\Rightarrow \quad x^2 + y^2 - 2hx - 2ky + h^2 + k^2 - a^2 = 0$

$\Rightarrow \quad x^2 + y^2 + 2gx + 2fy + c = 0$, where

$h = -g, k = -f$ and $c = h^2 + k^2 - a^2$

$\Rightarrow \quad x^2 + y^2 + 2gx + 2fy + c = 0$, where $h = -g$,

$k = -f$ & $a = \sqrt{h^2 + k^2 - c} = \sqrt{g^2 + f^2 - c}$

3.5 NATURE OF THE CIRCLE

Nature of the circle depends on the radius.

Let the equation of a circle is. Its radius is $\sqrt{g^2 + f^2 - c}$.

(i) If $(g^2 + f^2 - c) > 0$, then it represents a real circle.

(ii) If $(g^2 + f^2 - c) < 0$, then it represents a virtual circle or an imaginary circle.

(iii) If $(g^2 + f^2 - c) = 0$, then it represents a point circle.

3.6 CONCENTRIC CIRCLES

Two circles having the same centre, say, (h, k) and different radii say, r_1 and r_2 respectively are called concentric circles.

Thus $(x-h)^2+(y-k)^2=r_1^2$

and $(x-h)^2+(y-k)^2=r_2^2$ are two concentric circles.

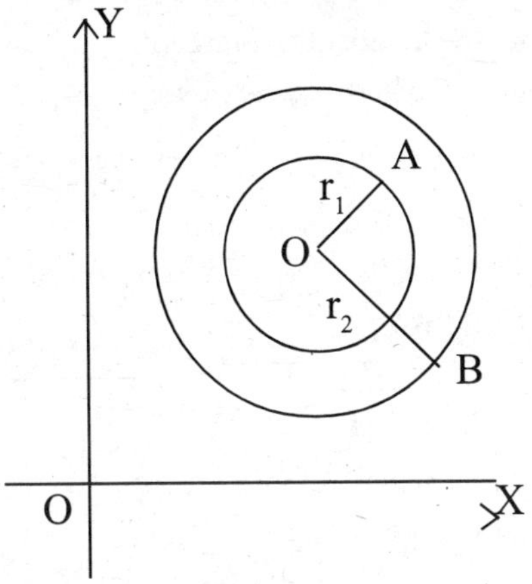

3.7 CONCYCLIC POINTS

If P, Q, R and S lie on the same circle, then P, Q, R and S known as concyclic points.

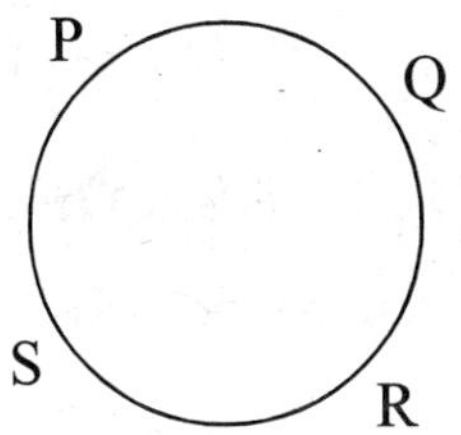

3.8 PARAMETRIC EQUATION OF A CIRCLE

If the radius of a circle, whose centre is origin, makes an angle θ with the +ve direction of x-axis, then θ is called a parameter and $0 \le \theta < 2\pi$.

(i) If the equation of a circle be $x^2+y^2=a^2$, then its parametric equations are $x = a\cos\theta,\ y = a\sin\theta$, where θ is a parameter

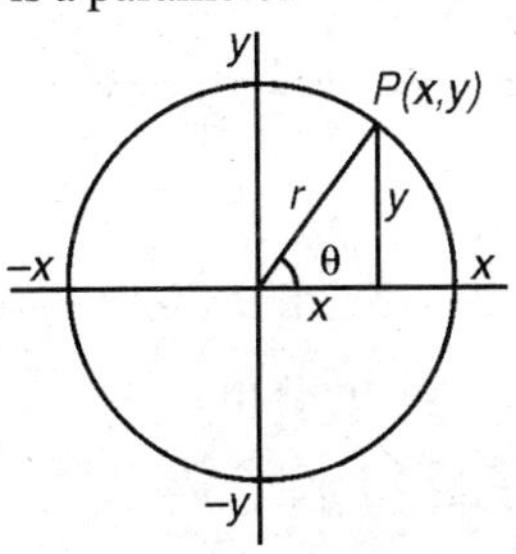

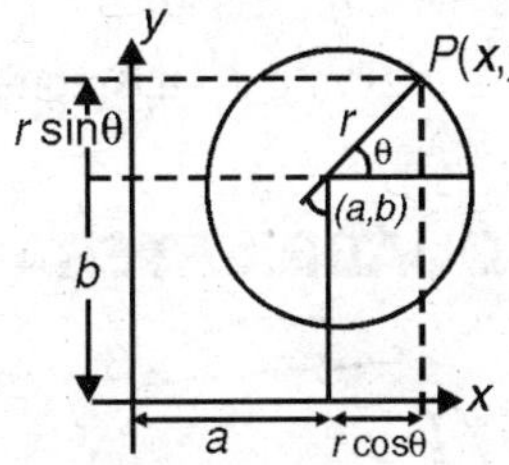

(ii) If the equation of a circle be $(x-h)^2+(y-k)^2=a^2$, then its parametric equations are

$x = h + a\cos?,\ y = k + a\sin?$, where θ is a parameter.

3.9 DIAMETRIC FORM OF A CIRCLE:

The equation of a circle, when the end points of a diameter are given (x_1, y_1) and (x_2, y_2), is

$(x-x_1)(x-x_2)+(y-y_1)(y-y_2)=0$.

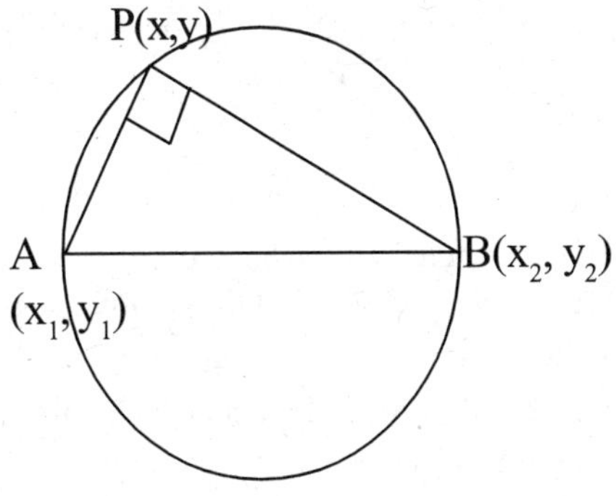

Now, $m(PA) = \dfrac{y-y_1}{x-x_1}$ and $m(PB) = \dfrac{y-y_2}{x-x_2}$.

As we know that, angle in a semi circle is a right angle.

Thus, $m(PA) \times m(PB) = -1$

$$\Rightarrow \left(\frac{y-y_1}{x-x_1}\right)\times\left(\frac{y-y_2}{x-x_2}\right) = -1$$

$$\Rightarrow (x-x_1)(x-x_2)+(y-y_1)(y-y_2) = -1.$$

Hence, the result.

3.10 EQUATION OF A CIRCLE PASSING THROUGH THREE NON COLLINEAR POINTS :

Let the equation of a circle be

$$x^2+y^2+2gx+2fy+c=0$$

If three points $(x_1, y_1), (x_2, y_2), (x_3, y_3)$ lie on a circle, then $x_1^2+y_1^2+2gx_1+2fy_1+c=0$,

$x_2^2+y_2^2+2gx_2+2fy_2+c=0$ and

$x_3^2 + y_3^2 + 2gx_3 + 2fy_3 + c = 0$.

Eliminating g, f and c, we get the required equation of a circle.

3.11 CYCLIC QUADRILATERAL

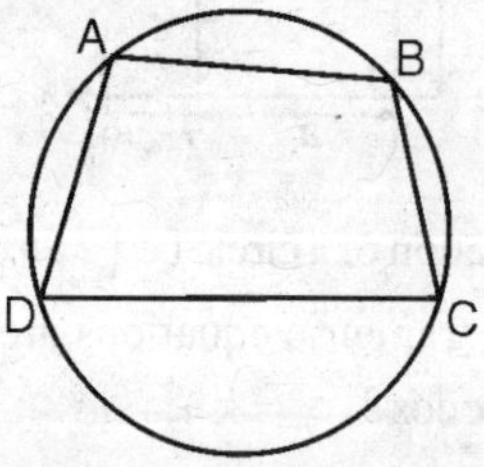

If all the vertices of a quadrilateral lie on a circle, then the quadrilateral is called a cyclic quadrilat eral. and the four vetices are known as concyclic points.

3.12 CONDICTION FOR CONCYCLIC POINTS

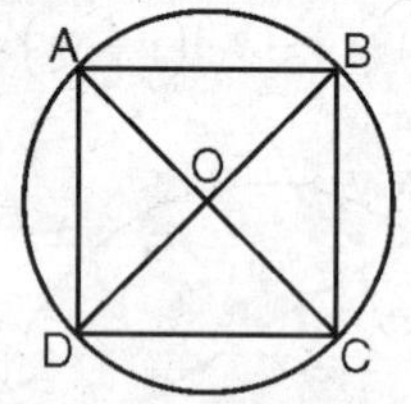

If A, B, C and D are concyclic points, then OA . OD = OB. OC, where O is the point of intersection of the chords AD and BC. O is not the centre of a circle.

If the lines $a_1x + b_1y + c_1 = 0$ and $a_2x + b_2y + c_2 = 0$ cut the x-axis and y-axis in four concyclic points, then $a_1 a_2 = b_1 b_2$. If two conics

$$a_1x^2 + 2h_1xy + b_1y^2 + 2g_1x + 2f_1y + c_1 = 0 \text{ and}$$

$$a_2x^2 + 2h_2xy + b_2y^2 + 2g_2x + 2f_2y + c_2 = 0$$

will intersect each other in four concyclic points,

then $\dfrac{a_1 - b_1}{a_2 - b_2} = \dfrac{h_1}{h_2}$

3.13 INTERCEPTS MADE ON THE AXES BY A CIRCLE

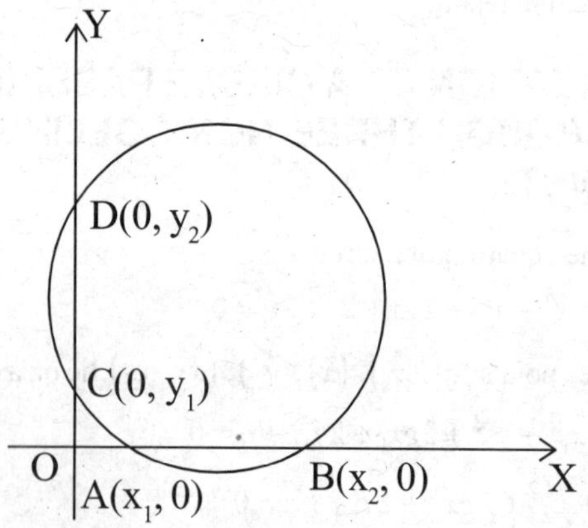

Let the circle be $x^2 + y^2 + 2gx + 2fy + c = 0$.

(i) the length of x-intercept = $2\sqrt{g^2 - c}$

(ii) the length of y-intercept = $2\sqrt{f^2 - c}$.

Let the circle be

$$x^2 + y^2 + 2gx + 2fy + c = 0 \qquad ...(i)$$

Case - I : The length of x-intercept.

Put x = 0 in (i), we get,

$x^2 + 2gx + c = 0$.

Let x_1, x_2 be its roots.

Thus, $x_1 + x_2 = -2g$ and $x_1x_2 = c$

Therefore,

$$x_1 - x_2 = \sqrt{(x_1 + x^2)^2 - 4x_1x_2} = \sqrt{4g^2 - 4c} = 2\sqrt{g^2 - c}$$

Case - II : The length of y-intercept.

Put y = 0 in (i), we

get, $y^2 + 2fy + c = 0$

Let y_1, y_2 be its roots.

Thus, $y_1 + y_2 = -2f$ and $y_1 y_2 = c$

Therefore,

$$y_1 - y_2 = \sqrt{(y_1 + y_2)^2 - 4y_1y_2} = \sqrt{4f^2 - 4c} = 2\sqrt{f^2 - c}$$

3.14 DIFFERENT FORMS OF A CIRCLE :

(i) **When the circle touches the x-axis**

The equation of a circle is $(x-h)^2 + (y-k)^2 = k^2$

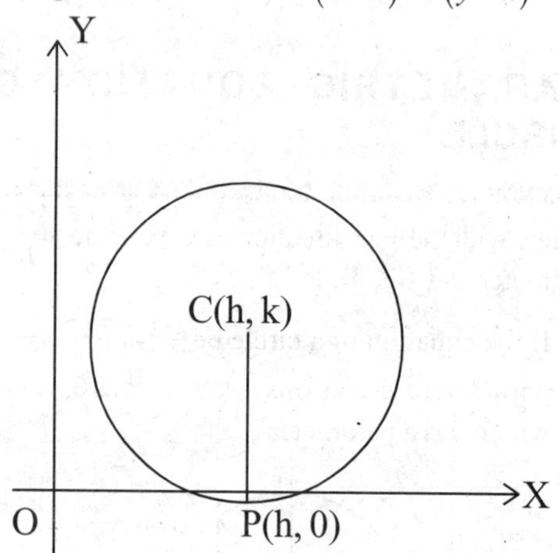

(ii) **When the circle touches the y-axis.**

The equation of a circle is

$(x-h)^2 + (y-k)^2 = h^2$.

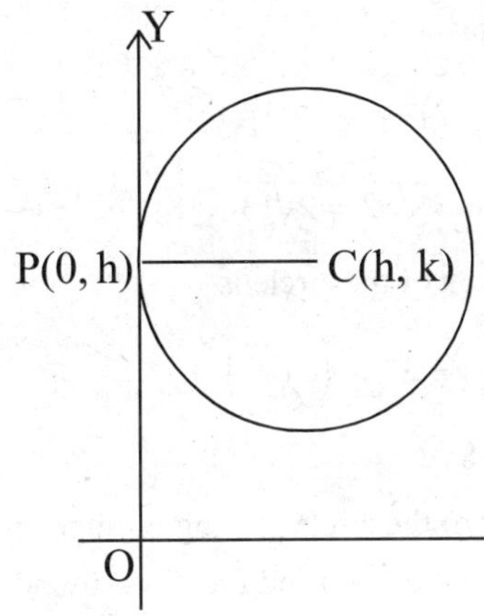

(iii) **When the circle touches bith the axes.**

The equation of a circle is

$(x-h)^2+(y-h)^2=h^2$ or $(x-k)^2+(y-k)^2=k^2$.

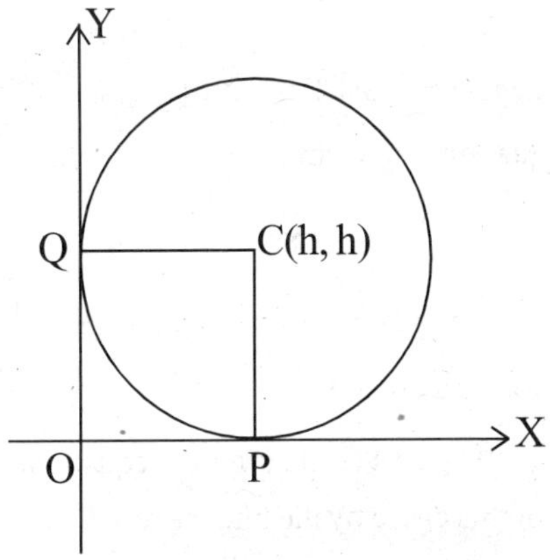

(iv) **When the circle passes through the origin and centre lies on x-axis.**

The equation of a circle is $(x-h)^2+y^2=h^2$ or

$x^2+y^2-2hx=0$

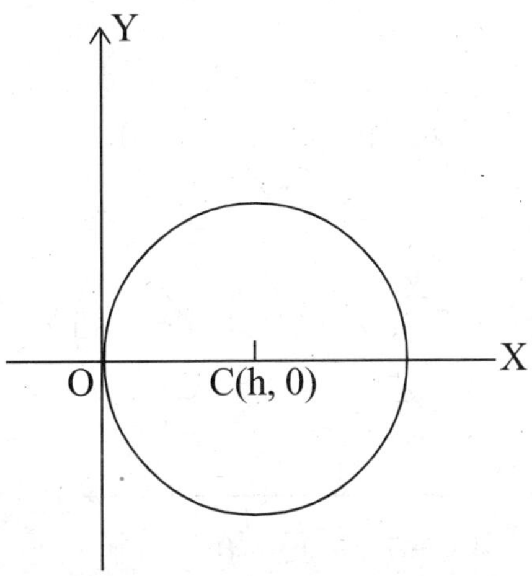

(v) **When the circle passes through the origin and centre lies on y-axis.**

The equation of a circle is $x^2+(y-k)^2=k^2$ or

$x^2+y^2-2ky=0$.

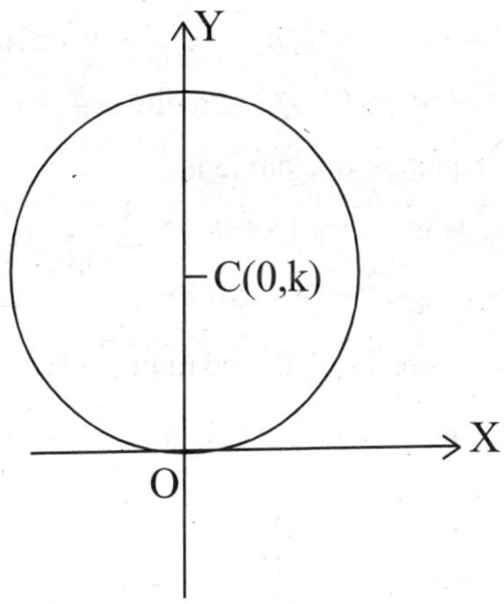

(vi) **When the circle passes through the origin and has intercepts a and b on the x and y axes respectively.**

The equation of the circle is $x^2+y^2-ax-by=0$.

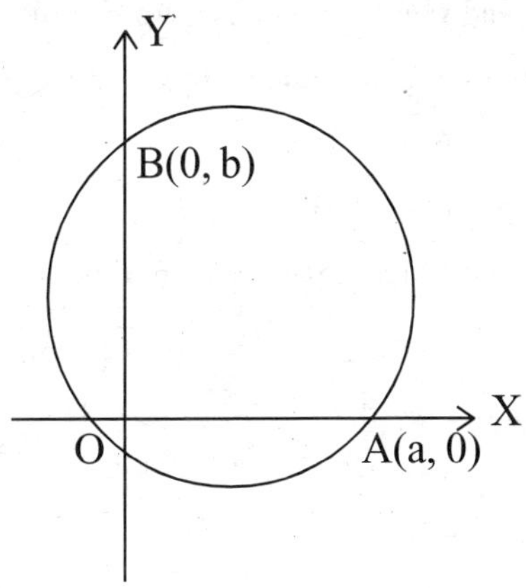

(vii) **When the circle passes through the origin**

The equation of a circle is $x^2+y^2+2gx+2fy=0$.

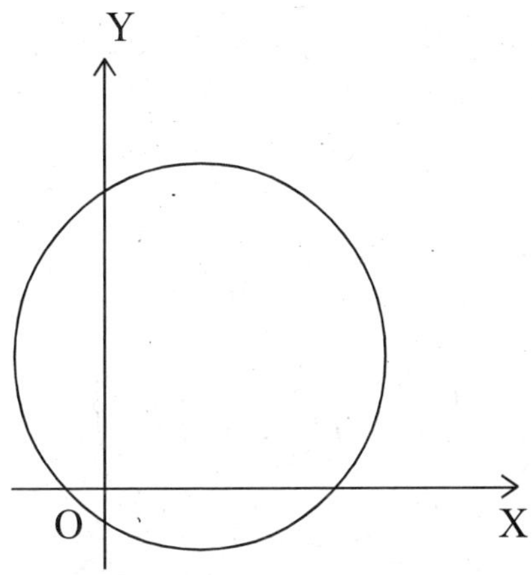

Ex-1. Find the centre and radius of the circles

(i) $x^2+y^2=16$

(ii) $x^2+y^2-8x+15=0$

(iii) $x^2+y^2-x-y=0$.

Sol. (i) The given equation of circle is $x^2+y^2=16$

Hence, the centre is (0, 0) and radius = 4.

(ii) The given equation of a circle is

$$x^2+y^2-8x+15=0$$

$$\Rightarrow \quad (x-4)^2+y^2=16-15=1$$

Hence, the centre is (4, 0) and radius = 1.

(iii) The given equation of a circle is $x^2+y^2-x-y=0$.

$$\Rightarrow \quad \left(x-\frac{1}{2}\right)^2+\left(y-\frac{1}{2}\right)^2=\frac{1}{4}+\frac{1}{4}=\frac{1}{2}=\left(\frac{1}{\sqrt{2}}\right)^2$$

Hence, the centre is $\left(\frac{1}{2},\frac{1}{2}\right)$ and radius is $\frac{1}{\sqrt{2}}$.

Ex-2. Prove that the radii of the circles $x^2+y^2=1$, $x^2+y^2-2x-6y=6$ and $x^2+y^2-4x-12y=9$ are in AP.

Sol. The equations of given circles are $x^2+y^2=1$ ...(i)

$x^2+y^2-2x-6y=6$ ...(ii)

and $x^2+y^2-4x-12y=9$ ...(iii)

Let r_1, r_2 and r_3 are the radii of (i), (ii) and (iii).

Then $r_1=1$, $r_2=\sqrt{g^2+f^2-c}=\sqrt{1+9+6}=4$ and

$r_3=\sqrt{4+36+9}=7$

Therefore, $r_1+r_3=7+1=8=2(4)=2r_2$.

Thys, r_1, r_2, r_3 are in A.P.

Ex-3. Find the equation of the circle concentric with the circle $x^2+y^2-8x+6y-5=0$ and passing through the point (–2, –7).

Sol. Since the circle is concentric, so the centre of the circle is same as $x^2+y^2-8x+6y-5=0$

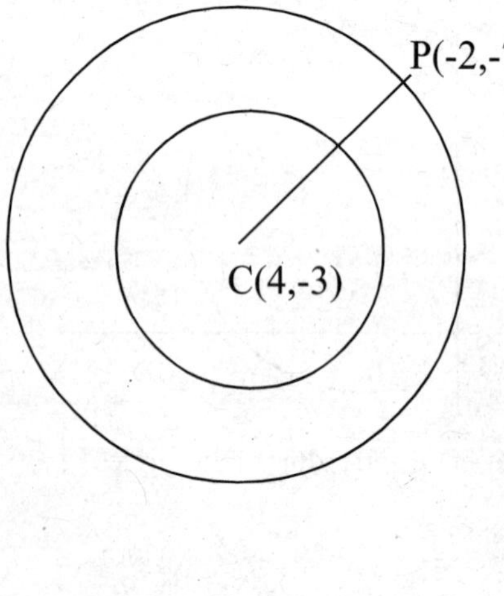

Let CP is the radius.

Then $CP=\sqrt{(-4-2)^2+(-7+3)^2}$

$=\sqrt{36+16}=\sqrt{52}=2\sqrt{13}$

Hence, the equation of the circle is

$$(x-4)^2+(y+3)^2=\left(2\sqrt{13}\right)^2$$

$$\Rightarrow \quad x^2+y^2-8x+6y=27.$$

Ex-4. Find the equation of the circle passing through the point of intersection of $x+3y=0$ and $2x-7y=0$ and whose center is the point of intersection of lines $x+y+1=0$ and $x-2y+4=0$.

Sol. The point of intersection of $x+3y=0$ and $2x-7y=0$ is P(0, 0) and the point of intersection of $x+y+1=0$ and $x-2y+4=0$ is C(-2, 1).

Thus, CP is the radius. i.e. $CP=\sqrt{4+1}=\sqrt{5}$

Hence, the equation of the circle is

$$(x+2)^2+(y-1)^2=\left(\sqrt{5}\right)^2$$

$$\Rightarrow \quad x^2+y^2+4x-2y=0.$$

Ex-5. Let the equation of a circle is $x^2+y^2-16x-24y+183=0$. Find the equation of the image of this circle by the line mirror- $4x+7y+13=0$.

Sol. The centre of the circle

$$x^2+y^2-16x-24y+183=0$$

is C (8, 12).

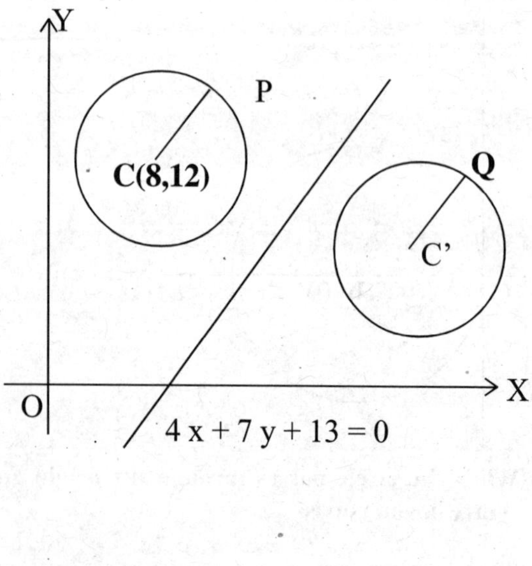

Let the centre of the new circle be C'(h, k)

Now, $\frac{h-8}{-4}=\frac{k-12}{7}=-\frac{2(-32+84+13)}{16+49}$

$\Rightarrow \quad h=0, k=-2$

Hence, the equation of the new circle is

$$x^2+(y+2)^2=\left(3\sqrt{3}\right)^2$$

$\Rightarrow \quad x^2+y^2+4y=23.$

Ex-6. Find the area of an equilateral triangle inscribed in the circle $x^2+y^2+2gx+2fy+c=0$.

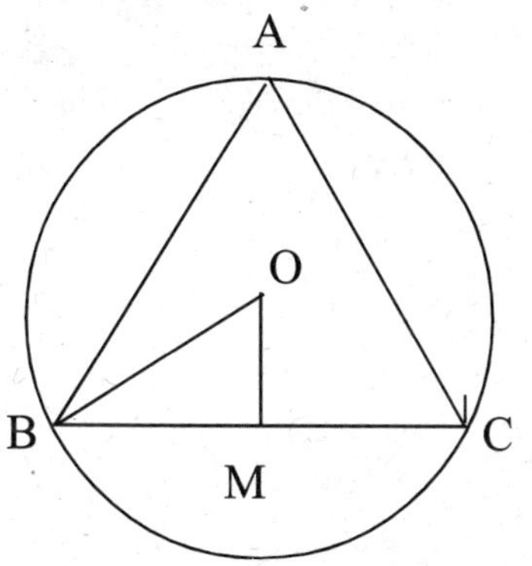

Sol. Let ABC be an equilateral triangle such that OM is perpendicular on BC.

Here, $OB=\sqrt{g^2+f^2-c}$

Clearly, $\angle BOM=60^?$.

Now, $\sin\left(\frac{p}{3}\right)=\frac{BM}{OB}$

$\Rightarrow \quad BM=\frac{\sqrt{3}}{2}OB=\frac{\sqrt{3}}{2}\times\sqrt{g^2+f^2-c}$

Thus, ar $(\Delta ABC)=\frac{\sqrt{3}}{4}\times(BC)^2=\frac{\sqrt{3}}{4}\times(2BM)^2$

$=\frac{3\sqrt{3}}{4}\times\left(g^2+f^2-c\right).$

Ex-7. A circle has radius 3 units and its centre lies on the line $y=x-1$. Find the equation of the circle if it passes through (7, 3).

Sol. Let the centre of the circle be (h, k) such that $k=h-1$.

We have, $(h-7)^2+(k-3)^2=3^2$

$\Rightarrow \quad (h-7)^2+(h-4)^2=3^2$

$\Rightarrow \quad h^2-11h+28=0$

$\Rightarrow \quad h=7, 4$ and $k=6, 3$.

Hence, the equation of a circle can be

$(x-7)^2+(y-6)^2=3^2$ & $(x-4)^2+(y-3)^2=3^2$

$\Rightarrow \quad x^2+y^2-8x-6y+16=0$

and $\quad x^2+y^2-14x-12y+76=0$.

Ex-8. Find the point P on the circle

$x^2+y^2-4x-6y+9=0$ such that $\angle POX$ is minimum, where O is the origin and OX is the x-axis.

Sol. Let $\angle POX=\theta$

Then $\angle NCP=\theta$

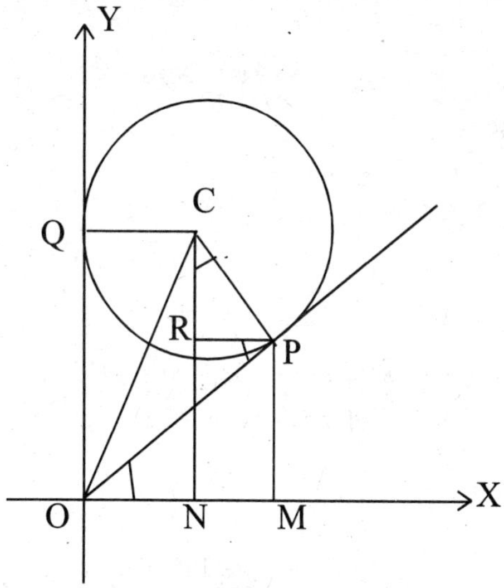

Here, $CP=2, OC=\sqrt{2^2+3^2}=\sqrt{13}$

$OP=\sqrt{OC^2-OP^2}=\sqrt{13-4}=\sqrt{9}=3$

$C=(2, 3)$ and $ON=2$

Now, $OM=ON+MN=ON+PR$

$\Rightarrow \quad OP\cos\theta=2+2\sin\theta$

$\Rightarrow \quad 3\cos\theta=2+2\sin\theta$

$\Rightarrow \quad 9\cos^2\theta=4+4\sin^2\theta+8\sin\theta$

$\Rightarrow \quad 9-9\sin^2\theta=4+4\sin^2\theta+8\sin\theta$

$\Rightarrow \quad 13\sin^2\theta+8\sin\theta-5=0$

$\Rightarrow \quad 13\sin^2\theta+13\sin\theta-5\sin\ -5=0$

$\Rightarrow \quad 13\sin\ (\sin\theta+1)-5(\sin\theta+1)=0$

$\Rightarrow \quad (\sin\theta+1)(13\sin\theta-5)=0$

$\Rightarrow \quad \sin\theta=\frac{5}{13}$ and $\Rightarrow \quad \cos\theta=\frac{12}{13}$

Therefore, $P=(OP.\cos\theta,\ OP.\sin\theta)=\left(\frac{36}{13},\frac{15}{13}\right)$

Ex-9. Find the equation of the circle when the end points of a diameter are (2, 3) and (6, 9)

Sol. Hence, the equation of the circle is

$$(x-2)(x-6)+(y-3)(y-9)=0$$

$\Rightarrow \quad x^2+y^2-8x-12y+39=0$

Ex-10. Find the equation of a circle passing through (1, 2), (4, 5) and (0, 9).

Sol. Hence, the equation of the circle be

$$x^2+y^2+2gx+2fy+c=0 \quad \text{...(i)}$$

Which is passing through (1, 2) , (4, 5) and (0, 9).

Thus, $1+4+2g+8f+c=0 \Rightarrow 2g+8f+c=-5$ ...(ii)

$16+25+8g+10f+c=0 \Rightarrow 8g+10f+c=-41$ ...(iii)

$0+81+18f+c=0 \Rightarrow 18f+c=-81$ ...(iv)

(iii) - (ii), we get, $6g+2f=-36$

$\Rightarrow \quad 3g+f=-18$ ...(v)

(iii) - (iv), we get, $8g-8f=40$

$\Rightarrow \quad g-f=5$ ...(vi)

From (v) and (vi), we get, $4g=-13 \Rightarrow g=-13/4$.

and $f=g-5=-13/4-5 \Rightarrow f=-33/4$

now, from (iv), we get, $c=-81-18f=-81-297/2=-135/2$

Put all these values of f, g and c in (i), we get,

$$x^2+y^2-\frac{13}{2}x-\frac{33}{2}y-\frac{135}{2}=0$$

$$\Rightarrow \quad 2\left(x^2+y^2\right)-13x-33y-135=0.$$

Ex-11. Find the equation of a circle passing through the point (1, 2) and (3, 4) and touching the line $3x+y=5$.

Sol. Let the equation of the circle is

$$x^2+y^2+2gx+2fy+c=0$$

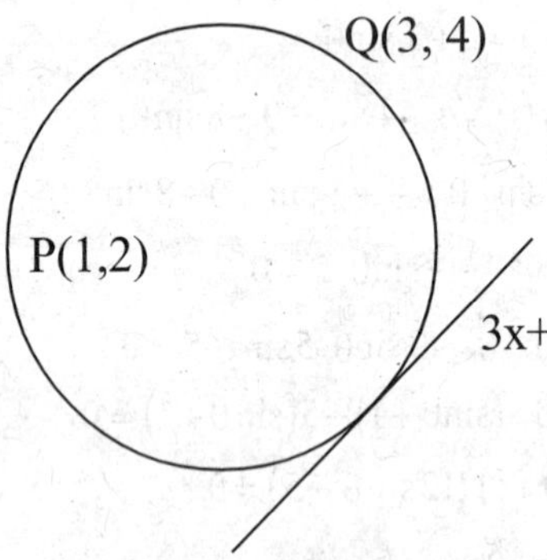

Which is passing through (1, 2) and (3, 4).

Therefore, $1+4+2g+4f+c=0$

$\Rightarrow \quad 2g+4f+c=-5$ ...(i)

And $9+16+6g+8f+c=0$

$\Rightarrow \quad 6g+8f+c=-25$ ...(ii)

(ii) - (i), we get, $4g+4f=-20$

$\Rightarrow \quad g+f=-5$ ...(iv).

Also, $\left|\dfrac{-3g-f-5}{\sqrt{3^2+1^2}}\right|=\sqrt{g^2+f^2-c}$

$$=\sqrt{(g+1)^2+(f+2)^2}$$

$\Rightarrow \quad (3g+f+5)^2=10\left\{(g+1)^2+(g+3)^2\right\}$

$\Rightarrow \quad (2g-5+5)^2=10(g^2+2g+1+g^2+6g+9))$.

$\Rightarrow \quad 4g^2=10(2g^2+8g+10)$

$\Rightarrow \quad 4g^2+20g+25=0$

$\Rightarrow \quad (2g+5)^2=0. \quad \Rightarrow \quad g=-5/2$

Thus, $f=-5-g=-5+\frac{5}{2}=-\frac{5}{2}$. and $c=10$

Hence, the equation of the required circle is

$$x^2+y^2-2\left(\frac{5}{2}\right)x-2\left(\frac{5}{2}\right)+10=0$$

$$\Rightarrow \quad x^2+y^2-5x-5y+10=0.$$

Ex-12. Find the length of intercepts to the circle $x^2+y^2+6x+10y+8=0$

Sol. The lengths of the x-intercept

$$=2\sqrt{g^2-c}=2\sqrt{9-8}=2$$

and the y-intercept $=2\sqrt{f^2-c}=2\sqrt{25-8}=2\sqrt{17}$

Ex-13. Find the length of y-intercept to the circle $x^2+y^2-x-y=0$

Sol. The length of the y-intercept

$$=2\sqrt{f^2-c}=2\sqrt{\frac{1}{4}-0}=2\times\frac{1}{2}=1$$

Ex-14. Show that the circle $x^2+y^2-2ax-2ay+a^2=0$ touches both the co-ordinate axes.

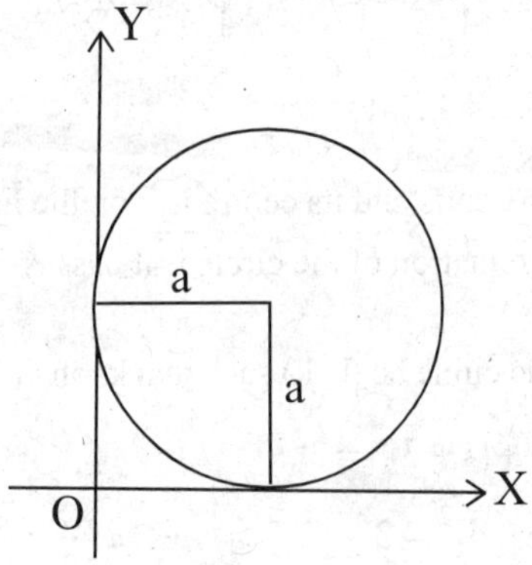

Sol. The given equation of a circle is

$$x^2+y^2-2ax-2by+a^2=0$$

$\Rightarrow \quad (x-a)^2+(y-a)^2=a^2$.

Thus, the centre is (a, a) and radius is a .

3.15 POSITION OF A POINT WITH RESPECT TO A CIRCLE

(i) A point (x_1, y_1) lies outside , on and inside of a circle

$x^2 + y^2 = a^2$

if $x_1^2 + y_1^2 - a^2 > 0, = 0, < 0$

(ii) A point (x_1, y_1) lies outside , on and inside of a circle

$x^2 + y^2 + 2gx + 2fy + c = 0$

if $x_1^2 + y_1^2 + 2g\,x_1 + 2f\,y_1 + c > 0,\ = 0,\ < 0$.

Ex-1. Discuss the position of the points (1, 2) and (6, 0) with respect to the circle $x^2 + y^2 - 4x + 2y - 11 = 0$.

Sol. Let $N = x^2 + y^2 - 4x + 2y - 11$.

The values of N at (1, 2) is $1 + 4 - 4 + 4 - 11 = 5 - 11 = -6 < 0$

and at (6, 0) is $36 + 0 - 0 + 12 - 11 = 37 > 0$.

Thus, the point (1, 2) lies inside of the circle and (6, 0) lies outside of the circle.

Ex-2. If the point $(\lambda, -\lambda)$ lies inside the circle $x^2 + y^2 - 4x + 2y - 8 = 0$, then find range of λ.

Sol. Since, the point $(\lambda, -\lambda)$ lies inside the circle $x^2 + y^2 - 4x + 2y - 8 = 0$, so

$$\lambda^2 + \lambda^2 - 4\lambda - 2\lambda - 8 < 0$$

$$\Rightarrow \quad 2\lambda^2 - 6\lambda - 8 < 0$$

$$\Rightarrow \quad \lambda^2 - 3\lambda - 4 < 0$$

$$\Rightarrow \quad (\lambda - 4)(\lambda + 1) < 0$$

$$\Rightarrow \quad -1 < \lambda < 4.$$

Thus, the range of λ is $(-1, 4)$.

3.16 SHORTEST AND LARGEST DISTANCE OF A CIRCLE FROM A POINT

Let $P(x_1, y_1)$ be any point and the circle be

$$x^2 + y^2 + 2gx + 2fy + c = 0$$

Case - I: When P lies inside the circle.

Draw a line through P passes through the centre and inetrsects the circle at Aand B respectively.

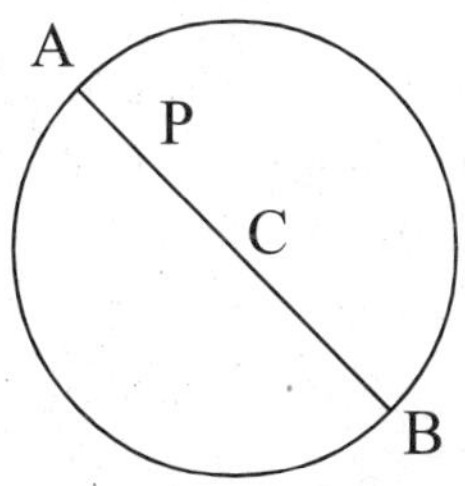

Shortest distance = PA = CA- CP

Largest distance = PB = CP + CB.

Case - II: When P lies outside on the circle

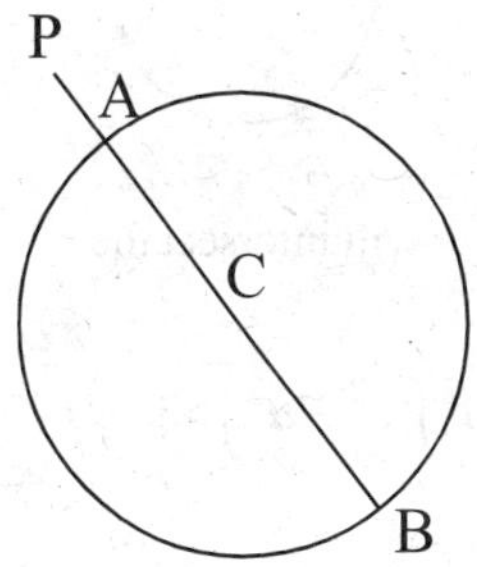

Draw a line through P passes through the center and intersçts the circle at A and B respectively .

Shortest distance = PA = CP - CA Largest distance = PB = CP + CB.

Case - III: When P lies on the circle Draw a line through P passes through the center and intersçts the circle at A and B respectively .

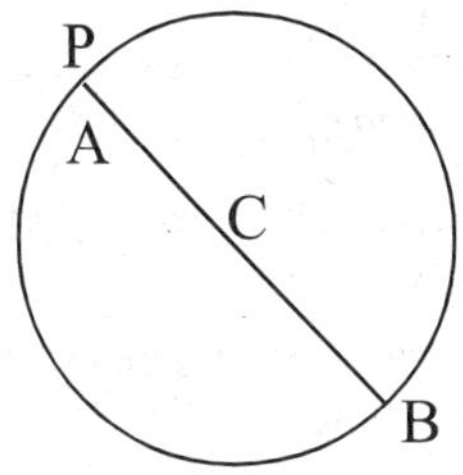

Shortest distance = 0 Largest distance = PB = 2 radius.

Ex-1. Find the shortest and largest distance from the point (2, –7) to the circle $x^2 + y^2 - 14x - 10y - 151 = 0$

Sol. Let $N = x^2 + y^2 - 14x - 10y - 151$.

The value of N at (2, -7) is $4 + 49 - 28 + 98 - 151$

$= 153 - 151 - 28 = 2 - 28 = -26$.

Thus, the point P(2, -7) lies inside of the circle.

The centre of the circle is C(7, 5) and the radius is $= CA = CB = 15$.

Now CP

$$= \sqrt{(7-2)^2 + (5+7)^2} = \sqrt{25 + 144} = \sqrt{169} = 13.$$

Hence, the chortest distance = PA = CA - CP = 15 - 13 = 2 and the largest distance = PB = CP + CB = 13 + 15 = 28.

3.17 INTERSECTION OF A LINE AND A CIRCLE

Let the circle be $x^2 + y^2 = a^2$ ...(i)

and the line be $y = mx + c$ ...(ii)

From (i) and (ii), we get, $x^2 + (mx + c)^2 = a^2$

$$\Rightarrow \quad (1 + m^2)x^2 + 2mcs + (c^2 - a^2) = 0$$

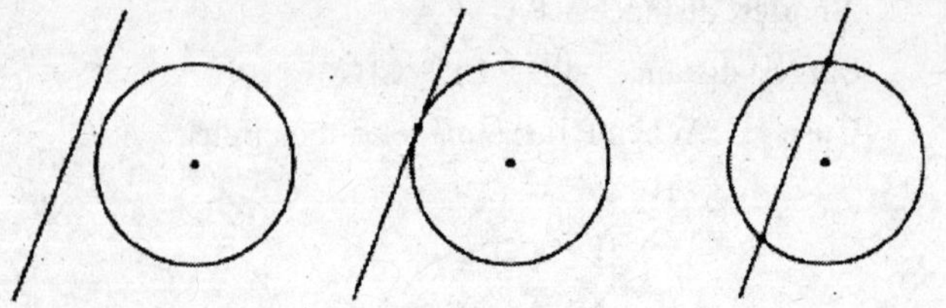

(i) The line y = m x + c will intersect the circle in two distinct points if D > 0

$$4m^2c^2 - 4\left(1+m^2\right)\left(c^2 - a^2\right) > 0$$

$$\Rightarrow \quad m^2c^2 - \left(c^2 + m^2c^2 - a^2\left(1+m^2\right)\right) > 0$$

$$\Rightarrow \quad c^2 - a^2\left(1+m^2\right) > 0$$

$$\Rightarrow \quad a^2\left(1+m^2\right) > c^2$$

$$\Rightarrow \quad a^2 > \frac{c^2}{\left(1+m^2\right)}$$

$$\Rightarrow \quad a > \frac{|c|}{\sqrt{\left(1+m^2\right)}}$$

⇒ radius > length of perpendicular from the origin to the line y = m x + c.

(ii) The line y = m x + c will intersect the circle in two coincident points if D = 0 .

$$\Rightarrow \quad 4m^2c^2 - 4\left(1+m^2\right)\left(c^2 - a^2\right) = 0$$

$$\Rightarrow \quad m^2c^2 - \left(1+m^2\right)\left(c^2 - a^2\right) = 0$$

$$\Rightarrow \quad c^2 = a^2\left(1+m^2\right)$$

$$\Rightarrow \quad a^2 = \frac{c^2}{\left(1+m^2\right)}$$

$$\Rightarrow \quad a = \frac{|c|}{\sqrt{\left(1+m^2\right)}}\cdot$$

⇒ radius = the length of perpendicular from the centre of a circle to the line y = m x + c.

(iii) The line y = m x + c will not intersect the circle if D < 0

$$\Rightarrow \quad 4m^2c^2 - 4\left(1+m^2\right)\left(c^2 - a^2\right) < 0$$

$$\Rightarrow \quad m^2c^2 - \left(c^2 + m^2c^2 - a^2\left(1+m^2\right)\right) < 0$$

$$\Rightarrow \quad c^2 - a^2\left(1+m^2\right) < 0$$

$$\Rightarrow \quad a^2\left(1+m^2\right) < c^2$$

$$\Rightarrow \quad a^2 < \frac{c^2}{\left(1+m^2\right)}$$

$$\Rightarrow \quad a < \frac{|c|}{\sqrt{\left(1+m^2\right)}}$$

⇒ radius < length of perpendicular from the origin to the line y = m x + c.

3.18 THE LENGTH OF INTERCEPT CUT OFF FROM A LINE BY A CIRCLE

The length of the intercept cut off from the line y = m x + c by the circle $x^2 + y^2 = a^2$ is

$$2\times\sqrt{\left(\frac{a^2\left(1+m^2\right)-c^2}{\left(1+m^2\right)}\right)}.$$

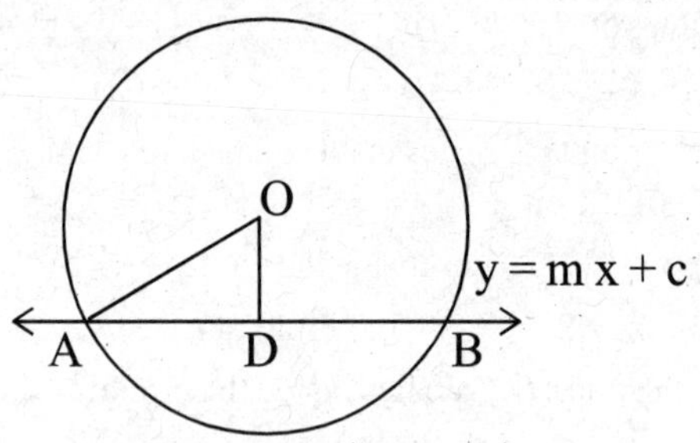

Proof: We have , $OD = \left|\frac{c}{\sqrt{1+m^2}}\right|$

In ? AOD, $AD^2 = OA^2 - OD^2 = a^2 - \frac{c^2}{\left(1+m^2\right)}$

$$= \frac{a^2\left(m^2+1\right)-c^2}{\left(1+m^2\right)}$$

$$\Rightarrow \quad AD = \sqrt{\frac{a^2\left(m^2+1\right)-c^2}{\left(1+m^2\right)}}$$

Thus, the length of intercept

$$= AB = 2\,AD = 2\times\sqrt{\frac{a^2\left(m^2+1\right)-c^2}{\left(1+m^2\right)}}.$$

Ex-1. Prove that the line $y = x + 2$ touches the circle $x^2 + y^2 = 2$. Find its point of contact.

Sol. The line y = x + 2 touches the circle $x^2 + y^2 = 2$, if the length of perpendicular from the centre to the given line is equal to the radius of a circle.

Thus, the radius of the circle is $\sqrt{2}$.

The length of perpendicular from the centre (0, 0) to the line x - y + 2 = 0 is

The length of perpendicular from the centre (0, 0) to the line x - y + 2 = 0 is

$$\left|\frac{0-0+2}{\sqrt{1^2+1^2}}\right| = \frac{2}{\sqrt{2}} = \sqrt{2} = \text{radius.}$$

Hence, the line y = x + 2 touches the circle $x^2 + y^2 = 2$.

On solving y = x + 2 and x 2 + y 2 = 2,

we get, $x^2 + (x+2)^2 = 2$

$\Rightarrow \quad x^2 + x^2 + 4x + 4 - 2 = 0$

$\Rightarrow \quad 2x^2 + 4x + 2 = 0$

$\Rightarrow \quad x^2 + 2x + 1 = 0$

$\Rightarrow \quad (x+1)^2 = 0$

$\Rightarrow \quad x = -1,\ y = -1 + 2 = 1$

Thus, the co-ordinates of the point of contact is (-1, 1).

Ex-2. Find the equation of the tangent to the circle $x^2 + y^2 = 4$ parallel to the line $3x + 2y + 5 = 0$

Sol. Equation of any line parallel to the line

3 x + 2 y + 5 = 0 is 3 x + 2 y + k = 0 ...(i)

The line (i) will be a tangent to the circle $x^2 + y^2 = 4$, if the length of perpendicular from the centre to the line (i) is equal to the radius of the circle.

Therefore, $\left|\frac{3.0+2.0+k}{\sqrt{3^2+2^2}}\right| = 2 \quad \Rightarrow \quad k = \pm\, 2\sqrt{13}$

Hence, the equation of tangents to the given circle are

$3x + 2y \pm 2\sqrt{13} = 0$.

Ex-3. Find the equation of the tangent to the circle $x^2 + y^2 = 9$ perpendicular to the line $4x + 3y = 0$.

Sol. Equation of any line perpendicular to the line

4 x + 3 y = 0 is 3 x - 4 y + k = 0...............(i)

The line (i) will be a tangent to the circle $x^2 + y^2 = 9$, if the length of perpendicular from the centre to the line (i) is equal to the radius of the circle.

Therefore, $\left|\frac{3.0-4.0+k}{\sqrt{3^2+4^2}}\right| = 3 \Rightarrow \quad k = \pm 15$.

Hence, the equation of tangents are 3 x - 4 y + 15 = 0 and 3 x - 4 y - 15 = 0.

Ex-4. Find the equation of tangent to the circle $x^2 + y^2 + 4x + 3 = 0$, which makes an angle of 60° with the +ve direction of x-axis.

Sol. Let the equation of line be

$y = mx + c = \sqrt{3}x + c \ (\because m = \tan(60^?) = \sqrt{3})$ ...(i)

The line (i), will be a tangent to the circle

$x^2 + y^2 + 4x + 3 = 0$, if the length of perpendicular from the centre (-2, 0) to the line (i) is equal to the radius (= 1) of a circle.

Therefore, $\left|\frac{-2\sqrt{3}-0+c}{\sqrt{3+1}}\right| = 1$

$\Rightarrow \quad c - 2\sqrt{3} = \pm 2 \quad \Rightarrow \quad c = 2\sqrt{3} \pm 2$.

Hence, the equation of tangents becomes

$y = \sqrt{3}x + (2\sqrt{3} \pm 2)$

Ex-5. If a tangent is equally inclined with the co-ordinate axes to the circle $x^2 + y^2 = 4$, then find its equation.

Sol. A line is equally inclined to the co-ordinate axes is

y = ± x + c ...(i)

The line (i) will be tangent to the circle $x^2 + y^2 = 4$, if the length of perpendicular from the centre (0, 0) to the circle is equal to the radius (=2) of the given circle.

Therefore, $\left|\frac{0+0+c}{\sqrt{1^2+1^1}}\right| = 2 \quad \Rightarrow c = \pm 4$

Hence, the equation of tangents becomes $y = \pm x \pm 4$.

Ex-6. Find the equation of the tangents to the circle $x^2 + y^2 = 25$ through (7, 1).

Sol. Equation of any line passing through (7, 1) is

y - 1 = m (x - 7) ...(i)

The line (i) will be a tangent to the circle $x^2 + y^2 = 25$, if the length of perpendicular from the centre of the given circle is equal to the radius of the same circle.

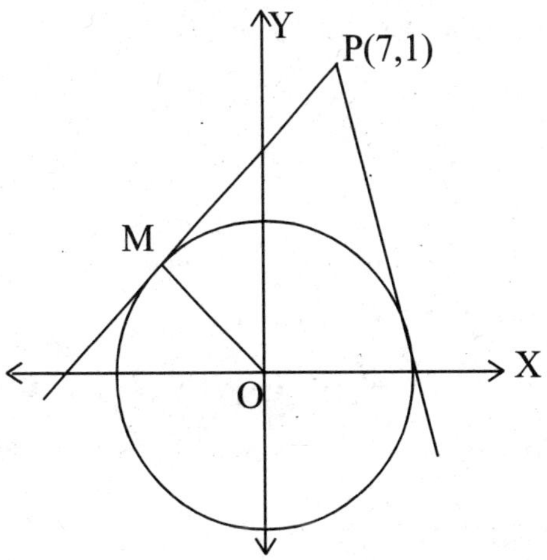

Therefore, $\left|\frac{0-0-(7m-1)}{\sqrt{m^2+1}}\right| = 5$

$\Rightarrow \quad (7m-1)^2 = 25\left(m^2+1\right)$

$\Rightarrow \quad 12m^2 - 7m - 12 = 0$

$\Rightarrow \quad 12m^2 - 16m + 9m - 12 = 0$

$\Rightarrow \quad (3m-4)(4m+3) = 0$

$\Rightarrow \quad m = \frac{4}{3}, -\frac{3}{4}$

Hence, the equation of tangents are

$$y-1 = \frac{4}{3}(x-7) \ \& \ y-1 = -\frac{3}{4}(x-7)$$

$\Rightarrow \quad 4x - 3y = 25 \ \& \ 3x + 4y = 25$

Ex-7. If the centre of a circle $x^2 + y^2 = 9$ is translated 2 units parallel to the line $x + y = 4$ where x increases, then find its equation

Sol. The centre of a circle is (0, 0) and raidus is 3 .
Here OC = 2 .

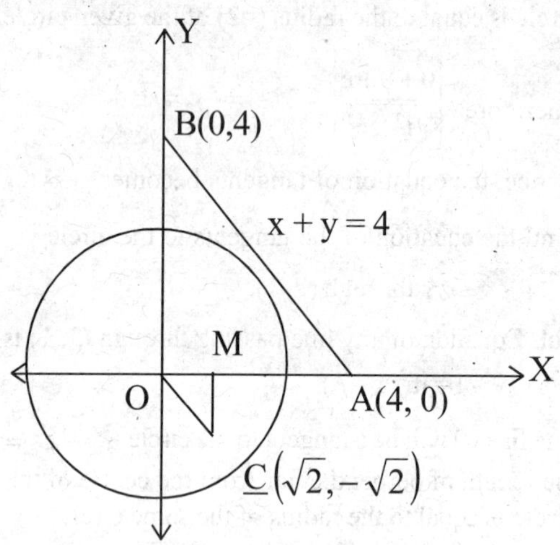

We shall find the co-ordinates of C.

Let C be (x, y) . Then $x = 2\cos\left(-45^?\right) = \sqrt{2}$

and $\quad y = 2\sin\left(-45^?\right) = -\sqrt{2}$.

Thus, the co-ordinates of C becomes $\left(\sqrt{2}, -\sqrt{2}\right)$.

Hence, the equation of a circle is

$$\left(x-\sqrt{2}\right)^2 + \left(y+\sqrt{2}\right)^2 = 3^2$$

$\Rightarrow \quad x^2 + y^2 - 2\sqrt{2}\,x - 2\sqrt{2}\,y - 5 = 0$.

3.19 TANGENT

If a line intersect the curve in two coincident points , then it is called a tangent and if a line intersects the curve in two distinct points, then it is called a secant.

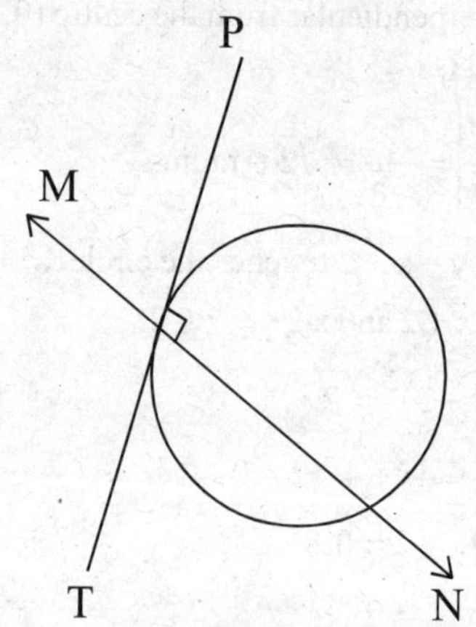

Here, PT is a tangent and MN be a secant.

3.20 DIFFERENT FORMS OF THE EQUATIONS OF TANGENTS

1. Point form :

(i) The equation of tangent to the circle $x^2 + y^2 = a^2$ at (x_1, y_1) is $xx_1 + yy_1 = a^2$.

Proof: Let C be the centre of the circle .

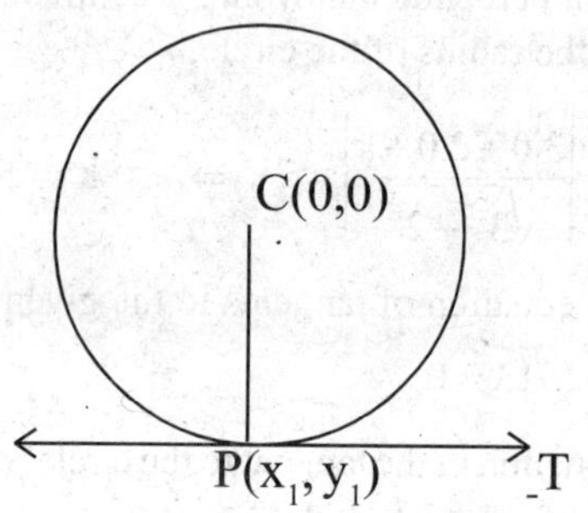

Now slope of CP = $\frac{y_1 - 0}{x_1 - 0} = \frac{y_1}{x_1}$.

Here , PT is perpendicular to CP.

Thus, slope of PT = $-\frac{x_1}{y_1}$.

Hence, the equation of tangent is

$$y - y_1 = -\frac{x_1}{y_1}(x - x_1)$$

$\Rightarrow \quad yy_1 - y_1^2 = -xx_1 + x_1^2$

$\Rightarrow \quad xx_1 + yy_1 = x_1^2 + y_1^2 = a^2$.

(ii) The equation of tangent to the circle $x^2 + y^2 + 2gx + 2fy + c = 0$ at (x_1, y_1) is $x^2 + y^2 + xx_1 + yy_1 + c = 0$.

Proof: Let C (-g, -f) be the centre of the circle.

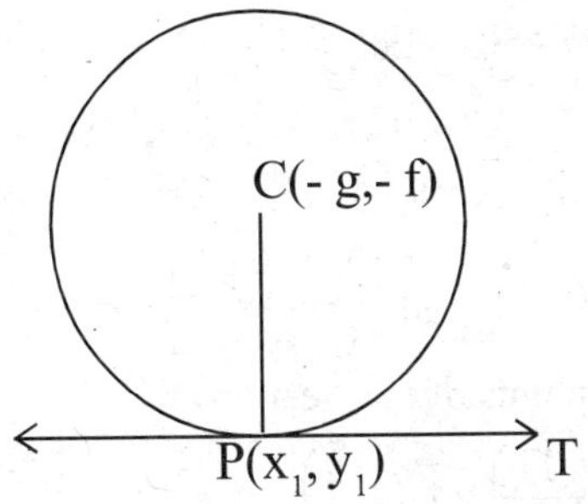

Now, slope of CP = $\dfrac{y_1+f}{x_1+g}$.

Here, PT is perpendicular to CP.

Thus, slope of PT = $-\dfrac{x_1+g}{y_1+f}$

Hence, the equation of the tangent at (x_1, y_1) is

$$y-y_1=-\frac{x_1+g}{y_1+f}(x-x_1)$$

$$\Rightarrow\ x^2+y^2+xx_1+yy_1+c=0.$$

Note : The equation of tangent to the 2nd degree curve

$$ax^2+2hxy+by^2+2gx+2fy+c=0$$

is $axx_1+h(xy_1+x_1y)+byy_1$

$$+g(x+x_1)+f(y+y_1)+c=0$$

In order to find out the equation of tangent to any 2nd degree curve, the following point must kept in your mind. x^2 is replaced by xx_1, y^2 is replaced by yy_1, xy is replaced by $\dfrac{xy_1+x_1y}{2}$, x is replaced by $\dfrac{x+x_1}{2}$, y is replaced by $\dfrac{y+y_1}{2}$, c will remain c.

This method is applicable only for a 2nd degree conic.

2. Parametric form

(i) The equation of tangent to the circle $x^2+y^2=a^2$ at $(a\cos\theta,\ a\sin\theta)$ is $x\cos\theta+y\sin\theta=a$

(ii) The equation of the tangent to the circle $(x-h)^2+(y-k)^2=a^2$ at $(h+a\cos\theta,\ k+a\sin\theta)$ is $(x-h)\cos\theta+(y-k)\sin\theta=a$

3. Condition of tangency

The line y = m x + c will be a tangent to the circle $x^2+y^2=a^2$ if $c^2=a^2\left(1+m^2\right)$.

Proof: The line y = m x + c will be a tangent to the circle $x^2+y^2=a^2$ if radius = the length of perpendicular from the centre of a circle to the line y = m x + c.

$$\Rightarrow\ a=\frac{|c|}{\sqrt{\left(1+m^2\right)}}.$$

$$\Rightarrow\ a^2=\frac{c^2}{\left(1+m^2\right)}$$

$\Rightarrow\ c^2=a^2\left(1+m^2\right)$. which is the required condition.

4. Slope form

The equation of tangent with slope m to a circle $x^2+y^2=a^2$ is $y \quad mx \quad a\sqrt{1+m^2}$ and the co-ordinates of the point of contact are

$$\left(\pm\frac{am}{\sqrt{\left(1+m^2\right)}},\ \mp\frac{a}{\sqrt{\left(1+m^2\right)}}\right)$$

5. Equation of any tangent to the circle can be considered as $y=mx+a\sqrt{1+m^2}$

6. Number of tangents

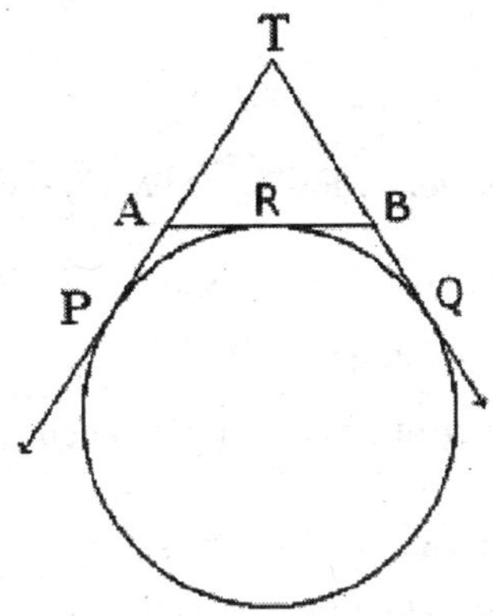

(i) If a point lies outside of a circle , then two tangents can be drawn.

Here, TP and TQ are two tangents .

(ii) If a point lies on the circle , then one tangent can be drawn.

Here, ARB be a tangent

(iii) If a point lies insdie the circle , then no tangent can be drawn.

3.21 Tangents from a point to a circle

Let the point be (x_1, y_1) and the circle be $x^2+y^2=a^2$

Equation of any tangent from a point (x_1, y_1) to a circle

$x^2+y^2=a^2$ is $(y-y_1)=m(x-x_1)$ ...(i)

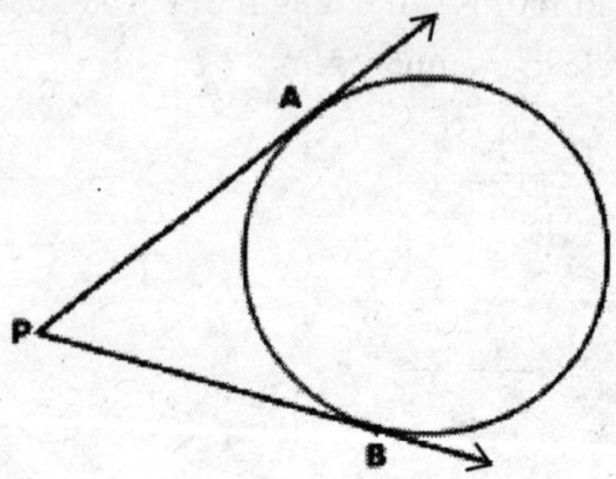

The line (i) will be tangent to the given circle if the length of perpendicular from the centre of a circle = radius of a circle

$$\left|\frac{(mx_1-y_1)}{\sqrt{1+m^2}}\right|=a$$

$\Rightarrow (mx_1-y_1)^2=a^2(1+m^2)$

$\Rightarrow m^2x_1^2-2mx_1y_1+y_1^2=a^2+a^2m^2$

$\Rightarrow m^2(x_1^2-a^2)-2mx_1y_1+(y_1^2-a^2)=0$

which is a quadratic in m, gives two values of m.
Put those values of m in (i), we get the required equations of tangents.

Ex-1. Find the equation of the tangents to the circle $x^2+y^2=9$ at $x=2$

Sol. When $x=2$, then $y=\pm\sqrt{5}$.

Therefore, the points are $(2,\sqrt{5})$ & $(2,-\sqrt{5})$.

Thus, the equation of tangents at $(2,\sqrt{5})$ & $(2,-\sqrt{5})$ are $2x+\sqrt{5}y=9$ & $2x-\sqrt{5}y=9$.

Ex-2. Find the equation of the tangent to the circle $x^2+y^2=16$ at $y=4$

Sol. When $y=4$, then $x=0$.
Therefore, the point is (0, 4).
Hence, the equation of the tangent to the given circle at (0, 4) is $x.0+y.4=16$
$\Rightarrow y=4$.

Ex-3. Find the points of intersection of the line $4x-3y=10$ and the circle $x^2+y^2-2x+4y-20=0$

Sol. The given equations are $4x-3y=10$ ...(i)
and $x^2+y^2-2x+4y-20=0$ ...(ii)
On solving (i) and (ii), we get,

$$x^2+\left(\frac{4x-3}{10}\right)^2-2x+4\left(\frac{4x-3}{10}\right)-20=0$$

$\Rightarrow 9x^2+(4x-10)^2-18x+48x-120-180=0$

$\Rightarrow 25x^2-50x-200=0$

$\Rightarrow x^2-2x-8=0$

$\Rightarrow (x-4)(x+2)=0$

$\Rightarrow x=-2,4$ and $y=-\frac{11}{10},\frac{13}{10}$.

Hence, the points of intersection are

$$\left(-2,-\frac{11}{10}\right)\&\left(4,\frac{13}{10}\right).$$

Ex-4. Find the equations of the pair of tangents drawn to the circle $x^2+y^2-2x+4y=0$ from (0, 1).

Sol. The given circle is $x^2+y^2-2x+4y=0$

$\Rightarrow (x-1)^2+(y+2)^2=5$ ...(i)

Equation of any line passing thorugh (0, 1) is

$y-1=m(x-0)$ ...(ii)

The line (ii) will be a tangent to the circle (i), then the length of perpendicular from the centre (1,- 2) to the line (ii) is equal to the radius of a circle (i).

Therefore, $\left|\frac{m+2+1}{\sqrt{m^2+1}}\right|=\sqrt{5}$

$\Rightarrow (m+3)^2=5(m^2+1)$

$\Rightarrow m^2+6m+9-5m^2-5=0$

$\Rightarrow 2m^2-3m-2=0$

$\Rightarrow (m-2)(2m+1)=0$

$\Rightarrow m=-\frac{1}{2},2$.

Hence, the equations of tangents are

$y-1=-\frac{1}{2}x$ & $y-1=2x$

$\Rightarrow x+2y-1=0$ & $2x-y+1=0$.

Ex-5. Find the equation of the common tangent to the curves $x^2+y^2=4$ and $y^2=4(x-2)$.

Sol. The given curves are $x^2+y^2=4$

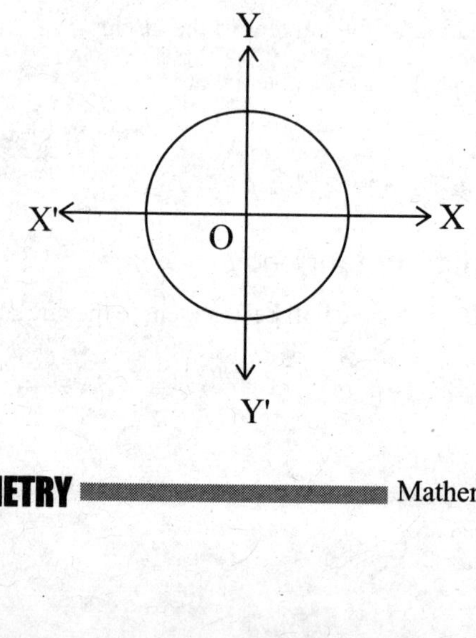

and $y^2 = 4(x-2)$.

From the graph, it is clear that, the equation of the common tangent is $x = 2$.

Ex-6. Find the shortest distance between the circle $x^2 + y^2 = 9$ and the line $y = x - 8$.

Sol. Let AB : $y = x - 4$ and CD be a tangent parallel to AB.

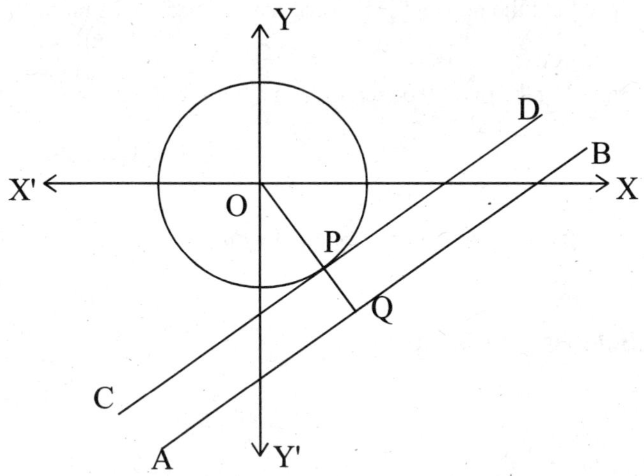

Now $OQ = \left|\dfrac{0-0-8}{\sqrt{1^2+1^2}}\right| = \dfrac{8}{\sqrt{2}} = 4\sqrt{2}$

and OP = radius of a circle = 3.

Thus, the shortest distance = PQ = OQ - OP

$= \left(4\sqrt{2}-3\right)$.

3.22 Length of tangent from a point to a circle :

(i) The length of tangent from a point (x_1, y_1) to the circle $x^2 + y^2 = a^2$ is $\sqrt{x_1^2 + y_1^2 - a^2}$.

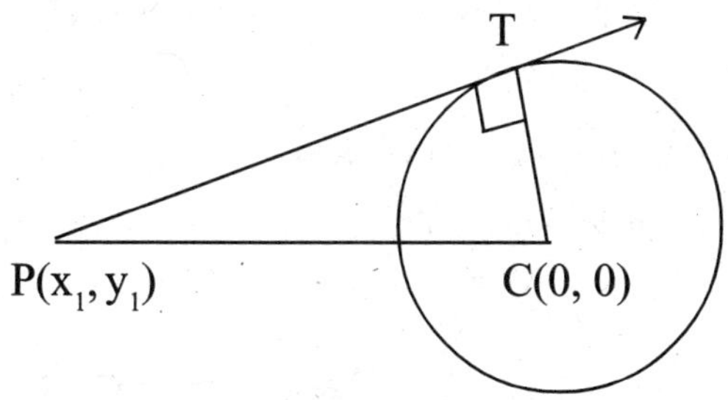

Proof: Let P be (x_1, y_1) and PT be tangent.

In Δ PCT, $CP^2 = PT^2 + CT^2$

$\Rightarrow \quad PT^2 = CP^2 - CT^2$

$\Rightarrow \quad PT^2 = x_1^2 + y_1^2 - a^2$

$\Rightarrow \quad PT = \sqrt{x_1^2 + y_1^2 - a^2}$.

(ii) The length of tangent from a point (x_1, y_1) to the circle $x^2 + y^2 + 2gx + 2fy + c = 0$ is

$$\sqrt{x_1^2 + y_1^2 + 2gx_1 + 2fy_1 + c}$$

Proof: Let P be (x1, y1) and PT be a tangent.

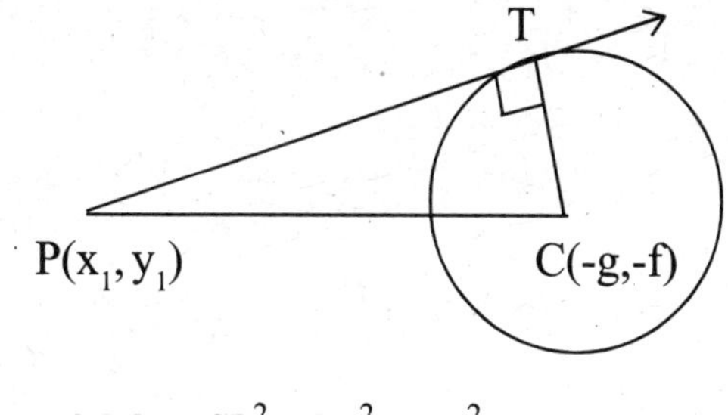

In ? PCT, $CP^2 = PT^2 + CT^2$

$\Rightarrow \quad PT^2 = CP^2 - CT^2$

$\Rightarrow \quad PT^2 = (x_1+g)^2 + (y_1+f)^2 - \left(g^2+f^2-c\right)$

$\Rightarrow \quad PT^2 = x_1^2 + y_1^2 + 2gx_1 + 2fy_1 + c$

$\Rightarrow \quad PT = \sqrt{x_1^2 + y_1^2 + 2gx_1 + 2fy_1 + c}$

Ex-1. Find the length of the tangents from the point (2, 3) to the circle $x^2 + y^2 = 4$.

Sol. Hence, the length of the tangent from the point (2, 3) to the circle $x^2 + y^2 = 4$ is

$= \sqrt{4+9-4} = \sqrt{9} = 3$

Ex-2. Find the length of the tangent from any point on the circle $x^2 + y^2 = a^2$ to the circle $x^2 + y^2 = b^2$

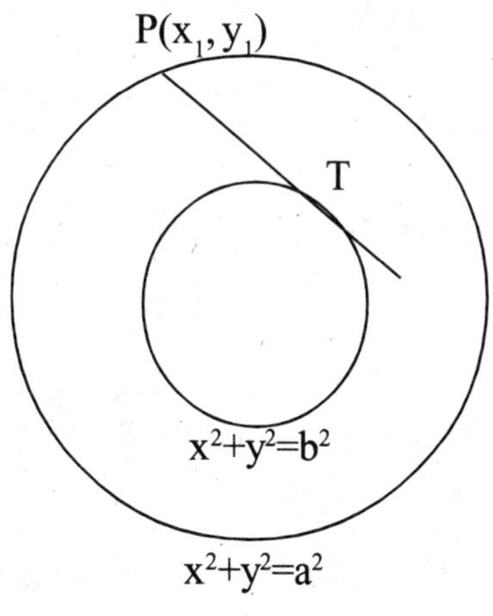

Sol. Let P (x_1, y_1) be any point on the circle $x^2 + y^2 - a^2$.

Therefore, $x_1^2 + y_1^2 = a^2$.

Now, the length of tangent from (x_1, y_1) to the circle $x^2 + y^2 = b^2$

is $\sqrt{x_1^2+y_1^2-b^2} = \sqrt{a^2-b^2}$.

Ex-3. Find the length of the tangent from any point on the circle $x^2+y^2+2011x+2012y+2013=0$ to the circle $x^2+y^2+2011x+2012y+2014=0$.

Sol. Let P be any point on

$x^2+y^2+2011x+2012y+2013=0$

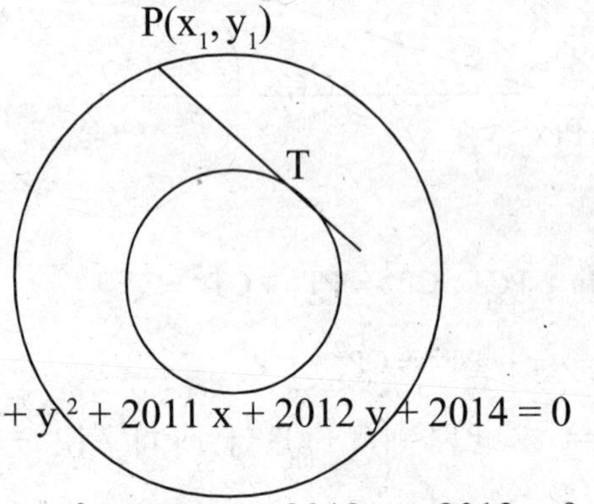

$$x^2+y^2+2011x+2012y+2013=0$$

Therefore,

$$x_1^2+y_1^2+2011x_1+2012y_1+2013=0$$

Now, the length of the tangent from (x_1, y_1) to the circle $x^2+y^2+2011x+2012y+2014=0$ is

$$= \sqrt{x_1^2+y_1^2+2011x_1+2012y_1+2014}$$

$$= \sqrt{-2013+2014}$$

$= 1$.

3.23 Power of a point with respect to a circle :

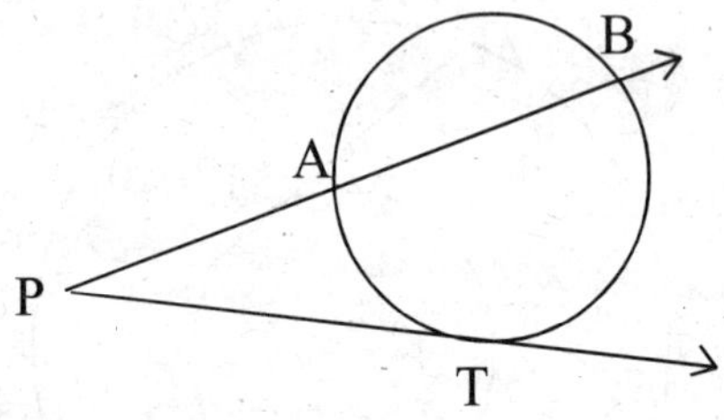

The power of a point P with respect to any circle is PA.PB. From the geometry, we can write , PA. PB = PT².
Thus, the power of a point is the square of the length of the tangent to a circle from that point.

(i) The power of a point (x_1, y_1) with respect to a circle $x^2+y^2=a^2$ is $\left(x_1^2+y_1^2-a^2\right)$.

(ii) The power of a point (x_1, y_1) with respect to a circle $x^2+y^2+2gx+2fy+c=0$ is $\left(x_1^2+y_1^2+2gx_1+2fy_1+c\right)$.

Ex-1. Find the power of a point (2, 5) with respect to the circle $x^2+y^2=16$

Sol. The power of a point (2, 5) with respect to a circle $x^2+y^2=16$ is $(4+25-16)=13$.

Ex-2. If a point P(1, 2) is rotated about the origin in an anti-clockwise sense through an angle of 90 say at Q, then find the power of a point Q with respect to the circle $x^2+y^2=4$.

Sol. Let the point P be represent a complex number Z .i.e. $Z=1+2i$
Then, from the rotation theorem , $Q=iZ=i(1+2i)$ $=i-2=-2+1.i=(-2, 1)$
Thus, the power of a point Q with respect to a circle is $(4+1-4)=1$.

3.24 Pair of tangents

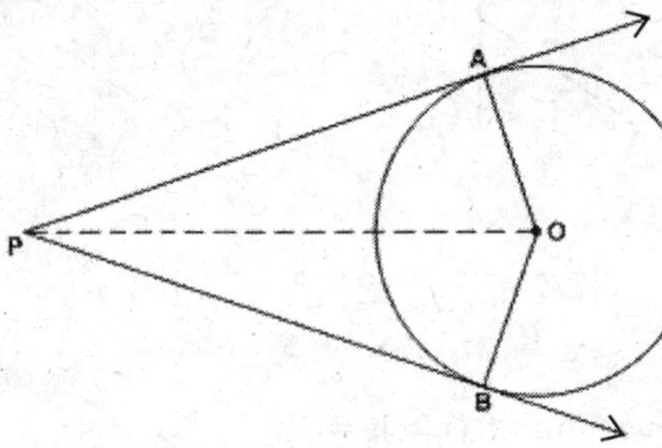

(i) The equation of a pair of tangents to a circle $x^2+y^2=a^2$ from a point (x_1, y_1) is $SS_1=T^2$,
where $S \equiv x^2+y^2-a^2$; $S_1 \equiv x_1^2+y_1^2-a^2$; $T \equiv xx_1+yy_1-a^2$.

(ii) The equation of a pair of tangents to a circle $x^2+y^2+2gx+2fy+c=0$ is
$SS_1=T^2$, where $S \equiv x^2+y^2+2gx+2fy+c$;
$S_1 \equiv x_1^2+y_1^2+2gx_1+2fy_1+c$
$T \equiv xx_1+yy_1+g(x+x_1)+f(y+y_1)+c$.

(iii) The angle between the pair of tangents from (x_1, y_1) to the circle $x^2+y^2=a^2$ is

$2\tan^{-1}\left(\frac{a}{\sqrt{S_1}}\right)$, where $S_1=x_1^2+y_1^2-a^2$.

Ex-1. Find the equation of the tangent from the point (1, 2) to the circle $x^2+y^2=4$

Sol. Hence, the equation of a pair of tangents to a circle $x^2+y^2=4$ from a point (1, 2) is S S1 = T2

$$\Rightarrow \left(x^2+y^2-4\right)(1+4-4)=(x+2y-4)^2$$

$$\Rightarrow \quad \left(x^2+y^2-4\right)=\left(x^2+4y^2+16+4xy-8x-16y\right)$$

$$\Rightarrow \quad 3y^2+4(x-4)y+4(5-2x)=0$$

$$\Rightarrow \quad y=\frac{-4(x-4)\pm\sqrt{16(x-4)^2-48(5-2x)}}{6}$$

$$\Rightarrow \quad y=\frac{-4(x-4)\pm 4\sqrt{x^2-8x+16-15+6x}}{6}$$

$$\Rightarrow \quad y=\frac{-4(x-4)\pm 4(x-1)}{6}$$

$$\Rightarrow \quad y=2,\ 4x-3y+2=0.$$

Ex-2. Find the equation of the tangent to the circle $x^2+y^2-4x+3=0$ from the point (2, 3).

Sol. Hence, the equation of the pair of tangents are $SS_1=T^2$

$$\Rightarrow \quad \left(x^2+y^2-4x+3\right)(4+9-8+3)$$

$$=\left(2x+3y-2(x+2)+3\right)^2$$

$$\Rightarrow \quad 8\left(x^2+y^2-4x+3\right)=(3y-1)^2$$

$$\Rightarrow \quad 8\left(x^2+y^2-4x+3\right)=9y^2-6y+1$$

$$\Rightarrow \quad y^2-8x^2+32x-6y-23=0$$

$$\Rightarrow \quad y^2-6y-\left(8x^2-32x+23\right)=0$$

$$\Rightarrow \quad y=\frac{6\pm\sqrt{36+4\left(8x^2-32x+23\right)}}{2}$$

$$\Rightarrow \quad y=\frac{6\pm\sqrt{32x^2-128x+128}}{2}$$

$$=\frac{6\pm\sqrt{32\left(x^2-4x+4\right)}}{2}=\frac{6\pm 4\sqrt{2}\,(x-2)}{2}$$

$$\Rightarrow \quad y=3\pm 2\sqrt{2}\,(x-2).$$

Ex-3. Find the angle between the tangent from the point (3, 5) to the circle $x^2+y^2=25$.

Sol. Hence, the angle between the tangent from the point (3, 5) to the circle $x^2+y^2=25$. is

$$=2\tan^{-1}\left(\frac{a}{\sqrt{S_1}}\right)=2\tan^{-1}\left(\frac{5}{\sqrt{9+25-25}}\right)=2\tan^{-1}\left(\frac{5}{3}\right)$$

Ex-4. If a point (1, 2) is translated 2 units through the positive direction of x-axis and then tangents drawn from that point to the circle $x^2+y^2=9$, then find the angle between the tangents.

Sol. After translation the point (1, 2) becomes $(1+2, 2)=(3, 2)$.

Hence, the angle between the tangent from the point (3, 2) to the circle $x^2+y^2=9$ is

$$=2\tan^{-1}\left(\frac{a}{\sqrt{S_1}}\right)=2\tan^{-1}\left(\frac{3}{\sqrt{9+4-9}}\right)=2\tan^{-1}\left(\frac{3}{2}\right).$$

3.25 Director circle :

The locus of the point of intersection of two perpendicular tangents to a circle is known as the director circle. Director circle of a circle is the concentric circle having radius $\sqrt{2}$ times the radius of the original circle

The equation of the director circle to the circle $x^2+y^2=a^2$ is $x^2+y^2=2a^2$.

Proof: Equation of any line passing through P(h, k)

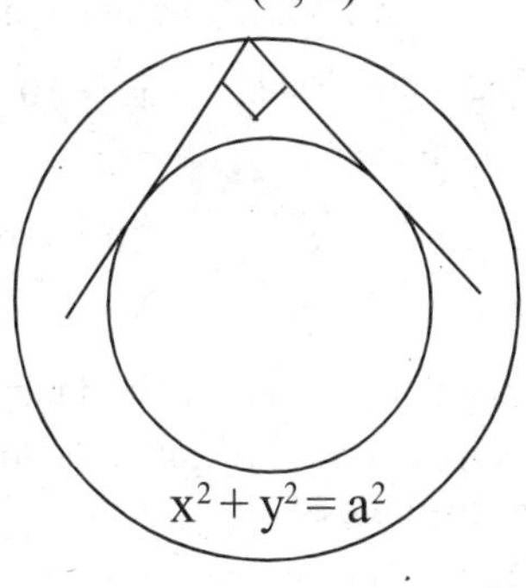

is $y-k=m(x-h)$.

$$\Rightarrow \quad mx-y=k-mh \text{ ....(i)}$$

The line (i) will be tangent to the circle $x^2+y^2=a^2$,

then $\left|\dfrac{0-0-(k-mh)}{\sqrt{m^2+1}}\right|=a$

$$\Rightarrow \quad (k-mh)^2=a^2\left(m^2+1\right)$$

$$\Rightarrow \quad \left(h^2-a^2\right)m^2-2kmh+\left(k^2-a^2\right)=0$$

Which is a quadratic equation of m.

Let its roots are m_1, m_2.

Thus, $m_1.m_2=\dfrac{\left(k^2-a^2\right)}{\left(h^2-a^2\right)} \quad \Rightarrow \quad \dfrac{\left(k^2-a^2\right)}{\left(h^2-a^2\right)}=-1$

$$\Rightarrow \quad \left(k^2-a^2\right)=-\left(h^2-a^2\right)$$

$$\Rightarrow \quad h^2+k^2=2a^2$$

Hence, the locus of P (h, k) is $x^2+y^2=2a^2$.

Ex-1. Find the locus of the point of intersection of two perpendicular tangents to a circle $x^2 + y^2 = 25$.

Sol. The locus of the point of intersection of two perpendicular tangents to a circle is the Director circle of the given circle.

Thus, the equation of the director circle to the circle $x^2 + y^2 = 25$ is $x^2 + y^2 = 2.25 = 50$

Ex-2. Tangents are drawn from an arbitrary point on the line $y = x + 1$ to the circle $x^2 + y^2 = 9$. If those tangents are orthogonal to each other, then find the locus of that point.

Sol. Clearly, the locus of the arbitrary point is the director circle of the given circle $x^2 + y^2 = 9$.

Hence, the equation of the director circle to the circle $x^2 + y^2 = 9$ is $x^2 + y^2 = 2.9 = 18$.

Ex-3. Tangents are drawn from any point on the circle $x^2 + y^2 = 20$ to the circle $x^2 + y^2 = 10$. Find the angle between their tangents.

Sol. Clearly, the equation $x^2 + y^2 = 20$ is the director circle of the circle $x^2 + y^2 = 10$.

Hence, the angle between the pair of tangents is = 90°.

Ex-4. Find the equation of the director circle to rach of the following given circles.

(i) $x^2 + y^2 + 2x = 0$

(ii) $x^2 + y^2 + 10y + 24 = 0$

(iii) $x^2 + y^2 + 16x + 12y + 99 = 0$

(iv) $x^2 + y^2 + 2gx + 2fy + c = 0$.

(v) $x^2 + y^2 - ax - by = 0$.

Sol. (i) The given circle $x^2 + y^2 + 2x = 0$ can be reduces to $(x+1)^2 + y^2 = 1$.

Hence, the equation of the director circle to the circle $(x+1)^2 + y^2 = 1$ is $(x+1)^2 + y^2 = 2.1 = 2$

$\Rightarrow \quad x^2 + y^2 + 2x - 1 = 0$

(ii) The given circle $x^2 + y^2 + 10y + 24 = 0$ can be reduces to $x^2 + (y+5)^2 = 1$

Hence, the equation of the director circle to the circle $x^2 + (y+5)^2 = 1$ is $x^2 + (y+5)^2 = 2.1 = 2$

$\Rightarrow \quad x^2 + y^2 + 10y + 23 = 0$.

(iii) The given circle $x^2 + y^2 + 16x + 12y + 99 = 0$ can be reduces to $(x+8)^2 + (y+6)^2 = 64 + 36 - 99 = 1$

Hence, the equation of the director circle to the circle $(x+8)^2 + (y+6)^2 = 1$ is $(x+8)^2 + (y+6)^2 = 2.1 = 2$

$\Rightarrow \quad x^2 + y^2 + 16x + 12y + 98 = 0$

(iv) The given eircle $x^2 + y^2 + 2gx + 2fy + c = 0$. can be reduces to $(x+g)^2 + (y+f)^2 = \left(\sqrt{g^2 + f^2 - c}\right)^2$

Hence, the equation of the director circle to the circle $(x+g)^2 + (y+f)^2 = \left(\sqrt{g^2 + f^2 - c}\right)^2$ is $(x+g)^2 + (y+f)^2 = 2.\left(\sqrt{g^2 + f^2 - c}\right)^2 = 2\left(g^2 + f^2 - c\right)$

$\Rightarrow \quad x^2 + y^2 + 2gx + 2fy - g^2 - f^2 + 2c = 0$.

(v) The given circle $x^2 + y^2 - ax - by = 0$ can be reduces to $\left(x - \frac{a}{2}\right)^2 + \left(y - \frac{b}{2}\right)^2 = \left(\frac{\sqrt{a^2 + b^2}}{2}\right)^2$

Hence, the equation of the director circle to the circle $\left(x - \frac{a}{2}\right)^2 + \left(y - \frac{b}{2}\right)^2 = \left(\frac{\sqrt{a^2 + b^2}}{2}\right)^2$ is $\left(x - \frac{a}{2}\right)^2 + \left(y - \frac{b}{2}\right)^2 = 2.\left(\frac{\sqrt{a^2 + b^2}}{2}\right)^2 = \left(\frac{a^2 + b^2}{2}\right)$

$\Rightarrow \quad x^2 + y^2 - ax - by - \frac{1}{4}\left(a^2 + b^2\right) = 0$.

3.26 NORMAL

If a line is perpendicular to the point of contact to the tangent is called a normal .

The relation between tangent and normal is $m(T) \times m(N) = -1$.

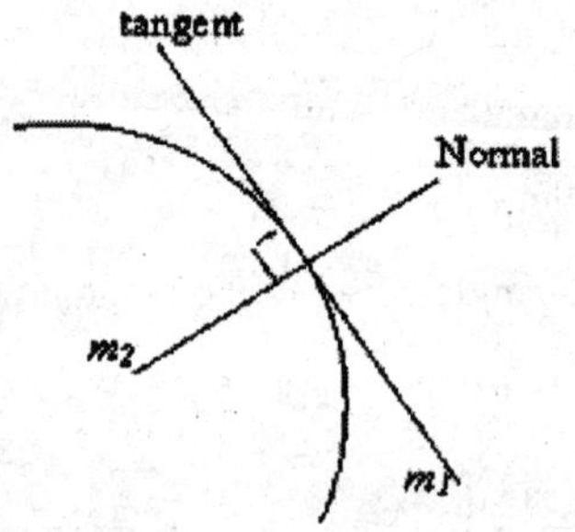

3.27 Different forms of the equation of normals

1. **Point form :**

(i) The equation of a normat to the circle $x^2 + y^2 = a^2$ at (x_1, y_1) is $\frac{x}{x_1} = \frac{y}{y_1}$.

Proof: Let PT be a tangent and PN be a normal.

PN be a perpendicular to PT.

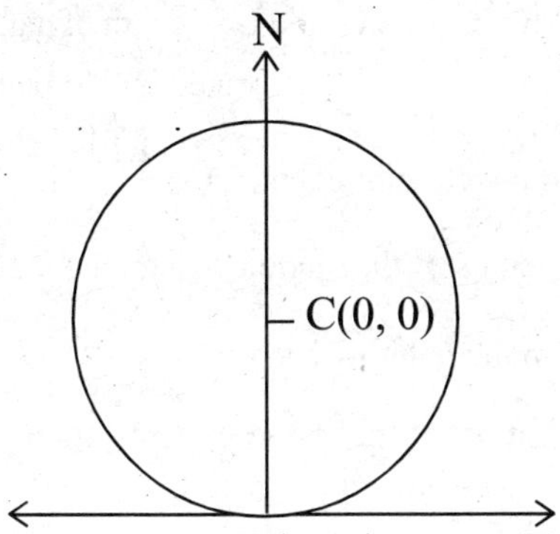

Equation of tangent at P is $x x_1 + y y_1 = a^2$ ...(i)

Equation of normal at P is $x y_1 - y x_1 + k = 0$ ...(ii)

Which is passing through (0, 0)

Therefore, $k = 0$.

Hence, the equation of normal is $x y_1 - y x_1 = 0$

$$\Rightarrow \quad \frac{x}{x_1} = \frac{y}{y_1}.$$

(ii) The equation of a normal to the circle $x^2 + y^2 + 2gx + 2fy + c = 0$ at (x_1, y_1) is

$$\frac{x - x_1}{x_1 + g} = \frac{y - y_1}{y_1 + f}$$

Proof: As we know that, normal always pass through the centre of a circle.

Thus, the equation of normal at P to the circle

$x^2 + y^2 + 2gx + 2fy + c = 0$ is $y - y_1 = \dfrac{y_1 + f}{x_1 + g}(x - x_1)$

$$\Rightarrow \quad \frac{x - x_1}{x_1 + g} = \frac{y - y_1}{y_1 + f}$$

(iii) The equation of a normal to a conic $ax^2 + 2hxy + by^2 + 2gx + 2fy + c = 0$ at (x_1, y_1) is

$$\frac{x - x_1}{a x_1 + h y_1 + g} = \frac{y - y_1}{h x_1 + b y_1 + f}$$

2. Parametric form :

The equation of normal to the circle $x^2 + y^2 = a^2$ at $(a\cos\theta, a\sin\theta)$ is $\dfrac{x}{\cos\theta} = \dfrac{y}{\sin\theta}$.

3. Slope form :

The equation of a normal to the circle $x^2 + y^2 = a^2$ is $y = mx$.

4. Normal always passes through the centre of a circle.

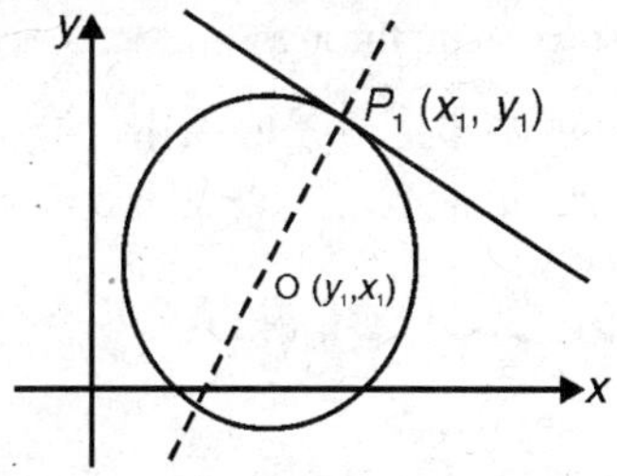

5. The line $y = mx + c$ will be a normal to the circle $x^2 + y^2 = a^2$ if $c = 0$.

Ex-1. Find the equation of normal to the circle $x^2 + y^2 = 9$ at $x = 2$

Sol. when $x = 2$, then $y = \pm\sqrt{5}$.

So, the points are $(2, \sqrt{5})$ & $(2, -\sqrt{5})$.

The equation of normal to the circle at

$(2, \sqrt{5})$ & $(2, -\sqrt{5})$ are $\dfrac{x}{2} = \dfrac{y}{\sqrt{5}}$ & $\dfrac{x}{2} = -\dfrac{y}{\sqrt{5}}$

$$\Rightarrow \quad y = \frac{\sqrt{5}}{2}x \;\&\; y = -\frac{\sqrt{5}}{2}x$$

Ex-2. Find the equation of normal to the circle $x^2 + y^2 + 2x + 4y + 4 = 0$ at (-2, 1)

Sol. Equation of normal to the given circle at (-2, 1) is

$$\frac{x - x_1}{x_1 + g} = \frac{y - y_1}{y_1 + f}$$

$$\Rightarrow \quad \frac{x + 2}{-2 + 1} = \frac{y - 1}{1 + 2}$$

$$\Rightarrow \quad 3x + 6 = -y + 1$$

$$\Rightarrow \quad 3x + y + 5 = 0$$

Ex-3. Find the equation of a normal to a circle $x^2 + y^2 - 4x - 6y + 4 = 0$, which is parallel to the line $y = x - 3$

Sol. The centre of a circle $x^2 + y^2 - 4x - 6y + 4 = 0$ is (2, 3).

Equation of a normal, parallel to $x - y - 3 = 0$ is $x - y + k = 0$ ...(i)

As we know that, normal always pass through the centre of a circle.

Therefore, $2 - 3 + k = 0 \Rightarrow k = 1$.

Hence, the equation of the normal is $x - y + 1 = 0$.

Ex-4. Find the equation of normal to a circle $x^2 + y^2 - 8x - 12y + 99 = 0$, which is perpendicular to the line $2x - 3y + 10 = 0$.

Sol. The centre of a circle $x^2 + y^2 - 8x - 12y + 99 = 0$ is (4, 6)

Equation of normal, which is perpendicular to

$2x - 3y + 10 = 0$ is $3x + 2y - k = 0$ ...(i)

Which is passing through (4, 6) .

Therefore, $12 + 12 - k = 0 \Rightarrow k = 24$.

Hence, the equation of normal is $3x + 2y = 24$.

3.28 CHORD OF CONTACT

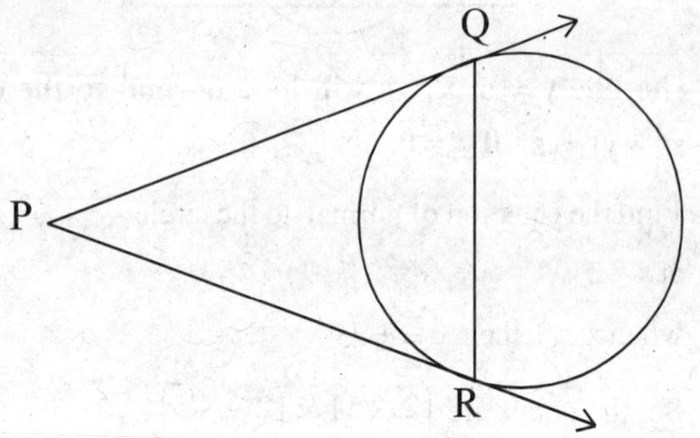

From any external point , two tangents can be drawn to a given circle . The chord joining the points of contact of the two tangents is called the chord of contact of tangents Here, QR is the chord of contact of tangents.

(i) The equation of the chord of contact of tangents drawn from a point (x_1, y_1) to the circle

$$x^2 + y^2 = a^2 \text{ is } xx_1 + yy_1 = a^2.$$

Proof: Tangent at Q is $xx_2 + yy_2 = a^2$ ...(i)

Tangent at R is $xx_3 + yy_3 = a^2$ ...(ii)

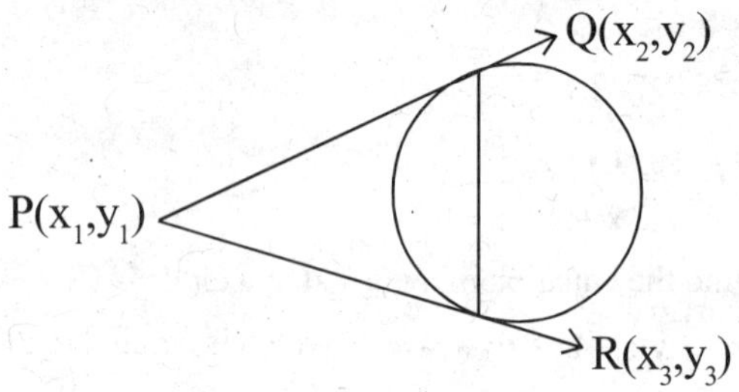

Equations (i) and (ii) , both are pass through the point (x_1, y_1).

Therefore, $x_1x_2 + y_1y_2 = a^2$ ...(iii)

and $x_1x_3 + y_1y_3 = a^2$ ...(iv)

From (iii) and (iv), it is clear that, $xx_1 + yy_1 = a^2$ passes through Q and R.

Hence, the chord of contact of tangents is $xx_1 + yy_1 = a^2$.

(ii) The equation of the chord of contact of tangents drawn from a point (x_1, y_1) to the circle

$$x^2 + y^2 + 2gx + 2fy + c = 0 \text{ is}$$

$$xx_1 + yy_1 + g(x + x_1) + f(y + y_1) + c = 0.$$

(iii) Chord of contact exists only when if the point P not lies inside of the circle.

(iv) Length of the chord of contact $T_1T_2 = \dfrac{2LR}{\sqrt{R^2 + L^2}}$, where R = radius and L = length of tangent.

(v) Area of the traingle formed by the pair of tangents and its chord of contact $= \dfrac{RL^2}{R^2 + L^2}$.

(vi) Tangents of the angle between the pair of tangents from the point $(x_1, y_1) = \dfrac{2RL}{L^2 - R^2}$.

(vii) Equation of the circle circumscribing the triangle $\Delta\, PT_1T_2$ is

$$(x - x_1)(x + g) + (y - y_1)(y + f) = 0.$$

(viii) The distance between the chord of contact of tangents to $x^2 + y^2 + 2gx + 2fy + c = 0$ from the origin and the point (g, f) is $\left|\dfrac{g^2 + f^2 - c}{2\sqrt{(g^2 + f^2)}}\right|$

Ex-1. Find the equation of the chord of contact of the tagents drawn from (5, 3) to the circle $x^2 + y^2 = 25$

Sol. Equation of the chord of contact of tangents from (5, 3) to the circle $x^2 + y^2 = 25$ is $5x + 3y = 25$.

Ex-2. Find the co-ordinates of the point of intersection of the tangents at the points where the line $2x + y + 12 = 0$ meets the circle

$$x^2 + y^2 - 4x + 3y - 1 = 0.$$

Sol. Let the point be (x_1, y_1).

Clearly, $2x + y + 12 = 0$................(i) is the chord of contact of the tangents to the circle $x^2 + y^2 - 4x + 3y - 1 = 0$ from (x_1, y_1).

Equation of the chord of contact of tangents to the circle $x^2 + y^2 - 4x + 3y - 1 = 0$ from the point (x_1, y_1) is

$$xx_1 + yy_1 - 2(x + x_1) + \frac{3}{2}(y + y_1) - 1 = 0 \quad \text{...(ii)}$$

Clearly (i) and (ii) are identical .

$$\text{Therefore, } \frac{x_1 - 2}{2} = \frac{y_1 + \frac{3}{2}}{1} = \frac{\frac{3}{2}y_1 - 2x_1 - 1}{12}$$

$\Rightarrow \quad x_1 - 2y_1 = 5 \;\&\; 4x_1 + 21y_1 = -38$

$\Rightarrow \quad x_1 = 1,\; y_1 = -2$

Hence, the point is (1, -2).

Ex-3. Find the condition that the chord of contact from an external point (h, k) to the circle $x^2 + y^2 = a^2$ subtends a right angle at the centre.

Sol. The equation of the chord of contact QR is

$$hx + ky = a^2 \qquad ...(i)$$

The chord of contact subtends a right angle at the centre. of the circle $x^2 + y^2 = a^2$

Therefore, $\dfrac{x^2 + y^2}{a^2} = \left(\dfrac{hx + ky}{a^2}\right)^2$

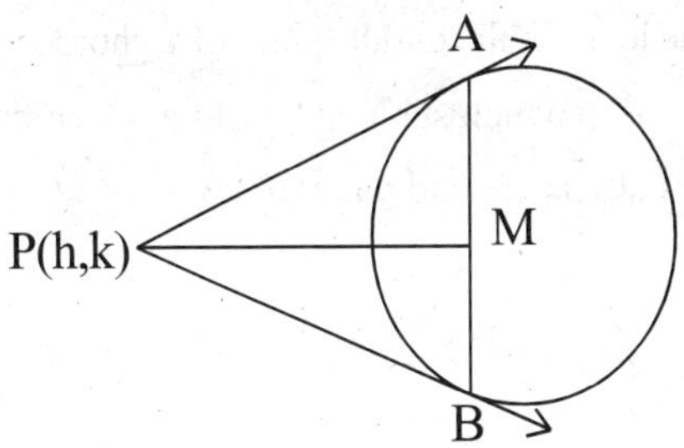

$\Rightarrow \quad a^2\left(x^2 + y^2\right) = (hx + ky)^2$

$\Rightarrow \quad x^2\left(a^2 - h^2\right) + y^2\left(a^2 - k^2\right) - 2hkxy = 0$

Since, the line (i) makes a right angle at the senctre, so

$\left(a^2 - h^2\right) + \left(a^2 - k^2\right) = 0 \quad \Rightarrow \quad h^2 + k^2 = 2a^2.$

Which is the required condition.

Ex-4. Tangents are drawn from the point (h, k) to the circle $x^2 + y^2 = a^2$. Prove that the area of the triangle formed by the tangents and their chord of contact is

$$a\left(\frac{\left(h^2 + k^2 - a^2\right)^{3/2}}{\left(h^2 + k^2\right)}\right).$$

Sol. Let AB be the chord of contact.

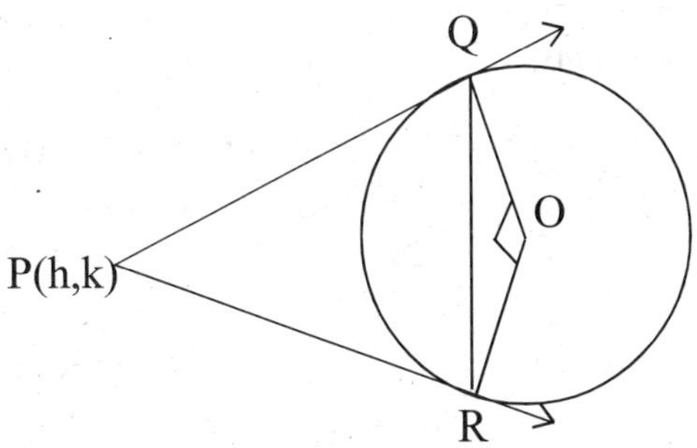

Then AB : $hx + ky = a2$.

Now, PM $= \left|\dfrac{h^2 + k^2 - a^2}{\sqrt{h^2 + k^2}}\right|$.

The length of the chord of contact = AB = $\dfrac{2LR}{\sqrt{L^2 + R^2}}$,

Where L = the length of the tangent and R be the radius of the circle.

Therefore,

$$AB = \frac{2a \times \sqrt{h^2 + k^2 - a^2}}{\sqrt{\left(h^2 + k^2 - a^2\right) + a^2}} = \frac{2a \times \sqrt{h^2 + k^2 - a^2}}{\sqrt{h^2 + k^2}}.$$

Thus, the area of the triangle PAB

$$= \frac{1}{2} \times \left(\frac{2a \times \sqrt{h^2 + k^2 - a^2}}{\sqrt{h^2 + k^2}}\right) \times \left(\frac{h^2 + k^2 - a^2}{\sqrt{h^2 + k^2}}\right)$$

$$= a\left(\frac{\left(h^2 + k^2 - a^2\right)^{3/2}}{\left(h^2 + k^2\right)}\right)$$

Ex-5. The chord of contact of tangents drawn from a point on the circle $x^2 + y^2 = a^2$ to the circle $x^2 + y^2 = b^2$ touches the circle $x^2 + y^2 = c^2$ such that $b^m = a^n c^p$, where $m, n, p \in N$, then find the value of $m + n + p + 10$.

Sol. Let $P(a\cos ?, a\sin ?)$ be any point on the circle $x^2 + y^2 = a^2$.

Therefore QR : $ax\cos\theta + ay\sin\theta = b^2 \qquad ...(i)$

Since (i) be a tangent to the circle $x^2 + y^2 = c^2$, so

$$\left|\frac{0 + 0 - b^2}{\sqrt{a^2\cos^2\theta + a^2\sin^2\theta}}\right| = c$$

$\Rightarrow \quad b^2 = ac$

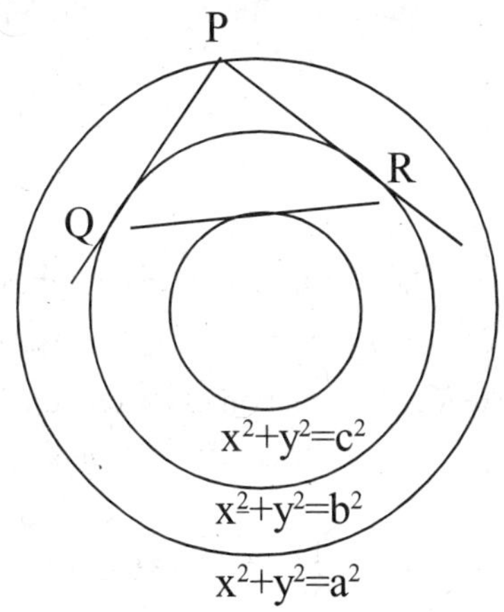

Thus, $m = 2$, $n = 1$ and $p = 1$.

Hence, the value of $m + n + p + 10 = 14$.

3.29 CHORD BISECTED AT A GIVEN POINT

(i) The equation of the chord of the circle $x^2 + y^2 = a^2$ bisected at a point (x_1, y_1) is given by $T = S_1$, where $S_1 \equiv x_1^2 + y_1^2 - a^2$ and $T \equiv xx_1 + yy_1 - a^2$.

Proof: Let C be (x_1, y_1).

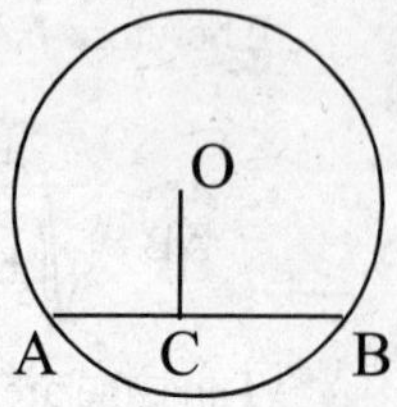

Slope of OC $= \frac{y_1 - 0}{x_1 - 0} = \frac{y_1}{x_1}$.

Here, AB is perpendicular to OC.

Thus, $m(AB) = -\frac{x_1}{y_1}$.

Hence, the equation of AB is $y - y_1 = -\frac{x_1}{y_1}(x - x_1)$

$\Rightarrow \quad yy_1 - y_1^2 = -xx_1 + x_1^2$

$\Rightarrow \quad xx_1 + yy_1 = x_1^2 + y_1^2$

$\Rightarrow \quad xx_1 + yy_1 - a^2 = x_1^2 + y_1^2 - a^2$

$\Rightarrow \quad T = S_1$, where $T \equiv xx_1 + yy_1 - a^2$ and

$$S_1 \equiv x_1^2 + y_1^2 - a^2.$$

(ii) The equation of the chord of the circle $x^2 + y^2 + 2gx + 2fy + c = 0$ bisected at a point (x_1, y_1) is given by $T = S_1$, where

$$S_1 \equiv x_1^2 + y_1^2 + 2gx_1 + 2fy_1 + c;$$

$$T \equiv xx_1 + yy_1 + g(x + x_1) + f(y + y_1) + c$$

Proof: Do yourself.

Ex-1. Find the equation of the chord of the circle $x^2 + y^2 = 25$, which is bisected at the point (-2, 3).

Sol. The equation of the chord of the circle $x^2 + y^2 = 25$ bisected at (-2, 3) is $T = S_1$

$\Rightarrow \quad -2x + 3y - 25 = 4 + 9 - 25$

$\Rightarrow \quad -2x + 3y = 13$

$\Rightarrow \quad 2x - 3y + 13 = 0.$

Ex-2. Find the equation of the chord of the circle $x^2 + y^2 + 6x + 8y - 11 = 0$, whose middle point is (1,-1)

Sol. Hence, the equation of the chord of the circle $x^2 + y^2 + 6x + 8y - 11 = 0$, whose middle point is (1, -1) is $T = S_1$

$\Rightarrow \quad x - y + 3(x + 1) + 4(y - 1) - 11 = 1 + 1 + 6 + 8 - 11$

$\Rightarrow \quad 4x + 3y - 1 = 16$

$\Rightarrow \quad 4x + 3y = 17.$

Ex-3. Find the locus of the middle points of the chords of the circle $x^2 + y^2 = a^2$ which pass through the fixed point (h, k).

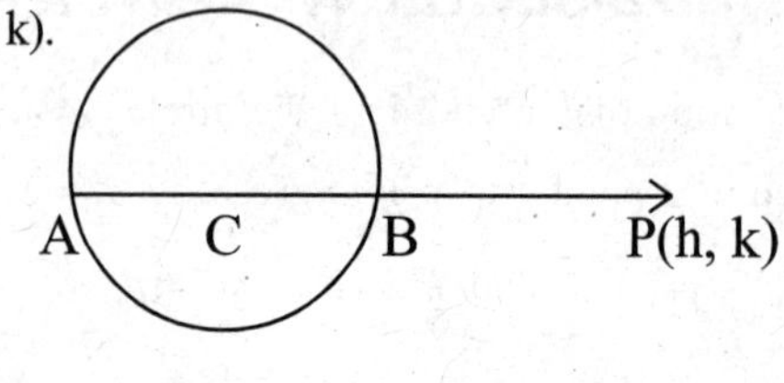

Sol. Let the chord AB bisected at C (x_1, y_1)

Equation of AB is $xx_1 + yy_1 = x_1^2 + y_1^2$

Which is passing through (h, k), so

$$hx_1 + ky_1 = x_1^2 + y_1^2$$

Thus, the locus of (x_1, y_1) is $x^2 + y^2 = hx + ky$.

Ex-4. Find the locus of the middle point of a chord of the circle $x^2 + y^2 = 4$ which subtend a right angle at the centre.

Sol. Let M(h, k) is the mid point of AB

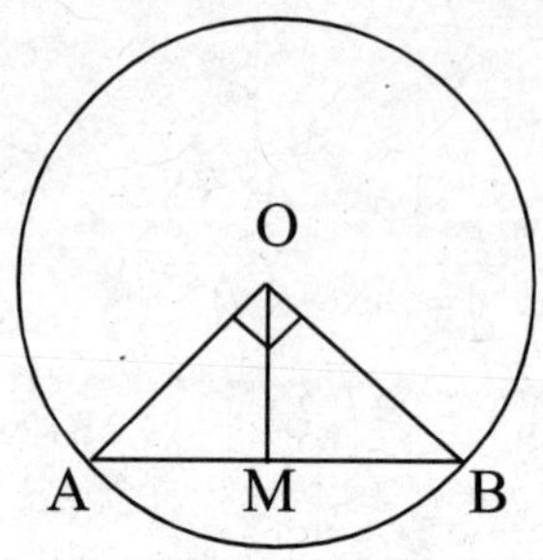

In ΔOAM, $\sin(45^o) = \frac{OM}{AM} = \frac{OM}{2}$.

$\Rightarrow \quad OM = 2\sin(45^o) = 2 \times \frac{1}{\sqrt{2}} = \sqrt{2}$

$\Rightarrow \quad OM^2 = 2$

$\Rightarrow \quad h^2 + k^2 = 2$

Hence, the locus of (h, k) is $x^2 + y^2 = 2$.

Ex-5. Let AB be a chord of the circle $x^2 + y^2 = 4$ such that $A = (\sqrt{3}, 1)$. If the chord AB makes an angle of 90° about the origin in anti-clock-wise sense, then find the co-ordinates of B.

Soln. Let A represent a complex number Z .ie. Z= $\sqrt{3} + i$.

Here, $\angle$ AOB = 90°.

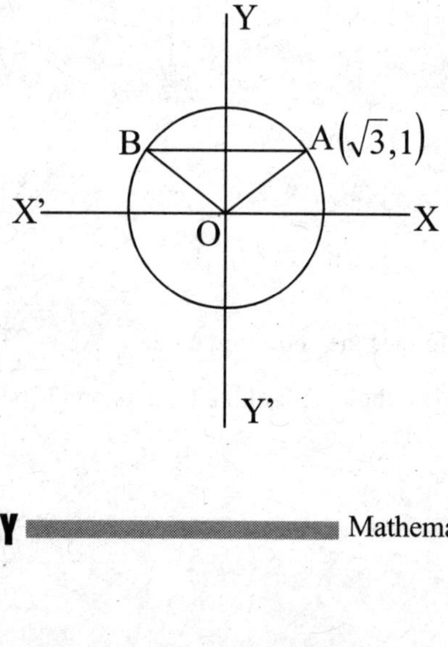

By rotation theorem, we can say that,

$$B = iZ = i\left(\sqrt{3}+i\right) = -1 + i\sqrt{3}$$

Hence, the point B is $\left(-1, \sqrt{3}\right)$.

Ex-6. Let CD be a chord of the circle $x^2 + y^2 = 9$ such that $C = \left(2\sqrt{2}, 1\right)$. If the chord CD makes an angle of $60°$ about the centre of the circle in clock-wise sense, then find the co-ordinates of D.

Sol. Let C represent a complex number Z and D be Z1.

Here, $\angle COD = 60°$

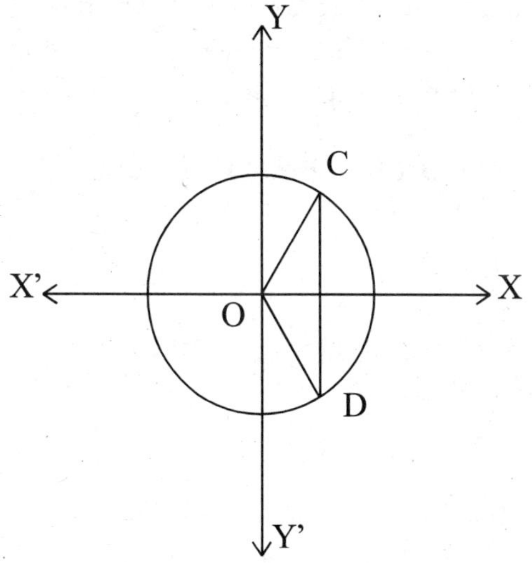

By rotation theorem, $\dfrac{Z_1 - 0}{Z - 0} = \left|\dfrac{Z_1 - 0}{Z - 0}\right| \times e^{-i\frac{p}{3}}$

$$\Rightarrow \frac{Z_1}{Z} = \frac{|Z_1|}{|Z|} \times e^{-i\frac{p}{3}} = e^{-i\frac{p}{3}}$$

$$\Rightarrow Z_1 = Z e^{-i\frac{p}{3}}$$

$$\Rightarrow Z_1 = \left(2\sqrt{2}+i\right)\left(\frac{1}{2} - i\frac{\sqrt{3}}{2}\right)$$

$$\Rightarrow Z_1 = \left(\sqrt{2} + \frac{\sqrt{3}}{2}\right) + i\left(\frac{1}{2} - \sqrt{3}\right)$$

Hence, the co-ordinates of D are

$$\left(\sqrt{2} + \frac{\sqrt{3}}{2}, \frac{1}{2} - \sqrt{3}\right).$$

3.30 DIAMMETER OF A CIRCLE

The locus of the mid points of a system of parallel chords of a circle is known as diameter of the circle.

The diammeter of a circle always passes through the centre of a circle and perpendicular to the parallel chords.

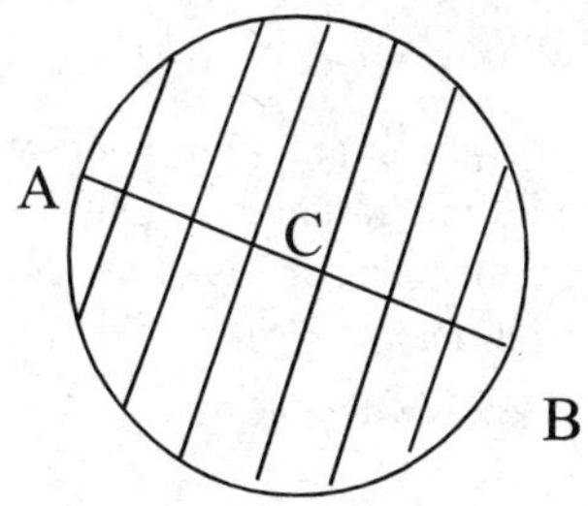

Let the circle be $x^2 + y^2 = a^2$ and parallel chord be $y = mx + c$.

Equation of any diameter to the given circle is perpendicualr to the given parallel chord is $my + x + ? = 0$ which is passes through the centre of a circle.

Thus $0 + 0 + \lambda = 0$

$\Rightarrow \lambda = 0$

Hence, the required equation of the diameter is $x + my = 0$.

Ex-1. Find the locus of the middle points of the chords of the circle $x^2 + y^2 = 9$ which are parallel to the line $2012x + 2013y + 2014 = 0$.

Sol. As we know that, the locus of the middle points of the chord of the circle is diameter of the circle.

Thus, the equation of diameter, which is parallel to $2012x + 2013y + 2014 = 0$.

is $2012x + 2013y + k = 0$.

Which is passing thorugh the centre of the circle $x^2 + y^2 = 9$.

Therefore, $k = 0$

Hence, the equation of the diameter is $2012x + 2013y = 0$.

Ex-2. Find the locus of the middle points of the chords of the circle $x^2 + y^2 - 4x - 6y = 0$, which are perpendicular to the line $4x + 5y + 10 = 0$.

Sol. Obviously, the locus of the mid-point of the chords of the circle is the diameter of the given circle.

Here, the centre of the circle $x^2 + y^2 - 4x - 6y = 0$ is $(2, 3)$.

Equation of the diameter of the circle, which is perpendicular to the line $4x + 5y + 10 = 0$ is $5x - 4y + k = 0$.

Which is passing thorugh $(2, 3)$.

Therefore, $k = 12 - 10 = 2$.

Hence, the equation of the diameter is $5x - 4y + 2 = 0$.

3.31 POLE AND POLAR

If from a point P any straight line is drawn to meet the circle in Q and R and if tangents to the circle at Q and R meet in T, then the locus of T is called the polar of P with respect to the circle.

The point P is known as pole of its polar.

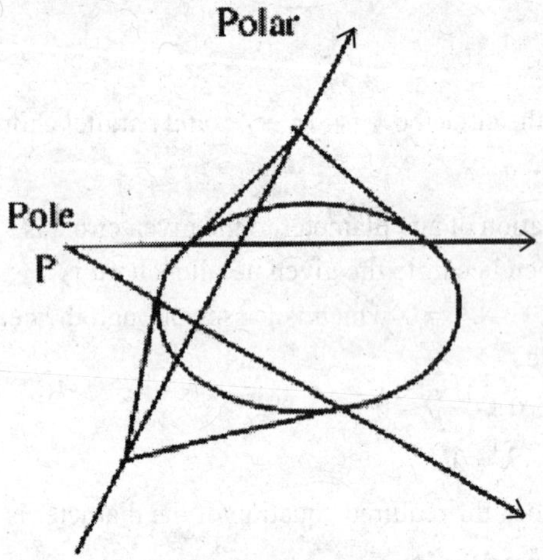

Polar of a circle is exists only when, the point P lies either outside or inside of the given circle.

(i) The equation of polar of the point (x_1, y_1) with respect to the circle $x^2 + y^2 = a^2$ is $xx_1 + yy_1 = a^2$

(ii) The equation of polar of the point (x_1, y_1) with respect to the circle $x^2 + y^2 + 2gx + 2fy + c = 0$ is $xx_1 + yy_1 + g(x + x_1) + f(y + y_1) + c = 0$.

(iii) If a point P lies outside of a circle, then the polar and the chord of contact of this point P are the same straight line.

(iv) If a point P lies on the circle, then the polar and the tangent to the circle at P are the same straight line.

(v) The pole of a line $lx + my + n = 0$ with respect to the circle $x^2 + y^2 = a^2$ is

$$\left(-\frac{a^2 l}{n}, -\frac{a^2 m}{n}\right).$$

(vi) If the polar of a point P with respect to a circle passes through Q, then the polar of Q with respect to the circle will pass through P.

Here, the points P and Q are called the **conjugate points.**

(vii) **Conjugate Points :** Two points are aid to be conjugate points with respect to a circle, if the polar of either passes thorugh the other.

(viii) If the pole of a line L_1 with respect to a circle lies on another line L_2, then the pole of the other line L_2 with respect to the same circle will lie on the first line L_1.

Here, the lines L_1 and L_2 are **conjugate lines.**

(ix) **Conjugate lines :** Two straight lines are said to be conjugate lines if the pole of either lies on the other.

(x) If the lines $a_1x + b_1y + c_1 = 0$ and $a_2x + b_2y + c_2 = 0$ are conjugate to each other with respect to the circle $x^2 + y^2 = c^2$,

then $a_1 a_2 + b_1 b_2 = \frac{c_1 c_2}{r^2}$.

(xi) If O be the centre of a circle and P be any point, OP is perpendicular to the polar of P.

(xii) If O be the centre of a circle and P be any point, then if OP (produced, if it is necessary) meet the polar of P in Q, then $OP.OQ = (\text{radius})^2$.

3.32 COMMON CHORD OF TWO CIRCLES

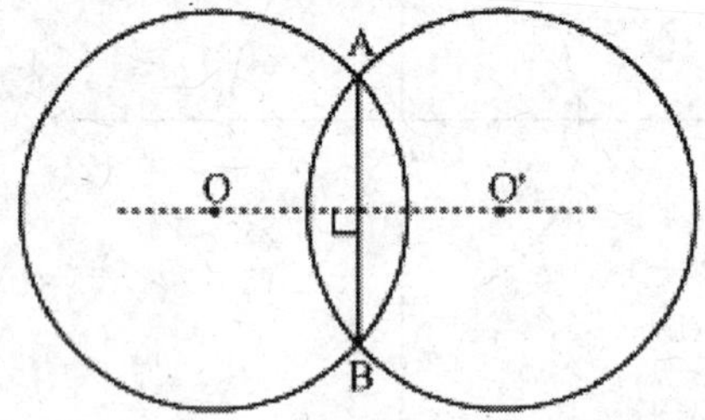

The chord joining the points of intersection of two given circles is called their common chord.

The equation of the common chord between two circles is $S_1 - S_2 = 0$

$\Rightarrow \quad 2(g_1 - g_2)x + 2(f_1 - f_2)y = c_1 - c_2$,

where $S_1 \equiv x^2 + y^2 + 2g_1x + 2f_1y + c_1 = 0$ and

$S_2 \equiv x^2 + y^2 + 2g_2x + 2f_2y + c_2 = 0$

(i) The length of the common chord = PQ = 2. PM = $2\sqrt{(C_1P)^2 - (C_1M)^2}$, where

C_1P = radius of the circle $S_1 = 0$ and C_1M = Length of perpendicular from C_1 on the common chord PQ.

(ii) The common chord PQ of two circles becomes of the maximum length, when it is a diam eter of the smaller one between them.

(iii) If the circle on the common chord be a diameter, then the centre of the circle passing through P and Q lie on the common chord of the two circles.

(iv) If the circle $S_1 = 0$, bisects the circumference of the circle $S_2 = 0$, then their common chord will be the diameter of the circle $S_2 = 0$.

Ex-1. Find the lengths of the common chord of the circles $x^2+y^2+3x+5y+4=0$ and $x^2+y^2+5x+3y+4=0$.

Sol. The equation of the common chord of the circle is

$2x-2y=0 \Rightarrow x=y$.

On solving y = x and the circle $x^2+y^2+3x+5y+4=0$, we get the points of intersection .

Thus, $x=-2+\sqrt{2}=y$ & $x=-2-\sqrt{2}=y$

Let the common chord be PQ, where

$P=\left(-2+\sqrt{2},-2+\sqrt{2}\right)$ and $Q=\left(-2-\sqrt{2},-2-\sqrt{2}\right)$

Thus, the length of the common chord

$$PQ=\sqrt{\left(-2-\sqrt{2}+2-\sqrt{2}\right)^2+\left(-2-\sqrt{2}+2-\sqrt{2}\right)^2}$$

$$=\sqrt{8+8}=\sqrt{16}=4.$$

Ex-2. Find the equation of the circle whose diameter is the common chord of the circles

$x^2+y^2+2x+3y+1=0$

and $x^2+y^2+4x+3y+2=0$.

Sol. The equation of the common chord of the given circles is $2x+1=0$.

On solving $2x+1=0$ and $x^2+y^2+2x+3y+1=0$, we get the points of intersection.

Thus, the points of intersection are

$$x=-\frac{1}{2} \;\&\; y=-\frac{3}{2}\pm\sqrt{2}.$$

Let PQ be the common chord, where

$$P=\left(-\frac{1}{2},-\frac{3}{2}+\sqrt{2}\right) \text{ and } Q=\left(-\frac{1}{2},-\frac{3}{2}-\sqrt{2}\right)$$

The mid-point of P and Q is the centre of the new circle .

Thus, centre is $C=\left(-\frac{1}{2},-\frac{3}{2}\right)$

Now, radius $r=CP=\sqrt{2}$.

Hence, the equation of the circle is

$$\left(x+\frac{1}{2}\right)^2+\left(y+\frac{3}{2}\right)^2=2$$

$$\Rightarrow \quad 2\left(x^2+y^2\right)+2x+6y+1=0$$

3.33 INTERSECTION BETWEEN TWO CIRCLES

Let the two circles be $(x-\alpha)^2+(y-\beta)^2=r_1^2$ and $(x-\gamma)^2+(y-\delta)^2=r_2^2$, where centres are $C_1(\alpha,\beta)$ and $C_2(\gamma,\delta)$ and radii are r_1 & r_2 respectively.

(i) When two circles do not intersect :

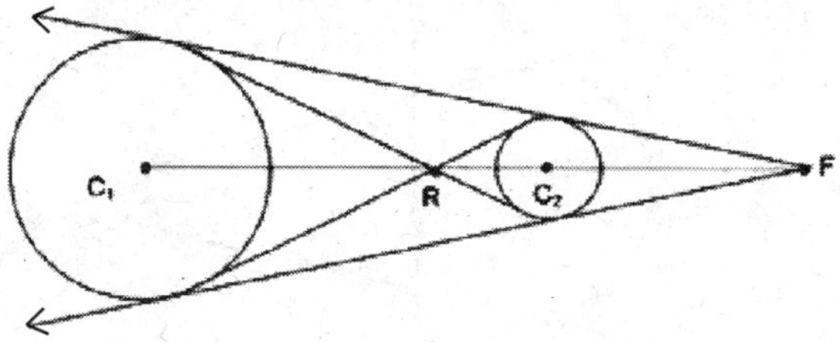

Then $C_1C_2>r_1+r_2$

Thus 4 common tangents can be drawn.

Let P be the point of intersection of two transeverse tangents and D be the point of intersection of two direct common tangents.

Then the co-ordinates of P and D are

$$\left(\frac{r_1x_2+r_2x_1}{r_1+r_2},\frac{r_1y_2+r_2y_1}{r_1+r_2}\right)=(h,k) \text{ and}$$

$$\left(\frac{r_1x_2-r_2x_1}{r_1-r_2},\frac{r_1y_2-r_2y_1}{r_1-r_2}\right)=(\lambda,\mu) \text{ respectively}$$

Then the equation of the transverse common tangents is $(y-k)=m_1(x-h)$ and the equation of direct common tangent is $(y-\mu)=m_2(x-\lambda)$.

Now values of m_1,m_2 can be obtained from the length of perpendicular from the center C_1 or C_2 on the tangent is equal to r_1 or r_2 .Put two values of m_1,m_2 on the common tangent equations, then we get the requred

(ii) when two circles intersect.

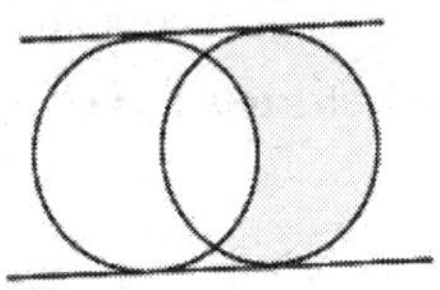

Then $|r_1-r_2|<C_1C_2<r_1+r_2$

Thus 2 common tangents can be drawn.

Let two direct common tangents intersect at D externally in the ratio $r_1:r_2$.

Then the co-ordinates of D are

$$\left(\frac{r_1x_2-r_2x_1}{r_1-r_2},\frac{r_1y_2-r_2y_1}{r_1-r_2}\right)=(h,k)$$

Hence the equation of the direct common tangent is

$y-k=m(x-h)$

Now values of m canbe obtained from the length of perpendicular from the center C_1 orC_2 on the tangent is equal to r_1 or r_2 put two values of m on the common tangent equation, then we get the requred equation of direct common tangents.

(iii) When two circles touch each other externally.

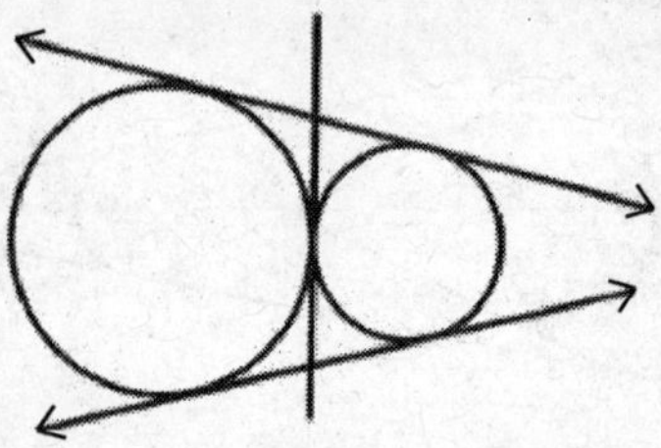

Then $C_1C_2 = r_1 + r_2$

Thus 3 common tangents can be drawn.

Let the point of contact be P.

Then the co-ordinates of P are $\left(\frac{r_1x_2 + r_2x_1}{r_1 + r_2}, \frac{r_1y_2 + r_2y_1}{r_1 + r_2}\right)$

Hence the equation of the common transeverse tangent is $S_1 - S_2 = 0$ which is the same as the equation of the common chord.

Let two direct common tangents intersect at D externally in the ratio $r_1 : r_2$

Then the co-ordinates of D are

$\left(\frac{r_1x_2 - r_2x_1}{r_1 - r_2}, \frac{r_1y_2 - r_2y_1}{r_1 - r_2}\right) = (h, k)$

Hence the equation of the direct common tangent is

$(y - k) = m(x - h)$

Now values of m canbe obtained from the length of perpendicular from the center C_1 or C_2 on the tangent is equal to r_1 or r_2 put two values of m on the common tangent equation , then we get the requred equation of direct common tangents.

(iv) When two circles touch each other internally.

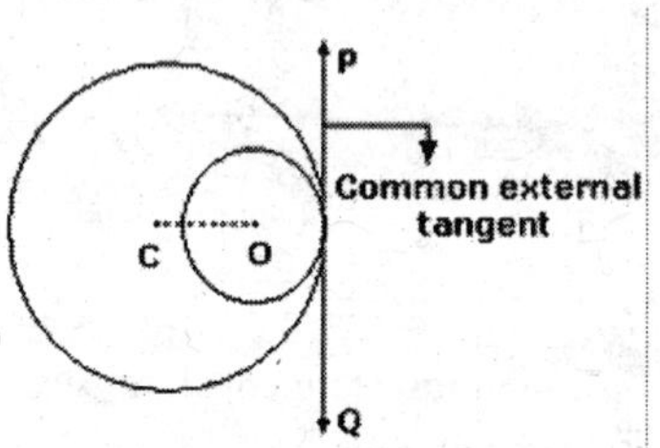

Then $C_1C_2 = |r_1 - r_2|$

Thus, only one tangent can be drawn.

Equation of the common transverse tangent is.

$S_1 - S_2 = 0$.

(v) When one circle lies inside the other one.

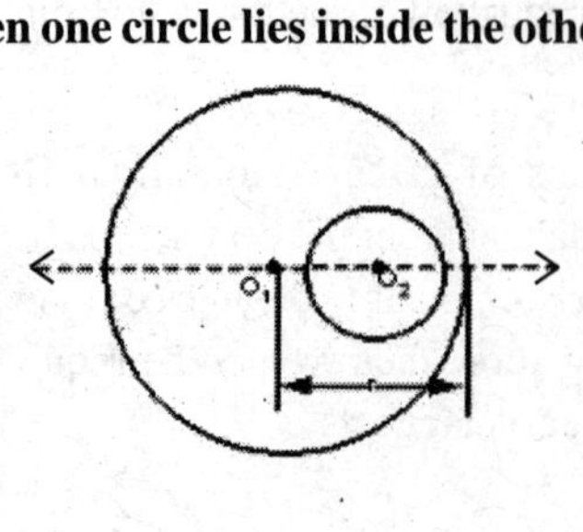

Then $C_1C_2 > |r_1 - r_2|$

Thus, no common tangent can be drawn.

(vi) The direct common tangents meet at a point which divideds the line joining the centres of the circles externally in the ratio of their radii.

(vii) Transverse common tangents meet at a point which divides the line joining the centres of the circles internally in the ratio of their radii.

(viii) Length of an external common tangent and internal common tangent to the two circles is given by the length of external common tangent $L_{ex} = \sqrt{d^2 - (r_2 - r_1)^2}$ and the length of internal common tangent $L_{in} = \sqrt{d^2 - (r_2 + r_1)^2}$, (it is applicable only when $d > r_1 + r_2$)

Where d is the distance between the centres of two circles and r_1 & r_2 are the radii of two circles where $C_1C_2 = d$

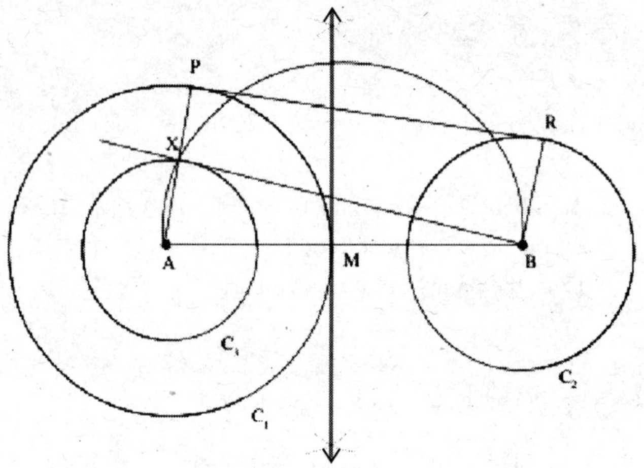

Ex-1. Find the number of tangents between the given circles

(i) $x^2 + y^2 = 4$ and $x^2 + y^2 - 2x = 0$

(ii) $x^2 + y^2 + 4x + 6y + 12 = 0$
and $x^2 + y^2 - 6x - 4y + 12 = 0$

(iii) $x^2 + y^2 - 6x - 6y + 9 = 0$
and $x^2 + y^2 + 6x + 6y + 9 = 0$

(iv) $x^2 + y^2 - 4x - 4y = 0$ and $x^2 + y^2 + 2x + 2y = 0$

(v) $x^2 + y^2 = 64$ and $x^2 + y^2 - 4x - 4y + 4 = 0$

(vi) $x^2 + y^2 - 2(1+\sqrt{2})x - 2y + 1 = 0$
and $x^2 + y^2 - 2x - 2y + 1 = 0$

Sol. (i) The given circles are $x^2 + y^2 = 4$ ...(i)

and $x^2 + y^2 - 2x = 0$ ...(ii)

Now, C_1 (0, 0) and C_2(1, 0) and $r_1 = 2$ and $r_2 = 1$
Thus, $C_1C_2 = 1 = r_2 - r_1$
Hence, both the circles touches each other internally.
Thus, the number of common tangent = 1.

(ii) The given circles are $x^2+y^2+4x+6y+12=0$

and $x^2+y^2-6x-4y+12=0$

Now, C_1 : (-2, -3), C_2 : (3, 2), $r_1 = 1$ and $r_2 = 1$
Therefore,

$$C_1C_2 = \sqrt{(3+2)^2+(-3-2)^2} = \sqrt{25+25} = \sqrt{50} = 5\sqrt{2}$$

and $r_1 + r_2 = 1 + 1 = 2$.
Thus, $C_1C_2 > r_1 + r_2$
Hence, the number of common tangents = 4 .

(iii) The given circles are $x^2+y^2-6x-6y+9=0$ and

$x^2+y^2+6x+6y+9=0$

Now, C_1 = (3, 3), C_2 = (-3, -3), $r_1 = 3$ and $r_2 = 3$
Therefore

$$C_1C_2 = \sqrt{(-3-2)^2+(-3-3)^2} = \sqrt{36+36} = \sqrt{72} = 6\sqrt{2}$$

and $r_1 + r_2 = 3 + 3 = 6$
Thus, $C_1C_2 > r_1 + r_2$
Hence, the number of common tangents = 4

(iv) The given circles are $x^2+y^2-4x-4y=0$ and

$x^2+y^2+2x+2y=0$

Now, C_1 = (2, 2), C_2 = (-1, -1), $r_1 = 2\sqrt{2}$ and $r_2 = \sqrt{2}$
Therefore,

$$C_1C_2 = \sqrt{(-1-2)^2+(-1-2)^2} = \sqrt{9+9} = \sqrt{18} = 3\sqrt{2}.$$

and $r_1 + r_2 = 2\sqrt{2}+\sqrt{2} = 3\sqrt{2}$
Thus, $C_1C_2 = r_1 + r_2$
Hence, the number of common tangents = 3 .

(v) The given circles are $x^2+y^2=64$

and $x^2+y^2-4x-4y+4=0$

Now, C_1 : (0, 0), C_2: (2, 2), $r_1 = 8$ and $r_2 = 2$
Therefore,

$$C_1C_2 = \sqrt{(2-0)^2+(2-0)^2} = \sqrt{4+4} = 2\sqrt{2}$$

and $r_1 + r_2 = 8 + 2 = 10$
Therefore, $C_1C_2 < r_1 + r_2$
Thus , one circle lies inside of the other .
Hence, the number of common tangents = 0 .

(vi) The given circles are

$$x^2+y^2-2\left(1+\sqrt{2}\right)x-2y+1=0$$

and $x^2+y^2-2x-2y+1=0$

Now $C_1 : \left(1+\sqrt{2}, 1\right)$, C_2 : (1, 1), $r_1 = \sqrt{2}+1$ and $r_2 = 1$.

Therefore, $C_1C_2 = \sqrt{\left(\sqrt{2}\right)^2} = \sqrt{2}$ and $r_1 - r_2 = \sqrt{2}$.

Thus, $C_1C_2 = r_1 - r_2$
Hence, the number of common tangents = 1 .

Ex-2. Find all the common tangents to the circles $x^2+y^2-2x-6y+9=0$ and $x^2+y^2+6x-2y+1=0$.

Sol. The given circles are

$x^2+y^2-2x-6y+9=0$

and $x^2+y^2+6x-2y+1=0$.

Now, C_1 : (1, 3), C_2 : (-3, 1), $r_1 = 1$ and $r_2 = 3$.
Therefore,

$$C_1C_2 = \sqrt{(-3-1)^2+(1-3)^2} = \sqrt{16+4} = \sqrt{20} = 2\sqrt{5}$$

and $r_1 + r_2 = 1 + 3 = 4$
Then, $C_1C_2 > r_1 + r_2$
Thus, both the circles do not intersect.
Hence, the number of common tangents = 4 , in which 2 are direct common tangents and another 2 are transverse common tangents.

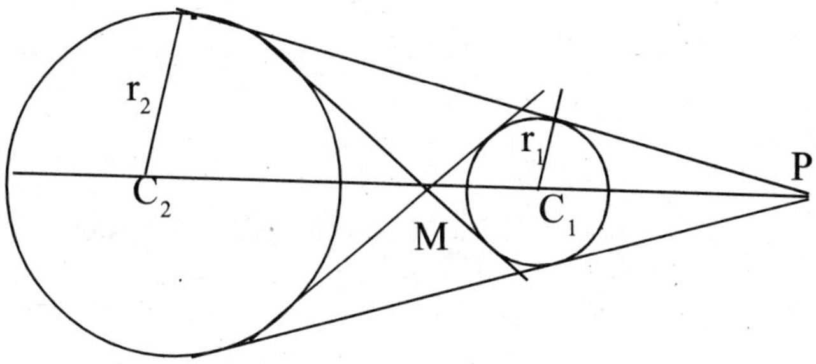

Here, the point M divide C_2 (-3, 1) and C_1(1, 3) internally in the ratio 3:1 .

Then, the co-ordinates of M are

$$\left(\frac{3.1-1.3}{3+1}, \frac{3.3.+1.1}{3+1}\right) = \left(0, \frac{5}{2}\right)$$

Also, the point P divide C_2 (-3, 1) and C_1 (1, 3) externally in the ratio 3 : 1.

Then, the co-ordinates of P are

$$\left(\frac{3.1+1.3}{3-1}, \frac{3.3.-1.1}{3-1}\right) = (3, 4)$$

Case - I: Direct common tangents.

Any line through (3, 4) is $y-4 = m(x-3)$ ...(i)

$\Rightarrow \quad mx - y + 4 - 3m = 0$

If it is a tangent to the circle, $\left|\frac{m-3+4-3m}{\sqrt{m^2+1}}\right| = 1$

$\Rightarrow \quad (1-2m)^2 = (m^2+1)$

$\Rightarrow \quad 3m^2 - 4m = 0$

$\Rightarrow \quad m(3m-4) = 0$

$\Rightarrow \quad m = 0, \frac{4}{3}$.

Hence, the direct common tangents are y = 4 , 4 x - 3 y = 0.`

Case - II : Transverse common tangents.

Any line through (0, 5/2) is $y - \frac{5}{2} = m(x-0)$ ...(i)

$\Rightarrow \quad 2mx - 2y + 5 = 0$

If it is a tangent to a circle, then $\left|\frac{m.1 - 3 + \frac{5}{2}}{\sqrt{m^2+1}}\right| = 1$

$\Rightarrow \quad (2m-1)^2 = 4(m^2+1)$

$\Rightarrow \quad 4m^2 - 4m + 1 = 4(m^2+1)$

$\Rightarrow \quad 4m + 3 = 0$

$\Rightarrow \quad m = \infty, \; m = -\frac{3}{4}$

Hence, the equation of transeverse tangents are $x = 0$ and $3x + 4y = 10$.

Ex-3. If two circles $x^2 + y^2 + c^2 = 2ax$ and $x^2 + y^2 + c^2 = 2by$ touches each other externally, then prove that $\frac{1}{a^2} = \frac{1}{b^2} + \frac{1}{c^2}$.

Sol. Given circles are $x^2 + y^2 + c^2 = 2ax$

$\Rightarrow \quad (x-a)^2 + y^2 = \left(\sqrt{a^2 - c^2}\right)^2$ ...(i)

and $x^2 + y^2 + c^2 = 2by$

$\Rightarrow \quad x^2 + (y\text{-}b)^2 = \left(\sqrt{b^2 - c^2}\right)^2$ ...(ii)

Now $C_1 : (a, 0), C_2 : (0, b)$, $r_1 = \sqrt{a^2 - c^2}$

and $r_2 = \sqrt{b^2 - c^2}$

Since both the circles touch each other expternally, then

$C_1C_2 = r_1 + r_2$

$\Rightarrow \quad \sqrt{a^2 + b^2} = \sqrt{a^2 - c^2} + \sqrt{b^2 - c^2}$

$\Rightarrow \quad a^2 + b^2 = a^2 - c^2 + b^2 - c^2 + 2\left(\sqrt{a^2 - c^2}\right)\left(\sqrt{b^2 - c^2}\right)$

$\Rightarrow \quad 2c^2 = 2\left(\sqrt{a^2 - c^2}\right)\left(\sqrt{b^2 - c^2}\right)$

$\Rightarrow \quad c^4 = (a^2 - c^2)(b^2 - c^2) = a^2b^2 - c^2(a^2 + b^2) + c^4$

$\Rightarrow \quad a^2b^2 - c^2(a^2 + b^2) = 0$

$\Rightarrow \quad \frac{1}{a^2} + \frac{1}{b^2} = \frac{1}{c^2}$

Ex-4. If two circles $x^2 + y^2 = 9$ and $x^2 + y^2 - 8x - 6y + n^2 = 0$, where n is any integer, have exactly two common tangents, then find the number of passible values of n.

Sol. The given circles are $x^2 + y^2 = 9$ ...(i)

and $x^2 + y^2 - 8x - 6y + n^2 = 0$

$\Rightarrow \quad (x-4)^2 + (y-3)^2 = \left(\sqrt{25 - n^2}\right)^2$ ...(ii)

Here, $C_1 : (0, 0)$, $C_2 : (4, 3)$, $r_1 = 3$ and $r_2 = \sqrt{25 - n^2}$

Since the circles have only tow common tangents , so we can write, $|r_1 - r_2| < C_1C_2 < r_1 + r_2$

$\Rightarrow \quad \left|3 - \sqrt{25 - n^2}\right| < 5 < 3 + \sqrt{25 - n^2}$

Case - I : When $\left|3 - \sqrt{25 - n^2}\right| < 5$

Then $\quad -5 < 3 - \sqrt{25 - n^2} < 5$

$\Rightarrow \quad -5 - 3 < -\sqrt{25 - n^2} < 5\text{-}3$

$\Rightarrow \quad -2 < \sqrt{25 - n^2} < 8$

$\Rightarrow \quad 4 < 25 - n^2 < 64$

$\Rightarrow \quad -21 < -n^2 < 39$

$\Rightarrow \quad -39 < n^2 < 21$

$\Rightarrow \quad 0 < n < \sqrt{21}$

$\Rightarrow \quad n = 1, 2, 3, 4$

Case - II : When $5 < 3 + \sqrt{25 - n^2}$

Then, $\quad \sqrt{25 - n^2} > 2$

$\Rightarrow \quad 25 - n^2 > 4$

$\Rightarrow \quad n^2 < 21$

$\Rightarrow \quad n < \sqrt{21}$

$\Rightarrow \quad n = 1, 2,, 3, 4$.

Hence, the number of integers = 4.

3.24 ANGLE OF INTERSECTION OF TWO CIRCLES

Let the two circles be $S_1 : x^2 + y^2 + 2g_1x + 2f_1y + c_1 = 0$

$S_2: x^2+y^2+2g_2x+2f_2y+c_2=0$

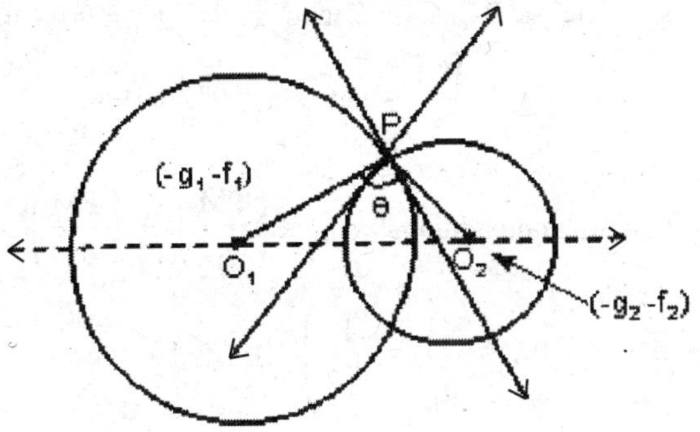

Let C_1 and C_2 are the centres of the given circles and r 1 and r 2 are the radii of the circles.

Thus $C_1=(-g_1,-f_1)$ and $C_2=(-g_2,-f_2)$ and

$r_1=\sqrt{g_1^2+f_1^2-c_1}$ and $r_2=\sqrt{g_2^2+f_2^2-c_2}$.

Let $d=C_1C_2=\sqrt{(g_1-g_2)^2+(f_1-f_2)^2}$

$=\sqrt{g_1^2+g_2^2+f_1^2+f_2^2-2(g_1g_2+f_1f_2)}$

In C_1PC_2, $\cos a=\left(\dfrac{r_1^2+r_2^2-d^2}{2r_1r_2}\right)$

$\Rightarrow \cos(180^? - ?)=\left(\dfrac{r_1^2+r_2^2-d^2}{2r_1r_2}\right)$.

3.35 Orthogonal circles

If the angle between two circles is 90°, then the circles are said to be orthogonal circles .

Condition of Orthogonality

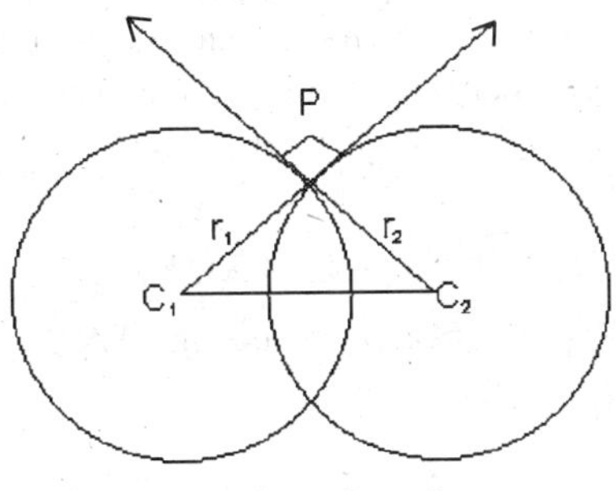

Here, $\theta=90°$, then $\dfrac{r_1^2+r_2^2-d^2}{2r_1r_2}=0$

$\Rightarrow r_1^2+r_2^2-d^2=0$

$\Rightarrow r_1^2+r_2^2=d^2$

$\Rightarrow g_1^2+f_1^2-c_1+g_2^2+f_2^2-c_2=g_1^2+f_1^2+g_2^2+f_2^2-2(g_1g_2+f_1f_2)$

$\Rightarrow 2(g_1g_2+f_1f_2)=c_1+c_2$

which is the required condition .

Ex-1. Find the angle at which the circles $x^2+y^2+x+y=0$ and $x^2+y^2+x-y=0$ intersect.

Sol. The given circles are $x^2+y^2+x+y=0$ and

$x^2+y^2+x-y=0$

Here, $g_1=-1/2, f_1=-1/2, g_2=-1/2, f_2=1/2, c_1=0, c_2=0$

Now, $2(g_1g_2+f_1f_2)=2(-1/4+1/4)=0$ and $c_1+c_2=0$.

Hence, the angle between the given circles is 90°.

Ex-2. If the circles $x^2+y^2+2a_1x+2b_1y+c_1=0$ and $x^2+y^2+a_2x+b_2y+c_2=0$ intersect othogonally, then prove that $a_1a_2+b_1b_2=c_1+c_2$.

Sol. The given circles are

$x^2+y^2+2a_1x+2b_1y+c_1=0$ and

$x^2+y^2+a_2x+b_2y+c_2=0$

Here, $g_1=a_1, f_1=b_1, g_2=a_2/2, f_2=b_2/2, c_1=c_1$ and $c_2=c_2$.

Since the given two circles are orthogonal , so

$2(g_1g_2+f_1f_2)=c_1+c_2$.

$\Rightarrow 2\left(a_1.\dfrac{a_2}{2}+b_1.\dfrac{b_2}{2}\right)=c_1+c_2$

$\Rightarrow (a_1.a_2+b_1.b_2)=c_1+c_2$

Hence, the result.

Ex-3. If two circles $2x^2+2y^2-3x+6y+k=0$ and $x^2+y^2-4x+10y+16=0$ cut orthogonally, then find the value of k.

Sol. The given circles are $2x^2+2y^2-3x+6y+k=0$

$\Rightarrow x^2+y^2-\dfrac{3}{2}x+3y+\dfrac{k}{2}=0$

and $x^2+y^2-4x+10y+16=0$

Since, the given two circles are orthogonal, then

$2(g_1g_2+f_1f_2)=c_1+c_2$

$\Rightarrow 2\left(-\dfrac{3}{4}\times-2+\dfrac{3}{2}\times5\right)=\dfrac{k}{2}+16$

$\Rightarrow \dfrac{k}{2}+16=18$

$\Rightarrow \dfrac{k}{2}=18\text{-}16$

$\Rightarrow k=4$

Hence, the value of k is 4 .

Ex-4. A circle passes through the origin and centre lies on the line y = x. If it cuts the circle $x^2+y^2-4x-6y+18=0$ orthogonally, then find its equation.

Sol. Let the equation of the circle be

$x^2+y^2+2gx+2fy=0$ ...(i)

Therefore, the centre of the circle is $(-g, -f)$.

Since, the centre lies on the line $y = x$,

so $-f = -g \Rightarrow f = g$.

The equation (i) is orthogonal to

$$x^2+y^2-4x-6y+18=0,$$

so $2(g(-2)+f(-3)) = 0+18$

$\Rightarrow 2(-5g) = 18$ (since, $f = g$)

$\Rightarrow g = -\frac{9}{5} = f$

Hence, the equation of the circle is

$$x^2+y^2-\frac{18}{5}x-\frac{18}{5}y=0$$

Ex-5. Find the locus of the centres of the circles which cut the circles $x^2+y^2+4x-6y+9=0$ and $x^2+y^2-5x+4y-2=0$ orthogonally.

Sol. Let the equation of the circle be

$$x^2+y^2+2gx+2fy+c=0 \quad \text{...(i)}$$

The equation of the circle (i) is orthogonal to

$x^2+y^2+4x-6y+9=0$ and

$x^2+y^2-5x+4y-2=0$

Thus, $(4g-6f) = c+9$ ...(ii)

and $(-5g+4f) = c-2$ ...(iii)

Subtracting $-9g+10f+11=0$

$\Rightarrow 9(-g)-10(-f)+11=0$

Hence, the locus of the centre is $9x - 10y + 11 = 0$.

Ex-6. If a circle passes through the point (a, b) and cuts the circle $x^2+y^2=4$ orthogonally, then find the locus of its centre.

Sol. Let the equation of the circle be

$$x^2+y^2+2gx+2fy+c=0 \quad \text{...(i)}$$

which is passing through (a, b)

Therefore, $a^2+b^2+2ga+2fb+c=0$ ...(ii)

It is given that, the circle (i) is orthogonal to $x^2+y^2=4$,

so $2(g.0+f.0) = c-4 \Rightarrow c = 4$.

From (ii), we get, $a^2+b^2+2g.a+2f.b+4=0$

Hence, the locus of $(-g, -f)$ is

$$2ax+2by-(a^2+b^2+4)=0.$$

Ex-7. Two circles having radii r_1 and r_2 intersect orthogonally, then find the length of the common chord.

Sol. Let C_1 and C_2 be the centres of the two orthogonal circles with radii r_1 and r_2 respectively.

Here $\angle C_1PC_2 = 90°$

and let $\angle PC_1C_2 = ?$ and $\angle PC_2C_1 = 90° - \theta$

Thus, $\sin(\theta) = \frac{PM}{r_1}$ and $\sin(90° - \theta) = \frac{PM}{r_2}$.

Squaring and adding, we get, $\left(\frac{PM}{r_1}\right)^2 + \left(\frac{PM}{r_2}\right)^2 = 1$

$$\Rightarrow PM^2\left(\frac{1}{r_1^2}+\frac{1}{r_2^2}\right)=1$$

$$\Rightarrow PM^2 = \frac{r_1^2 r_2^2}{r_1^2+r_2^2}$$

$$\Rightarrow PM = \frac{r_1 r_2}{\sqrt{r_1^2+r_2^2}}$$

Hence, the length of the common chord = PQ = 2 PM = $\frac{2r_1r_2}{\sqrt{r_1^2+r_2^2}}$

3.36 RADICAL AXIS

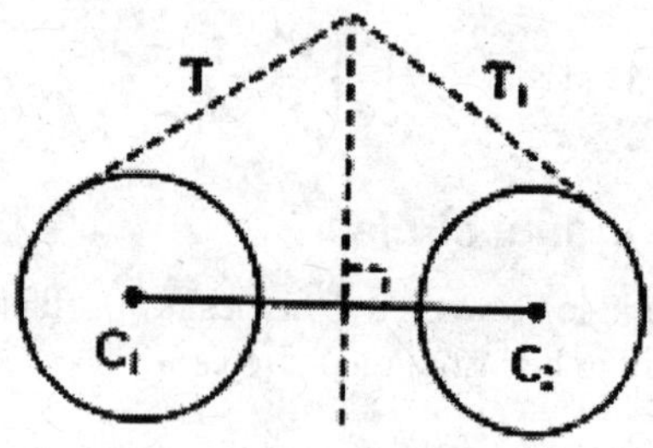

The radical axis of two circles is the locus of a point which moves in a plane in such a way that the lengths of the tangents drawn from it to the two circles are same.

Consider $S_1: x^2+y^2+2g_1x+2f_1y+c_1=0$

and $S_2: x^2+y^2+2g_2x+2f_2y+c_2=0$

Let $P(x_1, y_1)$ be a point such that PA = PB

Thus, $PA^2 = PB^2$

$$\Rightarrow x_1^2+y_1^2+2g_1x_1+2f_1y_1+c_1$$
$$= x_2^2+y_2^2+2g_2x_2+2f_2y_2+c_2$$

$$\Rightarrow 2(g_1-g_2)x+2(f_1-f_2)y = c_2-c_1$$

3.37 PROPERTIES OF THE RADICAL AXIS

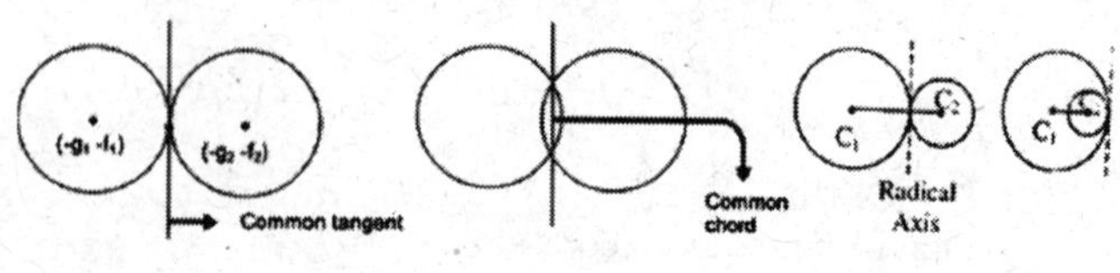

(i) **The radical axis and common chord are identical :**

Since the radical axis and common chord of two circles $S_1 = 0$ and $S_2 = 0$ are the same straight line $S_1 - S_2 = 0$, they are identical.

The only difference is that, the common chord exists only if the circles intersect in two real points, while the radical axis exists for all pair of circles irrespective of their position.

(ii) The radical axis is perpendicular to the straight line which joins the centres of the circles.

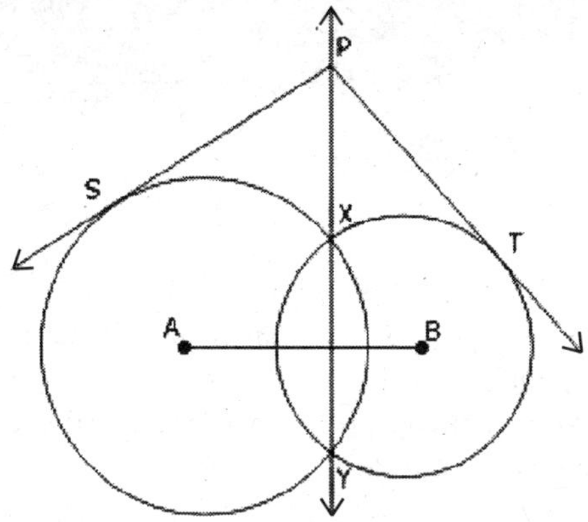

Consider $S_1 : x^2 + y^2 + 2g_1x + 2f_1y + c_1 = 0$

and $S_2 : x^2 + y^2 + 2g_2x + 2f_2y + c_2 = 0$

Here, $A(-g_1, -f_1)$ & $B(-g_2, -f_2)$ are the centres of the circles

Now slope of AB $= \dfrac{f_1 - f_2}{g_1 - g_2}$.

Equation of the radical axis is

$$2(g_1 - g_2)x + 2(f_1 - f_2)y = c_2 - c_1.$$

Slope of the radical axis is $-\dfrac{g_1 - g_2}{f_1 - f_2}$.

Clearly product of their slopes is -1.

Hence *AB* and radical axis are perpendicular to each other.

(iii) If two circles touch each other externally or internally.

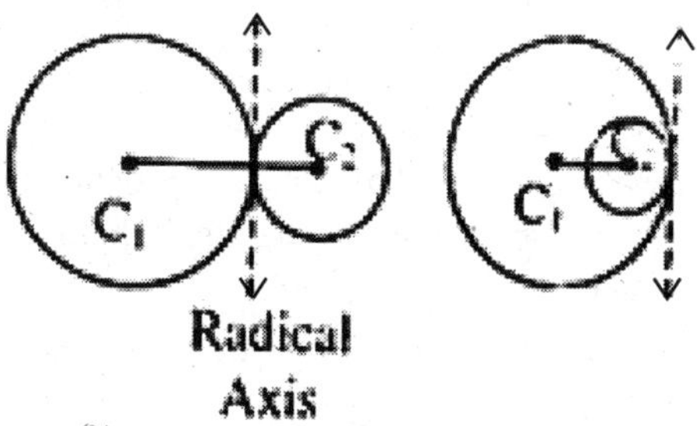

In this case, the common tangents itself becomes the radical axis.

(iv) The radical axis bisects common tangents of two circles

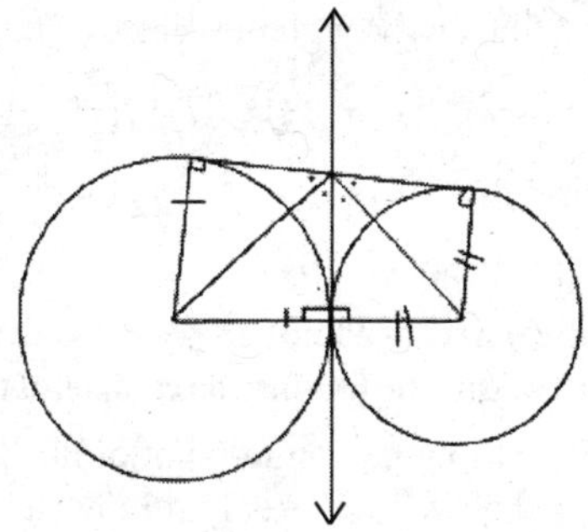

In this case radical axis bisects the common tangent

(v) Radical axis of three circles taken in pairs are concurrent.

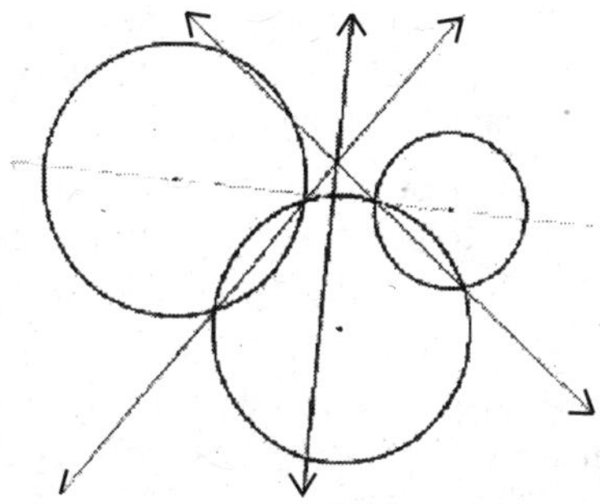

Let $S_1 : x^2 + y^2 + 2g_1x + 2f_1y + c_1 = 0$,

$S_2 : x^2 + y^2 + 2g_2x + 2f_2y + c_2 = 0$

and $S_3 : x^2 + y^2 + 2g_3x + 2f_3y + c_3 = 0$

Now $S_1 - S_2 : 2(g_1 - g_2)x + 2(f_1 - f_2)y = c_2 - c_1$

$S_2 - S_3 : 2(g_2 - g_3)x + 2(f_2 - f_3)y = c_3 - c_2$

$S_3 - S_1 : 2(g_3 - g_1)x + 2(f_3 - f_1)y = c_1 - c_3$

Adding above equations , we get , both the sides are identical.

Thus three radical axes are concurrent.

(vi) If two circles cut a third circle othogonally , the radical axis of the two circles will pass through the centre of the third circle.

Let $S_1 : x^2 + y^2 + 2g_1x + 2f_1y + c_1 = 0$ ...(i)

$S_2 : x^2 + y^2 + 2g_2x + 2f_2y + c_2 = 0$ ...(ii)

and $S_3 : x^2 + y^2 + 2g_3x + 2f_3y + c_3 = 0$ ...(iii)

Since (i) and (ii) both cut (iii) orthogonally , then

$$2(g_1g_3 + f_1f_3) = c_1 + c_3$$

$$2(g_2g_3 + f_2f_3) = c_2 + c_3$$

Subtracting, we get ,

$$2g_3(g_1 - g_2) + 2f_3(f_1 - f_2) = c_1 - c_2 \quad \text{...(iv)}$$

Also radical axis of (i) and (ii) is

$$S_1 - S_2 : 2(g_1 - g_2)x + 2(f_1 - f_2)y = c_2 - c_1$$

Since it will pass through the centre of third circle,

so we get, $-2g_3(g_1-g_2)-2f_3(f_1-f_2)=-c_1+c_2$

$\Rightarrow \quad 2g_3(g_1-g_2)+2f_3(f_1-f_2)=c_1-c_2$.

which is identical with (iv).

(vii) **Radical axis need not always pass through the mid point of the line joining the centres of the two circles.**

It will pass through the mid-point of the line joining the centres of the two circles only if they have equal radii.

(viii) The centre of a variable circle orthogonal to two fixed circles lies on the radical axis of two circles.

(ix) If two circles are orthogonal, then the polar of a point P on the first circle with respect to the second circle passes through the point Q, which is the other end of the diameter through P.

Hence locus ofa point which moves in such a way that, its polars with respect to the circles $S_1=0$, $S_2=0$ and $S_3=0$ are concurrent in a circle which is orthogonal to all the three circles.

(x) Pairs of circles which do not have radical axis are concurrent.

(xi) A system of circles, every two which have the same radical axis, is called a coaxial sysem.

3.38 RADICAL CENTER

The radical axes of three circles, taken in pairs, meet at a point, which is called their radical center

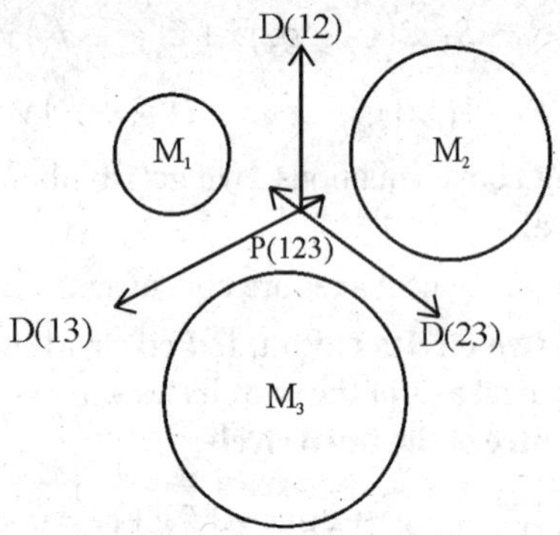

Let $S_1: x^2+y^2+2g_1x+2f_1y+c_1=0$,

$S_2: x^2+y^2+2g_2x+2f_2y+c_2=0$

and $S_3: x^2+y^2+2g_3x+2f_3y+c_3=0$

Equations of three radical axis are

$S_1-S_2: 2(g_1-g_2)x+2(f_1-f_2)y=c_2-c_1$

$S_2-S_3: 2(g_2-g_3)x+2(f_2-f_3)y=c_3-c_2$

and $S_3-S_1: 2(g_3-g_1)x+2(f_3-f_1)y=c_1-c_3$

Solve the three equations of radical axes, then we get the required radical center.

3.38 Properties of the Radical centres

1. The radical centre of the three circles described on the sides of a triangle as diameters is the ortho center of the triangle

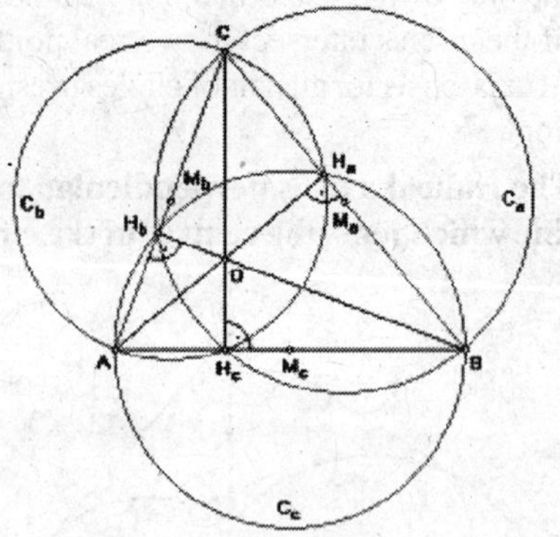

2. The radical centre of the three given circles will be the centre of a fourth circle, which cuts all the three circles orthogonally and the radius of the fourth circle is the length of the tangent drawn from radical centre of the three given circles to any of these circles.

1. The equation of the family of circles passing through the point of intersection of two given circles $S_1=0$ & $S_2=0$ is given by $S_1+\lambda S_2=0$, where λ is a parameter and $\lambda \neq -1$.

2. The equation of the family of circles passing through the point of intersection of a circle S = 0 and a line L = 0 is given by $S+\lambda L=0$, where λ is a parameter.

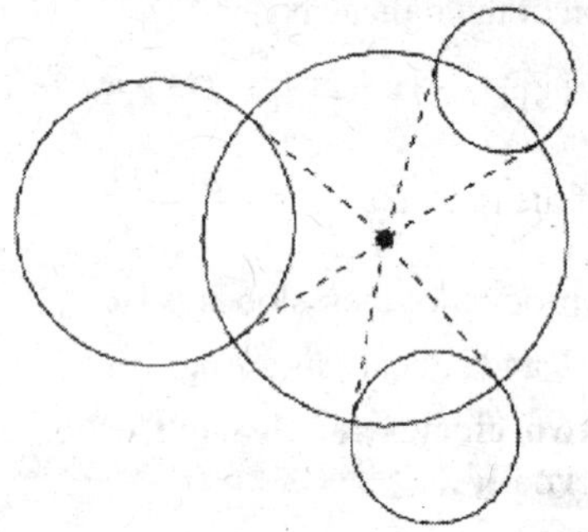

Let the fourth circle be $(x-h)^2+(y-k)^2=r^2$, where (h, k) is the centre of the circle and r be the radius. The centre of the circle is the radical centre of the given circles and r is the length of the tangent from (h, k) to any of the given three circles.

Ex-1. Find the radical axis of the two circles $x^2+y^2+4x+6y+9=0$ and $x^2+y^2+3x+8y+10=0$

Sol. Hence, the equation of the radical axis is

$$\left(x^2+y^2+4x+6y+9\right)-\left(x^2+y^2+3x+8y+10\right)=0$$

$\Rightarrow \quad (4x-3x)+(6y-8y)+(9-10)=0$

$\Rightarrow \quad x-2y-1=0$

Ex-2. Find the image of a point (2, 3) with respect to the radical axis of two circles $x^2+y^2+8x+2y+10=0$ and $x^2+y^2-2x-y-8=0$.

Sol. Hence, the equation of the radical axis is

$(x^2+y^2+8x+2y+10) - (x^2+y^2+7x+3y+10)=0$

$\Rightarrow \quad (8x-7x)+(2y-3y)=0$

$\Rightarrow \quad y=x$.

Hence, the image of (2, 3) with respect to the line $y=x$ is (3, 2).

Ex-3. Find the radical centre of the three circles $x^2+y^2=1$,

$x^2+y^2-8x+15=0$

and $x^2+y^2+10y+24=0$

Sol. Let $S_1: x^2+y^2=1$ ...(i)

$S_2: x^2+y^2-8x+15=0$ ...(ii)

and $S_3: x^2+y^2+10y+24=0$ ...(iii)

(i) - (ii), we get, $8x=16 \Rightarrow x=2$

(i) - (iii), we get, $-10y=25 \Rightarrow y=-5/2$

Hence, the radical centre is $\left(2, -\frac{5}{2}\right)$.

Ex-4. Find the equation of a circle, which cuts evvery member of the circles $x^2+y^2-3x-6y+14=0$,

$x^2+y^2-x-4y+8=0$

and $x^2+y^2+2x-6y+9=0$ orthogonally.

Sol. Let the equation of the circle be

$x^2+y^2+2gx+2fy+c=0$ ...(i)

The circle (i) is orthogonal to

$x^2+y^2-3x-6y+14=0$, $x^2+y^2-x-4y+8=0$

and $x^2+y^2+2x-6y+9=0$

Therefore, $2\left(g.\left(-\frac{3}{2}\right)-3f\right)=c+14$

$\Rightarrow \quad (-3g-6f)=c+14$ ...(ii)

$2\left(g.\left(-\frac{1}{2}\right)-2f\right)=c+8$

$\Rightarrow \quad (2g-4f)=c+8$ ...(iii)

and $2(g.1-3.f)=c+9$

$\Rightarrow \quad (2g-6f)=c+9$ ...(iv)

(iii) - (ii), we get, $5g+2f=-6$ ...(v)

(iii) - (iv), we get, $2f=-1 \Rightarrow f=-1/2$

Put the value of f in (v), we get, $g=-1$

Also, put the values of f and g in (iv), we get, $c=-8$.

Hence, the equation of the circle is

$x^2+y^2-2x-y-8=0$.

3.39 FAMILY OF CIRCLES

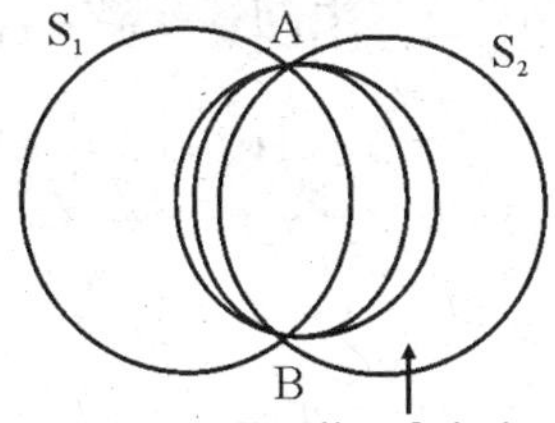

Family of circles

1. The equation of the family of circles passing through the point of intersection of two given circles $S_1=0$ & $S_2=0$ is given by $S_1+\lambda S_2=0$, where 1 is a parameter and $\lambda \neq -1$.
2. The equation of the family of circles passing through the point of intersection of a circle S = 0 and a line L = 0 is given by $S+\lambda L=0$, where λ is a parameter.
3. The equation of the family of circles touching the circle S = 0 and the line L = 0 is $S+\lambda L=0$ where λ is a parameter..
4. The equation of the family of circles passing through two given points $P(x_1, y_1)$ & $Q(x_2, y_2)$ can be written in the form

$$(x-x_1)(x-x_2)+(y-y_1)(y-y_2)+\lambda\begin{vmatrix} x & y & 1 \\ x_1 & y_1 & 1 \\ x_2 & y_2 & 1 \end{vmatrix}=0.$$

Ex-1. Find the equation of the circle passing through the points of intersection of the circles

$x^2+y^2+13x-3y=0$

and $2x^2+2y^2+4x-7y-25=0$ and the point (1, 1).

Sol. Equation of any circle passing through the point of intersect of the circles and $2x^2+2y^2+4x-7y-25=0$ is

$\Rightarrow \quad (4x^2+4y^2+30x-13y\text{-}25)=0$ ...(i)

Which is passing through (1, 1).

Therefore,

$(1+1+13-3)+\lambda(2+2+4-7-25)=0$

$\Rightarrow \quad 12-24\lambda=0 \quad \Rightarrow \quad \lambda=\frac{1}{2}$

Put the value of λ in (i), we get,

$(x^2+y^2+13x-3y)+\frac{1}{2}(2x^2+2y^2+4x-7y-25)=0$

$\Rightarrow \quad (2x^2+2y^2+26x-6y)$
$$+(2x^2+2y^2+4x-7y-25)=0$$
$\Rightarrow \quad (4x^2+4y^2+30x-13y\text{-}25)=0.$

Ex-2. If the circle $x^2+y^2+2x+3y+1=0$ cuts the circle $x^2+y^2+4x+3y+2=0$ in two points, say, A and B, then find the equation of the circle as AB as a diameter.

Sol. The equation of radical axis is

$(x^2+y^2+2x+3y+1)-(x^2+y^2+4x+3y+2)=0$

$\Rightarrow \quad (2x+3y+1)-(4x+3y+2)=0$

$\Rightarrow \quad 2x+1=0$

$\Rightarrow \quad x=-\frac{1}{2}.$

Thus, the equation of the circle is

$$(x^2+y^2+2x+3y+1)+\lambda(2x+1)=0$$

$\Rightarrow \quad (x^2+y^2+2(\lambda+1)x+3y+(1+\lambda))=0$

Since AB is diameter of the circle, so the centre lies on it.

Therefore, $-2?-2+1=0 \Rightarrow \lambda=-\frac{1}{2}.$

Hence, the equation of the circle is

$$(x^2+y^2+2x+3y+1)-\frac{1}{2}(2x+1)=0$$

$\Rightarrow \quad (x^2+y^2+2x+6y+1)=0$

Ex-3. Find the equation of the smallest circle passing through the intersection of the line x + y = 1 and the circle $x^2+y^2=9$.

Sol. Any circle passing through the point of intersection of the given line and the circle is

$x^2+y^2-9+?(x+y-1)=0$

$\Rightarrow \quad x^2+y^2+\lambda x+\lambda y-(9+\lambda)=0$

So the centre is $\left(-\frac{\lambda}{2},-\frac{\lambda}{2}\right)$.

Since , the circle is smallest, so the centre $\left(-\frac{\lambda}{2},-\frac{\lambda}{2}\right)$ lies on the chord $x+y=1$

Therefore, $-\frac{\lambda}{2}-\frac{\lambda}{2}=1 \Rightarrow \lambda=-1.$

Hence, the equation of the smallest circle is

$$x^2+y^2-9-(x+y-1)=0$$

$\Rightarrow \quad x^2+y^2-x-y-8=0$

Ex-4. Find the equation of the circle , which is passing through the point of intersection of the circles

$x^2+y^2-6x+2y+4=0$ and $x^2+y^2+2x-4y-6=0$ and its centre lies on the line y = x.

Sol. Equation of any circle passing through the point of intersection of the given circle is

$(x^2+y^2-6x+2y+4)+?(x^2+y^2+2x-4y-6)=0$

$\Rightarrow \quad (1+\lambda)x^2+(1+\lambda)y^2+2(\lambda-3)x+2$
$$(1-2\lambda)y+2(2-3\lambda)=0$$

$\Rightarrow \quad x^2+y^2+2\left(\frac{\lambda-3}{\lambda+1}\right)x+2\left(\frac{1-2\lambda}{\lambda+1}\right)y$
$$+\left(\frac{2(2-3\lambda)}{\lambda+1}\right)=0$$

So its centre is $\left(\frac{3\text{-}\lambda}{\lambda+1},\frac{2\lambda\text{-}1}{\lambda+1}\right)$.

Since, centre lies on the line y = x, $\frac{2\lambda\text{-}1}{\lambda+1}=\frac{3\text{-}\lambda}{\lambda+1}$

$\Rightarrow \quad 3\lambda=4 \quad \Rightarrow \quad \lambda=4/3$

Hence, the equation of the circle is

$$x^2+y^2-\frac{10}{7}x-\frac{10}{7}y-\frac{12}{7}=0.$$

Ex-5. Find the circle , whose diameter is the common chord of the circles $x^2+y^2+2x+3y+1=0$ and $x^2+y^2+4x+3y+2=0$.

Sol. The given circles are $x^2+y^2+2x+3y+1=0$ and $x^2+y^2+4x+3y+2=0$.

Hence, the equation of the common chord is $2x+1=0$

Therefore, the equation of the circle is

$x^2+y^2+2x+3y+1+?(x^2+y^2+4x+3y+2)=0$ ...(i)

$\Rightarrow \quad (1+\lambda)x^2+(1+\lambda)y^2+2(1+2\lambda)x+3$
$$(1+\lambda)y+(1+2\lambda)=0$$

$\Rightarrow \quad x^2+y^2+2\left(\frac{1+2\lambda}{(1+?)}\right)x+3y+\frac{(1+2\lambda)}{(1+\lambda)}=0$

So, its centre is $\left(-\frac{1+2\lambda}{\lambda+1},-\frac{3}{2}\right)$

Since $2x+1=0$ is the diameter , so centre lies on it .

Therefore, $2\left(-\frac{1+2\lambda}{\lambda+1}\right)+1=0$

$\Rightarrow \quad -2-4\lambda+\lambda+1=0$

$\Rightarrow \quad \lambda=-\frac{1}{3}.$

Hence, the equation of the circle (i) is

$$2(x^2+y^2)+2x+6y+1=0.$$

Level – I QUESTIONS BASED ON FUNDAMENTALS

ABC of Circles

1. Find the centre and radius of the following circles :
   (i) $x^2+y^2=4$
   (ii) $x^2+y^2+4x+6y=3$.
   (iii) $x^2+y^2+4x+6y+13=0$
   (iv) $x^2+y^2-x=0$
   (v) $x^2+y^2-2y-3=0$
   (vi) $x^2+y^2-x-y=0$
2. Find the centre and radius of the circle $2x^2+2y^2=3x-5y+7$
3. Prove that the radii of the circles $x^2+y^2=1, x^2+y^2-2x-6y=6$ and $x^2+y^2-4x-12y=9$ are in AP.
4. Find the equation of the circle whose centre is the point of intersection of the lines $2x-3y+4=0$ and $3x+4y-5=0$ and passes through the origin.
5. Find the equation of the circle concentric with the circle $x^2+y^2-8x+6y-5=0$ and passing through the point (–2, –7)
6. Find the equation of the circle passing through the center of the circle $x^2+y^2-4x-6y=8$ and being concentric with the circle $x^2+y^2-2x-8y=5$
7. Find the equation of the circle passing through the point of intersection of $x+3y=0$ and $2x-7y=0$ and whose center is the point of intersection of lines $x+y+1=0$ and $x-2y+4=0$.
8. Find the of the circle touching the lines $4x-3y=30$ and $4x-3y+10=0$ having the centre on the line $2x+y=0$.
9. A circle of radius 4 units touches the co-ordinate axes in the first quadrant. Find the equation of its image with respect to the line mirror $y=0$.
10. Let the equation of a circle is
    $$x^2+y^2+16x-24y+183=0.$$
    Find the equation of the image of this circle by the line mirror $4x+7y+13=0$.
11. Find the centre of the circle which is inscribed in the triangle formed by the lines $3x+4y=15, 3x-4y=7$ and $12x+5y=115$.
12. Find the area of an equilateral triangle inscribed in the circle $x^2+y^2+2gx+2fy+c=0$
13. Prove that the locus of the centre of the circle
    $$\frac{1}{2}(x^2+y^2)+x\cos\theta+y\sin\theta-4=0 \text{ is } x^2+y^2=1.$$
14. One of the diameters of the circle circumscribing the rectangle ABCD is $4y=x+7$. If A and B are the points (-3, 4) and (5, 4) respectively. , then find the area of the rectangle.
15. A circle has radius 3 units and its centre lies on the line $y=x-1$. Find the equation of the circle if it passes through (7, 3).
16. Show that the line $3x-4y=c$ will meet the circle having centre at (2, 4) and the radius 5 in real and distict points if $-35<c<15$.

Parametric Equation

17. Find the parametric equation of the following circles:
    (i) $x^2+y^2=4$ (ii) $x^2+y^2=9$
    (iii) $x^2+y^2-x=0$ (iv) $(x-h)^2+(y-k)^2=a^2$
    (v) $x^2+y^2+x+y=0$ (vi) $x^2+y^2-x-y=0$.
18. Find the point P on the circle $x^2+y^2-4x-6y+9=0$ such that $\angle POX$ is minimum, where O is the origin and OX is the x-axis.
19. Find the point Q on the circle $x^2+y^2-10y+24=0$ such that $\angle QOX$ is maximum, where O is the origin and OX is the x-axis.

Diametric form of a Circle

20. Find the equation of the circle when the end points of a diameter are (2, 3) and (6, 9)
21. Find the equation of the circle the end points of whose diameter are the centres of the circles
    $x^2+y^2+6x-14y=1$ and $x^2+y^2-4x+10y=2$.
22.. If (4, 1) be an extremity of a diameter of the circle $x^2+y^2-2x+6y-15=0$, find the co-ordinates of the other extremity of the diameter.
23. The sides of a square are $x=2, x=3, y=1$ and $y=2$. Find the equation of the circle drawn on the diagonals of the square as its diameter.

Equation of a circle passing through three non-collinear points :

24. Find the equation of the circle passing through (0, 0), (a, 0) and (0, b).
25. Find the equation of a circle passing through (1, 2), (4, 5) and (0, 9).
26. Find the equation of the circle passing through the three non-collinear points (1, 1) (2, –1) and (3, 2).
27. Find the equation of the circle which passes through the points (4, 1), (6, 5) and has its centre on the line $4x+y=16$.
28. Find the equation of the circle passing through (0, 0) and the points where the straight line $3x+4y=12$, meets the axes of co-ordinates.

29. Show that the four points (1, 0), (2, –7), (8, 1) and (9, –6) are concyclic.

30. If the points (2, 0), (0, 1), (4, 5) and (0, c) are concyclic, then the value of c.

31. Find the centre of the circle inscribed in the square formed by the lines $x^2 - 8x + 12 = 0$ and $y^2 - 14y + 45 = 0$.

32 Find the equationof the circle which passes through the points (1, 1), (2, 2) and whose radius is 1.

33 Find the equation of a circle passing through the point (1, 2) and (3, 4) and touching the line $3x + y = 3$.

34. Find the equation of the circles passing through (-4, 3) and touching the lines $x + y = 2$ and $x - y = 2$.

35. If $\left(m_i, \frac{1}{m_i}\right)$; i = 1, 2, 3, 4 are four distinct points on a circle, show that $m_1 m_2 m_3 m_4 = 1$.

Intercepts made on the axes by a circle:

36. Find the length of x-intercept to the circle $x^2 + y^2 + 4x + 6y - 7 = 0$

37. Find the length of y-intercept to the circle $x^2 + y^2 - x - y = 0$

38. Find the equation of the circle whose centre is (3, -1) and which cut off an intercept of length 6 from the line $2x - 5y + 18 = 0$.

39. Find the equations to the circles touching y-axis at (0, 3) and making intercepts of 8 units on the x-axis.

40. Find the equation of the circle whose diameter is the line joining the points (-4, 3) and (12, -1). Find also the intercept made by it on y-axis.

Various forms of a circle :

41. Find the equation of the circle which touches the axes and whose centre lies on the line $x - 2y = 3$.

42. Find the equation of the circle which passes through the origin and makes intercept of length of a and b on the x and y axes respectively.

43. Show that the circle $x^2 + y^2 - 2ax - 2by + a^2 = 0$ touches both the co-ordinate axes.

44. If a circle of constant radius 3k passes through the origin and meets the axes at A and B, then prove that the locus of the centroid of ? AOB is $x^2 + y^2 = 4k^2$.

45. A circle of radius 2 lies in the first quadrant and touches both the axes of co-ordinates. Find the equation of the circle with centre of (6, 5) and touching the above circle externally.

46. A circle of radius 5 units touches the co-ordinate axes in first quadrant. If the circle makes one complete roll on x-axis along the positive direction of x-axis, find its equation in the new position.

47. The circle $x^2 + y^2 - 4x - 8y + 16 = 0$ rolls up the tangent to it at $(2 + \sqrt{3}, 3)$ by 2 units, assuming the x-axis as horizontal, find the equation of the circle in the new position.

Position of a point w.r.t a circle:

48. Discuss the position of the points (1, 2) and (6, 0) with respect to the circle $x^2 + y^2 - 4x + 2y - 11 = 0$

49. Find the shortest and largest distance from the point (2, –7) to the circle $x^2 + y^2 - 14x - 10y - 151 = 0$

50. Find the greatest distance of the point (10, 7) from the circle $x^2 + y^2 - 4x - 2y - 20 = 0$.

51. If the point $(\lambda, -\lambda)$ lies inside the circle $x^2 + y^2 - 4x + 2y - 8 = 0$, then find range of λ.

Intersection of a line and a circle :

52. Find the points of intersection of the line $4x - 3y = 10$ and the circle $x^2 + y^2 - 2x + 4y = 20$.

53. Find the length of the chord $4x - 3y = 5$ of the circle $x^2 + y^2 + 3x - y = 10$.

54. Find the length of the chord of the circle $x^2 + y^2 = 16$ which bisects the join of the points (2, 3) and (1, 2) perpendicularity.

Tangents and tangency

55. Find the equation of the tangent to the circle at the indicated points :
    (i) $x^2 + y^2 = 5$ at the point (2, 1)
    (ii) $x^2 + y^2 = 9$ at the point $(1, 2\sqrt{2})$
    (iii) $x^2 + y^2 + 2x + 3y + 7 = 0$ at the point (2, 3)

56. Prove that the tangents to the circle $x^2 + y^2 = 25$ at (3, 4) and (4, –3) are perpendicular to each other.

57. Find the equation of tangent to the circle $x^2 + y^2 - 2ax = 0$ at the point $[a(1 + \cos\alpha), a\sin\alpha]$.

58. Find the equation of the tangents to the circle $x^2 + y^2 = 9$, which
    (i) are parallel to the line $3x + 4y - 5 = 0$
    (ii) are perpendicular to the line $2x + 3y + 7 = 0$
    (iii) make an angle of 60° witht the x-axis.

59. Find the area of the triangle formed by the tangent at the point (a, b) to the circle $x^2 + y^2 = r^2$ and the co-ordinate axes.

60. Find the equation of the tangent to the circle $x^2 + y^2 + 4x - 4y + 4 = 0$ which make equal intercepts on the positive co-ordinate axes.

61. The lines $3x - 4y = 6$ and $6x - 8y - 7 = 0$ are tangents to the same circle. Then find its radius.

62. Prove that the line $y = mx + c$ will be a tangent to the circle $x^2 + y^2 = a^2$ if $c^2 = a^2(1+m^2)$.

63. Find the value of λ so that the line $3x - 4y = \lambda$ may touch the circle $x^2 + y^2 - 4x - 8y - 5 = 0$.

64. Find the equations of the tangents to the circle $x^2 + y^2 = 16$ drawn from the point (1, 4).

65. Find the equation of the family of circle which touch the pair of straight lines $x^2 - y^2 + 2y - 1 = 0$

66. Find the equation of the tangent to the circle $x^2 + y^2 - 6x + 4y - 12 = 0$ which are parallel to the line $4x + 3y + 5 = 0$.

67. Find the equations of the pair of tangents drawn to the circle $x^2 + y^2 - 2x + 4y = 0$ from the pt (0, 1).

Length of the Tangents :

68. Find the length of tangents drawn from the point (3, –4) to the circle $2x^2 + 2y^2 - 7x - 9y - 13 = 0$.

69. If the length of tangent from (f, g) to the circle $x^2 + y^2 = 6$ be twice the length of the tangent from (f, g) to circle $x^2 + y^2 + 3x + 3y = 0$ then prove that $f^2 + g^2 + 4f + 4g + 2 = 0$.

70. Show that the length of the tangent from any point on the circle $x^2 + y^2 + 2gx + 2fy + c = 0$ to the circle $x^2 + y^2 + 2gx + 2fy + c_1 = 0$ is $\sqrt{(c_1 - c)}$.

71. Find the area of the quadrilateral formed by a pair of tangents from the point (4, 5) to the circle $x^2 + y^2 - 4x - 2y - 11 = 0$ and a pair of its radii.

Power of a Point

72. Find the power of point (2, 4) with respect to the circle $x^2 + y^2 - 6x + 4y - 8 = 0$.

73. Find the prower of the point (2, 3) with respect to the circle $(x-4)^2 + (y-5)^2 = 4$

Normals and normalcy

74. Find the equation of the normal to the circle $x^2 + y^2 - 5x + 2y - 48 = 0$ at the point (6, 6).

75. Find the equation of the normal to the circle $x^2 + y^2 = 2x$, which is parallel to the line $x + 2y = 3$.

76. Find the equation of the normal to the circle $x^2 + y^2 = 2x$ which is perpendicular to the line $x + 2y = 5$.

77. Find the condition when a line $y = mx + c$ will be a normal to the circle $x^2 + y^2 = a^2$.

78. Find the equation of a circle having the pair of lines $x^2 + 2xy + 3x + 6y = 0$ as its normals and having the size just sufficient to obtain the circle $x(x-4) + y(y-3) = 0$.

79. Show that the area of the triangle formed by the positive x-axis, the normal and the tangent to the circle $x^2 + y^2 = 4$ at $(1, \sqrt{3})$ is $2\sqrt{3}$.

80. The normal at the point (3, 4) on a circle cuts the circle at the point (-1, -2). Then find the equation of the circle.

Chord of Contact

81. Find the equation of the chord of contact to the circle $x^2 + y^2 = 9$ at the point (3, 4).

82. The chord of contact of tangents drawn from a point on the circle $x^2 + y^2 = a^2$ to the circle $x^2 + y^2 = b^2$ and touches the circle $x^2 + y^2 = c^2$. Show that a, b, c are in GP.

83. Find the condition that chord of contact of any external point (h, k) to the circle $x^2 + y^2 = a^2$ should subtend a right angle at the centre of the circle.

Chord Bisected at a point

84. Find the equation of the chord of $x^2 + y^2 - 6x + 10y - 9 = 0$ which is bisected at (–2, 4).

85. Through a fixed point (h, k), secants are drawn to the circle $x^2 + y^2 = r^2$. Show that the locus of mid point of the portion of secants intercepted by the circle is $x^2 + y^2 = hx + ky$.

86. Prove that the locus of the mid point of a chord of the circle $x^2 + y^2 = 4$, which subtends a right angle at the origin is $x^2 + y^2 = 2$.

Director Circle :

87. Find the angle between the two tangents from the origin to the circle $(x-7)^2 + (y+1)^2 = 25$.

88. If the tangents drawn from the origin to the circle $x^2 + y^2 - 2kx - 2ry + r^2 = 0$ are perpendicular, then find a relation between k and r.:

89 The perpendicular tangents to the circle $x^2 + y^2 = a^2$ meet at at P. Then prove taht the locus of P is $x^2 + y^2 = 2a^2$.

90. If P is the point of intersection of two perpendicular tangents to the circle $x^2 + y^2 - 2y = 0$, then find the locus of P.

91. Prove that the angle between the pair of tangents from the point (1, 1/2) to the circle

$x^2 + y^2 + 4x + 2y - 4 = 0$ is $\cos^{-1}\left(\frac{3}{5}\right)$ or $\sin^{-1}\left(\frac{4}{5}\right)$

Diameter :

92. Find the equation of the diameter of the circle $x^2 + y^2 = 9$ which corresponds to the chord $x + 2y = 5$..

93. Find the equation of the diameter of the circle $x^2+y^2+2gx+2fy+c=0$ which corresponds to the chord $ax+by+d=0$.

Pole and Polar :

94. Find the equation of the polar w.r.t the circle $x^2+y^2=9$ at the point (3, 5).

95 Find the locus of the pole of the line $lx+my+n=0$ with respect to the circle which touches y-axis at the origin.

96. Find the pole of the straight line $9x+y-28=0$ with respect to the circle $2x^2-2y^2-3x+5y-7=0$

When two circles touch each other :

97. Examine if the two circles $x^2+y^2-2x-4y=0$ and $x^2+y^2-8y-4=0$ touch each other externally or internally.

98. Prove that the circles $x^2+y^2+c^2=2ax$ and $x^2+y^2+c^2-2by=0$ will touch each other externally, if $\frac{1}{a^2}+\frac{1}{b^2}=\frac{1}{c^2}$.

The intersection of two Circles:

99. Find the number of common tangents that can be drawn to the circles $x^2+y^2-4x-6y-3=0$ and $x^2+y^2+2x+2y+1=0$.

100. Find all the common tangents to the circles $x^2+y^2-2x-6y+9=0$ and $x^2+y^2+6x-2y+1=0$.

Common Chord of two Circles:

101. Prove that the length of the common chord f the two circles:

$(x-a)^2+(y-b)^2=c^2$ and $(x-b)^2+(y-a)^2=c^2$ is $\sqrt{4c^2-2(a-b)^2}$.

find also the condition when the given circles touch.

102. Find the circle whose diameter is the common chord of the circles $x^2+y^2+2x+3y+1=0$ and $x^2+y^2+4x+3y+2=0$.

Family of Circles

103. Find the equation of the circle passing through (1, 1) and the point of intersection of the circles

$x^2+y^2+13x-3y=0$

and $2x^2+2y^2+4x-7y-25=0$

104. Find the equations of the circle passing through the point of intersection of the circles $x^2+y^2-6x+2y+4=0$, $x^2+y^2+2x-4y-6=0$ and with its centre on the line $y=x$.

105. Find the equation of the circle through points of intersection of the circle $x^2+y^2-2x-4y+4=0$ and the line $x+2y=4$ which touches the line $x+2y=0$.

106. Find the equation of the circle described on the common chord of the circles $x^2+y^2+2x=0$ and $x^2+y^2+2y=0$ as diameter.

107. Find the equation of the diameter of the circle $3(x^2+y^2)-2x+6y-9=0$ which is perpendicular to the line $2x+3y=12$.

108. If the circle $x^2+y^2+4x+22y+c=0$ bisects the circumference of the circle $x^2+y^2-2x+8y-d=0$, then find the value of $c+d+2012$.

Angle of intersection of two Circles/ Orthogonal Circles

109. Find the angle between the circles

$S: x^2+y^2-4x+6y+11=0$

and $S': x^2+y^2-2x+8y+13=0$

110. Show that the circles $x^2+y^2-6x+4y+4=0$ and $x^2+y^2+x+4y+1=0$ cut orthogonally.

111. Find the equations of the two circles which intersect the circles $x^2+y^2-6y+1=0$ and $x^2+y^2-4y+1=0$ orthogonally and touch the line $3x+4y+5=0$.

112. Prove that the two circles, which pass through (0, a), (0, -a) and touch the line $y=mx+c$ will cut orthogonally, if $c^2=a^2(2+m^2)$.

113. Find the equation of the circle which cuts orthogonally each of the three circles given below :

$x^2+y^2-2x+3y-7=0$, $x^2+y^2+5x-5y+9=0$ and $x^2+y^2+7x-9x+29=0$.

Radical Axis

114. Find the equation of the radical axis to the circles $x^2+y^2+4x+6y+9=0$ and $x^2+y^2+x+y-1=0$

115. Find the radical centre of circles $x^2+y^2+3x+2y+1=0$, $x^2+y^2-x+6y+5=0$ and $x^2+y^2+5x-8y+15=0$. Also find the equation of the circle cutting them orthogonally.

116. Find the radical centre of three circles described on the three sides $4x-7y+10=0$, $x+y-5=0$ and $7x+4y-15=0$ of a triangle as diameters.

117. Find the radical centre of the circles $x^2+y^2=1$, $x^2+y^2+10y+24=0$ and $x^2+y^2-8x+15=0$

118. Find the co-ordinates of the point from which the lengths of the tangents to the following three circles be equal $3x^2+3y^2+4x-6y-1=0$, $2x^2+2y^2-3x-2y-4=0$ and $2x^2+2y^2-x+y-1=0$.

Coaxial System of Circles/Limiting point

119. Find the equation of the system of circles co-axial with the circles $x^2+y^2+4x+2y+1=0$, $x^2+y^2-2x+6y-6=0$.

Also, find the equation of that particular circle whose centre lies on the radical axis.

120. Find the co-ordinates of the limiting points of the system of circles determined by the two circles

$x^2+y^2+5x+y+4=0$ and $x^2+y^2+10x-4y-1=0$

121. If the origin be one limiting point of a system of co-axial circles of which $x^2+y^2+3x+4y+25=0$ is a member, find the other limiting point.

122. If (1, 2) is a limiting point of the co-axial system of circles containing the circle

$x^2+y^2+x-5y+9=0$, then the equation of the radical axis is :

(a) $x-9y+4=0$ (b) $3x-y+4=0$

(c) $x+3y-4=0$ (d) $9x+y-4=0$

123. One of the limiting points of the co-axial system of circles containing the circles $x^2+y^2-4=0$ and $x^2+y^2-x-y=0$ is :

(a) $(\sqrt{2}, \sqrt{2})$ (b) $(-\sqrt{2}, \sqrt{2})$

(c) $(-\sqrt{2}, -\sqrt{2})$ (d) none of these

124 Find the equation of a circle which is co-axial with the circles $x^2+y^2+4x+2y+1=0$ and $x^2+y^2-x+3y=3/2$.

ANSWER

1. (i) (0, 0) ; 2 (ii) (-2, -3) ; 4

(iii) (-2, -3) ; 0 (iv) $\left(\frac{1}{2}, 0\right); \frac{1}{2}$

(v) (0, 1) ; 2 (vi) $\left(\frac{1}{2}, \frac{1}{2}\right); \frac{1}{\sqrt{2}}$

2. $\left(\frac{3}{4}, -\frac{5}{4}\right); \frac{3}{2}\sqrt{5}$

3. $x^2+y^2+\frac{2}{17}x+\frac{44}{17}y=0$

4. $(x-4)^2+(y+3)^2=52$

6. $x^2+y^2-2x-8y+15=0$

7. $x^2+y^2+4x-2y=0$

8. $x^2+y^2-2x-3y=\frac{51}{4}$

9. $x^2+y^2-8x+8y+16=0$

10. $x^2+y^2+32x+4y+235=0$

11. (7, 1)

12. $\frac{3\sqrt{3}}{4}\times\left(g^2+f^2-c\right)$

14. 32 s. u.

15. $x^2+y^2-8x-6y+16=0$ and $x^2+y^2-14x-12y+76=0$.

17. (i) $x=2\cos\theta$, $y=2\sin\theta$

(ii) $x=3\cos\theta$, $y=3\sin\theta$

(iii) $x=\frac{1}{2}+\frac{1}{2}\cos\theta$, $y=\frac{1}{2}\sin\theta$

(iv) $x=h+a\cos\theta$, $y=k+a\sin\theta$

(v) $x=-\frac{1}{2}+\frac{1}{\sqrt{2}}\cos\theta$, $y=-\frac{1}{2}+\frac{1}{\sqrt{2}}\sin\theta$

(vi) $x=\frac{1}{2}+\frac{1}{\sqrt{2}}\cos\theta$, $y=\frac{1}{2}+\frac{1}{\sqrt{2}}\sin\theta$

18. $P=\left(2+\frac{4}{\sqrt{13}}, 3+\frac{6}{\sqrt{13}}\right)$

19. $P=\left(-\frac{2\sqrt{6}}{5}, \frac{24}{5}\right)$

20. $x^2+y^2-8x-12y+39=0$

21. $x^2+y^2+x-2y-41=0$

22. $x^2+y^2-2x+6y-15=0$

23. $x^2+y^2-5x-3y+8=0$

24. $x^2+y^2-ax-by=0$

26. $x^2+y^2-5x-y+4=0$

27. $x^2+y^2-6x-8y+15=0$

28. $x^2+y^2-4x-3y=0$

29. $c=14/3$

31. (4, 7)

32. $x^2+y^2-4x-2y+4=0$

33. $x^2+y^2-8x-2y+7=0$

34. $x^2+y^2+2\left(10\pm3\sqrt{6}\right)x+\left(55\pm24\sqrt{6}\right)=0$.

and $x^2+y^2-3x-7y+12=0$.

36. 8

37. $\sqrt{2}$

38. $x^2+y^2-6x+2y-28=0$.

39. $x^2+y^2\pm10x-6y+9=0$.

40. $4\sqrt{13}$

41. $x^2+y^2+6x+6y+9=0$ or $x^2+y^2+2x-2y+1=0$ or $x^2+y^2-2x-2y+1=0$

42. $x^2+y^2 \pm ax \pm by = 0$.

45. $x^2+y^2-12x-10y+52=0$

46. $x^2+y^2-10(2p+1)x-10y+(100p^2+100p+25)=0$

47. $x^2+y^2-6x-2(4+\sqrt{3})y+(24+8\sqrt{3})=0$.

48. (1, 2) lies inside the circle and (6, 0) lies outside of the circle.

49. Shortest distance = 2 ; Largest distance = 28

50. Largest distance = 15

51. $-1<\lambda<4$

52. (4, 2), (-2, -6)

53. $5\sqrt{2}$

54. $4\sqrt{2}$

55. (i) $2x+y=5$ (ii) $x+2\sqrt{2}y=9$

(iii) $2x+3y+9=0$

57. $(1-a)(1+\cos\alpha)\,x+(\sin\alpha)\,y=0$

58. (i) $3x+4y\pm15=0$

(ii) $3x-2y\pm3\sqrt{13}=0$

(iii) $y=\sqrt{3}x+6$

59. $\dfrac{r^4}{2|ab|}$

60. $x+y=\pm2\sqrt{2}$

61. $\pi\times\left(\dfrac{19}{10}\right)^2$

63. 14, -36

64. $y=4,\ 8x+15y=68$

66. $4x+3y+19=0,\ 4x+3y-31=0$.

67. $2x-y+1=0,\ x+y-2=0$

68. $2\sqrt{13}$

71. 8 sq. units.

72. 16.

73. 4

74. $2x-y=6$

75. $x+2y=1$

76. $2x-y=2$

77. $c=0$

78. $x^2+y^2+6x-3y=45$

80. $x^2+y^2-2x-2y=11$

81. $3x+4y=9$

83. $h^2+k^2=2a^2$.

84. $5x-9y+46=0$

87. $\pi/2$

88. $k=r$, $k=-r$, $k^2=r^2$.

89. $x^2+y^2-2y-1=0$

92. $2x-y=0$

93. $bx-ay+bg-af=0$

94. $3x+5y=9$

96. $y(lx-n)=mx^2$

97. Internally

99. 3

100. $x=0,\ 3x+4y=10,\ y=4,\ 4x=3y$.

102. $2(x^2+y^2)+2x+6y+1=0$.

103. $4(x^2+y^2)+30x-13y-25=0$

104. $7(x^2+y^2)-10x-4y-12=0$.

105. $x^2+y^2-x-2y=0$

106. $x^2+y^2+x+y=0$

107. $3x-2y-3=0$

108. 2062.

109. 135°

111. $x^2+y^2-1=0$ and $4x^2+4y^2-15x-4=0$

113. $x^2+y^2-16x-18y-4=0$

114. $3x+5y+8=0$.

115. $x^2+y^2-6x-4y-14=0$

116. (1,2)

117. (2,3/2)

118. $\left(-\dfrac{16}{21},-\dfrac{31}{63}\right)$

119. $6x-4y+7=0$; $26(x^2+y^2)+98x+56y+9=0$

120. (-2,-1), (0,-3)

121. (-6,-8)

122. $3x-y+4=0$

123. $(-\sqrt{2},-\sqrt{2})$

124. $5(x^2+y^2)+6x+10y-3=0$

Level – II FOR JEE MAIN AND ADVANCED EXAMS ONLY

1. The equation $ax^2 + 2hxy + by^2 + 2gx + 2fy + c = 0$ represents a circle if
(a) a = b , c = 0 (b) a = b , h = 0
(c) a = b , g = 0 (d) a = b , f = 0

2. The equation of the circle passing through the points (0, 0), (1, 0) and (0, 1) is
(a) $x^2 + y^2 + x + y = 0$ (b) $x^2 + y^2 - x + y = 0$
(c) $x^2 + y^2 - x - y = 0$ (d) $x^2 + y^2 - x = 0$

3. The equation $x^2 + y^2 + 4x + 6y + 13 = 0$ represents a
(a) point
(b) circle
(c) pair of straight lines
(d) a pair of coincident lines.

4. The circle $x^2 + y^2 + 4x - 7y + 12 = 0$ cuts an intecept on y-axis is
(a) 7 (b) 4 (c) 3 (d) 1

5. The equation of the daimeter of the circle $x^2 + y^2 - 6x + 2y - 8 = 0$ is
(a) x + 3 y = 0 (b) x = 3y (c) x = 2 y (d) x + 2 y = 0.

6. The length of tangent drawn from any point on the circle
$$x^2 + y^2 + 4x + 6y + 4 = 0$$
to the circle $x^2 + y^2 + 4x + 6y + 11 = 0$ is
(a) 4 (b) $\sqrt{7}$ (c) $\sqrt{15}$ (d) $\sqrt{17}$

7. The value of c for which the points (2, 0), (0, 1) (0, 5) and (0, c) are concyclic, is
(a) 1 (b) 2 (c) 3 (d) 4

8. The equation of a circle passing through the origin is $x^2 + y^2 - 4x + 6y = 0$, then the equation of the diameter is
(a) x = y (b) 3 x + 2 y = 0
(c) y = 3 x (d) 3 x - 4 y = 0.

9. The equation of the common chord of the circles $x^2 + y^2 - 4x + 6y = 0$ and $x^2 + y^2 - 6x + 4y - 12 = 0$ is
(a) x + y + 6 = 0 (b) x - y + 6 = 0
(c) x - y - 6 = 0 (d) - x + y + 6 = 0

10. The circumcentre of the triangle whose vertices are (0, 0), (2, 0) and (0, 2) is
(a) (1, 2) (b) (2, 2) (c) (1, 1) (d) (-2, -2)

11. If the lines $a_1x + b_1y + c_1 = 0$ and $a_2x + b_2y + c_2 = 0$ cut the x-axis and y-axis in four concyclic points, then
(a) $a_1a_2 = b_1b_2$ (b) $a_1b_1 = a_2b_2$
(c) $a_1b_2 = a_2b_1$ (d) None.

12. If the circles $x^2 + y^2 + 2g_1x + 2f_1y = 0$ and $x^2 + y^2 + 2g_2x + 2f_2y = 0$ touch each other, then
(a) $g_1g_2 + f_1f_2 = 0$ (b) $g_1g_2 = f_1f_2$
(c) $g_1f_2 = f_1g_2$ (d) None.

13. Any point on the circle $x^2 + y^2 - 4x - 4y + 4 = 0$ can be taken as
(a) $(2 + 2\cos\theta,\ 2 + 2\sin\theta)$
(b) $(2 - 2\cos\theta,\ 2 - 2\sin\theta)$
(c) $(2 - 2\cos\theta,\ 2 + 2\sin\theta)$
(d) $(2 + 2\cos\theta,\ 2 - 2\sin\theta)$

14. The equation of the chord of the circle $x^2 + y^2 = 25$ whose mid-point is (2, -5) is
(a) 3 x - 2 y = 11 (b) 2 x - 3 y = 13
(c) 2 x + 3 y = 10 (d) 3 x + 2 y = 11

15. The value of λ for which the line $3x - 4y = \lambda$ touches the circle $x^2 + y^2 = 16$ is
(a) 4 (b) 20 (c) 15 (d) 10

16. The locus of the point of intersection of two perpendicular tangents to the circle $x^2 + y^2 = 1006$ is
(a) $x^2 + y^2 = 2012$ (b) $x^2 + y^2 = 2020$
(c) $x^2 + y^2 = 2010$ (d) $x^2 + y^2 = 2000$

17. The equation of the normal to the circle
$$x^2 + y^2 - 2x - 2y + 1 = 0,$$
which is parallel to the line 2 x + 4 y = 3 is
(a) x + 2 y = 3 (b) x + 2 y + 3 = 0
(c) 2 x + 4 y = - 3 (d) None.

18. The image of the center of the circle $x^2 + y^2 - 2x - 6y + 1 = 0$ to the line mirror y = x is
(a) (1, 3) (b) (3, 1) (c) (1, -3) (d) (-3, 1)

19. The length of the common chord of the circles $x^2 + y^2 + 2x + 3y + 1 = 0$ and $x^2 + y^2 + 3x + 2y + 1 = 0$ is
(a) $3\sqrt{2}$ (b) $\frac{1}{3\sqrt{2}}$ (c) $\frac{3}{\sqrt{2}}$ (d) $\frac{\sqrt{2}}{3}$

20. The number of common tangents to the circles $x^2 + y^2 + 2x - 8y - 23 = 0$ and $x^2 + y^2 - 4x - 10y + 19 = 0$ is

(a) 4 (b) 2 (c) 3 (d) 1.

21. The angle between the tangents drawn from the origin to the circle $(x-7)^2+(y+1)^2=25$ is

(a) $\pi/3$ (b) $\pi/6$ (c) $\pi/2$ (d) $\pi/4$

22. The ends of a quadrant of a circle have the co-ordinates (1, 3) and (3, 1), then the centre of such a circle is

(a) (1,1) (b) (2,2) (c) (2,6) (d) (4,4)

23. The line $2x-y+1=0$ is a tangent to the circle at the point (2, 5) and the centre of the circles lies on $x-2y=4$. The radius of the circle is

(a) $3\sqrt{5}$ (b) $5\sqrt{3}$ (c) $2\sqrt{5}$ (d) $5\sqrt{2}$

24. Two circles of radii 4 cms and 1 cm touch each other externally and θ is the angle contained by their direct common tangents. Then sin θ is

(a) 24/25 (b) 12/25 (c) 3/4 (d) None

25. The locus of poles whose polar with respect to $x^2+y^2=a^2$ always pass through (k, 0) is

(a) $kx-a^2=0$ (b) $kx+a^2=0$

(c) $ky+a^2=0$ (d) $ky-a^2=0$

26. The locus of the midpoints of the chords of the circle $x^2+y^2-ax-by=0$ which subtend a right angle at $\left(\frac{a}{2},\frac{b}{2}\right)$ is

(a) $ax+by=0$

(b) $ax+by=a^2+b^2$

(c) $x^2+y^2-ax-by+\frac{a^2+b^2}{8}=0$

(d) $x^2+y^2-ax-by-\frac{a^2+b^2}{8}=0$

27. From (3, 4) chords are drawn to the circle $x^2+y^2-4x=0$. The locus of the mid-points of the chords is

(a) $x^2+y^2-5x-4y+6=0$

(b) $x^2+y^2+5x-4y+6=0$

(c) $x^2+y^2-5x+4y+6=0$

(d) $x^2+y^2-5x-4y-6=0$

28. The lines $y-y_1=m(x-x_1)\pm a\sqrt{1+m^2}$ are tangents to the same circle. The radius of the circle is

(a) a / 2 (b) a (c) 2 a (d) None

29. The centre of the smallest circle touching to the circles $x^2+y^2-2y-3=0$ and $x^2+y^2-8x-18y+93=0$ is

(a) (3,2) (b) (4,4) (c) (2,7) (d) (2,5)

30. The ends of the base of an isosceles triangle are at (2, 0) and (0, 1) and the equation of one side is $x=2$, then the orthocenter of the triangle is

(a) $\left(\frac{3}{4},\frac{3}{2}\right)$ (b) $\left(\frac{5}{4},1\right)$ (c) $\left(\frac{3}{4},1\right)$ (d) $\left(\frac{4}{3},\frac{7}{12}\right)$

31. A rhombus is inscribed in the region common to the two circles $x^2+y^2-4x-12=0$ and $x^2+y^2+4x-12=0$ with two of its vertices on the line joining the centres of the circles. Then the area of the rhombus is

(a) $8\sqrt{3}$ sq. units (b) $4\sqrt{3}$ sq. units

(c) $16\sqrt{3}$ sq. units (d) None.

32. The angle between the two tangents from the origin to the circles $(x-7)^2+(y+1)^2=25$ is

(a) $\pi/4$ (b) $\pi/3$ (c) $\pi/2$ (d) None.

33. The equation of the circle having normal at (3, 3) as the straight line $y=x$ and passing through the point (2, 2) is

(a) $x^2+y^2-5x+5y+12=0$

(b) $x^2+y^2+5x-5y+12=0$

(c) $x^2+y^2-5x-5y-12=0$

(d) $x^2+y^2-5x-5y+12=0$

34. In a right triangle ABC, right angled at A, on the leg AC as diameter, a semi – circle is described. The chord joining A with the point of intersection D of the hypotenuse and the semi-circle, then the length AC equals to

(a) $\frac{AB.AD}{\sqrt{AB^2+AD^2}}$ (b) $\frac{AB.AD}{AB+AD}$

(c) $\sqrt{AB.AD}$ (d) $\frac{AB.AD}{\sqrt{AB^2-AD^2}}$

35. If the circle $C_1: x^2+y^2=16$ intersect another circle C_2 of radius 5 in such a manner that the common chord is of maximum length and has a slope 3/4, then the co-ordinates of the centre C_2 are

(a) $\left(\pm\frac{9}{5},\pm\frac{12}{5}\right)$ (b) $\left(\pm\frac{9}{5},\mp\frac{12}{5}\right)$

(c) $\left(\pm\frac{12}{5},\pm\frac{9}{5}\right)$ (d) $\left(\pm\frac{12}{5},\mp\frac{9}{5}\right)$

36. Two lines $p_1x+q_1y+r_1=0$ and $p_2x+q_2y+r_2=0$ are conjugates lines with respect to the circle $x^2+y^2=a^2$ if

(a) $p_1p_2+q_1q_2=r_1r_2$

(b) $p_1p_2+q_1q_2+r_1r_2=0$

(c) $a^2(p_1p_2+q_1q_2)=r_1r_2$

(d) $(p_1p_2+q_1q_2)=a^2r_1r_2$

37. If a circle passes through the point (a, b) cuts the circle $x^2+y^2=k^2$ orthogonally, then the equation of the locus of its centre is

(a) $2ax+2by-(a^2+b^2+k^2)=0$

(b) $2ax+2by-(a^2-b^2-k^2)=0$

(c) $x^2+y^2-3ax-4by-(a^2+b^2-k^2)=0$

(d) $x^2+y^2-2ax-3by-(a^2-b^2-k^2)=0$.

38. Consider the circle $S: x^2+y^2-4x-4y+4=0$. If another circle of radius 'r' less than the radius of the circle S is drawn , touching the circle S, and the co-ordinates axes, then the value of 'r ' is

(a) $3-2\sqrt{2}$ (b) $4-2\sqrt{2}$

(c) $7-4\sqrt{2}$ (d) $6-4\sqrt{2}$

39. The distance between the chords of contact of tangents to the circle $x^2+y^2+2gx+2fy+c=0$ from the origin and the point (g, f) is

(a) $\sqrt{g^2+f^2}$ (b) $\dfrac{\sqrt{g^2+f^2-c}}{2}$

(c) $\dfrac{g^2+f^2-c}{2\sqrt{g^2+f^2}}$ (d) $\dfrac{\sqrt{g^2+f^2-c}}{2\sqrt{g^2+f^2}}$

40. The locus of the centres of the circles which cut the circles $x^2+y^2+4x-6y+9=0$ and $x^2+y^2-5x+4y-2=0$ orthogonally is

(a) $9x+10y-7=0$ (b) $x-y+2=0$

(c) $9x-10y+11=0$ (d) $9x+10y+7=0$.

41. The locus of the centres of the circles such that the point (2, 3) is the mid-point of the chord $5x+2y+16=0$ is

(a) $2x-5y+11=0$ (b) $2x+5y-11=0$

(c) $2x+5y+11=0$ (d) None.

42. The locus of the mid-points of the chords of the circle $x^2+y^2+4x-6y-12=0$ which subtend an angle of $\frac{\pi}{3}$ radians at its circumcentre is

(a) $(x-2)^2+(y+3)^2=6.25$

(b) $(x+2)^2+(y-3)^2=6.25$

(c) $(x+2)^2+(y-3)^2=18.75$

(d) $(x+2)^2+(y+3)^2=18.75$.

43. If two chords of the circle $x^2+y^2-ax-by=0$ drawn from the point (a, b) is divided by the x-axis in the ratio 2 : 1 is

(a) $a^2>3b^2$ (b) $a^2<3b^2$

(c) $a^2>4b^2$ (d) $a^2<4b^2$.

44. The angle at which the circles $(x-1)^2+y^2=10$ and $x^2+(y-2)^2=5$ intersect is

(a) $\pi/6$ (b) $\pi/4$ (c) $\pi/3$ (d) $\pi/2$

45. Two congruent circles with centres at (2, 3) and (5, 6) which intersect at right angles has radius equal to

(a) $2\sqrt{2}$ (b) 3 (c) 4 (d) None

46. A circle of radius unity is centred at origin . Two particles start moving at the same time from the point (1, 0) and moves around the circle in opposite direction. One of the particle moves counterclockwise with constant speed 'v' and the other moves clock-wise with constant speed '3v'. After leaving (1, 0) , the two particles meet first at a point P and continue until they meet next at point Q. Then the co-ordinates of the point Q are

(a) (1, 0) (b) (0, 1) (c) (0, -1) (d) (-1, 0)

47. The value of 'c' for which the set

$$\{(x,y): x^2+y^2+2x\le 1\}\cap\{(x,y): x-y+c\ge 0\}$$

contains only one point in common is

(a) $(-\infty,-1]\cup[3,\infty)$ (b) {-1, 3}

(c) { - 3 } (d) { - 1 }

48. A circle is inscribed into a rhombus ABCD with one angle 60°. The distance from the centr of the circle to the nearest vertex is equal to 1. If P is any point of the circle, then $|PA|^2+|PB|^2+|PC|^2+|PD|^2$ is equal to

(a) 12 (b) 11 (c) 9 (d) None.

49. P is a point (a, b) in the first quadrant. If the two circles which pass through P and touch both the co-ordinates axes cut at right angles, then

(a) $a^2-6ab+b^2=0$ (b) $a^2+2ab-b^2=0$

(c) $a^2-4ab+b^2=0$ (d) $a^2-8ab+b^2=0$

50. The range of value of 'a' such that the angle θ between the pair of tangents drawn from the point Q (a, 0) to the circle $x^2+y^2=1$ satisfies $\pi/2<\theta<\pi$ is

(a) (1, 2) (b) $(1,\sqrt{2})$

(c) $(-\sqrt{2},-1)$ (d) $(-\sqrt{2},-1)\cup(1,\sqrt{2})$

51. Three concentric circles of which the biggest is $x^2+y^2=1$ have their radii in A.P . If the line y = x + 1 Cuts all the circles in real and distinct points . The interval in which the common difference of A.P. will lie is

(a) $\left(0,\frac{1}{4}\right)$ (b) $\left(0,\frac{1}{2\sqrt{2}}\right)$

(c) $\left(0,\frac{2-\sqrt{2}}{4}\right)$ (d) None

52. A tangent is a point on the circle $x^2+y^2=a^2$ intersects a concentric circle C at two points P and Q. The tangents to the circle C at P and Q meet at a point on the circle $x^2+y^2=b^2$, then the equation of the circle is

(a) $x^2+y^2=ab$ (b) $x^2+y^2=(a-b)^2$

(c) $x^2+y^2=(a+b)^2$ (d) $x^2+y^2=a^2+b^2$

53. AB is the diameter of a semicircle k, C is an arbitrary point on the semi-circle (other than A or B) and S is the

centre of the circle inscribed into triangle ABC , then measure of

(a) angle ASB changes as C moves on k

(b) angle ASB = 135 for all C

(c) angle ASB = 150 for all C

(d) angle ASB is the same for all positions of C, but r cannot be determined without knowing the radius.

54. Tangents are drawn to the circle $x^2+y^2=1$ at the points, where it is met by the circles,

$$x^2+y^2-(\lambda+6)x+(8-2\lambda)y-3=0,$$

λ being the variable. The locus of the point of intersection of these tangents is

(a) $2x-y+10=0$ (b) $x+2y-10=0$

(c) $x-2y+10=9$ (d) $2x+y-10=0$.

55. Given $\frac{a}{x}+\frac{b}{y}=1$ and $ax+by=1$ are two variable lines 'a' and 'b' being the parameters connected by the relation $a^2+b^2=ab$. The locus of the point of intersection has the equation

(a) $x^2+y^2+xy-1=0$ (b) $x^2+y^2-xy+1=0$

(c) $x^2+y^2+xy+1=0$ (d) $x^2+y^2-xy-1=0$

56. B and C are two fixed points having co-ordinates (3, 0) and (-3, 0) respectively. If the vertical angle BAC is 90°, then the locus of the centroid of the ΔABC has the equation

(a) $x^2+y^2=1$ (b) $x^2+y^2=2$

(c) $x^2+y^2=1/9$ (d) $x^2+y^2=4/9$.

57. If $\left(a,\frac{1}{a}\right),\left(b,\frac{1}{b}\right),\left(c,\frac{1}{c}\right)$ and $\left(d,\frac{1}{d}\right)$ are four distinct points on a circle of radius 4 units, then a b c d is equal to

(a) 4 (b) ¼ (c) 1 (d) 10

58. Triangle formed by the lines $x+y=0$, $x-y=0$ and $lx+my=1$. If l amd m vary subject to the condition $l^2+m^2=1$, then locus of its circum-centre is

(a) $(x^2-y^2)^2=x^2+y^2$ (b) $(x^2+y^2)^2=x^2-y^2$

(c) $(x^2+y^2)=4x^2y^2$ (d) $(x^2+y^2)^2=(x^2-y^2)$

59. tangents are drawn to a unit circle at the origin from each point on the line $2x+y=4$. Then the equation to the locus of the middle point of the chord of contact is

(a) $2(x^2+y^2)=x+y$ (b) $2(x^2+y^2)=x+2y$

(c) $4(x^2+y^2)=2x+y$ (d) None.

60. ABCD is a square of unit area. A circle is tangent to two sides of ABCD and passes through exactly one of its vertices. The radius of the circle is

(a) $2-\sqrt{2}$ (b) $\sqrt{2}-1$ (c) $\frac{1}{2}$ (d) $\frac{1}{\sqrt{2}}$

61. A pair of tangents are drawn to a unit circle with centre at the origin and these tangents intersect at A enclosing an angle of 60°. The area enclosed by these tangents and the arc of the circle is

(a) $\frac{2}{\sqrt{3}}-\frac{\pi}{6}$ (b) $\sqrt{3}-\frac{\pi}{3}$

(c) $\frac{\pi}{3}-\frac{\sqrt{3}}{6}$ (d) $\sqrt{3}\left(1-\frac{\pi}{6}\right)$

62. Two circles are drawn through the points (1, 0) and (2, -1) to touch the axis of y. They intersect at angle

(a) $\cot^{-1}\left(\frac{3}{4}\right)$ (b) $\cot^{-1}\left(\frac{4}{5}\right)$

(c) $\frac{\pi}{2}$ (d) $\tan^{-1}(1)$

63. If the line $x\cos\theta+y\sin\theta=2$ is the equation of transverse common tangent to the circles $x^2+y^2=4$ and $x^2+y^2-6\sqrt{3}x-6y+20=0$, then the value of θ is

(a) $5\pi/6$ (b) $2\pi/3$ (c) $\pi/3$ (d) $\pi/6$.

64. A circle of constant radius 'a' passes through the origin 'O' and cuts the axis of co-ordinates in points P and Q, then the equation of the locus of the foot of perpendicular from O to PQ is

(a) $(x^2+y^2)\left(\frac{1}{x^2}+\frac{1}{y^2}\right)=4a^2$

(b) $(x^2+y^2)^2\left(\frac{1}{x^2}+\frac{1}{y^2}\right)=a^2$

(c) $(x^2+y^2)^2\left(\frac{1}{x^2}+\frac{1}{y^2}\right)=4a^2$

(d) $(x^2+y^2)\left(\frac{1}{x^2}+\frac{1}{y^2}\right)=a^2$.

65. A square is inscribed in the circle $x^2+y^2-2x+4y+3=0$. Its sides are parallel to the co-ordinate axes. Then one vertex of the square is

(a) $(1+\sqrt{2},-2)$ (b) $(1-\sqrt{2},-2)$

(c) $(1,-2+\sqrt{2})$ (d) None.

66. The point of contact of the tangent to the circle $x^2+y^2=5$ at the point (1, -2) which touches the circle $x^2+y^2-8x+6y+20=0$, is

(a) (2, -1) (b) (3, -1) (c) (4, -1) (d) (5, -1)

67. The center of the circle passing through the point (0, 1) and touching the curve $y=x^2$ at (2, 4) is

(a) (-16/5, 27/10) (b) (-16/7, 53/10)
(c) (-16/5, 53/10) (d) None.

68. The locus of the middle points of the chords of the circle $x^2+y^2-2x-6y-10=0$ which passes through the origin is the circle

(a) $x^2+y^2+x+3y=0$

(b) $x^2+y^2-x+3y=0$

(c) $x^2+y^2+x-3y=0$

(d) $x^2+y^2-x-3y=0$

69. The equation of the circle through the points of intersection of $x^2+y^2=1$, $x^2+y^2-2x-4y+1=0$ and touching the line $x+2y=0$

(a) $x^2+y^2+x+2y=0$

(b) $x^2+y^2-x+2y=0$

(c) $x^2+y^2-x-2y=0$

(d) $2(x^2+y^2)-x-2y=0$

70. $y-x+1=0$ is the equation of normal at $\left(3+\frac{3}{\sqrt{2}}, \frac{3}{\sqrt{2}}\right)$ to which of the following circles ?

(a) $\left(x-3-\frac{3}{\sqrt{2}}\right)^2+\left(y-\frac{3}{\sqrt{2}}\right)^2=9$

(b) $\left(x-3-\frac{3}{\sqrt{2}}\right)^2+y^2=6$

(c) $(x-3)^2+y^2=6$

(d) $(x-3)^2+(y-3)^2=9$

71. Radical axis of two circles whose centers lie along x and y axes is

(a) $ax-by-\left(\frac{a^2+b^2}{4}\right)=0$

(b) $2g^2x+2f^2y-\left(\frac{g^2+f^2}{4}\right)=0$

(c) $gx+fy=g^4+f^4$

(d) $2gx-2fy+g^2-f^2=0$

72. A circle has its center in the first quadrant and passes through the point of intersections of the lines x = 2 and y = 3. If it makes intercepts of 3 and 4 units on these lines respectively, then its equation is

(a) $x^2+y^2-3x-5y+8=0$

(b) $x^2+y^2-4x-6y+13=0$

(c) $x^2+y^2-6x-8y+23=0$

(d) $x^2+y^2-8x-9y+30=0$

73. The radius of the circle passing through the points (1, 2), (5, 2) and (5, -2) is

(a) $5\sqrt{2}$ (b) $2\sqrt{5}$ (c) $3\sqrt{2}$ (d) $2\sqrt{2}$

74. Lines are drawn from the point (-2, -3) to meet the circle $x^2+y^2-2x-10y+1=0$.

The length of the line that meets the circle at two coincident point is

(a) $4\sqrt{3}$ (b) 16 (c) 48 (d) Cannot be Calculated unless coincident points are given

75. The equation of the circle , which touches both the axes and the straight line 4x+3y=6 in the first quadrant and lies below it is

(a) $4(x^2+y^2)-4x-4y+1=0$

(b) $x^2+y^2-6x-6y+9=0$

(c) $x^2+y^2-6x-y+9=0$

(d) $(x^2+y^2-x-6y)+4=0$

76. Circles are drawn through the point (2, 0) to cut intercepts of length 5 units on the x-axis. If their centers lie in the first quadrant , then their equation is

(a) $x^2+y^2-9x+2ky+14=0$

(b) $3x^2+3y^2+27x-2ky+42=0$

(c) $x^2+y^2-9x-2ky+14=0$

(d) $x^2+y^2-2kx-9y+14=0$, where k is a positive real number.

77. If the tangent to the circle $x^2+y^2=5$ at (1, -2) touches the circle $x^2+y^2-8x+6y+20=0$ at the point

(a) (2, -1) (b) (3, -1) (c) (4, -1) (d) (5, -1)

78. The center of the circle passing through the point (0, 1) and touching the curve $y=x^2$ at (2, 4) is

(a) (-16/5, 27/10) (b) (-16/7, 53/10)
(c) (-16/5, 53/10) (d) None.

79. If the lines $2x-4y=9$ and $6x-12y+7=0$ touch a circle, then the radius of the circle is

(a) $\frac{\sqrt{3}}{5}$ (b) $\frac{17}{6\sqrt{5}}$ (c) $\frac{2\sqrt{5}}{3}$ (d) $\frac{17}{3\sqrt{5}}$

80. If the co-ordinates at one end of a diameter of the circle $x^2+y^2-8x-4y+c=0$ are (-3, 2), then the co-ordinates of the other end are

(a) (5, 3) (b) (6, 2) (c) (1, -8) (d) (11, 2)

81. If a circle is inscribed in an equilateral triangle of side a, then the area of the square inscribed in the circle is

(a) $a^2/6$ (b) $a^2/3$ (c) $2a^2/5$ (d) $2a^2/3$

82. The equations of lines joining the origin to the point of intersection of circle $x^2+y^2=3$ and the line $x+y=2$ is

(a) $y-(3+2\sqrt{2})x=0$ (b) $x-(3+2\sqrt{2})y=0$

(c) $x-(3-2\sqrt{2})y=0$ (d) $y-(3-2\sqrt{2})x=0$

83. Two circles $x^2+y^2-10x+16=0$ and $x^2+y^2=r^2$ intersect each other at two distinct points if

(a) $r<2$ (b) $r>8$

(c) $2<r<8$ (d) $2\le r\le 8$.

84. If the equations of the tangents drawn from the origin to the circle $x^2+y^2-2rx-2hy+h^2=0$ are perpendicular, then

(a) $h=r$ (b) $h^2=r^2$

(c) $h=-r$ (d) $r^2+h^2=1$

85. If a circle C and $x^2+y^2=1$ are orthogonal and have radical axis parallel to y-axis , then C is

(a) $x^2+y^2-1+x=0$ (b) $x^2+y^2-1-x=0$

(c) $x^2+y^2+1-y=0$ (d) $x^2+y^2+1+x=0$

86. The equation of the line meeting the circle $x^2+y^2=a^2$, two points at equal distances 'd' from a point (x_1, y_1) on the circumference is

(a) $xx_1+yy_1-a^2+\frac{1}{2d^2}=0$

(b) $xx_1-yy_1-a^2+\frac{1}{2d^2}=0$

(c) $xx_1+yy_1+a^2-\frac{1}{2d^2}=0$

(d) $xx_1+yy_1-a^2+\frac{1}{2d^2}=0$

87. The equations of the tangents drawn from the origin to the circle $x^2+y^2-2rx-2hy+h^2=0$ are

(a) $x=0$ (b) $y=0$

(c) $(h^2-r^2)x-2rhy=0$ (d) $(h^2-r^2)x+2rhy=0$

88. Two circles $x^2+y^2=6$ and $x^2+y^2-6x+8=0$ are given. Then the equation of the circle through their points of intersection and the point (1, 1) is

(a) $x^2+y^2-6x+4=0$ (b) $x^2+y^2-3x+1=0$

(c) $x^2+y^2-4x+2=0$ (d) None.

89. The equation of the cir cle passing through (1, 1) and the points of intersection of

$x^2+y^2+13x-3y=0$, $2x^2+2y^2+4x-7y-25=0$ is

(a) $4x^2+4y^2-30x-10y-25=0$

(b) $4x^2+4y^2+30x-13y-25=0$

(c) $4x^2+4y^2-17x-10y-25=0$

(d) None

90. The center of the circle passing through the point (0, 1) and touching the curve $y=x^2$ at (2, 4) is

(a) $\left(-\frac{16}{5},\frac{27}{10}\right)$ (b) $\left(-\frac{16}{7},\frac{53}{10}\right)$

(c) $\left(-\frac{16}{5},\frac{53}{10}\right)$ (d) None.

91. AB is a diameter of a circle and C is any point on the circumference of the circle. Then

(a) The area of triangle ABC is maximum when it is isosceles.

(b) The area of triangle ABC is minimum when it is isosceles.

(c) The area of triangle ABC is minimum when it is isosceles.

(d) None.

92. The locus of the mid-point of a chord of the circle $x^2+y^2=4$, which subtends a right angle at the origin is

(a) $x+y=2$ (b) $x^2+y^2=1$

(c) $x^2+y^2=2$ (d) $x+y=1$

93. If a circle passes through the point (a, b) and cuts the circle $x^2+y^2=k^2$ orthogonally, then the equation of the locus of its center is

(a) $2ax+2by-(a^2+b^2+k^2)=0$

(b) $2ax+2by-(a^2-b^2+k^2)=0$

(c) $x^2+y^2-3ax-4by+(a^2+b^2-k^2)=0$

(d) $x^2+y^2-2ax-3by+(a^2+b^2-k^2)=0$

94. The equation of the tangents drawn from the origin to the circle $x^2+y^2+2rx-2hy+h^2=0$ are

(a) $x=0$

(b) $y=0$

(c) $(h^2-r^2)x-2rhy=0$

(d) $(h^2-r^2)x+2rhy=0$.

95. If the two circles $(x-1)^2+(y-3)^2=r^2$ and $x^2+y^2-8x+2y+8=0$ intersects in two distinct points, then

(a) $2<r<8$ (b) $r<2$ (d) $r=2$ (d) $r>2$.

96. The lines $2x-3y=5$ and $3x-4y=7$ are diameters of a circle of area 154 sq. units. Then the equation of the circle is

(a) $x^2+y^2+2x-2y-62=0$

(b) $x^2+y^2+2x-2y-47=0$

(c) $x^2+y^2-2x+2y-47=0$

(d) $x^2+y^2-2x+2y-62=0$

97. The center of a circle passing through the points (0, 0), (1, 0) and touching the circle $x^2+y^2=9$ is

(a) (3/2, ½) (b) (1/2, 3/2)

(c) (1/2, ½) (d) $\left(1/2, 1/\sqrt{2}\right)$

98. The locus of the center of a circle which touches externally the circle $x^2+y^2-6x-6y+14=0$ and also touches the y-axis is given by the equation

(a) $x^2-6x-10y+14=0$ (b) $x^2-10x-6y+14=0$

(c) $y^2-6x-10y+14=0$ (d) $y^2-10x+6y+14=0$

99. The circles $x^2+y^2-10x+16=0$ and $x^2+y^2=r^2$ intersect each other in distinct points if

(a) r<2 (b) r>8

(c) 2 <r<8 (d) $2\le r\le 8$

100. The angle between a pair of tangents drawn from a point P to the circle

$x^2+y^2+4x-6y+9\sin^2\alpha+13\cos^2\alpha=0$ is 2α. Then the locus of P is

(a) $x^2+y^2+4x-6y+4=0$

(b) $x^2+y^2+4x-6y-9=0$

(c) $x^2+y^2+4x-6y-4=0$

(d) $x^2+y^2+4x-6y+9=0$

101. The number of common tangents to the circles $x^2+y^2=4$ and $x^2+y^2-6x-8y-24=0$ is

(a) 0 (b) 1 (c) 3 (d) 4

102. Let $A_0A_1A_2A_3A_4A_5$ be a regular hexagon inscribed in a unit circle . Then the product of the lengths of line segments A_0A_1, A_0A_2 and A_0A_4 is

(a) 3/4 (b) $3\sqrt{3}$ (c) 3 (d) $3\sqrt{3}/2$.

103. If two distinct chords , drawn from the point (p, q) on the circle $x^2+y^2=px+qy$, where $pq\ne 0$ are bisected by the x-axis, then

(a) $p^2=q^2$ (b) $p^2=8q^2$

(c) $p^2<8q^2$ (d) $p^2>8q^2$.

104. The triangle PQR is inscribed in the circle $x^2+y^2=25$. If Q and R have co-ordinates (3, 4) and (-4, 3) respectively, then $\angle QPR$ is

(a) π/2 (b) π/3 (c) π/4 (d) π/6.

105. If the circles $x^2+y^2+2x+2ky+b=0$ and

$x^2+y^2+2ky+k=0$

intersect orthogonally, then k is

(a) 2 or -3/2 (b) - 2 or – 3/2 (c) 2 or 3/2 (d) - 2 or 3/2.

106. Let AB be a chord of the circle $x^2+y^2=r^2$ subtending right angle at the center , then the locus of the centroid of the triangle PAB as P moves on the circle is

(a) a parabola (b) a circle

(c) an ellipse (d) a pair of st lines.

107. Let PQ and Rs be tangents at the extremities of the diameter PR of a circle of radius r . If PS and RQ intersect a point x on the circumference of the circle, then 2 r equals

(a) $\sqrt{PQ.RS}$ (b) $\dfrac{PQ+RS}{2}$

(c) $\dfrac{2PQ+RS}{PQ+RS}$ (d) $\sqrt{\dfrac{PQ^2+RS^2}{2}}$

108. If the tangent at the point P on the circle $x^2+y^2+6x+6y=2$ meets the straight line $5x-2y+6=0$ at a point Q on the y-axis , then the length of PQ is

(a) 4 (b) $2\sqrt{5}$ (c) 5 (d) $3\sqrt{5}$.

109. If a > 2 b > 0 then the positive value of m for which $y=mx-b\sqrt{1+m^2}$ is a common tangent to $x^2+y^2=b^2$ and $(x-a)^2+y^2=b^2$ is

(a) $\dfrac{2b}{\sqrt{a^2-4b^2}}$ (b) $\dfrac{\sqrt{a^2-4b^2}}{2a}$

(c) $\dfrac{2b}{a-2b}$ (d) $\dfrac{b}{a-2b}$.

110. The center of the circle inscribed in square formed by the lines $x^2-8x+12=0$ and $y^2-14y+45=0$ is

(a) (4,7) (b) (7,4) (c) (9,4) (d) (4,9)

111. If one of the diameters of the circle

$x^2+y^2-2x-6y+6=0$

is a chord to the circle with center (2, 1), then the radius of the circle is

(a) $\sqrt{3}$ (b) $\sqrt{2}$ (c) 3 (d) 2.

112. A circle is given by $x^2+(y-1)^2=1$, another circle C touches it externally and also the x-axis, then the locus of its center is

(a) $\{(x,y): x^2=4y\}\cup\{(x,y): y\le 0\}$

(b) $\{(x,y): x^2+(y-1)^2=4\}\cup\{(x,y): y\le 0\}$

(c) $\{(x,y): x^2=y\}\cup\{(0,y): y<0\}$

(d) $\{(x,y): x^2=y\}\cup\{(0,y): y\le 0\}$

113. Tangent to the curve $y=x^2+6$ at a point P(1, 7) touches the circle $x^2+y^2+16x+12y+c=0$ at a point Q. Then the co-ordinates of Q are

(a) (-6, -7) (b) (-10, -15) (c) (-9, -13) (d) (-6, -11).

114. Let ABCD be a quadrilateral with area 18 , with side AB parallel to the side CD and AB = 2 CD.

Let AD be perpendicular to AB and CD . If a circle is drawn inside the quadrilateral ABCD touching all the sides, then its radius is

(a) 3 (b) 2 (c) 3/2 (d) 1.

115. Tangents drawn from the point P(1, 8) to the circle $x^2+y^2-6x-4y-11=0$ touch the circle at A and B. The equation of the circum-circle of the triangle PAB is

(a) $x^2+y^2+4x-6y+19=0$

(b) $x^2+y^2-4x-10y+19=0$

(c) $x^2+y^2-2x+6y-29=0$

(d) $x^2+y^2-6x-4y+19=0$

116. Two parallel chords of a circle of radius 2 are ata distance $\sqrt{3}+1$ apart. If the chords subtends at the center, angles of $\frac{\pi}{k}$ and $\frac{2\pi}{k}$, where $k>0$, then the value of [k] is, where [,]=G.I.F

(a) 1 (b) 2 (c) 3 (d) 4

117. The circle passing through the point (-1, 0) and touching the y-axis at (0, 2) , also passes through the point

(a) $\left(-\frac{3}{2},0\right)$ (b) $\left(-\frac{5}{2},2\right)$

(c) $\left(-\frac{3}{2},\frac{5}{2}\right)$ (d) (–4, 0)

ANSWER

1. (b)	2. (c)	3. (b)	4. ()	5. (a)	6. (b)	7. (a)	8. (b)	9. (a)	10.(c)
11. (a)	12. (a)	13.(a)	14. (b)	15.(b)	16.(a)	17. (a)	18. (b)	19.(c)	20. (c)
21.(c)	22. ()	23. ()	24. ()	25.()	26. ()	27.()	28.()	29. ()	30. ()
31.()	32. ()	33.()	34.()	35. ()	36. ()	37.()	38. ()	39.()	40.()
41. ()	42. ()	43.()	44. ()	45.()	46.()	47. ()	48. ()	49.()	50. ()
51.()	52.()	53. ()	54. ()	55.()	56. ()	57.()	58.()	59. ()	60. ()
61.()	62. ()	63.()	64.()	65. ()	66. (b)	67.(c)	68. (d)	69.(c)	70.(c)
71. (d)	72. (a)	73.(d)	74. (a)	75.(b)	76.(d)	77. (b)	78. (c)	79.(b)	80. (d)
81.(a)	82.(b)	83. (c)	84. (c)	85.(b,d)	86. (a)	87.(a,c)	88.(d)	89. (b)	90. (c)
91.(a)	92. (c)	93.(a)	94.(a, c)	95. (a)	96. (c)	97. (d)	98. (b)	99. (c)	100.(d)
101. (b)	102. (c)	103.(d)	104. (c)	105.(a)	106.(b)	107. (a)	108. (c)	109.(a)	110. (a)
111.(c)	112.(d)	113. (a)	114. (b)	115.(b)	116. (c)	117.(d)			

Level – III FOR JEE ADVANCE EXAM ONLY

1. Find the number of points with integral co-ordinates that are interrior to the circle $x^2+y^2=16$.

2. If the circle $x^2+y^2+2gx+2fy+c=0$ cuts each of the circles $x^2+y^2=4$, $x^2+y^2-6x-8y+10=0$ and $x^2+y^2+2x-4y-2=0$ at the extremities of a diameter, then prove that

(i) c = - 4

(ii) g + f + 1 = c

(iii) $g^2+f^2-17=c$

(iv) g f = 6.

3. The equations of four circles are $(x\pm a)^2+(y\pm a)^2=a^2$. Then find the radius of a circle which touching all the four circles.

4. A square is inscribed in the circle

$$x^2+y^2-10x-6y+30=0.$$

One side of the square is parallel to y = x + 3 , then one vertex of the square is .....

5. If a chord of the circle $x^2+y^2=8$ makes equal intercepts of length a on the co-ordinate axes, then $|a|<$...........

6. Origin is limiting point of co-axial system of which $x^2+y^2-6x-8y+1=0$ is a member. Then find the other limiting point.

7. If the circles $(x-a)^2+(y-b)^2=c^2$ and

$$(x-b)^2+(y-a)^2=c^2$$

touch each other, then find the value of a.

8. Find the locus of the mid points of the chords of the circle $x^2+y^2+4x-6y-12=0$, which subtends an angle of

π/3 radians at its circumference.

9. Find the equation of the largest circle passing from (1, 1) and (2, 2) and always in first quadrant.

10. Find the distance between the chord of contact of tangents to the circle $x^2+y^2+2gx+2fy+c=0$ from the origin and the point (g, f).

11. If $(1+\alpha x)^n = 1+8x+24x^2+$.......... and a line through $P(\alpha, n)$ cuts the circle $x^2+y^2=4$ in A and B, then PA. PB =..........................

12 The circle $x^2+y^2=4$ cuts the circle

$$x^2+y^2+2x+3y-5=0$$

in A and B , then the centre of the circle AB as diameter is............................

13. find the length of the tangents from any point of the circle $x^2+y^2+2gx+2fy+c=0$ to the circle $x^2+y^2+2gx+2fy+d=0$, (d > c).

14. If the points (4, -2) and (3, b) are conjugate with respect to the circle $x^2+y^2=24$, then find the value of b.

15. Find the equation of the image of the circle $(x-3)^2+(y-2)^2=1$ by the line mirror x + y = 19 .

16. Two circles $(x-1)^2+(y-3)^2=r^2$ and

$$x^2+y^2-8x+2y+8=0$$

intersects in two distinct points, then prove that $2 < r < 8$.

17. If exactly two real tangents can be drawn to the circles $x^2+y^2-2x-2y=0$ and $x^2+y^2-8x-8y+\lambda=0$, then prove that $0<\lambda<24$.

18. Two vertices of an equilateral triangle are (-1, 0) and (1, 0) and its third vertex lies above the x-axis. Then prove that the equation of the circum circle is

$$x^2+y^2-\frac{2}{\sqrt{3}}y-1=0.$$

19. A square is inscribed in the circle

$$x^2+y^2-2x+4y-93=0$$

with its sides parallel to the co-ordinate axes. Then find the co-ordinates of its vertices.

20. If the equation of incircle of an equilateral triangle is $x^2+y^2+4x-6y+4=0$, then prove that the equation of the circumcircle of the triangle is $x^2+y^2+4x-6y-23=0$.

21. If a square is inscribed in the circle $x^2+y^2+2gx+2fy+c=0$ of radius r, the prove that the length of its side is $r\sqrt{2}$.

22. If r be the radius , then prove that the area of the equilateral triangle inscribed in the circle

$$x^2+y^2+2gx+2fy+c=0 \text{ is } \frac{3\sqrt{3}}{4}\times r^2.$$

23. Prove that the equation of a circle with center at origin and passing through the vertices of an equilateral triangle whose median is of length 3a is $x^2+y^2=2a^2$.

24. A circle is inscribed in an equilateral triangle of side a . Prove that the area of any square inscribed in the circle is $\frac{a^2}{6}$.

25. Find the co-ordinates of the point on the circle $x^2+y^2-12x+4y+30=0$ which is farthest from the origin.

26. A diameter of $x^2+y^2-2x-6y+6=0$ is a chord to the circle with center (2, 1) , then find the radius of it.

27. Prove that angle between two tangents from the origin to the circle $(x-1)^2+(y+1)^2=25$ is $\frac{\pi}{2}$.

28. Prove that the tangents are drawn from the point (4, 3) to the circle $x^2+y^2-2x-4y=0$ are inclined at an angle is $\frac{\pi}{2}$.

29. Find the number of tangents that can be drawn from the point (0, 1) to the circle $x^2+y^2-2x-4y=0$.

30. Prove that the locus of the point of intersection of tangents to the circle $x^2+y^2=a^2$ at the points whose parametric angles differ by $\frac{\pi}{3}$ is $x^2+y^2=\frac{4a^2}{3}$.

31. Prove that the area of the triangle formed by +ve axis and the normal and tangent to the circle $x^2+y^2=4$ at $(1,\sqrt{3})$ is $2\sqrt{3}$.

Answer

1. 45.

3. $a(\sqrt{2}-1),\ 2\sqrt{2}a$

4. (3, 3) ; (7, 3)

5. 4

6. (3/25, 4/25)

7. $a=b\pm c\sqrt{2}$

8. $(x+2)^2+(y-3)^2=6.25$.

9. $x^2+y^2-2x-4y+4=0$

10. $\dfrac{\left(g^2+f^2-c\right)}{2\sqrt{g^2+f^2}}$

11. 16

12. (2/13, 3/13)

13. $\sqrt{d-c}$

14. -6

15. $(x-17)^2+(y-16)^2=1$

19. (-6, -9), (-6, 5), (8, -9), (8, 5).

25. (9, 3)

26. 3

29. 0.

Level – III COMPREHENSIVE LINK PASSAGE (FOR JEE MAIN AND ADVANCED EXAMS ONLY)

PASSAGE–1

If $7l^2-9m^2+8l+1=0$ and we have to find the equation of circle having $lx+my+1=0$ is a tangent and we can adjust the given condition as $16l^2+8l+1=9\left(l^2+m^2\right)$

or $(4l+1)^2=9\left(l^2+m^2\right)$

$\Rightarrow \left|\dfrac{(4l+1)}{\sqrt{\left(l^2+m^2\right)}}\right|=3$.

Thus centre of a circle = (4, 0) and radius = 3 .

Also when two non parallel lines touching a circle, then the centre of circle lies on angle bisector of lines.

1. If $16m^2-8l-1=0$, then the equation of a circle having $lx+my+1=0$ is a tangent is

(a) $x^2+y^2+8x=0$ (b) $x^2+y^2-8x=0$

(c) $x^2+y^2+8y=0$ (d) $x^2+y^2-8y=0$

2. If $4l^2-5m^2+6l+1=0$, then the centre and and the radius of the circle, which have $lx+my+1=0$ is a tangent, is

(a) $(0,4);\sqrt{5}$ (b) $(4,0);\sqrt{5}$

(c) $(0,3);\sqrt{5}$ (d) $(3,0);\sqrt{5}$

3. If $16l^2+9m^2=24lm+6l+8m+1$ and if S be the equation of the circle having $lx+my+1=0$ is a tangent , when the equation of director circle of S is

(a) $x^2+y^2+6x+8y=25$

(b) $x^2+y^2-6x+8y=25$

(c) $x^2+y^2-6x-8y=25$

(d) $x^2+y^2+6x-8y=25$.

PASSAGE - II

A circle C of radius 1 is inscribed in an equilateral triangle PQR. The points of contact of C with the side PQ, QR, RP are D, E, F respectively. The line PQ is given by the equation $\sqrt{3}x+y=6$ and the point D is $\left(\dfrac{3\sqrt{3}}{2},\dfrac{3}{2}\right)$. Further it is given that the origin and the centre C are on the same side PQ.

1. The equation of circle C is

(a) $\left(x-2\sqrt{3}\right)^2+(y-1)^2=1$

(b) $\left(x-2\sqrt{3}\right)^2+\left(y-\dfrac{1}{2}\right)^2=1$

(c) $\left(x-\sqrt{3}\right)^2+(y+1)^2=1$

(d) $\left(x-\sqrt{3}\right)^2+(y-1)^2=1$

2. Points E and F are given by

(a) $\left(\dfrac{\sqrt{3}}{2},\dfrac{3}{2}\right),\left(\sqrt{3},0\right)$ (b) $\left(\dfrac{\sqrt{3}}{2},\dfrac{1}{2}\right),\left(\sqrt{3},0\right)$

(c) $\left(\dfrac{\sqrt{3}}{2},\dfrac{3}{2}\right),\left(\dfrac{\sqrt{3}}{2},\dfrac{1}{2}\right)$ (d) $\left(\dfrac{3}{2},\dfrac{\sqrt{3}}{2}\right),\left(\dfrac{\sqrt{3}}{2},\dfrac{1}{2}\right)$

3. Equation of the sideS QR , PR are

(a) $y=\dfrac{2}{\sqrt{3}}x+1,\ y=-2\sqrt{3}x+1$

(b) $y=\dfrac{1}{\sqrt{3}}x+1;\ y=0$

(c) $y=\left(\dfrac{\sqrt{3}}{2}\right)x+1; y=\left(-\dfrac{\sqrt{3}}{2}\right)x-1$

(d) $y=\sqrt{3}\,x,\ y=0$.

PASSAGE -III

The euation of the tangent and normal to the circle $x^2+y^2+2gx+2fy+c=0$ at (x_1, y_1) are Tangent : $xx_1+yy_1+g(x+x_1)+f(y+y_1)+c=0$

Normal: $\dfrac{x-x_1}{x_1+g}=\dfrac{y-y_1}{y_1+f}$.

Clearly , normal is always passes through the centre of the circle.

1. Equation of the tangent to the circle $x^2+y^2+4x+6y-12=0$ at (1, 1) is
(a) $3x+4y=7$ (b) $3x-4y=7$
(c) $-3x+4y=7$ (d) $-3x-4y=7$.

2. The tangent to the circle $x^2+y^2=5$ at (1, -2) also touches the circle
(a) $x^2+y^2-8x+6y-20=0$
(b) $x^2+y^2+8x+6y-20=0$
(c) $x^2+y^2-8x+6y+20=0$
(d) $x^2+y^2-8x+9y+20=0$

3. The area of the triangle formed by the positive x-axis, the normal and the tangent to the circle $x^2+y^2=4$ at $(1,\sqrt{3})$ is
(a) $3\sqrt{3}$ s.u (b) $2\sqrt{3}$ s.u
(c) $4\sqrt{3}$ s.u. (d) $5\sqrt{3}$ s. u.

4. The extremities of a diagonal of a rectangle are (-4, 4) and (6, -1). A circle circumscribes the rectangle and cuts an intercept AB on the y-axis. The area of the triangle formed by AB and the tangents to the circle at A and B is
(a) $\frac{363}{8}$ s.u (b) $\frac{365}{8}$
(c) $\frac{363}{4}$ s.u. (d) $\frac{365}{4}$ s. u

5. The equation of the normal to the circle $x^2+y^2-5x+2y-48=0$ at the point (5, 6) is
(a) $14x+5y=10$ (b) $14x-5y=40$
(c) $5x-14y=40$ (d) None.

6. If the normal to the circle $x^2+y^2-6x+4y-50=0$ is parallel to the line $3x+4y+5=0$ then the equation of normal is
(a) $3x+4y+1=0$ (b) $3x+4y=2$
(c) $3x-4y=1$ (d) $3x+4y-2=0$

PASSAGE -IV

Let $P(x_1, y_1)$ be a point lying inside the circle $S: x^2+y^2+2gx+2fy+c=0$. If the tangents from P to the circle $S=0$ at A and B, then AB is called the chord of contact.

Then the equation of the chord of contact is $xx_1+yy_1+g(x+x_1)+f(y+y_1)+c=0$.

Let tangents PA and PB are drawn from P(0, -2) to the circle $x^2+y^2+2x-4y=0$. Then

1. The equation of the chord of contact is
(a) $x-4y+4=0$ (b) $x-3y-3=0$
(c) $x+4y+4=0$ (d) $x+5y+6=0$.

2. The length of the chord AB is
(a) $2\sqrt{\frac{60}{17}}$ (b) $2\sqrt{\frac{65}{17}}$ (c) $2\sqrt{\frac{12}{17}}$ (d) $2\sqrt{\frac{37}{17}}$

3. The area of a triangle PAB is
(a) $12\sqrt{\frac{5}{17}}$ (b) $12\sqrt{\frac{7}{17}}$ (c) $12\sqrt{\frac{11}{17}}$ (d) $6\sqrt{\frac{5}{17}}$

4. The area of a quadrilateral PACB is, where C is the centre of the circle
(a) $2\sqrt{15}$ (b) $3\sqrt{15}$ (c) $4\sqrt{15}$ (d) $5\sqrt{15}$

5. The angle between PA and PB is
(a) $\tan^{-1}\left(\frac{4\sqrt{15}}{7}\right)$ (b) $\tan^{-1}\left(\frac{8\sqrt{15}}{7}\right)$
(c) $\tan^{-1}\left(\frac{16\sqrt{15}}{7}\right)$ (d) $\tan^{-1}\left(\frac{6\sqrt{15}}{7}\right)$

6. The chord of contact of tangents drawn from a point on the circle $x^2+y^2=a^2$ to the circle $x^2+y^2=b^2$ touches the circle $x^2+y^2=c^2$. Then a, b, c are in
(a) A. P (b) G.P (c) H. P (d) A. G. P

PASSAGE-V

The line $y=mx+c$ will be a tangent to the circle $x^2+y^2=a^2$ if $c=\pm a\sqrt{1+m^2}$

Equation of any tangent to the circle $x^2+y^2=a^2$ can be considered as $y=mx+a\sqrt{1+m^2}$.

and the co-ordinates of the point of contacts are $\left(\pm\frac{am}{\sqrt{1+m^2}},\mp\frac{a}{\sqrt{1+m^2}}\right)$ and the length of the tangent from the point $P(x_1, y_1)$ to the circle $x^2+y^2+2gx+2fy+c=0$ is $\sqrt{x_1^2+y_1^2+2gx_1+2fy_1+c}$.

1. The equation of tangent to the circle $x^2+y^2+4x+2y=0$ from the point P(1, -2) is
(a) $x-2y-5=0$ (b) $x+2y+5=0$
(c) $x-2y=0$ (d) $y-3x=0$.

2. The equation of tangents from origin to the circle $x^2+y^2-2x-4y=0$ is
(a) $3x-4y=0$ (b) $4x-3y=0$
(c) $3x+4y=0$ (d) $4x+3y=0$.

3. The length of the tangent from any point on the circle $x^2+y^2-2009x-2010y+2012=0$ to the circle $x^2+y^2-2009x-2010y+2020=0$ is

(a) $2\sqrt{2}$ (b) $3\sqrt{2}$ (c) $5\sqrt{2}$ (d) $\sqrt{2}$

4. If the angle between a pair of tangents from a point P to the circle $x^2+y^2+4x-6y+13\cos^2\alpha+9\sin^2\alpha=0$ is 2α. then the equation of the locus of P is

(a) $(x+2)^2+(y-3)^2=1$ (b) $(x-2)^2+(y-3)^2=1$

(c) $(x-2)^2+(y+3)^2=1$ (d) $(x+2)^2+(y+3)^2=1$

5. Tangents PA and PB are drawn from P(-1, 2) to the circle $x^2+y^2-2x-4y+2=0$. The area of a triangle PAB is

(a) $\frac{\sqrt{3}}{4}$ (b) $\frac{\sqrt{3}}{2}$ (c) $\frac{2\sqrt{3}}{5}$ (d) $\frac{4\sqrt{3}}{5}$.

PASSAGE-VI

The equation of the chord of the circle $x^2+y^2=a^2$ bisected at the point (x_1, y_1) is $T=S_1$

i.e. $xx_1+yy_1-a^2=x_1^2+y_1^2-a^2$.

1. The equation of the chord of the circle $x^2+y^2-6x+10y-9=0$ bisected at the point (-2, 4) is

(a) 5x-9y+40=0 (b) 5x-9y+46=0

(c) 3x-4y+46=0 (d) 4x-5y+46=0.

2. The locus of the mid-point of a chord of the circle $x^2+y^2=4$, which subtends a right angle at the origin is

(a) x+y=1 (b) x+y=2

(c) $x^2+y^2=2$ (d) $x^2+y^2=1$

3. The equation of the locus of the mid-points of the chords of the circle $4x^2+4y^2-12x+4y+1=0$ that subtends an angle of $\frac{2\pi}{3}$ at its centre is

(a) $16(x^2+y^2)-48x+16y+31=0$

(b) $16(x^2+y^2)-16x+48y+31=0$

(c) $16(x^2+y^2)-16x-48y+31=0$

(d) $16(x^2+y^2)-16x-48y-31=0$

4. If two distinct chords, drawn from the point (p, q) on the circle $x^2+y^2=px+qy$ (where $pq\neq 0$) are bisected by the x-axis, then

(a) $p^2=q^2$ (b) $p^2=8q^2$

(c) $p^2>8q^2$ (d) $p^2<8q^2$.

5. Let a circle be given by $2x(x-a)+2y(y-b)=0$, $(a,b\neq 0)$. If two chords are bisected by the x - axis, can be drawn to the circle from the point $\left(a,\frac{b}{2}\right)$

(a) $a^2>b^2$ (b) $a^2>2b^2$

(c) $a^2<2b^2$ (d) $a^2<b^2$

6. The locus of the mid-points of the chords of the circle $x^2+y^2=a^2$, which subtend right angle at the point (c, 0) is

(a) $2(x^2+y^2)-2cx=a^2-c^2$

(b) $2(x^2+y^2)-2cx=a^2+c^2$

(c) $2(x^2+y^2)+2cx=a^2+c^2$

(d) $2(x^2+y^2)+2cx=a^2-c^2$.

PASSAGE-VII

The equation of the family of circles passing through the point of intersection of two given circles $S_1=0$ and $S_2=0$ is given by $S_1+\lambda S_2=0, \lambda\neq -1$, where λ is a parameter.

The equation of the family of circles passing through the point of intersection of circle S = 0 and a line L=0 is given by $S+\lambda L=0$, where λ is a parameter.

The equation of the family of circles touching the circle S= 0 and the line L=0 at their point of contact P is $S+\lambda L=0$, where λ is a parameter

1. The equation of the circle passing through (1, 1) and the points of intersection of the circles

$$x^2+y^2+13x-3y=0$$

and $2(x^2+y^2)+4x-7y-25=0$ is

(a) $4(x^2+y^2)+30x-13y=25$

(b) $4(x^2+y^2)-30x-13y=25$

(c) $4(x^2+y^2)-30x+13y=25$

(d) $4(x^2+y^2)+30x+13y=25$.

2. The equation of the circle passing through the point of intersection of the circles $x^2+y^2-6x+2y+4=0$, $x^2+y^2+2x-4y-6=0$ and with its center on the line y=x is

(a) $7(x^2+y^2)-10(x+y)=12$

(b) $7(x^2+y^2)-10(x-y)=12$

(c) $7(x^2+y^2)+10(x-y)=12$

(d) $7(x^2+y^2)+10(x+y)=12$.

3. The equation of the circle through the points of intersection of the circle $x^2+y^2-2x-4y+4=0$ and the line x + 2 y = 4 which touches the line x + 2 y = 0 is

(a) $x^2+y^2-x-2y=0$ (b) $x^2+y^2+x-2y=0$

(c) $x^2+y^2+x+2y=0$ (d) $x^2+y^2-x+2y=0$

4. The equation of the circle whose diameter is the common chord of the circles $x^2+y^2+2x+3y+1=0$ and $x^2+y^2+4x+3y+2=0$ is

(a) $2(x^2+y^2)+2x+6y+1=0$

(b) $2(x^2+y^2)+3x+6y+1=0$

(c) $2(x^2+y^2)+2x+5y+1=0$

(d) $2(x^2+y^2)+x+6y+1=0$.

For JEE- Main and Advanced Exams Only

1. Match the following columns :

Column-I	Column-II
(A) If the shortest and the largest distance from the point (10, 7) to the circle $x^2+y^2-4x-2y-2=0$ are L and M respectively, then	(P) L + M = 10
	(Q) L + M = 20
(B) If the shortest and the largest distance from the point (3,-6) to the circle $x^2+y^2-16x-12y-125=0$ are L and M respectively, then	(R) L + M = 30
(C) If the shortest and the largest distance from the point (6, -6) to the circle $x^2+y^2-4x+6y-12=0$ are L and M respectively, then	(S) M - L = 10
	(T) M - L = 26

2. Match the following columns :

Column-I	Column-II
(A) The radius of the circle $x^2+y^2-2x-2y=0$ is	(P) 2
(B) The radius of the circle $x^2+y^2-4x-4y+4=0$ is	(Q) 4
(C) The radius of the circle $x^2+y^2-6x-10y-18=0$ is	(R) $\sqrt{2}$
(D) The radius of the circle $2(x^2+y^2)-4x-6y+16=0$ is	(S) 3
(E) The radius of the circle $x^2+y^2-10x=0$ is	(T) 5

3. Match the following columns :

Column-I	Column-II
(A) The point $(\lambda, \lambda+2)$ lies inside the circle $x^2+y^2=4$, then the value of λ can be	(P) -1
(B) The point $(\lambda, \lambda+2)$ lies outside the circle $x^2+y^2-2x+4y=0$, then the value of λ can be	(Q) -1/2
	(R) 1
(C) If both the equations $x^2+y^2+2\lambda x+4=0$ and $x^2+y^2-4\lambda y+8=0$ represent real circles, then the value of λ can be	(S) 3
	(T) 5

4. Match the following columns :

Column-I	Column-II
(A) If the straight lines $y=a_1x+b$ and $y=a_2x+b$, $(a_1 \neq a_2)$ and $b \in R$ meet the co-ordinate axes in concyclic points, then	(P) $a_1^2+a_2^2=4$
	(Q) $a_1+a_2=3$
(B) If the chord of contact of the tangents drawn from any point on $x^2+y^2=a_1^2$ to $x^2+y^2=b^2$ touches the circle $x^2+y^2=a_2^2$, where $(a_1 \neq a_2)$, then	(R) $a_1a_2=b$
	(S) $a_1a_2=1$
(C) If the circles $x^2+y^2+2a_1x+b=0$ and $x^2+y^2+2a_2x+b=0$	(T) $a_1a_2=b^2$

where $(a_1 \neq a_2)$ and $b \in R$ cuts orthogonally, then

5. Match the following columns

Column-I	Column-II
(A) The lines $3x - 4y + 4 = 0$ and $6x - 8y - 7 = 0$ are the tangents to a circle, then its radius is	(P) 2
(B) The radius of the circle inscribed in the triangle formed by the lines $x = 0, y = 0$ and $4x + 3y = 24$ is	(Q) 3/4
(C) The radius of the circle $3x(x-2)+3y(y+1)=4$ is	(R) 7
(D) The lines $2x - 3y = 5$ and $3x - 4y = 7$ are the diameters of a circle of area 154 s.u., then its radius is	(S) $\sqrt{\frac{31}{12}}$

6. Match the following Columns .

Column-I	Column-II
(A) The length of the tangents from any point on the circle $x^2+y^2+4x+6y+2008=0$ to the circle $x^2+y^2+4x+6y+2012=0$ is	(P) $3/\sqrt{2}$
	(Q) 2
(B) The lengths of the common chord of the circles $x^2+y^2+2x+3y+1=0$ and $x^2+y^2+3x+2y+1=0$ is	(R) 1
(C) The number of tangents which can be drawn from the point (2, 3) to the circle $x^2+y^2=13$ is	(S) 5/3
(D) The radius of the circle $ax^2+(2a-3)y^2-4x-7=0$ is	(T) 4/3

7. Match the following columns :

Column-I	Column-II
(A) No. of common tangents to the circles $x^2+y^2-2x=0$ and $x^2+y^2+6x-6y+2=0$ is	(P) 1
(B) No. of common tangents to the circles $x^2+y^2-4x-10y+4=0$ and $x^2+y^2-6x-12y-55=0$ is	(Q) 2
(C) No. of common tangents to the circles $x^2+y^2-2x-4y=0$ and $x^2+y^2-8y-4=0$ is	(R) 3
(D) No. of common tangents to the circles $x^2+y^2+2x-8y+13=0$ and $x^2+y^2-6x-2y+6=0$ is	(S) 0

8. Match the following columns :

Column-I	Column-II
(A) If $\left(a,\frac{1}{a}\right),\left(b,\frac{1}{b}\right),\left(c,\frac{1}{c}\right)$ & $\left(d,\frac{1}{d}\right)$ are four distincts points on a circle of radius 2012 units then the value of abcd is	(P) 2
(B) If a circle passes through the point of intersection of axes with the lines $\lambda x - y + 1 = 0$ and $x - 2y + 3 = 0$, then the value of λ is	(Q) 1
	(R) -5
(C) If the curves $ax^2+4xy+2y^2+x+y+5=0$ and $ax^2+6xy+5y^2+2x+3y+8=0$ intersect at four concyclic points, then the value of a is	(S) -4
	(T) 3

9. Match the following columns :

Column-I	Column-II
(A) If one of the diamters of the circle $x^2+y^2-2x-6y+6=0$ is a chord to the circle with center (2, 1), then the radius of the circle is	(P) 7
	(Q) 9
(B) If the tangent at the point P on the circle $x^2+y^2+6x+6y=2$ meets the straight line 5x-2y+6=0 at a point Q on the y-axis, then the length of PQ is	(R) 5
	(S) 2
(C) If the angle between the tangents from a point P to the circle $x^2+y^2+4x-6y+4\cos^2\alpha+9=0$ is 2α, then the radius of the locus of P is	(T) 3

10. Match the following columns :

Column-I	Column-II
(A) The locus of the point of	(P) x^2+y^2-

intersection of two perpendicular tangents to a circle $x^2+y^2=10$ is	$10x-25=0$
(B) The equation of the director circle of the circle	(Q) $x^2+y^2-6y+1=0$

$x^2+y^2-10x=0$ is

(C) The equation of the director circle of the circle $x^2+y^2-6y+5=0$ is	(R) $x^2+y^2=20$

ANSWER

5. (A) $\to$ (Q); (B) $\to$ (P) ; (C) $\to$ (S) ; (D) $\to$ (R)
6. (A) $\to$ (Q); (B) $\to$ (P) ; (C) $\to$ (R) ; (D) $\to$ (R)
7. (A) $\to$ (R); (B) $\to$ (S) ; (C) $\to$ (P) ; (D) $\to$ (Q)
8. (A) $\to$ (Q); (B) $\to$ (P) ; (C) $\to$ (S)
9. (A) $\to$ (T); (B) $\to$ (R) ; (C) $\to$ (S)
10. (A) $\to$ (R); (B) $\to$ (P) ; (C) $\to$ (Q)

QESTIONS ASKED IN ROORKEE JEE EXAM

1. A circle of diameter 13 m with centre O coinciding with the origin of co-ordinates axes has diameter AB on the x-axis. If the length of the chord AC be 5 m find the followings:
   (i) Equations of the pair of line BC and BC'
   (ii) The area of the smaller portion bounded between the circle and the chord AC.

   [Roorkee – 1983]

2. A circle I of radius 5 m is having its centre A at the origin of the co-ordinate axes. Two circles II and III with centre's at B and C and radii 3 and 4 m respectively , touch the circle I and also touch the x-axis to the right of A . Find the equations of any two common tangents to the circles II and III.

   [Roorkee – 1983]

3. Find the equation of a circle which is co-axial with the circles $2x^2+2y^2-2x+6y-3=0$ and $x^2+y^2+4x+2y+1=0$

   [Roorkee – 1984]

4. Find the condition such that the four points in which the circles $x^2+y^2+ax+by+c=0$ and $x^2+y^2+a'x+b'y+c'=0$ are intersected by the straight lines Ax + By+C = 0 and A'x+B'y+C'=0respectively lie on another circle.

   [Roorkee – 1986]

5. Obtains the equation of the straight lines passing through the point A(2, 0) and making 45° angle with the tangent A to the circle $(x+2)^2+(y-3)^2=25$. Find the equations of the circles each of radius 3 whose centers are on these straight lines at a distance of $5\sqrt{2}$ from A.

   [Roorkee – 1987]

6. A circle has radius 3 units and its centre lies on the line y = x – 1 . Find the equation of this circle if it passes through (7,3) **[Roorkee – 1988]**

7. Find the equation of the circles passing through the point (2, 8) touching the lines 4x– 3y–24 = 0 and 4 x + 3 y – 42=0 and having x co-ordinate of the center of the circle less than or equal to 8.

   [Roorkee – 1988]

8. The abscissa of two points A and B are the roots of the equation $x^2+2x-a^2=0$ and the ordinates are the roots of the equation $y^2+4y-b^2=0$. Find the equation of the circle with AB as its diameter. Also find the co-ordinates of the center and the length of the radius of the circle.

   [Roorkee – 1989]

9. The point of contact of the tangent to the circle $x^2+y^2=5$ at the point (1, -2) which touches the circle $x^2+y^2-8x+6y+20=0$, is
   (a) (2, -1) (b) (3, -1) (c) (4, -1) (d) (5, -1)

   [Roorkee – 1989]

10. The center of the circle passing through the point (0, 1) and touching the curve $y=x^2$ at (2, 4) is
    (a) (-16/5, 27/10) (b) (-16/7, 53/10)
    (c) (-16/5, 53/10) (d) None.

    [Roorkee – 1989]

11. The locus of the middle points of the chords of the circle $x^2+y^2-2x-6y-10=0$ which passes through the origin is the circle.
    (a) $x^2+y^2+x+3y=0$ (b) $x^2+y^2-x+3y=0$
    (c) $x^2+y^2+x-3y=0$ (d) $x^2+y^2-x-3y=0$

    [Roorkee – 1989]

12. The equation of the circle through the points of intersection of $x^2+y^2=1$, $x^2+y^2-2x-4y+1=0$ and touching the line x + 2 y = 0
    (a) $x^2+y^2+x+2y=0$
    (b) $x^2+y^2-x+2y=0$

(c) $x^2+y^2-x-2y=0$

(d) $2(x^2+y^2)-x-2y=0$

[Roorkee – 1989]

13. y-x+1=0 is the equation of normal at $\left(3+\frac{3}{\sqrt{2}}, \frac{3}{\sqrt{2}}\right)$ to which of the following circles ?

(a) $\left(x-3-\frac{3}{\sqrt{2}}\right)^2+\left(y-\frac{3}{\sqrt{2}}\right)^2=9$

(b) $\left(x-3-\frac{3}{\sqrt{2}}\right)^2+y^2=6$

(c) $(x-3)^2+y^2=6$

(d) $(x-3)^2+(y-3)^2=9$

[Roorkee – 1990]

14. Radical axis of two circles whose centers lie along x and y axes is

(a) $ax-by-\left(\frac{a^2+b^2}{4}\right)=0$

(b) $2g^2x+2f^2y-\left(\frac{g^2+f^2}{4}\right)=0$

(c) $gx+fy=g^4+f^4$

(d) $2gx-2fy+g^2-f^2=0$

[Roorkee – 1990]

15. Find the equations of the circle having the lines $x+2xy+3x+6y=0$ as its normals and having size just sufficient to contain the circle $x(x-4)+y(y-3)=0$.

[Roorkee Main – 1990]

16. A circle has its center in the first quadrant and passes through the point of intersections of the lines x = 2 and y = 3 . If it makes intercepts of 3 and 4 units on these lines respectively, then its equation is

[Roorkee – 1991]

(a) $x^2+y^2-3x-5y+8=0$

(b) $x^2+y^2-4x-6y+13=0$

(c) $x^2+y^2-6x-8y+23=0$

(d) $x^2+y^2-8x-9y+30=0$

17. The radius of the circle passing through the points (1, 2), (5, 2) and (5, -2) is

(a) $5\sqrt{2}$ (b) $2\sqrt{5}$ (c) $3\sqrt{2}$ (d) $2\sqrt{2}$

[Roorkee – 1991]

18. Find the equations of the circle passing through the points A(4, 3) and B(2, 5) and touching the axis of y . Also find the point P on the y-axis such that the angle APB has largest magnitude.

[Roorkee Main – 1991]

19. Find the radius of the smallest circle which touches the straight line 3x-y=6 at (1, -3) and also touches the line y = x . Compute up to one place of decimal only.

[Roorkee Main – 1991]

20. Lines are drawn from the point (-2, -3) to meet the circle $x^2+y^2-2x-10y+1=0$. The length of the line that meets the circle at two coincident point is

(a) $4\sqrt{3}$ (b) 16 (c) 48 (d) Cannot be Calculated unless coincident points are given

[Roorkee – 1992]

21. The equation of the circle , which touches both the axes and the straight line 4x+3y=6 in the first quadrant and lies below it is

(a) $4(x^2+y^2)-4x-4y+1=0$

(b) $x^2+y^2-6x-6y+9=0$

(c) $x^2+y^2-6x-y+9=0$

(d) $(x^2+y^2-x-6y)+4=0$

[Roorkee – 1992]

22. Circles are drawn through the point (2, 0) to cut intercepts of length 5 units on the x-axis. If their centers lie in the first quadrant , then their equation is

(a) $x^2+y^2-9x+2ky+14=0$

(b) $3x^2+3y^2+27x-2ky+42=0$

(c) $x^2+y^2-9x-2ky+14=0$

(d) $x^2+y^2-2kx-9y+14=0$, where k is a positive real number.

[Roorkee – 1992]

23. From a point P tangents drawn to the circles $x^2+y^2+x-3=0$, $3x^2+3y^2-5x+3y=0$ and $4x^2+4y^2+8x+7y+9=0$ are of equal lengths . Find the equation of the circle through P which touches the line x+y=5 at the point (6, -1)

[Roorkee Main -1992]

24. Find the equation of the system of co-axial circles that are tangent at $(\sqrt{2}, 4)$ to the locus of the point of intersection of mutually perpendicular tangents to the conic $x^2+y^2=9$

[Roorkee Main – 1993]

25. If the tangent to the circle $x^2+y^2=5$ at (1, -2) touches the circle $x^2+y^2-8x+6y+20=0$ at the point

(a) (2, -1) (b) (3, -1) (c) (4, -1) (d) (5, -1)

[Roorkee – 1994]

26. The center of the circle passing through the point (0, 1) and touching the curve $y = x^2$ at (2, 4) is

(a) (-16/5, 27/10) (b) (-16/7, 53/10)

(c) (-16/5, 53/10) (d) None.

[Roorkee – 1994]

27. Find the equation of the circle which touches the circle $x^2 + y^2 - 6x + 6y + 17 = 0$ externally and to which the lines $x^2 - 3xy - 3x + 9y = 0$ are normal.

[Roorkee Main – 1994]

28. If the lines $2x - 4y = 9$ and $6x - 12y + 7 = 0$ touch a circle, then the radius of the circle is

(a) $\frac{\sqrt{3}}{5}$ (b) $\frac{17}{6\sqrt{5}}$ (c) $\frac{2\sqrt{5}}{3}$ (d) $\frac{17}{3\sqrt{5}}$

[Roorkee – 1995]

29. If the co-ordinates at one end of a diameter of the circle $x^2 + y^2 - 8x - 4y + c = 0$ are (-3, 2), then the co-ordinates of the other end are

(a) (5, 3) (b) (6, 2) (c) (1,-8) (d) (11, 2)

[Roorkee – 1995]

30. If a circle is inscribed in an equilateral triangle of side a, then the area of the square inscribed in the circle is

(a) $a^2/6$ (b) $a^2/3$ (c) $2a^2/5$ (d) $2a^2/3$

[Roorkee – 1995]

31. The equations of lines joining the origin to the point of intersection of circle $x^2 + y^2 = 3$ and the line x + y = 2 is

(a) $y - (3 + 2\sqrt{2})x = 0$ (b) $x - (3 + 2\sqrt{2})y = 0$

(c) $x - (3 - 2\sqrt{2})y = 0$ (d) $y - (3 - 2\sqrt{2})x = 0$

[Roorkee – 1995]

32. From a point on the line $4x - 3y = 6$, tangents are drawn to the circle $x^2 + y^2 - 6x - 4y + 4 = 0$ which make an angle of $\tan^{-1}\left(\frac{24}{7}\right)$ between them. Find the co-ordinates of all such points and the equations of tangents.

[Roorkee Main – 1995]

33. Two circles $x^2 + y^2 - 10x + 16 = 0$ and $x^2 + y^2 = r^2$ intersect each other at two distinct points if

(a) r < 2 (b) r > 8

(c) 2 < r < 8 (d) $2 \le r \le 8$.

[Roorkee – 1996]

34. A tangent is drawn from the point (4, 0) to the circle $x^2 + y^2 = 8$ touches at a point A in the first quadrant. Find the co-ordinates of another point B on the circle such that AB = 4.

[Roorkee Main – 1996]

35. If the equations of the tangents drawn from the origin to the circle $x^2 + y^2 - 2rx - 2hy + h^2 = 0$ are perpendicular, then

(a) h = r (b) $h^2 = r^2$

(c) h = - r (d) $r^2 + h^2 = 1$

[Roorkee – 1997]

36. If a circle C and $x^2 + y^2 = 1$ are orthogonal and have radical axis parallel to y-axis, then C is

(a) $x^2 + y^2 - 1 + x = 0$ (b) $x^2 + y^2 - 1 - x = 0$

(c) $x^2 + y^2 + 1 - y = 0$ (d) $x^2 + y^2 + 1 + x = 0$

[Roorkee – 1997]

37. The equation of the line meeting the circle $x^2 + y^2 = a^2$, two points at equal distances 'd' from a point (x_1, y_1) on the circumference is

(a) $xx_1 + yy_1 - a^2 + \frac{1}{2d^2} = 0$

(b) $xx_1 - yy_1 - a^2 + \frac{1}{2d^2} = 0$

(c) $xx_1 + yy_1 + a^2 - \frac{1}{2d^2} = 0$

(d) $xx_1 + yy_1 - a^2 + \frac{1}{2d^2} = 0$

[Roorkee – 1998]

38. The equations of the tangents drawn from the origin to the circle $x^2 + y^2 - 2rx - 2hy + h^2 = 0$ are

(a) x = 0 (b) y = 0

(c) $(h^2 - r^2)x - 2rhy = 0$ (d) $(h^2 - r^2)x + 2rhy = 0$

[Roorkee – 1998]

39. Find the equation of a circle which touches the line x + y = 5 at the point (-2, 7) and cuts the circle $x^2 + y^2 + 4x - 6y + 9 = 0$ orthogonally.

[Roorkee Main -1998]

40. Extremities of a diagonal of a rectangle are (0, 0) and (4, 3). Find the equations of the tangents to the circum-circle of the rectangle which are parallel to this diagonal.

[Roorkee Main 2000]

41. Find the point on the straight line y = 2 x + 11 which is nearest to the circle $16(x^2 + y^2) + 32x - 8y - 50 = 0$.

[Roorkee Main – 2000]

42. A circle of radius 2 units rolls on the outer side of the circle $x^2 + y^2 + 4x = 0$, touching it externally Find the locus of the center of this outer circle. Also find the equations of the common tangents of the two circles when the line joining the centers of the two circles makes an angle of 60° with x-axis.

[Roorkee Main – 2000]

43. 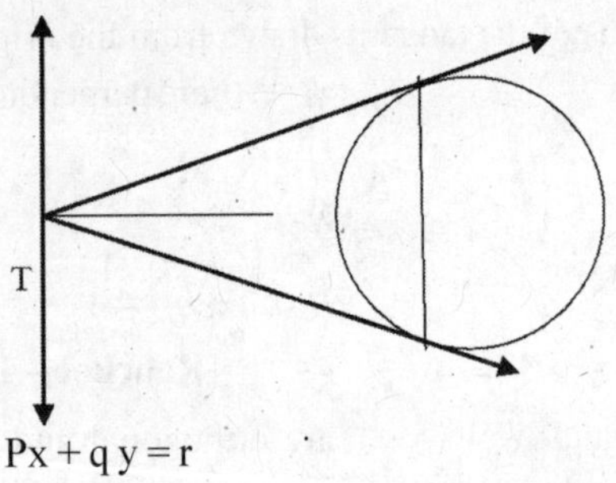

[Roorkee Main – 2001]

Tangents TP and TQ are drawn from a point T to the circle $x^2+y^2=a^2$. If the point T lies on the line $px+qy=r$, then find the locus of the center of the circumference of the triangle TPQ.

44. Find the equation of the circle which passes through the points of intersection of circles

$x^2+y^2-2x-6y+6=0$ and

$x^2+y^2+2x-6y+6=0$ and intersects the circle

$x^2+y^2+4x+6y+6=0$ orthogonally.

[Roorkee Main – 2001]

ANSWER

1. (i) $72y=\pm 15\,(2x+3)$;

(ii) $\left\{\frac{169}{8}\sin^{-1}\left(\frac{20}{169}\right)-15\right\}$ sq.m

2. $y=\frac{14\left(\sqrt{55}-\sqrt{65}\right)}{71-2\sqrt{(65\times 55)}}\left(x-\frac{3\sqrt{65}+4\sqrt{55}}{7}\right)$

3. $4x^2+4y^2+6x+10y-1=0$

4. $BA'(c-c')+CA'(b-b')-CB'(a-a')=0$

5. $x-7y-2=0$; $(x-1)^2+(y-7)^2=9$, $(x-9)^2+(y-1)^2=9$

6. $(x-7)^2+(y-6)^2=9$, $(x-4)^2+(y-3)^2=9$

7. $x^2+y^2-2x-6y-12=0$

8. $x^2+y^2+2x+4y-(a^2+b^2)=0$, $\sqrt{a^2+b^2+5}$

15. $x^2+y^2+6x-3y-45=0$

18. $x^2+y^2-4x-9y+9=0$

19. 1.9

23. $x^2+y^2-7x+7y+12=0$

24. $x^2+y^2-4\sqrt{2}x-42=0$

27. $x^2+y^2-6x-2y+1=0$

32. (0, -2), (6, 6)

34. (-2, 2), (2, -2)

39. $x^2+y^2+7x-11y+38=0$

40. $8y-6x\pm 25=0$

41. $\left(-\frac{9}{2},2\right)$

42. $x^2+y^2+4x-12=0$; $y+\frac{x}{\sqrt{3}}+C_1=0$, where $C_1=2\sqrt{3}$, $C_1=-\frac{2}{\sqrt{3}}$.

43. $(px+qy-r)^2=(p^2+q^2)(x^2+y^2)$

44. $x^2+y^2+\left(\frac{2\lambda-2}{1+\lambda^2}\right)x+\left(\frac{-6\lambda-6}{1+\lambda^2}\right)y+\left(\frac{6+6\lambda}{1+\lambda^2}\right)=0$, where λ = -2, -4.

QUESTIONS ASKED IN IIT-JEE EXAM

1. Find the equation of the circle which passes through the point (2, 0) and whose center is the limit of the point of intersection of the lines $3x+5y=1$, $(2+c)x+5c^2y=1$ as c tends to 1.

[IIT-JEE – 1979]

2. Two circles $x^2+y^2=6$ and $x^2+y^2-6x+8=0$ are given. Then the equation of the circle through their points of intersection and the point (1, 1) is

(a) $x^2+y^2-6x+4=0$ (b) $x^2+y^2-3x+1=0$

(c) $x^2+y^2-4x+2=0$ (d) None.

[IIT-JEE – 1980]

3. Let A be the center of the circle

$x^2+y^2-2x-4y-20=0$.

Suppose that the tangents at the points B(1, 7) and D(4, -2) on the circle meet at the point C, find the area of the quadrilateral ABCD.

[IIT-JEE – 1981]

4. Find the equations of the circles passing through (-4, 3) and touching the lines x + y = 4 and x – y = 2

[IIT-JEE – 1982]

5. If A nad B are point in the plane such that $\frac{PA}{PB}=k$ (constant) for all P on a given circle, then find the value of k cannot be equal to… **[IIT-JEE – 1982]**

6. The points of intersection of the line $4x-3y-10=0$ and the circle $x^2+y^2-2x+4y-20=0$, is ....

[IIT-JEE – 1983]

7. The equation of the cir cle passing through (1, 1) and the points of intersection of $x^2+y^2+13x-3y=0$,

$2x^2+2y^2+4x-7y-25=0$ is

(a) $4x^2+4y^2-30x-10y-25=0$

(b) $4x^2+4y^2+30x-13y-25=0$

(c) $4x^2+4y^2-17x-10y-25=0$

(d) None

[IIT-JEE – 1983]

8. The center of the circle passing through the point (0, 1) and touching the curve $y=x^2$ at (2, 4) is

(a) $\left(-\frac{16}{5},\frac{27}{10}\right)$ (b) $\left(-\frac{16}{7},\frac{53}{10}\right)$

(c) $\left(-\frac{16}{5},\frac{53}{10}\right)$ (d) None.

[IIT-JEE – 1983]

9. AB is a diameter of a circle and C is any point on the circumference of the circle . Then

(a) The area of triangle ABC is maximum when it is isosceles.

(b) The area of triangle ABC is minimum when it is isosceles.

(c) The area of triangle ABC is minimum when it is isosceles.

(d) None. [IIT-JEE – 1983]

10. Through a fixed point (h, k) secants are drawn to the circle $x^2+y^2=r^2$. Show that the locus of the middle points of the secants intercepted by the circle is $x^2+y^2=hx+ky$

[IIT-JEE1983]

11. The locus of the mid-point of a chord of the circle $x^2+y^2=4$, which subtends a right angle at the origin is

(a) $x+y=2$ (b) $x^2+y^2=1$

(c) $x^2+y^2=2$ (d) $x+y=1$

[IIT-JEE – 1984]

12. The abscissa of the two points A and B are the roots of the equation $x^2+2ax-b^2=0$ and their ordinates are the roots of the equation $y^2+2py-q^2=0$. Find the equation of the circle on AB as diameter.

[IIT-JEE – 1984]

13. The lines $3x-4y+4=0$ and $6x-8y-7=0$ are tangents to the same circle. The radius of the circle is ....

[IIT-JEE -1984]

14. From the origin chords are drawn to the circle $(x-1)^2+y^2=1$. The equation of the locus of the mid-points of these chords is........................

[IIT-JEE -1984]

15. Let $x^2+y^2-4x-2y-11=0$ be a circle. A pair of tangents from (4, 5) with a pair of radii form a quadrilateral of area....................

[IIT-JEE – 1985]

16. The equation of the line passing through the points of intersection of the circles $3x^2+3y^2-2x+12y-9=0$ and $x^2+y^2+6x+2y-15=0$ is...........

[IIT-JEE – 1986]

17. From the point A(0, 3) on the circle $x^2+4x+(y-3)^2=0$. A chord AB is drawn and extended to a point M such that AM = 2AB . The equation of the locus of M is..................

[IIT-JEE-1986]

18. Lines $5x+12y-10=0$ and $5x-12y-40=0$, touch a circle C_1 of diameter 6 . If the center of C_1 lies in the first quadrant , find the equation of the circle C_2 which is concentric with C_1 and cuts intercepts of length 8 on these lines.

[IIT-JEE – 1986]

19. Let a given line L_1 intersect the x and y axis at P and Q respectively. Let another line L_2 perpendicular to cut the x and y axes at R and S respectively . Show that the locus of the point of intersection of the lines PS and QR is a circle passing through the origin.

[IIT-JEE – 1987]

20. The circle $x^2+y^2-4x-4y+4=0$ is inscribed in a triangle which has two of its sides along the c o - ordinate axes. The locus of the circumcentre of the triangle is $x+y-xy+k\left(\sqrt{x^2+y^2}\right)=0$, then find the value of k.

[IIT-JEE – 1987]

21. The area of the triangle formed by tangents from the points (4, 3) to the circle $x^2+y^2=9$ and the line joining their points of contact is....................

[IIT-JEE -1987]

22. A Polygon of nine sides , each of length 2 , is inscribed in a circle. The radius of the circle is.............................

[IIT-JEE – 1987]

23. If the circle $C_1: x^2+y^2=16$ intersects another circle C2 of radius 5 in such a manner that the common chord is of maximum length and has a slope equal to 3 / 4 , then the co-ordinates of the center C2 are ....

[IIT-JEE – 1988]

24. If a circle passes through the point (a, b) and cuts the circle $x^2+y^2=k^2$ orthogonally, then the equation of the locus of its center is

(a) $2ax+2by-(a^2+b^2+k^2)=0$

(b) $2ax+2by-(a^2-b^2+k^2)=0$

(c) $x^2+y^2-3ax-4by+(a^2+b^2-k^2)=0$

(d) $x^2+y^2-2ax-3by+(a^2+b^2-k^2)=0$

[IIT-JEE – 1988]

25. The equation of the tangents drawn from the origin to the circle $x^2+y^2+2rx-2hy+h^2=0$ are

(a) x=0

(b) y=0

(c) $(h^2-r^2)x-2rhy=0$

(d) $(h^2-r^2)x+2rhy=0$.

[IIT-JEE – 1988]

26. Let $S=x^2+y^2+2gx+2fy+c=0$ be a given circle. Find the locus of the foot of the perpendicular drawn from the origin upon any chord of S which subtends a right angle at the origin.

[IIT-JEE – 1988]

27. If the two circles $(x-1)^2+(y-3)^2=r^2$ and

$x^2+y^2-8x+2y+8=0$

intersects in two distinct points, then

(a) 2<r<8 (b) r<2 (d) r=2 (d) r>2.

[IIT-JEE – 1989]

28. The lines 2 x – 3 y = 5 and 3 x – 4 y = 7 are diameters of a circle of area 154 sq. units . Then the equation of the circle is

(a) $x^2+y^2+2x-2y-62=0$

(b) $x^2+y^2+2x-2y-47=0$

(c) $x^2+y^2-2x+2y-47=0$

(d) $x^2+y^2-2x+2y-62=0$

[IIT-JEE – 1989]

29. If $\left(m_i, \frac{1}{m_i}\right)$ i= 1, 2, 3, 4 are four distinct points on a circle, then show that $m_1 m_2 m_3 m_4 = 1$.

[IIT-JEE – 1989]

30. The line x + 3 y = 0 is a diameter of the circle $x^2+y^2-6x+2y=0$. Is it true/ false?

[IIT-JEE – 1989]

31. ABC is an isosceles triangle inscribed in a circle of radius r . If AB = AC and h is the altitude from A to BC then the triangle ABC has perimeter

$P=2\left(\sqrt{2hr-h^2}+\sqrt{2hr}\right)$, then area

A = ...also find the limit of $\lim_{h\to 0}\left(\frac{A}{p^3}\right)$

[IIT-JEE – 1989]

32. The area of the triangle formed by the positive x-axis and the normal and the tangent to the circle $x^2+y^2=4$ at $(1,\sqrt{3})$ is..........................

[IIT-JEE – 1989]

33. A circle touches the line y = x at a point P such that $OP=\sqrt{2}$, where O is the origin. The circle contains the point (-10, 2) in its interior and the length of its chord on the line x + y = 0 is $6\sqrt{2}$. Determine the equation of the circle.

[IIT-JEE – 1990]

34. A point P is given on the circumference of a circle of radius r , Chord QR is parallel to the tangent at P. Determine the maximum possible area of the triangle PQR.

[IIT-JEE – 1990]

35. Two circles each of radius 5 units , touch each other at (1, 2) . If the equation of their common tangent is 4 x + 3 y = 10 . Find the equations of the circles.

[IIT-JEE – 1991]

36. If a circle passes through the points of intersection of the co-ordinate axes with the lines $\lambda x-y+1=0$ and x – 2 y + 3 = 0 , then the line passes through a fixed point , whose co-ordinates are..............

[IIT-JEE – 1991]

37. Three circles, each of radius 5 units , touch each other externally. The tangent at their points of contact meet at a point whose distance from a point of contact is 4. Find the ratio of the product of the radii to the sum of the radii of the circles.

[IIT-JEE-1992]

38. Let a circle be given by $2x(x-a)+y(2y-b)=0$, $(a, b\neq 0)$, find the condition on a and b if two chords , each bisects by the x-axis, can be drawn to the circle from $\left(a,\frac{b}{2}\right)$

[IIT-JEE – 1992]

39. The center of a circle passing through the points (0, 0) , (1, 0) and touching the circle $x^2+y^2=9$ is

(a) (3/2 , ½) (b) (1/2 , 3/2)

(c)(1/2, ½) (d) $(1/2, 1/\sqrt{2})$

[IIT-JEE – 1992]

40. The locus of the center of a circle which touches externally the circle $x^2+y^2-6x-6y+14=0$ and also touches the y-axis is given by the equation

(a) $x^2 - 6x - 10y + 14 = 0$

(b) $x^2 - 10x - 6y + 14 = 0$

(c) $y^2 - 6x - 10y + 14 = 0$

(d) $y^2 - 10x + 6y + 14 = 0$

[IIT-JEE – 1993]

41. Consider a family of circles passing through two fixed point A(3, 7) and B (6, 5). Show that the chords in which the circle $x^2 + y^2 - 4x - 6y - 3 = 0$ cuts the members of the family are concurrent at a point . Find the co-ordinates of this point.

[IIT-JEE – 1993]

42. Find the co-ordinates of the point at which the circle $x^2 + y^2 - 4x - 2y - 4 = 0$ and $x^2 + y^2 - 12x - 8y - 36 = 0$ touch each other . Also find equations of common tangents touching the circles in distinct points.

[IIT-JEE – 1993]

43. The equation of the locus of the mid-points of chords of the circle $4x^2 + 4y^2 - 12x + 4y + 1 = 0$ that subtend an angle of $\frac{2\pi}{3}$ at its center is..........................

[IIT-JEE – 1993]

44. The circles $x^2 + y^2 - 10x + 16 = 0$ and $x^2 + y^2 = r^2$ intersect each other in distinct points if

(a) r<2 (b) r>8

(c) 2 <r<8 (d) $2 \le r \le 8$

[IIT-JEE – 1994]

45. A circle is inscribed in an equilateral triangle of side. The area of any square inscribed in this circle is...

[IIT-JEE – 1994]

46. The angle between a pair of tangents drawn from a point P to the circle $x^2 + y^2 + 4x - 6y + 9\sin^2\alpha + 13\cos^2\alpha = 0$ is 2α . Then the locus of P is

(a) $x^2 + y^2 + 4x - 6y + 4 = 0$

(b) $x^2 + y^2 + 4x - 6y - 9 = 0$

(c) $x^2 + y^2 + 4x - 6y - 4 = 0$

(d) $x^2 + y^2 + 4x - 6y + 9 = 0$

[IIT-JEE – 1996]

47. A circle passes through three point A, B and C with the line segment AC as its diameter. A line passing through A intersects the chord BC at a point D inside the circle. If angles DAB and CAB are α and β respectively and the distance between the point A and the mid-point of the line segment DC is d. Prove that the area of the circle is

[IIT-JEE – 1996]

$$\frac{\pi d^2 \cos^2\alpha}{\cos^2\alpha + \cos^2\beta + 2\cos\alpha\cos\beta\cos(\beta - \alpha)}.$$

48. Find the interval in which ‘a’ lies for which the line y + x = 0 bisects two chords drawn from the point $\left(\frac{1+a\sqrt{2}}{2}, \frac{1-a\sqrt{2}}{2}\right)$ to the circle $2(x^2 + y^2) - (1 + a\sqrt{2})x - (1 - a\sqrt{2})y = 0$.

[IIT-JEE – 1996]

49. Intercepts on the line y = x by the circle $x^2 + y^2 - 2x = 0$ is AB. Equation of the circle with AB as diameters is ...

[IIT-JEE – 1996]

50. Let C be any circle with center $(0, \sqrt{2})$. Prove that at the most two rational points can be there on C. (A rational point is a point for which both the co-ordinates are rational numbers).

[IIT-JEE – 1997]

51. Consider a curve $ax^2 + 2hxy + by^2 = 1$ and a point P not on the curve . A line drawn from the point P intersects the curve at point Q and R. If the product PQ. PR is independent of the slope of the line, then show that the curve is a circle.

[IIT-JEE – 1997]

52. For each natural number k, let C k denotes the circle with radius k centimeters and center at the origin . On the circle C k , a particle moves k centimeters in the counter clockwise direction . After completing its motion on Ck , the particle moves to C k+1 in the radial direction. The particle starts at (1,0) . If the particle crosses the positive direction of the x-axis for the first time on the circle C n , then n = ...

[IIT-JEE – 1997]

53. The chords of contact of the pair of tangents drawn from each point on the line 2 x + y = 4 to the circle $x^2 + y^2 = 1$ pass through the point ....

[IIT-JEE – 1997]

54. Two vertices of an equilateral triangle are (-1, 0) and (1, 0) and its third vertex lies above the x-axis, the equation of its circum-circle is............................

[IIT-JEE – 1997]

55. The number of common tangents to the circles $x^2 + y^2 = 4$ and $x^2 + y^2 - 6x - 8y - 24 = 0$ is

(a) 0 (b) 1 (c) 3 (d) 4

[IIT-JEE – 1998]

56. C_1 and C_2 are two concentric circles, the radius of C_2 being twice that of C_1. From a point P on C_2 tangents PA and PB are drawn to C_1 . Prove that the centroid of the triangle PAB lies on C_1.

[IIT-JEE – 1998]

57. Let $A_0A_1A_2A_3A_4A_5$ be a regular hexagon inscribed in a unit circle. Then the product of the lengths of line segments A_0A_1, A_0A_2 and A_0A_4 is

[IIT-JEE – 1998]

(a) 3/4 (b) $3\sqrt{3}$ (c) 3 (d) $3\sqrt{3}/2$.

58. If two distinct chords, drawn from the point (p, q) on the circle $x^2+y^2=px+qy$, where $pq \neq 0$ are bisected by the x-axis, then

[IIT-JEE – 1999]

(a) $p^2=q^2$ (b) $p^2=8q^2$

(c) $p^2<8q^2$ (d) $p^2>8q^2$.

59. Consider the family of circles $x^2+y^2=r^2, 2<r<5$. If in the first quadrant, the common tangent to a circle of this family and the ellipse $4x^2+25y^2=100$ meets the co-ordinate axes at A and B, then find the equation of the locus of the mid-point of AB.

[IIT-JEE -1999]

60. Let T_1, T_2 be two tangents drawn from (-2, 0) on the circle C : $x^2+y^2=1$. Determine the circles touching C and having T_1, T_2 as their pairs of tangents. Furthers find the equations of all possible common tangents to these circles, when taken two at a time.

[IIT-JEE – 1999]

61. The triangle PQR is inscribed in the circle $x^2+y^2=25$. If Q and R have co-ordinates (3, 4) and (-4, 3) respectively, then $\angle QPR$ is

[IIT-JEE – 2000]

(a) π/2 (b) π/3 (c) π/4 (d) π/6.

62. If the circles $x^2+y^2+2x+2ky+b=0$ and $x^2+y^2+2ky+k=0$ intersect orthogonally, then k is

(a) 2 or -3/2 (b) - 2 or – 3/2

(c) 2 or 3/2 (d) - 2 or 3/2.

[IIT-JEE– 2000]

63. Let AB be a chord of the circle $x^2+y^2=r^2$ subtending right angle at the center, then the locus of the centroid of the triangle PAB as P moves on the circle is

(a) a parabola (b) a circle

(c) an ellipse (d) a pair of st lines

[IIT-JEE – 2000]

64. Let ABC be an equilateral triangle inscribed in the circle $x^2+y^2=a^2$, suppose perpendiculars from A, B, C to the major axis of the ellipse $\frac{x^2}{a^2}+\frac{y^2}{b^2}=1$; (a > b) meet the ellipse respectively at P, Q so that P, Q, R on the same side of the major axis as A, B, C respectively. Prove that the normals to the ellipse drawn at the points P, Q and R are concurrent.

[IIT-JEE – 2000]

65. Let $2x^2+y^2-3xy=0$ be the equation of pair of tangents drawn from the origin O to a circle of radius 3 with center is in the first quadrant. If A is one of the points of contact, find the length of OA.

[IIT-JEE – 2001]

66. Let PQ and Rs be tangents at the extremities of the diameter PR of a circle of radius r. If PS and RQ intersect a point x on the circumference of the circle, then 2 r equals

(a) $\sqrt{PQ.RS}$ (b) $\frac{PQ+RS}{2}$

(c) $\frac{2PQ+RS}{PQ+RS}$ (d) $\sqrt{\frac{PQ^2+RS^2}{2}}$

[IIT-JEE – 2001]

67. Let C1 and C2 be two circles with C2 lying inside C1. A circle C lying inside C1 touches C1 internally and C2 externally. Identify the locus of the center of C.

[IIT-JEE – 2001]

68. If the tangent at the point P on the circle

$$x^2+y^2+6x+6y=2$$

meets the straight line $5x-2y+6=0$ at a point Q on the y-axis, then the length of PQ is

[IIT-JEE – 2002]

(a) 4 (b) $2\sqrt{5}$ (c) 5 (d) $3\sqrt{5}$.

69. If a > 2 b > 0 then the positive value of m for which $y=mx-b\sqrt{1+m^2}$ is a common tangent to $x^2+y^2=b^2$ and $(x-a)^2+y^2=b^2$ is

[IIT-JEE – 2002]

(a) $\frac{2b}{\sqrt{a^2-4b^2}}$ (b) $\frac{\sqrt{a^2-4b^2}}{2a}$

(c) $\frac{2b}{a-2b}$ (d) $\frac{b}{a-2b}$.

70. Find the point on $x^2+2y^2=6$, which is nearest to the line x + y = 7.

[IIT-JEE – 2003]

71. Tangents are drawn from P(6, 8) to the circle $x^2+y^2=r^2$. Find the radius of the circle such that the area of the triangle formed by the tangents and the chord of contact is maximum.

[IIT-JEE – 2003]

72. If In represents area of n-sided regular polygon inscribed in a unit circle and On be the area of the n – sided regular polygon circumscribing it, prove that

$$I_n = \frac{O_n}{2}\left[1+\sqrt{1-\left(\frac{2\,I_n}{n}\right)^2}\,\right]$$

[IIT-JEE – 2003]

73. The center of the circle inscribed in square formed by the lines $x^2-8x+12=0$ and $y^2-14y+45=0$ is

[IIT-JEE – 2004]

(a) (4, 7) (b) (7,4) (c) (9,4) (d) (4,9)

74. If one of the diameters of the circle

$$x^2+y^2-2x-6y+6=0$$

is a chord to the circle with center (2, 1), then the radius of the circle is

[IIT-JEE – 2004]

(a) $\sqrt{3}$ (b) $\sqrt{2}$ (c) 3 (d) 2.

75. Find the center and radius of the circle formed by all the points represented by z = x + I y satisfying the relation $\frac{|z-\alpha|}{|z-\beta|}=k,\ (k\neq 1)$, where α and β are constant complex numbers given by $\alpha=\alpha_1=i\,\alpha_2, \beta=\beta_1+i\beta_2$.

[IIT-JEE – 2004]

76. Find the equation of the circle touches the line 2 x + 3 y + 1 = 0 at the point (1, -1) and is orthogonal to the circle which has the line segment having end points (0, -1) and (-2, 3) as the diameter.

[IIT-JEE – 2004]

77. Three circles of radii 3, 4 and 5 units touches each other externally and the tangents drawn at the point of contact intersect at P. Find distance between point P and point of contact.

[IIT-JEE – 2005]

78. A circle is given by $x^2+(y-1)^2=1$, another circle C touches it externally and also the x-axis, then the locus of its center is

[IIT-JEE – 2005]

(a) $\{(x,y): x^2=4y\}\cup\{(x,y): y\leq 0\}$

(b) $\{(x,y): x^2+(y-1)^2=4\}\cup\{(x,y): y\leq 0\}$

(c) $\{(x,y): x^2=y\}\cup\{(0,y): y<0\}$

(d) $\{(x,y): x^2=y\}\cup\{(0,y): y\leq 0\}$

79. Tangent to the curve $y=x^2+6$ at a point P(1, 7) touches the circle $x^2+y^2+16x+12y+c=0$ at a point Q. Then the co-ordinates of Q are

[IIT-JEE – 2005]

(a) (-6, -7) (b) (-10, -15) (c) (-9, -13) (d) (-6, -11).

80. Let ABCD be a quadrilateral with area 18 , with side AB parallel to the side CD and AB = 2 CD.

Let AD be perpendicular to AB and CD . If a circle is drawn inside the quadrilateral ABCD touching all the sides, then its radius is

[IIT-JEE – 2007]

(a) 3 (b) 2 (c) 3/2 (d) 1.

COMPREHENSION LINK PASSAGE

Let ABCD be a square of side length 2 units . C_2 is the circle through vertices A, B, C, D and C_1 in the circle touching all the sides of the square ABCD , L is a line through A

81. If P is a point on C_1 and Q in another point on C_2, then $\frac{PA^2+PB^2+PC^2+PD^2}{QA^2+QB^2+QC^2+QD^2}$ is equal to

(a) 0.75 (b) 1.25 (c) 1 (d) 0.5

82. A circle touches the line L and the circle C_1 externally such that both the circles are on the same side of the line, then the locus of center of the circle is

(a) ellipse (b) hyperbola

(c) parabola (d) pairs of st lines.

83. A line M through A is drawn parallel to BD. Point S moves such that its distances from the line BD and the vertex A are equal . If locus of S cuts M at T_2 and T_3 and AC at T_1, then the area of $\Delta T_1T_2T_3$ is

(a) 1/2 sq. unit (b) 2/3 sq. unit

(c) 1 sq. unit (d) 2 sq. unit.

[IIT-JEE – 2007]

84. Tangents are drawn from the point (17, 7) to the circle $x^2+y^2=169$

Statement - 1: The tangents are mutually perpendicular.

Satetement-2: The locus of the point from which mutually perpendicular tangents can be drawn to the given circle is $x^2+y^2=338$.

[IIT-JEE - 2007]

Ans. (a)

85. Consider $L_1: 2x+3y+(p-3)=0$

$L_2: 2x+3y+(p+3)=0$, where p is a real number and

$C: x^2+y^2+6x-10y+30=0$

Statement-1: If L1 is a chord of circle C , then L2 is not always diameter of circle C.

Statement-2: If L1 is a dimameter of circle C, the line L2 is not a chord of circle C.

[IIT-JEE-2008]

86. **Comprehension**

A circle C of radius 1 is inscribed in an equilateral triangle PQR. The points of contact of C with the side PQ, QR, RP are D, E, F respectively. The line PQ is given by the equation $\sqrt{3}x + y = 6$ and the point D is $\left(3\sqrt{3}/2,\ 3/2\right)$. Further it is given that the origin and the centre C are on the same side PQ.

1. The equation of circle C is

(a) $\left(x-2\sqrt{3}\right)^2+\left(y-1\right)^2=1$

(b) $\left(x-2\sqrt{3}\right)^2+\left(y-1/2\right)^2=1$

(c) $\left(x-\sqrt{3}\right)^2+\left(y+1\right)^2=1$

(d) $\left(x-\sqrt{3}\right)^2+\left(y-1\right)^2=1$

2. Points E and F are given by

(a) $\left(\sqrt{3}/2,\ 3/2\right),\left(\sqrt{3},\ 0\right)$

(b) $\left(\sqrt{3}/2,\ 1/2\right),\left(\sqrt{3},\ 0\right)$

(c) $\left(\sqrt{3}/2,\ 3/2\right),\left(\sqrt{3}/2,\ 1/2\right)$

(d) $\left(3/2,\ \sqrt{3}/2\right),\left(\sqrt{3}/2,\ 1/2\right)$

3. Equations of the sides QR, PR are

(a) $y=\left(2/\sqrt{3}\right)x+1,\ y=-\left(2/\sqrt{3}\right)x-1$

(b) $y=\left(1/\sqrt{3}\right)x+1,\ y=0$

(c) $y=\left(\sqrt{3}/2\right)x+1,\ y=\left(-\sqrt{3}/2\right)x-1$

(d) $y=\sqrt{3}x,\ y=0$

[IIT-JEE-2008]

87. Tangents are drawn from a point P(1, 8) to the circle $x^2+y^2-6x-4y-11=0$ touch the circle at the points A and B . The equation of the circumcircle of the traingle PAB is

(a) $x^2+y^2-6x-4y-19=0$

(b) $x^2+y^2-6x-10y-19=0$

(c) $x^2+y^2-2x+6y-29=0$

(d) $x^2+y^2-6x-4y+19=0$

[IIT-JEE-2009]

88. Two parallel chords of a circle of radius 2 are at a distance $\sqrt{3}+1$ apart. If the chords subtend at the centre , angles of $\frac{\pi}{k}$ and $\frac{3\pi}{k}$, where k > 0 , then the value of [k] is...., where [,] = G.I.F

[IIT-JEE-2010]

ANSWER

1. $25\left(x^2+y^2\right)-4x+2y-60=0$

3. 75 sq. units

4. $x^2+y^2+2\left(10\pm\sqrt{54}\right)x+\left(55\pm\sqrt{54}\right)=0$

5. 1

6. (4, 2) ; (-2, -6)

12. $x^2+y^2+2ax+2py-\left(b^2+q^2\right)=0$

13. 3/4

14. $x^2+y^2-x=0$

15. 8 sq. units

16. $10x-3y-18=0$

17. $x^2+y^2-8x-6y+9=0$

18. $x^2+y^2-10x-4y+4=0$

20. $k=\frac{xy+2}{2\sqrt{x^2+y^2}}$

21. 192/25

22. $\cos\left(\frac{\pi}{9}\right)$

23. $\left(-\frac{9}{5},\frac{12}{5}\right),\left(\frac{9}{5},-\frac{12}{5}\right)$

26. $x^2+y^2+gx+fy+\frac{C}{2}=0$

30. True

31. $h\sqrt{2hr-h^2},\ \frac{1}{128\,r}$

32. $2\sqrt{3}$

33. $x^2+y^2+18x-2y+32=0$

34. $\frac{3\sqrt{3}}{4}\times r^2$ sq. units

35. $x^2+y^2+6x+2y-15=0$

36. 1=2

37. 16:1

38. $a^2>2b^2$

41. $\left(2, \frac{23}{3}\right)$

42. $7y - 24x + 16 = 0$

43. $16(x^2 + y^2) - 48x + 16y + 31 = 0$

45. $\frac{a^2}{6}$ sq. units.

48. $a \in (-\infty, -2) \cup (2, \infty)$

49. $x^2 + y^2 - x - y = 0$

52. 7

53. $\left(\frac{1}{2}, \frac{1}{4}\right)$

54. $x^2 + y^2 - \frac{2}{\sqrt{5}} y - 1 = 0$

59. $4x^2 + 25y^2 = 4x^2y^2$

60. $x = \pm 1 = y;\ x = \pm\left(\frac{x+2}{\sqrt{3}}\right),\ y = 5\left(\frac{x + \frac{4}{5}}{\sqrt{39}}\right)$

65. $9 + 3\sqrt{10}$

67. The Ellipse

70. (2, 1)

71. 5

75. $\frac{\alpha - k^2\beta}{1-k^2},\ \left|\frac{k(\alpha-\beta)}{1-k^2}\right|$

76. $2x^2 + 2y^2 - 10x - 5y + 1 = 0$

77. $\sqrt{5}$

84. (a)

85. (c)

88. 3

SELF ASSESSMENT TEST-I

Time : 3 Hrs. **Ch: The Circle** **M.M. : 100**

Give answers the following questions

1. The chord of contact of tangents from a point on the circle $x^2 + y^2 = a^2$ to the circle $x^2 + y^2 = b^2$ touches the circle $x^2 + y^2 = c^2$. Show that a, b, c are in G.P

2. If the pole of a straight line with respect to the circle $x^2 + y^2 = c^2$ lies on the circle $x^2 + y^2 = 9c^2$, then prove that the line is a tangent to the circle $9x^2 + 9y^2 = c^2$.

3. A tangent drawn from the point (4, 0) to the circle $x^2 + y^2 = 8$ touches it a point A in the first quadrant. Find the co-ordinates of another point B on the circle such that AB = 4.

4. Find the area of an equilateral triangle inscribed in the circle $x^2 + y^2 + 2gx + 2fy + c = 0$.

5. Find the area of the square circumscribing the circle $3(x^2 + y^2) - 6x + 8y = 0$.

6. If the four distinct points $\left(m_r, \frac{1}{m_r}\right)$, r = 1, 2, 3, 4 are concyclic , then prove that the product of their ordinates is equal to 1.

7. Prove that the circle $x^2 + y^2 - 6x - 4y + 9 = 0$ bisects the circumference of the circle

$$x^2 + y^2 - 8x - 6y + 23 = 0.$$

8. Find the equation of the circle whose diameter is the common chord of the circles

$$x^2 + y^2 + 2x + 3y + 1 = 0,\ x^2 + y^2 + 4x + 3y + 2 = 0.$$

SELF ASSESSMENT TEST-II

Time : 3 Hrs. **Ch: The Circle** **M.M. : 100**

Give answers the following questions

1. The straight line $mx - y = 1 + 2m$ cuts the circle $x^2 + y^2 =$ 1 at one point at least. Then the set of values of m is

(a) [-4/3, 0] (b) [-4/3, 4/3] (c) [0, 4/3] (d) None

2. If (2, 5) is an interrior point of the circle $x^2 + y^2 - 8x - 12y + p = 0$ and the circle neither cuts nor touches any one of the axes of co-ordinates, then the value of p lies in

(a) (36, 47) (b) (16, 47) (c) (16, 36) (d) None.

3. The number of points (a+1, a) , where a is an integer , lying inside the region bounded by the circles

$x^2 + y^2 - 2x - 1 = 0$ and $x^2 + y^2 - 2x - 17 = 0$, is

(a) 2 (b) 4 (c) 1 (d) None.

4. Prove that one-third of the circumference of the circle $x^2 + y^2 - 2x = 0$ falls inside the circle

$$\sqrt{3}(x^2 + y^2) - 2\sqrt{3}\,x + 2y + 1 = 0.$$

5. If a vertex of an equilateral triangle is $(2\sqrt{2}, -1)$ and its centroid is (0, 0), then find the equation of its incircle.

6. P(2, 2) is a point on circle $x^2 + y^2 - 2x - 2y = 0$. If P travels on the circle and reaches Q such that arc

$PQ = \frac{1}{6} \times$ circumference of the circle, then find the co-ordinates of Q.

7. Find the range of values of 'a' such that the angle θ between the pair of tangents drawn from (a, 0) to the circle $x^2 + y^2 = 1$ satisfies $\frac{\pi}{2} < \theta < \pi$.

(a) $(1, 2)$ (b) $\left(1, \sqrt{2}\right)$

(c) $\left(-\sqrt{2}, -1\right)$ (d) $\left(-\sqrt{2}, -1\right) \cup \left(1, \sqrt{2}\right)$.

ANSWER

Self Assessment Test-I

3. (2, -2) ; (-2, 2)

4. $\frac{3\sqrt{3}}{4}\left(g^2 + f^2 - c\right)$ sq. unit.

5. 100/9 sq. units

8. $2\left(x^2 + y^2\right) + 2x + 6y + 1 = 0$.

Self Assessment Test-II

5. $4\left(x^2 + y^2\right) = 9$.

6. $\left(\frac{3}{2} \mp \frac{\sqrt{3}}{2}, \frac{3}{2} \pm \frac{\sqrt{3}}{2}\right)$.

❑❑❑

THE CONIC SECTIONS

4 The Parabola

CONCEPT BOOSTER

4.1 INTRODUCTION

It is believed that the first definition of a conic section is due to Menaechmus (died 320 BC). His work did not survive and is only known through secondary accounts. The definition used at that time differs from the one commonly used today in that it requires theplane cutting the cone to be perpendicular to one of the lines, (a generatrix), that generates the cone as a surface of revolution. Thus the shape of the conic is determined by the angle formed at the vertex of the cone (between two opposite generatrices): If the angle is acute then the conic is an ellipse; if the angle is right then the conic is a parabola; and if the angle is obtuse then the conic is a hyperbola. Note that the circle cannot be defined this way and wasnot considered a conic at this time.

Euclid (300 BC) is said to have written four books on conics but these were lost as well. Archimedes (died 212 BC) is known to have studied conics, having determined the a r e a bounded by a parabola and an ellipse. The only part of this work to survive is a book on the solids of revolution of conics.

Apollonius of Perga

The greatest progress in the study of conics by the ancient Greeks is due to Apollonius of Perga (died in 190 BC)), whose eight volume Conic Sections summarized the existing knowledge at the time and greatly extended it. Apollonius's major innovation was to characterize a conic using properties within the plane and intrinsic to the curve; this greatly simplified analy sis. With this tool, it was now possible to show that any plane cutting the cone, regardless of its angle, will produce a conic according to the earlier definition, leading to the definition commonly used today.

Pappus of Alexandria is credited with discovering importance of the concept of a focus of a conic, and the discovery of the related concept of a directrix.

Al-Kuhi

An instrument for drawing conic sections was first described in 1000 CE by the Islamic mathematician Al-Kuhi.

Omar Khayyám

Apollonius's work was translated into Arabic (the technical language of the time) and much of his work only survives through the Arabic version. Persians found applications to the theory; the most notable of these was the Persian mathematician and poet Omar Khayyám who used conic sections to solve algebraic equations.

Europe

Johannes Kepler extended the theory of conics through the "principle of continuity", a precur sor to the concept of limits. Girard Desargues and Blaise Pascal developed a theory of conics using an early form of projective geometry and this helped to provide impetus for the study of this new field. In particular, Pascal discovered a theorem known as the hexagrammum mysticum from which many other properties of conics can be deduced.

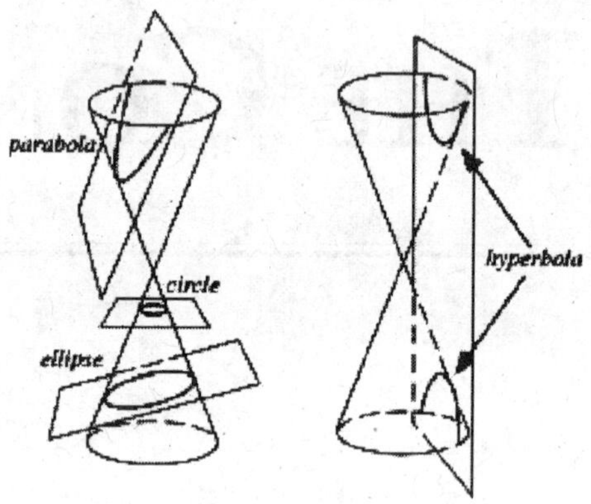

4.2 BASIC DEFINITIONS

(i) **Circle :** Section of a right circlular cone by a plane which parallel to its base is a circle.

(ii) **Parabola :** Section of a right circular cone by a plane which is parallel to a genrator of a cone.

(iii) **Ellipse:** Section of a right circular cone by a plane which is neither parallel to a generator of a cone nor parallel or perpendicular to the axis of a cone is an ellipse.

(iv) **Hyperbola :** Section of a right circular cone by a plane which is parallel to the axis of a cone is a hyperbola.

4.3 CONIC SECTION

It is the locus of a point which moves in a plane in such a way that its distance from a fixed point to its perpendicular distance from a fixed straight line is always constant.

The fixed point is called focus of the conic and this fixed straight line is called the directrix of the conic and this constant ratio is known as eccentricity of the conic. It is denoted as 'e'.

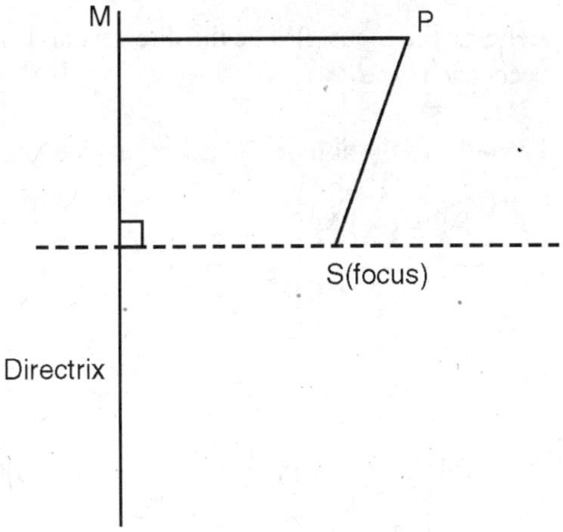

4.4 CONIC SECTION WITH RESPECT TO ECCENTRICITY

(i) If $e = 0$, the conic section is called a circle

(ii) If $e = 1$, the conic section is called a parabola.

(iii) If $e < 1$, the conic section is called an ellipse.

(iv) If $e > 1$, the conic section is called a hyperbola.

(v) If $e = \sqrt{2}$, the conic section is called a rectangular hyperbola.

4.5 SOME IMPORTANT DEFINITIONS TO REMEMBER :

Axis : The straight line passing through the focus and perpendicular to the directrix is called the axis of the conic section.

Vertex : The point of intersection of the conic section and the axis is called the vertex of the conic section .

Double Ordinate : Any chord , which is perpendicular to the axis of the conic section is called a double ordinate of the conic sections.

Focal chord : Any chord passing through the focus is called the focal chord of the conic section.

Focal distance: The distance between focus and any point on the conic is known as focal distance of the conic section.

Latus Rectum : Any chord passing thorugh the focus and perpendicular to the axis is known as latus rectum of the conic section.

Centre : The point which bisects every chord of the conic passing through it, is called the center of the conic section.

4.6 RECOGNIZATION OF CONICS :

A genral equation of 2nd degree is

$$ax^2 + 2hxy + by^2 + 2gx + 2fy + c = 0,$$

where ? $= \begin{vmatrix} a & h & g \\ h & b & f \\ g & f & c \end{vmatrix} = abc + 2fgh - af^2 - bg^2 - ch^2$

and $H = \begin{vmatrix} a & h \\ h & b \end{vmatrix} = ab - h^2$.

There are two types of conics .

(i) Degeerate conic and

(ii) Non-degenerate conic.

We use the term degenerate conic sections to describe the single point, single line and pair of lines and the term non-degenerate conic sections to describe those conic sections that are circles, parabolas, ellipses or hyperbolas.

A non degenrate conic represents

(i) a circle if, $\Delta \neq 0, h = 0, a = b$

(ii) a parabola if $\Delta \neq 0, H = 0$

(iii) an ellipse , if $\Delta \neq 0, H < 0$

(iv) a hyperbola , if $\Delta \neq 0, H > 0$

(v) a rectangular hyperbola , if $\Delta \neq 0, H > 0$ and $a + b = 0$.

Now, centre of the conics is obtained by

$$\frac{df}{dx} = 2ax + 2hy + 2g = 0 \text{ and}$$

$$\frac{df}{dy} = 2hx + 2by + 2f = 0.$$

$$\Rightarrow \quad ax + hy + g = 0, \; hx + by + f = 0.$$

Solve the above equations , then we get the required centre of the given conic.

4.7 EQUATION OF CONIC SECTION:

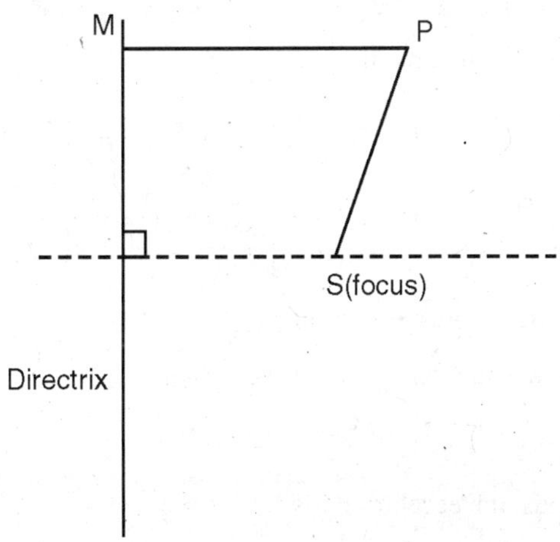

Let the focus be (h, k), directrix be $ax+by+c=0$ and the ececentricity is 'e' Then the equation of the conic sections is $\frac{SP}{PM}=e$

$$\Rightarrow \quad \sqrt{(x-h)^2+(y-k)^2}=e\left|\frac{ax+by+c}{\sqrt{a^2+b^2}}\right|$$

$$\Rightarrow \quad (x-h)^2+(y-k)^2=e^2\left(\frac{(ax+by+c)^2}{a^2+b^2}\right)$$

Which is the general equation of the conic section.

Ex-1. What conic does $\sqrt{ax}+\sqrt{by}=1$ represent ?

Sol. The given equation is $\sqrt{ax}+\sqrt{by}=1$

$\Rightarrow \left(\sqrt{ax}+\sqrt{by}\right)^2=1$

$\Rightarrow ax+by+2\sqrt{abxy}=1$

$\Rightarrow (ax+by-1)^2=\left(2\sqrt{abxy}\right)^2$

$\Rightarrow a^2x^2+b^2y^2+1+2abxy-2ax-2by=4abxy$

$\Rightarrow a^2x^2-2abxy+b^2y^2-2ax-2by+1=0$

Here A= a^2, B = b^2 and H = - ab.

Now, $H^2-AB=a^2b^2-a^2b^2=0$

Hence, it represents a parabola.

Ex-2. If the conic $x^2-4xy+\lambda y^2+2x+4y+10=0$ represents a parabola , then find the value of λ.

Sol. Here , a = 1 , h = - 2 and b = λ.

Since, it represents a parabola , so $h^2-ab=0$

$\Rightarrow \quad 4-\lambda=0$

$\Rightarrow \quad \lambda=4.$

Ex-3. If the conic $16\left(x^2+(y-1)^2\right)=\left(x+\sqrt{3}y-5\right)^2$ represents a non degenarate conic, then write its name and also find its eccentricity.

Sol. The given conic is

$$16\left(x^2+(y-1)^2\right)=\left(x+\sqrt{3}y-5\right)^2$$

$$\Rightarrow \quad \left(x^2+(y-1)^2\right)=\frac{1}{4}\left(\frac{x+\sqrt{3}y-5}{\sqrt{1+3}}\right)^2 \quad ...(i)$$

Which represents an ellipse

Now, equation (i) can aslo be written as $SP^2=e^2\times PM^2$

$\Rightarrow \quad SP=e\times PM$

Thus, the eccentricity is $\frac{1}{2}$.

Ex-4. If the focus and the directrix of a conic be (1, 2) and $x+3y+10=0$ respectively and the eccentricity be $\frac{1}{\sqrt{2}}$, then find its equation .

Sol. Let S be the focus, PM be the directrix and eccentricity = e

From the definition of conic section , we get, $\frac{SP}{PM}=e$

$\Rightarrow \quad SP=e\times PM$

$\Rightarrow \quad SP^2=e^2\times PM^2$

$\Rightarrow \quad (x-1)^2+(y-2)^2=\frac{1}{2}\times\left(\frac{x+3y+10}{\sqrt{1+9}}\right)^2$

$\Rightarrow \quad 20\left\{(x-1)^2+(y-2)^2\right\}=(x+3y+10)^2$

$\Rightarrow \quad 20\left\{x^2+y^2-2x-4y+5\right\}=\left(x^2+9y^2+100+6xy+20x+6y\right)$

$\Rightarrow \quad 19x^2-6xy+11y^2-60x-86y=0$

Ex-5. Find the equation of a parabola , whose focus is (1, 1) and directrix is $x-y+3=0$.

Sol. Let S be the focus , PM be the directrix From the definition of conic section , it is clear that , SP = PM

$\Rightarrow \quad SP^2=PM^2$

$\Rightarrow \quad (x-1)^2+(y-1)^2=\left(\frac{x-y+3}{\sqrt{1+1}}\right)^2$

$\Rightarrow \quad 2\left\{(x-1)^2+(y-1)^2\right\}=(x-y+3)^2$

$\Rightarrow \quad 2\left(x^2+y^2-2x-2y+2\right)=\left(x^2+y^2+9-2xy-6x-6y\right)$

$\Rightarrow \quad x^2+2xy+y^2+2x+2y+4=0$

PARABOLA

4.8 INTRODUCTION

The term parabola comes from Greek para "alongside, nearby, right up to," and -bola, from the verb ballein "to cast, to throw." Understandably, parallel and many of its derivatives start with the same root. The word parabola may thus mean "thrown parallel" in accordance with the definition.

4.9 MATHEMATICAL DEFINITIONS

Definition-1: It is the locus of a point which moves in a plane in such a way that its distance from a fixed point is equal its distance from a fixed straight line.

The fixed point is called focus and the fixed straight line is called directrix.

Definition-2: Let D be a line in the plane and F be a fixed point not on D. A parabola is the collection of points in the plane that are equidistant from F and D. The point F is called the focus and the line D is called the directrix.

Definition-3: In algebra, parabolas are frequently encountered as graphs of quadratic functions, such as $y = ax^2 + bx + c$ or $x = ay^2 + by + c$.

Definition-4: It is a section of a conic , whose eccentricity is '1'

Definition-5: A plane curve formed by the intersection of a right circular cone and a plane parallel to an element of the cone

Definition -6: A conic $ax^2 + 2hxy + by^2 + 2gx + 2fy + c = 0$ represents a parabola if

(i) $\Delta \neq 0$

(ii) $h^2 - ab = 0$, where

$$\Delta = abc + 2fgh - af^2 - bg^2 - ch^2.$$

4.10 STANDARD EQUATION OF A PARABOLA:

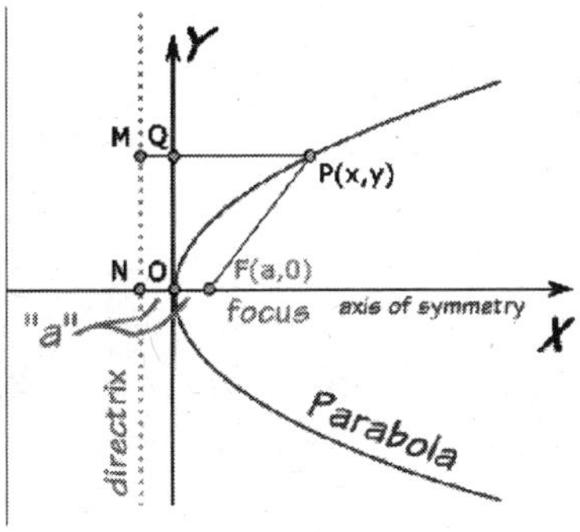

Let F be the focus and MN be the directrix of the parabola.

Draw FN perpendicular to MN and let O be the mid-point of FN .

Thus OF = ON

So O lies on the parabola . Consider O as the origin and OX and Oy as x and y axes respec tively.

Let OF = ON = a

Then the co-ordinates of F is (a, 0) and the equation of MN is x + a = 0.

Now from the definition of parabola , we get, PF = PM

$$\Rightarrow \quad PF^2 = MN^2$$

$$\Rightarrow \quad (x-a)^2 + (y-0)^2 = (x+a)^2$$

$$\Rightarrow \quad y^2 = 4ax.$$

Which is the required equation of a parabola.

This is also known as horizontal parabola or right-ward parabola.

4.11 IMPORTANT TERMS RELATED TO PARABOLA:

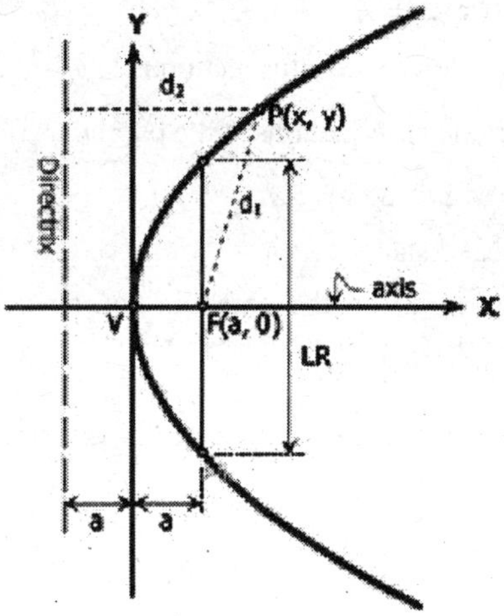

Focus: It is the fixed point with reference to which the parabola is constructed.

Directrix: It is a straight line outside the parabola.

Axis of symmetry: It is the line which is perpendicular to the Directrix and passes through the focus. It divides the parabola into two equal halves.

Vertex: It is the point on the axis of symmetry that intersects the parabola when the turn of the parabola is the sharpest. The vertex is halfway between the Directrix and the focus.

Focal chord: It is any chord that passes through the focus.

Latus rectum: It is that focal chord which is perpendicular to the axis of symmetry. The latus rectum is parallel to the directrix. Half of the latus rectum is called the semi-latus rectum.

Focal parameter: The distance from the focus to the directrix is called the focal parameter.

Focal distance : The distance between any point on the parabola to the focus is called the focal distance.

Parametric equation :From the equation of the parabola, we can write $\frac{y}{2a} = \frac{2x}{y} = t$

Then $x = at^2$, $y = 2at$, where t is a parameter.

The equations $x = at^2$, $y = 2at$ are called the parametric equations and the point $(at^2, 2at)$ is also referred to as the point 't' .

(i) Vertex is : (0, 0)

(ii) Focus is : (- a, 0)

(iii) Equation of the directrix is : x - a = 0.

(iv) Equation of the axis is : y = 0

(v) Equation of the tangent at the vertex is : x = 0

(vi) Length of the latus rectum : 4a

(vii) Extremities of the latus rectum are : L(- a, 2a),

L' (a, -2a)

(viii) Equation of the latus rectum is : x = - a

(ix) parametric equations of the parabola : $y^2 = 4ax$ are

$x = -at^2$ & $y = 2at$

(x) Focal distance : x - a

(xi) Any point on the parabola can be considered as $\left(-at^2, 2at\right)$.

Ex-1. Find the vertex, focus, latus rectum, directrix and axis of the parabolas.

(i) $y^2 = x + 2y + 2$

(ii) $y^2 = 3x + 4y + 2$

(iii) $x^2 = y + 4x + 2$

(iv) $x^2 + x + y = 0$

Sol. (i) The given equation is $y^2 = x + 2y + 2$

$\Rightarrow \quad y^2 - 2y = x + 2$

$\Rightarrow \quad (y-1)^2 = x + 3$

$\Rightarrow \quad Y^2 = X$, where $X = x + 3$, $Y = y - 1$

Vertex : V (0, 0) $\Rightarrow \quad X = 0,\ Y = 0$

$\Rightarrow \quad x + 3 = 0,\ y - 1 = 0$

$\Rightarrow \quad x = -3,\ y = 1$

Hence, the vertex is (-3, 1)

Focus : (a, 0) $\Rightarrow \quad X = a,\ Y = 0$

$\Rightarrow \quad x + 3 = \frac{1}{4},\ y - 1 = 0$

$\Rightarrow \quad x = \frac{1}{4} - 3,\ y = 1$

$\Rightarrow \quad x = -\frac{11}{4},\ y = 1$

Hence, the focus is $\left(-\frac{11}{4}, 1\right)$

Latus Rectum : 4a = 1

Directrix : $X + a = 0 \Rightarrow x + 3 = \frac{1}{4} \Rightarrow x = -\frac{11}{4}$

$\Rightarrow 4x + 11 = 0$

Axis : $Y = 0 \Rightarrow y - 1 = 0 \Rightarrow y = 1$.

(ii) The given equation is $y^2 = 3x + 4y + 2$

$\Rightarrow \quad y^2 - 4y = 3x + 2$

$\Rightarrow \quad y^2 - 4y + 4 = 3x + 6$

$\Rightarrow \quad (y-2)^2 = 3(x+2)$

$\Rightarrow \quad Y^2 = 3X$, where $X = x + 2$ and $Y = y - 2$.

Vertex : (0, 0) $\Rightarrow X = 0, Y = 0$

$\Rightarrow x + 2 = 0$ and $y - 2 = 0$

$\Rightarrow x = -2$ and $y = 2$.

Hence, the vertex is (-2, 2).

Focus : (a, 0) $\Rightarrow X = a, Y = 0$

$\Rightarrow x + 2 = \frac{3}{4},\ y - 2 = 0$

$\Rightarrow x = -\frac{5}{4}$ and $y = 2$

Hence, the focus is $\left(-\frac{5}{4}, 2\right)$

Latus Rectum : 4a = 3

Directrix : $X + a = 0 \Rightarrow x + 2 = 3/4$

$\Rightarrow x = -5/3 \Rightarrow 3x + 5 = 0$

Axis : $Y = 0 \Rightarrow y - 2 = 0 \Rightarrow y = 2$

(iii) The given equation is $x^2 = y + 4x + 2$

$\Rightarrow \quad x^2 - 4x = y + 2$

$\Rightarrow \quad x^2 - 4x + 4 = y + 6$

$\Rightarrow \quad (x-2)^2 = y + 6$

$\Rightarrow \quad X^2 = Y$, where $X = x - 2$ and $Y = y + 6$.

Vertex : (0, 0) $\Rightarrow X = 0, Y = 0$

$\Rightarrow x - 2 = 0$ and $y + 6 = 0$

$\Rightarrow x = 2$ and $y = -6$

Hence, the vertex is (2, -6)

Focus : (0, a) $\Rightarrow X = 0, Y = a$

$\Rightarrow x - 2 = 0$ and $y + 6 = 1/4$

$\Rightarrow x = 2$ and $y = -23/4$

Hence, the focus is $\left(2, -\frac{23}{4}\right)$

Latus Rectum : 4 a = 1

Directrix : $Y + a = 0 \Rightarrow y + 6 = 1/4 \Rightarrow 4y + 23 = 0$.

Axis : $X = 0 \Rightarrow x - 2 = 0 \Rightarrow x = 2$.

(iv) The given equation is $x^2 + x + y = 0$

$\Rightarrow \quad x^2 + x = -y$

$\Rightarrow \quad \left(x + \frac{1}{2}\right)^2 = -y + \frac{1}{4} = -\left(y - \frac{1}{4}\right)$

$\Rightarrow \quad X^2 = -Y$, where $X = x + \frac{1}{2},\ Y = y - \frac{1}{2}$

Vertex : (0, 0) $\Rightarrow$ X = 0 , Y = 0

$\Rightarrow \quad x+\frac{1}{2}=0,\ y-\frac{1}{2}=0$

$\Rightarrow \quad x=-\frac{1}{2},\ y=\frac{1}{2}$

Hence, the vertex is $\left(-\frac{1}{2}, \frac{1}{2}\right)$.

Focus : (0 , - a) $\Rightarrow$ X = 0 , Y = - a

$\Rightarrow$ x + 1/2 = 0 , y - 1/2 = 1/4

$\Rightarrow$ x = - 1/2 , y = 3/4

Hence, the focus is (-1/2, 3/4)

Latus Rectum : 4a = 1

Directrix : Y - a = 0

$\Rightarrow$ y - 1/2 - 1/4 = 0

$\Rightarrow$ y - 3/4 = 0

$\Rightarrow$ 4 y - 3 = 0

Axis : Y = 0 $\Rightarrow$ y - 1/2 = 0 $\Rightarrow$ 2 y - 1 = 0 .

Ex-2. If the focal distance on a point to a parabola $y^2=12x$ is 6, then find the co-ordinates of that point .

Sol. Let the point be (x, y)

The given equation is $y^2=12x$

$\Rightarrow$ 4a = 12

$\Rightarrow$ a = 12/4 = 3

Given focal distance = 6

$\Rightarrow$ x + a = 6

$\Rightarrow$ x + 3 = 6

$\Rightarrow$ x = 6-3 = 3

When x = 3 , $y^2=12\times 3=36 \Rightarrow y=\pm 6$

Hence, the co-ordinates of the points are (3, 6) and (3, -6)

Ex-3. Find the equation of a parabola , whose focus (-6, -6) and vertex is (-2, -2).

Sol. Let the vertex be V and the focus be S .

The equation of axis is x - y = 0 .

Let the point Q is the point of intersection of the axis and the directrix.

Clearly, V is the mid-point of Q and S

Then Q is (2. 2)

As we know that , the directrix is perpendicular to the axis of the parabola.

So, the equation of the directrix is x + y - k = 0

Which is passing through (2, 2)

Therefore, k = 4 .

Hence, the equation of the directrix is x + y - 4 = 0 .

Thus the equation of the parabola is

$$\sqrt{(x+6)^2+(y+6)^2}=\left(\frac{x+y-4}{\sqrt{1+1}}\right)$$

$$\Rightarrow \quad 2\left((x+6)^2+(y+6)^2\right)=(x+y-4)^2$$

$$\Rightarrow \quad 2\left(x^2+y^2+12x+12y+36\right)$$

$$=\left(x^2+y^2+16+2xy-8x-8y\right)$$

$$\Rightarrow \quad x^2-2xy+y^2+32x+32y+76=0$$

The Parabola opening upawards : $x^2=4ay$

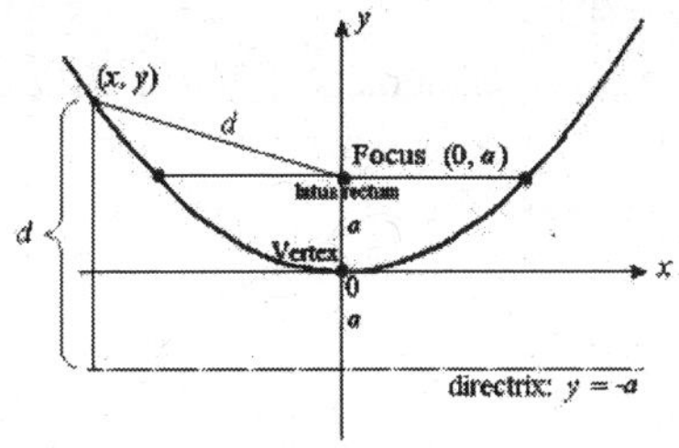

(i) Vertex is : (0, 0)

(ii) Focus is : (0, a)

(iii) Equation of the directrix is : y + a = 0.

(iv) Equation of the axis is : x = 0

(v) Equation of the tangent at the vertex is : y = 0

(vi) Length of the latus rectum : 4a

(vii) Extremities of the latus rectum are : L(2 a, a), L' (- 2a, a)

(viii) Equation of the latus rectum is : y = a

(ix) parametric equations of the parabola $x^2=4ay$ are $x=2at$ & $y=at^2$

(x) Focal distance: y + a

(xi) Any point on the parabola can be considered as $\left(2at, at^2\right)$.

The parabola opening downwards : $x^2=-4ay$

(i) Vertex is : (0, 0)

(ii) Focus is : (0, - a)

(iii) Equation of the directrix is : y - a = 0.

(iv) Equation of the axis is : x = 0

(v) Equation of the tangent at the vertex is : y = 0

(vi) Length of the latus rectum : 4a

(vii) Extremities of the latus rectum are : L(2 a, - a), L' (- 2a, - a)

(viii) Equation of the latus rectum is : y = - a

(ix) parametric equations of the parabola : $x^2=-4ay$ are $x=2at$ & $y=-at^2$

(x) Focal distance : y - a

(xi) Any point on the parabola can be considered as $\left(2at, -at^2\right)$.

Ex-1. The parametric equation of a parabola is $x = t^2 + 1$ and $y = 2t + 1$. Then find its directrix.

Sol. The given equations are $x = t^2 + 1$ and $y = 2t + 1$

On eliminating 't'. we get, $(y-1)^2 = 4(x-1)$

$\Rightarrow \quad Y^2 = 4X$, where X = (x-1) and Y = (y-1)

Hence, the equation of the directrix is $X + a = 0$

$\Rightarrow \quad x - 1 + 1 = 0$

$\Rightarrow \quad x = 0$.

Ex-2. If the vertex of a parabola be (-3, 0) and the directrx is $x + 5 = 0$, then find its equation.

Sol. Let the vertex be V and the focus be S

Let Q be the point of intersection of the axis and the directrix.

Clearly, Q be (-5, 0) and V be the mid - point of S and Q.

Then focus S is (-1, 0)

Hence, the equation of the parabola is

$$\sqrt{(x+1)^2 + y^2} = \left(\frac{x+5}{\sqrt{1^2}}\right)$$

$$\Rightarrow \quad (x+1)^2 + y^2 = (x+5)^2$$

$$\Rightarrow \quad y^2 = 8x + 24 = 8(x+3)$$

4.12 GENERAL EQUATION OF A PARABOLA:

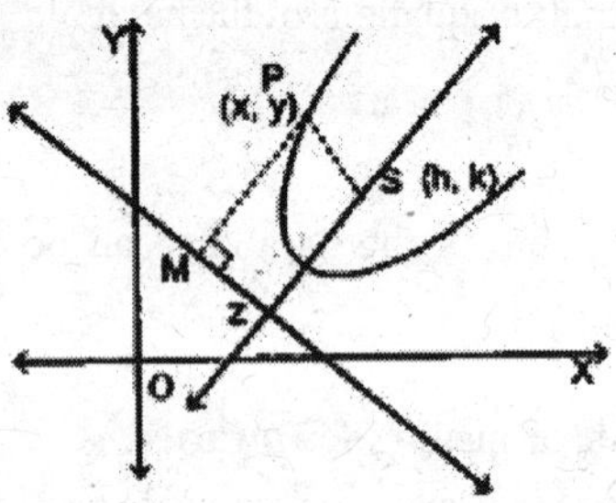

Let S (h, k) be the focus and $lx + my + n = 0$ is the equation of the directrix and P(x, y) be any point on the parabola.

Then SP = PM.

$$\Rightarrow \quad \sqrt{(x-h)^2 + (y-k)^2} = \left|\frac{lx + my + n}{\sqrt{(l^2 + m^2)}}\right|$$

$$\Rightarrow \quad (x-h)^2 + (y-k)^2 = \frac{(lx + my + n)^2}{(l^2 + m^2)}$$

$$\Rightarrow \quad m^2x^2 + l^2y^2 - 2lmxy + (\text{term})x + (\text{term})y + (\text{constant term}) = 0$$

$$\Rightarrow \quad (mx - ly)^2 + 2gx + 2fy + c = 0$$

Which is the general equation of a parabola.

4.13 EQUATION OF A PARABOLA WHEN VERTEX IS (H, K) AND AXIS IS PARALLEL TO X-AXIS.

$$(y - k)^2 = 4a(x - h)$$

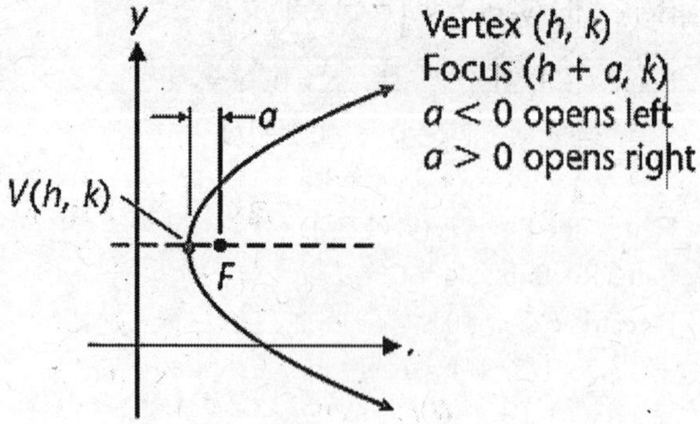

The equttion of the parabola $y^2 = 4ax$ can be written as

$(y-0)^2 = 4a(x-0)$

The vertex of the parabola is O (0, 0). Now origin is shifted to V(h, k) without changing the direction of axes, its equation becomes

$(y-k)^2 = 4a(x-h)$

Thus its focus is F (a + h, k) , latus rectum = 4 a and the equation of the directrix is x = h - a i.e. x + a - h = 0.

Parametric equation of the curve $(y-k)^2 = 4a(x-h)$ are $x = h + at^2$, $y = k + 2at$.

4.14 EQUATION OF A PARABOLA WHEN VERTEX IS (H, K) AND AXIS IS PARALLEL TO Y-AXIS.

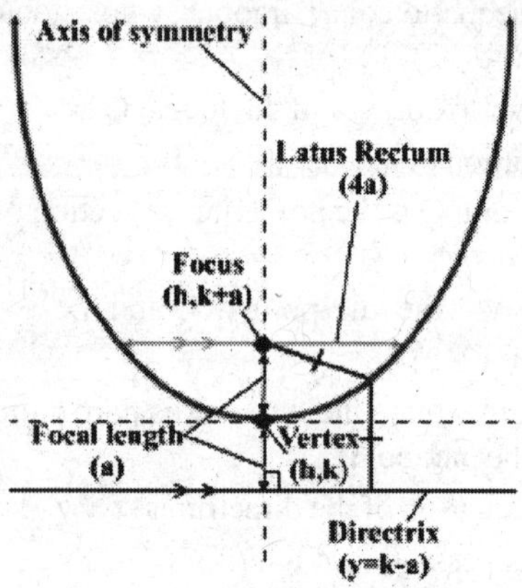

The equation of a parabola with vertex V(h, k) is

$(x-h)^2 = 4a(y-k)$

Thus, its focus is F (h, a + k) , latus rectum = 4a and the equation of the directrix is $y = k - a$ i.e. $y + a - k = 0$.

Parametric equation of the curve $(x-h)^2 = 4a(y-k)$

are $x = h + 2at,\ y = k + at^2$.

Note : 1. Equation of a parabola, whose axis is parallel to y - axis can aslo be considered as $y = ax^2 + bx + c$.

Polar form of a parabola:

In polar coordinates, the equation of a parabola with parameter r & θ and center (0, 0) is given by $r = -\dfrac{2a}{1+\cos?}$

Ex-1. Find the equation of parabola whose axis is parallel to y-axis and which passes through the points (0, 2) , (-1, 0) and (1, 6).

Sol. Let the equation of the parabola be

$$y = ax^2 + bx + c \quad ...(i)$$

Which is passing through (0, 2) , (-1. 0) and (1, 6) .

So, $c = 2$, $a + c = b$, $a + b + c = 6$.

On solving, we get, a = 1 , b = 3 and c = 2 .

Hence, the equation of the parabola is $y = x^2 + 3x + 2$.

Ex-2. Find the equation of a parabola whose vertex is (1, 2) and axis is parallel to x-axis and also passes through the point (3,4)

Sol. Let the equation of the parabola be

$(y-k)^2 = 4a(x-h)$, where vertex is (h, k)

Then the equation becomes $(y-2)^2 = 4a(x-1)$

Which is passing through (3, 4) .

Therefore, $8a = 4 \Rightarrow a = \dfrac{1}{2}$

Hence, the equation of the parabola is $(y-2)^2 = 2(x-1)$

Ex-3. If the axis of a parabola is parallel to y-axis , vertex and the length of the latus rectum are (3, 2) and 12 respectively, then find its equation.

Sol. Let the equation of the parabola be

$(x-h)^2 = 4a(y-k)$, where vertex is (h. k) .

The the equation becomes $(x-3)^2 = 4a(y-2)$.

Also it given that , the length of the latus rectum = 12

$\Rightarrow 4a = 12 \Rightarrow a = 3$.

Hence, the equation of the parabola is

$(x-3)^2 = 12(y-1)$.

4.15 FOCAL CHORD:

Any line passing through the focus and intersects the parabola in two distinct points , then it is known as focal chord of the parabola.

Any point on the parabola $y^2 = 4ax$ can be considered as $(at^2, 2at)$.

4.16 PROPERTIES OF THE FOCAL CHORD :

(i) If the chord joining $P(at_1^2, 2at_1)$ and $Q(at_2^2, 2at_2)$ is the focal chord , then $t_1t_2 = -1$.

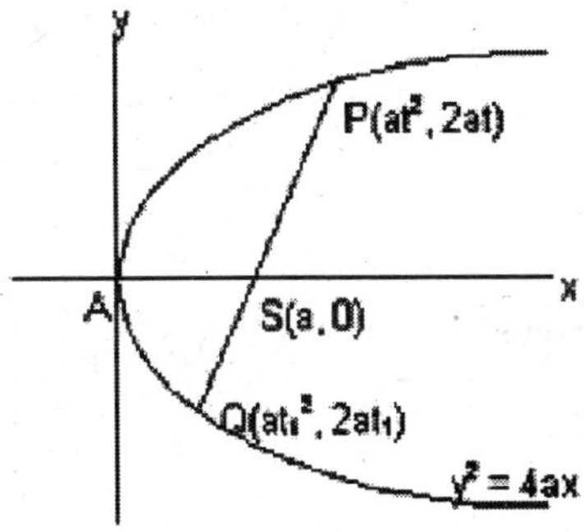

Let $y^2 = 4ax$ be a parabola , if PQ be a focal chord .

Consider any two point on the parabola are

$(at_1^2, 2at_1)$ & $(at_2^2, 2at_2)$.

Since PQ passes through the focus S(a, 0) , so P, S, Q are collinear.

Thus , $m(PS) = m(QS)$

$$\Rightarrow \frac{2at_1 - 0}{at_1^2 - a} = \frac{0 - 2at_2}{a - at_2^2}$$

$$\Rightarrow \frac{2at_1}{at_1^2 - a} = \frac{2at_2}{at_2^2 - a}$$

$$\Rightarrow \frac{2t_1}{t_1^2 - 1} = \frac{2t_2}{t_2^2 - 1}$$

$$\Rightarrow \frac{t_1}{t_1^2 - 1} = \frac{t_2}{t_2^2 - 1}$$

$$\Rightarrow t_1(t_2^2 - 1) = t_2(t_1^2 - 1)$$

$$\Rightarrow t_1t_2(t_2 - t_1) + (t_2 - t_1) = 0$$

$$\Rightarrow t_1t_2 + 1 = 0$$

$$\Rightarrow t_1t_2 = -1$$

Which is the required relation.

(ii) If the point $\left(at^2, 2at\right)$ be the extremity of a focal chord of the parabola $y^2 = 4ax$, then the length of the focal chord is $a\left(t+\frac{1}{t}\right)^2$.

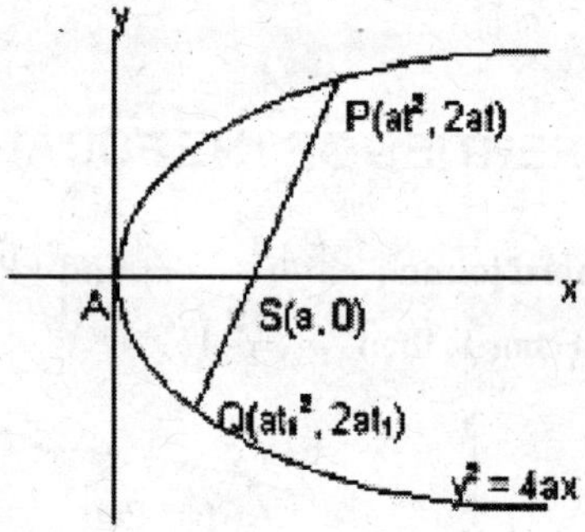

Since one extremity of the focal chord is $P\left(at^2, 2at\right)$,

then the other extremity will be I $Q\left(\frac{a}{t^2}, -\frac{2a}{t}\right)$.

Thus , PQ = SP + SQ

$$= \left(at^2 + a\right) + \left(\frac{a}{t^2} + a\right) = a\left(t^2 + \frac{1}{t^2} + 2\right) = a\left(t + \frac{1}{t}\right)^2.$$

(iii) If the length of the focal chord makes an angle θ with the +ve direction of x-axis , then its length is 4a cosec^2? .

Now, slope of $PQ = \frac{2}{t - \frac{1}{t}} = \tan\theta$

$\Rightarrow \quad 2\cot\theta = t - \frac{1}{t}$

Thus, $PQ = a\left(t + \frac{1}{t}\right)^2 = a\left[\left(t - \frac{1}{t}\right)^2 + 4\right]$

$$= a\left(4\cot^2\theta + 4\right) = 4a \ \operatorname{cosec}^2\theta.$$

(iv) Semi latus rectum of the parabola $y^2 = 4ax$ is the harmonic mean between the segments of any focal chord of the parabola.

Let the parabola be $y^2 = 4ax$ and SP and SQ are the focal chords , where

$S = (a, 0),\ P = \left(at^2, 2at\right) \& Q = \left(\frac{a}{t^2}, -\frac{2a}{t}\right)$.

Thus , $SP = a + at^2,\ SQ = a + \frac{a}{t^2}$

Now, Harmonic mean of SP and SQ

$$= \frac{2SP\ .SQ}{SP + SQ} = \frac{2}{\frac{1}{SP} + \frac{1}{SQ}}$$

$$\frac{1}{SP} + \frac{1}{SQ} = \frac{1}{a + at^2} + \frac{1}{a + \frac{a}{t^2}} = \frac{1 + t^2}{a\left(1 + t^2\right)} = \frac{1}{a}$$

Thus , $\frac{2}{\frac{1}{SP} + \frac{1}{SQ}} = \frac{2}{\frac{1}{a}} = 2a$ = semi latus rectum.

(v) The length of a focal chord of the parabola varies inversely as the square of its distance from the vertex.

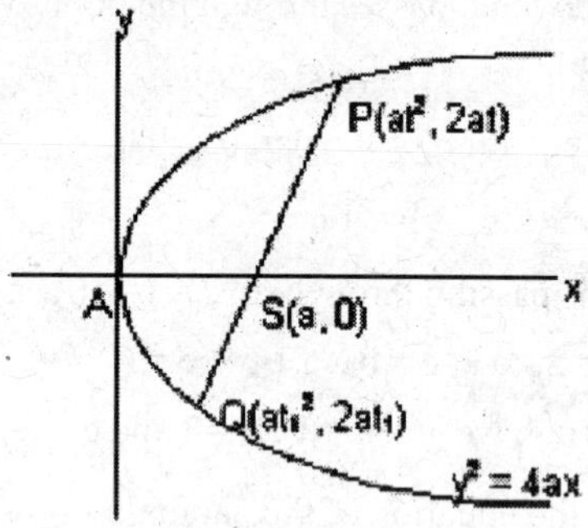

Equation of the focal chord SP :

$$y - 0 = \frac{2at - 0}{at^2 - a}(x - a)$$

$\Rightarrow \quad y\left(t^2 - 1\right) = 2tx - 2at$

$\Rightarrow \quad 2tx - \left(t^2 - 1\right)y - 2at = 0$

Let d be the distnace of the focal chord SP from the vertex (0, 0) to the parabola $y^2 = 4ax$.

Then , $d = \left|\frac{(0 - 0 - 2at)}{\sqrt{4t^2 + \left(t^2 - 1\right)^2}}\right| = \frac{2at}{\left(t^2 + 1\right)} = \frac{2a}{\left(t + \frac{1}{t}\right)}$.

Also , $PQ = a\left(t + \frac{1}{t}\right)^2 = a \times \frac{4a^2}{d^2} = \frac{4a^3}{d^2}$.

Thus, $PQ \ \alpha \ \frac{1}{d^2}$

Hence the length of the focal chord varies inversely as the square of its distance from the vertex of the given parabola.

(vi) Circle described on the focal chord as diameter touches the tangent to the parabola.

Let the circle described on the focal chord SP , where

S =(a, 0) and $P = \left(at^2, 2at\right)$.

Equation of the circle is

$$\left(x-at^2\right)(x-a)+(y-2at)(y-0)=0.$$

Solving it with y-axis, $x=0$, we have,

$y^2-2aty+a^2t^2=0$

Claearly, it has equal roots.

So circle touches the y-axis.

Also, the point of contact is (0, at).

(vii) **Circle described on the focal chord as diameter touches the directrix of the parabola.**

Equation of the circle described on AB as diameter is

$$\left(x-at^2\right)\left(x-\frac{a}{t^2}\right)+(y-2at)\left(y+\frac{2a}{t}\right)=0$$

Put x = a, we have, $y^2-2a\left(t-\frac{1}{t}\right)y+a^2\left(t-\frac{1}{t}\right)^2=0$

Clearly, it has equal roots.

Hence the circle touches the directrix at x = - a.

4.17 POSITION OF A POINT RELATIVE TO A PARABOLA :

Consider the parabola $y^2=4ax$ and the point be (x_1, y_1).

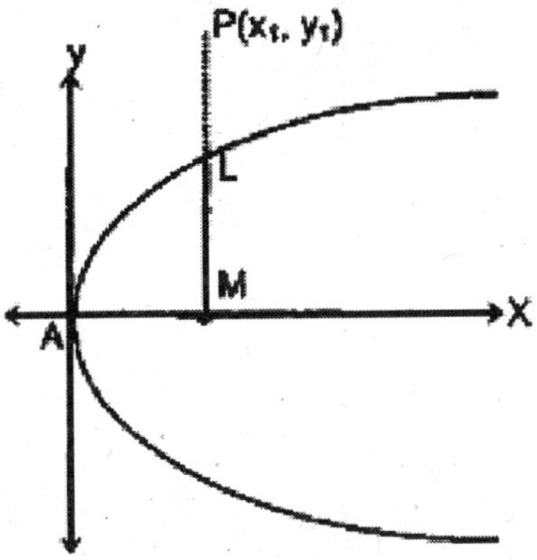

The point (x_1, y_1) lies outside, on and inside of the parabola $y^2=4ax$ acoording

as $y_1^2-4ax_1>0, =0, <0$.

Ex-1. If a point $(\lambda, -\lambda)$ lies in an interrior point of the parabola $y^2=4x$, then find the range of λ.

Sol. Since, the point $(\lambda, -\lambda)$ lies inside of the parabola $y^2=4x$, then $\lambda^2-4\lambda<0$

$\Rightarrow \quad \lambda(\lambda-4)<0$

$\Rightarrow \quad 0<\lambda<4$

Hence, the range of λ is $(0, 4)$.

Ex-2. If a point (λ, 2) is an exterrior point of both the parabolas $y^2=(x+1)$ and $y^2=-x+1$, then find the value of λ.

Sol. Since the point (λ, 2) $(\lambda, 2)$ is an exterrior point of both the parabolas $y^2=(x+1)$ & $y^2=-(x-1)$, so we have,

4 - x - 1 > 0 and 4 + x - 1 > 0

$\Rightarrow \quad 3-\lambda>0$ and $3+\lambda>0$

$\Rightarrow \quad \lambda-3<0$ and $\lambda+3>0$

$\Rightarrow \quad \lambda<3$ and $\lambda>-3$

$\Rightarrow \quad -3<\lambda<3$.

4.18 INTERSECTION OF A LINE AND A PARABOLA:

Let the parabola be $y^2=4ax$ and the line be $y=mx+c$.

Eliminating x between these two equations, we get,

$$y^2=4a\left(\frac{y-c}{m}\right)$$

$\Rightarrow \quad my^2-4ay+4ac=0$

The given line will cut the parabola in two distinct, coincident and imaginary points according as $D>0, =0, <0$.

$\Rightarrow \quad 16a^2-16amc>0, =0, <0$

$\Rightarrow \quad a>cm, a=cm, a<cm$.

Condition of tangency :

The line y = m x + c will be a tangent to the parabola $y^2=4ax$ if $c=\frac{a}{m}$.

Equation of any tangent to the parabola can be considered as $y=mx+\frac{a}{m}$.

The co-ordinates of the point of contact in terms of 'm' is $\left(\frac{a}{m^2}, \frac{2a}{m}\right)$

Ex-1. If $2x+3y+5=0$ is a tangent to the parabola $y^2=8x$, then find the co-ordinates of the point of contact..

Sol. The given line is $2x+3y+5=0$ ...(i)

and the parabola $y^2=8x$ ...(ii)

Since (i) be a tangent to the parabola $y^2=8x$,

so $\left(\frac{-2x-5}{3}\right)^2=8x$

$\Rightarrow \quad (2x+5)^2=72x$

$\Rightarrow \quad 4x^2+20x+25=72x$

$\Rightarrow \quad 4x^2-52x+25=0$

$\Rightarrow \quad 4x^2-2x-50x+25=0$

$\Rightarrow \quad 2x(2x-1)-25(2x-1)=0$

$\Rightarrow \quad (2x-1)(2x-25)=0$

$\Rightarrow \quad x=1/2,\ x=25/2$

When x = 1/2 , then $y=\left(\frac{-1-5}{3}\right)=-2$

Ans also, when x = 25 / 2 , then y = - 10

Hence, the points of contact are (1/2, -2) or (25/2, -10)

Ex-2. If $3x+4y+\lambda=0$ is a tangent to the parabola $y^2=12x$, then find the value of λ.

Sol. The given parabola is $y^2=12x$ ...(i)

$\Rightarrow \quad 4a=12$

$\Rightarrow \quad a=3$

The given line is $3x+4y+\lambda=0$

$\Rightarrow \quad y=-\frac{3}{4}x-\frac{\lambda}{4}$ ...(ii)

Since, the line (ii) is a tangent to a parabola (i), so $c=\frac{a}{m}$

$\Rightarrow \quad -\frac{\lambda}{4}=\frac{3}{\left(-\frac{3}{4}\right)}=-4$

$\Rightarrow \quad \lambda=16$

Hence, the value of λ is 16 .

4.19 THE LENGTH OF THE CHORD $y=mx+c$ INTER CEPTED BY THE PARABOLA $y^2=4ax$.

Let the equation of the parabola be $y^2=4ax$ and the line be $y=mx+c$.

we have solve the above equations we get,

$$(mx+c)^2=4ax$$

$\Rightarrow \quad m^2x^2+(2mc-4a)x+c^2=0$

Let the line $y=mx+c$ intersects the parabola in two real and distinct points, say, (x_1, y_1) and (x_2, y_2).

Thus $(x_1-x_2)^2=(x_1+x_2)^2-4x_1x_2$

$$=\frac{4(mc-2a)^2}{m^4}-\frac{4c^2}{m^2}=\frac{16a(a-mc)}{m^4}$$

and $y_1-y_2=m(x_1-x_2)$

Thus, the required length $=\sqrt{(y_1-y_2)^2+(x_1-x_2)^2}$

$$=\sqrt{(x_1-x_2)^2m^2+(x_1-x_2)^2}$$

$$=\sqrt{1+m^2}\,(x_1-x_2)$$

$$=\frac{4}{m^2}\sqrt{1+m^2}\sqrt{a(a-mc)}.$$

4.20 TANGENT

If a line intersects the parabola in two coincident points, then it is known as tangent to a parabola.

Equation of tangent to a parabola in different forms :

(i) Point form :

The equation of tangent to the parabola $y^2=4ax$ at (x_1, y_1) is $yy_1=2a(x+x_1)$.

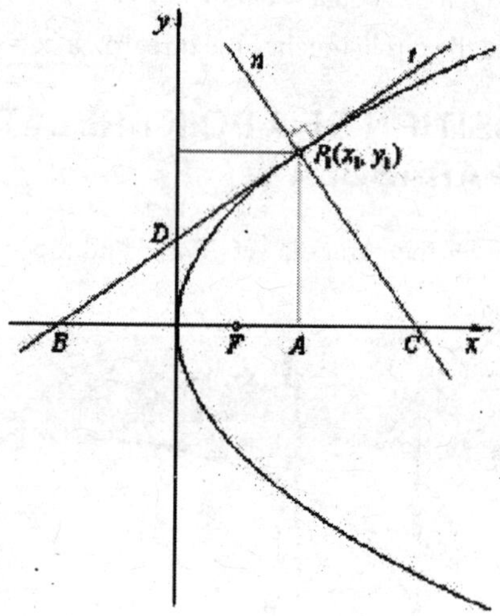

The equation of any tangent to the parabola at (x_1, y_1) is $(y-y_1)=m\ (x-x_1)$,

where $m=\left(\frac{dy}{dx}\right)_{(x_1,\ y_1)}$.

Now given equation is $y^2=4ax$.

Differentiating with respect to x, we get, $2y\frac{dy}{dx}=4a$

$\Rightarrow \quad \frac{dy}{dx}=\frac{2a}{y}$

Now $m=\left(\frac{dy}{dx}\right)_{(x_1,y_1)}=\frac{2a}{y_1}$.

Thus the equation of tangent is $y-y_1=\frac{2a}{y_1}(x-x_1)$

$\Rightarrow \quad yy_1-y_1^2=2ax-2ax_1$

$$\Rightarrow \quad yy_1 = 2ax - 2ax_1 + 4ax_1 = 2a(x+x_1)$$

$$\Rightarrow \quad yy_1 = 2a\,(x+x_1)$$

which is the required equation of tangent to the parabola $y^2 = 4ax$ at (x_1, y_1).

(ii) Parametric form :

The equation of the tangent to the parabola $y^2 = 4ax$ at (x_1, y_1) is $yy_1 = 2a(x+x_1)$.

$$\Rightarrow \quad y.2at = 2a\left(x+at^2\right)$$

$$\Rightarrow \quad yt = x + at^2.$$

(iii) Slope form :

The equation of tangent to the parabola $y^2 = 4ax$ at $\left(\frac{a}{m^2}, \frac{2a}{m}\right)$ is $y = mx + \frac{a}{m}$,

where m = slope.

The equation of the tangent to the parabola $y^2 = 4ax$ at (x_1, y_1) is $yy_1 = 2a(x+x_1)$ ...(i)

Here , $m = \frac{2a}{y_1} \Rightarrow y_1 = \frac{2a}{m}$

since the point (x_1, y_2) lies on the parabola $y^2 = 4ax$, we have, $y_1^2 = 4ax_1$.

$$\Rightarrow \quad 4ax_1 = \frac{4a^2}{m^2} \quad \Rightarrow \quad x_1 = \frac{a}{m^2}$$

Put the values of x_1 and y_1 in (i) , we get ,

$$y.\left(\frac{2a}{m}\right) = 2a\left(x + \frac{a}{m^2}\right)$$

$$\Rightarrow \quad y = mx + \frac{a}{m}.$$

(iv) Condition of tangency :

The line y = m x + c will be a tangent to the parabola $y^2 = 4ax$ is $c = \frac{a}{m}$.

Note : Any tangent to the parabola can be considered as $y = mx + \frac{a}{m}$.

(v) Point of intersection of tangents at any point on the parabola $y^2 = 4ax$.

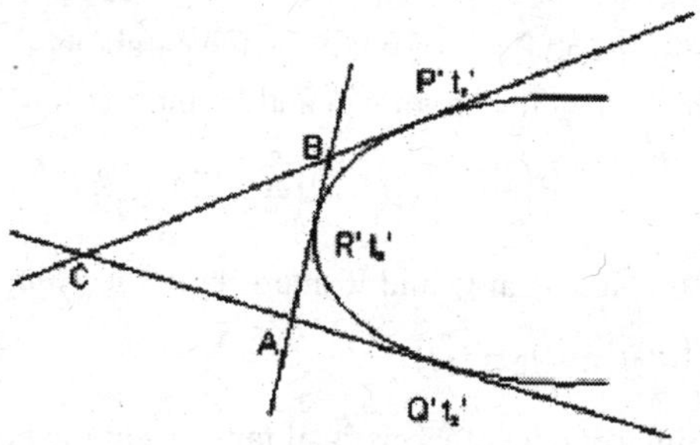

Let the parabola be $y^2 = 4ax$ and the two points on the parabola are $P\left(at_1^2, 2at_1\right)$ and $Q\left(at_2^2, 2at_2\right)$ respectively.

Equation of tangent at $P\left(at_1^2, 2at_1\right)$ and $Q\left(at_2^2, 2at_2\right)$ are $t_1\,y = x + at_1^2$ ....(i) and

$t_2 y = x + at_2$ ....(ii)

Solving these equations, we get,

$$x = at_1t_2, \quad y = a(t_1 + t_2).$$

Hence the co-ordinates of the point of intersection of the tangents are $\left(at_1t_2,\ a(t_1+t_2)\right)$.

Note : 1. Here x - co-ordinate is the geometric mean of the x co-ordinates of P and Q.

2. And y - co-ordinate is the arithemetic mean of the y-co-ordinates of P and Q.

(vi) The area of the triangle formed by three points on a parabola is twice the area of the triangle formed by the tangents at these points .

Let the three points of the parabola be

$$P\left(at_1^2, 2at_1\right), Q\left(at_2^2, 2at_2\right) \& R\left(at_3^2, 2at_3\right)$$

and the point of intersections of the tangents at these points are

$$A\left(t_2t_3, a(t_2+t_3)\right), B\left(t_1t_3, a(t_1+t_3)\right) \& A\left(t_1t_2, a(t_1+t_2)\right)$$

Now,

$$\text{ar}(\Delta PQR) = \frac{1}{2}\begin{vmatrix} at_1^2 & 2at_1 & 1 \\ at_2^2 & 2at_2 & 1 \\ at_3^2 & 2at_3 & 1 \end{vmatrix} = a^2(t_1-t_2)(t_2-t_3)(t_3-t_1)$$

$$\text{Also, } \text{ar}(\Delta ABC) = \frac{1}{2}\begin{vmatrix} at_2t_3 & a(t_2+t_3) & 1 \\ at_3t_1 & a(t_3+t_1) & 1 \\ at_1t_2 & a(t_1+t_2) & 1 \end{vmatrix}$$

$$= \frac{1}{2}a^2(t_1-t_2)(t_2-t_3)(t_3-t_1)$$

Hence , the result.

(vii) The circle circumscribing the triangle formed by any three tangents to a parabola passes through the focus.

Let P, Q and R be the points on the parabola $y^2 = 4ax$ at which tangents are drawn and let their co-ordinates be

$$P\left(at_1^2, 2at_1\right),\ Q\left(at_2^2, 2at_2\right) \& R\left(at_3^2, 2at_3\right).$$

The tangents at Q and R intersect in the point $A\left(at_2t_3,\ a\left(t_2+t_3\right)\right)$.

Similarly , the other pairs of tangents at the points $B\left(at_1t_3,\ a\left(t_1+t_3\right)\right)$ and $C\left(at_1t_2,\ a\left(t_1+t_2\right)\right)$

Let the equation to the circle be

$$x^2+y^2+2gx+2fy+c=0 \qquad ...(i)$$

since it passes through the above three points , we have,

$$a^2t_2^2t_3^2+a^2\left(t_2+t_3\right)^2+2gat_2t_3+2fa\left(t_2+t_3\right)+c=0 \qquad ...(ii)$$

$$a^2t_1^2t_3^2+a^2\left(t_1+t_3\right)^2+2gat_1t_3+2fa\left(t_1+t_3\right)+c=0 \qquad ...(iii)$$

and

$$a^2t_1^2t_2^2+a^2\left(t_1+t_2\right)^2+2gat_1t_2+2fa\left(t_1+t_2\right)+c=0 \qquad ...(iv)$$

subtracting (iii) from (ii) and dividing by $a\left(t_2-t_1\right)$, we get, $a\left(t_3^2\left(t_1+t_2\right)+t_1+t_2+2t_3\right)+2gt_3+2f=0$

similarly from (iii) and (iv) , we get,

$$a\left(t_1^2\left(t_3+t_2\right)+t_3+t_2+2t_1\right)+2gt_1+2f=0$$

From these two equations, we get,

$$2g=-a\left(1+t_2t_3+t_3t_1+t_1t_2\right),$$

$$2f=-a\left(t_1+t_2+t_3-t_1t_2t_3\right)$$

substituing these values of g and f in (ii), we get,

$$c=a^2\left(t_2t_3+t_3t_1+t_1t_2\right).$$

Thus, the equation of the circle is

$$x^2+y^2-a\left(1+t_2t_3+t_3t_1+t_1t_2\right)x-a$$

$$\left(t_1+t_2+t_3-t_1t_2t_3\right)y+a^2\left(t_2t_3+t_3t_1+t_1t_2\right)=0.$$

(viii) **The orthocentre of any triangle formed by three tangents to a parabola lies on the directrix.**

Let the equations to the three tangents be

$$y=m_1x+\frac{a}{m_1} \qquad ...(i)$$

$$y=m_2x+\frac{a}{m_2} \qquad ...(ii)$$

and $\quad y=m_3x+\dfrac{a}{m_3} \qquad ...(iii)$

The point of intersection of (ii) and (iii) is

$$\left(\frac{a}{m_2m_3},\ a\left(\frac{1}{m_2}+\frac{1}{m_3}\right)\right)$$

Equation of any line perpendicular to (i) and passes through the point of intersection of (ii) and (iii) is $y-a\left(\dfrac{1}{m_2}+\dfrac{1}{m_3}\right)=-\dfrac{1}{m_1}\left(x-\dfrac{a}{m_2m_3}\right)$

i.e $\quad y+\dfrac{x}{m_1}=a\left[\dfrac{1}{m_2}+\dfrac{1}{m_3}+\dfrac{1}{m_1m_2m_3}\right] \qquad ...(iv)$

Similarly the equation to the straight line through the point of intersection of (iii) and (i) and perpendicular to (ii) is

$$y+\frac{x}{m_2}=a\left[\frac{1}{m_3}+\frac{1}{m_1}+\frac{1}{m_1m_2m_3}\right] \qquad ...(v)$$

and the equation to the straight line through the point of intersection of (i) and (ii) and perpendicular to (iii) is

$$y+\frac{x}{m_3}=a\left[\frac{1}{m_1}+\frac{1}{m_2}+\frac{1}{m_1m_2m_3}\right] \qquad ...(vi)$$

The point which is common to the straight lines (iv), (v) and (vi) i.e. the orthocenter of the triangle is $\left(-a,\ a\left(\dfrac{1}{m_1}+\dfrac{1}{m_2}+\dfrac{1}{m_3}+\dfrac{1}{m_1m_2m_3}\right)\right)$

Hence, the point lies on the directrix.

(ix) **Director circle :**

The locus of the point of intersection of two perpendicular tangents to a parabola is known as director circle.

The equation of the director circle to the parabola $y^2=4ax$ is $x+a=0$.

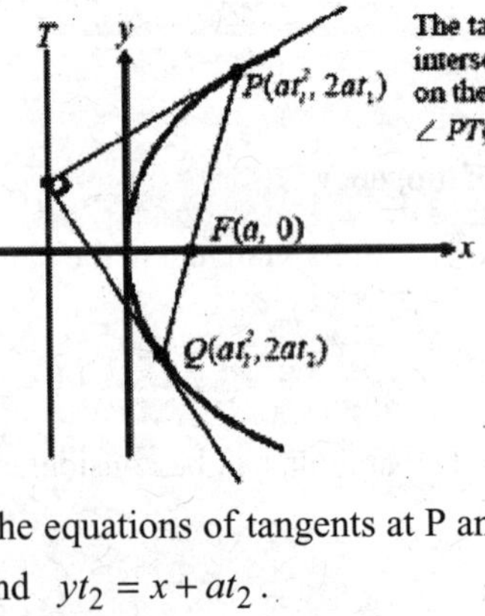

The tangents at P and Q intersect at right angles on the directrix, i.e $\angle PTQ = 90°$

The equations of tangents at P and Q are $yt_1=x+at_1^2$ and $yt_2=x+at_2$.

The point of intersection of these tangents is

$$\left(at_1t_2,\ a\left(t_1+t_2\right)\right).$$

Let this point be (h, k).

Slope of the tangents are $m_1 = \frac{1}{t_1}$ and $m_2 = \frac{1}{t_2}$.

Since these two tangents are perpendicular,

so $\quad m_1.m_2 = -a$

$\Rightarrow \quad \frac{1}{t_1}.\frac{1}{t_2} = -1$

$\Rightarrow \quad t_1 \,.\, t_2 = -1$

$\Rightarrow \quad h = -\,a$

Thus the locus of the points of intersection is x + a = 0 .

which is the directrix of the parabola $y^2 = 4ax$.

Ex-1. Find the equation of the director circle to the follwoing parabolas ;

(i) $y^2 = x+2$

(ii) $x^2 = 4x+4y$

(iii) $y^2 = 4x+4y-8$

Sol. (i) The given parabola is $y^2 = x+2$

$\Rightarrow \quad \mathrm{Y}^2 = \mathrm{X}$, where X = x + 2 and Y = y

We have , 4a = 1 $\Rightarrow$ $a = \frac{1}{4}$.

Hence, the equation of the director circle is $\mathrm{X} + \mathrm{a} = 0$

$\Rightarrow \quad \mathrm{x} + 2 + \frac{1}{4} = 0$

$\Rightarrow \quad 4\mathrm{x} + 9 = 0$.

(ii) The given parabola is $x^2 = 4x+4y$

$\Rightarrow \quad \left(x^2 - 4x + 4\right) = 4y + 4 = 4(y+1)$

$\Rightarrow \quad (x-2)^2 = 4(y+1)$

$\Rightarrow \quad \mathrm{X}^2 = 4\mathrm{Y}$, where X = x - 2 and Y = y + 1 .

We have , 4 a = 4 $\Rightarrow$ a = 1.

Hence, the equation of the director circle is $\mathrm{Y} + \mathrm{a} = 0$

$\Rightarrow \quad \mathrm{y} + 1 + 1 = 0$

$\Rightarrow \quad \mathrm{y} + 2 = 0$.

(iii) The given parabola is $y^2 = 4x+4y-8$

$\Rightarrow \quad \mathrm{y}^2 - 4\mathrm{y} + 4 = 4\mathrm{x} - 8 + 4$

$\Rightarrow \quad (\mathrm{y}-2)^2 = 4\mathrm{x} - 4 = 4(\mathrm{x}-1)$

$\Rightarrow \quad \mathrm{Y}^2 = 4\mathrm{X}$, where X = (x-1) and Y = (y - 2)

We have 4 a = 4 $\Rightarrow$ a = 1

Hence, the equation of the director circle is $\mathrm{X} + \mathrm{a} = 0$

$\Rightarrow \quad \mathrm{x} - 1 + 1 = 0$

$\Rightarrow \quad \mathrm{x} = 0$.

(x) The equation to the pair of tangents can be drawn to the parabola from the point (x_1, y_1).

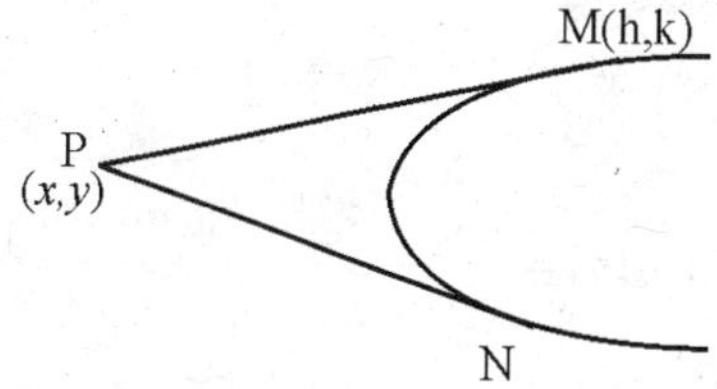

Let (h, k) be any point on either of the tangents drawn from (x_1, y_1) .

The equation to the line joining (x_1, y_1) and (h, k) is

$$y - y_1 = \frac{k - y_1}{h - x_1}(x - x_1)$$

$$\Rightarrow \quad y = \frac{k - y_1}{h - x_1}x + \frac{hy_1 - kx_1}{h - x_1}.$$

If this be a tangent , it must be of the form $y = mx + \frac{a}{m}$.

thus, $m = \frac{k - y_1}{h - x_1}$ and $\frac{a}{m} = \frac{hy_1 - kx_1}{h - x_1}$

Therefore, by multiplication , we get,

$$a = \left(\frac{k - y_1}{h - x_1}\right)\left(\frac{hy_1 - kx_1}{h - x_1}\right)$$

$$\Rightarrow \quad a(h - x_1)^2 = (k - y_1)(hy_1 - kx_1)$$

Hence , the locus of the point (h, k) is

$$a(x - x_1)^2 = (y - y_1)(xy_1 - yx_1)$$

$$\Rightarrow \quad \left(y^2 - 4ax\right)\left(y_1^2 - 4ax_1\right) = \{yy_1 - 2a(x + x_1)\}^2.$$

$\Rightarrow \quad SS_1 = T^2$, where,

$S : \left(y^2 - 4ax\right)$, $S_1 : \left(y_1^2 - 4ax_1\right)$

and $\quad T : \{yy_1 - 2a(x + x_1)\}$.

Ex-1. Two tangents are drawn from a point (-1, 2) to a parabola $y^2 = 4x$. Find the angle between the tangents.

Sol. The equation of line from (-1, 2) is

$$(\mathrm{y} - 2) = \mathrm{m}(\mathrm{x} + 1)$$

$$\Rightarrow \quad \mathrm{mx} - \mathrm{y} + (\mathrm{m} + 2) = 0$$

$$\Rightarrow \quad y = \mathrm{mx} + (\mathrm{m} + 2) \qquad \text{...(i)}$$

The line (i) will be a tangent to the parabola $y^2 = 4x$ if

$$(\mathrm{m} + 2) = \frac{1}{\mathrm{m}}$$

$$\Rightarrow \quad \mathrm{m}^2 + 2\mathrm{m} - 1 = 0$$

Which is a quadratic in m .

Let its roots are m_1, m_2

Thus, $m_1 + m_2 = -2$ and $m_1 m_2 = -1$

Let θ be the angle between them .

Then , $\tan(\theta) = \left|\frac{m_2 - m_1}{1+m_1m_2}\right| = \left|\frac{\sqrt{(m_1+m_2)^2 - 4m_1m_2}}{1+m_1m_2}\right|$

$\Rightarrow \quad \tan(\theta) = \infty$

$\Rightarrow \quad (\theta) = \frac{\pi}{2}$

Hence, the angle between the tangent is $\frac{\pi}{2}$

Ex-2. Find the equation of the tangent to the parabola $y^2 = 8x$ having slope 2 and also find its point of contact.

Sol. Let the equation of the tangent be

$y = 2x + c$ ...(i)

If the equation (i) be a tangent to the parabola , then

$c = \frac{a}{m} = \frac{2}{2} = 1$

Thus , the equation of tangent is $y = 2x + 1$ ...(ii)

The given parabola is $y^2 = 8x$ ...(iii)

On solving (ii) and (iii) , we get, $(2x+1)^2 = 8x$

$\Rightarrow \quad 4x^2 + 4x + 1 = 8x$

$\Rightarrow \quad 4x^2 - 4x + 1 = 0$

$\Rightarrow \quad (2x-1)^2 = 0$

$\Rightarrow \quad x = \frac{1}{2}$

When x = 1/2, then $y = \pm\ 2$

Hence, the point of contacts are $\left(\frac{1}{2}, 2\right)$ or $\left(\frac{1}{2}, -2\right)$.

Ex-3. Find the equation of tangent to the parabola $y^2 = 2x + 5y - 8$ at $x = 1$

Sol. The given parabola is $y^2 = 2x + 5y - 8$.

when $x = 1, y^2 = 5y - 6 \Rightarrow y^2 - 5y + 6 = 0$

$\Rightarrow (y-2)(y-3) \Rightarrow y = 2, 3$

Thus, the points are (1, 2) and (1, 3)

Hence, the equations of tangents can be at (1, 2) and (1, 3) be

$2y = (x+1) + \frac{5}{2}(y+2) - 8$ and

$3y = (x+1) + \frac{5}{2}(y+3) - 8$

$\Rightarrow \quad 2x + y - 4 = 0$ and $2x - y + 1 = 0$

Ex-4. Find the equation of the tangents to the parabola $y = x^2 - 3x + 2$ from the point (1, -1).

Sol. Let the equation of the tangent be $(y+1) = m(x-1)$

$\Rightarrow \quad y = mx - (m+1)$ ...(i)

Equation (i) be a tangent to the parabola $y = x^2 - 3x + 2$, then $mx - m - 1 = x^2 - 3x + 2$

$\Rightarrow \quad x^2 - (m+3)x + (m+3) = 0$

It has equal roots .

Therefore , $D = 0 \Rightarrow \quad (m+3)^2 - 4(m+3) = 0$

$\Rightarrow \quad (m+3)(m+3-4) = 0$

$\Rightarrow \quad (m+3)(m-1) = 0$

$\Rightarrow \quad m = 1, -3$

Hence, the equation of the tangents are $y = x - 2$ and $y = -3x + 2$.

Ex-5. Find the equation of the common tangent to the parabolas $y^2 = 4ax$ and $x^2 = 4ay$

Sol. The given parabolas are $y^2 = 4ax$ and $x^2 = 4ay$

Let the equation of the tangent be $y = mx + \frac{a}{m}$

If it is a tangent to the parabola $x^2 = 4ay$, then

$x^2 = 4a\left(mx + \frac{a}{m}\right)$

$\Rightarrow \quad mx^2 = 4am^2x + 4a^2$

$\Rightarrow \quad mx^2 - 4am^2x - 4a^2 = 0$

Now D = 0 gives , $16a^2m^4 + 16a^2m = 0$

$\Rightarrow \quad 16a^2m\left(m^3 + 1\right) = 0$

$\Rightarrow \quad m\left(m^3 + 1\right) = 0$

$\Rightarrow \quad m = 0\ \&\ -1$

$\Rightarrow \quad m = -1$, since m = 0 will not satisfy the given tangent.

Hence, the equation of the common tangent be $y = -x - a$

$\Rightarrow \quad x + y + a = 0$

Ex-6. Find the equation of the common tangent to the parabola $y^2 = 4ax$ and $x^2 = 4by$.

Sol. The given parabolas are $y^2 = 4ax$ and $x^2 = 4by$.

Let the equation of the tangent be $y = mx + \frac{a}{m}$ ....(i)

Equation (i) is also a tangent to the parabola $x^2 = 4by$

$\Rightarrow \quad x^2 = 4b\left(mx + \frac{a}{m}\right)$

$\Rightarrow \quad mx^2 = 4bm^2 x + 4ab$

$\Rightarrow \quad mx^2 - 4bm^2 x - 4ab = 0$

It has equal roots .

So, D = 0 gives $16b^2m^4 + 16abm = 0$

$\Rightarrow \quad 16bm(bm^3 + a) = 0$

$\Rightarrow \quad m^3 = -\frac{a}{b} \quad \Rightarrow \quad m = -\frac{a^{1/3}}{b^{1/3}}$

Hence, the equation of the common tangent be

$$y = \left(-\frac{a^{1/3}}{b^{1/3}}\right)x + a\left(-\frac{b^{1/3}}{a^{1/3}}\right).$$

Ex-7. Find the equation of the common tangent to the parabola $y^2 = 16x$ and the circle $x^2 + y^2 = 8$.

Sol. Let the equation of the tangent to the parabola $y^2 = 16x$ is $y = mx + \frac{4}{m}$

$\Rightarrow \quad m^2 x - my + 4 = 0$ ...(i)

If the equation (i) be a tangent to the circle $x^2 + y^2 = 8$, then the length of perpendicular from the centre to the tangent is equal to the radius of the circle.

Therefore, $\left|\frac{0 - 0 + 4}{\sqrt{m^4 + m^2}}\right| = 2\sqrt{2}$

$\Rightarrow \quad 8(m^4 + m^2) = 16$

$\Rightarrow \quad (m^4 + m^2 - 2) = 0$

$\Rightarrow \quad (m^4 + 2m^2 - m^2 - 2) = 0$

$\Rightarrow \quad (m^2 + 2)(m^2 - 1) = 0$

$\Rightarrow \quad (m^2 - 1) = 0$

$\Rightarrow \quad m = \pm 1$

Hence, the common tangents are $y = \pm x \pm 4$.

Ex-8. Find the equation of the common tangents to the parabolas $y = x^2$ and $y = -(x-2)^2$.

Sol. Any point on the parabola $y = x^2$ is (t, t^2)

Now tangent at (t, t^2) is $xx_1 = \frac{1}{2}(y + y_1)$

$\Rightarrow \quad tx = \frac{1}{2}(y + t^2)$

$\Rightarrow \quad 2tx - y - t^2 = 0$

If it is a tangent to the parabola, $y = -(x-2)^2$,

then $2tx - t^2 = -(x-2)^2$

$\Rightarrow \quad 2tx - t^2 = -x^2 + 4x - 4$

$\Rightarrow \quad x^2 + 2(2-t)x + (t^2 - 4) = 0$

It has equal roots .

So, D = 0 gives , $4(2-t)^2 - 4(t^2 - 4) = 0$

$\Rightarrow \quad (2-t)^2 - (t^2 - 4) = 0$

$\Rightarrow \quad t = 2$

Hence, the equation of the common tangent is $y = 4x - 4$.

Ex-9. Find the equation of the common tangents to the curves $y^2 = 8x$ and $xy = -1$.

Sol. Let the equation of the tangent to the parabola $y 2 = 8x$ is

$y = mx + \frac{2}{m}$ ...(i)

If it is a tangent to the curve $xy = -1$, then

$$x\left(mx + \frac{2}{m}\right) = -1$$

$\Rightarrow \quad m^2 x^2 + 2x + m = 0$

It has equal roots . So, D = 0

Then, $4 - 4m^3 = 0 \quad \Rightarrow \quad m^3 = 1$

$\Rightarrow \quad m = 1$

Hence, the equation of the common tangent is $y = x + 2$.

Ex-10. Find the equation of the common tangent to the circle $x^2 + y^2 - 6y + 4 = 0$ and the parabola $y^2 = x$.

Sol. Any point on the parabola $y^2 = x$ can be considered as (t^2, t)

Equation of the tangent to the parabola $y^2 = x$ at (t^2, t) is

$$yy_1 = \frac{1}{2}(x + x_1)$$

$\Rightarrow \quad yt = \frac{1}{2}(x + t^2)$

$\Rightarrow \quad x + 2yt - t^2 = 0$ ...(i)

If it is a tangent to the circle $x^2 + y^2 - 6y + 4 = 0$, then

$(2yt - t^2)^2 + y^2 - 6y + 4 = 0$

$\Rightarrow \quad 4y^2t^2 + t^4 - 4yt^3 + y^2 - 6y + 4 = 0$

$\Rightarrow \quad (4t^2 + 1)y^2 - 2(2t^3 + 3)y + (t^4 + 4) = 0$

It has equal roots .

So, D = 0 gives , $4\left(2t^3+1\right)^2-4\left(4t^2+1\right)\left(t^4+4\right)=0$

$\Rightarrow \quad \left(2t^3+1\right)^2-\left(4t^2+1\right)\left(t^4+4\right)=0$

$\Rightarrow \quad t^4-12t^3+16t^2-5=0$

$\Rightarrow \quad t=1$

Hence, the equation of the common tangent is $x+2y=1$.

Ex-11. Find the equation of the common tangent touching the circle $x^2+(y-3)^2=9$ and the pa rabola $y^2=4x$ above the x-axis.

Sol. Any tangent to the parabola $y^2=4x$ is

$$y=mx+\frac{a}{m} \Rightarrow y=mx+\frac{1}{m}$$

$\Rightarrow \quad m^2x-my+1=0 \qquad$ ...(i)

If it is a tangent to the circle $x^2+(y-3)^2=9$ is , then the length of the perpendicular from the centre to the tangent is equal to the radius of the circle

Therefore, $\left|\dfrac{3m^2+1}{\sqrt{m^4+m^2}}\right|=3$

$\Rightarrow \quad \left(3m^2+1\right)^2=9\left(m^4+m^2\right)$

$\Rightarrow \quad \left(9m^4+6m^2+1\right)=9\left(m^4+m^2\right)$

$\Rightarrow \quad 3m^2=1$

$\Rightarrow \quad m=\pm\left(\dfrac{1}{\sqrt{3}}\right)$

Since, the tangent touches the parabola above x-axis , so it will make an acute angle with x axis , so that m is +ve .

Thus $m=\dfrac{1}{\sqrt{3}}$.

Hence, the common tangent is $x-\sqrt{3}y+3=0$.

Ex-12. Find the points of intersection of the tangents at the ends of the latus rectum to the parabola $y^2=4x$

Sol. The equation of the given parabola is $y^2=4x$

We have , $4a=4 \Rightarrow a=1$

Let the end points of the latus rectum are L(a, 2a) and $L'(a,-2a)$

Therefore L = (1, 2) and L' = (1, -2)

As we know that, the point of intersection to the tangents at $\left(at_1^2, 2at_1\right)$ and $\left(at_2^2, 2at_2\right)$

to the parabola $y^2=4ax$ is $\left(at_1t_2, a\left(\dfrac{t_1+t_2}{2}\right)\right)$.

Thus, the point of intersection of the tangents at L(1, 2) and L`1, -2) is (1, 0) .

Ex-13. Find the angle between the tangents drawn from a point (1, 4) to the parabola $y^2=4x$.

Sol. Equation of tangent to the parabola $y^2=4x$ ....(i) from (1, 4) is $y-4=m(x-1)$

$\Rightarrow \quad y=mx+(4-m)$ ....(ii)

Since, (ii) is a tangent to the parabola $y^2=4x$, so $c=\dfrac{a}{m}$

$\Rightarrow \quad (4-m)=\dfrac{1}{m}$

$\Rightarrow \quad 4m-m^2-1=0$

$\Rightarrow \quad m^2-4m+1=0$

It has two roots, say, m_1 and m_2

Therefore, $m_1+m_2=4$ and $m_1m_2=1$

Let θ be the angle between the tangents

Then $\tan(\theta)=\left|\dfrac{m_2-m_1}{1+m_1m_2}\right|$

$$=\left|\frac{\sqrt{(m_1+m_2)^2-4m_1m_2}}{1+m_1m_2}\right|=\left|\frac{\sqrt{12}}{2}\right|=\sqrt{3}$$

$\Rightarrow \quad \theta=\dfrac{\pi}{3}$

Hence , the angle between the tangents is $\dfrac{p}{3}$.

Ex-14. Find the shortest distance between the line $y=x-2$ and the parabola $y=x^2+3x+2$.

Sol. The shotest distance between a line and the parabola means , the shortest distance between a line and a tangent to the parabola parallel to the given line .

Thus, slopes of the tangent and the line will be same.

Therefore, $2x+3=1 \Rightarrow x=-1$

when $x=-1$, then $y=0$.

Hence, the point on the parabola is (-1, 0)

Thus, the required shotest distance = $\left|\dfrac{-1-0-2}{\sqrt{1+1}}\right|=\dfrac{3}{\sqrt{2}}$

Ex-15. Find the shortest distance from the line $x+y=4$ and the parabola $y^2+4x+4y=0$.

Sol. The shotest distance between a line and the parabola means , the shortest distance between a line and a tangent to the parabola parallel to the given line .

Thus, slopes of the tangent and the line will be same.

Therefore , $-\dfrac{4}{2y+4}=-1 \Rightarrow y=0$

when $y=0$, then $x=0$.

Thus, the point on the parabola is (0, 0).

Hence, the required shortest distance

$$= \left|\frac{0+0-4}{\sqrt{1+1}}\right| = \frac{4}{\sqrt{2}} = 2\sqrt{2}.$$

Ex-16. If $y+b=m_1(x+a)$ and $y+b=m_2(x+a)$ are two tangents of the parabola $y^2=4ax$, then find the value of $m_1 m_2$.

Sol. The given tangents are $y+b=m_1(x+a)$ and $y+b=m_2(x+a)$

Therefore, both the tangents pass through (-a, - b).

Which is a point lying on the directrix .of the parabola.

Thus, the angle between them is 90°

Hence, the value of $m_1 m_2$ is - 1.

Ex-17. Tangent to the curve $y=x^2+6$ at a point (1, 7) touches the circle $x^2+y^2+16x+12y+c=0$ at Q. Then find the co-ordinates of Q.

Sol. The equation of the tangent to the curve y = x 2 + 6 at

$(1, 7)$ is $\frac{1}{2}(y+y_1) = x x_1 + 6$

$\Rightarrow \quad \frac{1}{2}(y+7) = x+6$

$\Rightarrow \quad 2x-y-5=0$ ...(i)

The given circle is

$$(x+8)^2+(y+6)^2=\left(\sqrt{100-c}\right)^2 \quad ...(ii)$$

If the line (i) be a tangent to the circle (ii), then the length of the perpendicular from thecentre of the circle is equal to the radius of the circle.

Therefore, $\left|\frac{-16+6-5}{\sqrt{2^2+1}}\right| = \sqrt{100-c}$

$\Rightarrow \quad 45 = 100-c$

$\Rightarrow \quad c = 100-45 = 55$

Thus, the equation of the circle is

$$(x+8)^2+(y+6)^2=45$$

$\Rightarrow \quad x^2+y^2+16x+12y+55=0$ ...(iii)

On solving (i) and (iii), we get,

$$x^2+(2x-5)^2+16x+12(2x-5)+55=0$$

$\Rightarrow \quad x^2+4x^2+25-20x+16x+24x-60+55=0$

$\Rightarrow \quad 5x^2+20x+20=0$

$\Rightarrow \quad x^2+4x+4=0$

$\Rightarrow \quad (x+2)^2=0$

$\Rightarrow \quad x=-2$

When $x=-2$, then $y=2x-5=-4-5=-9$.

Hence, the point Q is (-2, -9).

Ex-18. Two straight lines are perpendicular to each other. One of them touches the parabola $y^2=4a(x+a)$ and the other touches $y^2=4b(x+b)$. Prove that the point of intersection of the lines lie on the line $x+a+b=0$.

Sol. Any tangent to $y^2=4(x+a)$ is

$$y = m_1(x+a)+\frac{a}{m_1} \quad ...(i)$$

Also, any tangent to $y^2=4b(x+b)$ is

$$y = m_2(x+b)+\frac{b}{m_2} \quad ...(ii)$$

Since, two tangents are perpendicular, so $m_1 m_2 = -1$

$\Rightarrow \quad m_2 = -\frac{1}{m_1}$

From (ii), we get, $y = -\frac{1}{m_1}(x+b) - b m_1$ ...(iii)

Now subtracting (i) and (iii), we get,

$$m_1(x+a)+\frac{1}{m_1}(x+b)+\frac{a}{m_1}+bm_1=0$$

$$\Rightarrow \quad \left(m_1+\frac{1}{m_1}\right)x+\left(m_1+\frac{1}{m_1}\right)a+\left(m_1+\frac{1}{m_1}\right)b=0$$

$\Rightarrow \quad x+a+b=0$

Hence, the result.

4.21 NORMAL

It is a line, which is perpendicular to the point of contact to the tangent.

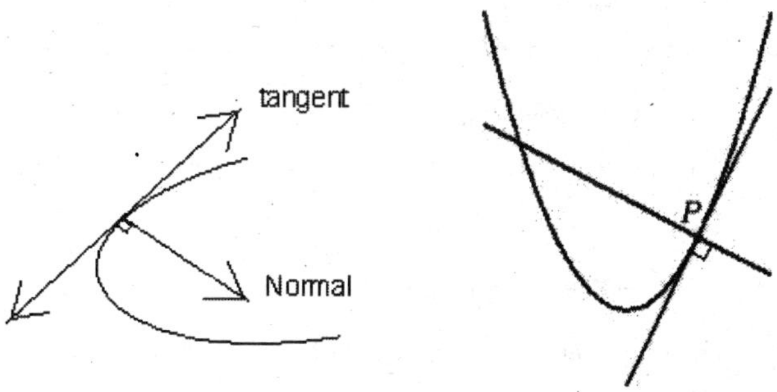

Equation of normals to the parabola in different forms :

(i) Point form :

The equation of normal to the parabola $y^2=4ax$ at

(x_1, y_1) is $\frac{y-y_1}{y_1} = \frac{x-x_1}{2a}$.

The equation of tangent to the parabola $y^2 = 4ax$ at (x_1, y_1) is $yy_1 = 2a(x + x_1)$ ...(i)

Slope of the tangent is $m(T) = \frac{2a}{y_1}$.

Slope of the normal is $m(N) = -\frac{y_1}{2a}$

Thus the equation of the normal is

$$y - y_1 = -\frac{y_1}{2a}(x - x_1).$$

(ii) Parametric form :

The equation of the normal to the parabola $y^2 = 4ax$ at $(at^2, 2at)$ is $y = -tx + 2at + at^3$.

As we know that, the equation of normal to the parabola $y^2 = 4ax$ at (x_1, y_1) is $\frac{y - y_1}{y_1} = -\frac{x - x_1}{2a}$

Replacing x_1 by at^2 and y_1 by 2 at, then we get,

$$\frac{y - 2at}{2at} = -\frac{x - at^2}{2a}.$$

$\Rightarrow y = -tx + 2at + at^3$.

which is the required equation of normal to the given parabola.

(iii) Slope form :

The equation of normal to the parabola $y^2 = 4ax$ at $(am^2, -2am)$ is $y = mx - 2am - am^3$.

As we know that the equation of normal to the parabola $y^2 = 4ax$ at $(at^2, 2at)$ is

$y = -tx + 2at + at^3$ ...(i)

slope of the normal is $m = -t \Rightarrow t = -m$

put the values of m in (i), we get,

$$y = mx - 2am - am^3.$$

which is the required equation of normal to the parabola $y^2 = 4ax$ at $(am^2, -2am)$.

(iv) Condition of normal :

The line $y = mx + c$ will be a normal to the parabola $y^2 = 4ax$ if $c = -2am - am^3$.

and the co-ordinates of the point of contact are $(am^2, -2am)$.

(v) Point of intersection of normals at any points on the parabola :

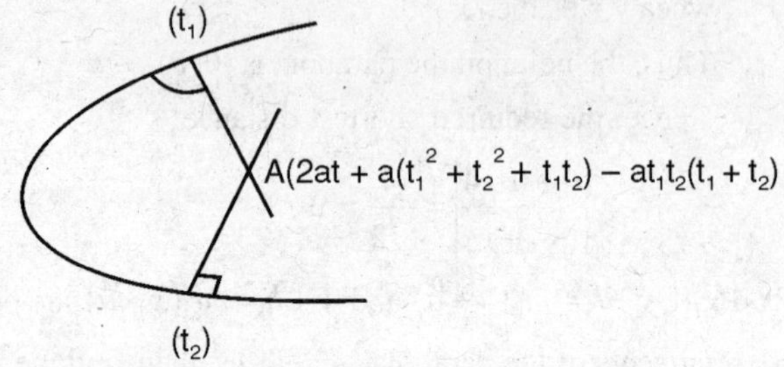

Let the parabola be $y^2 = 4ax$ and two points on the parabola are $P(at_1^2, 2at_1)$ and $Q(at_2^2, 2at_2)$.

Equation of normal at $P(at_1^2, 2at_1)$ and $Q(at_2^2, 2at_2)$ are

$y = -t_1x + 2at_1 + at_1^3$ ...(i)

and $y = -t_2x + 2at_2 + at_2^3$ ...(ii)

Solving (i) and (ii), we get, $x = 2a + a(t_1^2 + t_2^2 + t_1t_2)$

and $y = -at_1t_2(t_1 + t_2)$.

(vi) Relation between 't_1' and 't_2', where the normal at 't_1' to the parabola meets the parabola again at 't_2'.

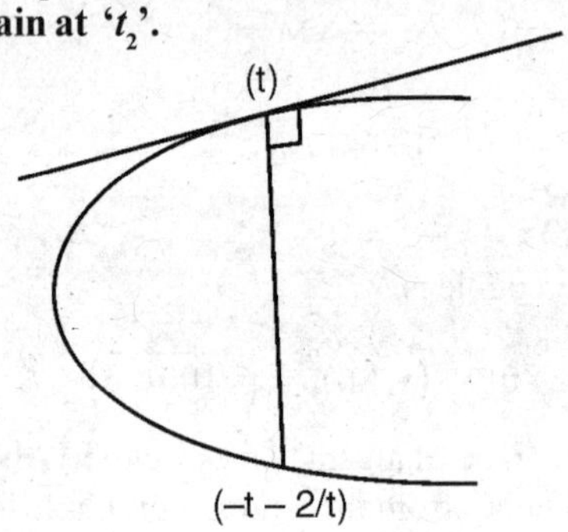

Let the parabola be $y^2 = 4ax$ and the two points on the parabola are

$P(at_1^2, 2at_1)$ & $Q(at_2^2, 2at_2)$

Equation of the normal to the parabola at $P(at_1^2, 2at_1)$ is $y = -t_1x + 2at_1 + at_1^3$

which is meets the parabola again at $Q(at_2^2, 2at_2)$.

Thus, $2at_2 = -at_1t_2^2 + 2at_1 + at_1^3$

$\Rightarrow \quad 2a(t_2 - t_1) + at_1(t_2^2 - t_1^2) = 0$

$\Rightarrow \quad (t_2 - t_1)(2a + at_1(t_2 + t_1)) = 0$

$\Rightarrow \quad (2 + t_1(t_2 + t_1)) = 0$

$\Rightarrow \quad t_1^2 + t_1t_2 + 2 = 0$

$\Rightarrow \quad t_2 = -t_1 - \dfrac{2}{t_1}$.

Which is the required condition.

Note : If the normal at 't_1' meets the parabola again at 't_2', then the minimum value of t_2^2 is 8 .

As we know that , if the normal at 't_1' meets the parabola again at 't_2' , then $t_2 = -t_1 - \dfrac{2}{t_1}$

$$\Rightarrow t_2^2 = \left(-t_1 - \frac{2}{t_1}\right)^2 = t_1^2 + \frac{4}{t_1^2} + 4 \geq 4 + 4 = 8$$

Hence, the result.

(vii) If two normals at t_1 and t_2 meet again the parabola at t_3 , then $t_1t_2 = 2$.

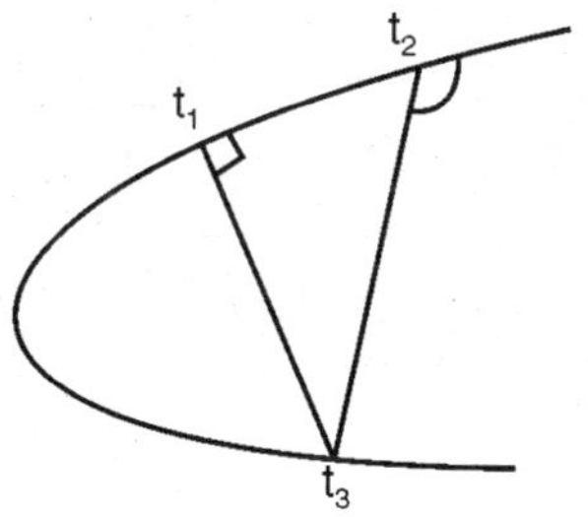

Since the normal at t_1 meets the parabola at t_3, so

$$t_3 = -t_1 - \frac{2}{t_1}$$

similarly , $t_3 = -t_2 - \dfrac{2}{t_2}$

Thus , $-t_1 - \dfrac{2}{t_1} = -t_2 - \dfrac{2}{t_2}$

$$\Rightarrow \quad (t_1 - t_2) = \left(\frac{2}{t_1} - \frac{2}{t_2}\right) = \frac{2(t_1 - t_2)}{t_1 t_2}$$

$\Rightarrow \quad t_1 t_2 = 2$.

(viii) Co-normal points :

In genral , three normals can be drawn from a point to a parabola and their feet points where they meet the parabola are called the co-normal points.

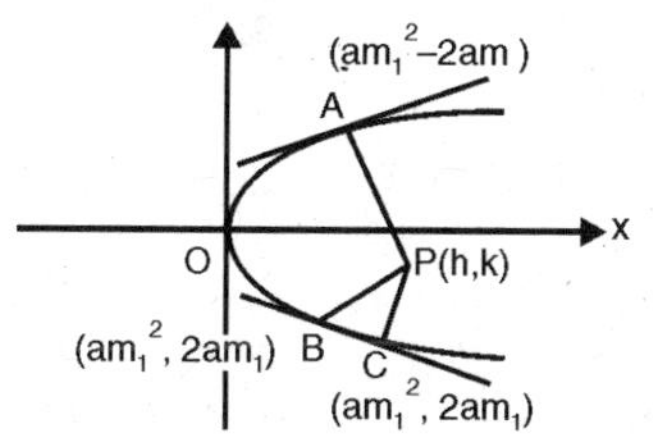

Here A, B and C are three co-normal points .

Let P(h , k) be any given point $y^2 = 4ax$ be a parabola

Equation of any normal to the parabola $y^2 = 4ax$ is $y = mx - 2am - am^3$.

which is passes through P(h, k) .

then, $k = mh - 2am - am^3$

$\Rightarrow \quad am^3 + (2a - h)m + k = 0$.

which is a cubic equation in m .

so, it has three roots .

Thus , in total three normals can be drawn from a point lies either outside or inside of a parabola.

Note : we can draw one and only one normal to a parabola, if a point lies on the parabola.

(ix) The algebraic sum of the three concurrent normals to a parabola is zero.

Equation of any normal to a parabola $y^2 = 4ax$ is

$y = mx - 2am - am^3$

which is meet at a point , say , (h, k).

Thus, $\quad am^3 + (2a - h)m + k = 0$.

which is a cubic equation in m .

So it has three roots, say, m_1, m_2 & m_3

Therefore, $\quad m_1 + m_2 + m_3 = 0$

Hence the result.

(x) The algebraic sum of the the ordinates of the feets of three normals drawn to a parabola from a given point is also zero.

Let the ordinates of A, B and C be y_1, y_2 , y_3 respectively.

Then , $y_1 = -2am_1$, $y_2 = -2am_2$, $y_3 = -2am_3$.

Thus, $\quad y_1 + y_2 + y_3 = -2am_1 - 2am_2 - 2am_3$

$$= -2a(m_1 + m_2 + m_3) = -2a.0 = 0 .$$

(xi) The centroid of the triangle formed by the feet of the three normals lies on the axis of the parabola. And, also find the centroid of the triangle.

If $A(x_1, y_1)$, $B(x_2, y_2)$ and $C(x_3, y_3)$ be the vertices of a triangle ABC , then its centroid is

$$\left(\frac{x_1 + x_2 + x_3}{3}, \frac{y_1 + y_2 + y_3}{3}\right) = \left(\frac{x_1 + x_2 + x_3}{3}, 0\right).$$

Hence the centriod lies on the axis of the parabola.

Also $\quad \dfrac{x_1 + x_2 + x_3}{3} = \dfrac{1}{3}\left(am_1^2 + am_2^2 + am_3^2\right)$

$$= \frac{a}{3}\left\{(m_1 + m_2 + m_3)^2 - 2(m_1m_2 + m_2m_3 + m_3m_1)\right\}$$

$$= \frac{a}{3}\left\{0 - 2\left(\frac{2a - h}{a}\right)\right\} = \frac{2h - 4a}{3}$$

Thus, the centroid of the triangle ABC is $\left(\frac{2h-4a}{3}, 0\right)$.

(xii) If three normals drawn from a given point (h, k) to any parabola be real, then h > 2 a.

When three normals are real, then all the three roots of $am^3+(2a-h)m+k=0$ are real.

Let its three roots are m_1, m_2, m_3.

For any real values of m_1, m_2, m_3,

$$m_1^2+m_2^2+m_3^2>0$$

$$\Rightarrow (m_1+m_2+m_3)^2-2(m_1m_2+m_2m_3+m_3m_1)>0$$

$$\Rightarrow 0-2\left(\frac{2a-h}{a}\right)>0$$

$$\Rightarrow h-2a>0$$

$$\Rightarrow h>2a.$$

(xiii) If three normals from a given point (h, k) to any parabola $y^2=4ax$ be real and distinct, then $27ak^2<4(h-2a)^3$.

Let $f(m)=am^3+(2a-h)m+k$.

$$\Rightarrow f'(m)=3am^2+(2a-h)$$

If f(m) has three distinct roots, so f'(m) has two distinct roots.

Let two distinct roots of f'(m) = 0 are α and β.

Thus, $\alpha=\sqrt{\left(\frac{h-2a}{3}\right)}$ and $\beta=-\sqrt{\left(\frac{h-2a}{3}\right)}$.

Now, $f(\alpha)f(\beta)<0$

$$\Rightarrow f(\alpha)f(-\alpha)<0$$

$$\Rightarrow \left(a\alpha^3+(2a-h)\alpha+k\right)\left(-a\alpha^3-(2a-h)\alpha+k\right)<0$$

$$\Rightarrow k^2-\left(\left(a\alpha^2+(2a-h)\right)^2\alpha^2\right)<0$$

$$\Rightarrow k^2-\left(\frac{h-2a}{3}+(2a-h)\right)^2\left(\frac{h-2a}{3}\right)<0$$

$$\Rightarrow k^2-\left(\frac{4a-2h}{3}\right)^2\left(\frac{h-2a}{3}\right)<0$$

$$\Rightarrow k^2-\frac{4(h-2a)^3}{27a}<0$$

$$\Rightarrow 27ak^2<4(h-2a)^3.$$

Hence, the result.

(xiv) From an external point to a parabola, only one normal can be drawn.

(xv) If a normal to a parabola $y^2=4ax$ makes an angle θ with the axis of the parabola, then it will cut the curve again at an angle of $\tan^{-1}\left(\frac{\tan\theta}{2}\right)$.

Let the normal at $P\left(at_1^2, 2at_1\right)$ be $y=-t_1x+2at_1+at_1^3$

Thus slope of the normal = tan θ = $-t_1$

It meets the parabola again at $Q\left(at_2^2, 2at_2\right)$

Then $t_2=-t_1-\frac{2}{t_1}$.

Now angle between the normal and parabola

= angle between the normal and the tangent at Q.

If φ be the angle between them, then

$$\tan\phi=\frac{m_1-m_2}{1+m_1m_2}=\frac{-t_1-\frac{1}{t_2}}{1+(-t_1)\left(\frac{1}{t_2}\right)}=-\frac{t_1t_2+1}{t_2-t_1}$$

$$=-\frac{t_1\left(-t_1-\frac{2}{t_1}\right)+1}{-t_1-\frac{2}{t_1}-t_1}=-\frac{-t_1^2-1}{-2\left(\frac{1+t_1^2}{t_1}\right)}=-\frac{t_1}{2}=\frac{\tan\theta}{2}$$

$$\Rightarrow \phi=\tan^{-1}\left(\frac{\tan\theta}{2}\right).$$

(xvi) The normal chord to a parabola $y^2=4ax$ at the point whose ordinate is equal to its abscissa, which subtends a right angle at the focus of the parabola.

Equation of normal to the parabola y2 = 4ax at $P\left(at^2, 2at\right)$ is $y=-tx+2at+at^3$.

It is given that $at^2=2at \Rightarrow t=2$.

Thus, the co-ordinates of P is (4a, 4a) and focus is S(a, 0)

Also, the normal chord meets the parabola at some point, say, at Q.

Then the co-ordinates of Q is (9a, -6a)

Now, Slope of SP = $m_1=\frac{4a}{3a}=\frac{4}{3}$ and the slope of SQ = $m_2=\frac{-6a}{8a}=-\frac{3}{4}$.

Thus, $m_1\times m_2=\frac{4}{3}\times-\frac{4}{3}=-1$

Hence, the result.

(xvii) Normals at the end points of the latus rectum of a parabola $y^2=4ax$ intersect at right angle on the

axis of the parabola and their point of intersection is $(3a, 0)$.

Let the latus rectum be LSL` , where L = (a, 2a) and L` = (a, -2a) .

Normal at L (a, 2a) is x + y = 3 a ...(i)

Normal at L`(a, -2a) is x - y = 3a ...(ii)

Clearly, (ii) is perpendicular to (i).

On solving , we get, x = 3a and y = 0

Hence, the point of intersection is (3a, 0).

(xviii) If S be the focus of the parabola and tangent and normal at any point P meet the axes in T and G respectively, then ST = SG = SP.

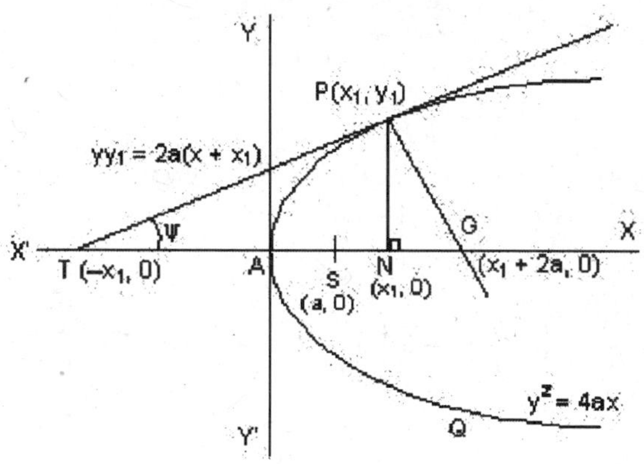

Let $P(x_1, y_1)$ be any point on the parabola $y^2 = 4ax$.

Equation of any tangent and normal at $P(x_1, y_1)$ are

$yy_1 = 2a(x + x_1)$

and $\dfrac{y - y_1}{y_1} = -\dfrac{x - x_1}{2a}$.

since the tangent and normal meet its axis at T and G respectively.

So the co-ordinates of T and G are $(-x_1, 0)$ and $(x_1 + 2a, 0)$.

Thus , $SP = PM = x_1 + a$, SG = AG - AS

$= x_1 + 2a - a = x_1 + a$.

and ST = AS + AT = $a + x_1$.

Hence , SP = SG = ST.

(xix) From any point P on the parabola $y^2 = 4ax$, perpendicular PN is drawn on the axis meeting at N , Normal at P meets the axis in G . Then the sub-normal NG = semi - latus rectum.

Normal at P(t) is $y = -tx + 2at + at^3$.

It meets the x-axis at G . Thus the co-ordinates of G be $(2a + at^2, 0)$

Also N is $(at^2, 0)$.

Thus $NG = 2a + at^2 - at^2 = 2a$ = semi - latus rectum.

(xx) The normal to the parabola $y^2 = 4ax$ at a point P on it, meets the x-axis in G , then P and G are equidistant from the focus S of the parabola.

Normal at P(t) is $y = -tx + 2at + at^3$.

Thus , S is (a, 0) , G is $(2a + at^2, 0)$ and P is $(at^2, 2at)$.

Now, $SP = a + x = a + at^2 = a(1 + t^2)$

$SG = 2a + at^2 - a = a + at^2 = a(1 + t^2) = SP$

Thus, P and G are equidistant from the focus.

(xxi) The normal at P to the parabola $y^2 = 4ax$ meets its axis at G . Q is another point on the parabola such that QG is perpendicular to the axis of the parabola. Then $QG^2 - PG^2$ = constant.

Normal at P (t) is $y = -tx + 2at + at^3$.

Thus G is $(2a + at^2, 0)$ and P is $(at^2, 2at)$.

Now , $PG^2 = 4a^2 + 4a^2t^2$ ...(i)

Q is a point on the parabola such that QG is perpendicular to axis , so that its ordinate is QG and abscissa is same as of G.

Hence, the point Q is $(2a + at^2, QG)$.

But Q lies on the parabola $y^2 = 4ax$.

$QG^2 = 4a(2a + at^2) = 8a^2 + 4a^2t^2$

$= (4a^2 + 4a^2t^2) + 4a^2 = PG^2 + 4a^2$

$\Rightarrow QG^2 - PG^2 = 4a^2$ = cosnstant.

Hence, the result.

Ex-1. Find the equation of the normal to the parabola $y^2 = 4x$ at the point (1, 2)

Sol. The equation of the normal

$$y - y_1 = -\frac{y_1}{2a}(x - x_1), \text{ where } a = 1$$

$$\Rightarrow \quad y - 2 = -\frac{2}{2}(x - 1) = -x + 1$$

$$\Rightarrow \quad x + y = 3$$

Ex-2. Find the equation of the normal to the parabola $y^2 = 8x$ at m = 2

Sol. Equation of the normal to the parabola $y^2 = 4ax$ is

$y = mx - 2am - am^3$

Here , a = 2 and m = 2 .

Therefore , y = 2 x - 8 - 16 = 2 x - 24

Hence, the equation of the normal is $y = 2x - 24$.

Ex-3. If $x + y = k$ is a normal to the parabola $y^2 = 12x$, then find the value of k.

Sol. The given parabola is $y^2 = 12x$

We have, $4a = 12 \Rightarrow a = 3$.

The given line $x + y = k \Rightarrow y = -x + k$ ....(i)

The line (i) will be a normal to the given parabola, if $k = -2am - am^3 = 6 + 3 = 9$.

Hence, the value of k is 9.

Ex-4. If the normal at P(18, 12) to the parabola $y^2 = 8x$ cuts it again at Q, then prove that $9PQ = 80\sqrt{10}$

Sol. The equation of the parabola is $y^2 = 8x$.

We have, $4a = 8 \Rightarrow a = 2$

The equation of the normal to the given parabola at

P(8, 12) is $y - y_1 = -\frac{y_1}{2a}(x - x_1)$

$$\Rightarrow \quad y - 12 = -\frac{12}{4}(x - 18)$$

$$\Rightarrow \quad y - 12 = -3x + 54$$

$$\Rightarrow \quad 3x + y = 66$$

On solving $y = 66 - 3x$ and the parabola $y^2 = 8x$, we get,

$$x = -\frac{44}{3},\ y = \frac{242}{9}$$

Hence, the co-ordinates of Q is $\left(-\frac{44}{3}, \frac{242}{9}\right)$

$$\text{Thus, PQ} = \sqrt{\left(\frac{242}{9} - 18\right)^2 + \left(-\frac{44}{3} - 12\right)^2}$$

$$= \sqrt{\frac{6400}{81} + \frac{6400}{9}}$$

$$= 80\sqrt{\frac{1}{81} + \frac{1}{9}}$$

$$= \frac{80}{9} \times \sqrt{10}$$

$$\Rightarrow \quad 9PQ = 80\sqrt{10}$$

Ex-5. Find the locus of the point of intersection of two normals to the parabola $y^2 = 4ax$, which are at right angles to one another.

Sol. The equations of normals at $P(t_1)$ and $Q(t_2)$ are $y = -t_1x + 2at_1 + at_1^3$ and $y = -t_2x + 2at_2 + at_2^3$.

Since these two normals are at right angles, so $t_1t_2 = -1$

Let M (h, k) be the point of intersection of two normals.

Then, $h = 2a + a\left(t_1^2 + t_1t_2 + t_2^2\right)$

and $k = -at_1t_2(t_1 + t_2)$

$$\Rightarrow \quad h = 2a + a\left\{(t_1 + t_2)^2 - 2t_1t_2\right\}$$

and $k = -at_1t_2(t_1 + t_2)$

$$\Rightarrow \quad h = 2a + a\left\{(t_1 + t_2)^2 + 2\right\} \text{ and } k = a(t_1 + t_2)$$

Eliminating t_1 and t_2, we get, $k^2 = a(h - 3a)$

Hence, the locus of M (h, k) is $y^2 = a(x - 3a)$.

Ex-6. If $lx + my + n = 0$ is a normal to the parabola $y^2 = 4ax$, prove that $al^3 + 2alm^2 + m^2n = 0$.

Sol. The given line is $lx + my + n = 0$

$$\Rightarrow \quad my = -lx - n$$

$$\Rightarrow \quad y = \left(-\frac{l}{m}\right)x + \left(-\frac{n}{m}\right)$$

As we know that, the line $y = mx + c$ will be a normal to the parabola $y^2 = 4ax$ if

$c = -2am - am^3$

$$\Rightarrow \quad \left(-\frac{n}{m}\right) = -2a\left(-\frac{l}{m}\right) - a\left(-\frac{l}{m}\right)^3$$

$$\Rightarrow \quad al^3 + 2alm^2 + nm^2 = 0.$$

Hence, the result.

Ex-7. If a normal chord subtends a right angle at the vertex of the parabola $y^2 = 4ax$. Prove that it is inclined at an angle of $\tan^{-1}(\sqrt{2})$ to the axis of the parabola.

Sol. The equation of the parabola is $y^2 = 4ax$.

If the normal at $P(t_1)$ meets the parabola again at $Q(t_2)$,

then $t_2 = -t_1 - \frac{2}{t_1}$

$$\Rightarrow \quad t_1t_2 = -t_1^2 - 2$$

$$\Rightarrow \quad t_1^2 + t_1t_2 + 2 = 0 \qquad ...(i)$$

The chord joining t_1, t_2 subtends a right angle at the vertex, so product of their slopes = -1

$$\Rightarrow \quad \frac{2}{t_1}.\frac{2}{t_2} = -1$$

$$\Rightarrow \quad t_1.t_2 = -4 \qquad ...(ii)$$

From (i) and (ii), we get, $t_1^2 - 4 + 2 = 0$

$$\Rightarrow \quad t_1^2 = 2$$

$$\Rightarrow \quad t_1 = \sqrt{2}$$

$$\Rightarrow \quad \tan\theta = \sqrt{2}$$

$$\Rightarrow \quad \theta = \tan^{-1}\left(\sqrt{2}\right).$$

Ex-8. At what point on the parabola $y^2=4x$, the normal makes equal angles with the axes?

Sol. The given equation of the parabola is $y^2=4x$.

We have $4a=4 \Rightarrow a=1$.

The equation of the normal to the parabola $y^2=4x$ at $(am^2, -2am)$ is $y=mx-2am-am^3=mx-2m-m^3$.

Since, the normal makes equal angles with the axes, so $m=\pm 1$

Thus, the points are $(m^2, -2m)=(1, \mp 2)$

Ex-9. Find the length of the normal chord which subtends an angle of 90° at the vertex of the parabola $y^2=4x$.

Sol. If the normal at P(t1) meets the parabola at Q(t2),

then, $t_2=-t_1-\dfrac{2}{t_1}$ ...(i)

Since, the normal chord subtends an angle of 90° at vertex, then $t_1t_2=-4$

From (i), we get, $t_1^2+t_1t_2+2=0$

$\Rightarrow \quad t_1^2-4+2=0$

$\Rightarrow \quad t_1^2=2$

Also, $t_2^2=\left(-t_1-\dfrac{2}{t_1}\right)^2=t_1^2+\dfrac{4}{t_1^2}+4=2+2+4=8.$

Therefore, $PQ^2=a^2\left(t_1^2-t_2^2\right)^2+4a^2\left(t_1-t_2\right)^2$

$=1.(2-8)^2+4\left(\sqrt{2}+2\sqrt{2}\right)^2=36+72=108$

$\Rightarrow \quad PQ=6\sqrt{3}$.

Ex-10. Prove that the normal chord of a parabola $y^2=4ax$ at the point (p, p) subtends a right angle at the focus.

Sol. The equation of the parabola is $y^2=4ax$.

Let the normal chord be PQ, where P (t_1) and Q(t_2)

Since the abscissa and ordinate of the point (p, p) are same, then $2at_1=at_1^2 \Rightarrow t_1=2$

If the normal at P(t_1) meets the parabola Q(t_2), then

$t_2=-t_1-\dfrac{2}{t_1}$.

$\Rightarrow \quad t_2=-2-1=-3$

Let S(a, 0) be the focus of the parabola $y^2=4ax$.

Then the slope of SP $=\dfrac{2at_1}{at_1^2-a}=\dfrac{4}{4-1}=\dfrac{4}{3}$

and the slope of SQ $=\dfrac{2at_2}{at_2^2-a}=\dfrac{-6}{9-1}=\dfrac{-6}{8}=-\dfrac{3}{4}$.

It is clear that, $m(SP)\times m(SQ)=\dfrac{4}{3}\times-\dfrac{3}{4}=-1$

Hence, the result.

Ex-11. Show that the locus of the mid-point of the portion of the normal to the parabola $y^2=4ax$ intercepted between the curve and the axis is another parabola.

Sol. The given equation of the parabola is $y^2=4ax$.

The equation of the normal at P(am^2, $-2am$) is

$y=mx-2am-am^3$ ....(i)

Let Q be a point on the axis of the parabola.

Put $y=0$ in (i), we get, $x=2a+am^2$.

Hence, the co-ordinates of the point Q is $(2a+am^2, 0)$

Let M (h, k) be the mid-point of the normal PQ.

Then, $h=\dfrac{am^2+2a+am^2}{2}$

and $k=-\dfrac{2am}{2}=-am$

Eliminating 'm', we get, $h=a+\dfrac{k^2}{a}$

$\Rightarrow \quad a^2+k^2=ah$

Hence, the locus of M (h, k) is $a^2+y^2=ax$

$\Rightarrow \quad y^2=a(x-a)$

Ex-12. Find the shortest distance between the curves $y^2=4x$ and $x^2+y^2-12x+31=0$.

Sol. The given equation of the parabola is $y^2=4x$.

The equation of the normal at P(m^2, $-2m$) to the parabola $y^2=4x$ is

$y=mx-2m-m^3$ ...(i)

The given equation of the circle is $x^2+y^2-12x+31=0$.

$\Rightarrow \quad (x-6)^2+y^2=5$ ...(ii)

The shotest distance between the parabola and the circle lies along the common normal.

Therefore, the centre of a circle passes through the normal, so we have, $0=6m-2m-m^3$

$\Rightarrow \quad m^3-4m=0$

$\Rightarrow \quad m=0, -2, 2$

Therefore, P is $(4, -4)$ or $(4, 4)$ and let C(6, 0) be the centre of the circle and Q be a point on the circle.

Therefore, CP $=\sqrt{(6-4)^2+(4-0)^2}=\sqrt{20}=2\sqrt{5}$

and CQ$=\sqrt{5}$

Thus , the shortest distance

$= CP - CQ = 2\sqrt{5} - \sqrt{5} = \sqrt{5}$

Ex-13. Find the shortest distance between the curves

$x^2 + y^2 + 12y + 35 = 0$ and $y^2 = 8x$.

Sol. The given equation of the parabola is $y^2 = 8x$.

We have, $4a = 8 \Rightarrow a = 2$.

The equation of the normal to the parabola y 2 = 8 x at $P(4m^2, -4m)$ is

$y = mx - 4m - 2m^3$ ...(i)

The given equation of the circle is

$$x^2 + y^2 + 12y + 35 = 0$$

$\Rightarrow \quad x^2 + (y+6)^2 = 1$

Thus , the centre of the circle is C(0, -6)

As we know that , the shotest distance between a circle and the parabola lies along the common normal .

Therefore , the normal always pass through the centre of the circle.

So, $-6 = -4m - 2m^3$

$\Rightarrow \quad m^3 + 2m - 3 = 0$

$\Rightarrow \quad m = 1$

Thus, the point P is (4, -4)

Let Q be any point on the circle .

Then CQ = 1

and CP $\sqrt{(4-0)^2 + (-4+6)^2} = \sqrt{20} = 2\sqrt{5}$

Hence, the shortest distance = PQ = CP - CQ = $2\sqrt{5} - 1$.

4.22 CHORD OF CONTACT

The chord joining the points of contact of two tangents drawn from an external point to a parabola is known as the chord of contact .

Equation of the chord of contact of tangents drawn from a point (x_1, y_1) to the parabola $y^2 = 4ax$ is

$yy_1 = 2a(x + x_1)$.

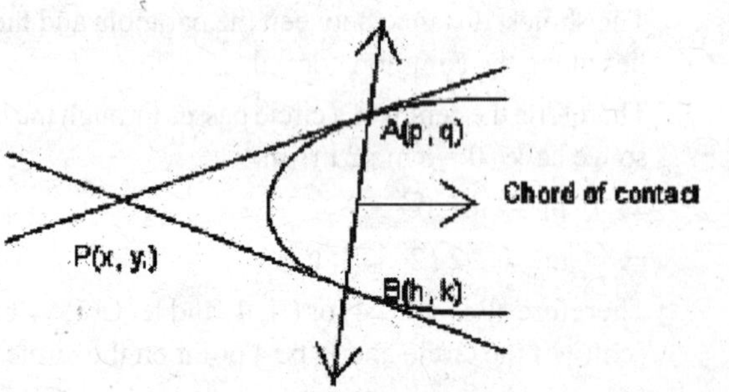

Ex-1. Find the equation of the chord of contact to the tangents from the point (2, 3) to the parabola $y^2 = 4x$

Sol. The equation of the chord of contact of the tangents from the point (2, 3) to the parabola $y^2 = 4x$ is

$yy_1 = 2(x + x_1)$

$\Rightarrow \quad 3y = 2(x+2)$

$\Rightarrow \quad 2x - 3y + 4 = 0$

Ex-2. Find the chord of contact of the tangents to the parabola $y^2 = 12x$ drawn through the (-1, 2)

Sol. The equation of the chord of contact of the tangents to the parabola $y^2 = 12x$ drawn through the point (-1, 2) is

$2y = 6(x - 1)$.

$\Rightarrow \quad y = 3x - 3$.

Ex-3. Prove that the locus of the point of intersection of two tangents to a parabola $y^2 = 4ax$ which makes a given angle θ with one another is $y^2 - 4ax = (x+a)^2 \tan^2\theta$

Sol. Let the point of intersection of the tangents be R(α,β)

Equations of the tangents to the parabola at $P(at_1^2, 2at_1)$ & $Q(at_2^2, 2at_2)$.

are $yt_1 = x + at_1^2$ & $yt_2 = x + at_2^2$

Thus, the slopes of the tangents are

$$m_1 = \frac{1}{t_1} \;\&\; m_2 = \frac{1}{t_2}$$

Then the point of intersection of the two tangents be

$(at_1t_2,\ a(t_1 + t_2))$

Therefore $a = at_1t_2$ & $ß = a(t_1 + t_2)$

Let θ be the angle between the two tangents .

$$\text{Then } \tan(?) = \left|\frac{\frac{1}{t_1} - \frac{1}{t_2}}{1 + \frac{1}{t_1t_2}}\right| = \left|\frac{t_2 - t_1}{t_1t_2 + 1}\right|$$

$$\Rightarrow \quad (1 + t_1t_2)\tan(?) = \left(\sqrt{(t_1+t_2)^2 - 4t_1t_2}\right)$$

$$\Rightarrow \quad (1 + t_1t_2)^2 \tan^2\theta = (t_1+t_2)^2 - 4t_1t_2$$

$$\Rightarrow \quad \left(1 + \frac{a}{a}\right)^2 \tan^2? = \frac{ß^2}{a^2} - \frac{4a}{a} = \frac{ß^2 - 4aa}{a^2}$$

$$\Rightarrow \quad (\alpha + a)^2 \tan^2? = \left(ß^2 - 4aa\right)$$

Hence, the locus of (α,β) is

$$\left(y^2 - 4ax\right) = (x+a)^2 \tan^2?$$

Ex-4. Prove that the length of the chord of contact of tangents drawn from (h, k) to the parabola $y^2 = 4ax$ is

$\frac{1}{a}\left|\left(k^2 + 4a^2\right)\left(k^2 - 4ah\right)\right|^{1/2}$

Sol. The equation of the parabola is $y^2 = 4ax$ and the point (h, k) be P

Let the tangents from P touch the parabola at $Q(at_1^2, 2at_1)$ and $R(at_2^2, 2at_2)$, then P is the point of intersection of the tangents.

Therefore, $h = at_1t_2$ & $k = a(t_1 + t_2)$

$$\Rightarrow \quad t_1t_2 = \frac{h}{a} \ \& \ (t_1 + t_2) = \frac{k}{a}$$

$$\text{Now, } QR = \sqrt{(at_1^2 - at_2^2)^2 + (2at_1 - 2at_2)^2}$$

$$= |a(t_1 - t_2)|\sqrt{(t_1 + t_2)^2 - 4}$$

$$= |a|\sqrt{\left(\frac{k^2}{a^2} - \frac{4h}{a}\right)}\sqrt{\left(\frac{k^2}{a^2} + 4\right)}$$

$$= \frac{1}{|a|} \times \sqrt{(k^2 - 4ah)(k^2 + 4a^2)}$$

Ex-5. Prove that the area of the triangle formed by the tangents from the point (h, k) to the parabola $y^2 = 4ax$ and a chord of contact is $\frac{(k^2 - 4ah)^{3/2}}{2a}$.

Sol. Let tangents are drawn from P (h, k) to the parabola $y^2 = 4ax$, intersects the parabola at Q and R.

Then the chord of contact of the tangents to the given parabola is QR.

Then QR is $yk = 2a(x + h)$

$$\Rightarrow 2ax - yk + 2ah = 0$$

Therefore PM = the length of perpendicular from P(h, k) to QR

$$= \left|\frac{2ah - k^2 + 2ah}{\sqrt{k^2 + 4a^2}}\right| = \left|-\frac{k^2 - 4ah}{\sqrt{k^2 + 4a^2}}\right| = \left|\frac{k^2 - 4ah}{\sqrt{k^2 + 4a^2}}\right|$$

Thus, the area of the triangle PQR $= \frac{1}{2}.QR.PM$

$$= \frac{1}{2}\cdot\frac{1}{|a|}\sqrt{(k^2 - 4ah)(k^2 + 4a^2)}\cdot\frac{(k^2 - 4ah)}{\sqrt{k^2 + 4a^2}}$$

$$= \frac{(k^2 - 4ah)^{3/2}}{2a}, \text{ if } a > 0.$$

4.23 CHORD BISECTED AT A GIVEN POINT

The equation of the chord of the parabola $y^2 = 4ax$ is bisected at the point (x_1, y_1) is $T = S_1$

$$\Rightarrow \quad yy_1 - 2a(x + x_1) = y_1^2 - 4ax_1,$$

where $T: yy_1 - 2a(x + x_1)$, $S: y_1^2 - 4ax_1$.

Ex-1. Find the equation of the chord of the parabola $y^2 = 8x$ which is bisected at (2, 3).

Sol. The equation of the chord of the parabola $y^2 = 4x$, which is bisected at (2, 3) is $T = S_1$

$$\Rightarrow \quad yy_1 - 2a(x + x_1) = y_1^2 - 4ax_1.$$

$$\Rightarrow \quad 3y - 4(x + 2) = 9 - 8.2 = -7.$$

$$\Rightarrow \quad 3y - 4x - 1 = 0$$

$$\Rightarrow \quad 4x - 3y + 1 = 0$$

Ex-2. Prove that the locus of the mid-points of the focal chord of the parabola is another parabola.

Sol. Let the equation of the parabola be $y^2 = 4ax$.

The equation of the chord of the parabola, whose middle point (x_1, y_1) is $T = S_1$.

$$\Rightarrow \quad yy_1 - 2a(x + x_1) = y_1^2 - 4ax_1$$

If it is a focal chord, then it will pass through the focus (a, 0) of the parabola.

Therefore, $0.y_1 - 2a(x + x_1) = y_1^2 - 4ax_1$

$$\Rightarrow \quad y_1^2 = -2a^2 - 2ax_1 + 4ax_1 = 2a(x_1 - a)$$

Hence, the locus of (x_1, y_1) is $y^2 = 2a(x - a)$.

Ex-3. Prove that the locus of the middle points of the chord of a parabola passes through the vertex is a parabola.

Sol. Let the equation of the parabola be $y^2 = 4ax$.

Let VP be any chord of the parabola through the vertex.and M(h, k) be the mid-pont of it.

Then, the co-ordinates of P becomes (2h, 2k)

Since P lies on the parabola, so $(2k)^2 = 4a.(2h)$

$$\Rightarrow \quad 4k^2 = 8ah$$

$$\Rightarrow \quad k^2 = 2ah$$

Hence, the locus of (h, k) is $y^2 = 2ax$

Ex-4. Prove that the locus of the middle points of a normal chords of the parabola $y^2 = 4ax$ is

$$y^4 - 2a(x - 2a)y^2 + 8a^4 = 0$$

Sol. Equation of the normal at any point $(at^2, 2at)$ of the parabola $y^2 = 4ax$ is

$$y = -tx + 2at + at^3 \quad \text{...(i)}$$

Lep PQ be the normal, whose mid-point is $M(\alpha, \beta)$

Therefore, $T = S_1$

$$\Rightarrow \quad y\beta - 2a(x + \alpha) = \beta^2 - 4a\alpha$$

$$\Rightarrow \quad y\beta = 2a(x + \alpha) - (\beta^2 - 4a\alpha) \quad \text{...(ii)}$$

Equations (i) and (ii) are identical.

$$\text{Therefore, } \frac{1}{\beta} = \frac{t}{-2a} = \frac{2at + at^3}{\beta^2 - 2a\alpha}$$

$$\Rightarrow \quad t = -\frac{2a}{\beta} \quad \text{and} \quad \frac{t}{-2a} = \frac{2at + at^3}{\beta^2 - 2aa}$$

From the above two relations, eliminating 't', we get,

$$\frac{\left(-\frac{2a}{\beta}\right)}{-2a} = \frac{2a\left(\frac{-2a}{\beta}\right) + a\left(\frac{-2a}{\beta}\right)^3}{\beta^2 - 2aa}$$

$$\Rightarrow \quad \left(\beta^2 - 2a\alpha\right) = -2a\left(2a + a\left(\frac{-2a}{\beta}\right)^2\right)$$

$$\Rightarrow \quad \beta^2\left(\beta^2 - 2aa\right) = -2a\left(2a\beta^2 + 4a^3\right)$$

$$\Rightarrow \quad \beta^2\left(\beta^2 - 2aa\right) = -4a^2\beta^2 - 8a^4$$

$$\Rightarrow \quad \beta^4 - 2a(a - 2a)\beta^2 + 8a^4 = 0$$

Hence the locus of $M(a, \beta)$

is $y^4 - 2a(x - 2a)y^2 + 8a^4 = 0$.

Ex-5. Prove that the locus of the middle point of a chord of a parabola $y^2 = 4ax$ which subtends a right angle at the vertex is $y^2 = 2a(x - 4a)$.

Sol. Let QR be the chord and $M(a, \beta)$ be the mid-point of it.

Then the equation of the chord of a parabola $y^2 = 4ax$ at $M(a, \beta)$ is $T = S1$

$$\Rightarrow \quad y\beta - 2a(x + a) = \beta^2 - 2aa$$

$$\Rightarrow \quad y\beta - 2ax = \beta^2 - 2aa \qquad \text{...(i)}$$

Let V (0, 0) be the vertex of the parabola.

Then, the combined equation of VQ and VR, making homogeneous by means of (i),

we have, $y^2 = 4ax \times \left(\frac{y\beta - 2ax}{\beta^2 - 2aa}\right)$

$$\Rightarrow \quad y^2\left(\beta^2 - 2aa\right) - 4a\beta xy + 8a^2x^2 = 0$$

Since, the chord QR subtends a right angle at the vertex, so we have, co-oefficient of x^2 + co-efficient of $y^2 = 0$

$$\Rightarrow \quad \left(\beta^2 - 2aa\right) + 8a^2 = 0$$

$$\Rightarrow \quad \beta^2 = 2a(\alpha - 4a)$$

Hence, the locus of $M(a, \beta)$ is $y^2 = 2a(x - 4a)$.

Ex-6. Prove that the locus of the middle points of chords of the parabola $y^2 = 4ax$ which touches the parabola

$y^2 = 4bx$ is $y^2(2a - b) = 4a^2x$.

Sol. Let QR be the chord of the parabola and $M(a, \beta)$ be its mid-point.

Then the equation of the chord QR bisected at $M(a, \beta)$ is $T = S_1$

$$\Rightarrow \quad y\beta - 2a(x + a) = \beta^2 - 4aa$$

$$\Rightarrow \quad y\beta = 2a(x + a) + \left(\beta^2 - 4aa\right)$$

$$\Rightarrow \quad y\beta = 2ax + \left(\beta^2 - 2aa\right) \qquad \text{...(i)}$$

If the equation (i) be a tangent to the parabola $y^2 = 4bx$,

then $c = \frac{b}{m}$

$$\Rightarrow \quad \left(\frac{\beta^2 - 2aa}{\beta}\right) = \frac{b}{(2a/\beta)} = \frac{b\beta}{2a}$$

$$\Rightarrow \quad (b - 2a)\beta^2 + 4a^2a = 0$$

Hence, the locus of $M(a, \beta)$ is $(2a-b)\,y^2 = 4a^2x$.

Ex-7. Find the locus of the mid-point of the chord of the parabola $y^2 = 4ax$, which pass through the point (3b, b)

Sol. Let the mid point of the chord be M(h, k).

Then the equation of the chord at M (h, k) is $T = S_1$

$$\Rightarrow \quad yk - 2a(x + h) = k^2 - 4ah$$

Which pass through the point (3b, b)

Then, $bk - 2a(3b + h) = k^2 - 4ah$.

$$\Rightarrow \quad k^2 - 2ah - bk + 6ab = 0$$

Hence, the locus of M (h, k) is $y^2 - 2ax - by + 6ab = 0$.

Ex-8. Prove that the locus of the middle points of all tangents drawn from points on the directrix to the parabola

$y^2 = 4ax$ is $y^2(2x + a) = a(3x + a)^2$.

Sol. The equation of the given parabola is $y^2 = 4ax$ ...(i)

Equation of the tangent at P $(at^2, 2at)$ is $yt = x + at^2$ ...(ii)

The equation of the directrix of the parabola $y^2 = 4ax$ is $x + a = 0$ ....(iii)

On solving (ii) and (iii), we get, $x = -a$ and $y = \frac{a\left(t^2 - 1\right)}{t}$.

Thus, the point on the directrix, say, Q, whose co-ordinates are $\left(-a, \frac{a\left(t^2 - 1\right)}{t}\right)$

Let M (h, k) be the mid-point of P and Q

Then, $h = \frac{at^2 - a}{2}$ and $k = \frac{a\left(t^2 - 1\right)}{2t} + \frac{2at}{2}$

$$\Rightarrow \quad t^2 = \frac{2h + a}{a} \quad \text{and} \quad 4k^2t^2 = a^2\left(3t^2 - 1\right)^2$$

Eliminating 't', we get,

$$4k^2\left(\frac{2h+a}{a}\right)=a^2\left(3\left(\frac{2h+a}{a}\right)-1\right)^2$$

$$\Rightarrow \quad 4k^2(2h+a)=a(6h+3a\text{-}a)^2$$

$$\Rightarrow \quad k^2(2h+a)=a(3h+a)^2$$

Hence, the locus of M (h, k) is $y^2(2x+a)=a(3x+a)^2$.

4.24 DIAMETER:

The locus of the mid-points of a system of parallel chords to a parabola is known as diameter of the parabola.

The equation of the diameter to the parabola $y^2=4ax$ bisecting a system of parallel chords with slope m is

$$y=\frac{2a}{m}.$$

Let (h, k) be the middle point of the chord $y=mx+c$ of the parabola $y^2=4ax$.

Then, $T=S_1$

$$\Rightarrow \quad ky-2a(x+h)=k^2-2ah.$$

Now slope $=\frac{2a}{k} \Rightarrow m=\frac{2a}{k} \Rightarrow k=\frac{2a}{m}$

Hence the locus of the mid-point (h, k) is $y=\frac{2a}{m}$.

Note: Any line which is parallel to the axis of the parabola drawn through any point on the parabola is called diameter of the parabola and its equation is the y-cordinate of that point.

4.25 PROPERTIES OF DIAMETER:

(i) The tangent at the extremity of a diameter of a parabola is parallel to the system of chords it bisects.

Let $y=mx+c$ represents the system of parallel chords.

Equation of diameter to the parabola $y^2=4ax$ is

$$y=\frac{2a}{m}.$$

The diameter meets the parabola $y^2=4ax$ at

$$\left(\frac{a}{m^2},\frac{2a}{m}\right)$$

Equation of tangent to the parabola $y^2=4ax$ at

$$\left(\frac{a}{m^2},\frac{2a}{m}\right) \text{ is } y=mx+\frac{a}{m}$$

which is parallel to $y=mx+c$.

(ii) Tangents at the end of any chord meet on the diameter which bisects the chords.

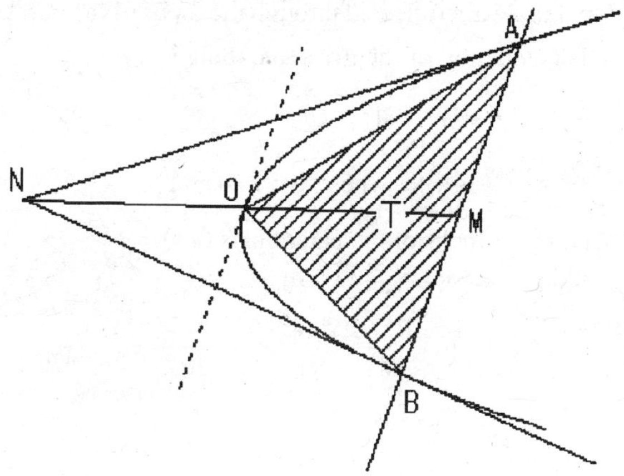

Let AB be the chord, where $A=\left(at_1^2,2at_1\right)$ and $B=\left(at_2^2,2at_2\right)$

Now slope of AB $=m(AB)=\frac{2a(t_2-t_1)}{a\left(t_2^2-t_1^2\right)}=\frac{2}{t_1+t_2}$.

Equation of diameter is

$$y=\frac{2a}{m} \Rightarrow y=a(t_1+t_2) \quad \text{...(i)}$$

Now tangents at $A=\left(at_1^2,2at_1\right)$

and $B=\left(at_2^2,2at_2\right)$ meet at $N\left(at_1t_2,\ a(t_1+t_2)\right)$.

Thus, N lies on $y=a(t_1+t_2)$.

4.26 REFLECTION PROPERTY OF A PARABOLA

All rays of light coming from the +ve direction of x-axis and parallel to the axis of the parabola are reflected through the focus of the parabola

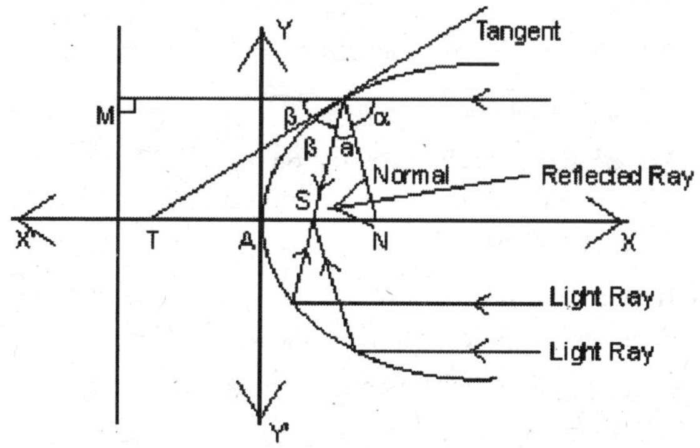

Ex-1. A ray of light moving parallel to the x-axis gets reflected from a parabolic mirror whose equation is $(y-4)^2=8(x+1)$. After reflection, the ray pass through the point (α, β), then find the value of $\alpha+\beta+10$.

Sol. As we know that, all rays of light parallel to x-axis of the parabola are reflected through the focus of the parabola.

The equation of the given parabola is

$$(y-4)^2 = 8(x+1)$$

$\Rightarrow \quad Y^2 = 8X$, where $Y = y - 4$ and $X = x + 1$.

Now the focus of the parabola is (a, 0)

Therefore, $X = a$ and $Y = 0$

$\Rightarrow \quad x + 1 = 2$ and $y - 4 = 0$

$\Rightarrow \quad x = 1$ and $y = 4$.

Hence, the focus is (1, 4)

Thus $\alpha = 1$ & $\beta = 4$

Now, $\alpha + \beta + 10 = 1 + 4 + 10 = 15$.

Ex-2. A ray of light is moving along the line $y = x + 2$, gets reflected from a parabolic mirrior whose equation is $y^2 = 4(x+2)$. After reflection, the ray does not pass through the focus of the parabola. Find the equation of the line which containg the reflected ray.

Sol. Let the line $y = x + 2$ intersects the parabola at P.

On solving the line $y = x + 2$ and the parabola $y^2 = 4(x+2)$, we get, the point P is (2, 4)

Now the equation of the tangent to the parabola $y^2 = 4(x+2)$ at P (2, 4) is

$$y y_1 = 2(x + x_1) + 8$$

$$\Rightarrow \quad 4y = 2(x+2) + 8$$

$$\Rightarrow \quad x - 2y + 6 = 0$$

Let IP be the incident ray, PM be the reflected ray and PN be the normal

As we know that, normal is equally inclined with the incident ray as well as the reflected ray.

Now the slope of IP = 1, slope of normal PN = -2 and let the slope of the reflected ray = m

Then, $\dfrac{1+2}{1-2} = \dfrac{-2-m}{1-2m}$

$$\Rightarrow \quad m = \frac{1}{7}$$

Hence, the equation of the reflected ray is

$$y - 4 = \frac{1}{7}(x - 2)$$

$$\Rightarrow \quad x - 7y + 26 = 0.$$

Level – I QUESTIONS BASED ON FUNDAMENTALS

ABC OF CONIC SECTION

1. Find the locus of a point which moves in such a way that its distance from the point (0, -1) is twice its distance from the line $3x + 4y + 1 = 0$.
2. What does the conic $25(x^2 + y^2 - 2x + 1) = (4x - 3y + 1)^2$ represent?
3. What conic does $13x^2 - 18xy + 37y^2 + 2x + 14y - 2 = 0$ represent?
4. What conic is represented by the equation $\sqrt{ax} + \sqrt{by} = 1$?
5. **For what value of** λ the equation of conic $2xy + 4x - 6y + \lambda = 0$ represents two intersecting straight lines? If $\lambda = 17$, then what does the equation represent?
6. If the equation $x^2 - y^2 - 2x + 2y + \lambda = 0$ represents a degenerate conic, then find the value of λ.
7. Find the centre of the conic $14x^2 + 11y^2 - 4xy - 44x - 58y + 71 = 0$.

THE PARABOLA

8. Find the equation of the parabola whose focus is at(-1, -2) and the directrix is the straight line $x - 2y + 3 = 0$.
9. The focal distance of a point on a parabola $y^2 = 8x$ is 8. Find the co-ordinates of that point.
10. Find the equation of the parabola whose focus is (4, -3) and vertex is (4, -1)
11. Find the length of the side of an equilateral triangle inscribed in the parabola $y^2 = 4ax$, so that one angular point is at the vertex.
12. Prove that the area of the triangle inscribed in the parabola $y^2 = 4ax$ is $\dfrac{1}{8a} \times (y_1 - y_2)(y_2 - y_3)(y_3 - y_1)$, where y_1, y_2, y_3 are the ordinates of the vertices.
13. (i) Find the equation of a parabola, when focus is the origin and the axis of the parabola is the x-axis.
    (ii) Find the equation of a parabola when the axis and the directrix are the co-ordinate axes.
    (iii) Find the equation of a parabola, when the vertex is (-3, 0) and directrix is $x + 5 = 0$.
14. Find the vertex, focus, latus rectum, axis and the directrix of each of the following parabolas:
    (i) $x^2 + 8x + 12y + 4 = 0$:
    (ii) $y = x^2 + 1$:
    (iii) $x^2 = 4y + 2$:
    (iv) $y = x^2 - 2x$:
    (v) $y^2 = y + x$:
    (vi) $y^2 + 8x + 12y + 4 = 0$:

(vii) $y^2+6x-2y+13=0$:

(viii) $y^2-4x-8y+12=0$:

(ix) $x^2-8x+2y+7=0$:

(x) $4y^2+4y+2x+3=0$. :

(xi) If the vertex of the parabola $y=x^2-8x+c$ lies on x-axis, then find the value of c.

15. If the vertex and focus of a parabola are (3, 3) and (-3, 3) respectively, then find its equation.

16. Find the equation of the latus rectum of the parabola $x^2+4x+2y=0$.

17. The equation $ax^2+4xy+y^2+ax+3y+2=0$ represents a parabola, then find the value of a.

18. Determine the nature of the curve described parametrically by the equations

$x=t^2+t+1$ and $x=t^2-t+1$

19. Prove that the equation of the parabola whose vertex and focus are on the x-axis at a distance 'a' and 'b' from the origin respectively, is, $y^2=4(a-b)(x-a)$.

POSITION OF A POINT W.R.T A PARABOLA

20. Find the position of the point (-2, 2) w. r. t. the parabola $y^2-4y+9x+13=0$.

21. Prove that the point (2, 3) lies inside the parabola $3y^2=10x$.

22. The point (a, 2a) is an interior point of the region bounded by the parabola $y^2=16x$ and the double ordinate through the focus. Find a.

23. Find the range of λ for which the point $(\lambda, -1)$ is exterior to both the parabola $y^2=|x|$.

PARAMETRIC RELATION BETWEEN THE CO-ORDINATES OF THE ENDS OF A FOCAL CHORD

24. If the point $(at^2, 2at)$ be the extremity of a focal chord of parabola $y^2=4ax$, then show that the length of the focal chord is $a\left(t+\frac{1}{t}\right)^2$.

25. Show that the focal chord of parabola $y^2=4ax$ makes an angle α with the x-axis is of length $4a\operatorname{cosec}^2\alpha$

26. Prove that the semi latus rectum of the parabola is the harmonic mean between the segments of any focal chord of the parabola.

27. Find the points on the parabola $y^2-2y-4x=0$, whose focal length is 6.

28. If the length of a focal chord of the parabola $y^2=4ax$ at a distance 'b' from the vertex is c.

Prove that $b^2c=4a^3$.

29. If (2, -8) is at an end of a focal chord of the parabola , then find the other end of the chord.

30. The co-ordinates of the ends of a focal chord of a parabola $y^2=4ax$ are (x_1, y_1) and (x_2, y_2), then find the value of $x_1x_2+y_1y_2$.

31. If the line passing through the focus S of the parabola meets the parabola $y=ax^2+bx+c$ at P and Q and if SP = 4 and SQ = 6, find the value of a.

32. Circles are drawn with diameter being any focal chord of the parabola $y^2-4x-y-4=0$ will always touch a fixed line, then find its equation.

33. If a focal chord of $y^2=4ax$ makes an angle $\alpha\in\left[0, \frac{\pi}{4}\right]$ with the +ve direction of x-axis, then find the minimum length of this focal chord.

INTERSECTION OF A LINE AND A PARABOLA

34. (i) Prove that the straight line $lx+my+n=0$ touches the parabola $y^2=4ax$ if $ln=am^2$.

(ii) Prove that the line y = m x + c is a tangent to the parabola $y^2=4a(x+a)$ if $c=\frac{a}{m}+am$.

35. Prove that the line $\frac{x}{l}+\frac{y}{m}=1$ touches the parabola $y^2=4a(x+b)$ if $al^2+m^2(l+b)=0$.

36. Find the equation of tangent to the parabola $y^2=8x$ having slope 5 and also find the point of contact

37. Find the equation of the tangent to the parabola $y^2=12x$, which is passing through (2, 5).

38. If the line y = 3 x + c touches the parabola $y^2=12x$ at a point P, find the equation of the tangent at the point Q, where PQ is a focal chord.

39. Find the equations of the straight line touching both $x^2+y^2=2a^2$ and $y^2=8ax$.

TANGENTS AND TANGENCY

40. Find the equation of the tangent to the parabola $y=x^2-2x+3$ at x = 1.

41. Find the equation of the tangent to the parabola $x=y^2+3y+2$ having slope 2.

42. Find the equation of tangents drawn to the parabola $y=x^2-3x+2$ from the point (1, -1).

43. Find the equations of the common tangents to the parabola $y^2 = 4ax$ and $x^2 = 4by$.

44. Find the common tangents to the parabolas $y^2 = 4ax$ and $x^2 = 4ay$.

45. Find the shortest distance between the line y = x – 2 and the parabola $y = x^2 + 3x + 2$.

46. A tangent to the parabola $y^2 = 8x$ makes an angle of 45° with the straight line y = 3 x + 5. Find the co-ordinates of the point of contact.

47. Parabola $y^2 = 4x$ and the circle having its center at (6, 5) intersect at right angle. Then find the possible points of intersection of these curves.

48. Two tangents are drawn from the point (-2, -1) to the parabola $y^2 = 4x$. If α is the angle between these tangents, then find α.

49. Tangents are drawn from the point (-1, 2) on the parabola $y^2 = 4x$. Find the length that these tangents will intercept on the line x = 2.

50. Find the slopes of the tangents to the parabola $y^2 = 8x$, which are normal to the circle $x^2 + y^2 + 6x + 8y - 24 = 0$.

51. Find the locus of the point of intersection of the perpendicular tangents of the curve $y^2 + 4y - 6x - 2 = 0$.

52. From a point P on the directrix, tangents PA and PB are drawn to the parabola $y^2 = 16x$. Find the minimum radius of the circle circumscribing ΔPAB.

53. Show that the locus of the points of intersection of the mutually perpendicular tangents to a parabola is the directrix of the parabola.

54. The tangents to the parabola $y^2 = 4ax$ at $P(at_1^2, 2at_1)$ and $Q(at_2^2, 2at_2)$ intersect at R. Prove that the area of the triangle is $\frac{1}{2} \times a^2 \times |(t_1 - t_2)|^3$.

55. The tangents to the parabola $y^2 = 4ax$ make angle θ_1 and θ_2 with x-axis. Find the locus of their point of intersection if $\cot\theta_1 + \cot\theta_2 = c$.

56. The angle between a pair of tangents drawn from a point P to the parabola $y^2 = 4ax$ is 45°. Prove that the locus of the point P is a hyperbola.

57. The product of the tangents drawn from a point P to the parabola $y^2 = 4ax$ is equal to the product of the focal distance of P and the latus rectum. Prove that the locus of P is $y^2 = 4a(x + a)$.

58. Prove that the orthocenter of the triangle formed by the tangents at the points t_1, t_2, t_3 to the parabola $y^2 = 4ax$ is $(-a,\ a(t_1 + t_2 + t_3 + t_1t_2t_3))$.

59. The sides of a triangle touch $y^2 = 4ax$ and two of its angular points are on $y^2 = 4b(x + c)$. Prove that the locus of the third angular point is $ax = \frac{y^2a^2}{4(2b - a)} - 4bc$.

NORMALS AND NORMALCY

60. If 2 x + y + k = 0 is a normal to the parabola $y^2 = -8x$, then find the value of k.

61. (i) If normal at 't_1' meets the parabola again at 't_2' then prove that $t_2 = -t_1 - \frac{2}{t_1}$.

(ii) If the normals at 't_1' and 't_2' meets the parabola $y^2 = 4ax$ at same point, then prove that $t_1 t_2 = 2$.

(iii) Show that the normal to the parabola $y^2 = 8x$ at the point (2, 4) meets it again at (18, -12). Find also the length of the normal chord.

62. Prove that the chord $y - x\sqrt{2} + 4a\sqrt{2} = 0$ is a normal chord of the parabola $y^2 = 4ax$.

63. If the normal to a parabola $y^2 = 4ax$ makes an angle ϕ with the axis, show that it will cut the curve again at an angle $\tan^{-1}\left(\frac{1}{2}\tan\phi\right)$.

64. Find the shortest distance between the curves $y^2 = 4x$ and $x^2 + y^2 - 12x + 31 = 0$.

65. Find the length of the normal chord which subtends an angle of 90° at the vertex of the parabola $y^2 = 4x$.

66. Find the locus of the point of intersection of the normals at the end of the focal chord of the parabola $y^2 = 4ax$.

67. The ordinates of points P and Q on the parabola $y^2 = 12x$ are in the ratio 1:2. Find the locus of the point of intersection of the normals to the parabola at P and Q.

68. Find the locus of the intersection of tangents to the parabola $y^2 = 4ax$ drawn at the extremities of the normal chords.

69. Prove that the two parabolas $y^2 = 4ax$ and $y^2 = 4c(x - b)$ cannot have a common normal other than the axis unless $\frac{b}{a - c} > 2$.

70. If the chord PQ of the parabola $y^2 = 4ax$ subtends a right angle at the vertex of the parabola, then prove that normal at P, Q will meet on the parabola $y^2 = 16a(x - 6a)$.

CO-NORMAL POINTS

71. (i) Prove that through any point three normals can be drawn to a parabola.

(ii) Prove that the algebraic sum of the slopes of three concurrent normals is zero.

(iii) Prove that the algebraic sum of the ordinates of the feet's of three normals drawn to a parabola from a given point is zero.

72. Find the number of distinct normals that can be drawn from (-2, 1) to the parabola $y^2-4x-2y-3=0$.

73. If two of the three feet of normals drawn from a point to the parabola $y^2=4x$ be (1, 2) and (1, -2), then find the third foot.

74. If three normals drawn to any parabola $y^2=4ax$ from a given point (h, k) be real then h > 2 a.

75. Prove that the centroid of the triangle formed by the feet of the three normals lies on the axis of the parabola . i.e. $\left(\frac{2h-4a}{3}, 0\right)$.

76. If three normals drawn to any parabola $y^2=4ax$ from a given point (h, k) be real and distinct , then $27ak^2<4(h-2a)^3$.

77. Prove that the locus of the points such that two of the three normals drawn from them to the parabola $y^2=4ax$ coincide is $27\,ay^2=4(x-2a)^3$.

78. Find the locus of the point through which pass three normals to the parabola $y^2=4ax$ such that two of them make angles α and β respectively with the axis such that $\tan\alpha.\tan\beta=2$.

79. Find the locus of the point of intersection of two normals to a parabola which are at right angles to one another.

80. If three distinct normals can be drawn to the parabola $y^2=2y+4x-9$ from the point (2a, b), then find the range of a.

81. Find the point on the axis of the parabola $3y^2+4y-6x+8=0$ from which three distinct normal's can be drawn.

82. Find the locus of the point of intersection of the normals at the end of the focal chord of the of the parabola $y^2=4ax$.

83. Find the locus of the point that three normals through it cut the axis in points whose distances from the vertex are in A.P.

CHORD OF CONTACT

84. Find the equation of the chord of contact to the parabola $y^2=10x$ at (1, 4)

85. Prove that the area of the triangle formed by the tangents drawn from (x_1,y_2) to $y^2=4ax$ and their chord of contact is $\frac{(y_1^2-4ax_1)^{3/2}}{2a}$.

86. If the chord of contact of tangents from a point P to the parabola $y^2=4ax$ touches the parabola $x^2=4by$, then find the locus of P.

87. If the distance of the point (a, 2) from its chord of contact w.r.t the parabola $y^2=4x$ is 4, then find the value of a.

88. From the point (–1, 2) tangents are drawn to the parabola $y^2=4x$. Find the area of the triangle formed by the chord of contact and tangents.

89. From a point a common tangents are drawn to the circle $x^2+y^2=\frac{a^2}{2}$ and the parabola $y^2=4ax$. Find the area of the quadrilateral formed by the common tangents , the chord of contact of the circle and the chord of contact to the parabola.

EQUATION OF THE CHORD BISECTED AT A POINT:

90. Find the equation of the chord to the parabola $y^2=6x$ is bisected at the point (2, 2).

91. Find the locus of the mid-point of chords of the parabola $y^2=4ax$ that pass through the point (3a, a).

92. If the tangent at P(2, 4) to the parabola $y^2=8x$ meets the parabola $y^2=8x+5$ at Q and R , then find the mid-point of the chord QR.

93. Find the locus of the middle points of the focal chord of the parabola $y^2=4ax$.

94. Prove that the locus of the middle points of the normal's chord of the parabola $y^2=4ax$ is $y^4-2a(x-2a)y^2+8a^4=0$.

95. If (a, b) is the mid-point of chord passing through the vertex of the parabola $y^2=4ax$, then prove that $b^2=2a^2$.

96. Prove that the locus of the middle points of all tangents drawn from points on the directrix to the parabola is $y^2(2x+a)=a(3x+a)^2$.

DIAMETER:

97. (i) Prove that the equation of the diameter to the parabola $y^2=4ax$ with slope m is $y=\frac{2a}{m}$.

(ii) Find the diameter of the parabola $y^2=6x$ corresponding to the system of parallel chords $3x-y+c=0$.

Director Circle :

98. (i) Prove that the equation of the director circle to the parabola $y^2=4ax$ is $x+a=0$

(ii) Find the equation of the director circle to the parabola $y^2 = x+2$.

(iii) Find the equation of the director circle to the parabola $y = x^2 + x + 1$.

POLE AND POLAR:

99. Prove that the polar of the parabola at focus is the directrix.

100. Find the pole of a given line $lx + my + n = 0$ with respect to the parabola $y^2 = 4ax$.

101. Show that the locus of the poles of normals chords of $y^2 = 4ax$ is $(x+2a)y^2 + 4a^3 = 0$.

102. If the polar of a point with respect to $y^2 = 4bx$ touch $x^2 = 4ay$, then prove that the locus of this point is a rectangular hyperbola.

REFLECTION PROPERTY OF A PARABOLA

103 A ray of light moving parallel to the x-axis gets reflected from a parabolic mirror whose equation is $(y-2)^2 = 4(x+1)$. After reflection , the ray pass through the point (α, β), then find the value of $\alpha + \beta + 10$.

104. A ray of light is coming along the line $y = b$ ($b > 0$) from the positive direction of the x-axis and strikes a concave mirror whose intersection with the x-y plane is the parabola $y^2 = 4ax$, ($a > 0$). Find the equation of the reflected ray and show that it passes through the focus of the parabola.

105. A ray of light travels along a line y = 4 and strikes the surface of a curve $y^2 = 4(x+y)$, then find the equation of the line along reflected ray travel .

106 A ray of light is coming along the line y = 2 from the positive direction of x-axis and strikes a concave mirror whose intersection with the x-y plane is a parabola $y^2 = 8x$, then find the equation of the reflected ray.

107. A ray of light moving parallel to the x-axis gets reflected from a parabolic mirror whose equation is $y^2 + 10y - 4x + 17 = 0$. A fter reflection, the ray must pass through the point $P(\alpha, \beta)$, then find the value of $\alpha + \beta +$ 2013.

108. A ray of light is coming along the line x = 2 from the positive direction of y – axis and strikes a concave mirror whose intersection with the x-y plane is a parabola $x^2 = 4y$, then find the equation of the reflected ray after second reflection .

109. Two rays of light coming along the line y = 1 and y = -2 from the positive direction of x-axis and strikes a concave mirror whose intersection with the x-y plane is a parabola $y^2 = x$ at A and B respectively. The reflected rays pass through a fixed point C , then find the area of the triangle ABC.

110. A ray of light is coming along the line $x = \lambda\ (\lambda < 0)$ from the positive direction of y-axis and strikes a concave mirror $x^2 = 4(y-1)$, the ray is reflected from it is $x + y = 2$, if this reflected ray again strikes , then find the equation of the new reflected ray .

ANSWER

1. $11x^2 + 39y^2 + 96xy + 24x - 18y - 21 = 0$
2. Parabola
3. Ellipse
4. Parabola
5. $l = -12$, Hyperbola
6. $\lambda \in R - \{2\}$
7. (2, 3)
8. $4x^2 + y^2 + 4xy + 4x + 32y + 16 = 0$
9. $\left(6, \pm 4\sqrt{3}\right)$
10. $x^2 - 8x + 8y + 24 = 0$
11. $8a\sqrt{3}$
13. (i) $y^2 = 4a(x+a)$
    (ii) $y^2 = 4a(x-a)$
    (iii) $y^2 = 4(x+4)$
14. (i) V(-4, 1) ; F(-4, -2) ; LR = 12 ; A: x+4=0; D : y- 4=0
    (ii) V(0, 1) ; F (0, 5/4) ; L .R = 1/4 ; Axis : x = 0, D: 4 y - 3 = 0.
    (iii) V(0, -1/2) ; F (0, 1/2) ; L .R = 1 ; Axis : x = 0, D: 2y+3 = 0.
    (iv) V(1, -1) ; F (1, 5/4) ; L .R = 1/4 ; Axis : x = 1, D: 4y - 3 = 0.
    (v) V(-1/4, 1/2) ; F (0, 1/4) ; L .R = 1/4 ; Axis : 4 y - 1 = 0, D: 2 x + 3 = 0 .
15. $y^2 - 6y + 24x - 63 = 0$
16. 2 y - 3 = 0
17. 4
18. Parabola
20. Outside
22. $0 < a < 4$.
23. $-1 < \lambda < 1$
27. $\left(4, 1 \pm \sqrt{17}\right)$

29. (32,32)

30.

31. a = 12/5

32. 16 x + 33 = 0

33.

36. y = 5 x + 2 / 5 ; (2/25, 4/5)

37. y = x + 3 ; 3 x - 2 y + 4 = 0

38. x + 3 y = 27

39. $x \pm y + 2a = 0$

40. y = 2

41. 16 x - 8 7 + 7 = 0.

42. x - 2 y - 1 = 0 ; 2 x - 2 y + 3 = 0 .

43. $a^{1/3} x + b^{1/3} y + a^{2/3} b^{2/3} = 0$

44. x + y + a = 0

45. $3/\sqrt{2}$

46. (8, 8) , (1/2, -2)

47. (4, 4) and (9, 6)

48. $\alpha = \tan^{-1}(3)$.

49. $6\sqrt{2}$.

50. $\left(2 \pm \sqrt{10}\right)$

51. 2 x + 5 = 0

52. min radius = a

55. y = a c

60. k = - 24

64. S.d = $\sqrt{5}$.

65. $\sqrt{85 + 16\sqrt{2}}$

66. $y^2 = a(x - 3a)$.

67. $\left(\frac{x}{3} - 2\right)^3 = 343 \times \left(\frac{y}{18}\right)^2$

68. $y^2(x + 2a) + 4a^3 = 0$.

72. 1

73. (0, 0)

78. $y^2 = 4ax$

79. $y^2 = a(x - 3a)$

80. $a > 2$.

81. (-2/3, 0)

82. $y^2 = a(x - 3a)$

83. $27ay^2 = 2(x - 2a)^3$.

84. 5 x - 4 y + 5 = 0

86. $xy = -2ab$.

87. $\left(1 \pm 4\sqrt{2}\right)$

88. 8 sq. u

89. $\frac{15a^2}{4}$

90. 3 x - 2 y - 2 = 0

91. $y^2 - 2ax - ay + 6a^2 = 0$.

92. (2, 4).

93. $y^2 = 2a(x - a)$

97. (ii) y = 1

98. (ii) 4 x + 9 = 0

(iii) 2 y - 1 = 0

103. 12

104. $(x - a) + \left(a^2 - b^2\right) y = 0$

105. y = 0

106. 4 x + 3 y = 8

107. 2011

108. y = 2

109. 21/ 8 sq. unit

110. $x + 2 = 2\sqrt{2}$.

Level – II FOR JEE MAIN AND ADVANCED EXAMS ONLY

1. Three normals to the parabola $y^2 = x$ are drawn through a point (c, 0) , then
   (a) c = ¼ (b) c = ½ (c) c > ½ (d) None.
2. The line which is parallel to x-axis and crosses the curve $y = \sqrt{x}$ at an angle of 45° is
   (a) x = ¼ (b) y = ¼ (c) y = ½ (d) y = 1.
3. Consider a circle with its centre lying on the focus of the parabola $y^2 = 2px$ such that it touches the directrix of the parabola , then a point of intersection of the circle and the parabola is
   (a) (p/2 , p) (b) (p/2, -p) (c) (-p/2, p) (d) (-p/2, -p)
4. If the line x – 1 = 0 is the directrix of the parabola $y^2 - kx + 8 = 0$, then one of the values of k is
   (a) 1/8 (b) 8 (c) 4 (d) ¼
5. If x + y = k is a normal to the parabola $y^2 = 12x$, then the value of k is
   (a) 9 (b) 3 (c) -9 (d) -3
6. The equation of the directrix of the parabola $y^2 + 4y + 4x + 2 = 0$ is

(a) x=-1 (b) x=1 (c) x=-3/2 (d) x=3/2

7. The equation of the common tangent touching the circle $(x-3)^2+y^2=9$ and the parabola $y^2=4x$ above the x-axis is

(a) $\sqrt{3}y=3x+1$ (b) $\sqrt{3}y=-(x+3)$

(c) $\sqrt{3}y=(x+3)$ (d) $\sqrt{3}y=-(3x+1)$.

8. The locus of the mid-point of the line segment joining the focus to a moving point on the parabola $y^2=4ax$ is another parabola with directrix

(a) x+a=0 (b) x=-a/2 (c) x=0 (d) x=a/2

9. The focal chord of $y^2=16x$ is tangent to $(x-6)^2+y^2=2$, then the possible values of the slope of this chord are

(a) (1,-1) (b) (-1/2, 2) (c) (-2, ½) (d) (1/2, 2)

10. Tangent to the parabola $y=x^2+6$ touches the circle $x^2+y^2+16x+12y+c=0$ at the point

(a) (-6,-9) (b) (-13,-9) (c) (-6,-7) (d) (13,7)

11. The axis of a parabola is along the line y = x and the distance of its vertex from origin is $\sqrt{2}$ and that from its focus is $2\sqrt{2}$. If vertex and focus both lie in the first quadrant, then the equation of the parabola is

(a) $(x+y)^2=(x+y-2)$ (b) $(x-y)^2=(x+y-2)$

(c) $(x-y)^2=4(x+y-2)$ (d) $(x-y)^2=8(x+y-2)$.

12. The equation of the common tangents to the parabola $y=x^2$ and $y=-(x-2)^2$ is /are

(a) y=4 (x-1) (b) y=0

(c) y=-4(x-1) (d) y=-10(3x+5)

13. The tangent PT and the normal PN to the parabola $y^2=4ax$ at a point P on it meet its axis at points T and N, respectively. The locus of the centroid of the triangle PTN is a parabola whose

(a) Vertex is (2a/3, 0) (b) directrix is x=0

(c) latus rectum is 2a (d) focus is (a, 0)

14. The normal at the point $(bt_1^2, 2bt_1)$ on a parabola meets the parabola again in the point $(bt_2^2, 2bt_2)$, then

(a) $t_2=-t_1+\frac{2}{t_1}$ (b) $t_2=t_1-\frac{2}{t_1}$

(c) $t_2=t_1+\frac{2}{t_1}$ (d) $t_2=-t_1-\frac{2}{t_1}$.

15. If $a\neq 0$ and the line 2 b x + 3 c y + 4 d = 0 passes through the points of intersection of the parabola $y^2=4ax$ and $x^2=4ay$, then

(a) $d^2+(2b-3c)^2=0$ (b) $d^2+(2b+3c)^2=0$

(c) $d^2+(3b+2c)^2=0$ (d) $d^2+(3b-2c)^2=0$.

16. The locus of the vertices of the family of parabolas $y=\frac{a^3x^2}{2}+\frac{a^2x}{2}-2a$ is

(a) x y=105/64 (b) x y=3/4

(c) x y=35/16 (d) x y=64/105.

17. Angle between the tangents to the curve $y=x^2-5x+6=0$ at the points (2, 0) and (3, 0) is

(a) π/2 (b) π/3 (c) π/6 (d) π/4.

18. The equation of a tangent to the parabola $y^2=8x$ is y = x+2. The point on this line from which the other tangent to the parabola is perpendicular to the given tangent is

(a) (-2, 0) (b) (-1, 1) (c) (0, 2) (d) (2, 4)

19. A parabola has the origin as its focus and the line x = 2 as the directrix. Then the vertex of the parabola is at

(a) (0, 1) (b) (2, 0) (c) (0, 2) (d) (1, 0).

20. The length of the chord of the parabola $y^2 = x$, which is bisected at the point (2, 1) is

(a) $2\sqrt{3}$ (b) $4\sqrt{3}$ (c) $3\sqrt{2}$ (d) $2\sqrt{5}$.

21. Two mutually perpendicular tangents of the parabola $y^2=4ax$ meet the axis in P_1 and P_2. If S is the focus of the parabola, then $\frac{1}{l(SP_1)}+\frac{1}{l(SP_2)}$ is equal to

(a) $\frac{4}{a}$ (b) $\frac{2}{a}$ (c) $\frac{1}{a}$ (d) $\frac{1}{4a}$.

22. Which of the following equations represented parametrically, represents equation to a parabolic profile?

(a) x = 3 cos t, y = 4 sin t

(b) $x^2-2=-2\cos t,\ y=4\cos^2\left(\frac{t}{2}\right)$

(c) $\sqrt{x}=\tan t,\ \sqrt{y}=\sec t$

(d) $x=\sqrt{1-\sin t},\ y=\sin\left(\frac{t}{2}\right)+\cos\left(\frac{t}{2}\right)$

23. The points of contact Q and R of tangent from the point P(2, 3) on the parabola $y^2=4x$ are

(a) (9, 6); (1, 2) (b) (1, 2); (4, 4)

(c) (4, 4); (9, 6) (d) (9, 6); (1/4, 1).

24. A tangent is drawn to the parabola $y^2 = 4x$ at the point P whose abscissa lies in the interval [1, 4]. The maximum possible area of the triangle formed by the tangent at P, ordinate of the point 'P' and the x-axis is equal to

(a) 8 (b) 16 (c) 24 (d) 32.

25. Length of the normal chord $y^2=4x$, which makes an angle of π/4 with the axis if x is

(a) 8 (b) $8\sqrt{2}$ (c) 4 (d) $4\sqrt{2}$.

26. The co-ordinates of the ends of a focal chord of a parabola $y^2 = 4ax$ are (x_1, y_1) and (x_2, y_2), then $x_1x_2 + y_1y_2$ has the value equal to

(a) $2a^2$ (b) $-3a^2$ (c) $-a^2$ (d) $4a^2$.

27. If the normal to a parabola $y^2 = 4ax$ at P meets the curve again at Q and if PQ and the normal at Q makes angles α and β respectively with the x-axis, then

$\tan\alpha(\tan\alpha + \tan\beta)$ is

(a) 0 (b) -2 (c) -1/2 (d) -1.

28. If the normal to the parabola $y^2 = 4ax$ at the point with parameter t_1, cuts the parabola again at the point with parameter t_2, then

(a) $2 \le t_2^2 \le 8$ (b) $2 \le t_2^2 \le 4$ (c) $t_2^2 \ge 4$ (d) $t_2^2 \ge 8$.

29. A parabola $y = ax^2 + bx + c$ crosses the x-axis at (α, 0) and (β, 0) both to the right of theorigin. A circle also passes through these two points. The length of a tangent from the origin to the circle is

(a) $\sqrt{\dfrac{bc}{a}}$ (b) ac^2 (c) $\dfrac{b}{a}$ (d) $\sqrt{\dfrac{c}{a}}$.

30. Two parabolas have the same focus . If their directrices are the x-axis and the y-axis are respectively , then the slope of their common chord is

(a) 1, -1 (b) 4/3 (c) ¾ (d) None.

31. The straight line joining the point P on the parabola $y^2 = 4ax$ to the vertex and perpendicular from the focus to the tangent at P intersect at R. Then the equation of the locus of R is

(a) $x^2 + 2y^2 - ax = 0$ (b) $2x^2 + y^2 - 2ax = 0$

(c) $2x^2 + 2y^2 - ax = 0$ (d) $2x^2 + y^2 - 2ay = 0$.

32. A normal chord of the parabola $y^2 = 4x$ subtending a right angle at the vertex makes an acute angle θ with the x-axis , then θ equals to

(a) $\tan^{-1} 2$ (b) $\sec^{-1}\sqrt{3}$ (c) $\cot^{-1}\sqrt{3}$ (d) none.

33. C is the centre of the circle with centre (0, 1) and radius unity. P is the parabola $y = ax^2$. The set of values of 'a' for which they meet at a point other than the origin is

(a) $a > 0$ (b) $a \in \left(0, \dfrac{1}{2}\right)$

(c) $a \in \left(\dfrac{1}{4}, \dfrac{1}{2}\right)$ (d) $a \in \left(\dfrac{1}{2}, \infty\right)$.

34. TP and TQ are the tangents to the parabola $y^2 = 4ax$ at P and Q . If the chord PQ passes through the fixed point (-a, b) , then the focus of T is

(a) ay = 2b (x-b) (b) bx=2a(y-a)

(c) by=2a(x-a) (d) ax=2b(y-b).

35. Through the vertex O of the parabola $y^2 = 4ax$ two chords OP and OQ are drawn and the circles on OP and OQ a s diameters intersect in R. If θ_1, θ_2 and ϕ are the angles made with the axis by the tangents at P and Q on the parabola and by OR, then the value of $\cot\theta_1 + \cot\theta_2$

(a) $-2\tan\phi$ (b) $-2\tan(\pi - \phi)$

(c) 0 (d) $2\cot\phi$.

36. The tangent at P to a parabola $y^2 = 4ax$ meets the directrix at U and the base of latus rectum at V, then SUV (where S is the focus) must be a / an

(a) a rt Δ (b) equilateral Δ

(c) isosceles Δ (d) rt isosceles Δ.

37. Two parabolas $y^2 = 4a(x - l_1)$ and $x^2 = 4a(y - l_2)$ always touch one another , the quantities l_1 and l_2 are both variable . Locus of their point of contact has the equation

(a) $xy = a^2$ (b) $xy = 2a^2$ (c) $xy = 4a^2$ (d) None.

38. If a normal to a parabola $y^2 = 4ax$ make an angle ϕ with its axis, then it will cut the curve again at an angle

(a) $\tan^{-1}(2\tan\phi)$ (b) $\tan^{-1}\left(\dfrac{1}{2}\tan\phi\right)$

(c) $\cot^{-1}\left(\dfrac{1}{2}\tan\phi\right)$ (d) None.

39. The vertex of a parabola is (2, 2) and the co-ordinates of its extremities of the latus rectum are (-2, 0) and (6,0) . The equation of the parabola is

(a) $y^2 - 4y + 8x - 12 = 0$ (b) $x^2 + 4x - 8y - 12 = 0$

(c) $x^2 - 4x + 8y - 12 = 0$ (d) $x^2 - 8y - 4x + 20 = 0$

40. The length of the chord of the parabola $y^2 =$ [illegible] which is bisected at the point (2, 1) is

(a) $2\sqrt{3}$ (b) $4\sqrt{3}$ (c) $3\sqrt{2}$ (d) $2\sqrt{5}$

41. If the tangents and normals at the extremities of a focal chord of a parabola intersect at

(x_1, y_1) and (x_2, y_2) respectively, then

(a) $x_1 = x_2$ (b) $x_1 = y_2$ (c) $y_1 = y_2$ (d) $x_2 = y_1$

42. If the chord of contact of tangents from a point P to the parabola $y^2 = 4ax$ touches the parabola $x^2 = 4by$, then the locus of P is

(a) Circle (b) Parabola

(c) Ellipse (d) Hyperbola.

43. The latus rectum of a parabola whose focal chord PSQ is such that SP = 3 and SQ = 2 is given by

(a) 24/5 (b) 12/5 (c) 6/5 (d) None.

44. If two normals to a parabola $y^2 = 4ax$ intersect at right angles, then the chord joining their feet passes through a fixed point whose co-ordinates are

(a) $(-2a, 0)$ (b) $(a, 0)$ (c) $(2a, 0)$ (d) None.

45. The equation of a straight line passing through the point $(3, 0)$ and cutting the curve $y = \sqrt{x}$ orthogonally is
(a) 4x+y=18 (b) x+y=9 (c) 4x-y=6 (d) None.

46. PQ is a normal chord of the parabola $y^2 = 4ax$ at P. A being the vertex of the parabola. Through P a line is drawn parallel to AQ meeting the x-axis in R. Then the length of AR is
(a) length of Latus Rectum
(b) Focal distance of the point P
(c) 2 × Focal distance of the point P
(d) distance of P from the directrix.

47. Locus of the point of intersection of the perpendicular tangents of the curve $y^2 + 4y - 6x - 2 = 0$ is
(a) $2x-1=0$ (b) $2x+3=0$ (c) $2y+3=0$ (d) $2x+5=0$.

48. Length of the focal chord of the parabola $y^2 = 4ax$ at a distance p from the vertex is
(a) $\frac{2a^2}{p}$ (b) $\frac{a^3}{p^2}$ (c) $\frac{4a^3}{p^2}$ (d) $\frac{p^2}{a}$.

49. The locus of a point such that two tangents drawn from it to the parabola $y^2 = 4ax$ are such that the slope of one is double the other is
(a) $y^2 = \frac{9}{2}ax$ (b) $y^2 = \frac{9}{4}ax$
(c) $y^2 = 9ax$ (d) $x^2 = 4ay$.

50. The triangle PQR of area 'A' is inscribed in the parabola $y^2 = 4ax$ such that the vertex P lies at the vertex of the parabola and the base QR is a focal chord. The modulus of the difference of the ordinates of the points Q and R is
(a) $\frac{A}{2a}$ (b) $\frac{A}{a}$ (c) $\frac{2A}{a}$ (d) $\frac{4A}{a}$.

51. The points on the parabola $y^2 = 4x$ which are closest to the circle $x^2 + y^2 - 24y + 128 = 0$ is/are
(a) $(0,0)$ (b) $(2, 2\sqrt{2})$ (c) $(4,4)$ (d) None

52. Tangents are drawn from the point (-1, 2) on the parabola $y^2 = 4x$. The length, these tangents will intercept on the line x=2 is
(a) 6 (b) $6\sqrt{2}$ (c) $2\sqrt{6}$ (d) None.

53. The curve describes parametrically by $x = t^2 - 2t + 2$, $y = t^2 + 2t + 2$ represents
(a) straight line (b) pair of st. lines
(c) circle (d) parabola.

54. The tangent and normal at P(t) for all real positive t, to the parabola $y^2 = 4ax$ meet the axis of the parabola in T and G respectively, then the angle at which the tangent at P to the parabola is inclined to the tangent at P to the circle passing through the point P, T and G is
(a) $\cot^{-1} t$ (b) $\cot^{-1} t^2$ (c) $\tan^{-1} t$ (d) $\tan^{-1} t^2$.

55. In a square matrix A of order 3, $a_{ii} = m_i + i$ where I = 1, 2, 3 and m_i's are the slopes (in increasing order of their absolute value) of the 3 normals concurrent at the point (9, -6) to the parabola $y^2 = 4x$. Rest all other entries of the matrix are one. The value of det (A) is equal to
(a) 37 (b) -6 (c) -4 (d) -9.

56. An equation for the line that passes through (10, -1) and is perpendicular to $y = \frac{x^2}{4} - 2$ is
(a) 4x+y=39 (b) 2x+y=19 (c) x+y=9 (d) x+2y=8.

Passage - I

A quadratic polynomial y = f(x) with absolute term 3 neither touches nor intersects the abscissa axis and is symmetric about the line x = 1. The co-efficient of the leading term of the polynomial is unity. A point $A(x_1, y_1)$ with abscissa $x_1 = 1$ and a point $B(x_2, y_2)$ with ordinate $y_2 = 11$ are given in a Cartesian rectangular system of co-ordinates OXY in the first quadrant on the curve y = f(x) where 'O' is the origin. Now answer the following questions:

57. Vertex of the quadratic polynomial is
(a) (1, 1) (b) (2, 3) (c) (1, 2) (d) None

58. The scaler product of the vectors $\vec{OA}$ and $\vec{OB}$ is
(a) -18 (b) 26 (c) 22 (d) -22.

59. The area bounded by the curve y = f(x) and a line y = 3 is
(a) 4/3 (b) 5/3 (c) 7/3 (d) 28/3

60 The graph of y = f(x) represents a parabola whose focus has the co-ordinates
(a) (1, 7/4) (b) (1, 5/4) (c) (1, 5/2) (d) (1, 9/4)

ANSWER

1.(c)	2.(c)	3.(b).	4.(c)	5.(a)	6.(d)	7.(c)	8.(c)	9.(a)	10.( )
11.(d)	12.(b)	13.(a)	14.(d)	15.(b)	16.(a)	17.(a)	18.(a)	19.( )	20.(d)
21.(c)	22.(b)	23.(b)	24.(b)	25.(b)	26.(b)	27.(b)	28.(d)	29.(d)	30.(a)
31.(b)	32.(b)	33.(d)	34.(c)	35.(a)	36.(c)	37.(c)	38.(b)	39.(c)	40.(d)
41.(c)	42.(d)	43.(a)	44.(b)	45.(a)	46.(c)	47.(d)	48.(c)	49.(a)	50.(c)
51(c)	52(b)	53.(d)	54.(c)	55.(c)	56.(d)	57.(c)	58.(b)	59.(a)	60.(d)

Level – III FOR JEE ADVANCE EXAM ONLY

1. If the two ends of a latus rectum of a parabola are the points (3, 6) and (-5, 6). Find the focus .
2. Find the locus of the vertices of the family of parabolas $y=\frac{a^3x^2}{3}+\frac{a^2x}{2}-2a$.
3 Find the equation of the parabola whose vertex and focus lie on the axis of x at distances a and a_1 from the origin respectively.
4. A square has one vertex at the vertex of the parabola $y^2=4ax$ and the diagonal through the vertex lies along the axis of the parabola. If the ends of the other diagonal lie on the parabola , then findthe co-ordinates of the vertices of the square.
5. Find the equation of the parabola whose axis is y = x distance from origin to vertex is $\sqrt{2}$ and distance from origin to focus is $2\sqrt{2}$.
6. If $a\neq 0$ and the line $2bx+3cy+4d=0$ passes through the points of intersection of the parabola $y^2=4ax$ and $x^2=4ay$, then prove that $d^2+(2b+3c)^2=0$.
7. Two straight lines are perpendicular to each other. One of them touches the parabola $y^2=4a(x+a)$ and the other $y^2=4b(x+b)$. Prove that their point of intersection lies on the line x + a + b = 0.
8. If the focal chord of $y^2=16x$ is a tangent to $(x-6)^2+y^2=2$, then find the possible values of the slope of this chord.
9. Find the point of intersection of the tangents at the ends of the latus rectum of the parabola $y^2=4x$.
10. If the tangent at the point P(2, 4) to the parabola $y^2=8x$ meets the parabola $y^2=8x+5$ at Q and R, then find the midpoint of QR.
11. If $y+b=m_1(x+a)$ and $y+b=m_2(x+a)$ are two tangents to the parabola $y^2=4ax$, then prove that $m_1m_2=-1$.
12. Find the equation of the common tangent to the circle $(x-3)^2+y^2=9$ and the parabola $y^2=4x$ above the x-axis.
13. Find the equation of the common tangent to the curves $y^2=8x$ and $xy=-1$.
14. Find the common tangents of $y=x^2$ and $y=-x^2+4x-4$.
15. Consider a circle with centre lying on the focus of the parabola $y^2=2px$ such that it touches the directrix of the parabola. Then find a point of intersection of the circle and the parabola.
16. If the normal drawn at a point $(at_1^2, 2at_1)$ of the parabola $y^2=4ax$ meets it again in the point $(at_2^2, 2at_2)$, then prove that $t_1^2+t_1t_2+2=0$.
17. Three normals to the parabola $y^2=x$ are drawn through a point (c, 0) , then find c.
18 A tangent to the parabola $y^2=8x$ makes an angle of 45° with the straight line y = 3 x + 5. Find the equation of the tangent and its point of contact.
19. Find the equations of the normals to the parabola $y^2=4ax$ at the ends of the latus rectum. If the normals again meet the parabola at Q, Q` , then prove that QQ` = 12 a.
20. Prove that from any point $P(at^2, 2at)$ on the parabola $y^2=4ax$, two normals can be drawn and their feet Q and R have the parameters satisfying the equation $\lambda^2+\lambda t+2=0$.
21. Find the locus of the point of intersection of those normals to the parabola $x^2=8y$ which are at right angles to each other.
22. Two lines are drawn at right angles , one being a tangent to $y^2=4ax$ and the other to $x^2=4by$. Show that the locus of their point of intersection is the curve $(ax+by)(x^2+y^2)+(bx-ay)^2=0$.
23. Prove that the locus of the centroid of equilateral triangles inscribed in the parabola $y^2=4ax$ is $9y^2=4a(x-8a)$.
24. Prove that the locus of the middle point of chords of the parabola $y^2=4ax$ which subtends a right angle at the vertex is $y^2=2a(x-a)$.
25. Prove that the locus of a point that divides a chord of slope 2 of the parabola $y^2=4x$ internally in the ratio 1 : 2 is a parabola . Find the vertex of the parabola.
26. From a point A, Common tangents are drawn to the circle $x^2+y^2=a^2/2$ and parabola $y^2=4ax$. Find the area of the quadrilateral formed by the common tangents, the chord of contact of the circle and the chord of contact of the parabola.
27. Normals are drawn from the point P with slopes m_1, m_2, m_3 to the parabola $y^2=4x$. If locus of P with $m_1 m_2=\alpha$ is a part of the parabola, then find the value of α.
28. The tangent at a point P to the parabola $y^2-2y-4x+5=0$ intersects the directrix at Q . Find thelocus of a point R such that it divides PQ externally in the ratio $\frac{1}{2}:1$.
29. Prove that the curve $y=-\frac{x^2}{2}+x+1$ is symmetric with respect to the line x = 1.
And also prove that it is symmetric about its axis.

ANSWER

1. (4,0)

2. $xy = \frac{105}{64}$.

3. $y^2 = 4(a_1 - a)(x - a)$.

4. (0, 0) ; (4a, 4a) ; (4a, -4a) ; (8a, 0)

5. $(x - y)^2 = 8(x + y - 2)$.

8. m = 1, -1

9. (-1, 0)

10. (2, 4)

11. $y\sqrt{3} = x + 3$ 12. Y = x + 2

13. Y=0, y=4 (x-1).

14. (p/2, p) ; (p/2, -p)

16. C > ½

17. x − 2 y + 8 = 0 , (8 , 8).

25. (2/9, 8/9)

26. 15/4 a^2 sq. u.

27. $\alpha = 2$.

28. $2(x - 2)(y - 1)^2 = (3x - 4)^2$

COMPREHENSIVE LINK PASSAGE(FOR JEE MAIN AND ADVANCED EXAM ONLY)

Passage – I

If a source of light is placed at the fixed point of a parabola and if the parabola is reflecting surface, then the ray will bounce back in a line parallel to the axis of the parabola.

1. A ray of light is coming along the line y = 2 from the positive direction of x-axis and strikes a concave mirror whose intersection with the x-y plane is a parabola $y^2 = 8x$, then the equation of the reflected ray is
(a) 2x+3y=4 (b) 3x+2y=6 (c) 4x+3y=8 (d) 5x+4y=10

2. A ray of light moving parallel to the x-axis gets reflected from a parabolic mirror whose equation is $y^2 + 10y - 4x + 17 = 0$. A fter reflection, the ray must pass through the point
(a) (-2, -5) (b) (-1, -5) (c) (-3, -5) (d) (-4, -5)

3. A ray of light is coming along the line x = 2 from the positive direction of y – axis and strikes a concave mirror whose intersection with the x-y plane is a parabola $x^2 = 4y$, then the equation of the reflected ray after second reflection is
(a) 2x+y=1 (b) 3x-2y+2=0 (c) y = 1 (d) None.

4. Two rays of light coming along the line y = 1 and y = -2 from the positive direction of x-axis and strikes a concave mirror whose intersection with the x-y plane is a parabola $y^2 = x$ at A and B respectively. The reflected rays pass through a fixed point C , then the area of the triangle ABC is
(a) 21/ 8 sq. unit (b) 19/2 sq. unit
(c) 17/2 sq unit (d) 15/2 sq unit.

5. A ray of light is coming along the line $x = \lambda$ ($\lambda < 0$) from the positive direction of y-axis and strikes aconcave mirror $x^2 = 4(y - 1)$, the ray is reflected from it is x + y = 2 , if this reflected ray again strikes, then the equation of the new reflected ray is
(a) $y + 1 = 2\sqrt{2}$ (b) $x + 1 = 2\sqrt{2}$
(c) $y + 2 = 2\sqrt{2}$ (d) $x + 2 = 2\sqrt{2}$.

Passage-II

y = x is a tangent to the parabola $y = ax^2 + c$.

6. If a = 2 , then the value of c is
(a) 1 (b) -1/2 (c) 1/ 2 (d) 1/8.

7. If (1, 1) is a point of contact , then the value of a is
(a) 1/ 4 (b) 1/3 (c) 1/ 2 (d) 1/6

8. If c = 2 , then the point of contact is
(a) (3, 3) (b) (2, 2) (c) (6, 6) (d) (4, 4).

Passage – III

Consider, the parabola whose focus is at (0, 0) and tangent at vertex is x – y + 1 = 0.

9. The length of the latus rectum is
(a) $4\sqrt{2}$ (b) $2\sqrt{2}$ (c) $8\sqrt{2}$ (d) $3\sqrt{2}$.

10. The length of the chord of parabola on the x-axis is
(a) $4\sqrt{2}$ (b) $2\sqrt{2}$ (c) $8\sqrt{2}$ (d) $3\sqrt{2}$.

11. Tangents drawn to the parabola at the extremities of the chord 3 x + 2 y = 0intersect at an angle
(a) $\frac{\pi}{6}$ (b) $\frac{\pi}{3}$ (c) $\frac{\pi}{2}$ (d) None.

Passage – IV

Two tangents on a parabola are x – y = 0 and x + y = 0. If (2, 3) is the focus of the parabola , then

12. The equation of the tangent at vertex is
(a) 4x-6y+5=0 (b) 4x-6y+3=0
(c) 4x-6y+1=0 (d) 4x-6y+3/2=0.

13. The length of the latus rectum of the parabola is

(a) $\frac{6}{\sqrt{3}}$ (b) $\frac{10}{\sqrt{13}}$ (c) $\frac{2}{\sqrt{13}}$ (d) $\frac{9\sqrt{2}}{\sqrt{13}}$.

14. If P and Q are ends of the focal chord of the parabola , then is

(a) $\frac{2\sqrt{13}}{3}$ (b) $2\sqrt{13}$ (c) $\frac{2\sqrt{13}}{5}$ (d) $\frac{2\sqrt{13}}{7}$.

Passage – V

If l, m are variable real numbers such that $5l^2+6m^2-4lm+3l=0$, then the variable line $lx+my=1$ always touches a fixed parabola , whose axes is parallel to x-axis. Then

15. The vertex of the parabola is

(a) $\left(-\frac{5}{3},\frac{4}{3}\right)$ (b) $\left(-\frac{7}{4},\frac{3}{4}\right)$

(c) $\left(\frac{5}{6},-\frac{7}{6}\right)$ (d) $\left(\frac{1}{2},-\frac{3}{4}\right)$

16. The focus of the parabola is

(a) $\left(\frac{1}{6},-\frac{7}{6}\right)$ (b) $\left(\frac{1}{3},\frac{4}{3}\right)$

(c) $\left(\frac{3}{2},-\frac{3}{2}\right)$ (d) $\left(-\frac{3}{4},\frac{3}{4}\right)$.

17. Equation of the directrix of the parabola is

(a) 6x+7=0 (b) 4x+11=0

(c) 3x+11=0 (d) 2x+13=0.

Passage – VI

Normals at three points P, Q, R on the parabola $y^2=4ax$ meet at (α,β). Then

18. The centroid of the triangle PQR is

(a) $\left(\frac{\alpha-2a}{3},0\right)$ (b) $\left(\frac{2\alpha-4a}{3},0\right)$

(c) $\left(\frac{\alpha}{3},\frac{\beta}{3}\right)$ (d) $\left(\frac{\alpha+\beta}{3},\frac{\beta-\alpha}{3}\right)$

19. The orthocenter of the triangle PQR is

(a) $\left(\alpha+6a,\frac{\beta}{2}\right)$ (b) $\left(\alpha+3a,\frac{\beta}{2}\right)$

(c) $\left(\alpha-6a,\frac{-\beta}{2}\right)$ (d) $\left(\alpha-3a,\frac{\beta}{2}\right)$.

20. The circum-center of the triangle PQR is

(a) $\left(\frac{\alpha+2a}{2},\frac{-\beta}{4}\right)$ (b) $\left(\frac{\alpha+2a}{4},\frac{\beta}{4}\right)$

(c) $\left(\frac{\alpha}{4},\frac{\beta}{4}\right)$ (d) $\left(\frac{\alpha}{2},\frac{\beta}{2}\right)$.

Passage- VII

Consider the circle $x^2+y^2=9$ and the parabola $y^2=8x$. They intersect at P and Q in the first and the fourth quadrants respectively. Tangents to the circle at P and Q intersect the x-axis at R and tangents to the parabola at P and Q intersect the x-axis at S.

21. The ratios of the areas of the triangles PQS and PQR is

(a) $1:\sqrt{2}$ (b) $1:2$

(c) $1:4$ (d) $1:8$

22. The radius of the circum-circle of the triangle PRS is

(a) 5 (b) $3\sqrt{3}$ (c) $3\sqrt{2}$ (d) $2\sqrt{3}$.

23. The radius of the incircle of the triangle PQR is

(a) 4 (b) 3 (c) 8/3 (d) 2.

Passage - VIII

If P is a point moving on a parabola $y^2=4ax$ and Q is a moving point on the circle $x^2+y^2-24ay+128a^2=0$. The point P and Q will be closest when they lie along the normal to the parabola $y^2=4ax$ passing through the centre of the circle.

24. If the normal at $(at^2, 2at)$ of the parabola passes through the centre of the circle , then the value of t must be

(a) 1 (b) 2 (c) 3 (d) 4

25. The shortest distance between P and Q must be

(a) $a(\sqrt{2}-1)$ (b) $2a(\sqrt{5}-1)$

(c) $4a(\sqrt{5}-1)$ (d) $4a(\sqrt{5}+1)$

26. When P and Q are closest , then the point P must be

(a) $(a, 2a)$ (b) $(2a, 2\sqrt{2}a)$

(c) $(4a, 4a)$ (d) $(5a, 4a)$.

27. When P and Q are closest . then the point Q must be

(a) $\left(\frac{4a}{\sqrt{5}}, 6a-\frac{8a}{\sqrt{5}}\right)$ (b) $\left(\frac{4a}{\sqrt{5}}, 12a-\frac{8a}{\sqrt{5}}\right)$

(c) $\left(\frac{4a}{\sqrt{5}}, -12a-\frac{8a}{\sqrt{5}}\right)$ (d) $\left(\frac{4a}{\sqrt{5}}, -8a-\frac{12a}{\sqrt{5}}\right)$.

28. When P and Q are closest and the diameter QR of the circle is drawn through Q, then the x - cordinate of Q is

(a) $-\frac{2a}{\sqrt{5}}$ (b) $-\frac{8a}{\sqrt{5}}$ (c) $-\frac{4a}{\sqrt{5}}$ (d) $-\frac{6a}{\sqrt{5}}$.

ANSWER

1.(c)	2.(b)	3.(d)	4.(a)	5.(d)	6.(d)	7.(c)	8.(d)	9.(b)	10.(a)
11.(c)	12.(a)	13.(b)	14.(c)	15.(a)	16.(b)	17.(c)	18.(b)	19.(c)	20.(a)
21.(c)	22.(b)	23.(d)	24.(b)	25.(c)	26.(c)	27.(b)	28.(c)		

MATCH MATRIX

1. AB is a chord of the parabola $y^2 = 4ax$ joining $A\left(at_1^2, 2at_1\right)$ and $B\left(at_2^2, 2at_2\right)$ then match the following columns

Column-I	Column-II
(A) AB is a normal chord if	(P) $t_2 = 2 - t_1$
(B) AB is a focal chord if	(Q) $t_1 t_2 = -4$
(C) AB subtends 90° at (0, 0) if	(R) $t_1 t_2 = -1$
(D) AB is inclined at 45° to the axis of the parabola	(S) $t_1^2 + t_1 t_2 + 2 = 0$

2. Match the following columns :

Column-I	Column-II
(A) The point from which perpendiculars tangents can be drawn to the parabola $y^2 = 4x$	(P) (-1, 2)
(B) The point from which only one normal can be drawn to the parabola $y^2 = 4x$	(Q) (3, 2)
(C) The point at which chord x - y + 1 = 0 of the parabola $y^2 = 4x$ is bisected	(R) (-1, -5)
(D) The point from which tangents can not be drawn to the parabola $y^2 = 4x$	(S) (5, -2)

3. Match the following columns :

Column-I	Column-II
(A) The equation of the director circle to the parabola $y^2 = 12x$ is	(P) 2 y - 1 = 0
(B) The equation of the director circle to the parabola $x^2 = 16y$ is	(Q) x - 2 = 0
(C) The equation of the director circle to the parabola $y^2 + 4x + 4y = 0$ is	(R) y + 4 = 0
(D) The equation of the director circle to the parabola $y = x^2 + x + 1$ is	(S) x + 3 = 0

4. Match the following columns :

Column-I	Column-II
(A) No. of distinct normals can be drawn from (-2, 1) to the parabola $y^2 - 4x - 2y - 3 = 0$ is	(P) 3
(B) No. of distinct normals can be drawn from (2, 3) to the parabola $y = x^2 + x + 1$ is	(Q) 1
(C) No. of distinct normals can be drawn from (-5, 3) to the parabola $y^2 - 4x - 6y - 11 = 0$ is	(R) 0
(D) No. of tangents can be drawn from (1, 2) to the parabola $y^2 - 2x - 2y + 1 = 0$ is	(S) 2

5. Match the following columns :

Normals are drawn at points P, Q and R lying on the parabola $y^2 = 4x$ which intersect at (3, 0). Then

Column-I	Column-II
(A) area of ΔPQR	(P) 2
(B) Radius of the circum-circle ΔPQR	(Q) 5/2
(C) Centroid of ΔPQR	(R) (5/2, 0)
(D) Circumcenter of ΔPQR	(S) (2/3, 0).

6. **Match the following columns :**

Column-I	Column-II
(A) If $y + 3 = m_1(x + 2)$ and $y + 3 = m_2(x + 2)$ are two tangents to the parabola $y^2 = 8x$ then	(P) $m_1 + m_2 = 0$
(B) If $y = m_1 x + c_1$ and $y = m_2 x + c_2$ are two tangents to a parabola $y^2 = 4a(x + a)$, then	(Q) $m_1 + m_2 = -1$
(C) If $y = m_1(x + 4) + 2013$ and $y + 1 = m_2(x + 4) + 2014$ are two tangents to the parabola $y^2 = 16x$, then	(R) $m_1 . m_2 = -1$
(D) If $y = m_1(x - 2) + 2010$ and $y = m_1(x - 2) + 2010$ are	(S) $m_1 - m_2 = 0$

two tangents to the parabola $y^2 = -8x$, then

7. Match the following columns :

Column-I	Column-II
(A) If $2x + y + \lambda = 0$ is a normal to the parabola $y^2 = -8x$, then λ is	(P) 9
(B) If $x + y = k$ is a normal to the parabola $y^2 = 12x$, then k is	(Q) 24
(C) If $2x - y - c = 0$ is a tangent to the parabola $y^2 = 16x$, then c is	(R) 17
(D) If $y = 4x + d$ is a tangent to the parabola $y^2 = 4(x+1)$, then 4d is	(S) 2

8. Match the following columns :

Column-I	Column-II
(A) The equation of the directrix of the parabola $y^2 + 4x + 4y + 2 = 0$ is	(P) $x - 2y + 4 = 0$
(B) The equation of the axis of the parabola $x^2 + 4x + 4y + 2013 = 0$ is	(Q) $2x - 3 = 0$
(C) The equation of the tangent to the parabola $y^2 = 4x$ from the point (2, 3) is	(R) $x + 3 = 0$
(D) The equation of the directrix of the parabola $y^2 = 4x + 8$ is	(S) $x + 2 = 0$

9. Match the following columns :

Column-I	Column-II
(A) The angle between the tangents drawn from the point (1, 4) to the parabola $y^2 = 4x$ is	(P) $\pi/2$
(B) The angle between the tangents drawn from the point (2, 3) to the parabola $y^2 = -8x$ is	(Q) $\pi/3$
(C) The angle between the tangents drawn from the point (4, 1) to the parabola $x^2 = 4y$ is	(R) $\pi/4$
(D) The angle between the tangents to the parabola $y = x^2 - 5x + 6$ at the points (2, 0) and (3, 0) is	(S) $\pi/12$

10. Match the following columns:

Column-I	Column-II
(A) Minimum area of the circle $y = x^2 + 1$ and $y^2 = x - 2$ is $\lambda\pi/32$, then λ is	(P) 2
(B) The shotest distance between the parabolas $2y^2 = 2x - 1$ and $2x^2 = 2y - 1$ is $1/\lambda\sqrt{2}$	(Q) 9
(C) Maximum number of common normals of the parabolas $y^2 = 4ax$ and $x^2 = 4by$ is	(R) 6
(D) The number of common chords of the parabolas $x = y^2 - 6y + 11$ and $y = x^2 - 6y + 11$ is	(S) 5

ANSWER

1. (A) → (S) ; (B) → (R) ; (C) → (Q) ; (D) → (P)
2. (A) → (P, R) ; (B) → (P, R) ; (C) → (Q) ; (D) → (Q, S)
3. (A) → (S) ; (B) → (R) ; (C) → (Q) ; (D) → (P)
4. (A) → (Q) ; (B) → (P) ; (C) → (Q) ; (D) → (R)
5. (A) → (P) ; (B) → (Q) ; (C) → (S) ; (D) → (R)
6. (A) → (R) ; (B) → (R) ; (C) → (R) ; (D) → (R)
7. (A) → (Q) ; (B) → (P) ; (C) → (S) ; (D) → (R)
8. (A) → (Q) ; (B) → (S) ; (C) → (P) ; (D) → (R)
9. (A) → (Q) ; (B) → (P) ; (C) → (Q); (D) → (P)
10. (A) → (Q) ; (B) → (P) ; (C) → (S); (D) → (R)

QUESTIONS ASKED IN ROORKEE EXAM

1. From the point (-1, 2) tangent lines are drawn to the parabola $y^2 = 4x$. Find the equation of the chord of contact. Also find the area of the triangle formed by the chord of contact and the tangents.

[**Roorkee Main 1994**]

2. The equation $y^2 - 2x - 2y + 5 = 0$ represents
(a) a circle with center (1, 1)
(b) a parabola with focus (1, 2)
(c) a parabola with directrix x = 3/2
(d) a parabola with directrix x = -1/2

[**Roorkee – 1995**]

3. A ray of light is coming along the line y = b from the positive direction of x-axis and strikes a concave mirror whose intersection with the xy-plane is a parabola

$y^2 = 4ax$. Find the equation of the reflected ray and show that it passes through the focus of the parabola. Both a and b are positive.

[Roorkee Main – 1995]

4. If tangent drawn at a point $(t^2, 2t)$ on the parabola $y^2 = 4x$ is same as the normal drawn at a point $(\sqrt{5}\cos\phi, 2\sin\phi)$ on the ellipse $4x^2 + 5y^2 = 20$, then find the values of t and ϕ.

[Roorkee – 1996]

5. The equations of normals to the parabola $y^2 = 4ax$ at the point (5a, 2a) are

(a) y = x – 3a (b) y = x + 3a

(c) y +2x=12a (d) 3x+y=33a

[Roorkee – 1997]

6. Find the locus of the point of intersection of those normals to the parabola $x^2 = 8y$ which are at right angles to each other.

[Roorkee Main – 1997]

7. The ordinates of points P and Q on the parabola $y^2 = 12x$ are in the ratio 1:2. Find the locus of the point of intersection of the normals to the parabola at P and Q.

[Roorkee Main – 1998]

8. Find the equations of the common tangents of the circle $x^2 + y^2 - 6y + 4 = 0$ and $y^2 = x$.

[Roorkee – 1999]

9. Find the locus of points of intersection of tangents drawn at the ends of all normals chords to the parabola $y^2 = 8(x-1)$

[Roorkee Main – 2001]

ANSWER

1. y = x – 1; $8\sqrt{2}$ sq. units
2. (c)
3. $(b^2 - 4a^2)y - 4abx + 4a^2b = 0$
4. $t = 0, \pm\frac{1}{\sqrt{5}}$; $f = \frac{p}{2}, \frac{3p}{2}$ or $\cos^{-1}\left(\frac{-1}{\sqrt{5}}\right)$
5. (a)
6. $x^2 - 2y + 12 = 0$
7. $y + 18\left(\frac{x-6}{21}\right)^{3/2} = 0$
8. $y = mx + \frac{1}{4m}$, where $m = -\frac{1}{2}, \pm\frac{\sqrt{30}}{10}$.
9. $y^2(1-x) = 5(y^2+32)$

QUESTIONS ASKED IN IIT-JEE EXAM

1. Suppose that the normals drawn at three different points on the parabola $y^2 = 4x$ pass through the point (h, 0). Show that h > 2. [IIT-JEE – 1981]

2. A is a point on the parabola $y^2 = 4ax$. The normal at A cuts the parabola again at B. If AB subtends a right angle at the vertex of the parabola, find the slope of AB.

[IIT-JEE -1982]

3. Find the equation of the normal to the curve $x^2 = 4y$ which pass through the point (1, 2)

[IIT-JEE – 1984]

4. Three normals are drawn from the point (c, 0) to the curve $y^2 = x$. Show that c must be greater than ½. One normal is always the x-axis. Find c for which the other two normals are perpendicular to each other.

[IIT-JEE – 1991]

5. Through the vertex 'O' of the parabola $y^2 = 4x$ chords OP and OQ are drawn at right angles, show that for all positions of P, PQ cuts the axis at the parabola at a fixed point. Also find the locus of the mid-point of PQ.

[IIT-JEE – 1994]

6. Consider a circle with its center lying on the focus of the parabola $y^2 = 2px$ such that it touches the directrix of the parabola. Then a point of intersection of the circle and the parabola is [IIT-JEE – 1995]

(a) $\left(\frac{p}{2}, p\right)$ or $\left(-\frac{p}{2}, p\right)$ (b) $\left(\frac{p}{2}, -\frac{p}{2}\right)$

(c) $\left(-\frac{p}{2}, p\right)$ (d) $\left(-\frac{p}{2}, -\frac{p}{2}\right)$.

7. Show that the locus of a point that divides a chord of slope 2 of the parabola $y^2 = 4x$ internally in the ratio 1 : 2 is parabola, find its vertex.

[IIT-JEE – 1995]

8. Points A, B, C lie on the parabola $y^2 = 4ax$. The tangent to the parabola at A, Band C taken in pair intersect at the points P, Q and R. Determine the ratio of the areas of the triangles ABC and PQR.

[IIT-JEE – 1996]

9. From a point A common tangents are drawn to the circle $x^2 + y^2 = \frac{a^2}{2}$ and the parabola $y^2 = 4ax$. Then find the

area of the quadrilateral formed by the common tangents drawn from A and the chord of contact of the circle and the parabola.

[IIT-JEE – 1996]

10. If x + y = k is normal to $y^2 = 12x$, then k is

(a) 3 (b) 9 (c) -9 (d) -3

[IIT-JEE – 2000]

11. If the line x – 1 = 0 is the directrix of the parabola $y^2 = kx - 8$, then one of the value of the k is

(a) 1/8 (b) 8 (c) 4 (d) ¼

[IIT-JEE – 2000]

12. The equation of the directrix of the parabola

$y^2 + 4y + 4x + 2 = 0$ in

(a) x = -1 (b) x = 1 (c) x = -3/2 (d) x = 3/2

[IIT-JEE – 2001]

13. The equation of the common tangent touching the circle $(x-3)^2 + y^2 = 9$ and the parabola $y^2 = 4x$ above the x-axis is **[IIT-JEE – 2001]**

(a) $y\sqrt{3} = 3x + 1$ (b) $y\sqrt{3} = -x - 3$

(c) $y\sqrt{3} = x + 3$ (d) $y\sqrt{3} = -(3x+1)$

14. The locus of the mid-point of the line segment joining the focus to a moving a point on the parabola $y^2 = 4x$ is another parabola with directrix

(a) x = - a (b) x = - a /2 (c) x = 0 (d) x = a/2

[IIT-JEE – 2002]

15. The equation of the common tangent to the curve $y^2 = 8x$ and $xy = -1$ is

(a) 3 y = 9 x + 2 (b) y = 2 x + 1

(c) 2 y = x + 8 (d) y = x + 2.

[IIT-JEE – 2002]

16. The focal chord to $y^2 = 16x$ is tangent to

$(x-6)^2 + y^2 = 2$, then the possible values of the slope of this chord, are,

(a) {-1, 1} (b) {-2, 2} (c) {-2, ½} (d) {2, -1/2}.

[IIT-JEE – 2003]

17. Let C_1 and C_2 be respectively, the parabolas $x^2 = y - 1$ and $y^2 = x - 1$, let P be any point on C_1 and Q be any point on C_2. Let P_1 and Q_1 be the reflections of P and Q respectively, with respect to the line y = x. Prove that P_1 lies on C_2, Q_1 lies on C_1 and PQ ≥ min $[PP_1, QQ_1]$. Hence or otherwise determine points P_0 and Q_0 on the parabolas C_1 and C_2 respectively such that $P_0 Q_0 \le PQ$ for all pairs of points (P_1, Q) with P on C_1 and Q on C_2.

[IIT-JEE – 2000]

18. Three normals with slopes m1, m2 and m3 are drawn from a point P not on the axis of the parabola $y^2 = 4x$. If $m_1 m_2 = \alpha$, results in the locus of P being a part of the parabola, then find the value of α.

[IIT-JEE – 2003]

19. The angle between the tangents drawn from the point (1, 4) to the parabola $y^2 = 4x$ is

(a) π/6 (b) π/4 (c) π/3 (d) π/2

[IIT-JEE – 2004]

20. At any point P on the parabola $y^2 - 2y - 4x + 5 = 0$, a tangent is drawn which meets the directrix at Q. Find the locus of point R which divides QP externally in the ratio $\frac{1}{2} : 1$

[IIT-JEE – 2004]

21. The axis of a parabola is along the line y = x and the distances of its vertex and focus from the origin are $\sqrt{2}$ and $2\sqrt{2}$ respectively. If vertex and focus both lie in the first quadrant , then the equation of the parabola is

(a) $(x-y)^2 = (x-y-2)$

(b) $(x-y)^2 = (x+y-2)$

(c) $(x-y)^2 = 4(x+y-2)$

(d) $(x-y)^2 = 8\,(x+y-2)$

[IIT-JEE-2006]

22. The equation of the common tangent to the parabola $y = x^2$ and $y = -(x-2)^2$ is / are

(a) y = 4 (x-1) (b) y = 0

(c) y = - 4(x-1) (d) y = - 30 x – 50.

[IIT-JEE – 2006]

23. Match the following :

Normals are drawn at points P, Q and R lying on the parabola $y^2 = 4x$ which intersect at (3, 0). Then

Column – I	Column – II
(i) Area of Δ PQR	(A) 2
(ii) Radius of circum-circle of Δ PQR	(B) 5/2
(iii) Centroid of Δ PQR	(C) (5/2 , 0)
(iv) Circum-center of Δ PQR	(D) (2/3, 0)

[IIT-JEE-2007]

24. Comprehension

Consider the circle $x^2 + y^2 = 9$ and the parabola $y^2 = 8x$. They intersect at P and Q in the first and the fourth quadrants respectively. Tangents to the circle at P and Q intersect the x-axis at R and tangents to the parabola at P and Q intersect the x-axis at S.

(i) The ratio of the areas of the triangles PQS and PQR

(a) $1:\sqrt{2}$ (b) $1:2$

(c) $1:4$ (d) $1:8$

(ii) The radius of the circum-circle of the triangle PRS is

(a) 5 (b) $3\sqrt{3}$

(c) $3\sqrt{2}$ (d) $2\sqrt{3}$

(iii) The radius of the incircle of the triangle PQR is

(a) 4 (b) 3

(c) 8/3 (d) 2.

[IIT-JEE – 2007]

25. Statement-1: The curve $y=-\frac{x^2}{2}+x+1$ is symmetric with respect to the line x = 1

Statement - 2: A parabola is symmetric about its axis.

[IIT-JEE-2007]

26. Let $P(x_1, y_1)$, $Q(x_2, y_2)$, $y_1<0$, $y_2<0$, be the end points of the latus rectum of the ellipse $x^2+4y^2=4$. The equation of the parabola with latus rectum PQ are

(a) $x^2+2\sqrt{3}y=3+\sqrt{3}$

(b) $x^2-2\sqrt{3}y=3+\sqrt{3}$

(c) $x^2+2\sqrt{3}y=3-\sqrt{3}$

(d) $x^2-2\sqrt{3}y=3-\sqrt{3}$

[IIT-JEE-2008]

27. The tangent PT and the normal PN to the parabola $y^2=4ax$ at a point P on it meet axes at points T and N respectively . The locus of the centroid of the triangle PTN is a parabola whose

(a) Vertex is (2a / 3, 0) (b) directrix is x = 0

(c) latus rectum is 2 a / 3 (d) focus is (a, 0)

[IIT-JEE-2009]

28. Let A and B be two distinct points on the parabola $y^2=4x$. If the axis of the parabola touches a circle of radius r having AB as the diameter, then the slope of the line joining A and B can be

(a) $-\frac{1}{r}$ (b) $\frac{1}{r}$ (c) $\frac{2}{r}$ (d) $-\frac{2}{r}$

[IIT-JEE-2010]

29. Let L be a normal to the parabola $y^2=4x$. If L passes through the point(9, 6) , then L is given by

(a) y - x + 3 = 0 (b) y + 3 x - 33 = 0

(c) y + x - 15 = 0 (d) y - 2 x + 12 = 0.

[IIT-JEE-2011]

30. Consider the parabola y 2 = 8 x , Let Δ_1 be the area of the triangle formed by the end points of its latus rectum and the point $P\left(\frac{1}{2},2\right)$ on the parabola, and Δ_1 be the area of the triangle formed by drawing tagents at P and at the end points of the latus rectum . Then $\frac{\Delta_1}{\Delta_2}$ .is........

[IIT-JEE-2011]

ANSWER

2. $\pm\sqrt{2}$

3. x + y = 3

4. 3/4

5. $y^2=2x-8$

6. (a)

7. $\left(\frac{2}{9},\frac{8}{9}\right)$

8. 2 : 1

9. $\frac{15}{4}\times a^2$

10. (b)

11. (c)

12. (d)

13. (d)

14. (c)

15. (d)

16. (a)

18. $\alpha=2$

19. (c)

20. $(y-1)^2(x+1)+4=0$

21. (d)

22. (a)

23. (i) $\rightarrow$ A; (ii) $\rightarrow$ B; (iii) $\rightarrow$ D; (iv) $\rightarrow$ C

24. (i).(c) (ii).(b) (iii).(d)

25. (a)

26. (b), (c)

27. (a), (d)

28. (c), (d)

29. (a), (b), (d)

30. 2

SELF ASSESSMENT TEST-I

Time : 3 Hrs. **Ch: The Parabola** **M.M. : 100**

Give answers the following questions. (Plz don't take any help from your teachers / friends).

1. A line L passing through the focus of the parabola $y^2 = 4(x-1)$ intersects the parabola in two distinct points. If 'm' be the slope of line L then

(a) $-1 < m < 1$ (b) $m > 1$ or $m < -1$ (c) $m \in R$ (d) None.

2. The range of values of λ for which the point $(\lambda, -1)$ is exterior to both the parabolas $y^2 = |x|$ is

(a) (0, 1) (b) (-1, 1) (c) (-1, 0) (d) None.

3. The number of distinct normals that can be drawn from (-2, 1) to the parabola $y^2 - 4x - 2y - 3 = 0$ is

(a) 1 (b) 2 (c) 3 (d) 0

4. The vertex of the parabola $y^2 = 8x$ is at the centre of a circle and the parabola cuts the circle at the ends of its latus rectum. Then the equation of the circle is

(a) $x^2 + y^2 = 4$ (b) $x^2 + y^2 = 20$

(c) $x^2 + y^2 = 90$ (d) None.

5. The locus of the point of trisection of the double ordinates of a parabola is

(a) pair of lines (b) circle

(c) parabola (d) st. line

6. The point (a, 2a) is an interior point of the region bounded by the parabola $y^2 = 16x$ and the double ordinate through the focus. Then a lies in

(a) $a \in (-\infty, 4)$ (b) $a \in (0, 4)$

(c) $a \in (0, 2)$ (d) $a \in (4, \infty)$.

7. If the tangents drawn from the point (0, 2) to the parabola $y^2 = 4ax$ are inclined at an angle $3\pi/4$, then the value of 'a' is

(a) 2 (b) -2 (c) 1 (d) None.

8. Minimum distance between the parabolas

$y^2 - 4x - 8y + 40 = 0$ and $x^2 - 8x - 4y + 40 = 0$ is

(a) 0 (b) $\sqrt{3}$ (c) $2\sqrt{2}$ (d) $\sqrt{2}$

SELF ASSESSMENT TEST-II

Time : 3 Hrs. **Ch: The Parabola** **M.M. : 100**

Give answers the following questions.

1. The length of each side of an equilateral triangle inscribed in the parabola $y^2 = 4x$ its vertex at with the vertex of the parabola is

(a) 8 (b) $8\sqrt{2}$ (c) $8\sqrt{3}$ (d) $8\sqrt{3}/3$

2. Parabola $y^2 = 4a(x - c_1)$ and $x^2 = 4a(y - c_1)$, where c1 and c2 are variables touch each other. Locus of their point of contact is

(a) $xy = a^2$ (b) $xy = 2a^2$ (c) $xy = 4a^2$ (d) None.

3. If the normal to the parabola $y^2 = 4ax$ at point t_1 cuts the parabola again at t_2, then

(a) $2 \le t_2^2 \le 8$ (b) $t_2^2 \le 2$

(c) $t_2^2 \ge 8$ (d) None.

4. The straight line $y = mx + c$ ($m > 0$) touches the parabola $y^2 = 8(x+2)$, then the minimum value taken by c is

(a) 4 (b) 8 (c) 12 (d) 6

5. The equation of the parabola to which the line $m^2(y-10) - mx - 1 = 0$ is a tangent for any real value of m is

(a) $y^2 = -4x$ (b) $x^2 = -4(y-10)$

(c) $y^2 = 4(x-4)$ (d) $x^2 = y - 10$.

6. The triangle formed by the tangent to the curve $f(x) = ax^2 + bx - b$ at the point (1, 1) and the co-ordinates axes lies in the first quadrant . If its area is 2, then the value of b is

(a) -1 (b) 3 (c) -3 (d) 1

7. A normal to the parabola $y^2 = 4ax$ with slope m touches the rectangular hyperbola $x^2 - y^2 = a^2$ if

(a) $m^6 + 4m^4 - 3m^2 + 1 = 0$

(b) $m^6 - 4m^4 + 3m^2 - 1 = 0$

(c) $m^6 + 4m^4 + 3m^2 + 1 = 0$

(d) $m^6 - 4m^4 - 3m^2 + 1 = 0$

8. Maximum number of common normal of $y^2 = 4ax$ and $x^2 = 4by$ may be equal to

(a) 2 (b) 4 (c) 5 (d) None.

9. Minimum distance between the curves $y^2 = 4x$ and $x^2 + y^2 - 12x + 31 = 0$ is

(a) $\sqrt{5}$ (b) $\sqrt{21}$

(c) $\sqrt{28} - \sqrt{5}$ (d) $\sqrt{21} = \sqrt{5}$

10. The mirror image of the parabola $y^2 = 4x$ in the tangent to the parabola at the point (1, 2) is

(a) $(x-1)^2 = 4(y+1)$ (b) $(x+1)^2 = 4(y+1)$

(c) $(x+1)^2 = 4(y-1)$ (d) $(x-1)^2 = 4(y-1)$

11. The number of points with integral co-ordinates that lie in the interior of the region common to the circle $x^2 + y^2 = 16$ and the parabola $y^2 = 4x$ is

(a) 8 (b) 10 (c) 16 (d) None

12. Consider a circle with its centre lying on the focus of the parabola $y^2 = 2px$ such that it touches the directrix of the parabola. Then a point of intersection of the circle and the parabola is

(a) $\left(\frac{p}{2}, p\right)$ (b) (2p, 2p)

(c) $\left(\frac{p}{2}, -p\right)$ (d) $\left(-\frac{p}{8}, \frac{p}{2}\right)$

ANSWER

Self Assessment Test-I

1.(c) 2.(b) 3.(d) 4.(a) 5.(d) 6.(d) 7.(c) 8.(d)

Self Assessment Test-II

1.(c) 2.(c) 3.(c) 4.(a) 5.(b) 6.(c) 7.(c) 8.(c) 9.(a) 10.(c)

11.(a) 12.(a)

□□□

5 The Ellipse

CONCEPT BOOSTER

5.1 INTRODUCTION

An oval is generally regarded as any ovum (egg)-shaped smooth, convex closed curve. Convex means that any chord connecting two points of the curve lies completely within the curve, and smooth means that the curvature does not change rapidly at any point. The ellipse is a typical oval, but a very particular one with a shape that is regular and can be exactly specified. It has two diameters at right angles that are lines of symmetry. It's best to reserve the word ellipse for real ellipses, and to call others ovals. A diameter is any chord through the center of the ellipse. The diameters that are lines of symmetry are called the major axis 2a, and the minor axis 2b, where $a > b$. If $a = b$, we have the very special ellipse, the circle, which has enough special properties that it should be distinguished from an ellipse, though, of course, it has all the properties of an ellipse in addition to its own remarkable properties. A vertex of a curve is a point of maximum or minimum radius of curvature. An ellipse has vertices at the ends of the major axis (minimum) and at the ends of the minor axis (maximum).

5.2 MATHEMATICAL DEFINITIONS:

Definition-1

It is the locus of a point which moves in a plane in such a way that its distance from a fixed point is a constant ratio from a fixed straight line. This ratio is always less than 1. This fixed point is called the focus and the fixed straight line is called directrix. The constant ratio is called eccentricity.

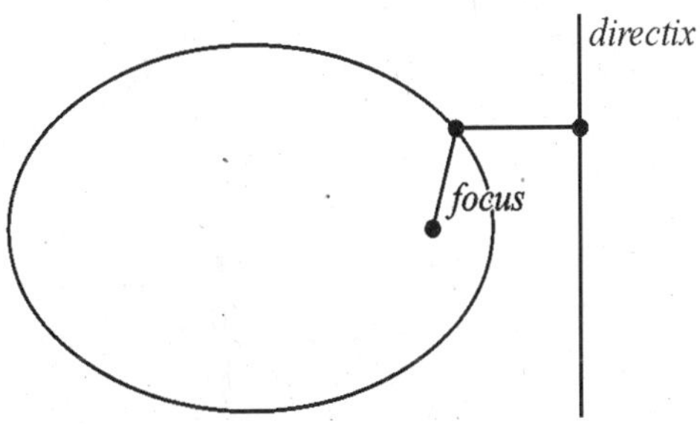

Definition-2

An ellipse is the set of all points in a plane , the sum of whose distances from two fixed points is a constant.

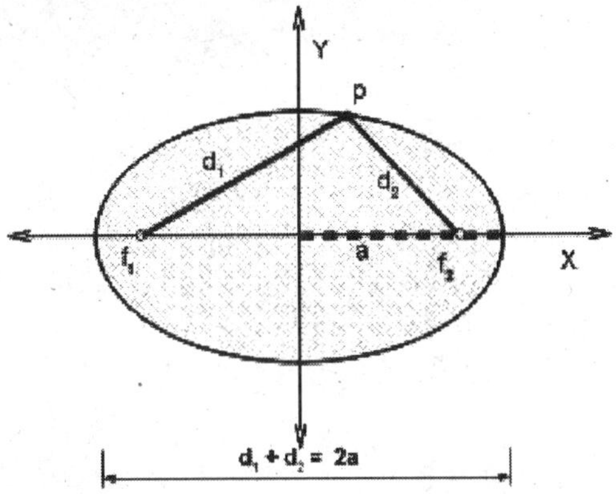

Definition-3

The ellipse is a conic section in which the eccentricity 'e' is less than unity .

Definition-4

In mathematics, an ellipse (from Greek elleipsis, a "falling short") is a plane curve that results from the intersection of a cone by a plane in a way that produces a closed curve.

Definition-5

Ellipses are closed curves and are the bounded case of the conic sections, the curves that result from the intersection of a circular cone and a plane that does not pass through its apex.

Definition-6

An ellipse is the set of points that are equidistant from one point in the plane (a focus) and a particular circle, the directrix circle (whose center is the other focus).

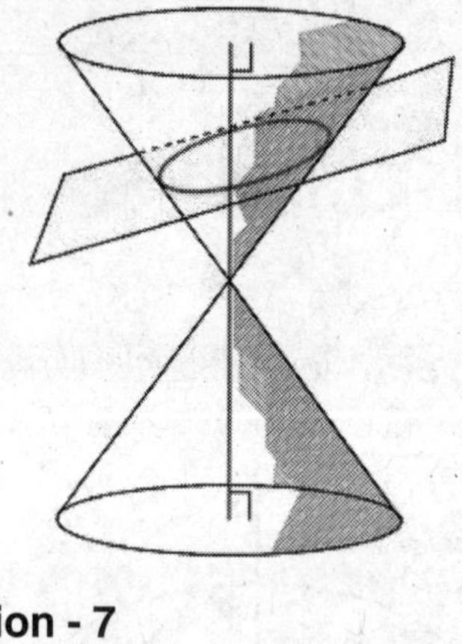

Definition - 7

The ellipse can also be defined as the set of points that are equidistant from one focus and a circle, the directrix circle, that is centered on the other focus. The radius of the directrix circle equals the ellipse's major axis, so the focus and the entire ellipse are inside the directrix circle.

Definition - 8

An ellipse is a smooth closed curve which is symmetric about its horizontal and vertical axes.

Definition - 9

In the parallelogram method, an ellipse is constructed point by point using equally spaced points on two horizontal lines and equally spaced points on two vertical lines.

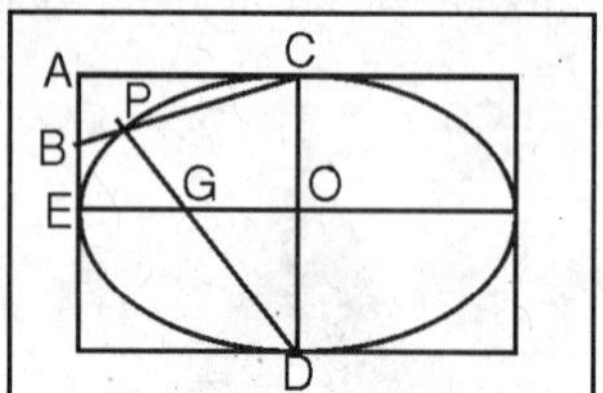

Parellelogram Method

Definition-10

A conic $ax^2 + 2hxy + by^2 + 2gx + 2fy + c = 0$ represents an ellipse if

(i) $\Delta \neq 0$ and

(ii) $h^2 - ab < 0$, where $\Delta = \begin{vmatrix} a & h & g \\ h & b & f \\ g & f & c \end{vmatrix}$.

Definition-11

Let z, z_1, z_3 be three complex numbers such that $|z - z_1| + |z - z_2| = k$, where $k > |z_1 - z_2|$ and k be a +ve real number, then the locus of z is an ellipse.

EQUATION OF AN ELLIPSE:

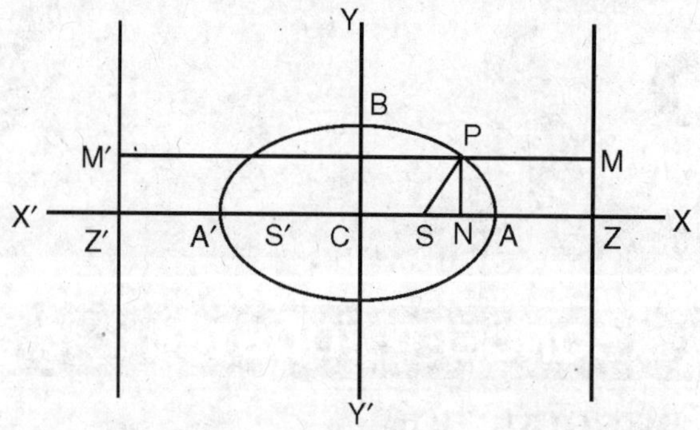

Let S be the focus and ZM be the directrix of the ellipse. Draw $SZ \perp ZM$. Divide SZ inter nally and externally in the ratio e : 1 (e<1) and let A and A' be these internal and external point of division.

Then SA = e SZ ....(i) and SA` = e A`Z ...(ii)

Clearly A and A' will lie on the ellipse.

Let AA` = 2a and take C be the mid - point of AA' as origin

Thus, CA = CA` = a ...(iii)

Let P(x, y) be any point on the ellipse referred to CA and CB as co-ordinate axes.

Adding (i) and (ii), we get, SA + SA` = e (AZ + A`Z)

$\Rightarrow$ AA` = e ( CZ-CA+CA`+CZ)

$\Rightarrow$ AA` = e (2 CZ)

$\Rightarrow$ 2a = 2e CZ

$\Rightarrow$ $CZ = \dfrac{a}{e}$

$\Rightarrow$ The directrix ZM is $x = CZ = \dfrac{a}{e}$.

Again subtracting (i) from (ii), we get,

SA - SA` = e ( A`Z - AZ)

$\Rightarrow$ (CA` + CS ) - (CA- CS) = e (AA`)

$\Rightarrow$ 2 CS = e (AA`)

$\Rightarrow$ 2 CS = e (2a)

$\Rightarrow$ CS = a e

$\Rightarrow$ The Focus is S(CS , 0) = S(ae, 0)

Now draw PM ⊥ ZM, $\dfrac{SP}{PM} = e$

$\Rightarrow$ $SP^2 = e^2\ PM^2$

$\Rightarrow$ $(x - ae)^2 + y^2 = e^2\left(\dfrac{a}{e} - x\right)^2$

$\Rightarrow$ $x^2 + a^2e^2 - 2aex + y^2 = a^2 - 2aex + e^2x^2$

$\Rightarrow$ $x^2\left(1 - e^2\right) + y^2 = a^2\left(1 - e^2\right)$

$$\Rightarrow \quad \frac{x^2}{a^2}+\frac{y^2}{a^2\left(1-e^2\right)}=1$$

$$\Rightarrow \quad \frac{x^2}{a^2}+\frac{y^2}{b^2}=1, \quad b^2=a^2\left(1-e^2\right)..$$

This is the standard equation of an ellipse.

5.3 PROPERTIES OF AN ELLIPSE

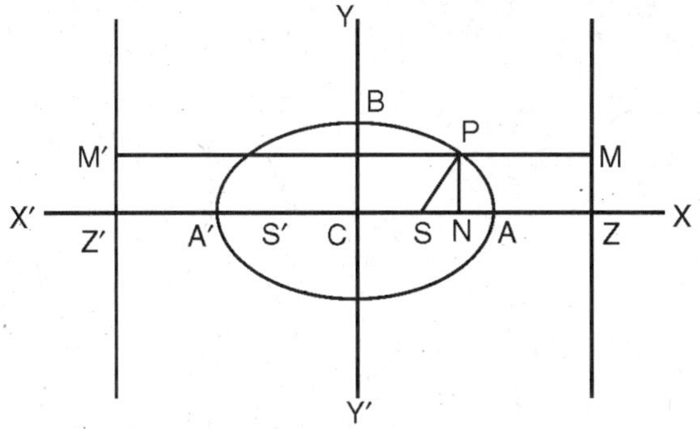

Center: A point inside the ellipse which is the midpoint of the line segment linking the two foci. The intersection of the major and minor axes. Here C = (0, 0).

Major / minor axis: The longest and shortest diameters of an ellipse.The length of the major axis is equal to the sum of the two generator lines.

Here , Major Axis = AA' = 2a, Minor Axis = BB' = 2b

Semi-major/semi-minor axis: The distance from the center to the furthest and closest point on the ellipse. Half the major / minor axis. See Semi-major/ Semi-minor axis of an ellipse.

Directrices:

ZM and Z'M' are two directrices of the ellipse .

Thus ZM : $x=\frac{a}{e}$ and Z'M' : $x=-\frac{a}{e}$.

Distance b/w two directrices : ZZ' = $\frac{2a}{e}$

Foci (Focus points): The two points that define the ellipse. Here S = (ae, 0) , S` = (-ae, 0).

Distance b/w to foci: SS` = 2 a e.

Perimeter: The perimeter is the distance around the ellipse.

Perimeter = $\pi\times\left[\frac{3}{2}(a+b)+\sqrt{ab}\right]$. It is not easy to calculate.

Area: The number of square units it takes to fill the region inside an ellipse.

If the equation of an ellipse is $\frac{x^2}{a^2}+\frac{y^2}{b^2}=1$, then its area is πab.

If the equation of ellipse is $Ax^2+Bxy+Cy^2=1$, then its area is $\frac{2p}{\sqrt{4AC-B^2}}$.

Chord: A line segment linking any two points on an ellipse.

Focal Chord: A chord of the ellipse passing through its focus is called a focal chord.

Focal Distances: Let P(x, y) be any point on the ellipse .

Here , SP = e PM = $e\left(\frac{a}{e}-x\right)=a-ex$

S`P = e PM` = $e\left(\frac{a}{e}+x\right)=a+ex$.

Now, SP + S`P = a - e x + a + e x = 2a = constant .

Thus the sum of the focal distances of a point on the ellipse is cosntant.

Note : Focal distances are also known as focal radii of the ellipse.

Vertices: The vertices of the ellipse are the points where the ellipse meets it major axis.

Here , A = (a, 0) and A` = (-a, 0) are the vertices of the given ellipse.

Co-vertices: The co-vertices of the ellipse are the points where the ellipse meets it minor axis. Here , B = (0, b) and B` = (0, -b) are the co-vertices of the given ellipse.

Double Ordinate :It is a chord perpendicular to the major axis and intersect the curve in two distinct points.

Latus rectum: It is a double ordinate , perpendicular to major axis and passing through the foci. Let LSL` and L_1SL_1' are two latus recta.

Length of the L.R: Let co-ordinates of L and L` be (ae, y_1) and (ae, -y_1)

Since L lies on the ellipse $\frac{x^2}{a^2}+\frac{y^2}{b^2}=1$

so we have, $\frac{a^2e^2}{a^2}+\frac{y_1^2}{b^2}=1$

$$\Rightarrow \quad y_1^2=b^2\left(1-e^2\right)=b^2\left(\frac{b^2}{a^2}\right)=\frac{b^4}{a^2}$$

$$\Rightarrow \quad y_1=b^2/a.$$

Thus the co-ordinates of L and L` are (ae, b^2/a) and (ae, $-b^2/a$).

Hence the length of the latus rectum = LL` = $\frac{2b^2}{a}$.

Relation amongst a, b, e : $b^2=a^2\left(1-e^2\right)$.

Eccentricity (e): $e=\sqrt{1-\frac{b^2}{a^2}}=\sqrt{\frac{a^2-b^2}{a^2}}$

Auxiliary circle : The circle described on the major axis of an ellipse as diameter is called the auxilliary circle.

Relation to a circle: A circle is actually a special case of an ellipse. In an ellipse, if you make the major and minor axis the same length, the result is a circle, with both foci at the center.

5.4 COMPARISION OF ELLIPSES

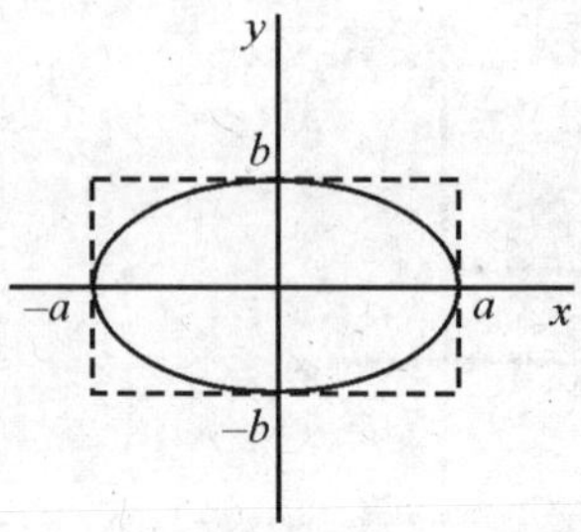

Horizontal ellipse

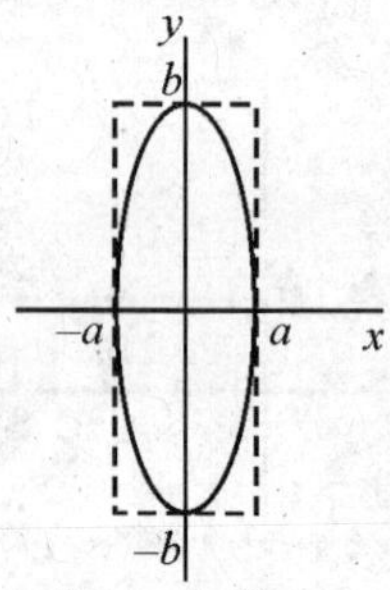

Vertical ellipse

		$\left(\frac{x^2}{a^2}+\frac{y^2}{b^2}=1,\ a>b\right)$	$\left(\frac{x^2}{a^2}+\frac{y^2}{b^2}=1,\ a<b\right)$
1. Centre	:	$(0,0)$	$(0,0)$
2. Vertices	:	$(\pm a, 0)$	$(0, \pm b)$
3. Length of major axis	:	2a	2b
4. Length of minor axis	:	2b	2a
5. Foci	:	$(\pm ae, 0)$	$(0, \pm be)$
6. Equation of directrices:	:	$x=\pm\frac{a}{e}$	$y=\pm\frac{b}{e}$
7. Relation in a , b, e	:	$b^2=a^2(1-e^2)$	$a^2=b^2(1-e^2)$
8. Eccentricity	:	$e=\sqrt{1-\frac{b^2}{a^2}}$	$e=\sqrt{1-\frac{a^2}{b^2}}$
9. Length of L.R	:	$\frac{2b^2}{a}$	$\frac{2a^2}{b}$
10. End points of L. R	:	$\left(\pm ae, \pm\frac{b^2}{a}\right)$	$\left(\pm\frac{a^2}{b}, \pm be\right)$
11. Parametric co-ordinates	:	$(a\cos\theta,\ b\sin\theta)$	$(a\cos\theta,\ b\sin\theta)$
12. Focal radii	:	SP= a - e x , S'P = a + e x	SP = b - e x, S'P = b+ e x.
13. Sum of focal radii	:	SP + S'P = 2a	SP + S'P = 2b
14. Distance between the foci:	:	2ae	2be
15. Distance between directrices:	:	2a / e	2b / e.
16. Equation of any tangent	:	$y=mx+\sqrt{a^2m^2+b^2}$	$y=mx+\sqrt{b^2m^2+a^2}$
17. Equation of director circle	:	$x^2+y^2=a^2+b^2$	$x^2+y^2=b^2+a^2$
18. Area	:	πab	πab

19. Equation of tangent :	:	$\frac{x}{a}\cos\theta+\frac{y}{b}\sin\theta=1$	$\frac{x}{a}\cos\theta+\frac{y}{b}\sin\theta=1$
20. Equation of axis :	:	y=0	x=0
21. Conjugate diameters	:	$m m_1=-\frac{b^2}{a^2}$	$m m_1=-\frac{a^2}{b^2}$
22. Tangent at vertices	:	$x=\pm a$	$y=\pm b$
23. Length of focal chord	:	$\frac{2ab^2}{a^2\sin^2\theta+b^2\cos^2\theta}$	$\frac{2a^2b}{b^2\sin^2\theta+a^2\cos^2\theta}$
24. Equation of diameter	:	$y=-\frac{b^2x}{a^2m}$	$y=-\frac{a^2x}{b^2m}$
25. Equation of latus rectum	:	$x=\pm ae$	$y=\pm be$
26. Polar form	:	$\frac{1}{r^2}=\frac{\cos^2\theta}{a^2}+\frac{\sin^2\theta}{b^2}$	$\frac{1}{r^2}=\frac{\cos^2\theta}{a^2}+\frac{\sin^2\theta}{b^2}$
27. Length of the radius vector	:	$r=\frac{ab}{\sqrt{a^2\sin^2\theta+b^2\cos^2\theta}}$	$r=\frac{ab}{\sqrt{a^2\sin^2\theta+b^2\cos^2\theta}}$
28. Perimeter of a triangle formed by Foci and a movable point P	:	4 a	4 b
29. Maximum number of normals can be drawn from a point	:	4	4
30. Maximum number of tangents can be drawn from a point	:	4	2

5.5 PARAMETRIC EQUATION OF AN ELLIPSE

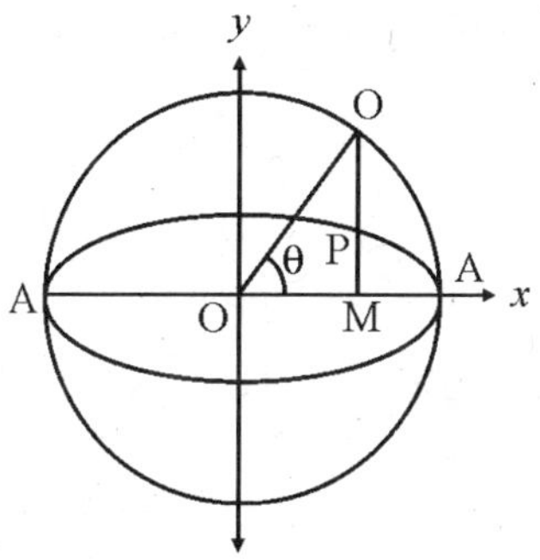

Let the equation of the ellipse be $\frac{x^2}{a^2}+\frac{y^2}{b^2}=1$

Then equation of its auxilliary circle is $x^2+y^2=a^2$. Let Q be a point on the auxilliary circle $x^2+y^2=a^2$ such QP produced is perpendicular to the x-axis.

Thus P and Q are the corresponding points on the ellipse and the auxilliary circle . Let $\angle QCA=\phi$, where $0\le\phi<2\pi$

Let Q = $(a\cos\phi,\ a\sin\phi)$ and P = $(a\cos\phi,\ y)$.

Since P lies on the ellipse $\frac{x^2}{a^2}+\frac{y^2}{b^2}=1$,

so we can write $\frac{a^2\cos^2\phi}{a^2}+\frac{y^2}{b^2}=1$

$\Rightarrow\quad y^2=b^2\sin^2\phi$

$\Rightarrow\quad y=b\sin\phi$, since P lies in the 1st quadrant.

Thus the parametric equations of the ellipse are

$$x=a\cos\phi,\ y=b\sin\phi.$$

Note : Any point , say , P, on the ellipse can be considered as $(a\cos\phi,\ b\sin\phi)$. Since the point is known when ϕ is given, then it is often called 'the point ϕ' or $P(f)$.

5.6 IMPORTANT PROPERTIES RELATED TO CHORD AND FOCAL CHORD:

(i) Equation of the chord joining the points $P(f_1)$ & $Q(f_2)$:

The equation of the chord joining the points

$P(a\cos f_1,\ b\sin f_1)$ and $Q(a\cos f_2,\ b\sin f_2)$ is

$$\frac{x}{a}\cos\left(\frac{f_1+f_2}{2}\right)+\frac{y}{b}\sin\left(\frac{f_1+f_2}{2}\right)=\cos\left(\frac{\phi_1-\phi_2}{2}\right)$$

(ii) The length of a radius vector from the center drawn in a given direction

As we know that, the equation of the ellipse is

$$\frac{x^2}{a^2}+\frac{y^2}{b^2}=1.$$

Put x = rcos?, y = rsin? , then we have

$$\frac{r^2\cos^2\theta}{a^2}+\frac{r^2\sin^2\theta}{b^2}=1.$$

$$\Rightarrow \quad r^2=\frac{a^2b^2}{b^2\cos^2\theta+a^2\sin^2\theta}$$

$$\Rightarrow \quad r=\frac{ab}{\sqrt{b^2\cos^2\theta+a^2\sin^2\theta}}.$$

Which is the required distance from centre of the point P(θ) on the ellipse $\frac{x^2}{a^2}+\frac{y^2}{b^2}=1$.

(iii) Product of the focal radii of an ellipse from any point P(θ) on the ellipse $\frac{x^2}{a^2}+\frac{y^2}{b^2}=1$ is a²sin²? + b²cos²? .

We have , SP = a - e x and S'P = a + e x .

Thus, $SP.\,S'P=\left(a^2-e^2x^2\right)=\left(a^2-a^2e^2\cos^2\theta\right)$

$$=\left(a^2+\left(b^2-a^2\right)\cos^2\theta\right)$$

$$=\left(a^2\left(1-\cos^2\theta\right)+b^2\cos^2\theta\right)$$

$$=a^2\sin^2\theta+b^2\cos^2\theta$$

(iv) If PQ be a focal chord and S , S` are the foci of an ellipse, then the perimeter of the triangle described by ? S'PQ is 4a.

We have , perimeter of the Δ S'PQ = S`P + S`Q + PQ

= (S`P + S`Q) + (SP + SQ)

= (S`P + SP ) + ( S`Q + S Q)

= 2 a + 2 a = 4 a.

(v) The length of the focal chord of an ellipse which makes an angle θ with the major axis is $\frac{2ab^2}{a^2\sin^2?+b^2\cos^2?}$.

Let the chord be PQ, where $P=(x_1, y_1)$ and $Q=(x_2, y_2)$ and S(ae, 0) be the focus.

The chord PQ be (y-0) = tan? (x – ae) ...(i)

Now PQ = SP + SQ = $a-ex_1+a-ex_2=2a-e(x_1+x_2)$

Let the equation of the ellipse be $\frac{x^2}{a^2}+\frac{y^2}{b^2}=1$ ...(ii)

From (i) and (ii), we get, $\frac{x^2}{a^2}+\frac{\tan^2?(x-ae)^2}{b^2}=1$

$$\Rightarrow \quad b^2x^2+a^2\tan^2\theta(x-ae)^2=a^2b^2$$

$$\Rightarrow \quad b^2x^2+a^2\tan^2\theta\left(x^2-2aex+a^2e^2\right)=a^2b^2$$

$$\Rightarrow \quad \left(b^2+a^2\tan^2\theta\right)x^2-2a^3e\tan^2\theta\, x+a^2\left(a^2e^2\tan^2\theta-b^2\right)=0$$

Let its roots are x_1 & x_2

Then $x_1+x_2=\frac{2a^3e\tan^2\theta}{b^2+a^2\tan^2\theta}$

Therefore, PQ = $2a-e(x_1+x_2)$

$$=2a-e\left(\frac{2a^3e\tan^2\theta}{b^2+a^2\tan^2\theta}\right)$$

$$=2a\left(\frac{b^2+a^2\tan^2\theta-a^2e^2\tan^2\theta}{b^2+a^2\tan^2\theta}\right)$$

$$=2a\left(\frac{b^2+a^2\left(1-e^2\right)\tan^2\theta}{b^2+a^2\tan^2\theta}\right)$$

$$=2a\left(\frac{b^2+b^2\tan^2\theta}{b^2+a^2\tan^2\theta}\right)$$

$$=2a\left(\frac{b^2\left(1+\tan^2\theta\right)}{b^2+a^2\tan^2\theta}\right)=\frac{2ab^2}{a^2\sin^2\theta+b^2\cos^2\theta}.$$

Hence the result.

(vi) If P(α) and P(β) are the extremities of a focal chord, then $\tan\left(\frac{a}{2}\right)\tan\left(\frac{ß}{2}\right)=\frac{e-1}{e+1}$.

Let the equation to the ellipse be $\frac{x^2}{a^2}+\frac{y^2}{b^2}=1$.

Equation of the chord PQ is

$$\frac{x}{a}\cos\left(\frac{\alpha+\beta}{2}\right)+\frac{y}{b}\sin\left(\frac{\alpha+\beta}{2}\right)=\cos\left(\frac{\alpha-\beta}{2}\right).$$

which is passing through the focus (ae, 0),

then $e\cos\left(\frac{\alpha+\beta}{2}\right)=\cos\left(\frac{\alpha-\beta}{2}\right)$

$$\Rightarrow \quad \frac{\cos\left(\frac{\alpha-\beta}{2}\right)}{\cos\left(\frac{\alpha+\beta}{2}\right)}=e$$

$$\Rightarrow \quad \frac{\cos\left(\frac{\alpha-\beta}{2}\right)+\cos\left(\frac{\alpha+\beta}{2}\right)}{\cos\left(\frac{\alpha-\beta}{2}\right)-\cos\left(\frac{\alpha+\beta}{2}\right)}=\frac{e-1}{e+1}$$

$$\Rightarrow \quad \tan\left(\frac{\alpha}{2}\right)\tan\left(\frac{\beta}{2}\right)=\frac{e-1}{e+1}.$$

Hence , the result.

(vii) If α and β are the eccentric angles of the extremities of a focal chord of the ellipse $\frac{x^2}{a^2}+\frac{y^2}{b^2}=1$, then the eccentricity of the ellipse is $\frac{\sin a+\sin ß}{\sin(a+ß)}$.

Equation of the chord joining the points $P(\alpha)$ and $P(\beta)$ is

$$\frac{x}{a}\cos\left(\frac{\alpha+\beta}{2}\right)+\frac{y}{b}\sin\left(\frac{\alpha+\beta}{2}\right)=\cos\left(\frac{\alpha-\beta}{2}\right)$$

Which is passing through (ae, 0),

we have , $e\cos\left(\frac{\alpha+\beta}{2}\right)=\cos\left(\frac{\alpha-\beta}{2}\right)$

$$\Rightarrow \quad e\times 2\sin\left(\frac{\alpha+\beta}{2}\right)\cos\left(\frac{\alpha+\beta}{2}\right)=2\sin\left(\frac{\alpha+\beta}{2}\right)\cos\left(\frac{\alpha-\beta}{2}\right)$$

$$\Rightarrow \quad e\times\sin(\alpha+\beta)=\sin\alpha+\sin\beta$$

$$\Rightarrow \quad e=\frac{\sin\alpha+\sin\beta}{\sin(\alpha+\beta)}$$

Hence , the result.

Ex-1: Find the centre, vertices, co-vertices, lengths of major and minor axes, eccentricity, lengths of latus rectum, equation of directrices and the end points of a latus recta of each of the following ellipses.

(i) $9x^2+16y^2=144$

(ii) $2x^2+3y^2-4x-12y+8=0$

Sol. (i) The given equation of the ellipse is

$$9x^2+16y^2=144$$

$$\Rightarrow \quad \frac{x^2}{16}+\frac{y^2}{9}=1$$

(a) Centre : C (0,0)

(b) Vertices : A (a, 0) A' (-a, 0) = A (4, 0) and A' (-4, 0)

(c) Co-vertices : B (0, b) and B' (0, -b) = B (0, 3) and (0, -3)

(d) Lengths of the major axis : 2a = 8

(e) Lengths of the minor axis : 2b = 6

(f) Eccentricity = $e=\sqrt{1-\frac{b^2}{a^2}}=\sqrt{1-\frac{9}{16}}=\frac{\sqrt{7}}{4}$

(g) Lengths of the latus rectum = $\frac{2b^2}{a}=\frac{18}{4}=\frac{9}{2}$

(h) Equations of the directrices : $x=\pm\frac{a}{e}$

$$\Rightarrow x=\pm\frac{4}{\frac{\sqrt{7}}{4}}=\pm\frac{16}{\sqrt{7}}$$

(i) End points of the latus recta : L(ae, $\frac{b^2}{a}$), L '(ae, -$\frac{b^2}{a}$)

$$=L(\sqrt{7},\frac{9}{4}),L'(\sqrt{7},-\frac{9}{4}).$$

(ii) The given equation of the ellipse is

$$2x^2+3y^2-4x-12y+8=0$$

$$\Rightarrow \quad 2\left(x^2-2x+1\right)+3\left(y^2-4y+4\right)=6$$

$$\Rightarrow \quad 2(x-1)^2+3(y-2)^2=6$$

$$\Rightarrow \quad \frac{(x-1)^2}{3}+\frac{(y-2)^2}{2}=1$$

$$\Rightarrow \quad \frac{X^2}{3}+\frac{Y^2}{2}=1,\text{ where } X=x-1,\ Y=y-2.$$

(a) Centre : $(0,0)\Rightarrow X=0, Y=0\Rightarrow x-1=0$ and $y-2=0\Rightarrow x=1$ and $y=2$

Hence, the centre is (1, 2) .

(b) Vertices : $(\pm a, 0)\Rightarrow X=\pm a,\ Y=0$

$\Rightarrow$ x-1 = ±3 , y-2 = 0

$\Rightarrow$ x = 1±3 , y = 2

$\Rightarrow$ x = 4, -2 , y = 2

Hence, the vertices are (4, 2) and (-2, 2)

(c) Co-vertices : $(0,\pm b)\Rightarrow X=0,\ Y=\pm 3$

$\Rightarrow$ x-1 = 0, y-2 = ± 3

$\Rightarrow$ x = 1, y = 2 ± 3

$\Rightarrow$ x = 1, y = 5, -1

Hence, the co-vertices are (1, 5) , (1, -1)

(d) The lengths of the major axis = 2a = 6

(e) The length of the minor axis = 2b = 4

(f) The length of the latus rectum = $\frac{2b^2}{a}=\frac{18}{4}=\frac{9}{2}$

(g) Eccentricity = $e=\sqrt{1-\frac{b^2}{a^2}}=\sqrt{1-\frac{2}{3}}=\frac{1}{\sqrt{3}}$

(h) Equations of the directrices :

$$X=\pm\frac{a}{e}=\pm\frac{3}{1/\sqrt{3}}=\pm3\sqrt{3}$$

$$\Rightarrow \quad x=1\pm3\sqrt{3}$$

(i) End points of the latus recta :

$$L\left(ae,\frac{b^2}{a}\right);\ L'\left(ae,-\frac{b^2}{a}\right)$$

$= L\left(\sqrt{3}, \frac{9}{2}\right); L'\left(\sqrt{3}, -\frac{9}{2}\right)$

Ex-2. Find the sum of the focal distances of any point on the ellipse $16x^2 + 25y^2 = 400$.

Sol. The given equation of the ellipse is

$$16x^2 + 25y^2 = 400$$

$$\Rightarrow \frac{x^2}{25} + \frac{y^2}{16} = 1$$

Thus, the sum of the focal distances = 2a = 10 units

Ex-3. If the equation $\frac{x^2}{10-a} + \frac{y^2}{4-a} = 1$ represents of an ellipse such that the length of the interval, where a lies is m, then find m.

Sol. The given equation of an ellipse is

$$\frac{x^2}{10-a} + \frac{y^2}{4-a} = 1$$

$$\Rightarrow (4-a)x^2 + (10-a)y^2 - (4-a)(10-a) = 0$$

Since, the given equation represents an ellipse,

$$h^2 - ab < 0$$

$$\Rightarrow 0 - (4-a)(10-a) < 0$$

$$\Rightarrow (a-4)\ (a-10) < 0$$

$$\Rightarrow 4 < a < 10$$

Thus, the length of the interval = 10 - 4 = 6

Hence, the value of m is 6

Ex-4. If (5, 12) and (24, 7) are the foci of an ellipse passing through the origin, find the eccentricity of the ellipse

Sol. Let the foci of the ellipse are S and S' respectively

Then S = (5, 12) and S ' = (24, 7).

Thus, the centre of the ellipse is $C\left(\frac{29}{2}, \frac{19}{2}\right)$.

Now $OC = \frac{1}{2} \times \sqrt{29^2 + 19^2} = \frac{1}{2} \times \sqrt{1202}$

We have, SS' = $\sqrt{386}$

$$\Rightarrow e = \frac{\sqrt{386}}{2a} = \frac{\sqrt{386}}{\sqrt{1202}} = \sqrt{\frac{386}{1202}} = \frac{1}{\sqrt{3}}$$

Ex-5. Find the equation of the ellipse whose axes are co-ordinate axes and foci are $(\pm 2, 0)$ and eccentricity is 1/2.

Sol. Let S (2, 0) and S`(-2, 0) are two foci of the ellipse and C(0, 0) be the centre of the ellipse.

We have , SS` = 4

$$\Rightarrow 2ae = 4 \Rightarrow 2a \times \frac{1}{2} = 4 \Rightarrow a = 4$$

Also, $b^2 = a^2\left(1-e^2\right) = 16\left(1-\frac{1}{4}\right) = 12$

$$\Rightarrow b = \sqrt{12} = 2\sqrt{3}$$

Hence, the equation of the ellipse is $\frac{x^2}{a^2} + \frac{y^2}{b^2} = 1$

$$\Rightarrow \frac{x^2}{16} + \frac{y^2}{12} = 1$$

Ex-6. If the distance between the foci of an ellipse is equal to the length of its latus rectum, then eccentricity is $\frac{\sqrt{5}-1}{2}$.

Sol. Given $2ae = \frac{2b^2}{a}$

$$\Rightarrow b^2 = a^2 e \Rightarrow a^2\left(1-e^2\right) = a^2 e$$

$$\Rightarrow \left(1-e^2\right) = e$$

$$\Rightarrow e^2 + e - 1 = 0 \Rightarrow e = \frac{\sqrt{5}-1}{2}.$$

Hence, the result

Ex-7. Find the eccentricity of the ellipse $\frac{x^2}{a^2} + \frac{y^2}{b^2} = 1$ whose latus rectum is half of its major axis.

Sol. The equation of the given ellipse is $\frac{x^2}{a^2} + \frac{y^2}{b^2} = 1$

It is given that , the length of the latus rectum = $\frac{1}{2} \times$ the length of the major axis.

$$\Rightarrow \frac{2b^2}{a} = a \Rightarrow b = a$$

As we know that, eccentricity = $\sqrt{1 - \frac{b^2}{a^2}} = \sqrt{1-1} = 0$

Ex-8. Find the eccentric angle of a point on the ellipse $\frac{x^2}{6} + \frac{y^2}{2} = 1$ whose distance from the centre of the ellipse is $\sqrt{5}$.

Sol. Let any point on the ellipse $\frac{x^2}{6} + \frac{y^2}{2} = 1$ is $P\left(\sqrt{6}\cos ?, \sqrt{2}\sin ?\right)$ and C be the centre of the ellipse.

Therefore, CP = $\sqrt{5}$

$$\Rightarrow 6\cos^2\theta + 2\sin^2\theta = 5$$

$$\Rightarrow 4\cos^2\theta = 3$$

$\Rightarrow \quad \cos\theta = \sqrt{\frac{3}{4}} = \frac{\sqrt{3}}{2}$

$\Rightarrow \quad \theta = \frac{\pi}{6}.$

Hence, the eccentric angle is $\frac{\pi}{6}$.

Ex-9. Find the area of the greatest rectangle thant can be inscribed in the ellipse $\frac{x^2}{16}+\frac{y^2}{9}=1$

Sol. Let Q be any poin on the given ellipse, whose co-ordinates are $(4\cos\theta, 3\sin\theta)$

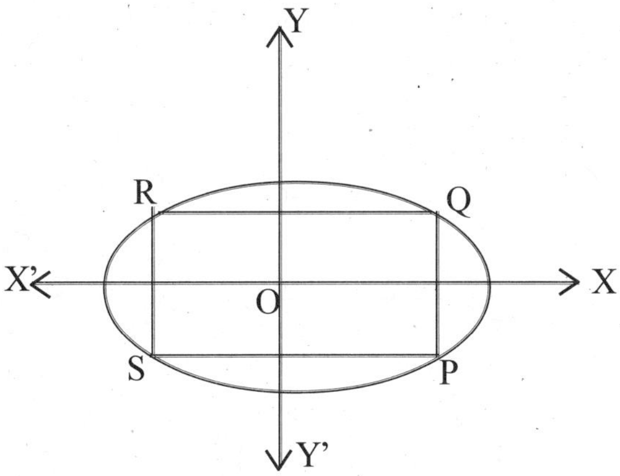

Thus, PQ $= 8\cos\theta$ and QR $= 6\sin\theta$

Thus, the area of the rectangle PQRS

$= PQ \times QR = 48\sin\theta\cos\theta$

$= 24\sin 2\theta$

Hence, the area of the greatest rectangle

$= 24$ sq. u. at $\theta = \frac{\pi}{4}$

Ex-10. Find the locus of a point whose co-ordinates are given by $x = 3+4\cos\theta.\ y = 2+3\sin\theta$.

Sol. The co-ordinates of the given point are

$x = 3+4\cos\theta,\ y = 2+3\sin\theta$

$\Rightarrow \quad \frac{(x-3)}{4} = \cos\theta,\ \frac{(y-2)}{3} = \sin\theta$

$\Rightarrow \quad \frac{(x-3)^2}{4^2}+\frac{(y-2)^2}{3^2} = \cos^2\theta + \sin^2\theta = 1$

$\Rightarrow \quad \frac{(x-3)^2}{16}+\frac{(y-2)^2}{9} = 1$

Which is the required locus.

Ex-11. If PSQ is a focal chord of an ellipse $16x^2+25y^2=400$ such that SP = 8, then find the length of SQ.

Sol. The equation of the ellipse is

$16x^2+25y^2 = 400$

$\Rightarrow \quad \frac{x^2}{25}+\frac{y^2}{16}=1$

As we know that , if SP and SQ are the focal segments of a focal chord PSQ,

then $\frac{1}{SP}+\frac{1}{SQ}=\frac{1}{a}$

$\Rightarrow \quad \frac{1}{8}+\frac{1}{SQ}=\frac{1}{5}$

$\Rightarrow \quad \frac{1}{SQ}=\frac{1}{5}-\frac{1}{8}=\frac{8-5}{40}=\frac{3}{40}$

$\Rightarrow \quad SQ = \frac{40}{3}$

Hence, the length of SQ is 40/3.

Ex-12. Find the area bounded by the curve $\frac{x^2}{16}+\frac{y^2}{9}\le 1$ and the line $\frac{x}{4}+\frac{y}{3}\le 1$

Sol. As we know that, the area of an ellipse $\frac{x^2}{a^2}+\frac{y^2}{b^2}=1$ is $=\pi ab$

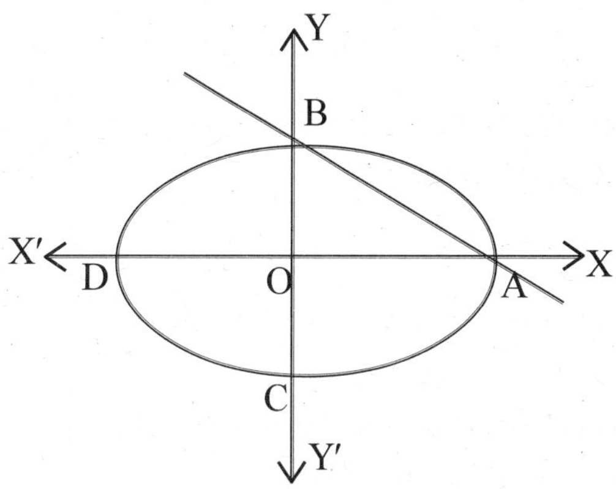

Thus, the area of ACDBA

$= \left(\frac{3}{4}\times p.4.3-\frac{1}{2}.4.3\right) = (9p-6)$ sq.u.

5.6 POSITION OF A POINT WITH RESPECT TO AN ELLIPSE

The point (x_1, y_1) lies outside, on or inside the ellipse $\frac{x^2}{a^2}+\frac{y^2}{b^2}=1$ according as $\frac{x_1^2}{a^2}+\frac{y_1^2}{b^2}-1 >,=,< 0$.

Ex-1. Find the location of the point (2, 3) with repect to the ellipse $\frac{x^2}{4}+\frac{y^2}{3}=1$.

Sol. Let $N=\frac{x_1^2}{4}+\frac{y_1^2}{3}-1$

Then, $N=\frac{4}{4}+\frac{9}{3}-1=1+3-1=3$

Since, the value of N is +ve at (2, 3), so the point (2, 3) lies outside of the ellipse $\frac{x^2}{4}+\frac{y^2}{3}=1$

Ex-2. If $(\lambda, -\lambda)$ be an interrior point of an ellipse $4x^2+5y^2=1$ such that the length of the interbal, where λ lies is m, where $m \in Q^+$, then find the value of $(3m-2)^{2013}+2013$.

Sol. Since the point $(\lambda, -\lambda)$ be an interrior point of an ellipse $4x^2+5y^2=1$, then $4\lambda^2+5\lambda^2-1<0$

$\Rightarrow \quad 9\lambda^2-1<0$

$\Rightarrow \quad (3\lambda+1)(3\lambda-1)<0$

$\Rightarrow \quad -\frac{1}{3}<\lambda<\frac{1}{3}$

Therefore, $m=\frac{2}{3}$

$\Rightarrow \quad (3m-2)^{2013}+2013=0+2013=2013$

5.7 INTERSECTION OF A LINE AND AN ELLIPSE

The line $y=mx+c$ intersect the ellipse $\frac{x^2}{a^2}+\frac{y^2}{b^2}=1$ into two

(i) real and distinct points if $c^2<a^2m^2+b^2$

(ii) coincident points if $c^2=a^2m^2+b^2$

(iii) imaginary points if $c^2>a^2m^2+b^2$.

(iv) the line $y=mx+c$ will be a tangent to the given ellipse if $c^2=a^2m^2+b^2$.

(v) the co-ordinates of the point of contact is $\left(\pm\frac{a^2m}{c}, \pm\frac{b^2}{c}\right)$. which is also known as the m-point on the ellipse.

(vi) Equation of any tangent to the ellipse can be considered as $y=mx+\sqrt{a^2m^2+b^2}$.

(vii) The line $lx+my+n=0$ will be a tangent to the ellipse $\frac{x^2}{a^2}+\frac{y^2}{b^2}=1$ if $a^2l^2+b^2m^2=n^2$

5.8 THE LENGTH OF THE CHORD INTERCEPTED BY THE ELLIPSE ON THE LINE $y=mx+c$.

Let the equation of the ellipse be $\frac{x^2}{a^2}+\frac{y^2}{b^2}=1$.

$$\Rightarrow \frac{x^2}{a^2}+\frac{(mx+c)^2}{b^2}=1$$

$$\Rightarrow \left(a^2m^2+b^2\right)x^2+2a^2mcx+a^2\left(c^2-b^2\right)=0$$

Let it roots are x_1, x_2.

Then $x_1+x_2=-\frac{2a^2mc}{a^2m^2+b^2}$ and $x_1.x_2=\frac{a^2\left(c^2-b^2\right)}{a^2m^2+b^2}$.

Thus, $x_1-x_2=\frac{2ab\sqrt{a^2m^2+b^2-c^2}}{a^2m^2+b^2}$.

Hence the length of the chord is

$$=\sqrt{(x_1-x_2)^2+(y_1-y_2)^2}=(x_1-x_2)\sqrt{1+m^2}$$

$$=\frac{2ab\times\sqrt{1+m^2}\sqrt{a^2m^2+b^2-c^2}}{a^2m^2+b^2}.$$

Ex.1. Find the no of tangents drawn from a point (2, 3) to an ellipse $4x^2+3y^2=12$.

Sol. We have, $4.4+3.3-12=16+9-12=25-12=13>0$

Thus, the point (2, 3) lies outside of the ellipse.

Thus, the number of tangents = 2

Ex.2. Find the equations of tangents drawn from the point (2, 3) to the ellipse $9x^2+16y^2=144$.

Sol. The given ellipse is $9x^2+16y^2=144$

$\Rightarrow \quad \frac{x^2}{16}+\frac{y^2}{9}=1$

Equation of any tangent to the given ellipse is

$y=mx+\sqrt{a^2m^2+b^2}$

$\Rightarrow \quad y=mx+\sqrt{16m^2+9}$

Which is passing through (2, 3),

so $3=2m+\sqrt{16m^2+9}$

$\Rightarrow \quad (3-2m)^2=16m^2+9$

$\Rightarrow \quad 9-6m+4m^2=16m^2+9$

$\Rightarrow \quad 12m^2+6m=0$

$\Rightarrow \quad 2m^2+m=0$

$\Rightarrow \quad m(2m+1)=0$

$\Rightarrow \quad m=0, -\frac{1}{2}$

Hence, the equation of tangents are $y = 3$

and $y = -\frac{1}{2}x + \sqrt{13}$

Ex.3. If the line $3x + 4y = 5$, touches the ellipse $9x^2 + 16y^2 = 144$, then find the points of contact.

Sol. The given line is $3x + 4y = 5 \Rightarrow 4y = -3x + 5$ and the ellipse is $9x^2 + 16y^2 = 144$

$$\Rightarrow \quad y = -\frac{3}{4}x + \frac{5}{4} \text{ and } \frac{x^2}{16} + \frac{y^2}{9} = 1$$

As we know that, the line $y = mx + c$ will be a tangent to the ellipse $\frac{x^2}{a^2} + \frac{y^2}{b^2} = 1$, then the points of contacts are

$$\left(\pm\frac{a^2 m}{c}, \pm\frac{b^2}{c}\right) = \left(\frac{\pm 16\left(-\frac{3}{4}\right)}{\frac{5}{4}}, \frac{\pm 9}{\frac{5}{4}}\right)$$

$$= \left(\frac{\pm(-48)}{5}, \frac{\pm 36}{5}\right)$$

Ex-4. For what value of λ does the line $y = x + \lambda$ touches the ellipse $9x^2 + 16y^2 = 144$?

Sol. The equation of the given ellipse is

$$9x^2 + 16y^2 = 144$$

$$\Rightarrow \quad \frac{x^2}{16} + \frac{y^2}{9} = 1$$

The line $y = x + ?$ will be a tangent to the ellipse if,

$$c^2 = a^2 m^2 + b^2$$

$$\Rightarrow \quad \lambda^2 = 16.1 + 9 = 25$$

$$\Rightarrow \quad \lambda = \pm 5$$

Hence, the values of λ are ± 5

Ex-5. Find the equations of tangents to the ellipse $\frac{x^2}{3} + \frac{y^2}{4} = 1$ having slope '2'.

Sol. The given ellipse is $\frac{x^2}{3} + \frac{y^2}{4} = 1$

Equation of any ellipse is $y = mx \pm \sqrt{a^2 m^2 + b^2}$

$$\Rightarrow \quad y = 2x \pm \sqrt{3.4 + 2} = 2x \pm \sqrt{14}$$

5.9 VARIOUS FORMS OF TANGENTS:

(i) **Point form**: Equation of tangent to the ellipse $\frac{x^2}{a^2} + \frac{y^2}{b^2} = 1$ at (x_1, y_1) is $\frac{xx_1}{a^2} + \frac{yy_1}{b^2} = 1$.

(ii) **Parametric form**: Equation of tangent to the ellipse $\frac{x^2}{a^2} + \frac{y^2}{b^2} = 1$ at $(a\cos ?, b\sin ?)$ is $\frac{x}{a}\cos\theta + \frac{y}{b}\sin\theta = 1$.

(iii) **Slope form** : Equation of tangent to the ellipse $\frac{x^2}{a^2} + \frac{y^2}{b^2} = 1$ in terms of slop m is $y = mx + \sqrt{a^2 m^2 + b^2}$.

(iv) The co-ordinates of the points of contact are

$$\left(\mp\frac{a^2 m}{\sqrt{a^2 m^2 + b^2}}, \pm\frac{b^2}{\sqrt{a^2 m^2 + b^2}}\right).$$

(v) The point of intersection of the tangents at $P(\theta)$ & $Q(\phi)$ is

$$\left(\frac{a\cos\left(\frac{\theta+\phi}{2}\right)}{\cos\left(\frac{\theta-\phi}{2}\right)}, \frac{b\sin\left(\frac{\theta+\phi}{2}\right)}{\cos\left(\frac{\theta-\phi}{2}\right)}\right).$$

Ex-1. The locus of the feet of perpendicular drawn from the centre upon any tangent to the given ellipse is $r^2 = a^2\cos^2\theta + b^2\sin^2\theta$

Sol. Equation of any tangent to the ellipse $\frac{x^2}{a^2} + \frac{y^2}{b^2} = 1$ at $P(\theta)$ is $\frac{x}{a}\cos\theta + \frac{y}{b}\sin\theta = 1$ ...(i)

Equation of perpendiculars from centre (0, 0) to tangent is $\frac{x}{b}\sin\theta - \frac{y}{a}\cos\theta = 0$ ...(ii)

From (ii) we get,

$$\frac{\sin\theta}{by} = \frac{\cos\theta}{ax} = \frac{1}{\sqrt{a^2x^2 + b^2y^2}} \quad \text{...(iii)}$$

Locus of the feet of perpendiculars is the point of intersection of (i) and (ii).

It is obtained by eliminating 'θ' between (i) and (ii).

squaring (i) and (ii) and adding, we get ,

$$\frac{x^2}{a^2}\cos^2\theta + \frac{y^2}{b^2}\sin^2\theta + \frac{x^2}{b^2}\sin^2\theta + \frac{y^2}{a^2}\cos^2\theta = 1$$

$$\Rightarrow \left(\frac{x^2}{a^2} + \frac{y^2}{a^2}\right)\cos^2\theta + \left(\frac{y^2}{b^2} + \frac{x^2}{b^2}\right)\sin^2\theta = 1$$

$$\Rightarrow (x^2 + y^2)\left(\frac{\cos^2\theta}{a^2} + \frac{\sin^2\theta}{b^2}\right) = 1$$

$$\Rightarrow (x^2 + y^2)(b^2\cos^2\theta + a^2\sin^2\theta) = a^2b^2$$

$$\Rightarrow (x^2 + y^2)\left(\frac{b^2a^2x^2}{a^2x^2 + b^2y^2} + \frac{b^2a^2y^2}{a^2x^2 + b^2y^2}\right) = a^2b^2$$

$$\Rightarrow (x^2 + y^2)^2 = (a^2x^2 + b^2y^2)$$

Now, put, $x = r\cos\theta$ & $y = r\sin\theta$, we get,

$r^2 = a^2\cos^2? + b^2\sin^2?$.

Hence, the result.

Ex-2. A circle of radius r is concentric with the ellipse $\frac{x^2}{a^2}+\frac{y^2}{b^2}=1$. Then the common tangent is inclined to the major axis at an angle of $\tan^{-1}\sqrt{\left(\frac{r^2-b^2}{a^2-r^2}\right)}$.

Sol. Equation of circle is $x^2+y^2=r^2$.

Equation of any tangent to the ellipse is

$y = mx + \sqrt{a^2m^2+b^2}$.

If it is tangent to a circle also, then the length of perpendicular from the centre (0, 0) of a circle is equal to the radius of a circle.

Thus, $\left|\frac{\sqrt{a^2m^2+b^2}}{\sqrt{1+m^2}}\right| = r$

$\Rightarrow a^2m^2+b^2 = r^2\left(1+m^2\right) = r^2+r^2m^2$

$\Rightarrow \left(a^2-r^2\right)m^2 = \left(r^2-b^2\right)$

$\Rightarrow m^2 = \left(\frac{r^2-b^2}{a^2-r^2}\right)$

$\Rightarrow m = \sqrt{\left(\frac{r^2-b^2}{a^2-r^2}\right)}$

$\Rightarrow \tan\theta = \sqrt{\left(\frac{r^2-b^2}{a^2-r^2}\right)}$

$\Rightarrow \theta = \tan^{-1}\left(\sqrt{\left(\frac{r^2-b^2}{a^2-r^2}\right)}\right)$.

Hence, the result.

Ex-3. The tangents at the extremities of latus rectum of an ellipse intersects on the corresponding directrix.

Sol. Let the end points of a latus rectum are

$L(ae, 0)$ & $L'(-ae, 0)$.

Tangent at L is $\frac{xe}{a}+\frac{y}{a}=1$ and tangent at L'is $\frac{xe}{a}-\frac{y}{a}=1$

On solving, we get, $x=\frac{a}{e}$ and $y = 0$.

$\Rightarrow x=\frac{a}{e}$ is the equation of directrix to the ellipse $\frac{x^2}{a^2}+\frac{y^2}{b^2}=1$.

Ex-4. The locus of the mid-points of the portion of the tangents to the given ellipse intercepted between the axes is $4r^2 = a^2\sin^2\theta + b^2\cos^2\theta$.

Sol. Equation of any tangent to the ellipse at $P(\theta)$ is AB :

$\frac{x}{a}\cos\theta+\frac{y}{b}\sin\theta = 1$.

Thus $A=(a\sec\theta, 0)$ and $A=(0, b\,\mathrm{cosec}\theta)$

Let (h, k) be the mid point of the tangent AB.

Therefore, $h=\frac{a\sec\theta}{2}$ & $k=\frac{b\,\mathrm{cosec}\theta}{2}$

$\Rightarrow \cos\theta=\frac{a}{2h}$ & $\sin\theta=\frac{b}{2k}$

Now squaring and adding, we get, $\frac{a^2}{4h^2}+\frac{b^2}{4k^2}=1$

$\Rightarrow \frac{a^2}{h^2}+\frac{b^2}{k^2}=4$

Hence the locus of (h, k) is $\Rightarrow \frac{a^2}{x^2}+\frac{b^2}{y^2}=4$

Now, put $x = r\cos\theta$, $y = r\sin\theta$,

we get, $4r^2 = a^2\sin^2\theta+b^2\cos^2\theta$,

Hence, the result.

Ex-5. A tangent to the ellipse $\frac{x^2}{a^2}+\frac{y^2}{b^2}=1$ meets the ellipse $\frac{x^2}{a}+\frac{y^2}{b}=a+b$ in the points P and Q, then the tangents at P and Q are at right angles.

Sol. Given ellipses are $\frac{x^2}{a^2}+\frac{y^2}{b^2}=1$ ...(i)

and $\frac{x^2}{a}+\frac{y^2}{b}=a+b \Rightarrow \frac{x^2}{a(a+b)}+\frac{y^2}{b(a+b)}=1$ ...(ii)

Let R(h, k) be the points of intersection of the tangents to the ellipse (ii) at P and Q. then PQ will be the chord of contact.

Thus its equation will be $\frac{hx}{a(a+b)}+\frac{ky}{b(a+b)}=1$

$\Rightarrow y=-\frac{bh}{ak}x+\frac{b(a+b)}{k}$ ...(iii)

since line (iii) is a tangent to the ellipse (i), so

we have, $\frac{b^2(a+b)^2}{k^2}=a^2\times\frac{b^2}{a^2}\times\frac{h^2}{k^2}+b^2$

$\Rightarrow b^2(a+b)^2 = b^2h^2+b^2k^2$

$$\Rightarrow \quad h^2+k^2=(a+b)^2.$$

Thus the locus of (h, k) is $x^2+y^2=(a+b)^2$.

which is the director circle of the ellipse

$$\frac{x^2}{a}+\frac{y^2}{b}=a+b.$$

Hence , the tangents at P and Q are at right angles.

Ex-6. The product of the perpendiculars drawn from the foci upon any tangent to an ellipse is constant. i.e. b^2.

Sol. Let two foci of an ellipse are

$$S(ae, 0) \ \& \ S'(-ae, 0).$$

Equation of tangent to the ellipse $\frac{x^2}{a^2}+\frac{y^2}{b^2}=1$ at $P(\theta)$ is

$$\frac{x}{a}\cos\theta+\frac{y}{b}\sin\theta=1.$$

Let p_1 & p_2 be the lengths of perpendicular from the given foci to the given ellipse.

$$\text{Thus, } p_1=\left|\frac{1-e\cos\theta}{\sqrt{\frac{\cos^2\theta}{a^2}+\frac{\sin^2\theta}{b^2}}}\right|$$

$$\text{and} \quad p_2=\left|\frac{1+e\cos\theta}{\sqrt{\frac{\cos^2\theta}{a^2}+\frac{\sin^2\theta}{b^2}}}\right|$$

$$\Rightarrow \quad p_1\times p_2=\left|\frac{1-e\cos\theta}{\sqrt{\frac{\cos^2\theta}{a^2}+\frac{\sin^2\theta}{b^2}}}\right|\left|\frac{1+e\cos\theta}{\sqrt{\frac{\cos^2\theta}{a^2}+\frac{\sin^2\theta}{b^2}}}\right|$$

$$=\left(\frac{1-e^2\cos^2\theta}{\frac{\cos^2\theta}{a^2}+\frac{\sin^2\theta}{b^2}}\right)$$

$$\Rightarrow \quad p_1\times p_2=\left(\frac{a^2b^2\left(1-e^2\cos^2\theta\right)}{b^2\cos^2\theta+a^2\sin^2\theta}\right)$$

$$=\left(\frac{a^2b^2\left(1-e^2\cos^2\theta\right)}{a^2\left(1-e^2\right)\cos^2\theta+a^2\sin^2\theta}\right)=b^2.$$

Ex-8. If an ellipse slides between two perpendicular straight lines, then the locus of its centre is a circle.

Sol. Consider P is the point of intersection of two perpendicular tangents.

Thus the locus of P is the director circle. Therefore the equation of a director circle is $x^2+y^2=a^2+b^2$. This means that the centre of the ellipse will always remain at a constant distance $\sqrt{a^2+b^2}$ from P.

Hence, the locus of the centre is a circle.

Ex-9. The locus of the feet of perpendiculars from foci upon any tangent to an ellipse is an auxiliary circle.

Sol. Equation of any tangent to the ellipse $\frac{x^2}{a^2}+\frac{y^2}{b^2}=1$

at $P(\theta)$ is $\frac{x}{a}\cos\theta+\frac{y}{b}\sin\theta=1$ ...(i)

Equation of perpendiculars from foci $(\pm ae, 0)$ to tangent

is $\frac{x}{b}\sin\theta-\frac{y}{a}\cos\theta=\pm\frac{ae\sin\theta}{b}$ ...(ii)

Locus of the feet of perpendiculars is the point of intersection of (i) and (ii).

It is obtained by eliminating 'θ' between (i) and (ii).

Squaring (i) and (ii) and adding, we get,

$$x^2\left(\frac{\cos^2\theta}{a^2}+\frac{\sin^2\theta}{b^2}\right)+y^2\left(\frac{\cos^2\theta}{a^2}+\frac{\sin^2\theta}{b^2}\right)=1+\frac{a^2e^2\sin^2\theta}{b^2}$$

$$\Rightarrow \quad \left(x^2+y^2\right)\left(\frac{\cos^2\theta}{a^2}+\frac{\sin^2\theta}{b^2}\right)=a^2\left(\frac{\cos^2\theta}{a^2}+\frac{\sin^2\theta}{b^2}\right)$$

$$\Rightarrow \quad \left(x^2+y^2\right)=a^2.$$

Hence , the result.

Ex-10. If p is the length of perpendicular from the focus S of the ellipse $\frac{x^2}{a^2}+\frac{y^2}{b^2}=1$ on the tangent at P,

then $\frac{b^2}{p^2}=\frac{2a}{SP}-1$.

Sol. Tangent at $P(\theta)$ is $\frac{x}{a}\cos\theta+\frac{y}{b}\sin\theta=1$.

Also SP = a - e x = $a(1-e\cos\theta)$.

p is the length of perpendicular from the focus S(ae, 0)

$$\text{Then, } p=\frac{e\cos\theta-1}{\sqrt{\left(\frac{\cos^2\theta}{a^2}+\frac{\sin^2\theta}{b^2}\right)}}$$

$$\Rightarrow \quad \frac{1}{p^2}=\frac{\left(b^2\cos^2\theta+a^2\sin^2\theta\right)}{a^2b^2\left(e\cos\theta-1\right)^2}$$

$$\Rightarrow \frac{b^2}{p^2} = \frac{\left(b^2\cos^2\theta + a^2\sin^2\theta\right)}{a^2(e\cos\theta-1)^2}$$

$$= \left[\frac{a^2\left(1-e^2\right)\cos^2\theta + a^2\sin^2\theta}{a^2(e\cos\theta-1)^2}\right]$$

$$\Rightarrow \frac{b^2}{p^2} = \left[\frac{\left(1-e^2\right)\cos^2\theta+\sin^2\theta}{(e\cos\theta-1)^2}\right] = \left[\frac{\left(1-e^2\cos^2\theta\right)}{(e\cos\theta-1)^2}\right]$$

$$\Rightarrow \frac{b^2}{p^2} = \left[\frac{1+e\cos\theta}{1-e\cos\theta}\right]$$

Also, $\frac{2a}{SP} - 1 = \frac{2a}{a(1-e\cos\theta)} - 1 = \frac{1+e\cos\theta}{1-e\cos\theta}$

Hence, $\frac{b^2}{p^2} = \frac{2a}{SP} - 1$.

Ex-11. If p be the perpendicular from the centre of an ellipse upon the tangent at any point P on it and r be the distance of P from the centre , then $\frac{a^2b^2}{p^2} = a^2+b^2-r^2$.

Sol. Let the point P be $(a\cos\theta, b\sin\theta)$

Eqution of tangent at P be $\frac{x}{a}\cos\theta + \frac{y}{b}\sin\theta = 1$

Now, $p = \left|\frac{0+0-1}{\sqrt{\frac{\cos^2\theta}{a^2}+\frac{\sin^2\theta}{b^2}}}\right|$

$$\Rightarrow \frac{1}{p^2} = \frac{\cos^2\theta}{a^2} + \frac{\sin^2\theta}{b^2}$$

$$\Rightarrow \frac{1}{p^2} = \frac{a^2\sin^2\theta + b^2\cos^2\theta}{a^2b^2}$$

$$\Rightarrow \frac{a^2b^2}{p^2} = a^2\sin^2\theta + b^2\cos^2\theta$$

$$\Rightarrow \frac{a^2b^2}{p^2} = a^2\left(1-\cos^2\theta\right) + b^2\left(1-\sin^2\theta\right)$$

$$= a^2+b^2-\left(a^2\cos^2\theta+b^2\sin^2\theta\right) = a^2+b^2-r^2.$$

Hence , the result.

Ex-12. The locus of the mid - points of the portion of the tangents to the ellipse $\frac{x^2}{a^2}+\frac{y^2}{b^2}=1$ intercepted between the axes is $\frac{a^2}{x^2}+\frac{b^2}{y^2}=4$.

Sol. Any tangent to the ellipse $\frac{x}{a}\cos\theta + \frac{y}{b}\sin\theta = 1$.

Let it meets the x-axis at A and y-axis at B. Then the co-ordinates of A and B are

$A = \left(\frac{a}{\cos\theta}, 0\right)$ & $B = \left(0, \frac{b}{\sin\theta}\right)$.

Let M(h, k) be the mid-point of AB.

Then $2h = \frac{a}{\cos\theta}$ & $2k = \frac{b}{\sin\theta}$

$\Rightarrow h = \frac{a}{2\cos\theta}$ & $k = \frac{b}{2\sin\theta}$

$\Rightarrow \cos\theta = \frac{a}{2h}$ & $\sin\theta = \frac{b}{2k}$

Squaring and adding, we get, $\frac{a^2}{4h^2}+\frac{b^2}{4k^2}=1$

$$\Rightarrow \frac{a^2}{h^2}+\frac{b^2}{k^2}=4$$

Hence , the locus of M(h, k) is $\frac{a^2}{x^2}+\frac{b^2}{y^2}=4$.

Ex-13. The portion of the tangent to the ellipse intercepted between the curve and the directrix subtends a right angle at the corresponding focus.

Sol. Tangent at $P(a\cos\theta, b\sin\theta)$ is

$$\frac{x}{a}\cos\theta + \frac{y}{b}\sin\theta = 1.$$

Let it meets the directrix $x = \frac{a}{e}$ at Q, where Q is

$$\left(\frac{a}{e}, \frac{b(e-\cos\theta)}{e\sin\theta}\right).$$

Slope of SP = $m_1 = \frac{b(e-\cos\theta)}{e\sin\theta}$

Slope of SQ

$$= m_2 = \frac{b(e-\cos\theta)}{e\sin\theta} / \left(\frac{a}{e} - ae\right) = \frac{b(e-\cos\theta)}{a\left(1-e^2\right)\sin\theta}$$

Thus $m_1 \times m_2 = \frac{b\sin\theta}{a(\cos\theta - e)} \times \frac{b(e-\cos\theta)}{a\left(1-e^2\right)\sin\theta}$

$$= -\frac{b^2}{a^2\left(1-e^2\right)} = -\frac{b^2}{b^2} = -1$$

$$m_1 \times m_2 = \frac{b\sin\theta}{a(\cos\theta - e)} \times \frac{b(e-\cos\theta)}{a\left(1-e^2\right)\sin\theta}$$

$$= -\frac{b^2}{a^2\left(1-e^2\right)} = -\frac{b^2}{b^2} = -1.$$

Hence, the result.

Ex-14. In an ellipse , the perpendicular from a focus upon any tangent and the line joining the centre of the ellipse to the point of contact meet on the corresponding directrix.

Sol. Any tangent to the ellipse is

$$\frac{x}{a}\cos\theta+\frac{y}{b}\sin\theta=1 \quad ...(i)$$

Its point of contact is $P(a\cos\theta, b\sin\theta)$ and its slope is

$$-\frac{b}{a}\cot\theta$$

Also the focus is S(ae, 0)

Any line through the focus S and perpendicular to tangent (i) is $y-0=\frac{a}{b}\tan\theta(x-ae)$ ...(ii)

Also equation of CP is $y-0=\frac{a}{b}\tan\theta(x-0)$ ...(iii)

Eliminating 'θ' between (ii) and (iii), we get,

$$\left(\frac{a^2}{b^2}\right)\left(\frac{x-ae}{x}\right)=1$$

$$\Rightarrow \left(\frac{x-ae}{x}\right)=\left(\frac{b^2}{a^2}\right)$$

$$\Rightarrow \left(1-\frac{ae}{x}\right)=\left(\frac{b^2}{a^2}\right)$$

$$\Rightarrow \left(1-\frac{b^2}{a^2}\right)=\left(\frac{ae}{x}\right)$$

$$\Rightarrow \left(1-\frac{a^2(1-e^2)}{a^2}\right)=\left(\frac{ae}{x}\right)$$

$$\Rightarrow e^2=\left(\frac{ae}{x}\right) \Rightarrow x=\frac{a}{e}$$

Hence, the result.

Ex-15. The co-rdinates of theose points on the ellipse $\frac{x^2}{a^2}+\frac{y^2}{b^2}=1$ tangents at which make equal angles with the axes is $\left(\pm\frac{a^2}{\sqrt{a^2+b^2}}, \pm\frac{b^2}{\sqrt{a^2+b^2}}\right)$

Sol. Consider any point on the ellipse is $P(a\cos\theta, b\sin\theta)$.

Equation of tangent at P is $\frac{x}{a}\cos\theta+\frac{y}{b}\sin\theta=1$.

Since the tangent makes equal angles with the axes, so its slope is ±1

Thus, $-\frac{b\cos\theta}{a\sin\theta}=\pm1$

$$\Rightarrow \frac{b^2\cos^2\theta}{a^2\sin^2\theta}=1$$

$$\Rightarrow \frac{\sin^2\theta}{a^2}=\frac{\cos^2\theta}{b^2}=\frac{1}{a^2+b^2}$$

$$\Rightarrow \sin^2\theta=\frac{a^2}{a^2+b^2} \;\&\; \cos^2\theta=\frac{b^2}{a^2+b^2}$$

Hence the point P is $\left(\pm\frac{a^2}{\sqrt{a^2+b^2}}, \pm\frac{b^2}{\sqrt{a^2+b^2}}\right)$.

DIRECTOR CIRCLE:

The locus of the point of intersection of two perpendicular tangents to an ellipse is known as director circle.

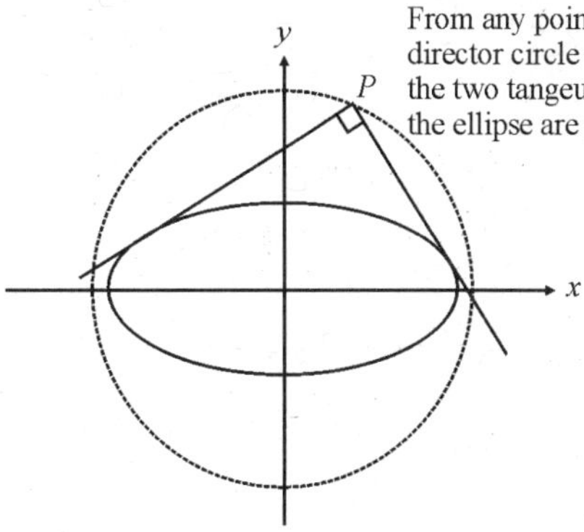

Equation of director circle to an ellipse $\frac{x^2}{a^2}+\frac{y^2}{b^2}=1$ is $x^2+y^2=a^2+b^2$.

Ex-1. Find the locus of the point of intersection of two perpendicular tangents to the ellipse

$$\frac{x^2}{16}+\frac{y^2}{9}=1.$$

Sol. As we know that , the locus of the point of intersection of two perpendicular tangents is the director circle.

Hence, the equation of the director circle to the given ellipse is $x^2+y^2=a^2+b^2=16+9=25$

$$\Rightarrow x^2+y^2=25$$

Ex.2. Tangents are drawn from any point P. on the parabola $(y-2)^2=4(x-1)$ to the ellipse $\frac{x^2}{4}+\frac{y^2}{1}=1$, which are mutually perpendicular to each other. Then find the locus of the point P.

Sol. As we know that, the locus of the point of intersection of two perpendicular tangents to an ellipse is the director circle.

Hence, the equation of the director circle is

$$x^2+y^2=a^2+b^2=4+1=5$$

$$\Rightarrow x^2+y^2=5$$

5.10 PAIR OF TANGENTS:

Equation of a pair of tangents from a point (x_1, y_1) to an ellipse $\frac{x^2}{a^2}+\frac{y^2}{b^2}=1$ is

$$\left(\frac{x^2}{a^2}+\frac{y^2}{b^2}-1\right)\left(\frac{x_1^2}{a^2}+\frac{y_1^2}{b^2}-1\right)=\left(\frac{xx_1}{a^2}+\frac{yy_1}{b^2}-1\right)^2.$$

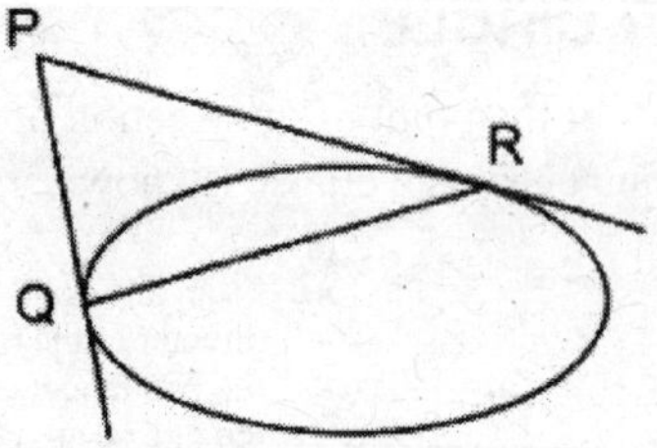

Ex-1. Find the equations of the pair of tangents to the ellipse $2x^2+3y^2=1$ from the point (1, 1).

Sol. Equations of the pair of tangents to the ellipse $2x^2+3y^2=1$ from the point (1, 1) is

$$\left(2x^2+3y^2-1\right)(2+3-1)=(2x+3y-1)^2$$

$$\Rightarrow \quad 4\left(2x^2+3y^2-1\right)=(2x+3y-1)^2$$

$$\Rightarrow \quad 4\left(2x^2+3y^2-1\right)=4x^2+9y^2+1+12xy-4x-6y$$

$$\Rightarrow \quad 4x^2+3y^2-12xy+4x+6y-3=0$$

Ex-2. If tangents are drawn from a point (1, 2) to the ellipse $3x^2+2y^2=5$, then find the angle between the tangents.

Sol. The equation of the given ellipse is $3x^2+2y^2=5$

$$\Rightarrow \quad \frac{x^2}{5/3}+\frac{y^2}{5/2}=1$$

Equation of any tangents to the ellipse are

$$y=mx\pm\sqrt{b^2m^2+a^2}$$

Which is passing through (1, 2), so $2=m\pm\sqrt{\frac{5}{2}m^2+\frac{5}{3}}$

$$\Rightarrow \quad (2\text{-}m)^2=\frac{5}{2}m^2+\frac{5}{3}$$

$$\Rightarrow \quad (2\text{-}m)^2=\frac{15m^2+6}{5}$$

$$\Rightarrow \quad 9m^2+24m-14=0$$

Let it roots are m_1, m_2

Then $m_1+m_2=-24/9$ and $m_1m_2=-14/9$

Let θ be the angle between them.

Then $\tan(?)=\left|\frac{m_2-m_1}{1+m_1m_2}\right|=\left|\frac{\sqrt{(m_1+m_2)^2-4m_1m_2}}{1+m_1m_2}\right|$

$$=\left|\frac{\sqrt{\frac{64}{9}+\frac{56}{9}}}{1-\frac{14}{9}}\right|=\frac{\sqrt{120}}{3}\times\frac{9}{5}=12\times\sqrt{\frac{5}{6}}$$

$$\Rightarrow \quad ?=\tan^{-1}\left(\frac{12\sqrt{6}}{\sqrt{5}}\right).$$

5.11 VARIOUS FORMS OF NORMALS:

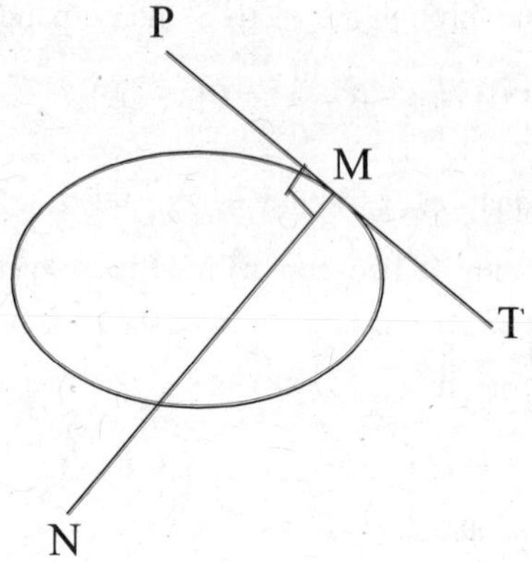

Here, PT be a tangent and MN be a normal.

Angle between the tangent and the normal is 90°.

(i) **Point form**: Equation of normal to the ellipse $\frac{x^2}{a^2}+\frac{y^2}{b^2}=1$ at the point (x_1, y_1) is $\frac{a^2x}{x_1}-\frac{b^2y}{y_1}=a^2-b^2$.

(ii) **Parametric form** : Equation of normal to an ellipse $\frac{x^2}{a^2}+\frac{y^2}{b^2}=1$ at the point $(a\cos\theta, b\sin?)$ is $ax\sec?-by\,\text{cosec}?=a^2-b^2$.

(iii) **Slope form** : Equation of normal in terms of slope is $y=mx\mp\frac{m\left(a^2-b^2\right)}{\sqrt{a^2+b^2m^2}}$.

(iv) The line $y=mx+c$ is a normal to an ellipse $\frac{x^2}{a^2}+\frac{y^2}{b^2}=1$ if $c^2=\frac{m^2\left(a^2-b^2\right)^2}{\left(a^2+b^2m^2\right)}$.

(v) The straight line $lx+my+n=0$ is a normal to an ellipse $\frac{x^2}{a^2}+\frac{y^2}{b^2}=1$ if $\frac{a^2}{l^2}+\frac{b^2}{m^2}=\frac{\left(a^2-b^2\right)^2}{n^2}$.

5.12 SOLVE EXAMPLES:

Ex-1. The normal at an end of a latus rectum of an ellipse $\frac{x^2}{a^2}+\frac{y^2}{b^2}=1$ passes through one extremity of the minor axis, then $e^4+e^2-1=0$.

Sol. Let one end of a latus rectum is $L\left(ae, \frac{b^2}{a}\right)$ and minor axis be $B(0, -b)$.

Equation of normal to the ellipse at L is

$$\frac{a}{e}x - ay = a^2 - b^2$$

Which is passing through B' (0, - b), so we have,

$$ab = a^2 - b^2$$

$$\Rightarrow ab = a^2 - a^2(1-e^2) = a^2e^2$$

$$\Rightarrow b = ae^2$$

$$\Rightarrow b^2 = a^2e^4$$

$$\Rightarrow a^2(1-e^2) = a^2e^4$$

$$\Rightarrow e^4 + e^2 - 1 = 0.$$

Hence, the result.

5.13 NUMBER OF NORMALS ARE DRAWN TO AN ELLIPSE FROM A POINT TO ITS PLANE

Equation of normal to the ellipse $\frac{x^2}{a^2}+\frac{y^2}{b^2}=1$ at $P(\theta)$ is

$$a\,x\sec\theta - b\,y\,\text{cosec}\,\theta = a^2 - b^2 \qquad \text{...(i)}$$

Let $Q(\alpha, \beta)$ be any point in the xy - plane.

Equation (i) passing through $Q(\alpha, \beta)$, so we have,

$$a\,a\sec\theta - b\,ß\,\text{cosec}\,\theta = a^2 - b^2$$

$$\Rightarrow a\,a\left(\frac{1+\tan^2\left(\frac{\theta}{2}\right)}{1-\tan^2\left(\frac{\theta}{2}\right)}\right) - bß\left(\frac{1+\tan^2\left(\frac{\theta}{2}\right)}{2\tan\left(\frac{\theta}{2}\right)}\right) = a^2 - b^2$$

$$\Rightarrow 2\,a\,a\left(1+\tan^2\left(\frac{\theta}{2}\right)\right)\tan\left(\frac{\theta}{2}\right) - bß\left(1-\tan^4\left(\frac{\theta}{2}\right)\right) = 2(a^2-b^2)\tan\left(\frac{\theta}{2}\right)\left(1-\tan^2\left(\frac{\theta}{2}\right)\right)$$

$$\Rightarrow 2\,a\,a\left(1+\tan^2\left(\frac{\theta}{2}\right)\right)\tan\left(\frac{\theta}{2}\right) - bß\left(1-\tan^4\left(\frac{\theta}{2}\right)\right) = 2(a^2-b^2)\tan\left(\frac{\theta}{2}\right)\left(1-\tan^2\left(\frac{\theta}{2}\right)\right)$$

$$\Rightarrow bßt^4 + 2(a^2-b^2+aa)t^3 - 2(a^2-b^2-aa)t - bß = 0,$$

where $t = \tan\left(\frac{\theta}{2}\right)$ ...(ii)

The above equation will give 4 values of t, say, t_1, t_2, t_3, t_4, Corresponding these four values of t, we will get 4 points, say, A, B, C, D on the ellipse, the normals to which pass through the point $Q(\alpha, \beta)$.

Hence, in genral 4 normals can be drawn from any point to an ellipse.

(i) Co-normal points : Let P, Q, R, S are four points on the ellipse. If the normals at these points meet at a point, say, M, then these four points are known as co - normal points.

(ii) If a, ß, ?, d be the eccentric angles of the four points on the ellipse such that the normals at these points are concurrent, then a + ß + ? + d = (2n + 1) p, n ∈ I

As we know that, if four normals are concurrent at a point, say, $M(\alpha,\beta)$, then

$$bßt^4 + 2(a^2-b^2+aa)t^3 - 2(a^2-b^2-aa)t - bß = 0,$$

where $t = \tan\left(\frac{\theta}{2}\right)$

Now, $\tan\left(\frac{\alpha}{2}+\frac{\beta}{2}+\frac{\gamma}{2}+\frac{\delta}{2}\right) = \frac{S_1 - S_3}{1 - S_2 + S_4}$

$$= \frac{\frac{-2\left(a\alpha + (a^2-b^2)\right)}{b\beta} + \frac{2\left(ab - (a^2-b^2)\right)}{b\beta}}{1-0-1} = \infty.$$

$$\Rightarrow \cot\left(\frac{\alpha}{2}+\frac{\beta}{2}+\frac{\gamma}{2}+\frac{\delta}{2}\right) = 0$$

$$\Rightarrow \cot\left(\frac{\alpha}{2}+\frac{\beta}{2}+\frac{\gamma}{2}+\frac{\delta}{2}\right) = 0 = \cot\left(\frac{2n+1}{2}\right)\pi$$

$$\Rightarrow \left(\frac{\alpha}{2}+\frac{\beta}{2}+\frac{\gamma}{2}+\frac{\delta}{2}\right) = \left(\frac{2n+1}{2}\right)\pi$$

$$\Rightarrow \alpha+\beta+\gamma+\delta = (2n+1)\pi.$$

Hence, the result.

Ex-2. The tangent and normal at any point of an ellipse bisects the the external and internal angles between the focal distances of the point.

Sol. Let the ellipse be $\frac{x^2}{a^2}+\frac{y^2}{b^2}=1$ and $P(a\cos\theta, b\sin\theta)$ be any point on the ellipse.

Then, $SP = a - ex = a - ae\cos\theta = a(1-e\cos\theta)$

and $S'P = a + ex = a + ae\cos\theta = a(1+e\cos\theta)$.

Equation of normal at P is $ax\sec\theta - by\,\text{cosec}\,\theta = a^2 - b^2$.

Now, $L = \left(\frac{a^2-b^2}{a}\cos\theta, 0\right) = \left(ae^2\cos\theta, 0\right)$

$\Rightarrow \quad OL = ae^2 \cos\theta$

Thus, $S'L = ae + ae^2 \cos\theta = ae(1 + e\cos\theta)$,

$$SL = ae - ae^2 \cos\theta = ae(1 - e\cos\theta)$$

Now, $\dfrac{S'P}{SP} = \dfrac{1+e\cos\theta}{1-e\cos\theta} = \dfrac{S'L}{SL}$

$\Rightarrow$ PL bisects the $\angle S'PS$ internally.

Since $PL \perp PT$, therefore, PT will bisect $\angle S'PS$ externally.

Ex-3. The normal at any point P on the ellipse $\dfrac{x^2}{a^2} + \dfrac{y^2}{b^2} = 1$ meets the major and minor axis at G and G' respectively and CF is perpendicular upon the normal from the centre C of the ellipse, then $PF.PG = b^2$ and $PF.PG' = a^2$.

Sol. Let the ellipse be $\dfrac{x^2}{a^2} + \dfrac{y^2}{b^2} = 1$ and $P(a\cos\theta,\, b\sin\theta)$ be any point on the ellipse.

Equation of normal at P is

$$ax\sec\theta - by\,\text{cosec}\theta = a^2 - b^2 \qquad ...(i)$$

Since line (i) meets the major axis and minor axis at G and G` respectively, then

$$G = \left(\frac{a^2 - b^2}{a}\cos\theta,\, 0\right) \text{ and } E = \left(0,\, -\frac{a^2 - b^2}{a}\sin\theta\right)$$

PF = CQ = length of perpendicular from C(0, 0) on the tangent $\dfrac{x}{a}\cos\theta + \dfrac{y}{b}\sin\theta = 1$ at P.

$$= \frac{ab}{\sqrt{a^2\sin^2\theta + b^2\cos^2\theta}}.$$

Also, $PG = \dfrac{b}{a}\sqrt{b^2\cos^2\theta + a^2\sin^2\theta}$

and $PG' = \dfrac{a}{b}\sqrt{b^2\cos^2\theta + a^2\sin^2\theta}$

Thus, $PF.PG = b^2$ and $PF.PG' = a^2$.

Ex-4. The normal at a point $P(\theta)$ on the ellipse $\dfrac{x^2}{a^2} + \dfrac{y^2}{b^2} = 1$ meets the axes of x and y at M and N respectively, then PM:PN $= a^2 : b^2$.

Sol. Equation of normal to the ellipse at $P(\theta)$ is

$$ax\sec\theta = by\,\text{cosec}\theta = a^2 - b^2$$

Thus the co-ordinates of M and N are

$$\left(0,\, \left(\frac{b^2 - a^2}{b}\right)\sin\theta\right) \text{ and } \left(\left(\frac{a^2 - b^2}{a}\right)\cos\theta,\, 0\right).$$

$$PM = \sqrt{a^2\cos^2\theta + \left(\frac{b^2 - a^2}{b} - b\right)^2 \sin^2\theta}$$

$$= \sqrt{a^2\cos^2\theta + \frac{a^4}{b^2}\sin^2\theta} = a^2\sqrt{\frac{\cos^2\theta}{a^2} + \frac{\sin^2\theta}{b^2}}$$

$$PN = \sqrt{\left(a - \frac{a^2 - b^2}{a}\right)^2 \cos^2\theta + b^2\sin^2\theta}$$

$$= \sqrt{\frac{b^4\cos^2\theta}{a^2} + b^2\sin^2\theta} = b^2\sqrt{\frac{\cos^2\theta}{a^2} + \frac{\sin^2\theta}{b^2}}$$

Thus, $PM : PN = a^2 : b^2$

Hence, the result.

Ex-5. An ordinate PN of an ellipse $\dfrac{x^2}{a^2} + \dfrac{y^2}{b^2} = 1$ meets the auxiliary circle in Q. Then the locus of the point of intersection of the normals at P and Q is the circle

$$x^2 + y^2 = (a+b)^2.$$

Sol. Since the ordinate P meets the circle at Q, then the co-ordinates of P and Q are $(a\cos\theta,\, b\sin\theta)$ and $(a\cos\theta,\, a\sin\theta)$ respectively.

Equation of normal to the ellipse at $P(\theta)$ is

$$ax\sec\theta - by\,\text{cosec}\theta = a^2 - b^2 \qquad ...(i)$$

Equation of normal to the auxiliary circle at

$$Q(a\cos\theta,\, a\sin\theta) \text{ is } y = (\tan\theta)\,x \qquad ...(ii)$$

On solving, we get, $\cos\theta = \dfrac{x}{(a+b)}$ & $\sin\theta = \dfrac{y}{(a+b)}$.

Squaring and adding, we get, $x^2 + y^2 = (a+b)^2$.

Ex-6. The tangent of the angle between CP and the normal at $P(\theta)$ is $\left(\dfrac{a^2 - b^2}{2ab}\right) \times \sin 2\theta$ and its greatest value is $\left(\dfrac{a^2 - b^2}{2ab}\right)$.

Sol. Equation of any normal at $P(\theta)$ is

$$ax\sec\theta - by\,\text{cosec}\theta = a^2 - b^2.$$

Slope of normal $= m_1 = \dfrac{a}{b}\tan\theta$ and slope of

$$\text{CP} = m_2 = \frac{b}{a}\tan\theta.$$

Let ϕ be the angle between CP and the normal at P.

$$\text{Then } \tan\phi = \left(\frac{\frac{a}{b}\tan\theta - \frac{b}{a}\tan\theta}{1 + \tan^2\theta}\right) = \left(\frac{a^2 - b^2}{ab}\right)\frac{\tan\theta}{\sec^2\theta}$$

$$=\left(\frac{a^2-b^2}{2ab}\right)\times\sin 2\theta.$$

Thus, it is maximum when $2\theta=90^\circ \Rightarrow \theta=45^\circ$.

Therefore, the maximum value is $\left(\frac{a^2-b^2}{2ab}\right)$.

Ex-7. In an ellipse, the distance between the centre and any normal does not exceed the difference between the semi axes of the curve.

Sol. Equation of any normal to the ellipse at $P(\theta)$ is

$$ax\sec\theta-by\,\text{cosec}\,\theta=a^2-b^2 \quad ...(i)$$

Let C be the centre of the ellipse .

Then CM = Length of perpendicular from the centre C to the normal is

$$\frac{\left(a^2-b^2\right)}{\sqrt{a^2\sec^2\theta+b^2\,\text{cosec}^2\theta}}$$

$$=\frac{\left(a^2-b^2\right)}{\sqrt{a^2+b^2+a^2\tan^2\theta+b^2\cot^2\theta}}$$

$$<\frac{\left(a^2-b^2\right)}{\sqrt{a^2+b^2+2ab}}=a-b.$$

Ex-8. The tangent and normal at any point P of an ellipse $\frac{x^2}{a^2}+\frac{y^2}{b^2}=1$ cut its major axis in point Q and R respectively. If QR = a , then the eccentric angle of the point P is satisfying the equation

$e^2\cos^2\phi+\cos\phi-1=0$.

Sol. Equation of tangent at P is $\frac{x}{a}\cos\phi+\frac{y}{b}\sin\phi=1 \quad ...(i)$

Equation of normal at P is

$$ax\sec\phi-by\,\text{cosec}\,\phi=a^2-b^2 \quad ...(ii)$$

Then Q = $(a\sec\phi,0)$ and R = $\left(\frac{\left(a^2-b^2\right)\cos\phi}{a},0\right)$.

Therefore, QR = a $\Rightarrow a\sec\phi-\frac{\left(a^2-b^2\right)\cos\phi}{a}=a$

$$\Rightarrow a^2\sin^2\phi+b^2\cos^2\phi=a^2\cos\phi$$

$$\Rightarrow a^2\sin^2\phi+a^2\left(1-e^2\right)\cos^2\phi=a^2\cos\phi$$

$$\Rightarrow a^2\left(\sin^2\phi+\cos^2\phi\right)-a^2e^2\cos^2\phi=a^2\cos\phi$$

$$\Rightarrow a^2-a^2e^2\cos^2\phi=a^2\cos\phi$$

$$\Rightarrow e^2\cos^2\phi+\cos\phi-1=0.$$

Ex-9. If the normals at $P(x_1,y_1)$, $Q(x_2,y_2)$ & $R(x_3,y_3)$ on the ellipse $\frac{x^2}{a^2}+\frac{y^2}{b^2}=1$ are concurrent,

then $\begin{vmatrix}x_1 & y_1 & x_1y_1\\ x_2 & y_2 & x_2y_2\\ x_3 & y_3 & x_3y_3\end{vmatrix}=0$ .and if points

$P(\alpha)$, $Q(\beta)$ & $R(\gamma)$, then $\begin{vmatrix}\sec\alpha & \text{cosec}\,\alpha & 1\\ \sec\beta & \text{cosec}\,\beta & 1\\ \sec\gamma & \text{cosec}\,\gamma & 1\end{vmatrix}=0$.

Sol. Equation of normal to the ellipse $\frac{x^2}{a^2}+\frac{y^2}{b^2}=1$ at $P(x_1,y_1)$, $Q(x_2,y_2)$ & $R(x_3,y_3)$ are

$$\frac{a^2x}{x_1}-\frac{b^2y}{y_1}=a^2-b^2 \quad ...(i)$$

$$\frac{a^2x}{x_2}-\frac{b^2y}{y_2}=a^2-b^2 \quad ...(ii)$$

and $$\frac{a^2x}{x_3}-\frac{b^2y}{y_3}=a^2-b^2 \quad ...(iii)$$

Eliminating 'x' and 'y' from (i), (ii) and (iii),

we get, $$\begin{vmatrix}\frac{a^2}{x_1} & -\frac{b^2}{y_1} & \left(a^2-b^2\right)\\ \frac{a^2}{x_2} & -\frac{b^2}{y_2} & \left(a^2-b^2\right)\\ \frac{a^2}{x_3} & -\frac{b^2}{y_3} & \left(a^2-b^2\right)\end{vmatrix}=0$$

$$\Rightarrow \begin{vmatrix}\frac{1}{x_1} & \frac{1}{y_1} & 1\\ \frac{1}{x_2} & \frac{1}{y_2} & 1\\ \frac{1}{x_3} & \frac{1}{y_3} & 1\end{vmatrix}=0 \Rightarrow \begin{vmatrix}x_1 & y_1 & x_1y_1\\ x_2 & y_2 & x_2y_2\\ x_3 & y_3 & x_3y_3\end{vmatrix}=0$$

Also $$\begin{vmatrix}a\cos\alpha & b\sin\alpha & ab\cos\alpha\sin\alpha\\ a\cos\beta & b\sin\beta & ab\cos\beta\sin\beta\\ a\cos\gamma & b\sin\gamma & ab\cos\gamma\sin\gamma\end{vmatrix}=0$$

$$\Rightarrow \begin{vmatrix}\text{cosec}\,\alpha & \sec\alpha & 1\\ \text{cosec}\,\beta & \sec\beta & 1\\ \text{cosec}\,\gamma & \sec\gamma & 1\end{vmatrix}=0$$

$$\Rightarrow \begin{vmatrix}\sec\alpha & \text{cosec}\,\alpha & 1\\ \sec\beta & \text{cosec}\,\beta & 1\\ \sec\gamma & \text{cosec}\,\gamma & 1\end{vmatrix}=0.$$

Hence the result.

5.14 CHORD OF CONTACT:

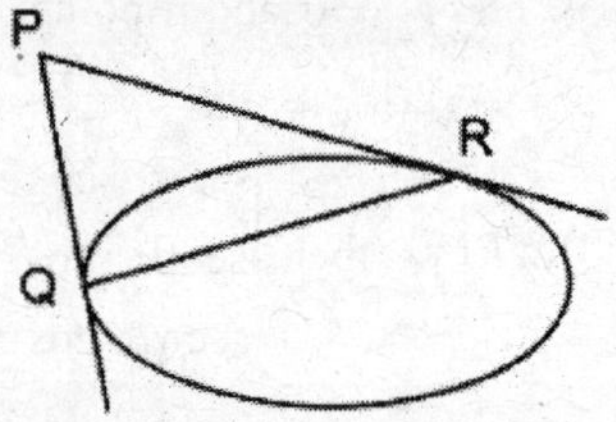

The equation of the chord of contact of tangents drawn from a point (x_1, y_1) to an ellipse

$\frac{x^2}{a^2}+\frac{y^2}{b^2}=1$ is $\frac{xx_1}{a^2}+\frac{yy_1}{b^2}=1$.

Ex-1. The locus of the point , the chord of contact of tangents from which to the ellipse $\frac{x^2}{a^2}+\frac{y^2}{b^2}=1$ subtends a right angle at the centre of the ellipse. is $\frac{x^2}{a^4}+\frac{y^2}{b^4}=\frac{1}{a^2}+\frac{1}{b^2}$.

Sol. Let the point from which tangents are drawn be (h, k)
Equation of the chord of contact from the point (h, k) to the given ellipse is $\frac{hx}{a^2}+\frac{ky}{b^2}=1$.
It subtends a right angle at the centre (0, 0) of the ellipse

$$\frac{x^2}{a^2}+\frac{y^2}{b^2}=1 \qquad ...(ii)$$

From (i) and (ii) , we get, $\frac{x^2}{a^2}+\frac{y^2}{b^2}=\left(\frac{xh}{a^2}+\frac{yk}{b^2}\right)^2$

$$\Rightarrow \left(\frac{1}{a^2}-\frac{h^2}{a^4}\right)x^2+\left(\frac{1}{b^2}-\frac{k^2}{b^4}\right)y^2-\frac{2hxky}{a^2b^2}=0$$

Since these lines are at right angles ,
therefore, sum of the co-efficient of x^2 and y^2 is zero.

$$\Rightarrow \left(\frac{1}{a^2}-\frac{h^2}{a^4}\right)+\left(\frac{1}{b^2}-\frac{k^2}{b^4}\right)=0$$

$$\Rightarrow \left(\frac{h^2}{a^4}+\frac{k^2}{b^4}\right)=\frac{1}{a^2}+\frac{1}{b^2}$$

Hence , the locus of (h, k) is $\left(\frac{x^2}{a^4}+\frac{y^2}{b^4}\right)=\frac{1}{a^2}+\frac{1}{b^2}$.

Ex-2. The locus of the point, from which the chord of contact of tangents are to be drawn to the ellipse touches the circle $x^2+y^2=a^2$ is $\frac{x^2}{a^4}+\frac{y^2}{b^4}=\frac{1}{c^2}$.

Sol. Let the point from which tangents are drawn be (h, k)
Equation of the chord of contact from the point (h, k) to the given ellipse is $\frac{hx}{a^2}+\frac{ky}{b^2}=1 \qquad ...(i)$

It touches the circle $x^2+y^2=c^2$.

Therefore, the length of perpendicular from the centre (0,0) to the chord of contact (i) is equal to the radius of the circle.

Thus, $\left|\frac{0+0-1}{\sqrt{\frac{h^2}{a^4}+\frac{k^2}{b^4}}}\right|=c \quad \Rightarrow \quad \frac{h^2}{a^4}+\frac{k^2}{b^4}=\frac{1}{c^2}$

Hence, the locus of (h, k) is $\frac{x^2}{a^4}+\frac{y^2}{b^4}=\frac{1}{c^2}$.

Ex-3. Perpendicular tangents are drawn to the ellipse $\frac{x^2}{a^2}+\frac{y^2}{b^2}=1$. Then the locus of the mid-point of the chord of contact is $\left(\frac{x^2}{a^2}+\frac{y^2}{b^2}\right)^2=\left(\frac{x^2+y^2}{a^2+b^2}\right)$.

Sol. Let (x_1, y_1) be the point of intersection of the perpendicular tangents, so that (x_1, y_1) lies on the director circle $x_1^2+y_1^2=a^2+b^2 \qquad ...(i)$

Equation of the chord of contact from (x_1, y_1) is

$$\frac{xx_1}{a^2}+\frac{yy_1}{b^2}=1 \qquad ...(ii)$$

Let its mid point be (h, k)
Equation of the chord bisected at (h, k) is

$$\frac{hx}{a^2}+\frac{ky}{b^2}=\frac{h^2}{a^2}+\frac{k^2}{b^2} \qquad ...(iii)$$

From (ii) and (iii) , we get, $\frac{x_1}{h}=\frac{y_1}{k}=\frac{1}{\left(\frac{h^2}{a^2}+\frac{k^2}{b^2}\right)}$

Now from (i), we get ,

$$\left(\frac{h}{\left(\frac{h^2}{a^2}+\frac{k^2}{b^2}\right)}\right)^2+\left(\frac{k}{\left(\frac{h^2}{a^2}+\frac{k^2}{b^2}\right)}\right)^2=\left(a^2+b^2\right)$$

$$\Rightarrow \left(a^2+b^2\right)\left(\frac{h^2}{a^2}+\frac{k^2}{b^2}\right)^2=\left(h^2+k^2\right)$$

Hence, the locus of (h, k) is

$$\left(a^2+b^2\right)\left(\frac{x^2}{a^2}+\frac{y^2}{b^2}\right)^2=\left(x^2+y^2\right).$$

Ex-4: Tangents are drawn from any point on the circle $x^2+y^2=c^2$ to the ellipse $\frac{x^2}{a^2}+\frac{y^2}{b^2}=1$. Then the locus of the mid points of the chord of contact is $\left(\frac{x^2}{c^2}+\frac{y^2}{b^2}\right)^2=\left(\frac{x^2+y^2}{c^2}\right)$.

Sol. Let the point be $(c\cos\theta, c\sin\theta)$

Equation of tangent to the ellipse at $(c\cos\theta, c\sin\theta)$ is

$$\frac{x.c\cos\theta}{a^2}+\frac{y.c\sin\theta}{b^2}=1 \quad ...(i)$$

Let the co-ordinates of the mid - point be (h, k)

Equation of the chord bisected at (h, k) is

$$\frac{hx}{a^2}+\frac{ky}{b^2}=\frac{h^2}{a^2}+\frac{k^2}{b^2} \quad ...(ii)$$

From (i) and (ii), we get, $\frac{h}{c\cos\theta}=\frac{k}{c\sin\theta}=\frac{1}{\frac{h^2}{a^2}+\frac{k^2}{b^2}}$

$$\Rightarrow \quad \cos\theta=\frac{h}{c}\left(\frac{h^2}{a^2}+\frac{k^2}{b^2}\right) \ \& \ \sin\theta=\frac{k}{c}\left(\frac{h^2}{a^2}+\frac{k^2}{b^2}\right)$$

Squaring and adding, we get,

$$\left(\frac{h}{c}\left(\frac{h^2}{a^2}+\frac{k^2}{b^2}\right)\right)^2+\left(\frac{k}{c}\left(\frac{h^2}{a^2}+\frac{k^2}{b^2}\right)\right)^2=1$$

$$\Rightarrow \quad \left(\frac{h^2}{a^2}+\frac{k^2}{b^2}\right)^2=\left(\frac{c^2}{h^2+k^2}\right)$$

Hence, the locus of (h, k) is $\left(\frac{x^2}{a^2}+\frac{y^2}{b^2}\right)^2=\left(\frac{c^2}{x^2+y^2}\right)$

Ex-5: PA and PB are tangents are drawn from a point P to the ellipse $\frac{x^2}{a^2}+\frac{y^2}{b^2}=1$. The area of the triangle formed by the chord of contact AB and axes of co-ordinates is constant. Then the locus of P is a hyperbola.

Sol. Let the co-ordinates of P be (h, k)

Equation of its chord of contact with respect to ellipse $\frac{x^2}{a^2}+\frac{y^2}{b^2}=1$ is $\frac{hx}{a^2}+\frac{ky}{b^2}=1$

It meets the axes in $A\left(\frac{a^2}{h}, 0\right)$ and $B\left(0, \frac{b^2}{k}\right)$.

Area of the triangle OAB

$$=\frac{1}{2}.OA.OB=\frac{1}{2}.\frac{a^2}{h}.\frac{b^2}{k}=\frac{a^2b^2}{2.h.k}=\text{constant}=\frac{\lambda}{2} \text{ (say)}$$

Hence , the locus of (h, k) is $x.y=\frac{a^2b^2}{\lambda}$

Which represents a hyperbola.

5.15 CHORD BISECTED AT A GIVEN POINT

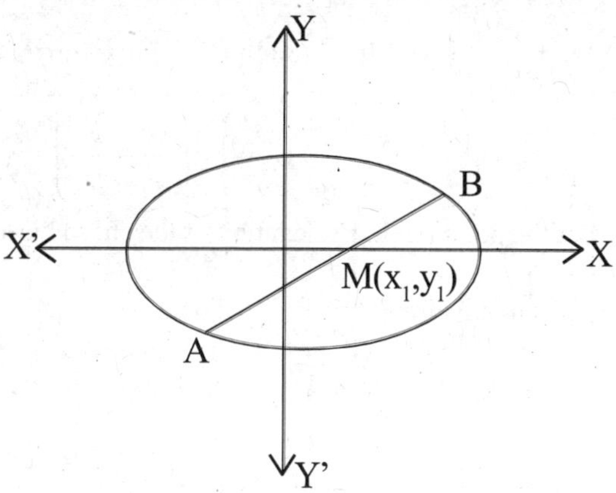

The equation of the chord bisected at a point (x_1, y_1) to an ellipse $\frac{x^2}{a^2}+\frac{y^2}{b^2}=1$ is

$$\frac{xx_1}{a^2}+\frac{yy_1}{b^2}-1=\frac{x_1^2}{a^2}+\frac{y_1^2}{b^2}-1 \text{ . ie. } T=S_1 .$$

Ex-1: The locus of the mid-points of the normal chords of the ellipse $\frac{x^2}{a^2}+\frac{y^2}{b^2}=1$ is

$$\left(\frac{a^6}{x^2}+\frac{b^6}{y^2}\right)\left(\frac{x^2}{a^2}+\frac{y^2}{b^2}\right)^2=\left(a^2-b^2\right)^2$$

Sol. Let The point P be $(a\cos\theta, b\sin\theta)$

Equation of normal at P to the ellipse is

$$a.x.\sec\theta-b.y.\operatorname{cosec}\theta=a^2-b^2 \quad ...(i)$$

Let its mid point be (h, k)

Equation of the chord bisected at (h, k) is

$$\frac{hx}{a^2}+\frac{ky}{b^2}=\frac{h^2}{a^2}+\frac{k^2}{b^2} \quad ...(ii)$$

From (i) and (ii), we get ,

$$\frac{a\sec\theta}{(h/a^2)}=\frac{b\operatorname{cosec}\theta}{(-k/b^2)}=\frac{a^2-b^2}{\left(\frac{h^2}{a^2}+\frac{k^2}{b^2}\right)}$$

$$\Rightarrow \quad \cos\theta=\left(\frac{h^2}{a^2}+\frac{k^2}{b^2}\right)/\left(\frac{h}{a^3\left(a^2-b^2\right)}\right)$$

$$\text{and} \quad \sin\theta=\left(\frac{h^2}{a^2}+\frac{k^2}{b^2}\right)/\left(\frac{-k}{b^3\left(a^2-b^2\right)}\right).$$

Squaring and adding, we get,

$$\left(\frac{a^6}{x^2}+\frac{b^6}{y^2}\right)\left(\frac{x^2}{a^2}+\frac{y^2}{b^2}\right)^2=\left(a^2-b^2\right)^2.$$

Ex-2: The locus of the midpoints of the chords of the ellipse $\frac{x^2}{a^2}+\frac{y^2}{b^2}=1$ which touch the auxiliary circle $x^2+y^2=a^2$ is $a^2\left(\frac{x^2}{a^4}+\frac{y^2}{b^4}\right)=\left(\frac{x^2}{a^2}+\frac{y^2}{b^2}\right)^2$

Sol. Let the point be (h, k) Equation of the chord bisected at (h, k) to the ellipse $\frac{x^2}{a^2}+\frac{y^2}{b^2}=1$ is

$$\frac{hx}{a^2}+\frac{ky}{b^2}=\frac{h^2}{a^2}+\frac{k^2}{b^2} \quad ...(i)$$

Equation of tangent to the auxiliary circle $x^2+y^2=a^2$ at $(a\cos\theta, a\sin\theta)$ is $x\cos\theta+y\sin\theta=a$ ...(ii)

From (i) and (ii), we get,

$$\frac{\cos\theta}{h/a^2}=\frac{\sin\theta}{k/b^2}=\frac{a}{\left(\frac{h^2}{a^2}+\frac{k^2}{b^2}\right)}$$

Squaring and adding, we get,

$$a^2\left(\frac{h^2}{a^4}+\frac{k^2}{b^4}\right)=\left(\frac{h^2}{a^2}+\frac{k^2}{b^2}\right)^2$$

Hence the locus of (h, k) is

$$a^2\left(\frac{x^2}{a^4}+\frac{y^2}{b^4}\right)=\left(\frac{x^2}{a^2}+\frac{y^2}{b^2}\right)^2.$$

Ex-3: The locus of the midpoints of the chords of the ellipse $\frac{x^2}{a^2}+\frac{y^2}{b^2}=1$ which subtend a right angle at the centre of the ellipse is $\left(\frac{x^2}{a^4}+\frac{y^2}{b^4}\right)=\left(\frac{x^2}{a^2}+\frac{y^2}{b^2}\right)^2\left(\frac{1}{a^2}+\frac{1}{b^2}\right)$.

Sol. Let the point be (h, k)

Equation of the chord bisected at (h, k) to the ellipse is

$$\frac{hx}{a^2}+\frac{ky}{b^2}=\frac{h^2}{a^2}+\frac{k^2}{b^2}$$

$$\Rightarrow \left(\frac{\left(\frac{hx}{a^2}+\frac{ky}{b^2}\right)}{\left(\frac{h^2}{a^2}+\frac{k^2}{b^2}\right)}\right)=1$$

Now we make it a homegenous equation of 2nd degree.

$$\text{Thus, } \left(\frac{x^2}{a^2}+\frac{y^2}{b^2}\right)=\left(\frac{\left(\frac{hx}{a^2}+\frac{ky}{b^2}\right)}{\left(\frac{h^2}{a^2}+\frac{k^2}{b^2}\right)}\right)^2$$

$$\Rightarrow \left(\frac{x^2}{a^2}+\frac{y^2}{b^2}\right)\left(\frac{h^2}{a^2}+\frac{k^2}{b^2}\right)^2=\left(\frac{hx}{a^2}+\frac{ky}{b^2}\right)^2$$

$$=\frac{h^2x^2}{a^4}+\frac{k^2y^2}{b^4}+\frac{2hkxy}{a^2b^2}$$

Since the chord subtends a right angle at the centre, so, co-efficient of x^2 + co-oefficient of $y^2=0$

$$\frac{\alpha^2x^2}{a^4}+\frac{\beta^2y^2}{b^4}=\left(\frac{x^2}{a^2}+\frac{y^2}{b^2}\right)^2$$

$$\Rightarrow \left(\frac{h^2}{a^2}+\frac{k^2}{b^2}\right)^2\left(\frac{1}{a^2}+\frac{1}{b^2}\right)=\left(\frac{h^2}{a^4}+\frac{k^2}{b^4}\right)$$

Hence, the locus of (h, k) is

$$\left(\frac{x^2}{a^2}+\frac{y^2}{b^2}\right)^2\left(\frac{1}{a^2}+\frac{1}{b^2}\right)=\left(\frac{x^2}{a^4}+\frac{y^2}{b^4}\right).$$

Ex-4: The eccentric angles of two points P and Q on the ellipse differ by $\pi/2$. Then the locus of the mid-point of PQ is $\frac{x^2}{a^2}+\frac{y^2}{b^2}=2$.

Sol. Let the point P be $(a\cos\theta, b\sin\theta)$ and Q be $\left(a\cos\left(\frac{\pi}{2}+\theta\right), b\sin\left(\frac{\pi}{2}+\theta\right)\right)$ .i.e $(-a\sin\theta, b\cos\theta)$

Let M(h, k) be the mid-point of PQ.

Then, $h=\frac{a}{2}(\cos\theta-\sin\theta)$ and $k=\frac{b}{2}(\cos\theta+\sin\theta)$

$$\Rightarrow \frac{2h}{a}=(\cos\theta-\sin\theta) \ \& \ \frac{2k}{b}=(\cos\theta+\sin\theta)$$

Squaring and adding, we get, $\left(\frac{4h^2}{a^2}+\frac{4k^2}{b^2}\right)=2$

$$\Rightarrow \left(\frac{h^2}{a^2}+\frac{k^2}{b^2}\right)=\frac{1}{2}$$

Hence, the locus of (h, k) is $\left(\frac{x^2}{a^2}+\frac{y^2}{b^2}\right)=\frac{1}{2}$.

Ex-5: The locus of the mid-point of the chord of contact of the perpendicular tangents to the ellipse $\frac{x^2}{a^2}+\frac{y^2}{b^2}=1$ is $\left(\frac{x^2}{a^2}+\frac{y^2}{b^2}\right)^2=\left(\frac{x^2+y^2}{a^2+b^2}\right)$.

Sol. Equation of the chord of contact to the tangents at (h, k) is

$$\frac{hx}{a^2}+\frac{ky}{b^2}=1 \quad ...(i)$$

Equation of the chord of the ellipse whose middle point

(α, β) is $\frac{\alpha x}{a^2}+\frac{\beta y}{b^2}=\frac{\alpha^2}{a^2}+\frac{\beta^2}{b^2}$ ...(ii)

Since (i) and (ii) are same, therefore,

$$\frac{h}{\alpha}=\frac{k}{\beta}=\frac{1}{\left(\frac{\alpha^2}{a^2}+\frac{\beta^2}{b^2}\right)}$$

$$\Rightarrow \quad h=\frac{\alpha}{\left(\frac{\alpha^2}{a^2}+\frac{\beta^2}{b^2}\right)} \ \& \ k=\frac{\beta}{\left(\frac{\alpha^2}{a^2}+\frac{\beta^2}{b^2}\right)}.$$

Also, (h, k) lies on the director circle of the given ellipse

$$x^2+y^2=a^2+b^2$$

Thus, $h^2+k^2=a^2+b^2$

$$\Rightarrow \quad \left(\frac{\alpha^2+\beta^2}{a^2+b^2}\right)=\left(\frac{\alpha^2}{a^2}+\frac{\beta^2}{b^2}\right)^2$$

Hence, the locus of (α,β) is $\left(\frac{x^2+y^2}{a^2+b^2}\right)=\left(\frac{x^2}{a^2}+\frac{y^2}{b^2}\right)^2$.

Ex-6. The locus of the mid-points of the focal chords of the ellipse $\left(\frac{x^2}{a^2}+\frac{y^2}{b^2}\right)=1$ is $b^2x^2+a^2y^2=ab^2xe$

Sol. Let the midpoint be (h, k)

Equation of the chord of the ellipse whose middle point

(h, k) is $\frac{hx}{a^2}+\frac{ky}{b^2}=\frac{h^2}{a^2}+\frac{k^2}{b^2}$.

Which is passes through the focus (ae, 0)

Thus, $\frac{hae}{a^2}=\frac{h^2}{a^2}+\frac{k^2}{b^2}$

$$\Rightarrow \quad \frac{he}{a}=\frac{b^2h^2+a^2k^2}{a^2b^2}$$

$$\Rightarrow \quad b^2h^2+a^2k^2=ab^2he$$

Hence, the locus of (h, k) is $b^2x^2+a^2y^2=ab^2xe$

Ex-7. The locus of the mid-points of the chords of the ellipse $\left(\frac{x^2}{a^2}+\frac{y^2}{b^2}\right)=1$ which are tangent to the ellipse

$\frac{x^2}{\alpha^2}+\frac{y^2}{\beta^2}=1$ is $\left(\frac{x^2}{a^2}+\frac{y^2}{b^2}\right)^2=\left(\frac{x^2\alpha^2}{a^4}+\frac{y^2\beta^2}{b^4}\right)$

Sol. Let the point be (h, k)

Equation of the chord of the ellipse whose middle point

(h, k) is $\frac{hx}{a^2}+\frac{ky}{b^2}=\frac{h^2}{a^2}+\frac{k^2}{b^2}$ ....(i)

Equation of tangent to the ellipse $\frac{x^2}{\alpha^2}+\frac{y^2}{\beta^2}=1$ at

$(\alpha\cos\theta, \beta\sin\theta)$ is $\frac{x}{\alpha}\cos\theta+\frac{y}{\beta}\sin\theta=1$

Both equations are identical.

Thus, $\frac{\cos\theta/\alpha}{h/a^2}=\frac{\sin\theta/\beta}{k/b^2}=\frac{1}{\left(\frac{h^2}{a^2}+\frac{k^2}{b^2}\right)}$

Squaring and adding, we get,

$$\frac{\alpha^2h^2}{a^4}+\frac{\beta^2k^2}{b^4}=\left(\frac{h^2}{a^2}+\frac{k^2}{b^2}\right)^2$$

Hence the locus of (h, k) is

$$\frac{\alpha^2x^2}{a^4}+\frac{\beta^2y^2}{b^4}=\left(\frac{x^2}{a^2}+\frac{y^2}{b^2}\right)^2$$

5.16 POLE AND POLAR:

The equation of polar of an ellipse $\frac{x^2}{a^2}+\frac{y^2}{b^2}=1$ from a point (x_1, y_1) is $\frac{xx_1}{a^2}+\frac{yy_1}{b^2}=1$, where (x_1, y_1) is the pole of polar.

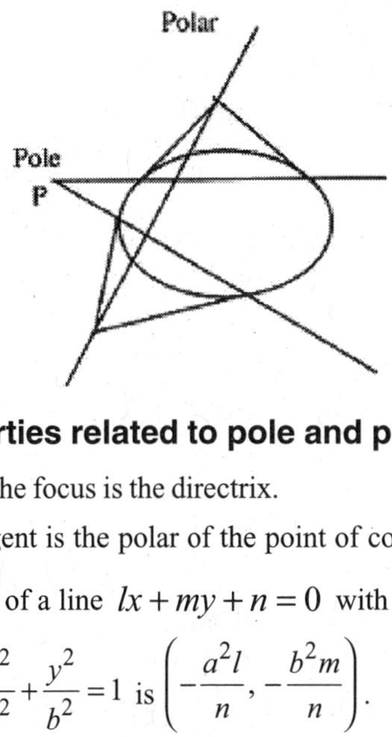

5.17 Properties related to pole and polar

(i) Polar of the focus is the directrix.

(ii) Any tangent is the polar of the point of contact.

(iii) The pole of a line $lx+my+n=0$ with respect to the ellipse $\frac{x^2}{a^2}+\frac{y^2}{b^2}=1$ is $\left(-\frac{a^2l}{n}, -\frac{b^2m}{n}\right)$.

(iv) Pole of a given line is same as point of intersection of tangents at its extremities.

(v) If the polar of $P(x_1, y_1)$ passes through $Q(x_2, y_2)$, then the polar of $Q(x_2, y_2)$ goes through

$P(x_1, y_1)$ and such points are said to be **conjugate points.**

(vi) If the pole of a line $lx + my + n = 0$ lies on the another line $l'x + m'y + n' = 0$, then pole of the second line will lie on the first and such lines are said to be **conjugate lines**.

5.18 DIAMETER:

The locus of the mid points of a system of parallel chords of an ellipse is called a diameter and the point where the diameter intersects the ellipse is called the vertex of the diameter.

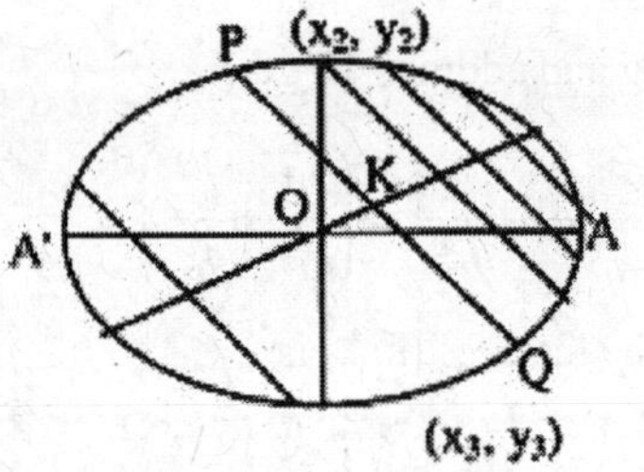

Let (h, k) be the mid point of the chord $y = mx + c$ of the ellipse $\frac{x^2}{a^2} + \frac{y^2}{b^2} = 1$.

Then $T = S_1 \quad \Rightarrow \quad \frac{xh}{a^2} + \frac{yk}{b^2} = \frac{h^2}{a^2} + \frac{k^2}{b^2}$.

$\Rightarrow \quad \text{slope} = m = -\frac{b^2h}{a^2k}$

$\Rightarrow \quad k = -\frac{b^2h}{a^2m}$

Hence, the locus of the mid point is $y = -\frac{b^2x}{a^2m}$.

5.19 CONJUGATE DIAMETERS:

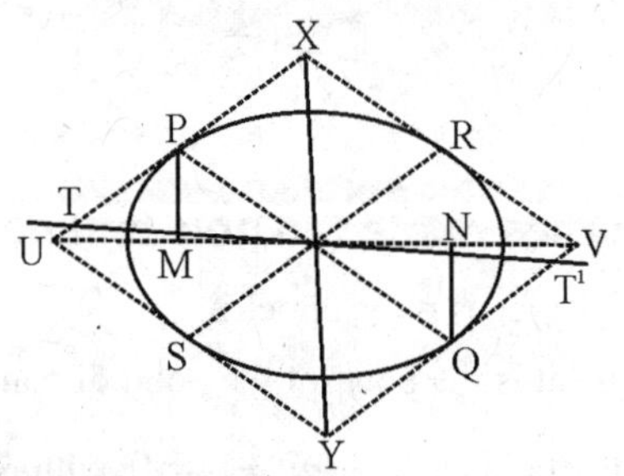

Two diameters are said to be conjugate when each bisects all chords parallel to the other.

If $y = m_1x$ and $y = m_2x$ be two conjugate diameters of an ellipse, then $m_1 m_2 = -\frac{b^2}{a^2}$.

Let PQ and RS be two conjugate diameters.

Then the co-ordinates of the four extremities of two conjugate diameters are

$P(a\cos\phi, b\sin\phi)$, $Q(-a\cos\phi, -b\sin\phi)$,

$R(-a\sin\phi, b\cos\phi)$ and $S(a\sin\phi, -b\cos\phi)$.

5.20 PROPERTIES OF CONJUGATE DIAMETERS

(i) The eccentric angles of the ends of a pair of conjugate diameters of an ellipse differ by a right angle.

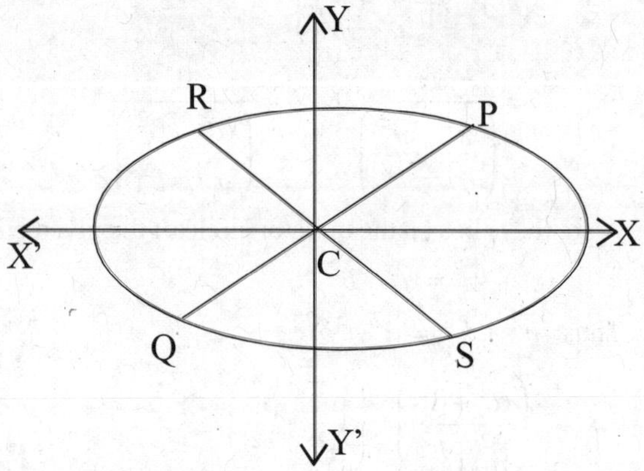

Let PCQ and RCS be two conjugate diameters of an ellipse $\frac{x^2}{a^2} + \frac{y^2}{b^2} = 1$.

Then the co-ordinates $P(a\cos\phi, b\sin\phi)$,
$R(a\cos\phi', b\sin\phi')$

Now, $m_1 = \text{Slope of CP} = \frac{b}{a}\tan f$ and

$m_2 = \text{Slope of CR} = \frac{b}{a}\tan\phi'$

Since the diameters PCQ and RCS are conjugate diameters,

then $m_1.m_2 = -\frac{b^2}{a^2}$

$\Rightarrow \quad \frac{b^2}{a^2}\tan\phi\tan\phi' = -\frac{b^2}{a^2}$

$\Rightarrow \quad \tan\phi\tan\phi' = -1$

$\Rightarrow \quad \tan\phi = -\cot\phi' = \tan\left(\frac{\pi}{2} + \phi'\right)$

$\Rightarrow \quad \phi = \frac{\pi}{2} + \phi'$

$\Rightarrow \quad \phi - \phi' = \frac{\pi}{2}$

Hence, the result.

(ii) The sum of the squares of any two conjugate semi diameters of an ellipse is constant and equal to the sum

of the squares of the semi axes of the ellipse.

i.e. $CP^2 + CD^2 = a^2 + b^2$.

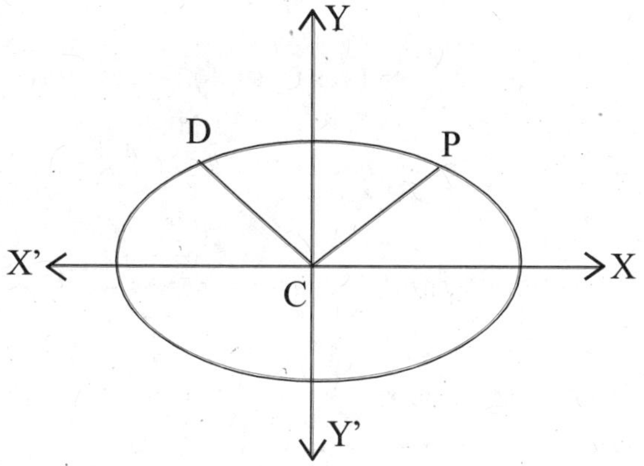

Let CP and CR be two conjugate semi diameters of an ellipse $\frac{x^2}{a^2}+\frac{y^2}{b^2}=1$. and let the eccentric angle of P is ϕ.

Thus the eccentric angle of R is $\frac{\pi}{2}+\phi$.

Therefore the co-ordinates of P and R are

$$(a\cos\phi,\ b\sin\phi) \text{ and } \left(a\cos\left(\frac{\pi}{2}+\phi\right),\ b\sin\left(\frac{\pi}{2}+\phi\right)\right)$$

i.e $(-a\sin\phi,\ b\cos\phi)$.

$$CP^2 + CR^2 = \left(a^2\cos^2\phi + b^2\sin^2\phi\right)$$

$$+\left(a^2\sin^2\phi + b^2\cos^2\phi\right) = a^2 + b^2.$$

(iii) The product of the focal distances of a point on an ellipse is equal to the square of the semi diameter, which is conjugate to the diameter through the point.

Let CP and CR be the conjugate diameters of the ellipse.

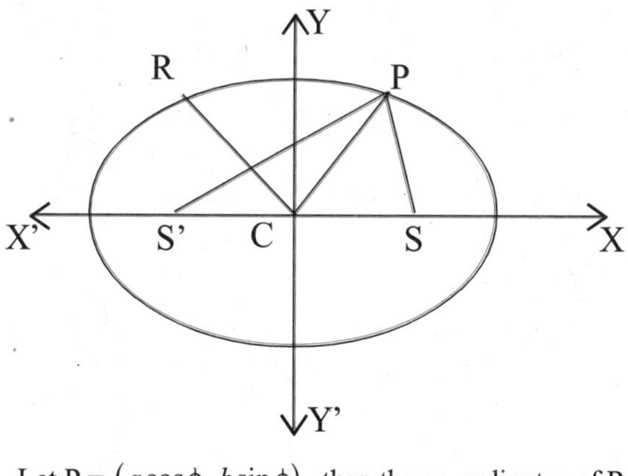

Let P = $(a\cos\phi,\ b\sin\phi)$. then the co-ordinates of R is $(-a\sin\phi,\ b\cos\phi)$.

Thus, $SP.S'P = (a - ae\cos\phi).(a + ae\cos\phi)$

$$= a^2 - a^2e^2\cos^2\phi$$

$$= a^2 - \left(a^2 - b^2\right)\cos^2\phi$$

$$= a^2\sin^2\phi + b^2\cos^2\phi$$

$= CP^2$

(iv) The tangent at the extremities of a pair of conjugate diameters form a parallelogram whosearea is constant and equal to the product of the axes.

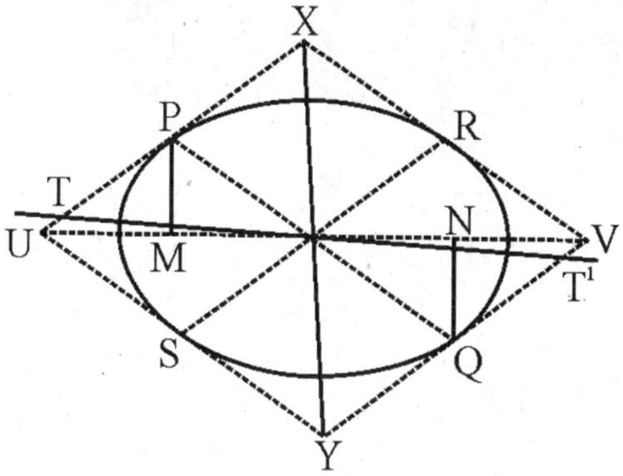

Let PCQ and RCS be two conjugate diameters of the ellipse $\frac{x^2}{a^2}+\frac{y^2}{b^2}=1$.

Then the co-ordinates of P, Q, R, and S are $P(a\cos\phi,\ b\sin\phi)$, $Q(-a\cos\phi,\ -b\sin\phi)$, $R(-a\sin\phi,\ b\cos\phi)$ and $S(a\sin\phi,\ -b\cos\phi)$ respectively.

Equations of tangents at P, R, Q and S are

$$\frac{x}{a}\cos\phi+\frac{y}{b}\sin\phi=1,\quad -\frac{x}{a}\sin\phi+\frac{y}{b}\cos\phi=1$$

$$-\frac{x}{a}\cos\phi-\frac{y}{b}\sin\phi=1 \text{ and } \frac{x}{a}\sin\phi-\frac{y}{b}\cos\phi=1.$$

Thus, the tangents at P and Q are parallel.

Also the tangent at R and S are are parallel

Hence, the tangents at P, R, Q, S form a parallelogram.

Area of the parallelogram = M N M' N' = 4 (the area of the paralleogram CPMR)

$$= 4\times\sqrt{a^2\cos^2\phi+b^2\sin^2\phi}\times\frac{ab}{\sqrt{a^2\cos^2\phi+b^2\sin^2\phi}}.$$

= 4 a b.

= constant.

Hence, the result.

(v) Equi conjugate diameters :

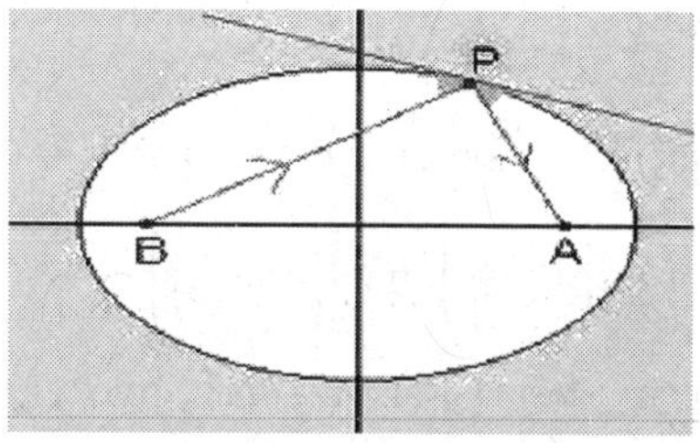

Two conjugate diameters are said to be equi-conjugate diameter if their lengths are equal.

i.e. $CP = CR = \sqrt{\dfrac{a^2+b^2}{2}}$.

Ex-1: Prove that the locus of the poles of the line joining the eccentricities of two conjugate diameters is the ellipse $\dfrac{x^2}{a^2}+\dfrac{y^2}{b^2}=2$.

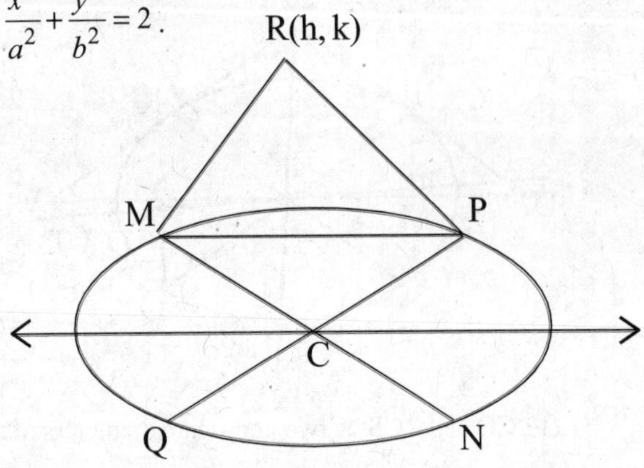

Sol. Let the eccentric angle of P is (ϕ) and the eccentric angle of M is $\left(f+\dfrac{p}{2}\right)$

Then the co-ordinates of P and M are $(a\cos f, b\sin f)$ and $\left(a\cos\left(f+\dfrac{p}{2}\right), b\sin\left(f+\dfrac{p}{2}\right)\right)$

i.e $(a\cos f, b\sin f)$ and $(-a\sin f, b\cos f)$

Equation of tangent at P is

$$\frac{x}{a}\cos f+\frac{y}{b}\sin f=1 \qquad \text{...(i)}$$

and the equation of tangent at M is

$$\frac{x}{-a}\sin f+\frac{y}{b}\cos f=1 \qquad \text{...(ii)}$$

Squaring and adding (i) and (ii), we get, $\dfrac{x^2}{a^2}+\dfrac{y^2}{b^2}=2$.

Ex-2. If P and D be the ends of the conjugate diameters of an ellipse, then find the locus of the mid-point of PD.

Sol. Let the equation of the ellipse be $\dfrac{x^2}{a^2}+\dfrac{y^2}{b^2}=1$.

Let the eccentric angle of P is (ϕ) and the eccentric angle of D is $\left(f+\dfrac{p}{2}\right)$

Then the co-ordinates of P and D are $(a\cos f, b\sin f)$ and $\left(a\cos\left(f+\dfrac{p}{2}\right), b\sin\left(f+\dfrac{p}{2}\right)\right)$

i.e $(a\cos f, b\sin f)$ and $(-a\sin f, b\cos f)$

Let M(h, k) be the mid-point of PD.

Then $h=\dfrac{a\cos f - a\sin f}{2}$ & $k=\dfrac{a\cos f + b\sin f}{2}$

$$\Rightarrow \frac{(2h)^2}{a^2}+\frac{(2k)^2}{b^2}=(\cos f-\sin f)^2+(\cos f+\sin f)^2$$

$$\Rightarrow \frac{h^2}{a^2}+\frac{k^2}{b^2}=\frac{1}{2}$$

Hence, the locus of (h, k) is $\dfrac{x^2}{a^2}+\dfrac{y^2}{b^2}=\dfrac{1}{2}$

Ex-3. For the ellipse $\dfrac{x^2}{a^2}+\dfrac{y^2}{b^2}=1$, find the equation of the diameter conjugate to $a x - b y = 0$.

Sol. The equation of the given diameter is $a x - b y = 0$

$$\Rightarrow y=\frac{a}{b}x \qquad \text{...(i)}$$

Thus, $m_1=\dfrac{a}{b}$

Let the diamter conjugate to (i) be $y=m_2 x$

As we know that, two diameters $y=m_1 x$ and $y=m_2 x$ are conjugate, if $m_1.m_2=-\dfrac{b^2}{a^2}$

$$\Rightarrow \frac{a}{b}\times m_2=-\frac{b^2}{a^2}$$

$$\Rightarrow m_2=-\frac{b^3}{a^3}$$

Hence, the required diameters is $y=-\dfrac{b^3}{a^3}x$

$$\Rightarrow a^3y+b^3x=0$$

Ex-4. If the point of intersection of the ellipses $\dfrac{x^2}{a^2}+\dfrac{y^2}{b^2}=1$ and $\dfrac{x^2}{c^2}+\dfrac{y^2}{d^2}=1$ be at the extremities of the conjugate diameters of the former, prove that $\dfrac{a^2}{c^2}+\dfrac{b^2}{d^2}=1$.

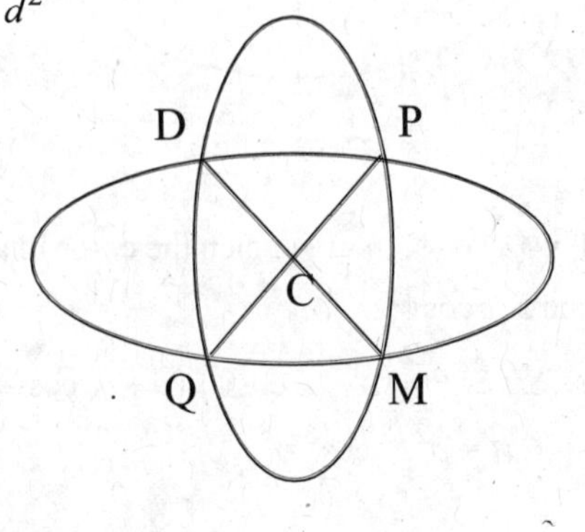

Sol. The given ellipses are $\frac{x^2}{a^2}+\frac{y^2}{b^2}=1$ ...(i)

and $\frac{x^2}{c^2}+\frac{y^2}{d^2}=1\pi$ ...(ii)

Equation of lines passing through the point of intersection of the ellipses are

$$x^2\left(\frac{1}{a^2}-\frac{1}{c^2}\right)+y^2\left(\frac{1}{b^2}-\frac{1}{d^2}\right)=0 \quad ...(iii)$$

Which represents a pair of lines through the origin.

If y = mx be one of the lines , then y = m x must satisfy (iii), then

$$\left(\frac{1}{a^2}-\frac{1}{c^2}\right)+m^2\left(\frac{1}{b^2}-\frac{1}{d^2}\right)=0$$

$$\Rightarrow \quad \left(\frac{1}{b^2}-\frac{1}{d^2}\right)m^2+\left(\frac{1}{a^2}-\frac{1}{c^2}\right)=0$$

which is a quadratic in m. Let it has roots m1 and m2.

$$\text{Then, } m1\,m2=-\frac{\left(\frac{1}{a^2}-\frac{1}{c^2}\right)}{\left(\frac{1}{b^2}-\frac{1}{d^2}\right)}.$$

$$\Rightarrow \quad -\frac{b^2}{a^2}=\frac{\left(\frac{1}{a^2}-\frac{1}{c^2}\right)}{\left(\frac{1}{b^2}-\frac{1}{d^2}\right)}$$

$$\Rightarrow \quad a^2\left(\frac{1}{a^2}-\frac{1}{c^2}\right)=-b^2\left(\frac{1}{b^2}-\frac{1}{d^2}\right)$$

$$\Rightarrow \quad 1-\frac{a^2}{c^2}=-1+\frac{b^2}{d^2}$$

$$\Rightarrow \quad \frac{a^2}{c^2}+\frac{b^2}{d^2}=2.$$

Hence, the result.

Ex-5. If CP and CD are the conjugate diameters of the ellipse $\frac{x^2}{a^2}+\frac{y^2}{b^2}=1$. Prove that the locus of the orthocentre of the ? PCD is

$$2\left(b^2y^2+a^2x^2\right)^2=\left(a^2-b^2\right)^2\left(b^2y^2-a^2x^2\right)^2.$$

Sol. Co-ordinates of P and D are (a cos f , b sin f) and (-a sin f , b cos f) Let PM is the normal at P and DN is the normal at D.

The equations of normal at P and D are

$$a\,x\,\text{sec}f - b\,y\,\text{cosec}f = a^2-b^2$$

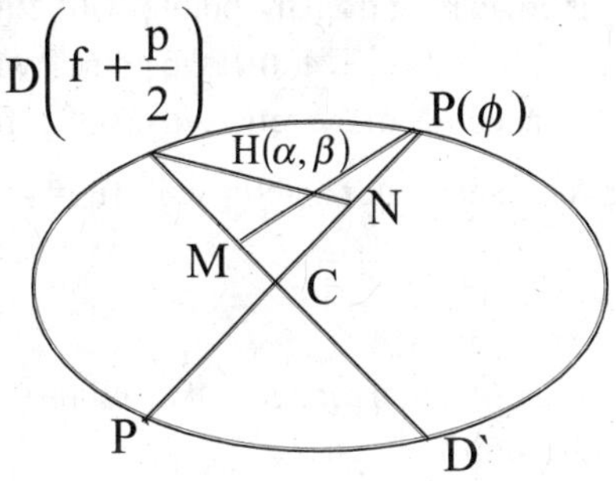

and $\quad -a\,x\,\text{cosec}f - b\,y\,\text{sec}f = a^2-b^2$

Since, H(α,β) is the point of intersection of the normals, so

$$a\,a\;\text{sec}f - bß\,\text{cosec}f - \left(a^2-b^2\right)=0 \quad ...(i)$$

and $\quad a\,a\,\text{cosec}f + bß\,\text{sec}f + \left(a^2-b^2\right)=0 \quad ...(ii)$

Eliminating ϕ from (i) and (ii)

we get, $\frac{\text{sec}f}{(aa-bß)}=\frac{\text{cosec}f}{-(aa+bß)}=\frac{\left(a^2-b^2\right)}{\left(a^2a^2+b^2ß^2\right)}$

$$\Rightarrow \quad \text{cos}f=\frac{\left(a^2a^2+b^2ß^2\right)}{\left(a^2-b^2\right)(aa-bß)}$$

$$\& \ \sin f=\frac{\left(a^2a^2+b^2ß^2\right)}{-\left(a^2-b^2\right)(aa+bß)}$$

Squaring and adding, we get,

$$2\left(a^2a^2+b^2ß^2\right)^3=\left(a^2-b^2\right)\left(a^2a^2-b^2ß^2\right)^2$$

Hence, the locus of H(α,β) is

$$2\left(a^2x^2+b^2y^2\right)^3=\left(a^2-b^2\right)\left(a^2x^2-b^2y^2\right)^2$$

5.20 REFLECTION PROPERTY OF AN ELLIPSE:

If an incoming light ray passes through one focus (S) strike the concave side of the ellipse, then it will get reflected towards other focus.

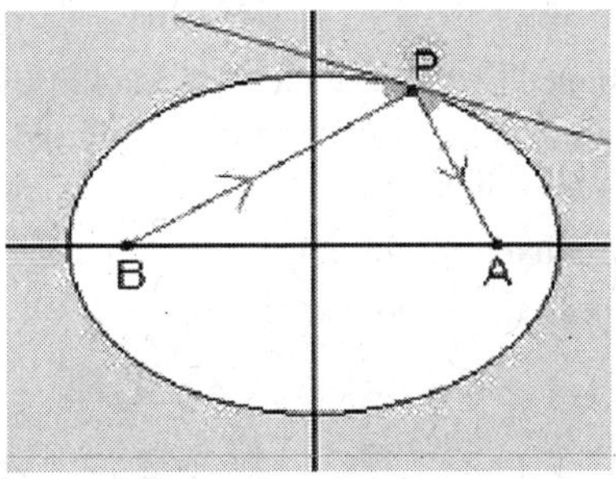

Ex-1. A ray is emanating from the point (-3, 0) is incident on the ellipse $16x^2+25y^2=400$ at the point P with ordinate 4. Find the equation of the reflected ray after first reflection.

Sol. The given equation of an ellipse is $16x^2+25y^2=400$

$$\Rightarrow \quad \frac{x^2}{25}+\frac{y^2}{16}=1$$

From the reflection property of an ellipse, reflection ray pass through thefocus.

Thus, the co-ordinates of the other focus = (3, 0)

When y = 4, then x = 0. So the point is (0, 4).

Equation of the reflection ray is $\frac{x}{3}+\frac{y}{4}=1$

$$\Rightarrow \quad 4x+3y=12.$$

Ex-2. A ray is coming along the line x - y + 2 = 0 on the ellipse $3x^2+4y^2=12$. After stricking the elliptic mirror, it is then reflected. Find the equation of line containg the reflected ray.

Sol. The equation of the incident ray is x - y + 2 = 0

$$\Rightarrow \quad \frac{x}{-2}+\frac{y}{2}=1$$

The equation of the ellipse is $3x^2+4y^2=12$

$$\Rightarrow \quad \frac{x^2}{4}+\frac{y^2}{3}=1$$

Clearly, the co-ordinates of the foci are (-2, 0) and (2, 0)

The incident ray x - y + 2 = 0 intersects the ellipse at (0, 2)

Hence, the equation of the reflection ray = the equation of the line joining (0, 2) and (2, 0)

$$\Rightarrow \quad \frac{x}{2}+\frac{y}{2}=1$$

$$\Rightarrow \quad x+y=2$$

Level – I QUESTIONS BASED ON FUNDAMENTALS

ABC OF ELLIPSE

1. Find the equation of an ellipse whose focus is (-1, 1), eccentricity is 1/2 and the directrix is x – y + 3 = 0.
2. The extremities of a line segment of length '*l*' move in two fixed perpendicular straight lines. Find the locus of that point which divides this line segment in the ratio 1 : 2
3. Show that the equation $(10x-5)^2+(10y-5)^2=(3x+4y-1)^2$ represents an ellipse. Find the eccentricity of an ellipse.
4. Find the centre, vertices, the length of the axes, eccentricity, foci, directrices, latus rectum, end points of latus recta of the ellipse

   (i) $\frac{x^2}{16}+\frac{y^2}{9}=1$

   (ii) $\frac{x^2}{4}+\frac{y^2}{9}=1$

   (iii) $25x^2+16y^2-150x=175$

   (iv) $4x^2+y^2-8x+2y+1=0$

   (v) $4x^2+9y^2-8x-54y+61=0$
5. The distance between the foci of an ellipse is 10 and its latus rectum is 15. Find its equation referred to its axes as axes of co-ordinates.
6. Find the equation of the ellipse whose foci are (2, 3), (-2, 3) and whose semi minor axes is $\sqrt{5}$.
7. If P(x, y), $F_1=(3,0)$, $F_2=(-3,0)$ and $16x^2+25y^2=400$, then find the value of PF_1+PF_2.
8. The eccentricity of an ellipse, with its centre at the origin, is 1/2. If one of the directrices is x = 4, then find the equation of the ellipse.
9. In an ellipse, the distance between its foci is 6 and minor axis is 8. Then find itseccentricity.
10. Find the centre of the ellipse
    $$14x^2-4xy+11y^2-44x-58y+71=0.$$
11. If the equation $\frac{x^2}{10-a}+\frac{y^2}{4-a}=1$ represents an ellipse, then find the value of a.
12. If the angle between the straight lines joining foci and the ends of the minor axis of the ellipse $\frac{x^2}{a^2}+\frac{y^2}{b^2}=1$ is 90°. Find its eccentricity.
13. Find the equation of the ellipse referred to its centre whose minor axis is equal to the distance between the foci and whose latus rectum is 10.
14. If a chord joining two points whose eccentric angles are α, β cut the major axis of an ellipse at a distance d from the centre. Prove that $\tan\left(\frac{\alpha}{2}\right)\tan\left(\frac{\beta}{2}\right)=\left(\frac{d-a}{d+a}\right)$, where 2a is the length of the major axis.
15. Find the eccentric angles of the ends of latus recta of the ellipse $\frac{x^2}{a^2}+\frac{y^2}{b^2}=1$.
16. Find the eccentric angle of a point on the ellipse $\frac{x^2}{5}+\frac{y^2}{4}=1$ at a distance 3 from the center.

17. Prove that the length of the focal chord of the ellipse $\frac{x^2}{a^2}+\frac{y^2}{b^2}=1$ which makes an angle θ with the major axis is $\frac{2ab^2}{a^2\sin^2\theta+b^2\cos^2\theta}$.

18. Find the locus of a variable point P whose co-ordinates are given by $(1+4\cos?, 2+3\sin?)$, where θ is a parameter.

19. Find the area of the greatest rectangle that can be inscribed in the ellipse $\frac{x^2}{a^2}+\frac{y^2}{b^2}=1$.

20. Find the area of the greatest isoceles triangle that can be inscribed in the ellipse $\frac{x^2}{a^2}+\frac{y^2}{b^2}=1$ having its vertex coincident with one extremity of the major axis.

21. Let P be a variable point on the ellipse $\frac{x^2}{25}+\frac{y^2}{16}=1$ with foci S_1 and S_2. If A be the area of the triangle ΔPS_1S_2, then find the maximum value of A.

22. An ellipse has OB as a semi minor axis, F and F' are its foci and the angle FBF' is a right angle. Then find the eccentricity of the ellipse.

23. P is a variable point on the ellipse $\frac{x^2}{a^2}+\frac{y^2}{b^2}=1$, whose foci are the points S1 and S2.
Prove that the locus of the incentre of ΔPS_1S_2 is an ellipse whose eccentricity is $\sqrt{\frac{2e}{1+e}}$

24. If the line $x+2y+4=0$ cutting the ellipse in points whose eccentric angles are 30° and 60° subtends a right angle at the origin, then prove that $\frac{x^2}{16}+\frac{y^2}{4}=1$.

25. Let $P(x_1, y_1)$ and $Q(x_2, y_2)$, $y_1<0, y_2<0$ be the end points of the latus rectum of the ellipse $x^2+4y^2=4$. Find the equations of the parabolas with latus rectum PQ.

26. The ellipse $x^2+4y^2=4$ is inscribed in a rectangle aligned with the co-ordinate axes, which in turn is inscribed in another ellipse that passes through the point (4, 0). Then prove that the equation of the ellipse is $x^2+12y^2=16$.

POSITION OF A POINT WITH RESPECT TO AN ELLIPSE

27. Find the position of a point (4, -3) relative to the ellipse $5x^2+7y^2=140$.

28. find the position of a point (1, 2) w. r. t. an ellipse $9x^2+16y^2=144$.

INTERSECTION OF A LINE AND AN ELLIPSE

29. Prove that the straight line $lx + my + n = 0$ touches the ellipse $\frac{x^2}{a^2}+\frac{y^2}{b^2}=1$ if $a^2l^2+b^2m^2=n^2$.

30. For what value of λ does the line $y=x+\lambda$ touches the ellipse $\frac{x^2}{25}+\frac{y^2}{9}=1$

31. Find the number of values of 'c' such that the straight line $y=4x+c$ touches the curve $\frac{x^2}{4}+y^2=1$.

32. Prove that the length of the chord intercepted by the ellipse $\frac{x^2}{a^2}+\frac{y^2}{b^2}=1$ on the line $y=mx+c$ is $\frac{2ab}{a^2+b^2}\left(\sqrt{1+m^2\left(a^2m^2+b^2-c^2\right)}\right)$.

TANGENTS AND TANGENCY

33. Find the equation of the tangents to the ellipse $\frac{x^2}{4}+\frac{y^2}{3}=1$ which are
    (i) perpendicular to the line $2x+y=4$
    (ii) parallel to the line $x+y=10$.

34. Find the number of tangents are drawn from the point
    (i) (2, 3) to the ellipse $3x^2+4y^2=12$
    (ii) (1, 2) to the ellipse $9x^2+16y^2=144$
    (iii) (2, 1) to the ellipse $2x^2+3y^2=12$

35. Find the equation of the tangents to the ellipse $\frac{x^2}{a^2}+\frac{y^2}{b^2}=1$ which are inclined
    (i) to the axis of x at an angle of 60° and
    (ii) which cut off equal intercepts on the axes.

36. Find the locus of the foot of the perpendicular drawn from centre upon any tangent to the ellipse $\frac{x^2}{a^2}+\frac{y^2}{b^2}=1$.

37. Tangents are drawn to an ellipse $x^2+2y^2=2$. Find the locus of the mid-point of intecept made by the tangents between the axes.

38. An ellipse passes through the point (4, -1) and its axes are along the axes of co-ordinates. If the line $x+4y-10=0$ is a tangent to it, then find its equation.

39. If p be the length of the perpendicular from the focus S of the ellipse $\frac{x^2}{a^2}+\frac{y^2}{b^2}=1$ on any tangent at P , then show that $\frac{b^2}{p^2}=\frac{2a}{SP}-1$.

40. A circle of radius r is concentric with the ellipse . Prove that the common tangent is inclined to the major axis at an angle $\tan^{-1}\sqrt{\left(\frac{r^2-b^2}{a^2-r^2}\right)}$.

41. The tangent at the point $\left(4\cos\phi, \frac{16}{\sqrt{11}}\sin\phi\right)$ to the ellipse $16x^2+11y^2=256$ is also a tangent to the circle $x^2+y^2-2x-15=0$, then find the value of ϕ.

42. Tangents are drawn to the ellipse $\frac{x^2}{9}+\frac{y^2}{5}=1$ at ends of a latus rectum . Find the area of the quadrilateral so formed.

43. Prove that the product of the perpendiculars from the foci of any tangent to an ellipse is equal to the square of the semi minor axis

44. Prove that the locus of the mid points of the portion of the tangents to the ellipse $\frac{x^2}{a^2}+\frac{y^2}{b^2}=1$ intercepted between the axes is $a^2y^2+b^2x^2=4x^2y^2$.

45 Prove that the tangents at the extremities of latus rectum of an ellipse intersect on the corresponding directrix.

46. If P is any point on the ellipse $\frac{x^2}{a^2}+\frac{y^2}{b^2}=1$ whose ordinate is y', then prove that the angle between the tangent at P and the focal distance of P is $\tan^{-1}\left(\frac{b^2}{aey'}\right)$.

47. Find the co-ordinates of those points on the eliipse $\frac{x^2}{a^2}+\frac{y^2}{b^2}=1$, tangents at which make equal angles with axes.

48. Find the number of values of $\theta\in[0, 2\pi]$ for which the line $2x\cos\theta+3y\sin\theta=6$ touches the ellipse $4x^2+9y^2=36$.

49. Prove that the product of the perpendiculars drawn from two foci of an ellipse to the tangent at any point of the ellipse is b^2.

50. Find the equations of the tangents to the ellipse $3x^2+y^2=3$ making equal intercepts on the axes.

51. P and Q are two points on the ellipse $\frac{x^2}{25}+\frac{y^2}{9}=1$ such that sum of their ordinate is 3 . Then prove that the locus of the point of intersection of tangents at at P and Q is $9x^2+25y^2=150y$.

52. Find the equation of the common tangent of

(i) $x^2+y^2=4$ and $2x^2+y^2=2$.

(ii) $x^2+y^2=9$ and $\frac{x^2}{9}+\frac{y^2}{4}=1$.

(iii) $x^2+y^2=4$ and $\frac{x^2}{4}+\frac{y^2}{9}=1$

(iv) $\frac{x^2}{16}+\frac{y^2}{9}=1$ and $\frac{x^2}{9}+\frac{y^2}{4}=1$

(v) $\frac{x^2}{9}+\frac{y^2}{4}=1$ and $\frac{x^2}{2}+\frac{y^2}{1}=1$.

53. Prove that the locus of the feet of the perpendicular drawn from the center upon any tangent to the ellipse is $r^2=a^2\cos^2\theta+b^2\sin^2\theta$.

54. Prove that the locus of the middle points of the portions of tangents included between the axes is the curve $\frac{a^2}{x^2}+\frac{b^2}{y^2}=1$.

55. A tangent to the ellipse $\frac{x^2}{a^2}+\frac{y^2}{b^2}=1$ meets the ellipse $\frac{x^2}{a}+\frac{y^2}{b}=a+b$ in the points P and Q . Prove that the tangents at P and Q are at right angles.

56. Prove that the angle between the tangents to the ellipse $\frac{x^2}{a^2}+\frac{y^2}{b^2}=1$ and the circle $x^2+y^2=ab$ at their points of intersection is $\tan^{-1}\left(\frac{a-b}{\sqrt{ab}}\right)$.

57. Find the locus of the point of intersection of the tangents to the ellipse if the difference of the eccentric angles of the points is $\frac{2\pi}{3}$.

PAIR OF TANGENTS:

58. Find the angle between the pair of tangents drawn from the point (1, 2) to the ellipse $3x^2+2y^2=5$.

59. Find the angle between the pair of tangents drawn to the ellipse $3x^2+2y^2=5$ from the point (1, 2).

60. Find the equation of tangents to the ellipse $9x^2+16y^2=144$ which pass through the point (2, 3).

61. Find the length of the common tangent to the circle $x^2+y^2=16$ and $9x^2+25y^2=225$.

DIRECTOR CIRCLE

62. Prove that the equation of the director circle with respect to an ellipse $\frac{x^2}{a^2}+\frac{y^2}{b^2}=1$ is $x^2+y^2=a^2+b^2$.

63. Find the locus of the point of intersection of two perpendicular tangents to the ellipse $\frac{x^2}{9}+\frac{y^2}{4}=1$.

NORMAL AND NORMALCY

64. Find the equation of the normal to the ellipse $4x^2+9y^2=20$ at $\left(1,\frac{4}{3}\right)$.

65. Find the equation of the normal to the ellipse $5x^2+3y^2=137$ at the point whose ordinate is 2.

66. Find the equation of normal to the ellipse $\frac{x^2}{9}+\frac{y^2}{4}=1$ at the -ve end of latus rectum.

67. Find the equation of the normal to the ellipse $\frac{x^2}{16}+\frac{y^2}{9}=1$ at (α, β).

68. Find the points on the ellipse $\frac{x^2}{4}+\frac{y^2}{9}=1$ for which the normals are parallel to the line 2 x - y = 1.

69. If the normals at $P(x_1, y_1)$, $Q(x_2, y_2)$ and $R(x_3, y_3)$ to the ellipse $\frac{x^2}{a^2}+\frac{y^2}{b^2}=1$ are concurrent, then prove that

$$\begin{vmatrix} x_1 & y_1 & x_1y_1 \\ x_2 & y_2 & x_2y_2 \\ x_3 & y_3 & x_3y_3 \end{vmatrix}=0$$

70. If the normal at an end of a latus rectum of an ellipse $\frac{x^2}{a^2}+\frac{y^2}{b^2}=1$ passes through one extremity of the minor axis, show that the eccentricity of the ellipse is given by $e^4+e^2-1=0$ or $e=\frac{\sqrt{5}-1}{2}$.

71. Prove that the straight line l x + m y + n = 0 is a normal to the ellipse $\frac{x^2}{a^2}+\frac{y^2}{b^2}=1$ if $\frac{a^2}{l^2}+\frac{b^2}{m^2}=\frac{\left(a^2-b^2\right)^2}{n^2}$.

72. If the normal at any point P on the ellipse meets the axes in G and g respectively, then prove that PG : Pg = $b^2 : a^2$.

73. Any ordinate NP of an ellipse meets the auxiliary circle in Q, prove that the locus of the intersection of the normals at P and Q is the circle $x^2+y^2=(a+b)^2$,

74. If the normal at the point $P(\theta)$ to the ellipse $5x^2+14y^2=70$ intersects it again at the point $Q(2\theta)$, then prove that $\cos\theta=-\frac{2}{3}$.

75. If the tangent drawn at point $(\lambda^2, 2\lambda)$ on the parabola $y^2=4x$ is same as the normal drawn at a point $(\sqrt{5}\cos\theta, 2\sin\theta)$ on the ellipse $4x^2+5y^2=20$. Find the values of λ and θ.

76. An ellipse slides between two straight lines at right angles to each other. Show that the locus of its centre is a circle.

77. Let 'e_1' be the eccentricity of an ellipse $\frac{x^2}{a^2}+\frac{y^2}{b^2}=1$, $a>b$. Normal at a variable point P meets the axes at Q and R. If the locus of the mid - point of QR is an ellipse whose eccentricity is e_2, then prove that $e_1 = e_2$.

78. The tangent and normal at any point of an ellipse $\frac{x^2}{a^2}+\frac{y^2}{b^2}=1$ cut its major axis in points P and Q respectively. If PQ = a, prove that the eccentric angle of the point P is given by $e^2\cos^2\phi+\cos\phi-1=0$

CHORD OF CONTACT

79. If chords of contact of tangents from two points (x_1, y_1) and (x_2, y_2) to the ellipse $\frac{x^2}{a^2}+\frac{y^2}{b^2}=1$ are at right angles, then find the value of $\frac{x_1x_2}{y_1y_2}$.

80. Prove that the chord of contact of tangents drawn from the point (h, k) to the ellipse $\frac{x^2}{a^2}+\frac{y^2}{b^2}=1$ will subtend a right angle at the centre, if $\frac{h^2}{a^4}+\frac{k^2}{b^4}=\frac{1}{a^2}+\frac{1}{b^2}$.

81. Tangents are drawn from a point on the ellipse $\frac{x^2}{a^2}+\frac{y^2}{b^2}=1$ to the circle $x^2+y^2=r^2$. Prove that the chord of contacts are tangents to the ellipse is $a^2x^2+b^2y^2=r^4$.

CHORD BISECTED AT A GIVEN POINT

82. Find the locus of the mid points of a focal chord of the ellipse $\frac{x^2}{a^2}+\frac{y^2}{b^2}=1$.

83. Find the locus of the mid points of chords of the ellipse $\frac{x^2}{a^2}+\frac{y^2}{b^2}=1$ (a> b) passing through the point (2a, 0).

84. Prove that the locus of the middle points of normals chords of the ellipse $\frac{x^2}{a^2}+\frac{y^2}{b^2}=1$ is the curve

$$\left(\frac{x^2}{a^2}+\frac{y^2}{b^2}\right)^2\left(\frac{a^6}{x^2}+\frac{b^6}{y^2}\right)=\left(a^2-b^2\right)^2.$$

85. Prove that the locus of the middle points of chords of an ellipse which pass through a fixed point, is another ellipse.

86. If the normal to an ellipse $\frac{x^2}{a^2}+\frac{y^2}{b^2}=1$ at any point P cuts the major axis at Q, find the locus of the middle point of PQ.

87. Find the length of the chord of the ellipse $\frac{x^2}{25}+\frac{y^2}{16}=1$ whose middle point is $\left(\frac{1}{2},\frac{2}{5}\right)$.

POLE AND POLAR

88. Prove that the polar of the focus is the directrix.

89. Find the pole of a given line $lx+my+n=0$ with respect to an ellipse $\frac{x^2}{a^2}+\frac{y^2}{b^2}=1$.

90. Prove that the pole of a given line is same as point of intersection of tangents at its extremities.

91. Find the pole of the straight line $x+4y=4$ with respect to the ellipse $x^2+4y^2=4$.

92. Find the locus of the poles of tangents to $\frac{x^2}{a^2}+\frac{y^2}{b^2}=1$ with respect to the concentric ellipse $c^2x^2+d^2y^2=1$.

93. The perpendicular from the centre of an ellipse $\frac{x^2}{a^2}+\frac{y^2}{b^2}=1$ on the polar of a point with respect to the ellipse is constant and equal to c. Prove that the locus of the point is the ellipse $\frac{x^2}{a^4}+\frac{y^2}{b^4}=\frac{1}{c^2}$.

94. Show that the equation of the locus of the poles of normals chords of the ellipse $\frac{x^2}{a^2}+\frac{y^2}{b^2}=1$ is
$$\left(a^2-b^2\right)^2\times x^2y^2=a^6y^2+b^6x^2.$$

95. If the polar with respect to $y^2=4x$ touches the ellipse $\frac{x^2}{\alpha^2}+\frac{y^2}{\beta^2}=1$, then find the locus of its pole.

DIAMETER/ CONJUGATE DIAMETERS/ EQUI–CONJUGATE DIAMTERS

96. Prove that the equation of the diameter of the ellipse $\frac{x^2}{a^2}+\frac{y^2}{b^2}=1$ is $y=-\frac{b^2x}{a^2m}$

97. Find the co-ordinates of the four extremities of two conjugate diameters of an ellipse $\frac{x^2}{a^2}+\frac{y^2}{b^2}=1$

98. Prove that the sum of the squares of any two conjugate semi diameters of an ellipse is constant and equal to the sum of the squares of the semi axes of the ellipse.
i.e. $CP^2+CD^2=a^2+b^2$.

99. Prove that the product of the focal distances of a point on an ellipse is equal to the square of the semi diameter, which is conjugate to the diameter through the point.
i.e. $SP.S'P=CD^2$.

100. Prove that the tangents at the extremities of a pair of conjugate diameters form a parallelogram whose area is constant and equal to the product of the axes.

101. Show that the tangents at the ends of conjugate diameters of the ellipse $\frac{x^2}{a^2}+\frac{y^2}{b^2}=1$ intersect on the ellipse $\frac{x^2}{a^2}+\frac{y^2}{b^2}=2$.

102. Find the eccentricity of the ellipse if $y=x$ and $2x+3y=0$ are the equations of a pair of its conjugate diameters.

REFLECTION PROPERTY OF AN ELLIPSE

103. A ray emanating from the point (-3, 0) is incident on the ellipse $16x^2+25y^2=400$ at the point P with ordinate 4. Find the equation of the reflected ray after first reflection.

104. A ray emanating from the point $\left(0,-\sqrt{5}\right)$ is incident on the ellipse $9x^2+4y^2=36$ at the point P with abscissa 2. Find the equation of the reflected ray after first reflection.

105. A ray is coming along the line $x-y+2=0$ on the ellipse $3x^2+4y^2=12$. After striking the elliptic mirror, it is then reflected. Find the equation of line containg the reflected ray.

ANSWER

1. $7x^2+7y^2+2xy+10x-10y+7=0$
2. $9x^2+36y^2=4l^2$
3. 1/4
4. (i) Centre : (0, 0) ; Vertices : (4, 0), (-4, 0); Length of the axes : 8, 6
Eccentricity $=e=\frac{\sqrt{7}}{4}$, Foci : $\left(\pm\sqrt{7},0\right)$;

Directrices : $x = \pm \dfrac{16}{\sqrt{7}}$; Latus rectum : $\dfrac{9}{2}$

End points of latus recta : $\left(\sqrt{7}, \pm \dfrac{9}{4}\right)$.

(ii) Centre : (0, 0) ; Vertices : (0, 3) , (0, -3); Length of the axes : 6, 4

Eccentricity = e = $\dfrac{\sqrt{5}}{3}$, Foci: $(\pm \sqrt{5}, 0)$; Directrices : $y = \pm \dfrac{9}{\sqrt{5}}$; Latus rectum : $\dfrac{8}{3}$

End points of latus recta : $\left(\pm \dfrac{4}{3}, \sqrt{5}\right)$.

(iii) Centre : (3, 0) ; Vertices : (3, 5) , (3, -5); Length of the axes : 8, 6

Eccentricity = e = $\dfrac{3}{5}$, Foci : $(3, \pm 3)$; Directrices : $y = \pm \dfrac{25}{3}$; Latus rectum : $\dfrac{32}{5}$

End points of latus recta : $\left(\pm \dfrac{16}{5}, 3\right)$.

(iv) Centre : (1, -1) ; Vertices : (1, -5) , (1, 3); Length of the axes : 4, 2

Eccentricity = e = $\dfrac{\sqrt{3}}{2}$, Foci : $(1, -1 \pm \sqrt{3})$;

Directrices : $y = -1 \pm \dfrac{4}{\sqrt{3}}$; Latus rectum : $\dfrac{1}{2}$

End points of latus recta : $\left(\dfrac{3}{2}, \sqrt{3}-1\right), \left(\dfrac{1}{2}, \sqrt{3}-1\right)$.

(v) Centre : (2, 3) ; Vertices : (5, 3) , (-1, 3); Length of the axes : 6, 4

Eccentricity = e = $\dfrac{\sqrt{5}}{3}$, Foci : $(2 \pm \sqrt{5}, 3)$;

Directrices : x $x = 2 \pm \dfrac{9}{\sqrt{5}}$; Latus rectum : $\dfrac{8}{3}$

End points of latus recta : $\left(2 + \sqrt{5}, 3 \pm \dfrac{4}{3}\right)$

5. $\dfrac{x^2}{65/2} + \dfrac{y^2}{45/2} = 1$

6. $5x^2 + 9y^2 - 54y + 36 = 0$

7. 10

8. $\dfrac{x^2}{4} + \dfrac{y^2}{3} = 1$

9. 3/5

10. $\left(\dfrac{11}{7}, \dfrac{29}{11}\right)$

11. $4 < a < 10$

12. $e = \dfrac{1}{\sqrt{2}}$

13. $x^2 + 2y^2 = 100$

15. $\sin^{-1}\left(\dfrac{b}{a}\right), \pi - \sin^{-1}\left(\dfrac{b}{a}\right)$.

16. $\dfrac{\pi}{4}, \dfrac{3\pi}{4}$.

18 $\dfrac{(x-1)^2}{16} + \dfrac{(y-2)^2}{9} = 1$.

19. 2ab

20. $\dfrac{3\sqrt{3}\,ab}{4}$.

21. 12 sq. u.

22. $e = \dfrac{1}{\sqrt{2}}$

25. 2

27. outside,

28. inside

30. $\lambda = \pm\sqrt{34}$

31. $\lambda = \pm 2\sqrt{5}$

33. (i) $x - 2y \pm 4 = 0$

(ii) $x + y \pm 4 = 0$

34. (i) 2, (ii) 1, (iii) 0.

35. (i) $y = x\sqrt{3} + \sqrt{(3a^2 + b^2)}$

(ii) $y = \pm x + \sqrt{(3a^2 + b^2)}$

36. $(x^2 + y^2)^2 = a^2x^2 + b^2y^2$

37. $\dfrac{1}{2x^2} + \dfrac{1}{4y^2} = 1$.

38. $\dfrac{x^2}{20} + \dfrac{y^2}{5} = 1$

41. $\phi = \pm \pi/3$.

42. 27 s. u.

47. $\left(\pm \dfrac{a^2}{\sqrt{a^2 + b^2}}, \pm \dfrac{b^2}{\sqrt{a^2 + b^2}}\right)$

52. (i) not defined (ii) $x = \pm 3$ (iii) $x = \pm 2$

(iv) not defined (v) not defined

57. $\frac{x^2}{a^2}+\frac{y^2}{b^2}=4$

58. $\frac{5}{\sqrt{2}}$

59. $\tan^{-1}(12/\sqrt{5})$

60. y = 3 and x + y = 5

61. $3\sqrt{7}/4$.

63. $x^2+y^2=13$

64. 9x - 3y = 5

65. 6x - 25y + 20 = 0

66. $9x+3\sqrt{5}y+13\sqrt{5}=0$

67. $\frac{a^2x}{a}-\frac{b^2y}{ß}=a^2-b^2$

68. $\left(\pm\frac{2}{\sqrt{10}},\pm\frac{9}{\sqrt{10}}\right)$.

75. $? = \cos^{-1}\left(-\frac{1}{\sqrt{5}}\right)$, $? = -\frac{1}{\sqrt{5}}$

79. $-\frac{a^4}{b^4}$

82. $\frac{\left(x+\frac{ae}{2}\right)^2}{a^2}+\frac{y^2}{b^2}=\frac{e^2}{4}$

83. $\left(\frac{x}{a}-1\right)^2+\frac{y^2}{b^2}=1$

86. $\left(\frac{2ax}{2a^2-b^2}\right)^2+\left(\frac{2y}{b}\right)^2=1$.

87. $\frac{7\sqrt{41}}{5}$.

89. $\left(-\frac{a^2l}{n},-\frac{b^2m}{n}\right)$

91. (1, 1)

92. $a^2c^4x^2+b^2d^4y^2=1$.

95. $2x^2-\beta^2y^2=4\alpha^2$

97. $P(a\cos\phi, b\sin\phi)$, $P'(-a\cos\phi, -b\sin\phi)$, Q(–asinf, bcosf), Q'(asinf, – bcosf)

102. $e=1/\sqrt{3}$

103. 4x + 3y = 12

104. $x\sqrt{5}+2y=2\sqrt{5}$.

105. x + y = 2

Level – II FOR JEE MAIN AND ADVANCED EXAMS ONLY

1. Tangents are drawn from a point on the circle $x^2+y^2=50$ to the ellipse $\frac{x^2}{30}+\frac{y^2}{20}=1$, then tangents are at angle is

(a) $\frac{\pi}{4}$ (b) $\frac{\pi}{3}$ (c) $\frac{\pi}{2}$ (d) $\frac{\pi}{8}$

2. The centre of the ellipse $4x^2+9y^2-8x-36y+4=0$ is

(a) (2,4) (b) (3,2) (c) (1,2) (d) (0,1)

3. The co-ordinates of the foci of the ellipse $4x^2+9y^2-8x-36y+4=0$ is

(a) $(1\pm\sqrt{5}, 2)$ (b) $(2\pm\sqrt{5}, 2)$

(c) $(\pm\sqrt{5}, 2)$ (d) $(1\pm\sqrt{5}, 3)$

4. The equation $\frac{x^2}{10-a}+\frac{y^2}{4-a}=1$ represents an ellipse if

(a) a < 4 (b) a > 4 (c) 4 < a < 10 (d) a > 10

5. Lep P be a variable point on the ellipse $\frac{x^2}{25}+\frac{y^2}{16}=1$ with foci at F and F'. If A is the area of the triangle PFF', then the maximum value of A is

(a) 12 s. u (b) 24 s. u (c) 36 s. u (d) 48 s. u.

6. The eccentricity of the ellipse $(10x-5)^2+(10y-5)^2=(3x+4y-1)^2$ is

(a) $\frac{1}{\sqrt{2}}$ (b) $\frac{1}{\sqrt{3}}$ (c) $\frac{1}{2}$ (d) $\frac{1}{4}$

7. If the line $y=x+\lambda$ touches the ellipse $9x^2+16y^2=144$, then the value of λ is

(a) ±5 (b) ±4 (c) ±7 (d) ±3

8. The equation of the tangent to the ellipse $3x^2+4y^2=12$ which are perpendicular to the line y + 2x = 4 is / are

(a) x - 2y + 4 = 0 (b) x - 2y + 7 = 0

(c) x - 2y - 4 = 0 (d) x - 2y - 7 = 0

9. The product of the perpendiculars from the foci of any tangent to an ellipse $b^2x^2+a^2y^2=a^2b^2$ is

(a) a^2 (b) b^2 (c) $2b^2$ (d) $2a^2$.

10. The number of tangents to the ellipse $\frac{x^2}{16}+\frac{y^2}{9}=1$ from the point (4, 3) is

(a) 0 (b) 1 (c) 2 (d) 3

11. If the normal at an end of a latus rectum of an ellipse $\frac{x^2}{a^2}+\frac{y^2}{b^2}=1$ passes through one extremity of the minor axis, then e^2 is

(a) $\frac{\sqrt{3}-1}{2}$ (b) $\frac{\sqrt{3}+1}{2}$ (c) $\frac{\sqrt{5}+1}{2}$ (d) $\frac{\sqrt{5}-1}{2}$.

12. The equation of common tangent between the ellipses $\frac{x^2}{9}+\frac{y^2}{4}=1$ and $\frac{x^2}{2}+\frac{y^2}{1}=1$ is

(a) x=3 (b) y=2
(c) x=1 (d) not defined.

13. If the equation of tangent to the ellipse $\frac{x^2}{a^2}+\frac{y^2}{b^2}=1$ is $\frac{x}{a}+\frac{y}{b}=\sqrt{2}$, then its eccentric angle is

(a) 45° (b) 60° (c) 90° (d) 22.5°

14. The equations of tangents to the ellipse $3x^2+y^2=3$ making equal intercepts on the axes are

(a) $y=\pm x\pm 2$ (b) $y=\pm x\pm 4$
(c) $y=\pm x\pm 5$ (d) $y=\pm x\pm 7$

15. The number of real tangents can be drawn from (3,5) to the ellipse $3x^2+5y^2=15$ is

(a) 4 (b) 2 (c) 1 (d) 0

16. The number of normals that can be drawn from a point to a given ellipse is

(a) 4 (b) 2 (c) 1 (d) 0

17. The set of possible values of 'm' for which a line with slope 'm' is a common tangent to the ellipse $\frac{x^2}{b^2}+\frac{y^2}{c^2}=1$ and the parabola $y^2=4ax$ is

(a) (3,5) (b) (2,3) (c) (1,3) (d) (0,1)

18. The angle between the normals of the ellipse $4x^2+y^2=5$, at the intersection of 2 x + y = 3 and ellipse is

(a) $\tan^{-1}(3/5)$ (b) $\tan^{-1}(3/4)$
(c) $\tan^{-1}(4/3)$ (d) $\tan^{-1}(4/5)$

19. If the latus rectum of an ellipse $x^2\tan^2\phi+y^2\sec^2\phi=1$ is 1/2, then ϕ is

(a) $\pi/2$ (b) $\pi/6$ (c) $\pi/3$ (d) $5\pi/12$

20. If pair of tangents are drawn to the ellipse $\frac{x^2}{16}+\frac{y^2}{9}=1$ from a point P, so that the tangents are at right angles to each other, then the possible co-ordinates of the point P are

(a) $(3\sqrt{2}, \sqrt{7})$ (b) (5,0)
(c) (3,4) (d) $(2\sqrt{5}, \sqrt{5})$

21. The eccentricity of the ellipse whose pair of a conjugate diameters are y = x and 3 y = - 2 x is

(a) $1/\sqrt{3}$ (b) 2/3 (c) 1/3 (d) 1/5

22. The minimum length of intercept of any tangent of ellipse $\frac{x^2}{a^2}+\frac{y^2}{b^2}=1$ between the axes is

(a) 2a (b) 2b (c) a + b (d) a - b.

23. The eccentric angle of a point on the ellipse $\frac{x^2}{6}+\frac{y^2}{2}=1$ whose distance from the centre is 2,is

(a) $\pi/4$ (b) $\pi/6$ (c) $\pi/2$ (d) $\pi/6$

24. If $\frac{x^2}{\lambda^2-\lambda-6}+\frac{y^2}{\lambda^2-6\lambda+5}=1$ represents an ellipse then λ lies in

(a) $(-\infty, -2)$ (b) $(1, \infty)$
(c) $(3, \infty)$ (d) $(5, \infty)$

25. The eccentricity of the ellipse $ax^2+by^2+2gx+2fy+c=0$, if its axis is parallel to X axis, is

(a) $\sqrt{\frac{a+b}{4}}$ (b) $\sqrt{\frac{a-b}{2}}$
(c) $\sqrt{\frac{b}{a}-1}$ (d) $\sqrt{1-\frac{a}{b}}$

26. S and T are the foci of an ellipse and B is an end of the minor axis. If STB is an equilateral triangle, the eccentricity of the ellipse is

(a) 1/4 (b) 1/3 (c) 1/2 (d) 2/3

27. The centre of the ellipse $\frac{(x+y-1)^2}{9}+\frac{(x-y)^2}{16}=1$ is

(a) (0,0) (b) (1,1) (c) (2,1) (d) (1,2)

28. Let P be a variable point on the ellipse $\frac{x^2}{a^2}+\frac{y^2}{b^2}=1$ with foci F_1 and F_2. If A is the area of the triangle PF_1F_2, then the max value of A is

(a) $\frac{ea}{b}$ (b) $\frac{ab}{e}$ (c) aeb (d) $\frac{e}{ab}$.

29. If the angle between the lines joining the foci of an ellipse to an extremity of a minor axis is 90°, then the eccentricity of the ellipse is

(a) 1/8 (b) 1/4 (c) $1/\sqrt{2}$ (d) $1/\sqrt{3}$.

30. On the ellipse $4x^2+9y^2=1$, the points at which the tangents are parallel to the line 8x = 9y are

(a) $\left(\frac{2}{5},\frac{1}{5}\right)$ (b) $\left(-\frac{2}{5},\frac{1}{5}\right)$

(c) $\left(-\frac{2}{5},-\frac{1}{5}\right)$ (d) $\left(\frac{2}{5},-\frac{1}{5}\right)$

31. The equation of the largest circle with centre (1, 0) that can be inscribed in the ellipse $x^2+4y^2=36$ is

(a) $3x^2+3y^2-6x-8=0$

(b) $3x^2+3y^2+6x-8=0$

(c) $2x^2+2y^2+5x-8=0$

(d) $2x^2+2y^2-5x-8=0$

32. Let E be the ellipse $\frac{x^2}{a^2}+\frac{y^2}{b^2}=1$ and C be the circle $x^2+y^2=9$. Let P and Q be the points (1, 2) and (2, 1) respectively. Then

(a) Q lies inside C but outside E

(b) Q lies outside both C and E

(c) P lies inside both C and E

(d) P lies inside C but outside E.

33. The radius of the circle passing through the foci of the ellipse $\frac{x^2}{16}+\frac{y^2}{9}=1$ and having its center at (0, 3) is

(a) 4 (b) 3 (c) 5 (d) 7.

34. An ellipse has OB as semi minor axis, F, F' are its foci and the engle FBF' is a right angle. Then the eccentricity of the ellipse is

(a) 1/2 (b) $1/\sqrt{2}$ (c) 1/3 (d) 1/4

35. The sum of the focal distances from any point on the ellipse $9x^2+16y^2=144$ is

(a) 32 (b) 18 (c) 16 (d) 8

36. If P = (x, y), $F_1=(3,0)$, $F_2=(-3,0)$ and $16x^2+25y^2=400$, then PF_1+PF_2 is equal to

(a) 8 (b) 6 (c) 10 (d) 12

37. The number of values of c such that the striaght line y = 4 x + c touches the ellipse $\frac{x^2}{4}+y^2=1$ is

(a) 0 (b) 1 (c) 2 (d) infinite.

38. The area of the quadrilateral formed by the tangents at the points of latus recta to the ellipse $\frac{x^2}{9}+\frac{y^2}{5}=1$ is

(a) 27/4 sq. u (b) 9 sq. u (c) 27/2 sq. u (d) 27 sq. u

39. Tangents is drawn to the ellipse $\frac{x^2}{27}+y^2=1$ at $(3\sqrt{3}\cos\theta, \sin\theta)$, where $0<\theta<\pi/2$. Then the value of θ for which the sum of intercepts on the axes made by this tangent is minimum is

(a) π/3 (b) π/4 (c) π/8 (d) π/6

40. If tangents are drawn to the ellipse $x^2+2y^2=2$, then the locus of the midpoint of the intercept made by the tangents between the co-ordinate axes is

(a) $\frac{1}{2x^2}+\frac{1}{4y^2}=1$ (b) $\frac{1}{4x^2}+\frac{1}{2y^2}=1$

(c) $\frac{x^2}{2}+\frac{y^2}{4}=1$ (d) $\frac{x^2}{4}+\frac{y^2}{2}=1$

41. The minimum area of the triangle formed by the tangent to the ellipse $\frac{x^2}{a^2}+\frac{y^2}{b^2}=1$ and the co-ordinate axes is

(a) ab sq. u (b) $\frac{a^2+b^2}{2}$ sq. u

(c) $\frac{(a+b)^2}{2}$ sq. u (d) $\frac{a^2+ab+b^2}{2}$ sq.u

42. The point on the curve $x^2+2y^2=6$ whose distance from the line x + y = 7 is min, is

(a) (1,2) (b) (1,3) (c) (2, 1) (d) (3, 1)

43. The equation of the common tangent in 1st quadrant to the circle $x^2+y^2=16$ and the ellipse $\frac{x^2}{25}+\frac{y^2}{4}=1$ is

(a) $2x+y\sqrt{3}=4\sqrt{7}$ (b) $2x-y\sqrt{3}=4\sqrt{7}$

(c) $3x-y\sqrt{3}=4\sqrt{7}$ (d) $3x+y\sqrt{3}=4\sqrt{7}$

44. Let $P(x_1, y_1)$ and $Q(x_2, y_2)$, $y_1<0$, be the end points of the latus rectum of the ellipse $x^2+4y^2=4$. The equation of parabolas with latus rectum PQ are

(a) $x^2+2\sqrt{3}\,y=3+\sqrt{3}$

(b) $x^2-2\sqrt{3}\,y=3+\sqrt{3}$

(c) $x^2+2\sqrt{3}\,y=3-\sqrt{3}$

(d) $x^2-2\sqrt{3}\,y=3-\sqrt{3}$

45. The line passing through the extremity A of the major axis and extremity B of the minor axis of the ellipse $x^2+9y^2=9$ meets the auxiliary circle at the point M. Then the area of the triangle with vertices at A, M and the origin is

(a) $\frac{31}{10}$ (b) $\frac{29}{10}$ (c) $\frac{21}{10}$ (d) $\frac{27}{10}$

46. The normal at a point P on the ellipse $x^2+4y^2=16$ meets the x-axis at Q. If M is the mid-point of the segment PQ, then the locus of M intersects the latus rectum of the given ellipse at the points

(a) $\left(\pm\frac{3\sqrt{5}}{2}, \pm\frac{2}{7}\right)$ (b) $\left(\pm\frac{3\sqrt{5}}{2}, \pm\frac{\sqrt{19}}{4}\right)$

(c) $\left(\pm 2\sqrt{3}, \pm\frac{1}{7}\right)$ (d) $\left(\pm 2\sqrt{3}, \pm\frac{4\sqrt{3}}{7}\right)$

47. Tangents are drawn from the point P(3, 4) to the ellipse $\frac{x^2}{9}+\frac{y^2}{4}=1$ touching the ellipse at A and B. Then the co-ordinates of A and B are

(a) (3. 0) & (0, 2) (b) $\left(-\frac{8}{5}, \frac{2\sqrt{161}}{15}\right)$&$\left(-\frac{9}{5}, \frac{8}{5}\right)$

(c) $\left(-\frac{8}{5}, \frac{2\sqrt{161}}{15}\right)$&(0, 2) (d) (3, 0) &$\left(-\frac{9}{5}, \frac{8}{5}\right)$

48. The maximum area of an isosceles triangle inscribed in the ellipse $\frac{x^2}{a^2}+\frac{y^2}{b^2}=1$ with its vertex at one end of the major axis is

(a) $\frac{3\sqrt{3}}{4}ab$ (b) $\frac{3\sqrt{2}}{4}ab$ (c) $\frac{2\sqrt{3}}{5}ab$ (d) $\frac{3\sqrt{3}}{5}ab$

49. The point (α, β) on the ellipse $4x^2+3y^2=12$, in the first quadrant, so that the area enclosed by the lines $y=x$ and $y=\beta, x=\alpha$ and the x-axis is maximum is

(a) $\left(\frac{3}{2}, 1\right)$ (b) $\left(1, \frac{3}{2}\right)$ (c) $\left(2, \frac{3}{2}\right)$ (d) $\left(3, \frac{3}{2}\right)$

50. Number of points on the ellipse $\frac{x^2}{50}+\frac{y^2}{20}=1$ from which pair of perpendicular tangents are drawn to the ellipse $\frac{x^2}{16}+\frac{y^2}{9}=1$ is

(a) 0 (b) 2 (c) 1 (d) 4

51. The eccentricity of the ellipse $(x-3)^2+(y-4)^2=\frac{y^2}{9}$ is

(a) $\frac{\sqrt{3}}{2}$ (b) $\frac{1}{3}$ (c) $\frac{1}{3\sqrt{2}}$ (d) $\frac{1}{\sqrt{3}}$

52. For an ellipse $\frac{x^2}{9}+\frac{y^2}{4}=1$ with vertices A and A', tangents are drawn at the point P in the first quadrant meets the y-axis in Q and the chord A'P meets the y-axis inM. If 'O' is the origin then OQ^2-MQ^2 is

(a) 9 (b) 13 (c) 4 (d) 5

53. The line lx+my+n=0 will cut the ellipse $\frac{x^2}{a^2}+\frac{y^2}{b^2}=1$ in points whose eccentric angles differ by $\pi/2$ if

(a) $a^2l^2+b^2n^2=2m^2$ (b) $a^2m^2+b^2l^2=2n^2$

(c) $a^2l^2+b^2m^2=2n^2$ (d) $a^2n^2+b^2m^2=2l^2$

54. A circle has the same centre as an ellipse and passes through the foci F_1 and F_2 of the ellipse such that two curves intersect in 4 points. Let P be any of their point of intersection. If the major axis of the ellipse is 17 and the area of the triangle PF_1F_2 is 30, then the distance between the foci is

(a) 11 (b) 12 (c) 13 (d) None

55. Point O is the centre of the ellipse with major axis AB and minor axis CD. Point F is one focus of the ellipse. If OF = 6 and the diameter of the inscribed circle of triangle OCF is 2, then the product of (AB)(CD) is

(a) 65 (b) 52 (c) 78 (d) None

56. A tangent having slope –4/3 to the ellipse $\frac{x^2}{18}+\frac{y^2}{32}=1$ intersects the major and minor axes in points A and B respectively. If C is the centre of the ellipse, then the area of the triangle ABC is

(a) 12 sq. units (b) 24 sq. units

(c) 36 sq. units (d) 48 sq. units.

57. The common tangent to the ellipse $\frac{x^2}{a^2+b^2}+\frac{y^2}{b^2}=1$ and $\frac{x^2}{a^2}+\frac{y^2}{a^2+b^2}=1$ is

(a) $ay=bx+\sqrt{a^4-a^2b^2+b^4}$

(b) $by=ax-\sqrt{a^4+a^2b^2+b^4}$

(c) $ay=bx-\sqrt{a^4+a^2b^2+b^4}$

(d) $by=ax+\sqrt{a^4-a^2b^2+b^4}$

58. The normal at a variable point P on an ellipse $\frac{x^2}{a^2}+\frac{y^2}{b^2}=1$ of eccentricity 'e' meets the axes of the ellipse in Q and R, then the locus of the mid point of QR is a conic with an eccentricity 'e' such that

(a) 'e' is independent of e (b) 'e' =1

(c) 'e' = e (d) 'e' = 1/e

59. An ellipse is drawn with major and minor axes of lengths 10 and 8 respectively. Using one focus as centre, a circle is drawn that is tangent to the ellipse, which no part of the circle being outside of the ellipse. The radius of the circle is

(a) $\sqrt{3}$ (b) 2 (c) $2\sqrt{2}$ (d) $\sqrt{5}$

60. A common tangent to $9x^2+16y^2=144$; $y^2=x-4$ and $x^2+y^2-12x+32=0$ is

(a) y=3 (b) x+4=0 (c) x=4 (d) y+3=0

61. The area of the rectangle formed by the perpendiculars from the centre of the standard ellipse to the tangent and normal at its point whose eccentric angle is $\pi/4$ is

(a) $\frac{(a^2-b^2)ab}{a^2+b^2}$ (b) $\frac{(a^2-b^2)}{(a^2+b^2)ab}$

(c) $\frac{(a^2+b^2)}{(a^2-b^2)ab}$ (d) $\frac{(a^2+b^2)ab}{(a^2-b^2)}$.

62. An ellipse having foci at (3, 3) and (-4, 4) and passing through the origin has eccentricity equal to

(a) 3/7 (b) 2/7 (c) 5/7 (d) 3/5

63. A bar of length 20 units moves with its ends on two fixed straight lines at right angles. A point P marked on the bar at a distance of 8 units from one and describes a conic whose eccentricity is

(a) 5/9 (b) $\frac{\sqrt{2}}{3}$ (c) $\frac{4}{9}$ (d) 3/5

64. If maximum distance of any point on the ellipse $x^2+2y^2+2xy=1$ from its center be r, then the value of r is

(a) $3+\sqrt{3}$ (b) $2+\sqrt{2}$

(c) $\frac{\sqrt{2}}{\sqrt{3}-\sqrt{5}}$ (d) $\sqrt{2-\sqrt{2}}$

65. If the ellipse $\frac{x^2}{a^2-7}+\frac{y^2}{13-5a}=1$ is inscribed in a square of side length $a\sqrt{2}$, then a is

(a) $\frac{6}{5}$

(b) $\left(-\infty,-\sqrt{7}\right)\cup\left(\sqrt{7},\frac{13}{5}\right)$

(c) $\left(-\infty,-\sqrt{7}\right)\cup\left(\sqrt{7},\frac{12}{5}\right)$

(d) No such value of a is exists.

66. If the ellipse $\frac{x^2}{a^2}+\frac{y^2}{b^2}=1$ is inscribed in a rectangle whose length : breadth is 2:1, then the area of the rectangle is

(a) $\frac{4}{7}\left(a^2+b^2\right)$ (b) $\frac{4}{3}\left(a^2+b^2\right)$

(c) $\frac{12}{5}\left(a^2+b^2\right)$ (d) $\frac{8}{5}\left(a^2+b^2\right)$.

67. The length of the side of the square which can be made by four perpendicular tangents to the ellipse $\frac{x^2}{7}+\frac{y^2}{11}=1$ is

(a) 10 (b) 8 (c) 6 (d) 5.

68. If the tangent to the ellipse $\frac{x^2}{a^2}+\frac{y^2}{b^2}=1$ make angles α and β with the major axis such that $\tan\alpha+\tan\beta=\lambda$, then the locus of their point of intersection is

(a) $x^2+y^2=a^2$ (b) $x^2+y^2=b^2$

(c) $x^2-2\lambda xy=a^2$ (d) $\lambda\left(x^2-a^2\right)=2xy$.

69. If $\alpha-\beta=c$, then the locus of the point of intersection of tangents at $P(a\cos\alpha, b\sin\alpha)$ and $Q(a\cos\beta, b\sin\beta)$ to the ellipse $\frac{x^2}{a^2}+\frac{y^2}{b^2}=1$ is

(a) a circle (b) a st. linq

(c) an ellipse (d) a parabola.

70. If the ececntricity of the ellipse $\frac{x^2}{a^2+1}+\frac{y^2}{a^2+2}=1$ is $\frac{1}{\sqrt{6}}$, then the latus rectum of the ellipse is

(a) $\frac{5}{\sqrt{6}}$ (b) $\frac{10}{\sqrt{6}}$ (c) $\frac{8}{\sqrt{6}}$ (d) $\frac{7}{\sqrt{6}}$.

ANSWER

1.(c)	2.(c)	3.(a)	4.(c)	5.(a)	6.(c)	7.(a)	8.(a)	9.(b)	10.(c)
11.(d)	12.(d)	13.(a)	14.(a)	15.(b)	16.(a,b)	17.(d)	18.(a)	19.(a)	20.(a,b,c,d)
21.(a)	22.(c)	23.(a)	24.(a)	25.(d)	26.(c)	27.(b)	28.(c)	29.(c)	30.(b)
31.(a)	32.(d)	33.(a)	34.(b)	35.(d)	36.(c)	37.(c)	38.(d)	39.(d)	40.(a)
41.(a)	42.(c)	43.(a)	44.(a)	45.(d)	46.(c)	47.(d)	48.(a)	49.(a)	50.(d)
51.(b)	52.(c)	53.(c)	54.(c)	55.(a)	56.(b)	57.(b)	58.(a)	59.(b)	60.(c)
61.(a)	62.(c)	63.(d)	64.(c)	65.(c)	66.(d)	67.(d)	68.(d)	69.(c)	70.(b)

Level – III FOR JEE ADVANCE EXAM ONLY

1. Let P be a variable point on the ellipse $\frac{x^2}{a^2}+\frac{y^2}{b^2}=1$ with foci F_1 and F_2. If A is the area of the triangle PF_1F_2, then find the maximum value of A.

2. Let d be the perpendicular distance from the centre of the ellipse $\frac{x^2}{a^2}+\frac{y^2}{b^2}=1$ to the tangent drawn at a point P on the ellipse. If F_1 and F_2 are the two foci of the ellipse, then prove that

$$(PF_1-PF_2)^2=4a^2\left(1-\frac{b^2}{d^2}\right).$$

3. Find the radius of the circle passing through the foci of the ellipse $\frac{x^2}{16}+\frac{y^2}{9}=1$ and having its centre at (0, 3).

4. If tangent drawn at a point $(t^2,2t)$ on the parabola $y^2=4x$ is same as the normal drawn at a point $(\sqrt{5}\cos\phi\ ,2\ \sin\phi)$ on the ellipse $4x^2+5y^2=20$. Find the values of t and ϕ.

5. An ellipse has OB as a minor axis. F, F' are its foci and the angle FBF' is a right angle Then find the eccentricity of the ellipse.

6. A tangent to the ellipse $x^2+4y^2=4$, $x^2+2y^2=6$ at P and Q. Prove that the tangentsat P and Q of the ellipse $x^2+2y^2=6$ are at right angles.

7. Find the co-ordinates of the points P on the ellipse $\frac{x^2}{a^2}+\frac{y^2}{b^2}=1$, for which the area of the triangle PON is maximum , where O denotes the origin and N, the foot of the perpendicular from O to the tangent at P.

8. Find the equation of the largest circle with centre (1, 0) that can be inscribed in the ellipse $x^2+4y^2=16$.

9. Find the condition so that the line px + q y = r intersects the ellipse $\frac{x^2}{a^2}+\frac{y^2}{b^2}=1$ in points whose eccentric angles differ by $\pi/4$.

10. Let ABC be an equilateral triangle inscribed in the circle $x^2+y^2=a^2$. Suppose perpendiculars from A, B, C to the major axis of the ellipse , (a > b) meet the ellipse respectively at P, Q, R, so that P, Q,R lie on the same side of the major axis as A, B, C respectively . Prove that the normals to the ellipse drawn at the points P, Q and R are collinear.

11. Prove that, in an ellipse , the perpendicular from a focus upon any tangent and the line joining the centre of the ellipse to the point of contact meet on the corresponding directrix.

12. Find the area of the quadrilateral formed by the tangents at the end points of latus rectum to the ellipse $\frac{x^2}{9}+\frac{y^2}{5}=1$.

13. Tangent is drawn to the ellipse $\frac{x^2}{27}+y^2=1$ at $(3\sqrt{3}\cos\theta,\ \sin\theta)$, where $0<\theta<\pi/2$. Then find the value of θ such that the sum of the intercepts on axes made by the tangent is minimum.

14. If tangents are drawn to the ellipse $x^2+2y^2=2$, then find the locus of the mid point of the intercept made by the tangents between the co-ordinate axes.

15. Find the minimum area of the triangle formed by the tangent to the ellipse $\frac{x^2}{a^2}+\frac{y^2}{b^2}=1$ and the co-ordinate axes.

16. Find the equation of the common tangent in 1st quadrant to the circle $x^2+y^2=16$ and the ellipse $\frac{x^2}{25}+\frac{y^2}{4}=1$. Also find the length of the intercept of the tangent between the co-ordinate axes.

17. If the curves $\frac{x^2}{4}+y^2=1$ and $\frac{x^2}{a^2}+y^2=1$ for suitable value of a cut on four concyclic points, then find the equation of the circle passing through these four points.

18. From any point P lying in the first quadrant on the ellipse $\frac{x^2}{25}+\frac{y^2}{16}=1$, PN is drawn perpendicular to the major axis and produced at Q so that NQ equals to PS, where S is a focus. Then Prove that the locus of Q is 3x + 5 y + 25 = 0.

19. If a tangent of slope 2 of the ellipse $\frac{x^2}{a^2}+\frac{y^2}{b^2}=1$ is normal to the circle $x^2+y^2+4x+1=0$, then find the maximum value of ab.

20. If maximum distance of any point on the ellipse $x^2+2xy+2y^2=1$ from its center ber, then find r.

21. The locus of the mid-points of the chords of the ellipse $\left(\frac{x^2}{a^2}+\frac{y^2}{b^2}\right)=1$ which are of constant length 2c is $\left(\frac{b^2x^2+a^2y^2}{a^4y^2+b^4x^2}\right)=\frac{1}{c^2}\left(1-\frac{x^2}{a^2}-\frac{y^2}{b^2}\right)$.

Answer

1. $b\sqrt{(a^2-b^2)}$

2. 4

4. $\phi=\pi-\tan^2 2,\quad t=-\frac{1}{\sqrt{5}};\phi=\pi+\tan^{-1}2,\quad t=\frac{1}{\sqrt{5}};$

$\phi=\pm\frac{\pi}{2}$, t=0.

5. $\frac{1}{\sqrt{2}}$

7. $\left(\frac{a^2}{\sqrt{(a^2+b^2)}},\frac{b^2}{\sqrt{(a^2+b^2)}}\right)$

8. $(x-1)^2+y^2=\frac{121}{9}$

9. $a^2p^2+b^2q^2=r^2\sec^2\left(\frac{\pi}{8}\right)$

12. 27 sq. units

13. $\pi/6$

14. $\frac{1}{2x^2}+\frac{1}{4y^2}=1$

15. ab sq. units

16. $Y=-\frac{2}{\sqrt{3}}x+4\sqrt{\frac{7}{3}};\ \frac{14}{\sqrt{3}}$

17. $x^2+y^2=1$.

19. 4.

20. $\frac{\sqrt{2}}{\sqrt{3}-\sqrt{5}}$.

Comprehensive Link Passage (For JEE Main and Advanced Exams Only)

PASSAGE - I

Let C : $x^2+y^2=r^2$ and E : $\frac{x^2}{16}+\frac{y^2}{9}=1$ intersect at four distinct points A, B, C, D . Their common tangents form a parallelogram EFGH.

1. If ABCD is a square then r is

(a) $\frac{12\sqrt{2}}{5}$ (b) $\frac{12}{5}$ (c) $\frac{12}{5\sqrt{5}}$ (d) None.

2. If EFGH is a square , then r is

(a) $\sqrt{20}$ (b) $\sqrt{12}$ (c) $\sqrt{15}$ (d) None.

3. If EFGH is a square , then the ratio of $\frac{\text{ar(Circle C)}}{\text{ar(circumcircle EFG)}}$ is

(a) $\frac{9}{16}$ (b) $\frac{3}{4}$ (c) $\frac{1}{2}$ (d) None.

PASSAGE - II

A curve is represented by C :

$21x^2-6xy+29y^2+6x-58y-151=0$.

1. The eccentricity of the given curve is

(a) $\frac{1}{3}$ (b) $\frac{1}{\sqrt{3}}$ (c) $\frac{2}{3}$ (d) $\frac{2}{\sqrt{5}}$

2. The length of axes are

(a) 6, $2\sqrt{6}$ (b) 5, $2\sqrt{5}$ (c) 4, $4\sqrt{5}$ (d) None.

3. The centre of the conic C is

(a) (1,0) (b) (0,0) (c) (0,1) (d) None.

PASSAGE - III

Let F , F' be the foci of the ellipse $\frac{x^2}{a^2}+\frac{y^2}{b^2}=1$ whose eccentricity is e, P is a variable point on the ellipse.

1. Then the locus of the incentre of the $\Delta PFF'$ is

(a) ellipse (b) hyperbola (c) parabola (d) circle.

2. The eccentricity of the locus of P is

(a) $\sqrt{\frac{2e}{1-e}}$ (b) $\sqrt{\frac{2e}{1+e}}$ (c) 1 (d) None.

3. Maximum area of the rectangle inscribed in the ellipse is

(a) $\frac{2abe^2}{1+e}$ (b) $\frac{2abe}{1+e}$ (c) $\frac{abe}{1+e}$ (d) None.

PASSAGE - IV

The ellipse $\frac{x^2}{a^2}+\frac{y^2}{b^2}=1$ is such that it has the least area but contains the circle $(x-1)^2+y^2=1$.

1. The eccentricity of the ellipse is

(a) $\sqrt{\frac{2}{3}}$ (b) $\frac{1}{\sqrt{3}}$ (c) $\frac{1}{2}$ (d) None.

2. Equation of the auxiliary circle of the ellipse is

(a) $x^2+y^2=\frac{13}{2}$ (b) $x^2+y^2=5$

(c) $x^2+y^2=\frac{9}{2}$ (d) None.

3. The length of the latus rectum of the ellipse is

(a) 2 (b) 1 (c) 3 (d) 5/2

PASSAGE - V

The conic section is the locus of a point which moves in a plane in such a way that, the ratio of its distance from a fixed point to a fixed striaght line is constant. The fixed point is called focus and the fixed straight line is called directrix. The constant ratio is called eccentricity. It is denoted as 'e'. If e is less that 1, then the conic section is called an ellipse. A line joining two points on the ellipse is called the chord of the ellipse. If through a point C any chord of an ellipse is bisected, then the point C is called centre of the ellipse.

Let the equation of the curve is

$ax^2 + 2hxy + by^2 + 2gx + 2fy + c = 0$.

It will represents an ellipse if $h^2 < ab$ and $\Delta \neq 0$, where

$$\Delta = \begin{vmatrix} a & h & g \\ h & b & f \\ g & f & c \end{vmatrix}$$

1. The length of the longest chord of the liipse $x^2 + xy + y^2 = 1$ is

(a) $\sqrt{2}$ (b) $\frac{1}{\sqrt{2}}$ (c) $2\sqrt{2}]$ (d) 1

2. The length of the chord passing through the centre and perpendicular to the longest chord of the ellipse $x^2 + xy + y^2 = 1$ is

(a) $\frac{1}{\sqrt{2}}$ (b) $\frac{\sqrt{3}}{2}$ (c) $2\sqrt{\frac{2}{3}}$ (d) $\frac{1}{\sqrt{3}}$

3. There are exactly n integral values of λ for which the equation $x^2 + \lambda xy + y^2 = 1$ represents an ellipse, then must be

(a) 0 (b) 1 (c) 2 (d) 3

4. The center of the ellipse $x^2 + xy + 2y^2 = 1$ is

(a) (0,0) (b) (1,1) (c) (1,2) (d) (2,1)

PASSAGE - VI

Tangents are drawn from the point P(3, 4) to the ellipse $\frac{x^2}{9} + \frac{y^2}{4} = 1$ touching the ellipse at points A and B.

1. The co-ordinates of Aand B are

(a) $(3, 0) \& (0, 2)$

(b) $\left(-\frac{8}{5}, \frac{2\sqrt{161}}{15}\right) \& \left(-\frac{9}{5}, \frac{8}{5}\right)$

(c) $\left(-\frac{8}{5}, \frac{2\sqrt{161}}{15}\right) \& (0, 2)$

(d) $(3, 0) \& \left(-\frac{9}{5}, \frac{8}{5}\right)$

2. The orthocenter of the triangle PAB is

(a) $\left(5, \frac{8}{7}\right)$ (b) $\left(\frac{7}{5}, \frac{25}{8}\right)$

(c) $\left(\frac{11}{5}, \frac{8}{5}\right)$ (d) $\left(\frac{8}{25}, \frac{7}{5}\right)$

3. The equation of the locus of the point whose distances from the point P and the line AB are equal is

(a) $9x^2 + y^2 - 6xy - 54x - 62y + 241 = 0$

(b) $9x^2 + y^2 + 6xy - 54x + 62y + 241 = 0$

(c) $9x^2 + 9y^2 - 6xy - 54x - 62y - 241 = 0$

(d) $x^2 + y^2 - 2xy + 27x + 31y - 120 = 0$.

MATCH MATRIX (FOR JEE ADVANCED EXAM ONLY)

1. Match the following columns :

Let the equation of the curve is $x^2 + 2y^2 + 4x + 12y = 0$. Then

Column-I	Column-II
(A) centre is	(P) $\left(-2-\sqrt{11}, -\right)$
(B) Focus is	(Q) $(-2, -3)$
(C) one extremity of the major axis is	(R) $\left(\sqrt{11}-2, -3\right)$
(D) Latus rectum is	(S) $\left(-2+\frac{\sqrt{11}}{2}, -2\right)$
	(T) $\sqrt{22}$

2. Match the following columns :

Let the equation of the ellipse is $\frac{(x-3)^2}{25} + \frac{(y-2)^2}{16} = 1$.

Then

Column-I	Column-II
(A) Centre is	(P) (8,2)
(B) One extremity of major axis is	(Q) (3,2)
(C) One of focus is	(R) (6,2)
(D) One extremity of minor axis is	(S) (3,6)
(E) Length of latus rectum is	(T) 10
(F) Focal distance is	(U) 6.4

3. Match the following columns :

For all real p , the line $2px+2\sqrt{1-p^2}=1$ touches a fixed ellipse . Then

Column - I	Column - II
(A) The eccentricity is	(P) 1/2
(B) The latus rectum is	(Q) $\sqrt{3}/2$
(C) The focal distance is	(R) 2
(D) One extremity of major axis is	(S) (0, 1)
(E) One of focus is	(T) $(0, \sqrt{3}/2)$

4. Match the following columns :

A tangent having slope - 4/3 touches the ellipse $\frac{x^2}{18}+\frac{y^2}{32}=1$ at point P and intersects the major and minor axes at A and B respectively, where O is the center of the ellipse. Then

Column - I	Column - II
(A) Distance between the parallel tangents having slopes - 4/3 is	(P) 24
(B) Area of $\Delta AOB$is	(Q) 7/24
(C) If the tangent in first quadrant touches the ellipse at (h, k), then the value of hk is	(R) 48/5
(D) If equation of the tangent intersecting +ve axes is $lx+my=1$, then the value of $l+m$ is	(S) 12

5. Match the following columns :

Let M(t, t+1) is a point moving in a straight line and C_1, C_2, C_3 be three conics whose equations are $x^2+y^2=2$, $y^2=8x$ and $x^2+2y^2=1$, If M lies within the interrior of C_1,C_2, C_3, then

Column - I	Column - II
(A) C1 is	(P) $\left(3-2\sqrt{2}, 3+2\sqrt{2}\right)$
(B) C2 is	(Q) $\left(-1, -\frac{1}{3}\right)$
(C) C3 is	(R) $\left(\frac{-1-\sqrt{3}}{2}, \frac{-1+\sqrt{3}}{2}\right)$

6. Match the following columns :

Tangents are drawn from (2, 3) to the ellipse $\frac{x^2}{4}+\frac{y^2}{3}=1$. Then

Column - I	Column - II
(A) the equation of PQ is	(P) $3\times\sqrt{\frac{3}{2}}$
(B) the length of PQ is	(Q) $12\sqrt{3}$
(C) Area of ΔTPQ is	(R) $9\sqrt{3}$
(D) Area of quadrilateral OPTQ is	(S) $x+2y=2$
	(T) $2x+y=1$

ANSWER

1. (A)→(Q) ; (B)→(P, R) ; (C)→(S); (D)→(T).
2. (A)→(Q) ; (B)→(P) ; (C)→(R); (D)→(S); (E)→(U); (F) →(T).
3. (A)→(Q) ; (B)→(P) ; (C)→(R); (D)→(S); (E)→(T);
4. (A)→(R) ; (B)→(P) ; (C)→(S); (D)→(Q);
5. (A)→(R) ; (B)→(Q) ; (C)→(P);
6. (A)→(S) ; (B)→(P) ; (C)→(R); (D)→(Q)

QUESTIONS ASKED IN ROORKEE EXAM

1. Find the maximum area of an isosceles triangle inscribed in the ellipse $\frac{x^2}{a^2}+\frac{y^2}{b^2}=1$ with its vertex at one end of the major axis.

[Roorkee Main – 1994]

2. Find the point (α,β) on the ellipse $4x^2+3y^2=12$, in the first quadrant, so that the area enclosed by the lines y = x and y = β, x = α and the x-axis is maximum.

[Roorkee Main – 1995]

3. Find the equation of the largest circle with center (1, 0) that can be inscribed in the ellipse $x^2+4y^2=16$.

[Roorkee – 1999]

4. Find the condition so that the line p x + q y = r intersects the ellipse $\frac{x^2}{a^2}+\frac{y^2}{b^2}=1$ in points whose eccentric angles differ by $\pi/4$.

[Roorkee Main – 2001]

ANSWER

1. $\frac{3\sqrt{3}}{4}ab$

2. Area = 1 sq. unit, $\left(\frac{3}{2},1\right)$

3. $(x-1)^2+y^2=\frac{11}{3}$

4. $r^2=\cos^2\left(\frac{\pi}{8}\right)\times\left(a^2p^2+b^2q^2\right)$

QUESTIONS ASKED IN IIT-JEE EXAM

1. The locus of a point whose distance from (-2, 0) is 2/3 times its distance from the line $x=-\frac{9}{2}$ is

(a) ellipse (b) parabola (c) hyperbola (d) none.

[IIT-JEE – 1994]

2. Let E be the ellipse $\frac{x^2}{9}+\frac{y^2}{4}=1$ and C be the circle $x^2+y^2=9$. Let P and Q be the points (1, 2) and (2, 1) respectively, then

(a) Q lies inside C but outside E

(b) Q lies outside both C and E

(c) P lies inside both C and E

(d) P lies inside C but outside E [IIT-JEE – 1994]

3. Let P be a variable point on the ellipse $\frac{x^2}{a^2}+\frac{y^2}{b^2}=1$. With foci F_1 and F_2. If A is the area of the triangle PF_1F_2, then find the maximum value of A.

[IIT-JEE – 1994]

4. The radius of the circle passing through the foci of the ellipse $\frac{x^2}{16}+\frac{y^2}{9}=1$, and having its center at (0, 3) is

(a) 4 (b) 3 (c) $\sqrt{\frac{1}{2}}$ (d) $\frac{7}{2}$

[IIT-JEE – 1995]

5. Let d be the perpendicular distance from the center of the ellipse $\frac{x^2}{a^2}+\frac{y^2}{b^2}=1$ to the tangent drawn at a point P on the ellipse. If F_1 and F_2 are the two foci of the ellipse, then show that $(PF_1-PF_2)^2=4a^2\left(1-\frac{b^2}{d^2}\right)$

[IIT-JEE – 1995]

6. An ellipse has eccentricity $\frac{1}{2}$ and one focus at the point $P\left(\frac{1}{2},1\right)$. Its one directrix is the common tangent, nearer to the point P to the circle $x^2+y^2=1$ and the hyperbola $x^2-y^2=1$. Then find the equation of the ellipse in its standard form. [IIT-JEE – 1996]

7. A tangent to the ellipse $x^2+4y^2=4$ meets the ellipse $x^2+2y^2=6$ at P and Q. Prove that the tangents at P and Q of the ellipse $x^2+2y^2=6$ are at right angles.

[IIT-JEE – 1997]

8. An ellipse has OB as a semi minor axis. F, F' are its foci, and the ellipse FBF' is a right angle. Then find the eccentricity of the fllipse.

[IIT-JEE – 1997]

9. If P = (x, y) be any point on $16x^2+25y^2=400$ with foci $F_1=(3,0)$, $F_2=(-3,0)$ and then PF_1+PF_2 is

[IIT-JEE – 1998]

(a) 8 (b) 6 (c) 10 (d) 12

10. Find the co-ordinates of all points P on the ellipse $\frac{x^2}{a^2}+\frac{y^2}{b^2}=1$, for which the area of the triangle PON is maximum, where O denotes the origin and N, the foot of the perpendicular from O to the tangent at P.

[IIT-JEE – 1999]

11. On the ellipse $4x^2+9y^2=1$, the points at which the tangents are parallel to the line 9y = 8 x are

(a) $\left(\frac{2}{5},\frac{1}{5}\right)$ (b) $\left(-\frac{2}{5},\frac{1}{5}\right)$

(c) $\left(-\frac{2}{5},-\frac{1}{5}\right)$ (d) $\left(\frac{2}{5},-\frac{1}{5}\right)$

[IIT-JEE – 1999]

12. Let P be a point on the ellipse $\frac{x^2}{a^2}+\frac{y^2}{b^2}=1,\ 0<b<a$. Let the line parallel to y-axis. Passing through P meet the circle $x^2+y^2=a^2$ at the point Q such that P and Q are on the same side of x-axis. For two positive real numbers r and s, find the locus of the point R on PQ such that PR : RQ = r : s and p varies over the two ellipse.

[IIT-JEE – 2001]

13. Prove that, in an ellipse, the perpendicular from a focus upon any tangent and the line joining the centerof the ellipse to the point of contact meet on the corresponding directrix.

[IIT-JEE – 2002]

14. The area of the quadrilateral formed by the tangents at the end points of latus rectum to the ellipse

$$\frac{x^2}{9}+\frac{y^2}{5}=1, \text{ is}$$

(a) 27/4 sq. units (b) 9 sq. units

(c) 27/2 sq. units (d) 27 sq. units.

[IIT-JEE – 2003]

15. If tangents are drawn to the ellipse $x^2+2y^2=2$, then the locus of the mid point of the intercept made by the tangents between the co-ordinate axes is

(a) $\frac{1}{2x^2}+\frac{1}{4y^2}=1$ (b) $\frac{1}{4x^2}+\frac{1}{2y^2}=1$

(c) $\frac{x^2}{2}+\frac{y^2}{4}=1$ (d) $\frac{x^2}{4}+\frac{y^2}{2}=1$

[IIT-JEE – 2004]

16. Find the equation of the common tangent in ist quadrant to the circle $x^2+y^2=16$ and the ellipse $\frac{x^2}{25}+\frac{y^2}{4}=1$. Also find the length of the intercept of the tangent between the co-ordinate axes.

[IIT-JEE – 2005]

17. A triangle is formed by a tangent to the ellipse $\frac{x^2}{a^2}+\frac{y^2}{b^2}=1$ and the co-ordinate axes . The area of the triangle cannot be less than

(a) $\frac{1}{2}\left(a^2+b^2\right)$ sq u. (b) $\frac{1}{3}\left(a^2+b^2+ab\right)$ sq.u.

(c) $\frac{1}{2}(a+b)^2$ (d) ab sq u.

[IIT-JEE-2005]

18. Let $P(x_1, y_1)$, $Q(x_2, y_2)$, $y_1<0$, $y_2<0$, be the end points of the latus rectum of the ellipse $x^2+4y^2=4$. The equation of the parabola with latus rectum PQ are

(a) $x^2+2\sqrt{3}y=3+\sqrt{3}$

(b) $x^2-2\sqrt{3}y=3+\sqrt{3}$

(c) $x^2+2\sqrt{3}y=3-\sqrt{3}$

(d) $x^2-2\sqrt{3}y=3-\sqrt{3}$

[IIT-JEE-2008]

19. The line passing through the extremity A of the major axis and extremity B of the minor axis of the ellipse $x^2+9y^2=9$ meets it auxiliary circle at the point M. Then the area of the triangle with vertices at A, M and the origin O is

(a) 31/10 (b) 29/10

(c) 21/10 (d) 27/10

[IIT-JEE-2009]

20. The normal at P on the ellipse $x^2+4y^2=16$ meets the x-axis at Q. If M is the mid-point of the line segment PQ, then the locus of M intersects the latus rectums of the given ellipse at the points

(a) $\left(\pm 3\sqrt{5}/2, \pm 2/7\right)$ (b) $\left(\pm 3\sqrt{5}/2, \pm \sqrt{19}/7\right)$

(c) $\left(\pm 2\sqrt{3}, \pm 1/7\right)$ (d) $\left(\pm 2\sqrt{3}, \pm 4\sqrt{3}/7\right)$

[IIT-JEE-2009]

COMPREHENSION

21. Tangents are drawn from the point P(3, 4) to the ellipse $\frac{x^2}{9}+\frac{y^2}{4}=1$ touching the ellipse at Points A and B

1. The co-ordinates of A and B are

(a) (3, 0) and (0, 2) (b) $\left(-\frac{8}{5}, \frac{2\sqrt{16}}{15}\right)\&\left(-\frac{9}{5}, \frac{8}{5}\right)$

(c) $\left(-\frac{8}{5}, \frac{2\sqrt{16}}{15}\right)\&(0,2)$ (d) $(3, 0)\&\left(-\frac{9}{5}, \frac{8}{5}\right)$

2. The orthocentre of the triangle PAB is

(a) $\left(5, \frac{8}{7}\right)$ (b) $\left(\frac{7}{5}, \frac{25}{8}\right)$

(c) $\left(\frac{11}{5}, \frac{8}{5}\right)$ (d) $\left(\frac{8}{25}, \frac{7}{5}\right)$

3. The equation of the locus of the point whose distances from the point P and the line AB are equal, is

(a) $9x^2+y^2-6xy-54x-62y+241=0$

(b) $x^2+9y^2+6xy-54x+62y-241=0$

(c) $9x^2+9y^2-6xy-54x-62y-241=0$

(d) $x^2+y^2-2xy+27x+31y-120=0$

[IIT-JEE-2010]

22. The ellipse $E_1 : \frac{x^2}{9}+\frac{y^2}{4}=1$ is inscribed in a rectangle R whose sides are parallel to co-ordinate axes another ellipse E_2 : passing through the point (0, 4) circumscribes the rectangle R. The eccentricity of the ellipse E_2 is

(a) $\frac{\sqrt{2}}{2}$ (b) $\frac{\sqrt{3}}{2}$ (c) $\frac{1}{2}$ (d) $\frac{3}{4}$

[IIT-JEE-2012]

ANSWER

3. $ab\sqrt{a^2-b^2}$

6. $\dfrac{\left(x-\frac{1}{3}\right)^2}{\frac{1}{9}}+\dfrac{(y-1)^2}{\frac{1}{12}}=1$

8. $\dfrac{1}{\sqrt{2}}$.

10. $\left(\pm\dfrac{a^2}{\sqrt{a^2+b^2}}, \pm\dfrac{b^2}{\sqrt{a^2+b^2}}\right)$

12. $\dfrac{x^2}{a^2}+\dfrac{(r+s)^2\, y^2}{(ra+sb)^2}=1$

16. $y=-\dfrac{2}{\sqrt{3}}x+4\sqrt{\dfrac{7}{3}}, \dfrac{14}{\sqrt{3}}$

SELF ASSESSMENT TEST

Time : 2 Hrs. **Ch: The Ellipse** **M.M. : 100**

Give answers the following questions :

1. Let (a, β) be a point from which two perpendicular tangent can be drawn to the ellipse $4x^2+5y^2=20$. If $F=4\alpha+3\beta$, then find the range of F.
2. If $\dfrac{x^2}{f(4x)}+\dfrac{y^2}{f(a^2-5)}=1$ represents an ellipse with major axis as y-axis and f is a decreasing function , then find a.
3. The point, as shortest distance from the line x + y = 7 and lying on an ellipse $x^2+2y^2=6$, has co-ordinates..........
4. The equation $\dfrac{x^2}{10-a}+\dfrac{y^2}{4-a}=1$ represent an ellipse if

   (a) a<4 (b) a>4 (c) 4<a<10 (d) a>10
5. Find the set of values of a fror which $(13x-1)^2+(13y-2)^2=a(5x+12y-1)^2$ represents an ellipse.
6. If α and β are eccebtric angles of the ends of a focal chord of the ellipse $\dfrac{x^2}{\lambda^2}+\dfrac{y^2}{b^2}=1$, then find the value of $\tan\left(\dfrac{\alpha}{2}\right)\times\tan\left(\dfrac{\beta}{2}\right)$.
7. Find the radius of the circle passing through the foci of the ellipse $\dfrac{x^2}{16}+\dfrac{y^2}{9}=1$ and having its centre (0, 3)
8. If the normals at the four points (x_i, y_i), I = 1, 2, 3, 4 on the ellipse $\dfrac{x^2}{a^2}+\dfrac{y^2}{b^2}=1$ are concurrent, then find the value of $(x_1+x_2+x_3+x_4)\left(\dfrac{1}{x_1}+\dfrac{1}{x_2}+\dfrac{1}{x_3}+\dfrac{1}{x_4}\right)$.
9. If the centre of an ellipse $\dfrac{(x-2)^2}{16}+\dfrac{(y-3)^2}{9}=1$ moves about the origin in anticlockwise sense through an angle of 90°, say, at P and then it moves $\sqrt{2}$ units along the direction of the north east, say at Q and then it is translated along the x-axis through 4 units , say , at R, then find the co-ordinates of R.

SELF ASSESSMENT TEST

6 The Hyperbola

CONCEPT BOOSTER

6.1 INTRODUCTION

The word "hyperbola" derives from the Greek , meaning "over-thrown" or "excessive", from which the English term hyperbole also derives. The term hyperbola is believed to have been coined by Apollonius of Perga (c. 262–c. 190 BC), who was a Greek geometer and astronomer noted for his writings on conic sections. His innovative methodology and terminology, especially in the field of the conic sections, the Conics. According to him, hyperbola, the inclination of the plane to the base of the cone exceeds that of the side of the cone

6.2 MATHEMATICAL DEFINITIONS

Definition-1:

A hyperbola is a symmetrical open curve formed by the intersection of a cone with a plane at a smaller angle with its axis than the side of the cone.

Definition-2:

A hyperbola is the pair of such curves formed by the intersection of a plane with two equal cones on opposites of the same vertex.

Definition -3:

A hyperbola is a conic section defined as the locus of all points P in the plane the difference of whose distances from two fixed points (the foci S and S') is a constant,

i.e. S'P - SP = 2a.

Definition-4:

It is the locus of a point, which moves in a plane in such a way that its distance from a fixed point (focus) to a fixed straight line (directrix) is constant (> 1) .

$$\text{i.e. } \frac{SP}{PM} = e\ (>1)$$

Definition-5 :

A conic section is said to be a hyperbola , if its eccentricity is more than 1.

Definition-6:

A conic $ax^2 + 2hxy + by^2 + 2gx + 2fy + c = 0$

represents a hyperbola if

(i) $\Delta \neq 0$

(ii) $h^2 - ab > 0$,

$$\text{where } \Delta = \begin{vmatrix} a & h & g \\ h & b & f \\ g & f & c \end{vmatrix}$$

$$= abc + 2fgh - af^2 - bg^2 - ch^2$$

Definition-7 :

Section of a double right circular cone and a plane is said to be a hyperbola if the plane is parallel to the axis of a double right circular cone.

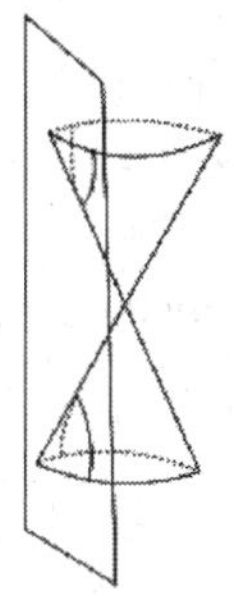

Definition-8:

If a circle touches both the circles ,which are neither touching nor intersecting, externally, then the locus of the first circle is a hyperbola w. r. to the given two circles.

Definition - 9:

If base of a triangle and the ratio of tangents of half of the base angles are given, then the locus of the opposite vertex is also a hyperbola.

Definitio-10:

Let z, z_1 & z_2 be three complex numbers such that $|z - z_1| - |z - z_2| = k$, where $k < |z_1 - z_2|$ Then the locus of 'z' is also known as hyperbola.

6.3 STANDARD EQUATION OF A HYPERBOLA

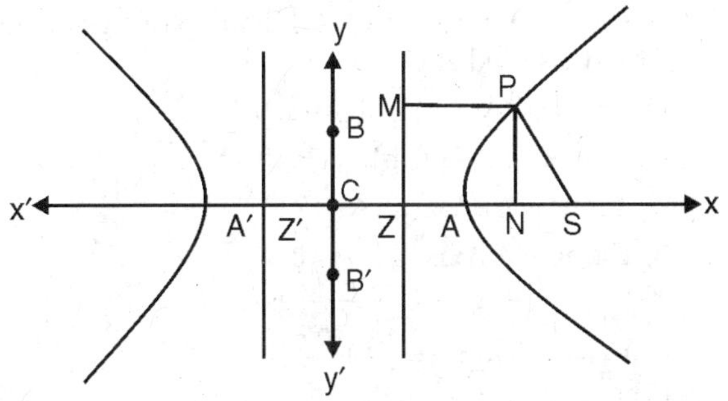

Let ZM be the directrix , S be the focus and SZ be the perpendicular to the directrix.

From the definition of hyperbola, we can write,

SA = e. AZ ...(i)

and SA` = e A`Z ...(ii)

Let the length of AA` = 2a and C be the middle point of AA` .

Adding (i) and (ii), we get, $SA + SA' = e(AZ + A'Z)$

$\Rightarrow \quad (CS - CA) + (CS + CA') = e(AZ + AA' - AZ)$

$\Rightarrow \quad 2CS = e(AA') = 2ae$

$\Rightarrow \quad CS = ae$ ...(iii)

Subtracting (i) from (ii), we get,

$(SA' - SA) = e(A'Z - AZ)$

$\Rightarrow \quad AA' = e((CA' + CZ) - (CA - CZ))$

$\Rightarrow \quad 2a = e.2CZ$

$\Rightarrow \quad CZ = \frac{a}{e}$ ...(iv)

Let P(x, y) be any point on the curve and PM be perpendicular to the directrix.

Now from the definiton of hyperbola, we get,

$SP^2 = e^2.PM^2$

$\Rightarrow \quad (x - ae)^2 + y^2 = e^2\left(\frac{ex - a}{\sqrt{e^2}}\right)^2 = (ex - a)^2$

$\Rightarrow \quad x^2 - 2aex + a^2e^2 + y^2 = (e^2x^2 - 2aex + a^2)$

$\Rightarrow \quad x^2(e^2 - 1) - y^2 = a^2(e^2 - 1)$

$\Rightarrow \quad \frac{x^2(e^2-1)}{a^2(e^2-1)} - \frac{y^2}{a^2(e^2-1)} = 1$

$\Rightarrow \quad \frac{x^2}{a^2} - \frac{y^2}{b^2} = 1$, where, $b^2 = a^2(e^2 - 1)$

Which is the standard equation of a hyperbola.

6.4 DEFINITION AND BASIC TERMILOGY OF THE HYPERBOLA $\frac{x^2}{a^2} - \frac{y^2}{b^2} = 1$

(i) **Centre:** Here, C (0, 0). All chords passing through C and bisected at C.

(ii) **Vertices:** A(a, o) and A`(-a, 0)

(iii) **Co-vertices:** B(0, b) and B`(0, -b)

(iv) **Transverse Axis:** AA` = 2 a

(v) **Conjugate Axis:** BB` = 2 b

(vi) **Eccentricity:** $e = \sqrt{1 + \frac{b^2}{a^2}}$

(vii) **Latus Rectum:** Any chord passing through the focus and perpendicular to the axis is known as latus rectum.

The length of the latus rectum is $\frac{2b^2}{a}$

(viii) **End points of a latus recta :**

Let LL` and $L_1L_1$` be two latus recta passes through the focus S(ae, o) and S`(-ae, 0)

Then,

$L\left(ae, \frac{b^2}{a}\right); L'\left(ae, -\frac{b^2}{a}\right); L_1\left(-ae, \frac{b^2}{a}\right) L_1'\left(-ae, -\frac{b^2}{a}\right)$

(ix) **Equation of the latus recta are :** $x = \pm\, ae$

(x) **Co-ordinates of Foci:** S (ae, 0) and S`(-ae, 0)

(xi) **Distances between two foci (/Focal length):** 2 a e

(xii) **Equation of directrices:** $x = \pm\,\frac{a}{e}$

(xiii) **Distance between the directrices:** $\frac{2a}{e}$

(xiv) **Focal distances :** $SP = ex - a$ and $S'P = ex + a$

(xv) $|S'P - SP| = 2a$.

(xvi) **Diameter:** Any chord passing through the centre of the hyperbola is known as diameter.

(xvii) **Focal chord:** Any chord passing through the focus is called focal chord.

(xviii) **Auxiliary Circle:** Any circle is drawn with centre C and transverse axis as a diameter is called the auxiliary circle.

Equation of the auxiliary circle is $x^2 + y^2 = a^2$.

(xix) **Parametrics Equations :**

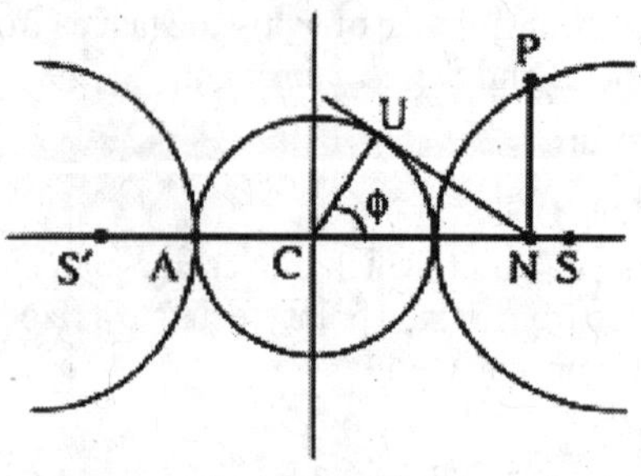

Let the auxiliary circle be $x^2 + y^2 = a^2$ and U be any point on the auxiliary circle be $(a\cos\phi,\ b\sin\phi)$

Let P(x, y) be any point on the hyperbola $\frac{x^2}{a^2} - \frac{y^2}{b^2} = 1$.

Draw PN be the perpendicular to x-axis

Let NU ba a tangent to the auxiliary circle. Join NU.

Let $\angle$ UCN = ϕ

Here P and U are the corresponding points of the hyper bola and the auxiliary circle and ϕ is the eccentric angle of P., where $0 \le \phi < 2\pi$.

Now, $U = (a\cos\phi,\ a\sin\phi)$

Now, $x = CN = \dfrac{CN}{CQ}.CQ = a.\sec\phi$.

Thus the co-ordinates of P be $(a\ \sec\phi,\ y)$. Since the point P lies on the hyperbola,

so $\dfrac{a^2\sec^2\phi}{a^2} - \dfrac{y^2}{b^2} = 1$

$\Rightarrow\ \sec^2\phi - \dfrac{y^2}{b^2} = 1 \Rightarrow \dfrac{y^2}{b^2} = \sec^2\phi - 1 = \tan^2\phi$

$\Rightarrow\ y^2 = b^2\tan^2\phi$

$\Rightarrow\ y = \pm\ b\ \tan\phi$.

$\Rightarrow\ y = b\ \tan\phi$ (since P lies in the first quadrant)

Hence, the parametric equation of the hyperbola are

$x = a\sec f$ & $y = b\tan f$.

(xx) Any point on the hyperbola can be considered as $(a\sec f,\ b\tan f)$

(xxi) **Eccentric angle:** If two points $P(a\sec f,\ b\tan f)$ and $Q(a\cos\phi,\ a\sin\phi)$ are the corresponding points on the hyperbola and the auxiliary circle, then ϕ is called the eccentric angle of the point P. on the hyperbola, where $0 \le \phi < 2\pi$.

(xxii) **Conjugate hyperbola:** Corresponding to every hyperbola, there exists a hyperbola in which the conjugate and transverse axes of one is equal to tansverse and conjugate axes of the other. Such type of hyperbolas are known as conjugate hyperbola.

Equation of conjugate hyperbola to the hyperbola $\dfrac{x^2}{a^2} - \dfrac{y^2}{b^2} = 1$ is $\dfrac{x^2}{a^2} - \dfrac{y^2}{b^2} = -1$

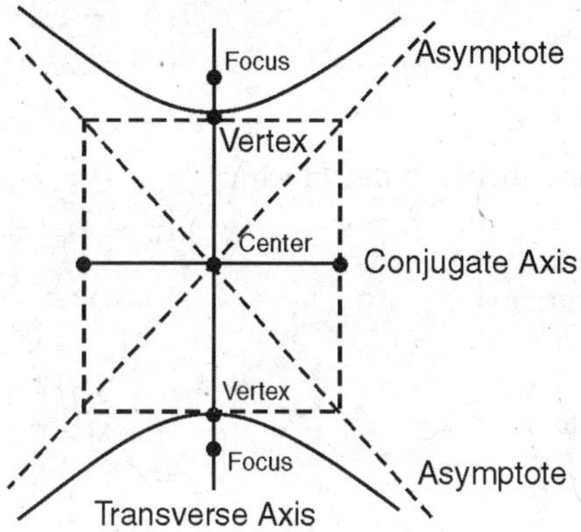

It is also known as vertical hyperbola.

(xxiii) **Rectangular or Equilateral hyperbola :** If the semi tansverse axis is equal to semi conjugate axis of a hyperbola i.e. $a = b$, then it is known as rectangular hyperbola or equilateral hyperbola.

Equation of a rectangular hyperbola is

$x^2 - y^2 = a^2$.

Clearly its eccentricity (e)

$= \sqrt{1+\dfrac{b^2}{a^2}} = \sqrt{1+\dfrac{a^2}{a^2}} = \sqrt{1+1} = \sqrt{2}$.

(xxiv) Equation of a hyperbola whose axes are parallel to the co-ordinate axes and centre (h, k)

is $\dfrac{(x-h)^2}{a^2} - \dfrac{(y-k)^2}{b^2} = 1$, where foci are $(h \pm ae,\ k)$

and directrix is $x = h \pm \dfrac{a}{e}$.

(xxv) **Comparision between hyperbola and its conjugate:**

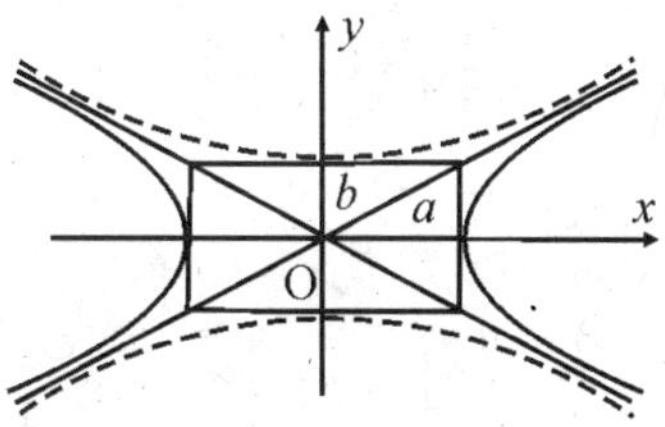

Fundamentals	**Hyperbola**	**Conjugate Hyperbola**
1. Std equation	$\dfrac{x^2}{a^2} - \dfrac{y^2}{b^2} = 1$	$\dfrac{x^2}{a^2} - \dfrac{y^2}{b^2} = -1$
2. Centre	(0, 0)	(0, 0)
3. Vertoces	$(\pm a,\ 0)$	$(0, \pm b)$
4. Co-vertices	$(0, \pm b)$	$(\pm a,\ 0)$
5. Length of transverse axis	2 a	2 b
6. Length of conjugate axis	2 b	2 a
7. Co-ordinates of foci	$(\pm ae,\ 0)$	$(0,\ \pm be)$

8. Focal length	2 a e	2 b e
9. Equation of directrices	$x = \pm \frac{a}{e}$	$y = \pm \frac{b}{e}$
10. Distance between the directrices	$\frac{2a}{e}$	$\frac{2b}{e}$
11. Eccentricity	$e = \sqrt{1 + \frac{b^2}{a^2}}$	$e = \sqrt{1 + \frac{a^2}{b^2}}$
12. Length of latus rectum	$\frac{2b^2}{a}$	$\frac{2a^2}{b}$
13. Focal radii :	SP = ex - a, S'P = ex + a	SP = ey - b, S'P = ey + b
14. Difference of focal radii:	2 a	2 b
15. Parametric equations	$x = a\sec\phi,\ y = b\tan\phi$	$x = b\sec\phi,\ y = a\tan\phi$

(xxvi) **Equation of the chord joining the points $P(f_1)$ & $Q(f_2)$:**

Equation of the chord joining the points $P(a\sec f_1, b\tan f_1)$ & $Q(a\sec f_2, b\tan f_2)$

is $\frac{x}{a}\cos\left(\frac{\phi_1 - \phi_2}{2}\right) - \frac{y}{b}\sin\left(\frac{\phi_1 + \phi_2}{2}\right) = \cos\left(\frac{\phi_1 + \phi_2}{2}\right)$

(xxvii) **Condition of a focal chord :**

Equation of the chord joining the points $P(a\sec f_1, b\tan f_1)$ & $Q(a\sec f_2, b\tan f_2)$

is $\frac{x}{a}\cos\left(\frac{\phi_1 - \phi_2}{2}\right) - \frac{y}{b}\sin\left(\frac{\phi_1 + \phi_2}{2}\right) = \cos\left(\frac{\phi_1 + \phi_2}{2}\right)$

Which is passing through the focus S(ae, 0)

So, $e\cos\left(\frac{\phi_1 - \phi_2}{2}\right) = \cos\left(\frac{\phi_1 + \phi_2}{2}\right)$

$$\Rightarrow \frac{\cos\left(\frac{\phi_1 - \phi_2}{2}\right)}{\cos\left(\frac{\phi_1 + \phi_2}{2}\right)} = \frac{1}{e}$$

$$\Rightarrow \frac{\cos\left(\frac{\phi_1 - \phi_2}{2}\right) - \cos\left(\frac{\phi_1 + \phi_2}{2}\right)}{\cos\left(\frac{\phi_1 - \phi_2}{2}\right) + \cos\left(\frac{\phi_1 + \phi_2}{2}\right)} = \frac{1-e}{1+e}$$

$$\Rightarrow \tan\left(\frac{\phi_1}{2}\right)\tan\left(\frac{\phi_2}{2}\right) = \frac{1-e}{1+e}$$

(xxviii) **Condition of a focal chord with respect to eccentricity (e) :**

As we know that, if the chord passing through the focus, then

$$e\cos\left(\frac{\phi_1 - \phi_2}{2}\right) = \cos\left(\frac{\phi_1 + \phi_2}{2}\right)$$

$$\Rightarrow e \times 2\sin\left(\frac{\phi_1 + \phi_2}{2}\right)\cos\left(\frac{\phi_1 - \phi_2}{2}\right) = 2\sin\left(\frac{\phi_1 + \phi_2}{2}\right)\cos\left(\frac{\phi_1 + \phi_2}{2}\right)$$

$$\Rightarrow e \times (\sin\phi_1 + \sin\phi_2) = \sin(\phi_1 + \phi_2)$$

$$\Rightarrow e = \frac{\sin(\phi_1 + \phi_2)}{(\sin\phi_1 + \sin\phi_2)}$$

Which is the required condition.

(xxix) **Rule to find out the centre of the hyperbola :**

If $f(x, y) = 0$ is the equation of a hyperbola , then the centre of the hyperbola is obtained by the relation

$$\frac{\delta f}{dx} = 0 \text{ and } \frac{\delta f}{dy} = 0.$$

Let $f(x, y) = ax^2 + 2hxy + by^2 + 2gx + 2fy + c = 0$ be the equation of a hyperbola.

Then, $\frac{\delta f}{dx} = 0$ gives

$$2ax + 2hy + 2g = 0 \Rightarrow ax + hy + g = 0 \quad \text{...(i)}$$

and $\frac{\delta f}{\delta y} = 0$ gives

$$2hx + 2by + 2f = 0 \Rightarrow hx + by + f = 0 \quad \text{...(ii)}$$

Solve (i) and (ii), we get the required centre.

(xxx) **Polar form of a hyperbola :**

Equation of hyperbola is $\frac{x^2}{a^2} - \frac{y^2}{b^2} = 1$

Pur x = r cos?, y = r sin? ,

we get, $\frac{1}{r^2} = \frac{\cos^2\theta}{a^2} - \frac{\sin^2\theta}{b^2}$

$$\Rightarrow \quad r^2 = \frac{a^2b^2}{b^2\cos^2? - a^2\sin^2?} = \frac{a^2(e^2-1)}{(e^2\cos^2\theta - 1)}.$$

(xxxi) **Polar form of a hyperbola if centered at focus :**

Equation of hyperbola is $\frac{x^2}{a^2} - \frac{y^2}{b^2} = 1$

If centered C(0, 0) at Focus (ae, 0), then the polar form of hyperbola becomes

$$r = \frac{a(e^2-1)}{1 - e\cos\theta}.$$

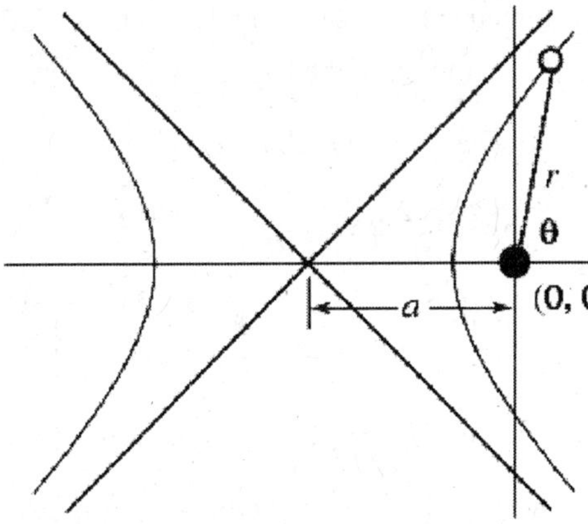

(xxxii) **Polar form of a rectangular hyperbola :**

Equation of rectangular hyperbola is $x^2 - y^2 = a^2$

Put $x = r\cos\theta$ & $y = r\sin\theta$, we get, $r^2 \cos 2? = a^2$

EXERCISE

1. Find the centre, vertices, co-vertices, length of tansverse axis, conjugate axis and latus rectum, eccentricity, foci and the equation of directrices of each of the following hyperbo las.

(i) $\frac{x^2}{9} - \frac{y^2}{4} = 1$

(ii) $\frac{x^2}{16} - \frac{y^2}{9} = -1$

(iii) $9x^2 - 16y^2 - 36x + 96y - 252 = 0$

Sol. (i) The equation of the given hyperbola is $\frac{x^2}{9} - \frac{y^2}{4} = 1$

(a) Centre : (0, 0)

(b) vertices : A(a, 0) = A(3, 0) and A (-a, 0) = A(-3, 0)

(c) co-vertices : B (0, b) = B (0, 2) and B'(0, -b) = B'(0, -2)

(d) The length of the transverse axis = 2a = 6

(e) The length of the conjugate axis = 2b = 4

(f) The length of the latus rectum = $\frac{2b^2}{a} = \frac{8}{3}$

(g) Eccentricity = e = $\sqrt{1+\frac{b^2}{a^2}} = \sqrt{1+\frac{4}{9}} = \frac{\sqrt{13}}{3}$

(h) Equation of the directrices :

$$x = \pm\frac{a}{e} = \pm\frac{2}{\sqrt{13}/3} = \pm\frac{6}{\sqrt{13}}$$

(ii) The equation of the given hyperbola is $\frac{x^2}{16} - \frac{y^2}{9} = -1$

(a) Centre : (0, 0)

(b) Vertices : A(0, b) = A(0, 3) and A (0, -b) = A(0, -3)

(c) Co-vertices : B (a, 0) = B (4, 0) and B`(-a, 0) = B`(-4, 0)

(d) The length of the transverse axis = 2a = 6

(e) The length of the conjugate axis = 2b = 8

(f) The length of the latus rectum = $\frac{2a^2}{b} = \frac{16}{3}$

(g) Eccentricity = e = $\sqrt{1+\frac{a^2}{b^2}} = \sqrt{1+\frac{9}{16}} = \frac{5}{4}$

(h) Equation of the directrices :

$$y = \pm\frac{b}{e} = \pm\frac{3}{5/4} = \pm\frac{12}{5}.$$

(iii) The equation of the hyperbola is

$$9x^2 - 16y^2 - 36x + 96y - 252 = 0$$

$$\Rightarrow \quad 9(x^2 - 4x) - 16(y^2 - 6y) = 252$$

$$\Rightarrow \quad 9(x-2)^2 - 16(y-3)^2 = 252 + 36 - 144 = 144$$

$$\Rightarrow \quad \frac{9(x-2)^2}{144} - \frac{16(y-3)^2}{144} = 1$$

$$\Rightarrow \quad \frac{(x-2)^2}{16} - \frac{(y-3)^2}{9} = 1$$

(a) Centre : (0, 0) $\Rightarrow$ X = 0, Y = 0

$\Rightarrow$ x-2 = 0, $y - 3 = 0$

$\Rightarrow$ x = 2 & $y = 3$

Hence, the centre is (2, 3)

(b) Vertices : $(\pm a,\ 0)$

$\Rightarrow$ X = ± a, Y = 0

$\Rightarrow$ x-2 = ± 4, $y - 3 = 0$

$\Rightarrow$ x = 2± 4, $y = 3$

Hence, the vertices are (6, 3) and (-2, 3)

(c) Co-vertices : $(0, \pm \mathbf{b})$

$\Rightarrow$ X = 0, Y = ± b

$\Rightarrow$ x-2 = 0, $y-3=\pm 3$

$\Rightarrow$ x = 2, $y=3\pm 3$

Hence, the co-vertices are (2, 6) and (2, 0)

(d) The length of the transverse axis = 2a = 8

(e) The length of the conjugate axis = 2 b = 6

(f) Eccentricity $= e = \sqrt{1+\frac{9}{16}} = \frac{5}{4}$

(g) Co-ordinates of Foci : $(\pm\, ae\, , 0)$

$\Rightarrow X = \pm 5,\ Y = 0$

$\Rightarrow X-2 = \pm 5,\ y-3=0$

$\Rightarrow X = 2\pm 5,\ y=3$

Hence, the co-ordinates of the foci are (7, 3) and (-3, 3)

Ex-2. Find the equation of the hyperbola, whose centre is (1, 0), one focus is (6, 0) and the length of transverse axis is 6.

Sol. The equation of the hyperbola with centre (1, 0) is

$$\frac{(x-1)^2}{a^2}-\frac{y^2}{b^2}=1$$

Here, 2a = 6 $\Rightarrow$ a = 3

Also, one focus = (6, 0) $\Rightarrow$ 1 + ae = 6

$\Rightarrow$ ae = 5

$\Rightarrow$ 3e = 5

$\Rightarrow$ e = 5/3

Therefore, $b^2 = a^2\left(e^2-1\right) = 9\left(\frac{25}{9}-1\right) = 16$

Hence, the equation of the hyperbola is

$$\frac{(x-1)^2}{9}-\frac{y^2}{16}=1$$

Ex-3. Find the equation of the hyperbola, whose centre is (3, 2), one focus is (5, 2) and one vertex is (4, 2)

Sol. Since the focus is (5, 2) and the vertex is (4, 2), so the axis of the hyperbola is parallel to x-axis and a = 1, ae = 2

Let the equation of the hyperbola be

$$\frac{(x-3)^2}{a^2}-\frac{(y-2)^2}{b^2}=1 \qquad ...(i)$$

As we know that, the relation in a, b and e with respect to a hyperbola is

$$b^2 = a^2\left(e^2-1\right) = a^2e^2 - a^2 = 4-1=3$$

Now from (i), we get, $\frac{(x-3)^2}{1}-\frac{(y-2)^2}{3}=1$

Ex-4. Find the equation of the hyperbola, whose centre is (-3, 2), one vertex is (-3, 4) and eccentricity is 5/2

Sol. Since the focus is (-3, 2) and the vertex is (-3,4), so the axis of the hyperbola is parallel to y-axis and be = 2

$$\Rightarrow\ b\times\frac{5}{2}=2 \Rightarrow\ b=\frac{4}{5}$$

Also, $a^2 = b^2\left(e^2-1\right) = \frac{16}{25}\left(\frac{25}{4}-1\right)=\frac{84}{25}$

Hence, the equation of the hyperbola is

$$\frac{(x+3)^2}{a^2}-\frac{(y-2)^2}{b^2}=1$$

$$\Rightarrow \frac{(x+3)^2}{84}-\frac{(y-2)^2}{16}=\frac{1}{25}$$

Ex-5. Find the equation of the hyperbola, whose one focus is (2, 1), directrix is x + 2 y = 1 and eccentricity is 2.

Sol. From the definition of the hyperbola, we can write,

$\frac{SP}{PM} = e$, where S = Focus, P = (x, y)

$$\Rightarrow\ SP^2 = e^2\ PM^2$$

$$\Rightarrow\ (x-2)^2+(y-1)^2 = 4\left\{\left(\frac{x+2y-1}{\sqrt{1+4}}\right)^2\right\}$$

$$\Rightarrow\ 5\left\{(x-2)^2+(y-1)^2\right\} = 4(x+2y-1)^2$$

Ex-6. Find the equation of the hyperbola, whose distance between foci is 16 and eccentricity is 2

Sol. Given relation is 2 a e = 16 $\Rightarrow$ a e = 8

$\Rightarrow$ a = 8 / e $\Rightarrow$ a = 4

Now, $b^2 = a^2\left(e^2-1\right) = a^2e^2 - a^2 = 64-4=60$

Hence, the equation of the hyperbola is $\frac{x^2}{a^2}-\frac{y^2}{b^2}=1$

$$\Rightarrow\ \frac{x^2}{4}-\frac{y^2}{60}=1$$

Ex-7. Find the equation of the hyperbola, whose foci are (6, 4) and (-6, 4) and eccentricity is 2.

Sol. Since foci are (6, 4) and (-6, 4), so the axis of the hyperbola is parallel to x-axis.

It is given that, distiance between two foci is 12

$\Rightarrow$ 2 a e = 12

$\Rightarrow$ a e = 6

$\Rightarrow$ 2 a = 6

$\Rightarrow$ a = 3

Also, $b^2 = a^2\left(e^2-1\right) = a^2e^2 - a^2 = 36-9=27$

Hence, the equation of the hyperbola is $\frac{x^2}{a^2}-\frac{y^2}{b^2}=1$

$$\Rightarrow \quad \frac{x^2}{9}-\frac{y^2}{27}=1$$

Ex-8. Find the eccentricity of the hyperbola whose latus rectum is half of its transverse axis.

Sol. Given relation is the length of the latus rectum

$$=\frac{1}{2}\times(2a)=a$$

$$\Rightarrow \quad \frac{2b^2}{a}=a$$

$$\Rightarrow \quad 2b^2=a^2$$

Also, relation in a, b and e is $b^2=a^2(e^2-1)$

$$\Rightarrow \quad \frac{a^2}{2}=a^2(e^2-1)$$

$$\Rightarrow \quad (e^2-1)=\frac{1}{2}$$

$$\Rightarrow \quad e=\sqrt{\frac{3}{2}}$$

Ex-9. If e_1 and e_2 be the eccentricities of a hyperbola and its conjugate, then prove that

$$\frac{1}{e_1^2}+\frac{1}{e_2^2}=1$$

Sol. Let the equation of the hyperbola is $\frac{x^2}{a^2}-\frac{y^2}{b^2}=1$ and its

conjugate is $\frac{x^2}{a^2}-\frac{y^2}{b^2}=-1$

Therefore, $e_1=\sqrt{1+\frac{b^2}{a^2}}$ and $e_2=\sqrt{1+\frac{a^2}{b^2}}$

$$\Rightarrow \quad e_1^2=\left(\frac{a^2+b^2}{a^2}\right) \;\&\; e_2^2=\left(\frac{a^2+b^2}{b^2}\right)$$

$$\Rightarrow \quad \frac{1}{e_1^2}+\frac{1}{e_2^2}=\left(\frac{a^2}{a^2+b^2}\right)+\left(\frac{b^2}{a^2+b^2}\right)=\left(\frac{a^2+b^2}{a^2+b^2}\right)=1$$

Ex-10. An ellipse and hyperbola are confocal (have the same focus) and the conjugate axis of the hyperbola is equal to the minor axis of the ellipse. If e_1 and e_2 are the eccentricities of the ellipse and the hyperbola, then prove that $e_1^2+e_2^2=2$.

Sol. Let the equation of the ellipse be $\frac{x^2}{a^2}+\frac{y^2}{b^2}=1$ and the

equation of the hyperbola is $\frac{x^2}{a^2}-\frac{y^2}{b^2}=1$

Also, it is given that, $2b=2a \Rightarrow b=a$

Let e_1 and e_2 be the eccentricities of the ellipse and the hyperbola.

Then $e_1=\sqrt{1-\frac{b^2}{a^2}}=\sqrt{1-\frac{a^2}{a^2}}=0$

and $e_2=\sqrt{1+\frac{b^2}{a^2}}=\sqrt{1+\frac{a^2}{a^2}}=\sqrt{2}$

Thus, $e_1^2+e_2^2=2$

Ex-11. Find the centre of the hyperbola

$$4(2y-x-3)^2-9(2x+y-1)^2=80$$

Sol. The equation of the hyperbola is

$$4(2y-x-3)^2-9(2x+y-1)^2=80$$

The centre of the hyperbola is obtained from the equations

$$2y-x-3=0 \text{ and } 2x+y-1=0$$

On solving, we get, $x=-2/5$ and $y=13/10$

Hence, the centre is $\left(-\frac{2}{5},\frac{13}{10}\right)$

Ex-12. Find the centre of the hyperbola

$$3x^2-5y^2-6x+20y-32=0$$

Sol. The equation of the given hyperbola is

$$3x^2-5y^2-6x+20y-32=0$$

$$\Rightarrow \quad 3(x^2-2x)-5(y^2-4y)=32$$

$$\Rightarrow \quad 3(x-1)^2-5(y-2)^2=32+3-20=15$$

$$\Rightarrow \quad \frac{3(x-1)^2}{15}-\frac{5(y-2)^2}{15}=1$$

$$\Rightarrow \quad \frac{(x-1)^2}{5}-\frac{(y-2)^2}{3}=1$$

Ex-13. Prove that the straight lines $\frac{x}{a}-\frac{y}{b}=2013$ and $\frac{x}{a}+\frac{y}{b}=\frac{1}{2013}$ always meet on a hyperbola.

Sol. The given straight lines are $\frac{x}{a}-\frac{y}{b}=2013$ ...(i)

and $\frac{x}{a}+\frac{y}{b}=\frac{1}{2013}$ ...(ii)

Multiplying (i) and (ii), we get,

$$\left(\frac{x}{a}-\frac{y}{b}\right)\left(\frac{x}{a}+\frac{y}{b}\right)=2013\times\frac{1}{2013}=1$$

$$\Rightarrow \quad \frac{x^2}{a^2}-\frac{y^2}{b^2}=1$$

Which represents a hyperbola.

Ex-14. Prove that the locus represented by $x=3\left(\frac{1+t^2}{1-t^2}\right)$ and $y=\frac{4t}{t^2-1}$ is a hyperbola.

Sol. We have, $x = 3\left(\frac{1+t^2}{1-t^2}\right)$ and $y = \frac{4t}{t^2-1}$

$$\Rightarrow \quad \frac{x^2}{9} - \frac{y^2}{4} = \left(\frac{1+t^2}{1-t^2}\right)^2 - \left(\frac{2t}{1-t^2}\right)^2$$

$$\Rightarrow \quad \frac{x^2}{9} - \frac{y^2}{4} = \frac{\left(1+t^2\right)^2 - 4t^2}{\left(1-t^2\right)^2} = \left(\frac{1-t^2}{1-t^2}\right)^2 = 1$$

$$\Rightarrow \quad \frac{x^2}{9} - \frac{y^2}{4} = 1$$

Which represents a hyperbola.

Ex-15. Prove that the locus represented by $x = \frac{1}{2}\left(e^t + e^{-t}\right)$ and $y = \frac{1}{2}\left(e^t - e^{-t}\right)$ is a hyperbola.

Sol. We have, $x = \frac{1}{2}\left(e^t + e^{-t}\right)$ and $y = \frac{1}{2}\left(e^t - e^{-t}\right)$

$$\Rightarrow \quad 2x = \left(e^t + e^{-t}\right) \ \& \ 2y = \left(e^t - e^{-t}\right)$$

$$\Rightarrow \quad 4x^2 - 4y^2 = \left(e^t + e^{-t}\right)^2 - \left(e^t - e^{-t}\right)^2$$

$$\Rightarrow \quad 4x^2 - 4y^2 = 2 + 2$$

$$\Rightarrow \quad x^2 - y^2 = 1$$

Which represents a rectangular hyperbola.

Ex-16. If the equation $\frac{x^2}{2014-\lambda} + \frac{y^2}{2013-\lambda} = 1$ represents a hyperbola, then find λ.

Sol. The given equation of the hyperbola is

$$\frac{x^2}{2014-\lambda} + \frac{y^2}{2013-\lambda} = 1$$

$$\Rightarrow \quad (2013-\lambda)\, x^2 + (2014-\lambda) y^2 - (2013-\lambda)(2014-\lambda) = 0$$

$$\Rightarrow \quad (2013-\lambda)\, x^2 + (\lambda\text{-}2014) y^2 - (2013-\lambda)(2014-\lambda) = 0$$

The given equation represents a hyperbola if

$$h^2 - ab > 0$$

$$\Rightarrow \quad 0 - (2013-\lambda)(\lambda-2014) > 0$$

$$\Rightarrow \quad (2013-\lambda)\,(\lambda-2014) < 0$$

$$\Rightarrow \quad 2013 < \lambda < 2014$$

$$\Rightarrow \quad \lambda \in (2013,\ 2014)$$

Ex-17. If the foci of the ellipse $\frac{x^2}{16} + \frac{y^2}{b^2} = 1$ and the hyperbola $\frac{x^2}{144} - \frac{y^2}{81} = \frac{1}{25}$ coincide, then find the value of b^2.

Sol. The given equation of the hyperbola is $\frac{x^2}{144} - \frac{y^2}{81} = \frac{1}{25}$

We have,

$$e = \sqrt{1 + \frac{b^2}{a^2}} = \sqrt{1 + \frac{81}{144}} = \sqrt{\frac{225}{144}} = \frac{15}{12} = \frac{5}{4}$$

Also, $a^2 = \frac{144}{25}$

Thus, the foci are $(\pm\, ae,\, 0)$

$$= \left(\pm \frac{12}{5} \times \frac{5}{4},\ 0\right) = (\pm\, 3,\, 0).$$

Now, for the ellipse, $ae = 3 \Rightarrow a^2e^2 = 9$

Thus, $b^2 = a^2\left(1\text{-}e^2\right) = a^2\text{-}a^2e^2 = 16\text{-}9 = 7$

Hence, the value of b^2 is 7.

Ex-18. If the latus rectum subtends a right angle at the centre of the hyperbola $\frac{x^2}{a^2} - \frac{y^2}{b^2} = 1$, then find its eccentricity.

Sol. Let LL` be the latus rectum of the given hyperbola.

Therefore, $L = \left(ae,\ \frac{b^2}{a}\right)$ and $L` = \left(ae,\ -\frac{b^2}{a}\right)$ and the centre of the hyperbola is C(0, 0)

Now, slope of $CL = m_1 = \frac{\left(b^2/a\right)}{ae} = \frac{b^2}{a^2e}$ and

the slope of $CL` = m_2 = \frac{\left(-b^2/a\right)}{ae} = -\frac{b^2}{a^2e}$

Since, the latus rectum subtends a right angle at the centre, so $m_1 \times m_2 = -1$

$$\Rightarrow \quad \left(\frac{b^2}{a^2e}\right) \times \left(-\frac{b^2}{a^2e}\right) = -1$$

$$\Rightarrow \quad \left(\frac{b^4}{a^4e^2}\right) = 1$$

$$\Rightarrow \quad b^4 = a^4e^2$$

$$\Rightarrow \quad a^4\left(e^2-1\right)^2 = a^4e^2$$

$$\Rightarrow \quad \left(e^2-1\right)^2 = e^2$$

$$\Rightarrow \quad e^4 - 3e^2 + 1 = 0$$

$$\Rightarrow \quad e^2 = \frac{3 \pm \sqrt{5}}{2}$$

$$\Rightarrow \quad e^2 = \frac{3 + \sqrt{5}}{2}$$

$$\Rightarrow \quad e^2 = \frac{3 + \sqrt{5}}{2} = \frac{6 + 2\sqrt{5}}{4} = \left(\frac{\sqrt{5}+1}{2}\right)^2$$

$$\Rightarrow \quad e = \left(\frac{\sqrt{5}+1}{2}\right)$$

6.6 POSITION OF A POINT WITH RESPECT TO A HYPERBOLA

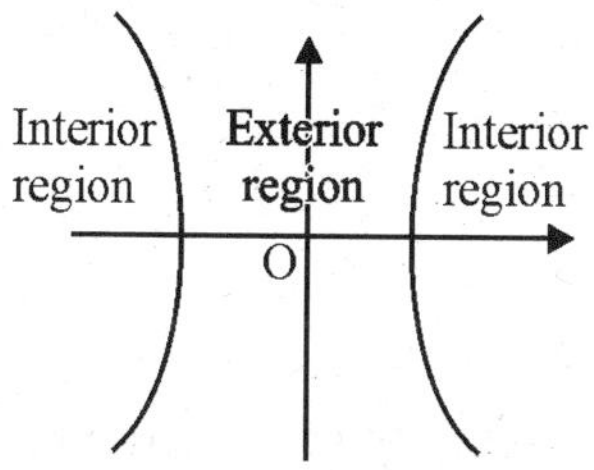

The point (x_1, y_1) lies outside, on or inside the hyperbola $\frac{x^2}{a^2} - \frac{y^2}{b^2} = 1$ according as

$$\frac{x_1^2}{a^2} - \frac{y_1^2}{b^2} - 1 < 0, = 0, > 0$$

Ex-1. Find the location of point (1, 4) w.r.t the hyperbola $2x^2 - 3y^2 = 6$.

Sol. We have, $2x_1^2 - 3y_1^2 - 1 = 2 - 48 - 1 = -47 < 0$

Thus , the point (1, 4) lies outside of the hyperbola.

Ex-2. If $(\lambda, -1)$ is an exterrior point of the curve $4x^2 - 3y^2 = 1$ such that the length of the interval where λ lies is 'm' , then find the value of m + 10.

Sol. Since , the point $(\lambda, -1)$ is an exterrior point of the curve $4x^2 - 3y^2 = 1$, so $4\lambda^2 - 3 - 1 < 0$

$$\Rightarrow \quad 4\lambda^2 - 4 < 0$$

$$\Rightarrow \quad \lambda^2 - 1 < 0$$

$$\Rightarrow \quad (\lambda+1)(\lambda-1) < 0$$

$$\Rightarrow \quad -1 < \lambda < 1$$

$$\Rightarrow \quad \lambda \in (-1, 1)$$

Thus , the length of the interval, where λ lies is 2

Therefore, m = 2

Hence, the value of m + 10 = 2 + 10 = 12 .

6.7 INTERSECTION OF A LINE AND A HYPERBOLA

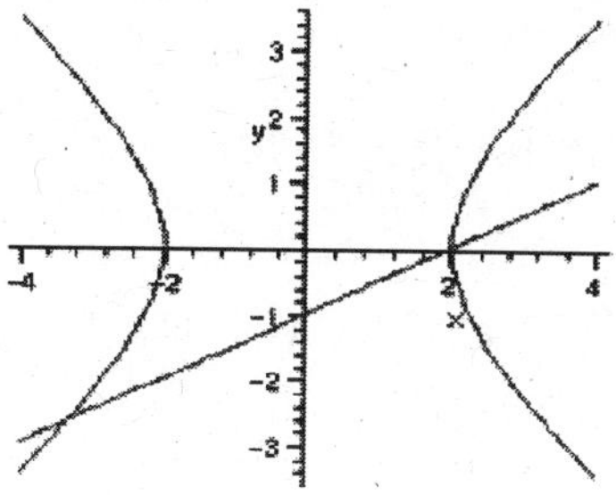

Let the hyperbola be $\frac{x^2}{a^2} - \frac{y^2}{b^2} = 1$ ...(i)

and the line be y = m x + c ...(ii)

From (i) and (ii), we get , $\frac{x^2}{a^2} - \frac{(mx+c)^2}{b^2} = 1$

$$\Rightarrow \quad b^2x^2 - a^2(mx+c)^2 = a^2b^2$$

$$\Rightarrow \quad (a^2m^2 - b^2)x^2 + 2mca^2x + a^2(b^2 + c^2) = 0$$

Now, $D = 4m^2c^2a^4 - 4a^2(a^2m^2 - b^2)(b^2 + c^2)$

$$= 4(m^2c^2a^4 - a^4m^2b^2 - a^4m^2c^2 + a^2b^4 + a^2b^2c^2)$$

$$= 4(-a^4m^2b^2 + a^2b^4 + a^2b^2c^2)$$

$$= 4a^2b^2(b^2 + c^2 - a^2m^2)$$

(i) The line y = m x + c will never intersect the hyperbola if D < 0

$$\Rightarrow \quad c^2 < a^2m^2 - b^2$$

(ii) The line y = m x + c will be a tangent to the hyperbola if D = 0

$$\Rightarrow \quad c^2 = a^2m^2 - b^2$$

This is known as condition of tangency .

(iii) The line y = m x + c will be intersect the hyperbola in two real and distinct points if D > 0

$$\Rightarrow \quad c^2 > a^2m^2 - b^2$$

(iv) Any tangent to the hyperbola can be considered as $y = mx + \sqrt{a^2m^2 - b^2}$.

(v) Co-ordinates of the point of contact :

If the line y = m x + c be a tangent to the hyperbola $\frac{x^2}{a^2} - \frac{y^2}{b^2} = 1$, then the co-ordinates of the point of contact is $\left(\pm \frac{a^2m}{c}, \pm \frac{b^2}{c}\right)$

Which is also known as **'m-point'** on the hyperbola.

(vi) No. of tangents : If a point lies out side, on and inside of a hyperbola , then the number of tangents are 2, 1 and 0 respectively.

(vii) If the line $lx+my+n=0$ be a tangent to the hyperbola $\frac{x^2}{a^2}-\frac{y^2}{b^2}=1$, then $a^2l^2-b^2m^2=n^2$.

Ex-1. Find the points common to the hyperbola $25x^2-9y^2=225$ and the straight line $25x+12y-45=0$

Sol. As we know that, if the line $y=mx+c$ be a tangent to the hyperbola $\frac{x^2}{a^2}-\frac{y^2}{b^2}=1$, then the co-ordinates of the point of contact is $\left(\pm\frac{a^2m}{c},\pm\frac{b^2}{c}\right)$.

The equation of the given hyperbola is

$$25x^2-9y^2=225$$

$$\Rightarrow \quad \frac{x^2}{9}-\frac{y^2}{25}=1 \quad ...(i)$$

Also , the given line is $25x+12y=45$

$$\Rightarrow \quad 12y=-25x+45$$

$$\Rightarrow \quad y=-\frac{25}{12}x+\frac{45}{12} \quad ...(ii)$$

Here, $a=3$, $b=5$ and $m=-25/12$

Thus, the common point is

$$\left(\pm\frac{a^2m}{c},\pm\frac{b^2}{c}\right)=\left(\mp 5,\pm\frac{20}{3}\right)$$

Ex-2. For what value of λ, does the line $y=3x+\lambda$ touch the hyperbola $9x^2-5y^2=45$.

Sol. As we know that , the line $y=mx+c$ will be a tangent to the hyperbola $\frac{x^2}{a^2}-\frac{y^2}{b^2}=1$

if $c^2=a^2m^2-b^2$ ...(i)

The equation of the hyperbola is $9x^2-5y^2=45$

$$\Rightarrow \quad \frac{x^2}{5}-\frac{y^2}{9}=1$$

Here, $a^2=5$, $b^2=9$, $m=3$, $c=\lambda$

Therefore, from (i), we get, $?^2=a^2m^2-b^2=15-9=6$

$$\Rightarrow \quad ?=\pm\sqrt{6}$$

Ex-3. For all real values of 'm' the striaght line $y=mx+\sqrt{9m^2-4}$ is a tangent to a hyperbola, find the equation of the hyperbola.

Sol. Equation of any tangent to the hyperbola $\frac{x^2}{a^2}-\frac{y^2}{b^2}=1$ is

$$y=mx+\sqrt{a^2m^2-b^2} \quad ...(i)$$

The equation of the given tangent is

$$y=mx+\sqrt{9m^2-4} \quad ...(ii)$$

Since (i) and (ii) are identical, so $a^2=9$, $b^2=4$

Hence, the equation of the hyperbola is $\frac{x^2}{9}-\frac{y^2}{4}=1$

$$\Rightarrow \quad 4x^2-9y^2=36$$

Ex-4. Find the equations of tangents to the curve $4x^2-9y^2=36$, which is parallel to $5x-4y+7=0$

Sol. Equation of any tangent to the parallel to $5x-4y+7=0$ is $5x-4y+\lambda=0$

$$\Rightarrow \quad 4y=5x+\lambda$$

$$\Rightarrow \quad y=\frac{5}{4}x+\frac{\lambda}{4} \quad ...(i)$$

The equation of the given hyperbola is $4x^2-9y^2=36$

$$\Rightarrow \quad \frac{x^2}{9}-\frac{y^2}{4}=1 \quad ...(ii)$$

Since, the line (i) be a tangent to the hyperbola (ii),

so $\frac{\lambda^2}{16}=9\left(\frac{25}{16}\right)-4$

$$\Rightarrow \quad \frac{\lambda^2}{16}=\frac{225-64}{16}$$

$$\Rightarrow \quad ?^2=161$$

$$\Rightarrow \quad ?=\pm\sqrt{161}$$

Hence, the equations of the tangents are

$$5x-4y\pm\sqrt{161}=0$$

Ex-5. Find the equations of tangents to the curve $9x^2-16y^2=144$, which is perpendicular to the straight line $3x+4y+10=0$.

Sol. Equation of any line perpendicular to $3x+4y+10=0$ is $4x-3y+\lambda=0$

$$\Rightarrow \quad y=\left(\frac{4}{3}\right)x+\frac{?}{3} \quad ...(i)$$

The equation of the given hyperbola is

$$9x^2-16y^2=144$$

$$\Rightarrow \quad \frac{x^2}{16}-\frac{y^2}{9}=1 \quad ...(ii)$$

The line (i) will be a tangent to the hyperbola (ii),

if $\left(\frac{\lambda}{3}\right)^2=16\left(\frac{4}{3}\right)^2-9$

$\Rightarrow \quad \lambda^2 = 256 - 81 = 175$

$\Rightarrow \quad \lambda = \pm\sqrt{175} = \pm\, 5\sqrt{7}$

Hence, the equation of the tangents are

$4x - 37 \pm 5\sqrt{7} = 0$.

Ex-6. If the line $5x + 12y - 9 = 0$ touches the hyperbola $x^2 - 9y^2 = 9$, then find its point of contact.

Sol. The given hyperbola is $x^2 - 9y^2 = 9$

$$\Rightarrow \quad \frac{x^2}{9} - \frac{y^2}{1} = 1 \qquad \text{...(i)}$$

The given line is $5x + 12y - 9 = 0$

$$\Rightarrow \quad y = \left(-\frac{5}{12}\right)x + \frac{3}{4} \qquad \text{...(ii)}$$

If the line (ii) be a tangent to the hyperbola (i), then the co-ordinates of the point of contact can be

$$\left(\pm\frac{a^2 m}{c}, \pm\frac{b^2}{c}\right) = \left(\pm(-5), \pm\frac{4}{3}\right)$$

Ex-7. Find the equation of tangents to the curve $4x^2 - 9y^2 = 36$ from the point (3, 2).

Sol. The equation of the given hyperbola is $4x^2 - 9y^2 = 36$

$$\Rightarrow \quad \frac{x^2}{9} - \frac{y^2}{4} = 1$$

Here, $a^2 = 9$, $b^2 = 4$.

Equation of any tangent to the hyperbola $\frac{x^2}{a^2} - \frac{y^2}{b^2} = 1$

is $y = mx + \sqrt{a^2 m^2 - b^2}$

$\Rightarrow \quad y = mx + \sqrt{9m^2 - 4}$

which is passing through (3, 2).

Therefore, $(2 - 3m)^2 = 9m^2 - 4$

$\Rightarrow \quad 4 - 12m + 9m^2 = 9m^2 - 4$

$\Rightarrow \quad 4 - 12m = -4$

$\Rightarrow \quad m = \frac{2}{3}, \; m = \infty$

Hence, the equations of the tangents are $x + 3 = 0$

and $\quad y = \frac{2}{3}x$.

Ex-8. Find the number of tangents from the point (1, -2) to the curve $2x^2 - 3y^2 = 12$.

Sol. We have, $2x_1^2 - 3y_1^2 - 12 = 2.1 - 3.4 - 12$

$= 2 - 12 - 12 = 2 - 24 = -22 < 0$

So, the point (1, -2) lies outside of the hyperbola.

Thus, the number of tangents is 2.

Ex-9. Find the equation of the tangent to the curve $3x^2 - 4y^2 = 12$ having slope '4'.

Sol. The equation of the given hyperbola is $3x^2 - 4y^2 = 12$

$$\Rightarrow \quad \frac{x^2}{4} - \frac{y^2}{3} = 1 \qquad \text{...(i)}$$

Here, $a^2 = 4$, $b^2 = 3$ and $m = 4$

Equation of any tangent to the hyperbola (i) is

$y = mx + \sqrt{a^2 m^2 - b^2}$

$\Rightarrow \quad y = 4x \pm \sqrt{64 - 3}$

$\Rightarrow \quad y = 4x \pm \sqrt{61}$

Hence, the equations of tangents are

$y = 4x + \sqrt{61}$ & $y = 4x - \sqrt{61}$.

4.8 DIFFERENT FORMS OF TANGENTS

(i) **Point form :** Equation of tangent to the hyperbola $\frac{x^2}{a^2} - \frac{y^2}{b^2} = 1$ at the point (x_1, y_1) is $\frac{xx_1}{a^2} - \frac{yy_1}{b^2} = 1$.

(ii) **Parametric form :** Equation of tangent to the hyperbola $\frac{x^2}{a^2} - \frac{y^2}{b^2} = 1$ at $(a\sec\phi, b\tan\phi)$

is $\frac{x}{a}\sec\phi - \frac{y}{b}\operatorname{cosec}\phi = 1$

(iii) The point of intersection of tangents at $P(\theta)$ & $Q(\phi)$ on the hyperbola $\frac{x^2}{a^2} - \frac{y^2}{b^2} = 1$

$$\text{is} \left(\frac{a\cos\left(\frac{\theta-\phi}{2}\right)}{\cos\left(\frac{\theta+\phi}{2}\right)}, \frac{b\sin\left(\frac{\theta+\phi}{2}\right)}{\cos\left(\frac{\theta+\phi}{2}\right)}\right)$$

(iv) **Slope form :** The equation of tangent to the hyperbola $\frac{x^2}{a^2} - \frac{y^2}{b^2} = 1$ in terms of slope 'm' is

$$y = mx + \sqrt{a^2 m^2 - b^2}.$$

The co-ordinates of the point of contact are

$$\left(\pm\frac{a^2 m}{\sqrt{a^2 m^2 - b^2}}, \pm\frac{b^2}{\sqrt{a^2 m^2 - b^2}}\right)$$

(v) The equation of tangent to the conjugate hyperbola $\frac{x^2}{a^2} - \frac{y^2}{b^2} = -1$

is $y = mx + \sqrt{b^2 - a^2m^2}$

The co-ordinates of the point of contact are

$$\left(\pm\frac{a^2 m}{\sqrt{b^2 - a^2m^2}}, \pm\frac{b^2}{\sqrt{b^2 - a^2m^2}}\right).$$

(vi) The line y = m x + c be a tangent to the hyperbola. $\frac{x^2}{a^2} - \frac{y^2}{b^2} = 1$ if $c^2 = a^2m^2 - b^2$.

(vii) **Director circle :** The locus of the point of intersection of two perpendicular tangents to a hyperbola is known as director circle of the hyperbola.

Equation of the director circle to the hyperbola $\frac{x^2}{a^2} - \frac{y^2}{b^2} = 1$ is $x^2 + y^2 = a^2 - b^2$.

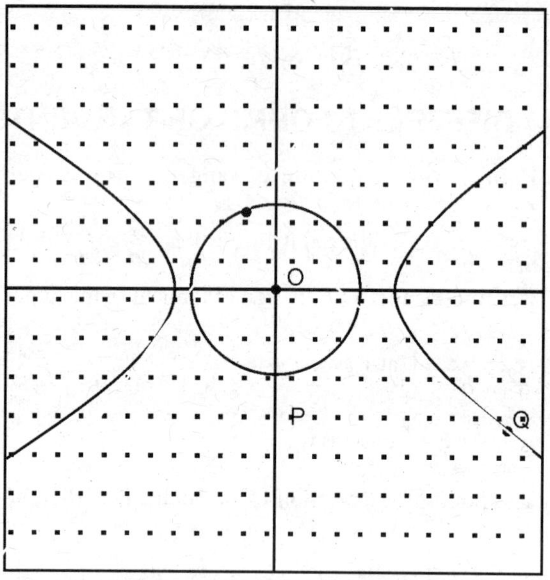

Equation of any tangent to a hyperbola is $y = mx + \sqrt{a^2m^2 - b^2}$.

Let it passes through the point (h, k).

Then $k = mh + \sqrt{a^2m^2 - b^2}$

$$\Rightarrow \quad (k - mh)^2 = \left(\sqrt{a^2m^2 - b^2}\right)^2$$

$$\Rightarrow \quad k^2 + m^2h^2 - 2kmh = a^2m^2 - b^2$$

$$\Rightarrow \quad \left(h^2 - a^2\right)m^2 - 2khm + \left(k^2 + b^2\right) = 0$$

It has two roots, say, m_1 & m_2

Thus, $m_1.m_2 = \frac{k^2 + b^2}{h^2 - a^2}$

$$\Rightarrow \quad \frac{k^2 + b^2}{h^2 - a^2} = -1$$

$$\Rightarrow \quad k^2 + b^2 = -h^2 + a^2$$

$$\Rightarrow \quad h^2 + k^2 = a^2 - b^2.$$

Hence, the locus of (h, k) is $x^2 + y^2 = a^2 - b^2$.

Note: 1. Director circle of a hyperbola $\frac{x^2}{a^2} - \frac{y^2}{b^2} = 1$ is exist only when a > b

2. If a < b, then the equation of director circle $x^2 + y^2 = a^2 - b^2$ does not exis.

3. The equation of the director circle to the conjugate hyperbola $\frac{x^2}{a^2} - \frac{y^2}{b^2} = -1$ is $x^2 + y^2 = b^2 - a^2$. It exists only when b > a

4. If b < a, then the equation of director circle does not exist.

(viii) Pair of tangents :

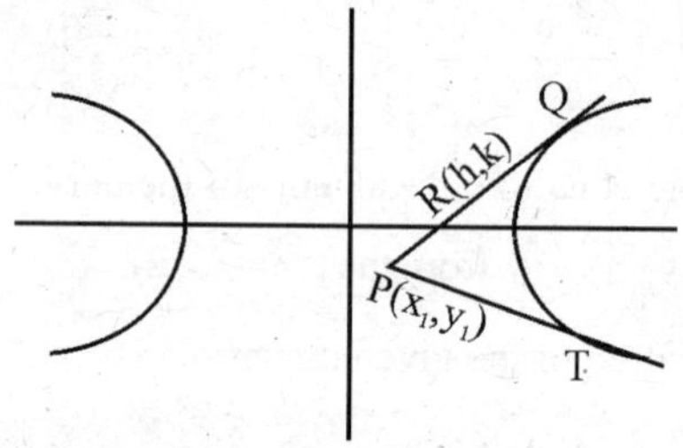

The combined equation of the pair of tangents drawn from a point P(x $_1$, y $_1$) lies outside of the hyperbola $\frac{x^2}{a^2} - \frac{y^2}{b^2} = 1$ to the hyperbola $\frac{x^2}{a^2} - \frac{y^2}{b^2} = 1$ is $SS_1 = T^2$

$$\Rightarrow \quad \left(\frac{x^2}{a^2} - \frac{y^2}{b^2} - 1\right)\left(\frac{x_1^2}{a^2} - \frac{y_1^2}{b^2} - 1\right) = \left(\frac{xx_1}{a^2} - \frac{yy_1}{b^2} - 1\right)^2$$

Ex-1. Find the equation of the tangent to the curve $x^2 - y^2 - 8x + 2y + 11 = 0$ at (2, 1).

Sol. Equation of tangent to the curve

$$x^2 - y^2 - 8x + 2y + 11 = 0 \text{ is}$$

$$xx_1 - yy_1 - 4(x + x_1) + (y + y_1) + 11 = 0$$

$$\Rightarrow \quad 2x - y - 4(x + 2) + (y + 1) + 11 = 0$$

$$\Rightarrow \quad -2x + 4 = 0$$

$$\Rightarrow \quad x - 2 = 0$$

Ex-2. Find the equation of tangent to the curve $4x^2 - 3y^2 = 24$ at y = 2.

Sol. when y = 2, then $4x^2 = 36 \Rightarrow x = \pm 3$

Hence, the points are (3, 2) and (-3, 2)

Equation of the tangent at (3, 2) is 12 x - 6 y = 24

$\Rightarrow 2x - y = 4$.

Also, the equation of the tangent at (-3, 2) is

$-12x - 6y = 24 \Rightarrow 2x + y + 4 = 0$.

Ex-3. Find the angle between the tangents to the curve $9x^2 - 16y^2 = 144$ drawn from the point (4, 3).

Sol. The equation of the given hyperbola is $9x^2 - 16y^2 = 144$

$$\Rightarrow \quad \frac{x^2}{16} - \frac{y^2}{9} = 1 \qquad ...(i)$$

Equation of any tangent to the hyperbola (i) can be considered as

$y = mx + \sqrt{16m^2 - 9}$

which is passing through (4, 3)

Therefore, $(3 - 4m)^2 = 16m^2 - 9$.

$\Rightarrow \quad 9 - 24m + 16m^2 = 16m^2 - 9$

$\Rightarrow \quad 24m = 18$

$\Rightarrow \quad m = \frac{3}{4}$ & $m = \infty$

Let θ be the angle between them.

$$\text{Then } \tan(?) = \left|\frac{\frac{3}{4} - \infty}{1 + \frac{3}{4}.\infty}\right| = \left|\frac{\frac{3}{4\infty} - 1}{\frac{1}{\infty} + \frac{3}{4}}\right| = \frac{4}{3}$$

$$\Rightarrow \quad ? = \tan^{-1}\left(\frac{4}{3}\right)$$

Hence, the angle between the tangents is $\tan^{-1}\left(\frac{4}{3}\right)$.

Ex-4. Find the equations of the common tangent to the curves $\frac{x^2}{a^2} - \frac{y^2}{b^2} = 1$ and $\frac{x^2}{b^2} - \frac{y^2}{a^2} = -1$

Sol. Equation of any tangent to the hyperbola $\frac{x^2}{a^2} - \frac{y^2}{b^2} = 1$

is $y = m_1 x + \sqrt{a^2 m_1^2 - b^2}$ ...(i)

Equation of any tangent to the hyperbola

$$\frac{x^2}{(-b^2)} - \frac{y^2}{(-a^2)} = 1 \text{ is}$$

$$y = m_2 x + \sqrt{(-b^2)m_2^2 - (-a^2)} \qquad ...(ii)$$

Equations (i) and (ii) are identical.

So, $a^2 m_1^2 - b^2 = (-b^2)m_2^2 - (-a^2)$

$\Rightarrow \quad m_1^2 = 1$ & $m_2^2 = 1$

Thus, $m_1 = \pm 1 = m_2$

Hence, the equations of the common tangents are

$y = \pm x + \sqrt{a^2 - b^2}$

Ex-5. Find the equations of the common tangents to the curves $\frac{x^2}{9} - \frac{y^2}{4} = 1$ and $\frac{x^2}{9} + \frac{y^2}{4} = 1$

Sol. Equation of the given curves are $\frac{x^2}{9} - \frac{y^2}{4} = 1$

and $\frac{x^2}{9} + \frac{y^2}{4} = 1$

Here, the length of the major axis of the ellipse is equal to the length of the transverse axis and also the length of the minor axis is equal to the length of the conjugate axis Thus, the equations of the common tangents are $x = \pm 3$ & $y = \pm 2$.

Ex-6. Find the equation of the common tangents to the curves $\frac{x^2}{16} - \frac{y^2}{9} = 1$ and $x^2 + y^2 = 9$.

Sol. Equation of any tangent to the hyperbola $\frac{x^2}{16} - \frac{y^2}{9} = 1$ is

$y = mx + \sqrt{16m^2 - 9}$

$$\Rightarrow \quad mx - y + \sqrt{16m^2 - 9} = 0 \qquad ...(i)$$

If the tangent (i) is also tangent to the circle $x^2 + y^2 = 9$, then the length of perpen dicular from the centre of the circle is equal to the radius of the circle.

$$\text{Therefore, } \left|\frac{0 - \sqrt{16m^2 - 9}}{\sqrt{m^2 + 1}}\right| = 3$$

$\Rightarrow \quad 16m^2 - 9 = 9(m^2 + 1)$

$\Rightarrow \quad 16m^2 - 9m^2 = 9 + 1 = 10$

$\Rightarrow \quad 7m^2 = 10$

$\Rightarrow \quad m = \pm\sqrt{\frac{7}{10}}$

Hence, the equation of tangents are $y = \pm\sqrt{\frac{7}{10}}x + \sqrt{\frac{11}{5}}$.

Ex-7. Find the equation of the common tangents to the curves $y^2 = 8x$ and $\frac{x^2}{9} - \frac{y^2}{5} = 1$

Sol. Equation of any tangent to the parabola $y^2 = 8x$ is

$$y = mx + \frac{2}{m} \qquad ...(i)$$

Since the tangent to the parabola is also a tangent to the hyperbola $\frac{x^2}{9}-\frac{y^2}{5}=1,$

so $5x^2-9\left(mx+\frac{2}{m}\right)^2=45$

$\Rightarrow \quad 5x^2-9\left(m^2x^2+\frac{4}{m^2}+4m\right)=45$

$\Rightarrow \quad \left(5-9m^2\right)x^2-36x-9\left(\frac{4}{m^2}+5\right)=0$

Therefore, D= 0 gives,

$$(36)^2+36\left(5-9m^2\right)\left(\frac{4}{m^2}+5\right)=0$$

$\Rightarrow \quad 36+\frac{20}{m^2}+25-36-45m^2=0$

$\Rightarrow \quad \frac{4}{m^2}+5-9m^2=0$

$\Rightarrow \quad 9m^4-5m^2-4=0$

$\Rightarrow \quad \left(m^2-1\right)\left(9m^2+4\right)=0$

$\Rightarrow \quad \left(m^2-1\right)=0$

$\Rightarrow \quad m=\pm1$

Hence, the equations of the common tangents are $y=\pm\ x\pm2$.

Ex-8. Find the locus of the point of intersection of the perpendicular tangents to the curve $\frac{x^2}{16}-\frac{y^2}{9}=1$.

Sol. As we know that, the locus of the perpendicular tangents is the director circle.

Hence, the equation of the director circle is

$$x^2+y^2=a^2-b^2=16-9=7$$

$\Rightarrow \quad x^2+y^2=7$

Ex-9. Find the product of the perpendiculars from foci upon any tangent to the hyperbola $\frac{x^2}{a^2}-\frac{y^2}{b^2}=1$.

Sol. Let F_1 and F_2 be two foci of the hyperbola $\frac{x^2}{a^2}-\frac{y^2}{b^2}=1$.

Then $F_1=(ae, 0)$ and $F_2=(-ae, 0)$.

Equation of any tangent to the hyperbola is

$$\frac{x}{a}\sec ?-\frac{y}{b}\tan ?=1 \qquad ...(i)$$

Let p_1 and p_2 be two the length of perpendiculars from foci upon the tangent (i).

Then, $p_1=\left|\frac{e\sec\theta-1}{\sqrt{\frac{\sec^2\theta}{a^2}+\frac{\tan^2\theta}{b^2}}}\right|$

and $p_2=\left|\frac{e\sec\theta+1}{\sqrt{\frac{\sec^2\theta}{a^2}+\frac{\tan^2\theta}{b^2}}}\right|$

$\Rightarrow \quad p_1p_2=\frac{(e\sec\theta-1)(e\sec\theta+1)}{\frac{\sec^2\theta}{a^2}+\frac{\tan^2\theta}{b^2}}=\frac{a^2b^2\left(e^2\sec^2\theta-1\right)}{\left(b^2\sec^2\theta+a^2\tan^2\theta\right)}$

$\Rightarrow \quad p_1p_2=\frac{a^4\left(e^2-1\right)\left(e^2\sec^2\theta-1\right)}{\left(a^2\left(e^2-1\right)\sec^2\theta+a^2\tan^2\theta\right)}$

$\Rightarrow \quad p_1p_2=\frac{a^2\left(e^2-1\right)\left(e^2\sec^2\theta-1\right)}{\left(\left(e^2-1\right)\sec^2\theta+\tan^2\theta\right)}$

$\Rightarrow \quad p_1p_2=\frac{a^2\left(e^2-1\right)\left(e^2\sec^2\theta-1\right)}{\left(\left(e^2-1\right)\sec^2\theta+\left(\sec^2\theta-1\right)\right)}$

$\Rightarrow \quad p_1p_2=\frac{a^2\left(e^2-1\right)\left(e^2\sec^2\theta-1\right)}{\left(e^2\sec^2\theta\text{-}1\right)}$

$\Rightarrow \quad p_1p_2=a^2\left(e^2-1\right)$

$\Rightarrow \quad p_1p_2=b^2$

Hence, the product of the lengths of the perpendiculars is b^2.

Ex-10. If tangents to the parabola $y^2=4ax$ intersect the hyperbola $\frac{x^2}{a^2}-\frac{y^2}{b^2}=1$ at A and B respectively. Find the locus of the points of intersectio of tangents at A and B.

Sol. Let $P(a, ß)$ be the point of intersection of tangents at A and B.

Clearly, the point of intersection of the tangents at A and B is the chord of contact.

Therefore, the chord of contact AB is $\frac{ax}{a^2}-\frac{ßy}{b^2}=1$

$\Rightarrow \quad y=\frac{b^2x\ a}{a^2yß}-\frac{b^2}{ß}$

Which is a tangent to the parabola $y^2=4ax$

Therefore, $-\frac{b^2}{ß} = \frac{a}{\left(\frac{b^2 a}{a^2 ß}\right)} \Rightarrow ß^2 = \left(-\frac{b^4}{a^3}a\right)$

Hence, the locus of $P(a, ß)$ is $y^2 = \left(-\frac{b^4}{a^3}x\right)$

6.8 DIFFERENT FORMS OF NORMALS

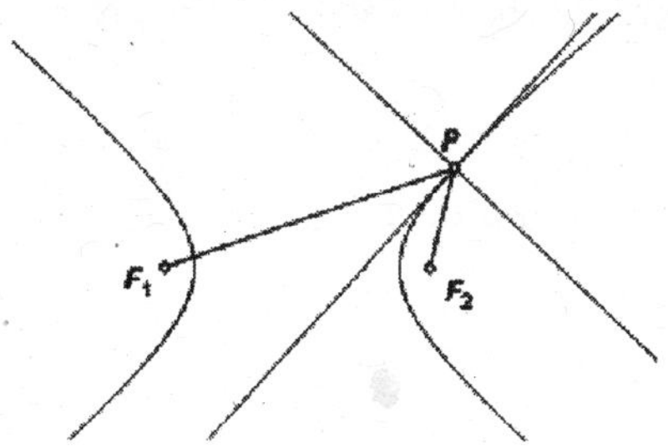

(i) **Point form:** Equation of normal to the hyperbola $\frac{x^2}{a^2} - \frac{y^2}{b^2} = 1$ at (x_1, y_1) is $\frac{a^2 x}{x_1} + \frac{b^2 y}{y_1} = a^2 + b^2$

(ii) **Parametric form :** Equation of normal to the hyperbola $\frac{x^2}{a^2} - \frac{y^2}{b^2} = 1$ at $(a \sec\phi, b\tan\phi)$ is

$$a x \cos\phi + b y \cot\phi = a^2 + b^2$$

(iii) **Slope form :** The equation of normal to the hyperbola $\frac{x^2}{a^2} - \frac{y^2}{b^2} = 1$ in terms of slope 'm' is

$$y = mx \mp \frac{m\left(a^2 + b^2\right)}{\sqrt{a^2 - m^2 b^2}}$$

The co-ordinates of the point of contact are

$$\left(\pm\frac{a^2}{\sqrt{a^2 - b^2 m^2}}, \mp\frac{m b^2}{\sqrt{a^2 - b^2 m^2}}\right).$$

(iv) The line y = m x + c will be a normal to the hyperbola if

$$c^2 = \left(\frac{m^2\left(a^2 + b^2\right)^2}{\left(a^2 - m^2 b^2\right)}\right)$$

Which is also known as condition of normalcy to a hyperbola.

Ex-1. Find the equation of the normal to the curve $\frac{x^2}{16} - \frac{y^2}{9} = 1$ at $(8, 3\sqrt{3})$.

Sol. The equation of the normal to the curve $\frac{x^2}{16} - \frac{y^2}{9} = 1$ at $(8, 3\sqrt{3})$ is

$$\frac{a^2 x}{x_1} + \frac{b^2 y}{y_1} = a^2 + b^2$$

$$\Rightarrow \frac{16x}{8} + \frac{9y}{3\sqrt{3}} = 16 + 9$$

$$\Rightarrow 2x + \sqrt{3}y = 25$$

Hence, the required equation of the normal is

$$2x + \sqrt{3}y = 25.$$

Ex-2. Normal is drawn at one end of the latus rectum of the hyperbola $\frac{x^2}{a^2} - \frac{y^2}{b^2} = 1$ which meets the axes at points A and B respectively . Then find the area of the ? OAB .

Sol. Let , one end of the latus rectum of the given hyperbola is $L\left(ae, \frac{b^2}{a}\right)$

Equation of the normal to the given hyperbola at L is

$$\frac{a^2 x}{x_1} + \frac{b^2 y}{y_1} = a^2 + b^2$$

$$\Rightarrow \frac{ax}{e} + ay = a^2 + b^2$$

$$\Rightarrow \frac{x}{\left(\frac{e\left(a^2 + b^2\right)}{a}\right)} + \frac{y}{\left(\frac{a^2 + b^2}{a}\right)} = 1$$

Hence, the area of the triangle OAB

$$= \frac{1}{2} \times \frac{e\left(a^2 + b^2\right)}{a} \times \left(\frac{a^2 + b^2}{a}\right)$$

$$= \frac{1}{2} \times \frac{e\left(a^2 + b^2\right)^2}{a^2} = \frac{1}{2} \times a^2 e^5$$

Ex-3. Prove that the locus of the foot of perpendicular from the centre upon any normal to the hyperbola $\frac{x^2}{a^2} - \frac{y^2}{b^2} = 1$. is. $\left(x^2 + y^2\right)^2\left(a^2 y^2 - b^2 x^2\right) = \left(a^2 + b^2\right)^2 x^2 y^2$.

Sol. Equation of any normal at $(a \sec f, b \tan f)$ to the hyperbola $\frac{x^2}{a^2} - \frac{y^2}{b^2} = 1$ is

$$a x \cos f + b y \cot f = a^2 + b^2 \quad ...(i)$$

Equation of any line perpendicular to (i) and passing through the origin is

$$(b \cot f)x - (a \cos f)y = 0$$

$\Rightarrow \quad bx - a \sin f \; y = 0$ ...(ii)

If we eliminate ϕ between (i) and (ii), we get, the required locus of the foot of perpendicular.

From (ii), we get, $\sin(f) = \dfrac{bx}{ay}$

Therefore, $\cos(f) = \dfrac{\sqrt{(a^2y^2 - b^2x^2)}}{ay}$

and $\cot(f) = \dfrac{\sqrt{(a^2y^2 - b^2x^2)}}{bx}$

From (i), we get,

$$ax \times \frac{\sqrt{(a^2y^2 - b^2x^2)}}{ay} + by \times \frac{\sqrt{(a^2y^2 - b^2x^2)}}{bx} = a^2 + b^2$$

$$\Rightarrow \quad (x^2 + y^2)\left(\sqrt{(a^2y^2 - b^2x^2)}\right) = (a^2 + b^2)xy$$

$$\Rightarrow \quad (x^2 + y^2)^2 (a^2y^2 - b^2x^2) = (a^2 + b^2)^2 x^2 y^2$$

Which is the required locus of the foot of perpendicular.

Ex-4. A normal to the hyperbola $\dfrac{x^2}{a^2} - \dfrac{y^2}{b^2} = 1$ meets the axes in M and N and lines MP and NP are drawn perpendiculars to the axes meeting at P. Prove that the locus of P is the hyperbola $a^2x^2 - b^2y^2 = (a^2 + b^2)^2$.

Sol. Equation of any normal to the hyperbola $\dfrac{x^2}{a^2} - \dfrac{y^2}{b^2} = 1$ is

$$ax \cos f + by \cot f = (a^2 + b^2) \quad \text{...(i)}$$

Normal (i) meets the x-axis at M and y-axis at N respectively.

Then, $M = \left(\dfrac{a^2 + b^2}{a \cos f}, 0\right)$ and

$$N = \left(0, \left(\frac{a^2 + b^2}{b}\right)\tan f\right)$$

Let the co-ordinates of the point P be $(a, ß)$

Since PM and PN are perpendicular to the axes, so the co-ordinates of P are

$$\left(\left(\frac{a^2 + b^2}{a}\right)\sec\varphi, \left(\frac{a^2 + b^2}{b}\right)\tan\varphi\right)$$

Therefore, $a = \left(\dfrac{a^2 + b^2}{a}\right)\sec\varphi$ & $ß = \left(\dfrac{a^2 + b^2}{b}\right)\tan\varphi$

$$\Rightarrow \quad a\left(\frac{a}{a^2 + b^2}\right) = \sec\varphi \;\; \& \;\; ß\left(\frac{b}{a^2 + b^2}\right) = \tan\varphi$$

As we know that, $\sec^2\varphi - \tan^2\varphi = 1$

$$\Rightarrow \quad a^2\left(\frac{a}{a^2 + b^2}\right)^2 - ß^2\left(\frac{b}{a^2 + b^2}\right)^2 = 1$$

$$\Rightarrow \quad a^2a^2 - ß^2b^2 = (a^2 + b^2)^2$$

Hence, the locus of $(a, ß)$ is

$$a^2x^2 - b^2y^2 = (a^2 + b^2)^2$$

Ex-5. If the normal at 'ϕ' on the hyperbola $\dfrac{x^2}{a^2} - \dfrac{y^2}{b^2} = 1$ meets the transverse axis at G such that

$AG.A'G = a^m(e^n \sec^p\theta - 1)$,

where A, A` are the vertices of the hyperbola and m, n and p are +ve integers, then find the value of $(m + n + p)^2 + 36$.

Sol. Equation of any normal to the hyperbola $\dfrac{x^2}{a^2} - \dfrac{y^2}{b^2} = 1$ at (ϕ) is $ax\cos\varphi + by\cot\varphi = a^2 + b^2$

Thus, the co-ordinates of $G = \left(\dfrac{a^2 + b^2}{a\cos\varphi}, 0\right)$

Clearly, the vertices, A = (a, 0) and A` = (-a, 0)

Now, $AG = \left(\dfrac{a^2 + b^2}{a\cos\varphi} - a\right)$

and $A'G = \left(\dfrac{a^2 + b^2}{a\cos\varphi} + a\right)$

Therefore, $AG.A`G = \left(\dfrac{a^2 + b^2}{a\cos\varphi} - a\right)\left(\dfrac{a^2 + b^2}{a\cos\varphi} + a\right)$

$$= \left(\left(\frac{a^2 + b^2}{a}\right)^2 \sec^2\phi - a^2\right)$$

$$= (a^2e^2\sec^2\phi - a^2) = a^2(e^2\sec^2\phi - 1)$$

$\Rightarrow \quad m = 2, n = 2, p = 2$

Hence, the value of $(m + n + p)^2 + 36 = 36 + 36 = 72$.

Ex-6. If the normals at (x_i, y_i), i = 1, 2, 3, 4 on the rectangular hyperbola $xy = c^2$ meet at the point (α, β), then prove that

(i) $x_1 + x_2 + x_3 + x_4 = \alpha$

(ii) $y_1 + y_2 + y_3 + y_4 = \beta$

(iii) $x_1^2 + x_2^2 + x_3^2 + x_4^2 = \alpha^2$

(iv) $y_1^2 + y_2^2 + y_3^2 + y_4^2 = \beta^2$

(v) $x_1.x_2.x_3.x_4 = -c^4$

(vi) $y_1.y_2.y_3.y_4 = -c^4$

Sol. Equation of the normal to the hyperbola $xy = c^2$ at $\left(ct, \frac{c}{t}\right)$ is $xt^3 - yt - ct^4 + c = 0$

$\Rightarrow \quad ct^4 - xt^3 + yt - c = 0$

Which is passing through (α, β), so

$$ct^4 - at^3 + ßt - c = 0$$

Let its four roots are t_1, t_2, t_3, t_4.

Therefore, $t_1 + t_2 + t_3 + t_4 = \frac{a}{c}$,

$$\sum (t_1t_2) = 0, \quad \sum (t_1t_2t_3) = -\frac{ß}{c}$$

and $\sum (t_1t_2t_3t_4) = -1$.

(i) $x_1 + x_2 + x_3 + x_4 = c(t_1 + t_2 + t_3 + t_4) = c\left(\frac{a}{c}\right) = a$

(ii) $y_1 + y_2 + y_3 + y_4 = c\left(\frac{1}{t_1} + \frac{1}{t_2} + \frac{1}{t_3} + \frac{1}{t_4}\right)$

$$= c\left(\frac{\sum (t_1t_2t_3)}{\sum (t_1t_2t_3t_4)}\right) = c\left(\frac{\left(-\frac{ß}{c}\right)}{-1}\right) = ß$$

(iii) $x_1^2 + x_2^2 + x_3^2 + x_4^2 = c^2\left(t_1^2 + t_2^2 + t_3^2 + t_4^2\right)$

$$= c^2\left\{\left(\sum t_1\right)^2 - 2\sum (t_1t_2)\right\}$$

$$= c^2\left\{\left(\frac{a}{c}\right)^2 - 0\right\} = a^2$$

(iv) $y_1^2 + y_2^2 + y_3^2 + y_4^2 = \left(\sum y_1\right)^2 - 2\sum (y_1y_2)$

$$= (ß)^2 - 2c^2 \sum \left(\frac{1}{t_1t_2}\right)$$

$$= (ß)^2 - 2c^2\left(\frac{\sum t_1t_2}{t_1t_2t_3t_4}\right) = (ß)^2$$

(v) $x_1.x_2.x_3.x_4 = c^4(t_1t_2t_3t_4) = -c^4$

(vi) $y_1.y_2.y_3.y_4 = c^4\left(\frac{1}{t_1t_2t_3t_4}\right) = c^4\left(\frac{1}{-1}\right) = -c^4$

Ex-7. If the normals at (x_i, y_i), i = 1, 2, 3, 4 on the hyperbola $\frac{x^2}{a^2} - \frac{y^2}{b^2} = 1$ are concurrent. Then prove that

(i) $(x_1 + x_2 + x_3 + x_4)\left(\frac{1}{x_1} + \frac{1}{x_2} + \frac{1}{x_3} + \frac{1}{x_4}\right) = 4$

(ii) $(y_1 + y_2 + y_3 + y_4)\left(\frac{1}{y_1} + \frac{1}{y_2} + \frac{1}{y_3} + \frac{1}{y_4}\right) = 4$

Sol. Equation of any normal to the given hyperbola at (x, y) is

$\Rightarrow \quad \frac{x}{a^2}(k - y) = \frac{y}{b^2}(x - b)$

$\Rightarrow \quad \left(\frac{1}{a^2} + \frac{1}{b^2}\right)xy - \frac{y}{b} - \frac{kx}{a^2} = 0$

$\Rightarrow \quad y = \frac{b^2kx}{a^2\left(e^2x - b\right)} \qquad ...(i)$

The equation of the hyperbola is

$$\frac{x^2}{a^2} - \frac{y^2}{b^2} = 1 \qquad ...(ii)$$

On solving (i) and (ii), we get,

$$\frac{x^2}{a^2} - \frac{b^4k^2x^2}{b^2a^4\left(e^2x - b\right)^2} = 1$$

$\Rightarrow \quad a^2e^4x^4 - 2ba^2e^2x^3 - \left(a^2b^2 + b^2k^2 + a^4e^4\right)$

$$x^2 + 2ba^4e^2x + a^4b^2 = 0 \qquad ...(iii)$$

Let x_1, x_2, x_3, x_4 are the roots of (iii).

Then, $x_1 + x_2 + x_3 + x_4 = \frac{2b}{e^2}$,

$$\sum (x_1x_2) = -\frac{a^2b^2 + b^2k^2 + a^4e^2}{a^2e^4}$$

$$\sum (x_1x_2x_3) = -\frac{2ba^2}{e^2}$$

and $\sum (x_1x_2x_3x_4) = \frac{a^2b^2}{e^4}$

Therefore, $\sum\left(\frac{1}{x_1}\right) = \frac{\sum (x_1x_2x_3)}{x_1x_2x_3x_4} = \frac{2e^2}{b}$

(i) $(x_1 + x_2 + x_3 + x_4)\left(\frac{1}{x_1} + \frac{1}{x_2} + \frac{1}{x_3} + \frac{1}{x_4}\right)$

$$= \left(\sum x_1\right)\left(\sum\left(\frac{1}{x_1}\right)\right) = \frac{2b}{e^2} \times \frac{2e^2}{b} = 4$$

similarly, (ii) $(y_1 + y_2 + y_3 + y_4)\left(\frac{1}{y_1} + \frac{1}{y_2} + \frac{1}{y_3} + \frac{1}{y_4}\right)$

$$= \left(\sum y_1\right)\left(\sum\left(\frac{1}{y_1}\right)\right)$$

$=4.$

6.9 CHORD OF CONTACT

If the tangent is drawn from a point $P(x_1, y_1)$ to the hyperbola $\frac{x^2}{a^2}-\frac{y^2}{b^2}=1$ touch the hyperbola at Q and R, then the equation of the chord of contact QR is

$$\frac{xx_1}{a^2}-\frac{yy_1}{b^2}=1.$$

6.10 EQUATION OF THE CHORD BI SECTED AT A POINT

The equation of the chord of the hyperbola $\frac{x^2}{a^2}-\frac{y^2}{b^2}=1$ bisected at the point (x_1, y_1)

is $SS_1 = T^2$

$$\text{i.e} \left(\frac{x^2}{a^2}-\frac{y^2}{b^2}-1\right)\left(\frac{x_1^2}{a^2}-\frac{y_1^2}{b^2}-1\right)=\left(\frac{xx_1}{a^2}-\frac{yy_1}{b^2}-1\right)^2.$$

Ex-1. Find the equation of the chord of contact of tangents from the point (2, 3) to the hyperbola $\frac{x^2}{9}-\frac{y^2}{4}=1$.

Sol. The equation of the chord of contact of tangents drawn from the point (2, 3) is

$$\frac{2x}{9}-\frac{y}{2}=1$$

$$\Rightarrow \quad 4x-9y=18$$

Ex-2. Find the locus of the middle points of the portions of the tangents to the hyperbola

$\frac{x^2}{9}-\frac{y^2}{4}=1$ included between the axes.

Sol. Any tangent to the hyperbola $\frac{x^2}{9}-\frac{y^2}{4}=1$ is

$$\frac{x}{3}\sec\theta-\frac{y}{2}\tan\theta=1 \qquad ...(i)$$

Let the tangent intersects the x-axis at A and y-axis at B respectively.

Then $A=(3\cos\theta, 0)$ and $B=(0, -2\cot\theta)$

Let (h, k) be the mid-point of AB.

Therefore, $2h=3\cos\theta$ & $2k=-2\cot\theta$

$$\Rightarrow \quad \sec\theta=\frac{3}{2h} \;\&\; \tan\theta=-\frac{1}{k}$$

As we know that, $\sec^2\theta-\tan^2\theta=1$

$$\Rightarrow \quad \frac{9}{4h^2}-\frac{1}{k^2}=1$$

Hence, the locus of (h, k) is $\frac{9}{4x^2}-\frac{1}{y^2}=1$.

Ex-3. From the points on the circle $x^2+y^2=a^2$, tangents are drawn to the hyperbola $x^2-y^2=a^2$. Prove that the locus of the middle points of the chord of contact is $\left(x^2-y^2\right)^2=a^2\left(x^2+y^2\right)$

Sol. Any point on the circle $x^2+y^2=a^2$ be $(a\cos\theta, a\sin\theta)$.

Equation of the chord of contact from the point $(a\cos\theta, a\sin\theta)$ to the hyperbola

$x^2-y^2=a^2$ is $(a\cos\theta)x-(a\sin\theta)y=a^2$

$$\Rightarrow \quad x\cos\theta-y\sin\theta=a \qquad ...(i)$$

Let the mid-point be (h, k)

Equation of the chord bisected at (h, k) to the hyperbola $x^2-y^2=a^2$ is $hx-ky=h^2-k^2$ ...(ii)

Equations (i) and (ii) are identical.

$$\text{Therefore,} \quad \frac{h}{\cos\theta}=\frac{-k}{\sin\theta}=\frac{h^2-k^2}{a}$$

$$\Rightarrow \quad \cos\theta=\frac{ah}{h^2-k^2} \;\&\; \sin\theta=\frac{-ak}{h^2-k^2}$$

Squaring and adding, we get,

$$\left(\frac{ah}{h^2-k^2}\right)^2+\left(\frac{-ak}{h^2-k^2}\right)^2=1$$

$$\Rightarrow \quad a^2\left(h^2+k^2\right)=\left(h^2-k^2\right)^2$$

Hence, the locus of (h, k) is

$$a^2\left(x^2+y^2\right)=\left(x^2-y^2\right)^2.$$

Ex-4. Prove that the locus of the mid-points of the hyperbola $\frac{x^2}{a^2}-\frac{y^2}{b^2}=1$ which subtend a right angle at the centre is

$$\left(\frac{x^2}{a^2}-\frac{y^2}{b^2}\right)^2\left(\frac{1}{a^2}-\frac{1}{b^2}\right)=\left(\frac{x^2}{a^4}+\frac{y^2}{b^4}\right).$$

Sol. Let the mid-point be (h, k)

Equation of the chord bisected at (h, k) to the given hyperbola is $T=S_1$

$$\Rightarrow \quad \frac{hx}{a^2}-\frac{ky}{b^2}=\frac{h^2}{a^2}-\frac{k^2}{b^2} \qquad ...(i)$$

The equation of the hyperbola is

$$\frac{x^2}{a^2}-\frac{y^2}{b^2}=1 \quad ...(ii)$$

Since the chord (i) subtends a right angle at the centre , so we can write,

$$\frac{x^2}{a^2}-\frac{y^2}{b^2}=\frac{\left(\frac{hx}{a^2}-\frac{ky}{b^2}\right)^2}{\left(\frac{h^2}{a^2}-\frac{k^2}{b^2}\right)^2}$$

$$\Rightarrow \frac{1}{a^2}\left(\frac{h^2}{a^2}-\frac{k^2}{b^2}\right)^2 x^2-\frac{1}{b^2}\left(\frac{h^2}{a^2}-\frac{k^2}{b^2}\right)^2$$

$$y^2=\frac{h^2}{a^4}x^2+\frac{k^2}{b^4}y^2-\frac{2hk}{a^2b^2}xy \quad ...(iii)$$

Equation (iii) will be a right angle if

co-efficient of x^2 + co-efficent of $y^2=0$

$$\Rightarrow \frac{1}{a^2}\left(\frac{h^2}{a^2}-\frac{k^2}{b^2}\right)^2-\frac{h^2}{a^4}-\frac{1}{b^2}\left(\frac{h^2}{a^2}-\frac{k^2}{b^2}\right)^2-\frac{k^2}{b^4}=0$$

$$\Rightarrow \left(\frac{h^2}{a^2}-\frac{k^2}{b^2}\right)^2\left(\frac{1}{a^2}-\frac{1}{b^2}\right)=\left(\frac{h^2}{a^4}+\frac{k^2}{b^4}\right)$$

Hence, the locus of (h, k) is

$$\left(\frac{x^2}{a^2}-\frac{y^2}{b^2}\right)^2\left(\frac{1}{a^2}-\frac{1}{b^2}\right)=\left(\frac{x^2}{a^4}+\frac{y^2}{b^4}\right).$$

Ex-5. Tangents are drawn from a point P to the parabola $y^2=4ax$. If the chord of contact of the parabola be a tangent to the hyperbola $\frac{x^2}{a^2}-\frac{y^2}{b^2}=1$, then find the locus of the point P.

Sol. Let the point on the parabola be (h, k) .

Equation of the chord of contact of the parabola is

$$yk=2a(x+h) \quad ...(i)$$

$$\Rightarrow \quad y=\frac{2a}{k}x+\frac{2ah}{k} \quad ...(ii)$$

Since, the line (ii) is a tangent to the hyperbola

$$\frac{x^2}{a^2}-\frac{y^2}{b^2}=1,$$

so $\quad c^2=a^2m^2-b^2$

$$\Rightarrow \left(\frac{2ah}{k}\right)^2=a^2\left(\frac{2a}{k}\right)^2-b^2$$

$$\Rightarrow \quad 4a^2h^2=4a^4-k^2b^2$$

Hence, the locus of (h, k) is $4a^2x^2=4a^4-y^2b^2$

Ex-6. A tangent to the hyperbola $\frac{x^2}{a^2}-\frac{y^2}{b^2}=1$ cuts the ellipse $\frac{x^2}{a^2}+\frac{y^2}{b^2}=1$ in points P and Q .

Find the locus of the mid-point PQ.

Sol. Any tangent to the hyperbola $\frac{x^2}{a^2}-\frac{y^2}{b^2}=1$ at (θ) is

$$\frac{x}{a}\sec\theta-\frac{y}{b}\tan\theta=1 \quad ...(i)$$

Let the mid point of PQ be (h, k)

Then the equation of the chord bisected at (h, k) to the ellipse $\frac{x^2}{a^2}+\frac{y^2}{b^2}=1$ is

$$\frac{hx}{a^2}+\frac{ky}{b^2}=\frac{h^2}{a^2}+\frac{k^2}{b^2} \quad ...(ii)$$

Therefore, the equations (i) and (ii) are identical

Thus, $\quad \frac{\sec\theta/a}{\frac{h}{a^2}}=\frac{-\tan\theta/b}{\frac{k}{b^2}}=\frac{1}{\left(\frac{h^2}{a^2}+\frac{k^2}{b^2}\right)}$

$$\Rightarrow \quad \frac{\sec\theta}{\frac{h}{a}}=\frac{-\tan\theta}{\frac{k}{b}}=\frac{1}{\left(\frac{h^2}{a^2}+\frac{k^2}{b^2}\right)}$$

$$\Rightarrow \quad \sec\theta=\frac{\frac{h}{a}}{\left(\frac{h^2}{a^2}+\frac{k^2}{b^2}\right)} \;\&\; \tan\theta=\frac{\frac{k}{b}}{\left(\frac{h^2}{a^2}+\frac{k^2}{b^2}\right)}$$

we have, $\sec^2\theta-\tan^2\theta=1$

$$\Rightarrow \frac{\left(\frac{h}{a}\right)^2}{\left(\frac{h^2}{a^2}+\frac{k^2}{b^2}\right)^2}-\frac{\left(\frac{k}{b}\right)^2}{\left(\frac{h^2}{a^2}+\frac{k^2}{b^2}\right)^2}=1$$

$$\Rightarrow \left(\frac{h^2}{a^2}-\frac{k^2}{b^2}\right)=\left(\frac{h^2}{a^2}+\frac{k^2}{b^2}\right)^2$$

Hence, the locus of (h, k) is

$$\left(\frac{x^2}{a^2}-\frac{y^2}{b^2}\right)=\left(\frac{x^2}{a^2}+\frac{y^2}{b^2}\right)^2.$$

Ex-7. Chords of the hyperbola $x^2-y^2=a^2$ touch the parabola $y^2=4ax$. Prove that the locus of their middle points is the curve $y^2(x-a)=x^3$.

Sol. If (h, k) be the mid-point of the chord of the hyperbola

$x^2 - y^2 = a^2$, then $T = S_1$

$\Rightarrow \quad hx - ky = h^2 - k^2$

$\Rightarrow \quad ky = hx + (k^2 - h^2)$

$\Rightarrow \quad y = (h/k)x + (k^2 - h^2)/k \qquad ...(i)$

If the line (i) touches the parabola $y^2 = 4ax$, so $c = \frac{a}{m}$

$$\Rightarrow \quad \left(\frac{h^2 - k^2}{k}\right) = \frac{a}{(h/k)} = \frac{ak}{h}$$

$$\Rightarrow \quad h\left(h^2 - k^2\right) = ak^2$$

Hence, the locus of (h, k) is $x\left(x^2 - y^2\right) = ay^2$

Ex-8. A variable chord of the hyperbola $\frac{x^2}{a^2} - \frac{y^2}{b^2} = 1$ is a tangent to the circle $x^2 + y^2 = c^2$.

Prove that the locus of its middle points is

$$\left(\frac{x^2}{a^2} - \frac{y^2}{b^2}\right)^2 = c^2\left(\frac{x^2}{a^4} + \frac{y^2}{b^4}\right)$$

Sol. If (h, k) be the mid-point of the chord of the hyperbola

$\frac{x^2}{a^2} - \frac{y^2}{b^2} = 1$, then $T = S_1$

$$\Rightarrow \quad \frac{hx}{a^2} - \frac{ky}{b^2} = \frac{h^2}{a^2} - \frac{k^2}{b^2}$$

$$\Rightarrow \quad \frac{ky}{b^2} = \frac{hx}{a^2} - \left(\frac{h^2}{a^2} - \frac{k^2}{b^2}\right)$$

$$\Rightarrow \quad y = \left(\frac{b^2h}{a^2k}\right)x - \frac{b^2}{k}\left(\frac{h^2}{a^2} - \frac{k^2}{b^2}\right) \qquad ...(i)$$

If the line (i) be a tangent to the circle $x^2 + y^2 = c^2$, then

$$C^2 = A^2\left(1 + m^2\right)$$

$$\Rightarrow \quad \frac{b^4}{k^2}\left(\frac{h^2}{a^2} - \frac{k^2}{b^2}\right)^2 = c^2\left(1 + \frac{b^4h^2}{a^4k^2}\right)$$

$$\Rightarrow \quad \left(b^2h^2 - a^2k^2\right)^2 = c^2\left(a^4k^2 + b^4h^2\right)$$

Hence, the locus of (h, k) is

$$\left(b^2x^2 - a^2y^2\right)^2 = c^2\left(a^4y^2 + b^4x^2\right).$$

$$\Rightarrow \quad \left(\frac{x^2}{a^2} - \frac{y^2}{b^2}\right)^2 = c^2\left(\frac{x^2}{a^4} + \frac{y^2}{b^4}\right)$$

Ex-10. A variable chord of the circle $x^2 + y^2 = a^2$ touch the hyperbola $\frac{x^2}{a^2} - \frac{y^2}{b^2} = 1$. Prove that the locus of its middle points is $\left(x^2 + y^2\right)^2 = a^2x^2 - b^2y^2$..

Sol. If (h, k) be the mid-point of the chord of the circle $x^2 + y^2 = a^2$, then T = S1

$\Rightarrow \quad hx + ky = h^2 + k^2$

$$\Rightarrow \quad y = \left(-\frac{h}{k}\right)x + \left(\frac{h^2 + k^2}{k}\right) \qquad ...(i)$$

If the line (i) be a tangent to the hyperbola $\frac{x^2}{a^2} - \frac{y^2}{b^2} = 1$,

so $c^2 = a^2m^2 - b^2$

$$\Rightarrow \quad \left(\frac{h^2 + k^2}{k}\right)^2 = a^2\left(\frac{h^2}{k^2}\right) - b^2$$

$$\Rightarrow \quad \left(h^2 + k^2\right)^2 = \left(a^2h^2 - b^2k^2\right)$$

Hence, the locus of (h, k) is

$$\left(x^2 + y^2\right)^2 = \left(a^2x^2 - b^2y^2\right)$$

Ex-11. A tangent to the parabola $y^2 = 4ax$ meets the hyperbola $xy = c^2$ in two points P and Q.Prove that the locus of the middle point of PQ lies on a parabola.

Sol. Any tangent to the parabola $y^2 = 4ax$ at $(at^2, 2at)$ is

$yt = x + at^2 \qquad ...(i)$

If (h, k) be the mid - point of the chord of the hyperbola $xy = c^2$, then $xk + yh = c^2 \qquad ...(ii)$

Therefore, the equations (i) and (ii) are identical.

Thus, $\frac{k}{1} = \frac{-h}{t} = \frac{-c^2}{at^2}$

$$\Rightarrow \quad t = \frac{-h}{k}, \quad t^2 = \frac{-c^2}{ak}$$

Eliminating 't', we get, $h^2a = -kc^2$

Hence n the locus of (h, k) is $yc^2 + x^2a = 0$

$$\Rightarrow \quad y = \left(-\frac{a}{c^2}\right)x^2.$$

Ex-12. From a point P tangents are drawn to the circle $x^2 + y^2 = a^2$. If the chord of contact of the circle is a normal chord of a hyperbola $\frac{x^2}{a^2} - \frac{y^2}{b^2} = 1$, then prove that the locusof the point P is $\left(\frac{a^2}{x^2}-\frac{b^2}{y^2}\right)=\left(\frac{a^2+b^2}{a^2}\right)^2$.

Sol. Let the point P be (h, k)

Then the equation of the chord of contact of the circle

$x^2+y^2=a^2$ is $hx+ky=a^2$ ...(i)

Equation of the normal chord of the hyperbola

$\frac{x^2}{a^2}-\frac{y^2}{b^2}=1$ at (ϕ) is $ax\cos f - by\cot f = a^2+b^2$ ...(ii)

Equations (i) and (ii) are identical .

Therefore, $\frac{a\cos f}{h}=-\frac{b\cot f}{k}=\frac{(a^2+b^2)}{a^2}$

$$\Rightarrow \quad \sec f=\frac{a^3}{h(a^2+b^2)} \ \& \ \tan f=-\frac{a^2b}{k(a^2+b^2)}$$

We have, $\sec^2\phi-\tan^2\phi=1$

$$\Rightarrow \quad \left(\frac{a^3}{h(a^2+b^2)}\right)^2-\left(-\frac{a^2b}{k(a^2+b^2)}\right)^2=1$$

$$\Rightarrow \quad \left(\frac{a^6}{h^2}-\frac{a^4b^2}{k^2}\right)=(a^2+b^2)^2$$

$$\Rightarrow \quad \left(\frac{a^2}{h^2}-\frac{b^2}{k^2}\right)=\left(\frac{a^2+b^2}{a^2}\right)^2$$

Hence, the locus of (h, k) is $\left(\frac{a^2}{x^2}-\frac{b^2}{y^2}\right)=\left(\frac{a^2+b^2}{a^2}\right)^2$

Ex-13. Prove that the locus of the middle points of the focal chord of the hyperbola

$\frac{x^2}{a^2}-\frac{y^2}{b^2}=1$ is $\frac{x^2}{a^2}-\frac{y^2}{b^2}=\frac{ex}{a}$

Sol. If (h, k) be the mid-point of the chord of the hyperbola

$\frac{x^2}{a^2}-\frac{y^2}{b^2}=1$, then $T=S_1$

$$\Rightarrow \quad \frac{hx}{x^2}-\frac{ky}{b^2}=\frac{h^2}{a^2}-\frac{k^2}{b^2} \quad ...(i)$$

Which is passing through the focus (ae, 0) of the given hyperbola.

Therefore, $\frac{aeh}{a^2}=\frac{h^2}{a^2}-\frac{k^2}{b^2}$

$$\Rightarrow \quad \frac{h^2}{a^2}-\frac{k^2}{b^2}=\frac{eh}{a}$$

Hence, the locus of (h, k) is $\frac{x^2}{a^2}-\frac{y^2}{b^2}=\left(\frac{e}{a}\right)x$

Ex-14. If the chords of contact of tangents from two points (x_1, y_1) and (x_2, y_2) to the hyperbola $\frac{x^2}{a^2}-\frac{y^2}{b^2}=1$ are at right angles such that $\frac{x_1x_2}{y_1y_2}=-\frac{a^m}{b^n}$, where m, n are +ve integers, the find the value of $\left(\frac{m+n}{4}\right)^{10}$.

Sol. Equations of the chord of contact of the tangents to the given hyperbola at (x_1, y_1)

and (x_2, y_2) are $\frac{xx_1}{a^2}-\frac{yy_1}{b^2}=1$ ...(i)

and $\frac{xx_2}{a^2}-\frac{yy_2}{b^2}=1$ ...(ii)

The slopes of (i) and (ii) are

$$m_1=\left(\frac{b^2x_1}{a^2y_1}\right) \ \& \ m_2=\left(\frac{b^2x_1}{a^2y_1}\right)$$

Since, (i) and (ii) are meet at right angles, so $m_1m_2=-1$

$$\Rightarrow \quad \left(\frac{b^2x_1}{a^2y_1}\right)\times\left(\frac{b^2x_1}{a^2y_1}\right)=-1$$

$$\Rightarrow \quad \frac{x_1x_2}{y_1y_2}=-\frac{a^4}{b^4}$$

Thus, $m=4$ and $n=4$

Hence, the value of $\left(\frac{m+n}{4}\right)^{10}$

$$=\left(\frac{4+4}{4}\right)^{10}=2^{10}=1024.$$

6.11 POLE AND POLAR

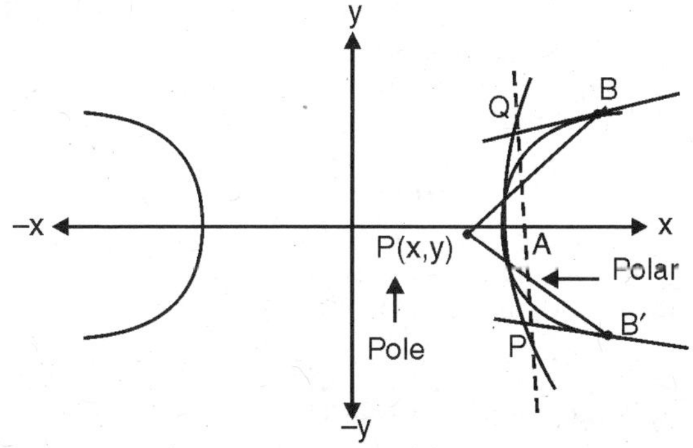

Let P be any point inside or outside of the hyperbola. Suppose any straight line through P intersects the hyperbola at A and B . Then the locus of the point of inter section of the tangents to the hyperbola at A and B is called the polar of the given point P with respect to the hyperbola and the point P is called the pole of the polar.

Equation of polar from a point (x_1, y_1) to the hyperbola

$\frac{x^2}{a^2}-\frac{y^2}{b^2}=1$ is $\frac{xx_1}{a^2}-\frac{yy_1}{b^2}=1$

4.12 Properties related to pole and polar

(i) Polar of the focus is the directrix.

(ii) Any tangent is the polar of the point of contact.

(iii) The pole of a line $lx+my+n=0$ with respect to the ellipse $\frac{x^2}{a^2}-\frac{y^2}{b^2}=1$ is $\left(-\frac{a^2 l}{n}, -\frac{b^2 m}{n}\right)$.

(iv) Pole of a given line is same as point of intersection of tangents at its extremities.

(v) If the polar of $P(x_1, y_1)$ passes through $Q(x_2, y_2)$, then the polar of $Q(x_2, y_2)$ goes through $P(x_1, y_1)$ and such points are said to be **conjugate points.**

(vi) If the pole of a line $lx+my+n=0$ lies on the another line $l'x+m'y+n'=0$, then pole of the second line will lie on the first and such lines are said to be **conjugate lines**.

Ex-1. Find the polar of the focus (-ae, 0) with respect to the hyperbola $\frac{x^2}{a^2}-\frac{y^2}{b^2}=1$.

Sol. Equation of the polar with respect to the hyperbola

$\frac{x^2}{a^2}-\frac{y^2}{b^2}=1$ is $\frac{xx_1}{a^2}-\frac{yy_1}{b^2}=1$

$$\Rightarrow \quad \frac{x(-ae)}{a^2}-\frac{y.0}{b^2}=1$$

$$\Rightarrow \quad x=-\frac{a}{e}$$

Ex-2. If the polars of (x_1, y_1) and (x_2, y_2) with respect to the hyperbola $\frac{x^2}{a^2}-\frac{y^2}{b^2}=1$ are at right angles, then prove that $\frac{x_1x_2}{y_1y_2}+\frac{a^4}{b^4}=0$.

Sol. Equation of the polars from points (x_1,y_1) and (x_2,y_2) to the hyperbola

$\frac{x^2}{a^2}-\frac{y^2}{b^2}=1$ are $\frac{xx_1}{a^2}-\frac{yy_1}{b^2}=1$ ...(i)

and $\frac{xx_2}{a^2}-\frac{yy_2}{b^2}=1$ ...(ii)

Now, slopes of (i) and (ii) are $m_1=\frac{b^2x_1}{a^2y_1}$ & $m_2=\frac{b^2x_2}{a^2y_2}$

Since the polars of the given points are perpendicular, so $m_1\times m_2=-1$

$$\Rightarrow \quad \left(\frac{b^2x_1}{a^2y_1}\right)\times\left(\frac{b^2x_2}{a^2y_2}\right)=-1$$

$$\Rightarrow \quad \frac{x_1x_2}{y_1y_2}=-\frac{a^4}{b^4}$$

$$\Rightarrow \quad \frac{x_1x_2}{y_1y_2}+\frac{a^4}{b^4}=0$$

Ex-3. Find the pole of the line x - y = 3 w. r. t. the hyperbola $x^2-3y^2=3$

Sol. Let (x1, y1) be the pole of the hyperbola.

Then the equation of the polar from a point (x1, y1) w.r.t the hyperbola $x^2-3y^2=3$

is $xx_1-3yy_1=3$ ...(i)

The equation of the given polar is $x-y=3$ ....(ii)

Therefore, the equations (i) and (ii) are identical

$$\Rightarrow \quad \frac{x_1}{1}=\frac{-3y_1}{-1}=\frac{3}{3}$$

$$\Rightarrow \quad x_1=1,\ y_1=\frac{1}{3}$$

Hence, the pole is $\left(1, \frac{1}{3}\right)$

Ex-4. Prove that the locus of the poles of the normal chords with respect to the hyperbola

$\frac{x^2}{a^2}-\frac{y^2}{b^2}=1$ is the curve

$$y^2a^6-x^2b^6=\left(a^2+b^2\right)^2x^2y^2$$

Sol. Let the pole be (h, k)

Equation of the polar from the point (h, k) w.r.t the hyperbola $\frac{x^2}{a^2}-\frac{y^2}{b^2}=1$ is $\frac{hx}{a^2}-\frac{ky}{b^2}=1$ ...(i)

Equation of the normal chord of the given hyperbola at (ϕ) is $ax\cos f - by\cot f=\left(a^2+b^2\right)$ ...(ii)

Equations (i) and (ii) are identical.

Therefore, $\frac{a\cos f}{(h/a^2)} = \frac{b\cot f}{(k/b^2)} = \frac{(a^2+b^2)}{1}$

$$\Rightarrow \quad \cos f = (a^2+b^2)\frac{h}{a^3}, \quad \cot f = (a^2+b^2)\frac{k}{b^3}$$

$$\Rightarrow \quad \sec f = \frac{a^3}{(a^2+b^2)h}, \quad \tan f = \frac{b^3}{(a^2+b^2)k}$$

We have, $\sec^2\phi - \tan^2\phi = 1$

$$\Rightarrow \quad \left(\frac{a^3}{(a^2+b^2)h}\right)^2 - \left(\frac{b^3}{(a^2+b^2)k}\right)^2 = 1$$

$$\Rightarrow \quad \left(\frac{a^3}{h}\right)^2 - \left(\frac{b^3}{k}\right)^2 = (a^2+b^2)^2$$

Hence, the locus of (h, k) is

$$(a^6y^2 - b^6x^2) = (a^2+b^2)^2(x^2y^2).$$

Ex-5. Prove that the locus of the poles with respect to the parabola $y^2 = 4ax$ of tangent to the hyperbola $x^2 - y^2 = a^2$ is the ellipse $4x^2 + y^2 = 4a^2$.

Sol. Let (h, k) be the pole.

Equation of the polar from the point (h, k) w.r.t the parabola $y^2 = 4ax$ is

$$yk = 2a(x+h). = 2ax + 2ah$$

$$\Rightarrow \quad y = \left(\frac{2a}{k}\right)x + \left(\frac{2ah}{k}\right) \qquad \text{...(i)}$$

If the line (i) be a tangent to the hyperbola $x^2 - y^2 = a^2$, then $c^2 = a^2m^2 - a^2$

$$\Rightarrow \quad \left(\frac{2ah}{k}\right)^2 = a^2\left(\frac{2a}{k}\right)^2 - a^2$$

$$\Rightarrow \quad 4h^2 = 4a^2 - k^2$$

$$\Rightarrow \quad h^2 + \frac{k^2}{4} = a^2$$

Hence, the locus of (h, k) is $x^2 + \frac{y^2}{4} = a^2$

$$\Rightarrow \quad 4x^2 + y^2 = 4a^2$$

Ex-6. Prove that the locus of the pole with respect to the hyperbola $\frac{x^2}{a^2} - \frac{y^2}{b^2} = 1$ of any tangent to the circle, whose diameter is the line joining the foci, is the ellipse $\frac{x^2}{a^4} + \frac{y^2}{b^4} = \frac{1}{a^2+b^2}$.

Sol. Let (h, k) be the pole.

Then the equation of the polar w.r.t the hyperbola

$$\frac{x^2}{a^2} - \frac{y^2}{b^2} = 1 \text{ is } \frac{hx}{a^2} - \frac{ky}{b^2} = 1$$

$$\Rightarrow \quad y = \left(\frac{b^2h}{a^2k}\right)x + \left(-\frac{b^2}{k}\right) \qquad \text{...(i)}$$

The foci of the given hyperbola are (ae, 0) and (-ae, 0)

The equation of the circle is $(x-ae)(x+ae) + y^2 = 0$

$$\Rightarrow \quad x^2 + y^2 = (ae)^2 \qquad \text{...(ii)}$$

If the line (i) be a tangent to the circle (ii), then

$$c^2 = a^2(1+m^2)$$

$$\Rightarrow \quad \frac{b^4}{k^2} = (ae)^2\left(1 + \frac{b^4k^2}{a^4h^2}\right)$$

$$\Rightarrow \quad \frac{b^4}{k^2} = e^2\left(\frac{a^4h^2 + b^4k^2}{a^2k^2}\right)$$

$$\Rightarrow \quad \frac{a^2b^4}{e^2} = (a^4h^2 + b^4k^2)$$

$$\Rightarrow \quad (a^4h^2 + b^4k^2) = \frac{a^4b^4}{(a^2+b^2)}$$

$$\Rightarrow \quad \left(\frac{h^2}{a^4} + \frac{k^2}{b^4}\right) = \frac{1}{(a^2+b^2)}$$

Hence, the locus of (h, k) is $\left(\frac{x^2}{a^4} + \frac{y^2}{b^4}\right) = \frac{1}{(a^2+b^2)}$

6.13 DIAMETER

The locus of the middle points of a syatem of parallel chords of a hyperbola is called a diameter of the hyperbola.

Equation of a diameter to a hyperbola $\frac{x^2}{a^2} - \frac{y^2}{b^2} = 1$ is

$$y = \frac{b^2}{a^2m}x.$$

Let (h, k) be the middle point of the chord $y = mx + c$ of the hyperbola $\frac{x^2}{a^2} - \frac{y^2}{b^2} = 1$.

Then, $T = S_1$

$$\Rightarrow \quad \frac{xh}{a^2} - \frac{yk}{b^2} - 1 = \frac{h^2}{a^2} - \frac{k^2}{b^2} - 1$$

$$\text{Slope} = \frac{b^2h}{a^2k}$$

Hence , the locus of the mid-point is $y=\frac{b^2 x}{a^2 m}$.

Ex-1. Prove that the equation of the diameter , which bisects the chord $7x+y-2=0$ of the hyperbola $\frac{x^2}{3}-\frac{y^2}{7}=1$ is $x+3y=0$.

Sol. The equation of the chord is $7x+y=2$

$\Rightarrow \quad y=-7x+2 \qquad ...(i)$

Hence, the equation of the diameter is

$$y=\frac{b^2x}{a^2m}=\frac{7x}{3\times(-7)}=-\frac{x}{3}$$

$\Rightarrow \quad x+3y=0$.

Ex-2. Find the equation of the diameter of the hyperbola $\frac{x^2}{9}-\frac{y^2}{4}=1$, which corresponds the line 3x+4y+10=0

Sol. The given line is $3x+4y+10=0$

$\Rightarrow \quad y=\left(-\frac{3}{4}\right)x+\left(-\frac{5}{2}\right) \qquad ...(i)$

Hence, the equation of the diameter corresponds to the line (i) is

$$y=\frac{b^2x}{a^2m}=\frac{4x}{9\left(-\frac{3}{4}\right)}=-\frac{16}{27}x$$

$\Rightarrow \quad 16x+27y=0$

6.14 CONJUGATE DIAMETERS

Two diameters are said to be conjugate when each bisects all chords parallel to the others.

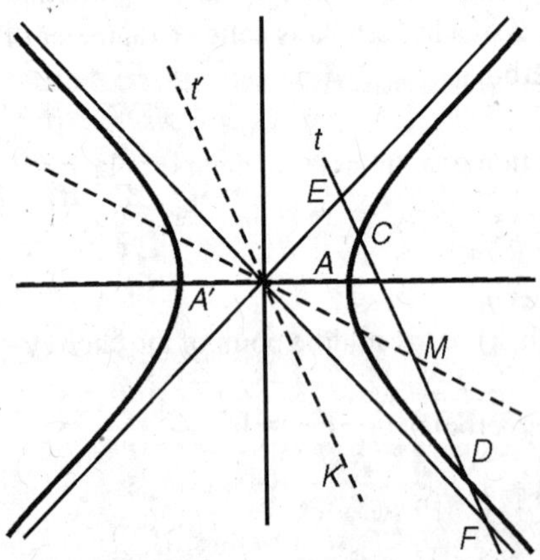

If $y=m_1x$ & $y=m_2x$ be two conjugate diameters ,

then , $m_1.m_2=\frac{b^2}{a^2}$.

6.15 PROPERTIES OF DIAMETERS

Prop-I: If a pair of diameters be conjugate with respect to a hyperbola, they are conjugate with respect to its conjugate hyperbola also.

Prop-II: The parallelogram formed by the tangents at the extremities of conjugate diameters of a hyperbola has its certices lying on the asymptotes and is of conjugate area.

Prop-III: If the normal at P meets the transverse axis in G, then SG = e. SP Also, that the tangent and normal bisects the angle between the focal distances of P.

Prop-IV: If a pair of conjugate diameters meet the hyperbola in P, P' and its conjugate in D, D\` then the asymptotes bisect PD, PD\`, P\`D and P\`D\`

Ex-1. Find the equation of the diameter to the hyperbola $\frac{x^2}{9}-\frac{y^2}{4}=1$ paralell to the chord $2x+3y+5=0$.

Sol. The slope of the given chord is $m=\left(-\frac{2}{3}\right)$.

Hence, the equation of the diameter parallel to the given chord is

$$y=\frac{b^2x}{a^2m}=\frac{4x}{9\left(-\frac{2}{3}\right)}=-\frac{2}{3}x$$

$\Rightarrow \quad 2x+3y=0$

Ex-2. In the hyperbola $16x^2-9y^2=144$, find the equation to the diameter which is conjugate to the diameter whose equation is $x=2y$.

Sol. Let the equation of the diameter , which is conjugate to $x=2y$ is $y=m_1x$.

As we know that , two diametrs $y=\left(\frac{1}{2}\right)x$ and $y=m_1x$ are conjugates, if $m_1 m_2=\frac{b^2}{a^2}$

$\Rightarrow \quad m_1\times\frac{1}{2}=\frac{16}{9} \quad\Rightarrow\quad m_1=\frac{32}{9}$

Hence, the equation of the conjugate diameter is

$y=\frac{32}{9}x \quad\Rightarrow\quad 32x=9y$

6.16 ASYMPTOTES

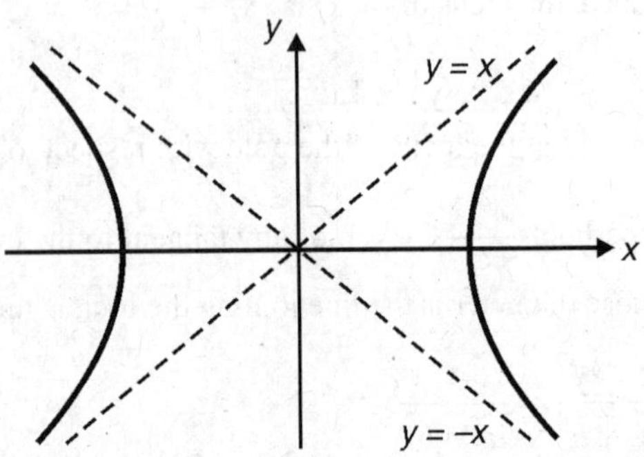

An asymptotes of any hyperbola or a curve is a straight line which touches in it two points at infinity

The equation of the asymptotes of the hyperbola $\frac{x^2}{a^2}-\frac{y^2}{b^2}=1$ are $y=\pm\frac{b}{a}x$.

As we know that, the difference between the 2nd degree curve and pair of asymptotes is constant.

Given hyperbola is $\frac{x^2}{a^2}-\frac{y^2}{b^2}=1$

Equation of the pair of asymptotes are

$$\frac{x^2}{a^2}-\frac{y^2}{b^2}+\lambda=0 \qquad ...(i)$$

Equation (i) represents a pair of straight lines, then $\Delta=0$

$$\Rightarrow \frac{1}{a^2}\left(-\frac{1}{b^2}\right).\lambda+0-0-0-\lambda.0=0$$

$$\Rightarrow \lambda=0$$

From (i) we get , the equation of asymptotes are

$$\frac{x^2}{a^2}-\frac{y^2}{b^2}=0.$$

$$\Rightarrow \quad y=\pm\frac{b}{a}x$$

4.17 Important points related to asymptotes:

(i) The asymptotes pass through the centre of the hyperbola.

(ii) A hyperbola and its conjugate have the same asymptotes.

(iii) The equation of the hyperbola and its asymptotes differ by a constant only.

(iv) Equation of the asymptotes of the rectangular hyperbola $x^2-y^2=a^2$ are $y=\pm x$

(v) The angle between the asymptotes of the hyperbola $\frac{x^2}{a^2}-\frac{y^2}{b^2}=1$ is $2\tan^{-1}\left(\frac{b}{a}\right)$.

(vi) The bisectors of the angles between the asymptotes are the co-ordinate axes.

(vii) No tangent to the hyperbola can be drawn from its centre.

(viii) Only one tangent to the hyperbola can be drawn from a point lying on its asymptotes other than its centre.

(ix) Two tangents can be drawn to the hyperbola from any of its external points which does not lie at its asymptotes.

(x) Let H : $\frac{x^2}{a^2}-\frac{y^2}{b^2}-1=0$, A : $\frac{x^2}{a^2}-\frac{y^2}{b^2}=0$ and C : $\frac{x^2}{a^2}-\frac{y^2}{b^2}+1=0$ be the equations of the hyperbola, its asymptote and its conjugate, then we can write from the above equations $C+H=2A$.

Ex-1. Find the asymptotes of the curve

$$xy-3y-2x=0$$

Sol. Equations of the asymptotes to the hyperbola $xy-2x-3y=0$ is $xy-2x-3y+\lambda=0$, where λ is any constant such that it represents two straight lines.

Therefore, $abc+2fgh-af^2-bg^2-ch^2=0$

$$\Rightarrow \quad 0+2\times\left(\frac{-3}{2}\right)\times(-1)\times\left(\frac{1}{2}\right)-0-0-?\left(\frac{1}{2}\right)^2=0$$

$$\Rightarrow \quad ?=6$$

Hence, the required asymptotes are $xy-2x-3y+6=0$

$$\Rightarrow \quad (x-2)(y-3)=0$$

$$\Rightarrow \quad x=2 \ \& \ y=3.$$

Ex-2. Find the equations of the asymptotes of the curve

$$3x^2+10xy+8y^2+14x+22y+2013=0$$

Sol. Equations of the asymptotes of the given curve is $3x^2+10xy+8y^2+14x+22y+\lambda=0$, where λ is any constant such that it represents two straight lines.

Therefore, $abc+2fgh-af^2-bg^2-ch^2=0$.

$$\Rightarrow 3.8.?-+2.7.11.5-3.121-8.49-?.25=0$$

$$\Rightarrow 24?-+770-363-392-25?=0$$

$$\Rightarrow \quad \lambda=15$$

Hence, the combined equation of the given asymptotes is

$$3x^2+10xy+8y^2+14x+22y+15=0$$

Ex-3. Find the eccentricty of the hyperbola , whose asymptotes are $3x+4y=10$ and $4x-3y=5$.

Sol. Since the asymptotes are perpendicular to each other, so the hyperbola is rectangular .

Hence , its eccentricity is $\sqrt{2}$.

Ex-4. Find the equation of a hyperbola whose asymptotes are $2x-y=3$ and $3x+y=7$ and which pass throgh the point (1, 1).

Sol. The combined equation of the asymptotes is $(2x-y-3)(3x+y-7)=0$

$$\Rightarrow \quad 6x^2-xy-y^2-23x+4y+21=0$$

Let the equation of the hyperbola be

$6x^2-xy-y^2-23x+4y+\lambda=0$, where λ is any constant such that it represents two straight lines.

Which passes through (1, 1), so $\lambda = 15$, Hence, the equation of the hyperbola becomes

$$6x^2 - xy - y^2 - 23x + 4y + 15 = 0.$$

Ex-5. The asymptotes of a hyperbola having centre at the point(1, 2) are parallel to the lines $2x+3y=0$ and $3x+2y=0$. If the hyperbola passes through the point (5, 3), prove that its equation is

$$(2x+3y-8)(3x+2y-7)-154=0.$$

Sol. The combined equation of the asymptotes, parallel to the lines $2x+3y=0$ and

$3x+2y=0$ is $(2x+3y+\lambda)(3x+2y+\mu)=0$

which is passing through (1, 2)

Therefore, $(2.1+3.2+\lambda)\ (3.1+2.2+\mu)=0$

$\Rightarrow \quad (8+\lambda)(\ +\mu)=0$

$\Rightarrow \quad \lambda=-8,\ \mu=-7.$

Thus, the combined equation of the assymptotes is $(2x+3y-8)(3x+2y-7)=0$

Let the equation of the hyperbola be

$\Rightarrow \quad 2x+3y=0\ \&\ 2x-3y=0$

Which is passing through (5, 3).

So, $(2.5+3.3-8)(3.5+2.3-7)+\lambda=0$

$\Rightarrow \quad 11\times 14+\lambda=0$

$\Rightarrow \quad \lambda=-154$

Hence, the equation of the hyperbola is

$$(2x+3y-8)(3x+2y-7)-154=0.$$

Ex-6. Find the product of the lengths of perpendiculars from any point on the hyperbola $x^2-2y^2=2$ to its asymptotes.

Sol. The equation of the given hyperbola is $x^2-2y^2=2$.

So, the equations of its asymptotes are

$$x-\sqrt{2}\,y=0\ \&\ x+\sqrt{2}\,y=0.$$

Let any point on the hyperbola be $P\left(\sqrt{2}\sec f,\ \tan f\right)$

Let PM and PN are two perpendiculars from the point P to the asymptotes.

Then, PM . PN

$$=\left|\frac{\sqrt{2}\sec\phi-\sqrt{2}\tan\phi}{\sqrt{1+2}}\right|\times\left|\frac{\sqrt{2}\sec\phi+\sqrt{2}\tan\phi}{\sqrt{1+2}}\right|$$

$$=\frac{2}{3}\times(\sec\varphi-\tan\varphi)\times(\sec\varphi+\tan\varphi)$$

$$=\frac{2}{3}\times\left(\sec^2\varphi-\tan^2\varphi\right)$$

$$=\frac{2}{3}.$$

Ex-7. Find the area of the triangle formed by any tangent to the hyperbola $\frac{x^2}{9}-\frac{y^2}{4}=1$ and its asymptotes.

Sol. The equation of the given hyperbola is $\frac{x^2}{9}-\frac{y^2}{4}=1$.

Thus, the equations of the asymptotes are

$$\left(\frac{x}{3}+\frac{y}{2}\right)\left(\frac{x}{3}-\frac{y}{2}\right)=0$$

$\Rightarrow \quad \left(\frac{x}{3}+\frac{y}{2}\right)=0\ \&\ \left(\frac{x}{3}-\frac{y}{2}\right)=0$

$\Rightarrow \quad 2x+3y=0\ \&\ 2x-3y=0$

Equation of any tangent to the hyperbola $\frac{x^2}{9}-\frac{y^2}{4}=1$

is $\frac{x}{3}\sec f-\frac{y}{2}\tan f=1$

Let the points of intersection of $2x+3y=0$,

$2x-3y=0$ and $\frac{x}{3}\sec f-\frac{y}{2}\tan f=1$ are O, P and Q respectively.

Therefore, $O=(0,0)$,

$$P=\left(\frac{3}{\sec\phi+\tan\phi},-\frac{2}{\sec\phi+\tan\phi}\right)$$

and $Q=\left(\frac{3}{\sec\phi-\tan\phi},\frac{2}{\sec\phi-\tan\phi}\right)$.

Hence, the area of the triangle OPQ

$$=\frac{1}{2}\begin{vmatrix}0 & 0\\ \frac{3}{\sec\varphi+\tan\varphi} & -\frac{2}{\sec\varphi+\tan\varphi}\\ \frac{3}{\sec\varphi-\tan\varphi} & \frac{2}{\sec\varphi-\tan\varphi}\\ 0 & 0\end{vmatrix}$$

$$=\frac{1}{2}(6+6)=6 \text{ sq. u.}$$

Ex-8. Let P be a variable point on the hyperbola $\frac{x^2}{a^2}-\frac{y^2}{b^2}=1$ such that its distance from the transverse axis is equal to its distance from an asymtote to the given hyperbola. Prove that the locus of P is

$$\left(x^2-y^2\right)^2=4x^2\left(x^2-a^2\right).$$

Sol. Let the point P be $(a\sec f,\ b\tan f)$

The equations of the asymptotes of the given hyperbola $\frac{x^2}{a^2}-\frac{y^2}{b^2}=1$ are

$bx - ay = 0$ & $bx + ay = 0$

Let PM and PN be two perpendiculars from the point P to the transverse axis and the asymptote $bx - ay = 0$.

Thus, $PM = b\tan\varphi$ and $PN = \left|\dfrac{ab\sec\varphi - ab\tan\varphi}{\sqrt{b^2+a^2}}\right|$.

It is given that, PM = PN

$$\Rightarrow \quad b\tan\varphi = \left|\frac{ab\sec\varphi - ab\tan\varphi}{\sqrt{b^2+a^2}}\right|$$

$$\Rightarrow \quad \tan\varphi = a\left|\frac{\sec\varphi - \tan\varphi}{\sqrt{b^2+a^2}}\right|.$$

Ex-9. Show that the tangent at any point of a hyperbola cuts off a triangle of constant area from the asymptotes and that the portion of it intercepted between the asymptotes is bisected at the point of contact.

Sol. Let the equation of the hyperbola be

$$\frac{x^2}{a^2} - \frac{y^2}{b^2} = 1 \qquad \text{...(i)}$$

and any point on the hyperbola (i) be $P(a\sec\phi, b\tan\phi)$

Equation of the tangent to the hyperbola (i) at P is

$$\frac{x}{a}\sec\varphi - \frac{y}{b}\tan\varphi = 1 \qquad \text{...(ii)}$$

The equations of the asymptotes of the hyperbola (i) are $bx - ay = 0$ and $bx + ay = 0$

Let the points of the intersection of the asymptotes and the tangent are O, Q, R resp.

Then, $O = (0, 0)$, $Q =$

$$\left(a(\sec\varphi + \tan\varphi), b(\sec\varphi + \tan\varphi)\right) \text{ and}$$

$$R = \left(a(\sec\varphi - \tan\varphi), -b(\sec\varphi - \tan\varphi)\right)$$

Clearly, mid-point of QR is $(a\sec\varphi, b\tan\varphi)$, which is co-ordinates of P.

Thus, the area of ΔOQR

$$= \frac{1}{2}\left\|\begin{matrix} 0 & 0 \\ a(\sec\phi + \tan\phi) & b(\sec\phi + \tan\phi) \\ a(\sec\phi - \tan\phi) & -b(\sec\phi - \tan\phi) \\ 0 & 0 \end{matrix}\right\|$$

$$= \frac{1}{2}\left|-ab - ab\right|$$

$$= ab.$$

Ex-10. If p_1 and p_2 are the perpendiculars from any point on the hyperbola $\dfrac{x^2}{a^2} - \dfrac{y^2}{b^2} = 1$ on its asymptotes, then prove that $\dfrac{1}{p_1 p_2} = \dfrac{1}{a^2} + \dfrac{1}{b^2}$.

Sol. The equations of the asymptotes of the given hyperbola $\dfrac{x^2}{a^2} - \dfrac{y^2}{b^2} = 1$ are $bx - ay = 0$ and $bx + ay = 0$.

Let P be any point on the given hyperbola be $(a\sec\varphi, b\tan\varphi)$

It is given that, p_1 and p_2 be the lengths of perpendiculars from the point P to the asymptotes $bx - ay = 0$ and $bx + ay = 0$.

$$\text{Thus,} \quad p_1 = \left|\frac{ab\sec\varphi - ab\tan\varphi}{\sqrt{b^2+a^2}}\right|$$

$$\text{and} \quad p_2 = \left|\frac{ab\sec\varphi + ab\tan\varphi}{\sqrt{b^2+a^2}}\right|$$

Therefore,

$$\frac{1}{p_1 p_2} = \left(\frac{a^2+b^2}{(ab\sec\varphi - ab\tan\varphi)(ab\sec\varphi + ab\tan\varphi)}\right)$$

$$= \left(\frac{a^2+b^2}{a^2b^2}\right) = \frac{1}{a^2} + \frac{1}{b^2}$$

Hence, the result.

6.18 RECTANGULAR HYPERBOLA

A hyperbola is said to be rectangular if the angle between its asymptote is 90°.

$$\text{Thus, } 2\tan^{-1}\left(\frac{b}{a}\right) = 90° \Rightarrow \tan^{-1}\left(\frac{b}{a}\right) = 45°$$

$$\Rightarrow \frac{b}{a} = \tan 45° \Rightarrow b = a$$

Hence, the equation of the rectangular hyperbola is $x^2 - y^2 = a^2$

Eccentricity of the rectangular hyperbola is

$$e = \sqrt{1 + \frac{a^2}{a^2}} = \sqrt{1+1} = \sqrt{2}$$

6.19 RECTANGULAR HYPERBOLA $xy = c^2$

Equation of rectangular hyperbola is $x^2 - y^2 = a^2$ and its asymptote are $x - y = 0$ and $x + y = 0$, where asymptotes are inclined at 45° and 135° respectively.

If we rotate the axes through an angle of 45° in clockwise sense without changing the origin, then we replace x by $[x\cos(-45°) - y\sin(-45°)]$ and y by $[x\sin(-45°) + y\cos(-45°)]$

i.e. x by $\left(\dfrac{x+y}{\sqrt{2}}\right)$ and y by $\left(\dfrac{-x+y}{\sqrt{2}}\right)$

Then the equation, $x^2 - y^2 = a^2$ reduces to

$$\left(\frac{x+y}{\sqrt{2}}\right)^2 - \left(\frac{-x+y}{\sqrt{2}}\right)^2 = a^2$$

$$\Rightarrow \quad \frac{1}{2}(2xy+2xy) = a^2$$

$$\Rightarrow \quad xy = \frac{a^2}{2} = c^2 \text{ (say)}$$

$$\Rightarrow \quad xy = c^2$$

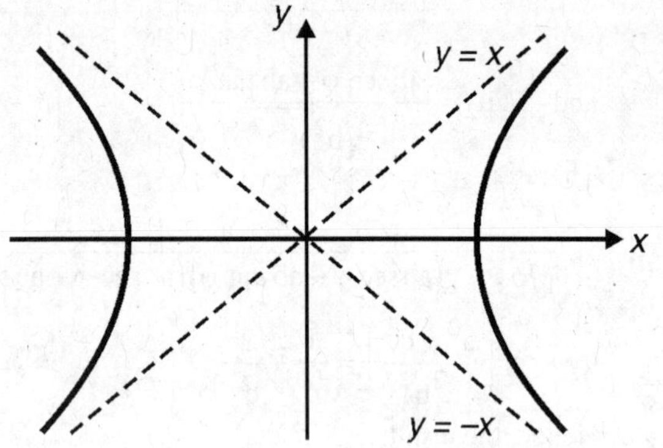

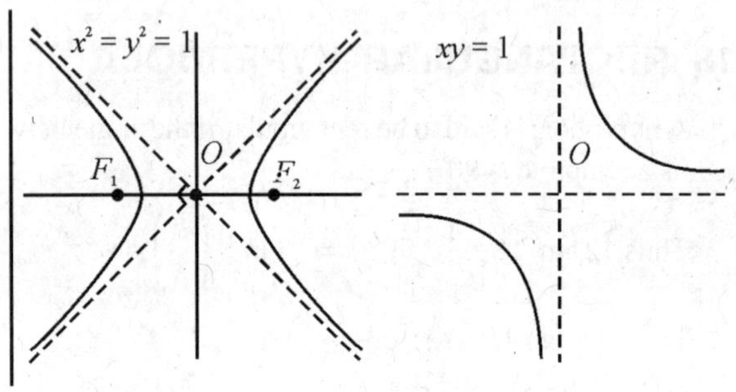

4.20 Properties of rectangular hyperbola

(i) The asymptotes of the rectangular hyperbola $xy = c^2$ are $x = 0$ and $y = 0$

(ii) The parametric equation of the rectangular hyperbola $xy = c^2$ are $x = ct$ & $y = \frac{c}{t}$

(iii) Any point on the rectangular hyperbola $xy = c^2$ can be considered as $\left(ct, \frac{c}{t}\right)$.

(iv) Equation of the chord joining the points 't_1' and 't_2' is $x + yt_1t_2 - c(t_1+t_2) = 0$

(v) Equation of tangent to the rectangular hyperbola $xy = c^2$ at (x_1, y_1) is $xy_1 + x_1y = c^2$

(vi) Equation of tangent at $\left(ct, \frac{c}{t}\right)$ to the hyperbola $xy = c^2$ is $\frac{x}{t} + yt = 2c$

(vii) Equation of normal at (x_1, y_1) to the hyperbola $xy = c^2$ is $xx_1 - yy_1 = x_1^2 - y_1^2$

(viii) Equation of the normal at 't' to the hyperbola $xy = c^2$ is $xt^3 - yt - ct^4 + c = 0$.

Ex-1. If the normal at 't_1' to the hyperbola $xy = c^2$ meets it again at 't_2', prove that $t_1^3 t_2 = -1$

Sol. Equation of the normal at

$$\left(ct_1, \frac{c}{t_1}\right) \text{ is } t_1^3x - t_1y - ct_1^4 + c = 0 \quad \text{...(i)}$$

Also it meets the hyperbola again at $\left(ct_2, \frac{c}{t_2}\right)$.

Therefore, $ct_2t_1^3 - c\frac{t_1}{t_2} - ct_1^4 + c = 0$

$$\Rightarrow \quad t_2t_1^3 - \frac{t_1}{t_2} - t_1^4 + 1 = 0$$

$$\Rightarrow \quad t_2^2t_1^3 - t_1 - t_1^4t_2 + t_2 = 0$$

$$\Rightarrow \quad t_2t_1^3(t_2 - t_1) + (t_2 - t_1) = 0$$

$$\Rightarrow \quad (t_2t_1^3 + 1)(t_2 - t_1) = 0$$

$$\Rightarrow \quad (t_2t_1^3 + 1) = 0 \quad (\because t_1 \neq t_2)$$

$$\Rightarrow \quad t_2t_1^3 = -1$$

Hence, the result.

Ex-2. A triangle has its vertices on a rectangular hyperbola. Prove that the orthocenter of the triangle also lies on the same hyperbola.

Sol. Let P, Q, R are the vertices of a triangle such that

$$P = \left(ct_1, \frac{c}{t_1}\right), \; Q = \left(ct_2, \frac{c}{t_2}\right), \; R = \left(ct_3, \frac{c}{t_3}\right)$$

Now, slope of QR $= \dfrac{\frac{c}{t_3} - \frac{c}{t_2}}{ct_3 - ct_2} = -\dfrac{1}{t_2t_3}$

Therefore, slope of PM is t_2t_3.

Equation of the perpendicular PM on QR is

$$y - \frac{c}{t_1} = t_2t_3(x - ct_1) \quad \text{...(i)}$$

Similarly, the equation of the perpendicular BN on PR is

$$y - \frac{c}{t_2} = t_1t_3(x - ct_2) \quad \text{...(ii)}$$

On solving (i) and (ii),

we get, $x = -\dfrac{c}{t_1t_2t_3}$ & $y = -ct_1t_2t_3$.

Thus, the point $\left(-\frac{c}{t_1t_2t_3}, -ct_1t_2t_3\right)$ lies on the rectangular hyperbola $xy = c^2$.

Hence, the result.

Ex-3. Find the locus of the poles of the normal chords of the rectangular hyperbola $xy = c^2$

Sol. Equation of the normal to the rectangular hyperbola $xy = c^2$ at 't' is

$$xt^2 - y = ct^3 - \frac{c}{t} \quad \text{...(i)}$$

Let the pole be (h, k)

Then the equation of the polar from the point (h, k) to the rectangular hyperbola $xy = c^2$ is

$$xk + yh = 2c^2 \quad \text{...(ii)}$$

Therefore, the equations (i) and (ii) are identical.

So, $\frac{k}{t^2} = \frac{h}{-1} = \frac{2c^2}{ct^3 - \frac{c}{t}}$

$\Rightarrow \quad t^2 = -\frac{k}{h}$ & $h = -\frac{2ct}{t^4 - 1}$

Eliminating 't', we get, $\left(h^2 - k^2\right)^2 + 4c^2 hk = 0$

Hence, the locus of (h, k) is $\left(x^2 - y^2\right)^2 + 4c^2 xy = 0$

Ex-4. If the angle between the asymptote is 2α, prove that the eccentricity of the hyperbola is sec α

Sol. The equations of the asymptotes of the rectangular hyperbola $xy = c^2$ are $x = 0$ and $y = 0$

Claearly, angle between the asymptotes $= \frac{\pi}{2}$

$\Rightarrow \quad 2a = \frac{p}{2}$

$\Rightarrow \quad a = \frac{p}{4}$

Thus, the eccentricity $= e = \sqrt{2} = \sec\left(\frac{p}{4}\right) = \sec a$.

Ex-5. A circle cuts the rectangular hyperbola x y = 1 in points (x_r, y_r), r = 1, 2, 3, 4, prove that $x_1 x_2 x_3 x_4 = 1$ and $y_1 y_2 y_3 y_4 = 1$

Sol. Let the equation of the circle be

$$x^2 + y^2 + 2gx + 2fy + c = 0 \quad \text{...(i)}$$

and the equation of the given hyperbola be

$$xy = 1 \quad \text{...(ii)}$$

On solving, we get, $x^2 + \frac{1}{x^2} + 2gx + \frac{2f}{x} + c = 0$

$\Rightarrow \quad x^4 + 2gx^3 + cx^2 + 2fx + 1 = 0$

Let its roots are x_1, x_2, x_3 and x_4

Then, $x_1 x_2 x_3 x_4 = 1$.

Similarly, we can easily prove that, $y_1 y_2 y_3 y_4 = 1$

Ex-6. If the tangent and normal to a rectangular hyperbola $xy = c^2$ at a point cuts of intercepts a_1 and a_2 on one axis and b_1, b_2 on the other axis, then prove that $a_1 a_2 + b_1 b_2 = 0$.

Sol. Any point on the rectangular hyperbola $xy = c^2$ is $P\left(ct, \frac{c}{t}\right)$

Equation of any tangent to the rectangular hyperbola

$xy = c^2$ at 't' is $\frac{x}{t} + yt = 2c$ ...(i)

Equation of any normal to the rectangular hyperbola $xy = c^2$ at 't' is

$$xt^3 - yt - ct^4 + c = 0 \quad \text{...(ii)}$$

Therefore,

$a_1 = 2ct$, $a_2 = \frac{2c}{t}$ & $b_1 = c\left(t - \frac{1}{t^3}\right)$, $b_2 = c\left(\frac{1}{t} - t^3\right)$

Now, $a_1a_2 + b_1b_2 = 2c^2 t\left(t - \frac{1}{t^3}\right) + \frac{2c^2}{t}\left(\frac{1}{t} - t^3\right)$

$= 2c^2\left(t^2 - \frac{1}{t^2} + \frac{1}{t^2} - t^2\right) = 0$.

Ex-7. If e_1 and e_2 are the eccentricities of the hyperbola $xy = c^2$ and $x^2 - y^2 = a^2$, then find the value of $(e_1 + e_2)^2$.

Sol. We have, $e_1 = \sqrt{2}$ & $e_2 = \sqrt{2}$

Now, $(e_1 + e_2)^2 = \left(\sqrt{2} + \sqrt{2}\right)^2 = \left(2\sqrt{2}\right)^2 = 8$

Ex-8. Find the product of the lengths of perpendiculars drawn from any point on the hyperbola $\frac{x^2}{2} - y^2 = 1$ to its asymptote.

Sol. Any point on the given hyperbola $\frac{x^2}{2} - y^2 = 1$ be $P\left(\sqrt{2}\sec\phi, \tan\phi\right)$

The equations of the asymptotes of the given hyperbola are $x - \sqrt{2}y = 0$ & $x + \sqrt{2}y = 0$.

Let PM and PN be the lengths of perpendiculars from the point P on the asymptotes.

Thus, PM. PN =

$$\left|\frac{\sqrt{2}\sec\phi-\sqrt{2}\tan\phi}{\sqrt{1+2}}\right|\times\left|\frac{\sqrt{2}\sec\phi+\sqrt{2}\tan\phi}{\sqrt{1+2}}\right|=\frac{2}{3}$$

Ex-9. A, B , C are the three points on the rectangular hyperbola $xy = c^2$. Then find

(i) the area of the triangle ABC

(ii) the area of the triangle formed by the tangents at A, B,C.

Sol. Let the points A, B, C be

$$\left(ct_1, \frac{c}{t_1}\right), \left(ct_2, \frac{c}{t_2}\right), \left(ct_3, \frac{c}{t_3}\right).$$

(i) Then the area of the triangle ABC

$$\frac{1}{2}\begin{vmatrix} ct_1 & \frac{c}{t_1} & 1 \\ ct_2 & \frac{c}{t_2} & 1 \\ ct_3 & \frac{c}{t_3} & 1 \end{vmatrix} = \frac{1}{2}\frac{c^2}{t_1t_2t_3}\begin{vmatrix} t_1^2 & 1 & t_1 \\ t_2^2 & 1 & t_2 \\ t_3^2 & 1 & t_3 \end{vmatrix}$$

$$=\frac{c^2}{2}\times\frac{(t_1-t_2)(t_2-t_3)(t_3-t_1)}{t_1t_2t_3}$$

(ii) Equations of the tangents at A, B and C are

$$\frac{x}{t_1}+yt_1 = 2c \qquad ...(i)$$

$$\frac{x}{t_2}+yt_2 = 2c \qquad ...(ii)$$

and $\frac{x}{t_3}+yt_3 = 2c$ ...(iii)

Thus, the points of intersections of (i) and (ii) , (i) and (iii), (ii) and (iii) meet at P, Q, R respectively.

Thus, $P = \left(\frac{2ct_1t_2}{t_1+t_2}, \frac{2c}{t_1+t_2}\right)$,

$Q = \left(\frac{2ct_1t_3}{t_1+t_3}, \frac{2c}{t_1+t_3}\right)$

and $R = \left(\frac{2ct_2t_3}{t_2+t_3}, \frac{2c}{t_2+t_3}\right)$ resp.

Hence, the area of the triangle PQR

$$=\frac{1}{2}\begin{vmatrix} \frac{2ct_1t_2}{t_1+t_2} & \frac{2c}{t_1+t_2} & 1 \\ \frac{2ct_1t_3}{t_1+t_3} & \frac{2c}{t_1+t_3} & 1 \\ \frac{2ct_2t_3}{t_2+t_3} & \frac{2c}{t_2+t_3} & 1 \end{vmatrix}$$

$$=\left(1\pm2\sqrt{2}, 2\right)$$

$$=\frac{2c^2(t_1-t_2)(t_2-t_3)(t_3-t_1)}{(t_1+t_2)(t_1+t_2)(t_1+t_2)}.$$

Ex-10. Find the length of the transverse axis of the rectangular hyperbola xy = 18.

Sol. The given rectangular hyperbola is x y = 18 ...(i)

Replacing x by $x\cos(45°)+y\sin(45°)$ and y by $-x\sin(45°)+y\cos(45°)$ in (i),

we get, $\left(\frac{x}{\sqrt{2}}+\frac{y}{\sqrt{2}}\right)\left(-\frac{x}{\sqrt{2}}+\frac{y}{\sqrt{2}}\right)=18$

$\Rightarrow \quad x^2-y^2=-18$

Hence, the length of the transverse axis = 2 a = 2 . 6 = 12 units.

Ex-11. Prove that the locus of a point whose chord of contact with respect to the circle $x^2+y^2=4$ is a tangent to the hyperbola xy = 1is a hyperbola.

Sol. Let (h, k) be any point.

Equation of the chord of contact of the tangents from

= (h, k) to the cirrcle $x^2+y^2=4$ is

$hx+ky=4$.

Also, the given hyperbola is $xy = 1$

$\Rightarrow \quad x\left(\frac{4-hx}{k}\right)=1$

$\Rightarrow \quad 4x-hx^2=k$

$\Rightarrow \quad hx^2-4x+k=0$

Thus, its roots are equal .

So, D = 0 gives, $16-4hk=0$

$\Rightarrow \quad hk=4$

Hence, the locus of (h, k) is $xy=4$.

Ex-12. Find the asymptotes of the hyperbola $xy=hx+ky$.

Sol. The combined equation of the asymptotes of the given hyperbola is $xy-hx-ky+?=0$

where λ is any constant such that it represents two straight lines.

Therefore, $abc+2fgh-af^2-bg^2-ch^2=0$.

$\Rightarrow \quad 0+2\left(-\frac{k}{2}\right)\left(-\frac{h}{2}\right)\left(\frac{1}{2}\right)-\frac{?}{4}=0$

$\Rightarrow \quad ?=hk$

Hence, the asymptotes are $xy-hx-ky+hk=0$

$\Rightarrow \quad (x-h)(y-k)=0$

$\Rightarrow \quad (x-h)=0 \;\&\; (y-k)=0$

Ex-13. If 'e' is eccentricity of the hyperbola $\frac{x^2}{a^2}-\frac{y^2}{b^2}=1$ and θ is the angle between the asymptotes, then find $\cos(\theta/2)$.

Sol. We have, $? = 2\tan^{-1}\left(\frac{b}{a}\right)$

$$\Rightarrow \quad \tan\left(\frac{\theta}{2}\right)=\frac{b}{a}$$

Also, $e=\sqrt{1+\frac{b^2}{a^2}}=\sqrt{1+\tan^2\left(\frac{\theta}{2}\right)}=\sec\left(\frac{\theta}{2}\right)$

$$\Rightarrow \quad \cos\left(\frac{\theta}{2}\right)=\frac{1}{e}$$

6.21 REFLECTION PROPERTY OF A HYPERBOLA

If an incoming light ray passing through one focus, after striking the convex side of the hyperbola then it will get reflected towards other focus.

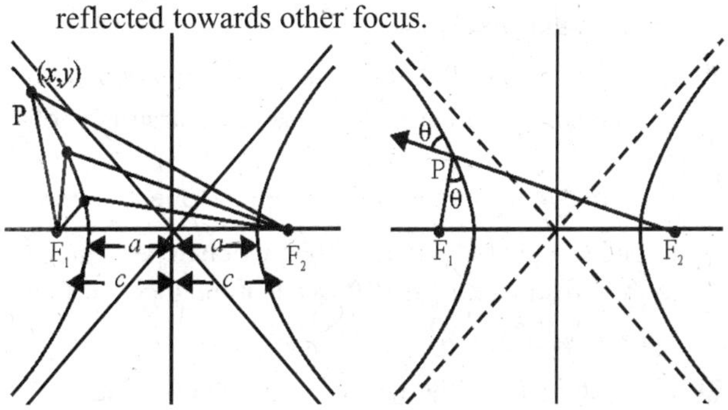

Ex-1. A ray is emanating from the point (5, 0) is incident on the hyperbola $9x^2-16y^2=144$ at the point P with abscissa 8. Find the equation of the reflected ray after first reflection and point P lies in first quadrant.

Sol. The equation of the given hyperbola is $9x^2-16y^2=144$

$$\Rightarrow \quad \frac{x^2}{16}-\frac{y^2}{9}=1 \qquad \text{...(i)}$$

Let any point on the given hyperbola be P $(8, k)$.

since the point P lies on (i), so $\frac{64}{16}-\frac{k^2}{9}=1$

$$\Rightarrow \quad k^2=27$$

$$\Rightarrow \quad k=3\sqrt{3}$$

Hence, the co-ordinates of P be $(8, 3\sqrt{3})$.

Thus, the equation o f the reflected ray is

$$y-3\sqrt{3}=\frac{0-3\sqrt{3}}{-5-8}(x-8)$$

$$\Rightarrow \quad 3\sqrt{3}\,x-13y+15\sqrt{3}=0$$

Ex-2. A ray is coming along the line $2x-y+3=0$ (not through the focus) to the hyperbola $\frac{x^2}{4}-\frac{y^2}{3}=1$. After striking the hyperbolic mirror it is reflected (not through the other focus).Then find the equation of the line containg the reflected ray.

Level – I QUESTIONS BASED ON FUNDAMENTALS

ABC OF HYPERBOLA

1. Find the locus of a point which moves in a plane in such way that the difference of its distances from two fixed point (foci) is always constant.
2. Find the equation of the hyperbola whose directrix is 2 x + y = 1 , focus is (1, 2) and eccentricity is $\sqrt{3}$.
3. Find the eccentricity of the hyperbola whose latus rectum is half of its transverse axis.
4. Prove that the point $\left\{\frac{a}{2}\left(t+\frac{1}{t}\right), \frac{b}{2}\left(t-\frac{1}{t}\right)\right\}$ lies on the hyperbola for all values of t, $(t \neq 0)$.
5. Find the equation of the hyperbola whose foci are (6, 4) and (-4, 4) and eccentricity is 2.
6. The foci of a hyperbola coincide with the foci of the ellipse $\frac{x^2}{25}+\frac{y^2}{9}=1$. Find the equation of the hyperbola if its eccentricity is 2.
7. If the equation $\frac{x^2}{10-\lambda}+\frac{y^2}{6-\lambda}=1$ represents a hyperbola, then find λ.
8. If e_1 and e_2 are the eccentricities of the conic section $16x^2+9y^2=144$ and $16x^2-9y^2=144$, then prove that $e_1^2+e_2^2<3$.
9. If e_1 and e_2 are the eccentricities of the hyperbola $\frac{x^2}{a^2}-\frac{y^2}{b^2}=1$ and $\frac{x^2}{b^2}-\frac{y^2}{a^2}=1$, then prove that the point $(1/e_1, 1/e_2)$ lies on the circle $x^2+y^2=1$.
10. Prove that the straight line $\frac{x}{a}-\frac{y}{b}=m$ and $\frac{x}{a}+\frac{y}{b}=\frac{1}{m}$ always meet on a hyperbola.
11. If e_1 and e_2 are the eccentricities of a hyperbola and its conjugate , then prove that $\frac{1}{e_1^2}+\frac{1}{e_2^2}=1$.

12. Find the equation of the hyperbola whose foci are $(0, \pm\sqrt{10})$ and which pass through the point (2, 3).

13. If the foci of an ellipse $\frac{x^2}{a^2}+\frac{y^2}{b^2}=1$ and the hyperbola $\frac{x^2}{144}-\frac{y^2}{81}=\frac{1}{25}$ coincide , then find the value of b^2.

14. Find the co-ordinates of the centre ,vertices lengths of the transverse and conjugate axes, eccentricity, latus rectum, co-ordinate of foci, and the equation of directrices of the following hyperbolas:

(i) $9x^2-y^2=1$

(ii) $7y^2-9x^2+54x-28y-116=0$

(iii) $3x^2-5y^2-6x+20y-32=0$.

(iv) $9x^2-16y^2-18x-64y-199=0$

(v) $16x^2-9y^2+32x+36y-164=0$.

(vi) $3x^2-3y^2-18x+12y=0$.

POSITION OF A POINT W. R. T A HYPERBOLA

15. Find the position of a point (5, -4) relative to the hyperbola $9x^2-y^2=1$.

16. Find the position of a point (5, 3) w.r.t a hyperbola $2x^2-3y^2=6$. Intersection of a line and a hyperbola:

17. Prove that the straight line l x + m y + n = 0 touches the hyperbola $\frac{x^2}{a^2}-\frac{y^2}{b^2}=1$ if $a^2l^2-b^2m^2=n^2$.

18. For what values of λ does the line $y=2x+\lambda$ touches the hyperbola $16x^2-9y^2=144$.

19. Find the equation of the tangent to the hyperbola $4x^2-9y^2=1$ which is parallel to the line $4y=5x+7$.

20. Find the equation of the tangent to the hyperbola $\frac{x^2}{16}-\frac{y^2}{9}=1$ which is perpendicular to the line 3 x + 2 y = 6.

TANGENTS AND NORMALS

21. Find the equation of the common tangents to the hyperbolas $\frac{x^2}{a^2}-\frac{y^2}{b^2}=1$ and $\frac{y^2}{a^2}-\frac{x^2}{b^2}=1$.

22. If the line $y=mx+\sqrt{a^2m^2-b^2}$ touches the hyperbola $\frac{x^2}{a^2}-\frac{y^2}{b^2}=1$ at the point $(a\sec\theta, b\tan\theta)$, then show that $\theta = \sin^{-1}\left(\frac{b}{am}\right)$.

23. Prove that the product of the length of the perpendiculars from the foci of the tangents to the hyperbola is constant.

24. Prove that the line lx + my = n will be a normal to the hyperbola $\frac{x^2}{a^2}-\frac{y^2}{b^2}=1$ if $\frac{a^2}{l^2}-\frac{b^2}{m^2}=\frac{(a^2+b^2)^2}{n^2}$.

25. If the normal at ϕ on the hyperbola $\frac{x^2}{a^2}-\frac{y^2}{b^2}=1$ meet transverse axis G, then prove that $AG.A'G=a^2(e^4\sec^2\phi-1)$, where A and A' are the vertices of the hyperbola.

26. If $a^2>b^2$, show that the locus of the point of intersection of mutually perpendicular tangents to the hyperbola $\frac{x^2}{a^2}-\frac{y^2}{b^2}=1$ is the circle $x^2+y^2=a^2-b^2$.

27. Show that the locus of the foot of perpendicular drawn from foci on any tangent to the hyperbola $\frac{x^2}{a^2}-\frac{y^2}{b^2}=1$ is $x^2+y^2=a^2$.

28. Show that the locus of the middle points of portions of the tangents to the hyperbola $\frac{x^2}{a^2}-\frac{y^2}{b^2}=1$ intercepted between the axes is $4x^2y^2=a^2y^2-b^2x^2$.

29. Find the locus of the point , tangents from which to the rectangular hyperbola $x^2-y^2=a^2$ contain an angle of 45°.

30. A normal to the hyperbola $\frac{x^2}{a^2}-\frac{y^2}{b^2}=1$ meets the axes in M and N and lines MP and NP are drawn perpendiculars to the axes meeting at P. Prove that the locus of P is the hyperbola $a^2x^2-b^2y^2=(a^2+b^2)^2$.

31. Find the locus of the foot of the perpendicular from the centre upon on any normal to the hyperbola $\frac{x^2}{a^2}-\frac{y^2}{b^2}=1$.

32. Prove that the locus of the point of intersection of the tangents at the ends of normal chords of the hyperbola $x^2-y^2=a^2$ is $a^2(y^2-x^2)=4x^2y^2$.

33. Find the common tangent to $9x^2-16y^2=144$ and $x^2+y^2=9$

CHORD OF CONTACT/ CHORD BISECTED AT A GIVEN POINT

34. Chords of the hyperbola $y^2=4ax$ touch the hyperbola $x^2-y^2=a^2$. Find the locus of the points of intersection of tangents to the parabola drawn at the extremities of such chords.

35. Find the equation of the chord of hyperbola $25x^2-16y^2=400$ whose mid point is (5, 3).

36. Find the locus of the midpoints of the chords of the hyperbola $\frac{x^2}{a^2}-\frac{y^2}{b^2}=1$ which subtends a right angle at the origin.

37. From the points on the circle $x^2+y^2=a^2$, tangents are drawn to the hyperbola $x^2-y^2=a^2$, then prove that the locus of the middle points of the chords of contact is the curve $\left(x^2-y^2\right)^2=a^2\left(x^2+y^2\right)$.

38. Prove that the locus of the middle points of the chords of the hyperbola which pass through a fixed point is a hyperbola whose centre is .

39. If the chord through the points $(a\sec\theta, b\tan\theta)$ and $(a\sec\phi, b\tan\phi)$ on the hyperbola $\frac{x^2}{a^2}-\frac{y^2}{b^2}=1$ passes through a focus, then prove that $\tan\left(\frac{\theta}{2}\right)\tan\left(\frac{\phi}{2}\right)=\frac{1-e}{1+e}$.

40. Prove that the locus of the middle points of the chords of contact of the tangents drawn from any point on the circle $x^2+y^2=c^2$ to the hyperbola $\frac{x^2}{a^2}-\frac{y^2}{b^2}=1$ is $\left(\frac{x^2}{a^2}-\frac{y^2}{b^2}\right)^2=\frac{x^2+y^2}{c^2}$.

POLE AND POLAR

41. Prove that the polar of the focus is the directrix

42. Find the pole of a given line $lx+my+n=0$ with respect to the hyperbola $\frac{x^2}{a^2}-\frac{y^2}{b^2}=1$.

43. Find the pole of a line $x-y=3$ w.r.t the hyperbola $x^2-3y^2=3$.

44. Prove that pole of a given line is same as the point of intersection of tangents at its extremities.

45. Find the locus of the poles of normals chords of the hyperbola $\frac{x^2}{a^2}-\frac{y^2}{b^2}=1$.

46. Prove that the polar of any point on the ellipse $\frac{x^2}{a^2}+\frac{y^2}{b^2}=1$ w.r.t the hyperbola $\frac{x^2}{a^2}-\frac{y^2}{b^2}=1$ will touch the ellipse at the other end of the ordinate through the point.

47. Show that the locus of the poles of the chords of the hyperbola $\frac{x^2}{a^2}-\frac{y^2}{b^2}=1$ which subtends a right angle at the centre is $\frac{x^2}{a^4}+\frac{y^2}{b^4}=\frac{1}{a^2}-\frac{1}{b^2}$.

48. If the polars of (x_1, y_1) and (x_2, y_2) with respect to the hyperbola $\frac{x^2}{a^2}-\frac{y^2}{b^2}=1$ are at right angles, then prove that $\frac{x_1x_2}{y_1y_2}+\frac{a^4}{b^4}=0$.

DIAMETER / CONJUGATE DIAMETERS

49. Prove that the diameter of a hyperbola $\frac{x^2}{a^2}-\frac{y^2}{b^2}=1$ is $y=\frac{b^2}{a^2m}x$

49. Prove that, if a pair of diameters be conjugate w.r.t a hyperbola, they are conjugate w.r.t its conjugate hyperbola also.

50. Prove that, the parallelogram formed by the tangents at the extremities of conjugate diameters of a hyperbola has its vertices lying on the asymptotes and is of constant area.

51. If a pair of conjugate diameters meets the hyperbola and its conjugate in P and D respectively, then prove that $CP^2-CD^2=a^2-b^2$.

52. For the hyperbola $x^2-y^2=a^2$, prove that the triangle CPD is isosceles and has constant area , where CP and CD are a pair of its conjugate diameters.

53. Find the diameter of $16x^2-9y^2=144$, which is conjugate to $x=2y$.

54. If $H=\frac{x^2}{a^2}-\frac{y^2}{b^2}-1=0$, $C=\frac{x^2}{a^2}-\frac{y^2}{b^2}+1=0$ and $A=\frac{x^2}{a^2}-\frac{y^2}{b^2}=0$, then prove that, H, A and C are in A.P

DIRECTOR CIRCLE

55. Find the equation of the director circle w.r.t the hyperbola is $\frac{x^2}{a^2}-\frac{y^2}{b^2}=1$

ASYMPTOTES

56. Find the equation of asymptotes w.r.t the hyperbola $\frac{x^2}{a^2}-\frac{y^2}{b^2}=1$.

57. Find the equation of the asymptotes w.r.t the rectangular hyperbola $x^2-y^2=a^2$.

58. Prove that a hyperbola and its conjugate have the same asymptotes.

59. Prove that the angle between the asymptotes to the hyperbola $\frac{x^2}{a^2}-\frac{y^2}{b^2}=1$ is $2\tan^{-1}\left(\frac{b}{a}\right)$.

60. Find the asymptotes of the hyperbola $xy-3y-2x=0$.

61. Find the equation of the asymptotes of the hyperbola $3x^2+10xy+8y^2+14x+22y+7=0$.

62. Find the equation of the conjugate hyperbola of the hyperbola $3x^2-5xy-2y^2+5x+11y-8=0$.

RECTANGULAR HYPERBOLA

63. Prove that the equation of a rectangular hyperbola is $xy=c^2$.

64. If the circle $x^2+y^2=a^2$ intersects the hyperbola $xy=c^2$ in four points $(x_1, y_1), (x_2, y_2), (x_3, y_3)$ and (x_4, y_4), then prove that
   (i) $x_1+x_2+x_3+x_4=0$
   (ii) $y_1+y_2+y_3+y_4=0$
   (iii) $x_1.x_2.x_3.x_4=c^4$
   (iv) $y_1.y_2.y_3.y_4=c^4$.

65. If the normal at the point 't_1' to the rectangular hyperbola $xy=c^2$ meets it again at the point 't_2', then prove that $t_1^3.t_2=-1$.

66. A triangle has its vertices on a rectangular hyperbola. Prove that the orthocenter of the triangle alsolies on the same hyperbola.

67. Prove that the area of the triangle cut off from the asymptotes by a tangent to a hyperbola is constant.

68. Find the locus of the poles of the normal chords of the rectangular hyperbola $xy=c^2$.

REFLECTION PROPERTY OF A HYPERBOLA

69. A ray emanating from the point (5, 0) is incident on the hyperbola $9x^2-16y^2=144$ at the point P with abscissa 8. Find the equation of the reflected ray after first reflection and the point P lies in first quadrant.

70. A ray emanating from the point $\left(-\sqrt{41},0\right)$ is incident on the hyperbola $16x^2-25y^2=400$ at the point P with abscissa 10. Find the equation of the reflected ray after first reflection and the point P lies in 2nd quadrant.

ANSWER

1. Hyperbola
2. $7x^2-2y^2+12xy-2x+14y-22=0$
3. $\sqrt{\frac{3}{2}}$
5. $12x^2-4y^2-24x+32y-127=0$
6. $3x^2-y^2=12$
7. $6<\lambda<10$.
13. 7
14. (i) Centre : (0, 0) Vertices : $\left(\pm\frac{1}{3}, 0\right)$, Length of transverse axis : $\frac{2}{9}$

   Lengths of conjugate axis : 2, Eccentricity = e = $\sqrt{10}$; Latus rectum : 18;

   Foci : $\left(\pm\frac{\sqrt{10}}{9}, 0\right)$; Directrices : $x=\pm\frac{1}{9\sqrt{10}}$

   (ii) Centre : (2, 3) Vertices :(3, 5), (3, -1), Length of transverse axis : = 6

   Lengths of conjugate axis : = $2\sqrt{7}$, Eccentricity = e = 4/3; Latus rectum : 14/3;

   Foci : (3, 6), (3, -2); Directrices : $y=\frac{17}{4}, \frac{1}{4}$

   (iii) Centre : (1, 2) Vertices : $\left(1\pm\sqrt{5}, 2\right)$, Length of transverse axis : = $2\sqrt{5}$

   Lengths of conjugate axis : = $2\sqrt{3}$,

   Eccentricity = e = $\frac{2\sqrt{2}}{\sqrt{5}}$; Latus rectum : $\frac{6}{\sqrt{5}}$;

   Foci : $\left(1\pm2\sqrt{2}, 2\right)$; Directrices : $x=1\pm\frac{5}{2\sqrt{2}}$

   (vi) Centre : (3, 2) Vertices : $\left(3\pm\sqrt{5}, 2\right)$, Length of transverse axis : = $2\sqrt{5}$

   Lengths of conjugate axis : = $2\sqrt{5}$, Eccentricity = e = $\sqrt{2}$; Latus rectum : $2\sqrt{5}$;

   Foci : $\left(3\pm\sqrt{10}, 2\right)$; Directrices : $x=3\pm\sqrt{\frac{5}{2}}$

15. inside
16. Outside.
18. $\lambda=\pm2\sqrt{5}$
19. $30x-24y\pm\sqrt{161}=0$.
21. $x\mp y=\pm\sqrt{(a^2-b^2)}$.
29. $\left(x^2+y^2\right)^2+4a^2\left(x^2-y^2\right)=4a^4$.
32. $\left(x^2+y^2\right)^2\left(a^2y^2-b^2x^2\right)=\left(a^2+b^2\right)^2x^2y^2$.
33. $\sqrt{7}y=\pm3\sqrt{2}x\pm15$.
34. $4x^2+y^2=4a^2$.
36. $\left(\frac{x^2}{a^2}-\frac{y^2}{b^2}\right)^2\left(\frac{1}{a^2}-\frac{1}{b^2}\right)=\frac{x^2}{a^4}+\frac{y^2}{b^4}$.
45. $a^6y^2-b^6x^2=\left(a^2+b^2\right)^2\times x^2y^2$.

60. $x-3=0, y-2=0$

61. $3x+4y+5=0, x+2y+3=0.$

62. $3x^2-5xy-2y^2+5x+11y-16=0.$

68. $(x^2-y^2)^2+4c^2xy=0.$

69. $3\sqrt{3}x-13y+15\sqrt{3}=0.$

70. $4\sqrt{3}x+(10-\sqrt{41})y-4\sqrt{123}=0.$

Level – II (For JEE Mains and Advanced Exams Only)

1. The magnitude of the gradient of the tangent at extremity latus rectum of the hyperbola $\frac{x^2}{a^2}-\frac{y^2}{b^2}=1$ is equal to

(a) b e (b) e (c) a b (d) a e

2. Eccentricity of the hyperbola conjugate to the hyperbola $\frac{x^2}{4}-\frac{y^2}{12}=1$ is

(a) $\frac{2}{\sqrt{3}}$ (b) 2 (c) $\sqrt{3}$ (d) $\frac{4}{3}$

3. The asymptote of the hyperbola $\frac{x^2}{a^2}-\frac{y^2}{b^2}=1$ form with any tangent to the hyperbola a triangle whose area is $a^2\times\tan\lambda$ in magnitude, then its eccentricity is

(a) $\sec\lambda$ (b) $\operatorname{cosec}\lambda$ (c) $\sec^2\lambda$ (d) $\operatorname{cosec}^2\lambda$

4. The equation $\frac{x^2}{29-p}+\frac{y^2}{4-p}=1$ ($p\neq 4, 29$) represents

(a) an ellipse if p is any constant greater than 4

(b) a hyperbola is any constant b/w 4 and 29

(c) a rectangular hyperbola if p is any constant greater than 29

(d) no real curve if p is less than 29.

5. Locus of the feet of the perpendiculars drawn from either foci on a variable tangent to the hyperbola $16y^2-9x^2=1$

(a) $x^2+y^2=9$ (b) $x^2+y^2=\frac{1}{9}$

(c) $x^2+y^2=\frac{7}{144}$ (d) $x^2+y^2=\frac{1}{16}$.

6. The locus of the point of intersection of the lines $\sqrt{3}x-y-4\sqrt{3}t=0$ and $\sqrt{3}tx+ty-4\sqrt{3}=0$ (where t is a parameter) is a hyperbola, whose eccentricity is

(a) $\sqrt{3}$ (b) 2 (c) $2/\sqrt{3}$ (d) 4/3

7. If the eccentricity of the hyperbola $x^2-y^2\sec^2\alpha=5$ is $\sqrt{3}$ times the eccentricity of the ellipse $x^2\sec^2\alpha+y^2=25$, then a value of α is

(a) π/6 (b) π/4 (c) π/4 (d) π/2

8. For all real values of m, the straight line $y=mx+\sqrt{9m^2-4}$ is a tangent to the curve

(a) $9x^2+4y^2=36$ (b) $4x^2+9y^2=36$

(c) $9x^2-4y^2=36$ (d) $4x^2-9y^2=36$

9. The foci of the ellipse $\frac{x^2}{16}+\frac{y^2}{b^2}=1$ and the hyperbola $\frac{x^2}{144}-\frac{y^2}{81}=\frac{1}{25}$ coincide. Then the value of b^2 is

(a) 5 (b) 7 (c) 9 (d) 4

10. Locus of the middle points of the parallel chords with gradient m of the rectangular hyperbola $xy=c^2$ is

(a) $mx+y=0$ (b) $y-mx=0$

(c) $my-x=0$ (d) $my+x=0$

11. The locus of the foot of the perpendicular from the centre of the hyperbola $xy=c^2$ on a variable tangent is

(a) $(x^2-y^2)^2=4c^2xy$ (b) $(x^2+y^2)^2=2c^2xy$

(c) $(x^2+y^2)=4c^2xy$ (d) $(x^2+y^2)^2=4c^2xy$

12. P is a point on the hyperbola $\frac{x^2}{a^2}-\frac{y^2}{b^2}=1$, N is the foot of the perpendicular from P on the transverse axis. The tangent to the hyperbola at P meets transverse axis at T. If O is the centre of the hyperbola, then OT.ON is

(a) e^2 (b) a^2 (c) b^2 (d) b^2/a^2

13. If PN is the perpendicular from a point on the rectangular hyperbola $x^2-y^2=a^2$ on any on its asymptotes, then the locus of the mid-point of PN is

(a) a circle (b) a parabola

(c) an ellipse (d) a hyperbola.

14. The equation to the chord joining two points (x_1, y_1) and (x_2, y_2) on the rectangular hyperbola $xy=c^2$ is

(a) $\frac{x}{x_1+x_2}+\frac{y}{y_1+y_2}=1$ (b) $\frac{x}{x_1-x_2}+\frac{y}{y_1-y_2}=1$

(c) $\frac{x}{y_1+y_2}+\frac{y}{x_1+x_2}=1$ (d) $\frac{x}{y_1-y_2}+\frac{y}{x_1-x_2}=1$

15. If $P(x_1, y_1)$, $Q(x_2, y_2)$, $R(x_3, y_3)$ and $S(x_4, y_4)$ are 4 concyclic points on the rectangular hyperbola $xy=c^2$, the co-ordinates of the orthocenter of the triangle PQR is

(a) (x_4-y_4) (b) (x_4, y_4)

(c) $(-x_4, -y_4)$ (d) $(-x_4, y_4)$.

16. The chord PQ of the rectangular hyperbola $xy = a^2$ meets the axis of x at A, C is the mid point of PQ and O is the origin . Then the ΔACO is

(a) equilateral (b) isosceles
(c) rt angled (d) right isosceles.

17. A conic passes through the point (2, 4) and is such that the segment of any of its tangents at any point contained between the co-ordinates is bisected at the point of tangency. Then the foci of the conic are

(a) $(2\sqrt{2},0)$ & $(-2\sqrt{2},0)$
(b) $(2\sqrt{2},2\sqrt{2})$ & $(-2\sqrt{2},-2\sqrt{2})$
(c) $(4,4)$ & $(-4,-4)$
(d) $(4\sqrt{2},4\sqrt{2})$ & $(-4\sqrt{2},-4\sqrt{2})$

18. Latus rectum of the conic satisfying the differential equation, $x\,dy + y\,dx = 0$ and passing through the point (2, 8) is

(a) $4\sqrt{2}$ (b) 8 (c) $8\sqrt{2}$ (d) 16

19. If the normal to the rectangular hyperbola $xy = c^2$ at the point 't' meets the curve again at t_1, then the value of $t^3 t_1$ is

(a) 1 (b) -1 (c) 0 (d) None

20. With one focus of the hyperbola $\frac{x^2}{9}-\frac{y^2}{16}=1$ as the centre, a circle is drawn which is tangent to the hyperbola with no part of the circle being outside the hyperbola. The radius of the circle is

(a) <2 (b) 2 (c) 11/3 (d) None

21. AB is a double ordinate of the hyperbola $\frac{x^2}{a^2}-\frac{y^2}{b^2}=1$ such that ΔAOB (where 'O' is the origin) is an equilateral triangle , then the eccentricity of the hyperbola satisfies

(a) $e>\sqrt{3}$ (b) $1<e<\frac{2}{\sqrt{3}}$
(c) $e=\frac{2}{\sqrt{3}}$ (d) $e>\frac{2}{\sqrt{3}}$

22. If the product of the perpendicular distances from any point on the hyperbola of eccentricity from its asymptotes is equal to 6, then the length of the transverse axis of the hyperbola is

(a) 3 (b) 6 (c) 8 (d) 12

23. If $x+iy=\sqrt{\phi+i\psi}$ where $i=\sqrt{-1}$ and f and ? are non zero real parameters, then f = constant and ? = constant , represents two systems of rectangular hyperbola which intersect at an angle of

(a) $\pi/6$ (b) $\pi/3$ (c) $\pi/4$ (d) $\pi/2$

24. The tangent to the hyperbola $xy = c^2$ at the point P intersect the x-axis at T and the y-axis at T'. The normal to the hyperbola at P intersects the x-axis at N and the y-axis at N'. The area of the triangles PNT and PN'T' are Δ and Δ' respectively, then $\frac{1}{\Delta}+\frac{1}{\Delta'}$ is

(a) equal to 1 (b) depends on t
(c) depends on c (d) equal to 2.

25. The ellipse $4x^2+9y^2=36$ and the hyperbola $4x^2-y^2=4$ have the same foci and they intersect at right angles , then the equation of the circle through the points of intersection of two conics is

(a) $x^2+y^2=5$
(b) $\sqrt{5}(x^2+y^2)-3x-4y=0$
(c) $\sqrt{5}(x^2+y^2)+3x+4y=0$
(d) $x^2+y^2=25$

26. At the point of intersection of the rectangular hyperbola $xy=c^2$ and the parabola $y^2=4ax$ tangents to the rectangular hyperbola and the parabola make an angle θ and ϕ respectively with the axis of X, then

(a) $\theta=\tan^{-1}(-2\tan\phi)$ (b) $\phi=\tan^{-1}(-2\tan\theta)$
(c) $\theta=\frac{1}{2}\tan^{-1}(-\tan\phi)$ (d) $\phi=\frac{1}{2}\tan^{-1}(-\tan\theta)$

27. Area of the quadrilateral formed with the foci of the hyperbola $\frac{x^2}{a^2}-\frac{y^2}{b^2}=1$ and $\frac{x^2}{a^2}-\frac{y^2}{b^2}=-1$ is

(a) $4(a^2+b^2)$ (b) $2(a^2+b^2)$
(c) (a^2+b^2) (d) $\frac{1}{2}(a^2+b^2)$.

28. The eccentricity of the hyperbola whose latus rectum is 8 and conjugate axis is equal to half the distance between the foci is

(a) $\frac{4}{3}$ (b) $\frac{4}{\sqrt{3}}$ (c) $\frac{2}{\sqrt{3}}$ (d) None.

29. If $P(\sqrt{2}\sec\theta, \sqrt{2}\tan\theta)$ is a point on the hyperbola whose distance from the origin is $\sqrt{6}$, where P is in the first quadrant, then θ

(a) $\frac{\pi}{4}$ (b) $\frac{\pi}{3}$ (c) $\frac{\pi}{6}$ (d) None.

30. An ellipse and a hyperbola have same centre origin , the same foci and the minor axis of the one is the same as the conjugate axis of the other. If e_1, e_2 be their eccentricities respectively, $\frac{1}{e_1^2}+\frac{1}{e_2^2}$

(a) 1 (b) 2 (c) 3 (d) None.

31. The number of possible tangents can be drawn to the curve $4x^2-9y^2=36$, which are perpendicular to the straight line $5x+2y-10=0$ is

(a) 0 (b) 1 (c) 2 (d) 4

32. Equation of tangent passing through (2, 8) to the hyperbola $5x^2 - y^2 = 5$ is

(a) $3x - y + 2 = 0$ (b) $3x + y - 14 = 0$

(c) $23x - 3y - 22 = 0$ (d) $3x - 23y + 178 = 0$.

33. If $P(x_1, y_1), Q(x_2, y_2), R(x_3, y_3)$ & $S(x_4, y_4)$ are four concyclic points on the rectangular hyperbola $xy = c^2$, the co-ordinates of the othocentre of the triangle PQR are

(a) (x_4, y_4) (b) $(x_4, -y_4)$

(c) $(-x_4, -y_4)$ (d) $(-x_4, y_4)$.

34. If the hyperbolas $x^2 + 3xy + 2y^2 + 2x + 3y + 2 = 0$ and $x^2 + 3xy + 2y^2 + 2x + 3y + c = 0$ are conjugate of each other, then the value of 'c' is

(a) -2 (b) 0 (c) 4 (d) 1

35. A rectangular hyperbola circumscribes a triangle ABC, then it will always pass through its

(a) orthocentre (b) circum-centre

(c) centroid (d) in-centre

36. The co-ordinates of a point on the hyperbola $\frac{x^2}{24} - \frac{y^2}{18} = 1$, which is nearest to the line $3x + 2y + 1 = 0$ are

(a) (6, 3) (b) (-6, -3) (c) (6, -3) (d) (-6, 3)

37. The latus rectum of the hyperbola

$9x^2 - 16y^2 - 18x - 32y - 151 = 0$ is

(a) 9/4 (b) 9 (c) 3/2 (d) 9/2

38. If the eccentricity of the hyperbola $x^2 - y^2 \sec^2 \alpha = 5$ is $\sqrt{3}$ times the eccentricity of the ellipse

$x^2 \sec^2 \alpha + y^2 = 25$, then the value of α can be

(a) $\frac{\pi}{6}$ (b) $\frac{\pi}{4}$ (c) $\frac{\pi}{3}$ (d) $\frac{\pi}{2}$

39. If values of m for which the line $y = mx + 2\sqrt{5}$ touches the hyperbola $16x^2 - 9y^2 = 144$ are the roots of $x^2 - (a+b)x - 4 = 0$, then the value of $(a+b)$ is

(a) 2 (b) 4 (c) 0 (d) None.

40. Locus of the feet of the perpendiculars drawn from either focus on a variable tangent to the hyperbola

$16x^2 - 9y^2 = 1$ is

(a) $x^2 + y^2 = 9$ (b) $x^2 + y^2 = 1/9$

(c) $x^2 + y^2 = 7/144$ (d) $x^2 + y^2 = 1/16$.

41. The locus of foot of the perpendicular from the centre of the hyperbola $xy = 1$ on a variable tangent is

(a) $(x^2 - y^2)^2 = 4xy$ (b) $(x^2 - y^2)^2 = 2xy$

(c) $(x^2 + y^2)^2 = 2xy$ (d) $(x^2 + y^2)^2 = 4xy$

42. The tangent at a point P on the hyperbola $\frac{x^2}{a^2} - \frac{y^2}{b^2} = 1$ meets one of the directrix in F. If PF subtends an angle θ at the corresponding focus, then the value of θ is

(a) $\frac{\pi}{4}$ (b) $\frac{\pi}{2}$ (c) $\frac{3\pi}{4}$ (d) None.

43. Number of points on the hyperbola $\frac{x^2}{a^2} - \frac{y^2}{b^2} = 3$, from which mutually perpendicular tangents can be drawn to the circle $x^2 + y^2 = a^2$, is

(a) 0 (b) 2 (c) 3 (d) 4

44. If the sum of the slopes of the normal from a point P to the hyperbola $xy = c^2$ is equal to λ, where $\lambda \in R^+$, then the locus of the point P is

(a) $x^2 = \lambda c^2$ (b) $y^2 = \lambda c^2$

(c) $xy = \lambda c^2$ (d) $x/y = \lambda c^2$.

45. If two distinct tangents can be drawn from the point $(\alpha, 2)$ on different branches of the hyperbola

$\frac{x^2}{9} - \frac{y^2}{16} = 1$, then

(a) $|\alpha| < \frac{3}{2}$ (b) $|\alpha| > \frac{2}{3}$

(c) $|\alpha| > 3$ (d) $|\alpha| > 5$

46. From any point on the hyperbola $\frac{x^2}{a^2} - \frac{y^2}{b^2} = 1$ tangents are drawn to the hyperbola $\frac{x^2}{a^2} - \frac{y^2}{b^2} = 2$. Then the area cut - off by the chord of contact on the asymptotes is

(a) a/2 (b) ab (c) 2ab (d) 4ab

47. A hyperbola passes through (2, 3) and has asymptotes $3x - 4y + 5 = 0$ and $12x + 5y = 40$, then the equation of its transverse axis is

(a) $77x - 21y - 265 = 0$ (b) $21x - 77y + 265 = 0$

(c) $21x - 77y - 265 = 0$ (d) $21x + 77y - 273 = 0$

48. The centre of a rectangular hyperbola lies on the line $y = 2x$. If one of the asymptotes is $x + y + c = 0$, then the other asymptote is

(a) $x - y - 3c = 0$ (b) $2x - y + c = 0$

(c) $x - y - c = 0$ (d) None.

49. Equation of a rectangular hyperbola, whose asymptotes are x = 3 and y = 5 and passing through (7, 8) is

(a) $xy-3y+5x+3=0$ (b) $xy+3y+4x+3=0$

(c) $xy-3y+5x-3=0$ (d) $xy-3y-5x+5=0$

50. Equation of conjugate axis of the hyperbola $xy-3y-4x+7=0$ is

(a) x + y = 3 (b) x + y = 7

(c) y - x = 3 (d) None.

51. The curve x y = c (c > 0) and the circle $x^2+y^2=1$ touch at two points, then the distnace between the points of contact is

(a) 2 (b) 3 (c) 4 (d) $2\sqrt{2}$

52. Let the curves $(x-1)(y-2)=5$ and $(x-1)^2+(y-2)^2=r^2$ intersect at four points P, Q, R, S. If the centroid of the triangle ΔPQR lies on the line y = 3 x - 4 , then the locus of S is

(a) $y=3x$ (b) $x^2+y^2+3x+1=0$

(c) $3y=x+1$ (d) $y=3x+1$

53. The ellipse $4x^2+9y^2=36$ and the hyperbola $a^2x^2-y^2=4$ intersect at right angles, then the equation of the circle through the point of intersection of two conic is

(a) $x^2+y^2=5$

(b) $\sqrt{5}\left(x^2+y^2\right)=3x+4y$

(c) $\sqrt{5}\left(x^2+y^2\right)+3x+4y=0$

(d) $x^2+y^2=25$

54. The angle between the lines joining the origin to the points of intersection of the line $\sqrt{3}x+y=2$ and the curve $\sqrt{3}x+y=2$ is

(a) $\tan^{-1}\left(\frac{2}{\sqrt{3}}\right)$ (b) $\frac{\pi}{6}$

(c) $\tan^{-1}\left(\frac{\sqrt{3}}{2}\right)$ (d) $\frac{\pi}{2}$

55. If S = 0 be the equation of the hyperbola $x^2+4xy+3y^2-4x+2y+1=0$, then the value of k for which S + k = 0 represents its asymptotes is

(a) 20 (b) -16 (c) -22 (d) 18.

ANSWER

1(b)	2(a)	3.(a)	4.(b)	5.(d)	6.(b)	7.(b)	8.(d)	9.(b)	10.(a)
11.(d)	12.(b)	13.(d)	14.(a)	15.(c)	16.(b)	17.(c)	18.(c)	19.(b)	20.(b)
21.(d)	22.(b)	23.(d)	24.(c)	25.(a)	26.(a)	27.(b)	28 (c)	29.(a)	30.(b)
31.(a)	32.()	33 (c)	34.(b)	35.(a)	36.(c)	37.(d)	38 (b)	39.(c)	40.(d)
41.(d)	42.(b)	43 (a)	44.(a)	45.(a)	46.(a)	47.(d)	48 (c)	49.(d)	50.(b)
51.(a)	52.(a)	53 (a)	54.(c)	55.(c)					

Level – III FOR JEE-ADVANCED EXAM ONLY

1. For all real values of 'm' the striaght line $y=mx+\sqrt{9m^2-4}$ is a tangent to a hyperbola , find the equation of the hyperbola.

2. Find the equations of the common tangent to the curves $\frac{x^2}{a^2}-\frac{y^2}{b^2}=1$ and $\frac{x^2}{b^2}-\frac{y^2}{a^2}=-1$ and also find its length

3. Find the equation of the common tangents to the curves $\frac{x^2}{16}-\frac{y^2}{9}=1$ and $x^2+y^2=9$

4. If the normal at 'ϕ' on the hyperbola $\frac{x^2}{a^2}-\frac{y^2}{b^2}=1$ meets the transverse axis at G such that $AG.A'G=a^m\left(e^n\sec^p?-1\right)$, where A, A' are the vertices of the hyperbola and m, n and p are +ve integers, then find the value of $(m+n+p)^2+36$.

5. If the normals at (x_i, y_i) , i = 1, 2, 3, 4 on the rectangular hyperbola $xy=c^2$ meet at the point (α, β) , then prove that

(i) $x_1+x_2+x_3+x_4=\alpha$

(ii) $y_1+y_2+y_3+y_4=\beta$

(iii) $x_1^2+x_2^2+x_3^2+x_4^2=\beta^2$

(iv) $y_1^2+y_2^2+y_3^2+y_4^2=\beta^2$

(v) $x_1.x_2.x_3.x_4=-c^4$

(vi) $y_1.y_2.y_3.y_4=-c^4$

6. If the normals at (x_i, y_i) , i = 1, 2, 3, 4 on the hyperbola $\frac{x^2}{a^2}-\frac{y^2}{b^2}=1$ are concurrent. Then prove that

(i) $(x_1+x_2+x_3+x_4)\left(\frac{1}{x_1}+\frac{1}{x_2}+\frac{1}{x_3}+\frac{1}{x_4}\right)=4$.

(ii) $(y_1+y_2+y_3+y_4)\left(\frac{1}{y_1}+\frac{1}{y_2}+\frac{1}{y_3}+\frac{1}{y_4}\right)=4$.

7. The perpendicular from the centre upon the normal at any point of the hyperbola $\frac{x^2}{a^2}-\frac{y^2}{b^2}=1$ meets at Q. Prove that the locus of Q is

8. From the points on the circle $x^2+y^2=a^2$, tangents are drawn to the hyperbola $x^2-y^2=a^2$. Prove that the locus of the middle points of the chord of contact is

$$\left(x^2-y^2\right)^2=a^2\left(x^2+y^2\right)$$

9. Prove that the locus of the mid-points of the hyperbola $\frac{x^2}{a^2}-\frac{y^2}{b^2}=1$ which subtend a right angle at the centre is

$$\left(\frac{x^2}{a^2}-\frac{y^2}{b^2}\right)^2\left(\frac{1}{a^2}-\frac{1}{b^2}\right)=\left(\frac{x^2}{a^4}+\frac{y^2}{b^4}\right).$$

10. Tangents are drawn from a point P to the parabola $y^2=4ax$. If the chord of contact of the parabola be a tangent to the hyperbola $\frac{x^2}{a^2}-\frac{y^2}{b^2}=1$, then find the locus of the point P.

11. Chords of the hyperbola $x^2-y^2=a^2$ touch the parabola $y^2=4ax$. Prove that the locus of their middle points is the curve $y^2(x-a)=x^3$.

12. Prove that the locus of the middle points of the rectangular hyperbola $xy=c^2$ of constant length 2d is

$$\left(x^2+y^2\right)\left(xy-c^2\right)=d^2xy.$$

13. A variable chord of the hyperbola $\frac{x^2}{a^2}-\frac{y^2}{b^2}$ 1 is a tangent to the circle x^2+y^2 c^2. Prove that the locus of its middle points is $\left(\frac{x^2}{a^2}-\frac{y^2}{b^2}\right)^2=c^2\left(\frac{x^2}{a^4}+\frac{y^2}{b^4}\right)$

14. A variable chord of the circle x^2+y^2 a^2 touch the hyperbola $\frac{x^2}{a^2}-\frac{y^2}{b^2}$ 1 . Prove that the locus of its middle points is

$$\left(x^2+y^2\right)^2=a^2x^2-b^2y^2.$$

15. A tangent to the parabola $y^2=4ax$ meets the hyperbola $xy=c^2$ in two points P and Q.
Prove that the locus of the middle point of PQ lies on a parabola.

16. From a point P tangents are drawn to the circle $x^2+y^2=a^2$. If the chord of contact of the circle is a normal chord of a hyperbola $\frac{x^2}{a^2}-\frac{y^2}{b^2}=1$, then prove that the locus of the point P is $\left(\frac{a^2}{x^2}-\frac{b^2}{y^2}\right)=\left(\frac{a^2+b^2}{a^2}\right)^2$.

17. The normal to the hyperbola $\frac{x^2}{a^2}-\frac{y^2}{b^2}=1$ meets the axes in M and N , and lines MP and NP are drawn at right angles to the axes. Prove that the locus of P is the hyper bola $a^2x^2-b^2y^2=\left(a^2+b^2\right)^2$.

18. Prove that the locus of the point of intersection of tangents to a hyperbola which meet at a constant angle β is the curve

$$\left(x^2+y^2+b^2-a^2\right)^2=4\cot^2\beta\left(a^2b^2-b^2x^2+a^2b^2\right)$$

19. Prove that chords of a hyperbola, which touch the conjugate hyperbola, are bisected at the point of contact.

20. A straight line is drawn parallel to the conjugate axis of a hyperbola to meet it and the conjugate hyperbola in the points P and Q. Show that the tangents at P and Q meet on the curve $\frac{y^4}{b^4}\left(\frac{y^2}{b^2}-\frac{x^2}{a^2}\right)=\frac{4x^2}{a^2}$ .and the normals meet on the axis of x.

21. Prove that the locus of the middle points of the chords of the circle $x^2+y^2=16$, which are tangent to the hyperbola $9x^2-16y^2=144$ is

$$\left(x^2+y^2\right)^2=16x^2-9y^2.$$

22. Find the asymptotes of the curve $2x^2+5xy+2y^2+4x+5y=0$. Find the general equation of all hyperbolas having the same asymptotes.

23. Find the equation of the hyperbola , whose asymptotes are the straight lines $x+2y+3=0$ and $3x+4y+5=0$ and which pass through the point (1, -1).

24. Let C is the centre of the hyperbola $\frac{x^2}{a^2}-\frac{y^2}{b^2}=1$ and the

tangent at any point P meets the asymptotes in the points Q and R . Prove that the equation to the locus of the centre of the circle circumscribing, the triangle CQR is

$$4(a^2x^2 - b^2y^2) = (a^2 + b^2)^2.$$

25. If P, Q, R be three points on the rectangular hyperbola $xy = c^2$, whose abscissae are x_1, x_2, x_3, then prove that the area of the triangle ΔPQR is

$$\frac{c^2}{2} \times \frac{(x_1 - x_2)(x_2 - x_3)(x_3 - x_1)}{x_1 x_2 x_3}$$

26. A tangent to the parabola $x^2 = 4ay$ meets the hyperbola $xy = k^2$ in two points P and Q. Prove that the locus of the middle point of PQ lies on the parabola.

ANSWER

1. $\frac{x^2}{9} - \frac{y^2}{4} = 1$
2. $y = \pm x \pm \sqrt{a^2 - b^2}$
3. $y = \pm\sqrt{\frac{7}{10}}x + \sqrt{\frac{11}{5}}$
4. 72
10. $4a^2x^2 + b^2y^2 = 4a^4$
22. $2x^2 + 5xy + 2y^2 + 4x + 5y + 2 = 0$
23. $3x^2 + 10xy + 8y^2 + 4x + 6y + 1 = 0$

COMPREHENSION LINK PASSAGE(FOR JEE ADVANCED EXAM ONLY)

PASSAGE - I

The locus of the foot of perpendicular from any focus of a hyperbola upon any tangent to the hyperbola is an auxiliary circle of the hyperbola.

Consider the foci of a hyperbola as (-3, -2) and (5, 6) and the foot of perpendicular from the focus (5, 6) upon a tangent to the hyperbola as (2, 5).

1. The conjugate axis of the hyperbola is

(a) $4\sqrt{11}$ (b) $2\sqrt{11}$ (c) $4\sqrt{22}$ (d) $2\sqrt{22}$

2. The directrix of the hyperbola corresponding to the focus (5, 6) is

(a) $2x + 2y - 1 = 0$ (b) $2x + 2y - 11 = 0$

(c) $2x + 2y - 7 = 0$ (d) $2x + 2y - 9 = 0$

3. The point of contact of the tangent with the hyperbola is

(a) $\left(\frac{2}{9}, \frac{31}{3}\right)$ (b) $\left(\frac{7}{4}, \frac{23}{4}\right)$ (c) $\left(\frac{2}{3}, 9\right)$ (d) $\left(\frac{7}{9}, 7\right)$.

PASSAGE - II

The portion of tangent intercepted between the asymptotes of the hyperbola is bisected at the point of contact.

Consider a hyperbola whose centre is at origin . A line x + y = 2 touches this hyperbola at $P(1,1)$ and intersects the asymptotes at A and B such that $AB = 6\sqrt{2}$.

1. Equation of asymptotes are

(a) $5xy + 2x^2 + 3y^2 = 0$ (b) $3x^2 + 4y^2 + 6xy = 0$

(c) $2x^2 + 2y^2 - 5xy = 0$ (d) $2x^2 + y^2 - 5xy = 0$

2. Angle subtended by AB at centre of the hyperbola is

(a) $\sin^{-1}\left(\frac{4}{5}\right)$ (b) $\sin^{-1}\left(\frac{2}{5}\right)$

(c) $\sin^{-1}\left(\frac{3}{5}\right)$ (d) $\sin^{-1}\left(\frac{1}{5}\right)$

3. Equation of the tangent to the hyperbola at $\left(-1, \frac{7}{2}\right)$ is

(a) $5x + 2y = 2$ (b) $3x + 2y = 4$

(c) $3x + 4y = 11$ (d) $3x - 4y = 10$.

PASSAGE - III

A point P moves such that the sum of the slopes of the normals drawn from it to the hyperbola x y = 16 is equal to the sum of the ordinates of the feet of normals. Then the locus of the P is a curve C.

1. The equation of the curve C is

(a) $x^2 = 4y$ (b) $x^2 = 16y$

(c) $x^2 = 12y$ (d) $y^2 = 8x$

2. If the tangent to the curve C cuts the co-ordinate axes at A and B , then the locus of the middle point of AB is

(a) $x^2 = 4y$ (b) $x^2 = 2y$

(c) $x^2 + 2y = 0$ (d) $x^2 + 4y = 0$

3. Area of the equilateral triangle, inscribed in the curve C, having one vertex as the vertex of curve C is

(a) $772\sqrt{3}$ sq. u (b) $776\sqrt{3}$ sq. u

(c) $760\sqrt{3}$ sq. u (d) $768\sqrt{3}$ sq. u

PASSAGE - IV

The vertices of DABC lie on a rectangular hyperbola such that the orthocentre of the triangle is (3, 2) and the asymptotes of the rectangular hyperbola are parallel to the co-ordinate axes. The two perpendicular tangents of the hyperbola intersect at the point (1, 1)

1. The equation of the asymptotes is

(a) $xy-x+y-1=0$ (b) $xy-x-y+1=0$

(c) $2xy=x+y$ (d) $2xy=x+y+1$

2. Equation of the rectangular hyperbola is

(a) $xy=2x+y-2$ (b) $xy=2x+y+5$

(c) $xy=x+y+1$ (d) $xy=x+y+10$

3. Number of real tangents that can be drawn from the point (1, 1) to the rectangular hyperbola is

(a) 4 (b) 0 (c) 3 (d) 2

PASSAGE - V

A line is drawn through the point P(-1, 2) meets the hyperbola $xy=c^2$ at the (points

A and B lie on the same side of P) and Q is a point on the line segment AB.

1. If the point Q be chosen such that PA, PQ, and PB are in A.P, then the locus of the point Q is

(a) $x=y+2xy$ (b) $x=y+xy$

(c) $2x=y+2xy$ (d) $2x=y+xy$

2. If the point Q be chosen such that PA, PQ,and PB are in G.P, then the locus of the point Q is

(a) $xy-y+2x-c^2=0$ (b) $xy+y-2x+c^2=0$

(c) $xy+y+2x+c^2=0$ (d) $xy-y-2x-c^2=0$

3. If the point Q is chosen such that PA, PQ, and PB are in H.P, then the locus of the point Q is

(a) $2x-y=2c^2$ (b) $x-2y=2c^2$

(c) $2x+y+2c^2=0$ (d) $x+2y=2c^2$

PASSAGE-VI

The graph of the conic $x^2-(y-1)^2=1$ has one tangent line with positive slope that passes through the origin, the point of tangency being (a, b). Then

1. The value of $\sin^{-1}\left(\frac{a}{b}\right)$ is

(a) $5\pi/12$ (b) $\pi/6$ (c) $\pi/3$ (d) $\pi/4$

2. Length of the latus rectum of the conic is

(a) 1 (b) $\sqrt{2}$ (c) 2 (d) None.

3. Eccentricity of the conic is

(a) 4/3 (b) $\sqrt{3}$ (c) 2 (d) None.

MATCH MATRIX

1. Match the following columns :

Let z, z_1, z_2 be three complex numbers and b, c $\in R^+$. Then the locus of z

Column-I	Column-II
(A) is an ellipse if	(P) $\lvert z-c\rvert=b$
(B) is a hyperbola , if	(Q) $\lvert z-z_1\rvert+\lvert z-z_2\rvert=2b$, where $2b>\lvert z_1-z_2\rvert$
(C) is a straight line , if	(R) $\lvert z-z_1\rvert-\lvert z-z_2\rvert=2b,\ 2b<\lvert z_1-z_2\rvert$
(D) circle , if	(S) $\lvert z-z_1\rvert+\lvert z-z_2\rvert=\lvert z_1-z_2\rvert$.

2. Match the following columns :

The locus of a variable point P , whose co-ordinates are given by .

Column - I	Column - II
(A) $x=3\left(\frac{1-t^2}{1+t^2}\right)$ and $y=\left(\frac{8t}{1-t^2}\right)$ is	(P) an ellipse
(B) $x=\frac{1}{2}\left(e^t+e^{-t}\right)$ and $y=\frac{1}{2}\left(e^t-e^{-t}\right)$ is	(Q) a hyperbola
(C) $x=\frac{2}{\left(e^{i\theta}+e^{-i\theta}\right)}$ and $y=i\times\left(\frac{e^{i\theta}-e^{-i\theta}}{e^{i\theta}+e^{-i\theta}}\right)$ is	(R) a circle
(D) $x=\frac{i}{2}\left(e^{-i\theta}-e^{i\theta}\right)$ and $y=\left(\frac{e^{i\theta}+e^{-i\theta}}{\sin 2\theta}\right)$ is	(S) a parabola.

3. Match the following columns :

The locus of the point of intersection of two perpendicular tangents to a conic is a director circle to the given conic.

Column - I	Column - II
(A) Director circle of $\frac{x^2}{16}-\frac{y^2}{9}=1$ is	(P) $x^2+y^2=45$
(B) Director circle of $\frac{x^2}{20}+\frac{y^2}{25}=1$ is	(Q) $x^2+y^2=7$
(C) Director circle of $x^2-y^2=16$ is	(R) $x^2+y^2=0$
(D) Director circle of $x^2+y^2=25$ is	(S) $x+2=0$
(E) Director circle of $y^2=8x$ is	(T) $x^2+y^2=50$
(F) Director circle of xy = 1 is	(U) $x+4=0$

4. Match the following columns :

Equation of the common tangent between the given curves

Column - I	Column - II
(A) $x^2+y^2=9$ and $\frac{x^2}{16}-\frac{y^2}{9}=1$ is	(P) y = x + 7
(B) $\frac{x^2}{25}-\frac{y^2}{9}=1$ and $\frac{x^2}{9}-\frac{y^2}{25}=1$ is	(Q) $y=3\sqrt{\frac{2}{7}}x+\frac{16}{\sqrt{7}}$
(C) $y^2=8x$ and $xy=-1$ is	(R) y = x + 2
(D) $x^2-y^2=9$ and $x^2+y^2=4$	(S) $y=\sqrt{\frac{3}{5}}x+6\sqrt{\frac{2}{3}}$

5. Match the follwoing columns:

Column - I	Column - II
(A) The product of the perpendiculars from the foci of any tangent to the hyperbola $\frac{x^2}{16}-\frac{y^2}{9}=1$ is	(P) 16
(B) The product of the perpendiculars the foci of any tangent to the ellipse $\frac{x^2}{25}+\frac{y^2}{16}=1$ is	(Q) 9
(C) The product of the perpendiculars from any point on the on the hyperbola $\frac{x^2}{9}-\frac{y^2}{16}=1$ upon its asymptotes is	(R) 144/25
(D) The product of the perpendiculars from any point on the hyperbola $\frac{x^2}{2}-y^2=1$ to its asymptotes is	(S) 2/3

6. Match the following columns :

Column - I	Column - II
(A) Two intersecting circles	(P) have a common tangent
(B) Two mutually external circles	(Q) have a common normal
(C) Two circles , one strictly inside the other	(R) do not have a common tangent.
(D) Two branches of a hyperbola	(S) do not have a common normal.

7. Match the following columns :

Column - I	Column - II
(A) Tangents are drawn from a point on the circle $x^2+y^2=11$ to the hyperbola $\frac{x^2}{25}-\frac{y^2}{14}=1$, then angle between the tangent is	(P) $\sin^{-1}\left(\frac{3}{5}\right)$
(B) Tangents are drawn from a point (4, 3) to the hyperbola $\frac{x^2}{16}-\frac{y^2}{9}=1$, then the angle between their tangents is	(Q) $\frac{\pi}{2}$
(C) The angle between the asymptotes to the hyperbola $\frac{x^2}{16}-\frac{y^2}{9}=1$ is	(R) $\sin^{-1}\left(\frac{24}{25}\right)$
(D) The angle between the asymptotes to the rectangular hyperbola $x^2-y^2=2013$ is	(S) $\frac{\pi}{3}$

ANSWER

1. (A) $\rightarrow$ (Q) ; (B) $\rightarrow$ (R) ; (C) $\rightarrow$ (S) ; (D) $\rightarrow$ (P) .

2. (A) $\rightarrow$ (P) ; (B) $\rightarrow$ (Q) ; (C) $\rightarrow$ (Q) ; (D) $\rightarrow$ (Q) .

3. (A) $\rightarrow$ (Q) ; (B) $\rightarrow$ (P) ; (C) $\rightarrow$ (R) ; (D) $\rightarrow$ (T); (E) $\rightarrow$ (S); (F) $\rightarrow$ (R).

4. (A) $\rightarrow$ (Q) ; (B) $\rightarrow$ (P) ; (C) $\rightarrow$ (R) ; (D) $\rightarrow$ (S).

5. (A) $\rightarrow$ (Q) ; (B) $\rightarrow$ (P) ; (C) $\rightarrow$ (R) ; (D) $\rightarrow$ (S).

6. (A) $\rightarrow$ (P, Q) ; (B) $\rightarrow$ (P, Q) ; (C) $\rightarrow$ (Q, R) ; (D) $\rightarrow$ (Q, R).

7. (A) $\rightarrow$ (Q) ; (B) $\rightarrow$ (P) ; (C) $\rightarrow$ (R) ; (D) $\rightarrow$ (S).

QUESTIONS ASKED IN ROORKEE EXAM.

1. Find the locus of the mid-points of the chords of the circle $x^2 + y^2 = 16$, which are tangent to the hyperbola $9x^2 - 16y^2 = 144$.

Ans. $(x^2 + y^2)^2 = 16x^2 - 9y^2$

[Roorkee Main – 1997]

QUESTIONS ASKED IN IIT-JEE EXAMS

1. The equation $\frac{x^2}{1-r} - \frac{y^2}{1-r} = 1,\ r > 1$ represents

(a) an ellipse (b) a hyperbola

(c) a circle (d) None.

[IIT-JEE-1981]

2. Each of the four inequalities given below defines a region in the xy - plane. One of these four regions does not have the following property. For any two points (x_1, y_1) and (x_2, y_2) in the region, the point $\left(\frac{x_1 + x_2}{2}, \frac{y_1 + y_2}{2}\right)$ is also in the region. The in equality defining the region is

(a) $x^2 + 2y^2 \le 1$ (b) $\max\{|x|, |y|\} \le 1$

(c) $x^2 - y^2 \le 1$ (d) $y^2 - x \le 0$

[IIT-JEE-1981]

3. No questions asked from **1982 to 1993**.

4. The equation $2x^2 + 3y^2 - 8x - 18y + 35 = k$ represents

(a) no locus if $k > 0$ (b) an ellipse if $k < 0$

(c) a point if $k = 0$ (d) a hyperbola if $k > 0$

[IIT-JEE-1994]

5. No questions asked in 1995.

6. An ellipse has eccentricity 1/2 and one focus at S (1/2, 1). Its one directrix is the common tangent (nearer to S) to the circle $x^2 + y^2 = 1$ and $x^2 - y^2 = 1$. The equation of the ellipse in standard form is ....

[IIT-JEE-1996]

7. A variable straight line of slope 4 intersects the hyperbola x y = 1 at two points. Find the locus of the point which divides the line segment between these two points in the ratio 1 : 2.

[IIT-JEE-1997]

8. If the circle $x^2 + y^2 = a^2$ intersect the hyperbola $xy = c^2$ in four points $P(x_1, y_1)$, $Q(x_2, y_2)$, $R(x_3, y_3)$ and $S(x_4, y_4)$, then

(a) $x_1 + x_2 + x_3 + x_4 = 0$ (b) $y_1 + y_2 + y_3 + y_4 = 0$

(c) $x_1.x_2.x_3.x_4 = c^4$ (d) $y_1.y_2.y_3.y_4 = c^4$

[IIT-JEE-1998]

9. If x = 9 is the chord of contact of the hyperbola $x^2 - y^2 = 9$, then the equation of the corresponding pair of tangents is

(a) $9x^2 - 8y^2 + 18x - 9 = 0$

(b) $9x^2 - 8y^2 - 18x - 9 = 0$

(c) $9x^2 - 8y^2 - 18x + 9 = 0$

(d) $9x^2 - 8y^2 + 18x + 9 = 0$

[IIT-JEE-1999]

10. Let $P(a\sec\theta, b\tan\theta)$ and $Q(a\sec\phi, b\tan\phi)$, where $\theta + \phi = \frac{\pi}{2}$, be two points on the hyperbola $\frac{x^2}{a^2} - \frac{y^2}{b^2} = 1$. If (h, k) is the point of the intersection of the normals at P and Q, then k is

(a) $\left(\frac{a^2 + b^2}{a}\right)$ (b) $-\left(\frac{a^2 + b^2}{a}\right)$

(c) $\left(\frac{a^2+b^2}{b}\right)$ (d) $-\left(\frac{a^2+b^2}{b}\right)$

[IIT-JEE-1999]

11. No questions asked in **2000, 2001, 2002**.

12. For hyperbola $\frac{x^2}{\cos^2\alpha}-\frac{y^2}{\sin^2\alpha}=1$, which of the following remains constant with change of α

(a) abscissae of vertices (b) abscissae of foci

(c) eccentricity (d) directrix

[IIT-JEE-2003]

13. The point of contact of the line $2x+\sqrt{6}y=2$ and the hyperbola $x^2-2y^2=4$ is

(a) $(4,-\sqrt{6})$ (b) $(\sqrt{6},1)$

(c) $(1/2, 1/\sqrt{6})$ (d) $(1/6, 3/2)$

[IIT-JEE-2004]

14. Tangents are drawn to the circle $x^2+y^2=9$ from a points on the hyperbola $\frac{x^2}{9}-\frac{y^2}{4}=1$. Find the locus of the mid-point of the chord of contact.

[IIT-JEE-2005]

15. Let a hyperbola passes through the focus of the ellipse $\frac{x^2}{25}+\frac{y^2}{16}=1$. The transverse and conjugate axis of this hyperbola coincide with the major and minor axes of the given ellipse, also the product of eccentricities of the given ellipse and hyperbola is 1, then

(a) the of hyperbola is $\frac{x^2}{9}-\frac{y^2}{16}=1$

(b) the hyperbola is $\frac{x^2}{9}-\frac{y^2}{25}=1$

(c) focus of hyperbola is (5, 0)

(d) vertex of hyperbola is $(5\sqrt{3}, 0)$

[IIT-JEE-2006]

16. A hyperbola, having the transverse axis of length $2\sin\theta$ is confocal with the ellipse $3x^2+4y^2=12$, then its equation is

(a) $x^2\,\mathrm{cosec}^2\theta-y^2\sec^2\theta=1$

(b) $x^2\sec^2\theta-y^2\,\mathrm{cosec}^2\theta=1$

(c) $x^2\sin^2\theta-y^2\cos^2\theta=1$

(d) $x^2\cos^2\theta-y^2\sin^2\theta=1$

[IIT-JEE-2007]

17. Consider a branch of the hyperbola $x^2-2y^2-2\sqrt{2}x-4\sqrt{2}y-6=0$ with vertex at the point A. Let B be one of the end points of its latus rectum. If C is the focus of the hyperbola nearest to the point A, then area of the triangle ABC is

(a) $\left(1-\sqrt{\frac{2}{3}}\right)$ (b) $\left(\sqrt{\frac{3}{2}}-1\right)$

(c) $\left(1+\sqrt{\frac{2}{3}}\right)$ (d) $\left(\sqrt{\frac{3}{2}}+1\right)$

[IIT-JEE-2008]

18. An ellipse intersects the hyperbola $2x^2-y^2=1$ orthogonally. The eccentricity of the ellipse is reciprocal of that of the hyperbola. If the axes of the ellipse are along the co-ordinate axes, then

(a) the ellipse is $x^2+2y^2=2$

(b) the ellipse is $x^2+2y^2=4$

(c) the foci of the ellipse are $(\pm 1, 0)$

(d) the foci of the ellipse are $(\pm\sqrt{2}, 0)$.

[IIT-JEE-2009]

19. Match the following columns :

Column - I	**Column - II**
(A) Circle	(P) The locus of the point (h, k) for which the line h x + k y = 1 touches the circle $x^2+y^2=4$.
(B) Parabola	(Q) Point z in the complex plane satisfying $\lvert z+2\rvert-\lvert z-2\rvert=\pm 3$
(C) Ellipse	(R) Points of the conic have parametric representations $x=\sqrt{3}\left(\frac{1-t^2}{1+t^2}\right)$ and $y=\left(\frac{2t}{1+t^2}\right)$
(D) Hyperbola	(S) The eccentricity of the conic lies in the interval $1\le x<\infty$.
	(T) Points z in the complex plane satisfying $\mathrm{Re}(z+1)^2=\lvert z\rvert^2+1$

[IIT-JEE-2009]

20. **Comprehension**

The circle $x^2+y^2-8x=0$ and the hyperbola $\frac{x^2}{9}-\frac{y^2}{4}=1$ intersect at the points A and B

1. Equation of common tangent with +ve slope to the circle as well as to the hyperbola is

(a) $2x-\sqrt{5}y-20=0$

(b) $2x-\sqrt{5}y+4=0$

(c) $3x-4y+8=0$

(d) $4x-3y+4=0$

2. Equation of circle with AB as its diameter is

(a) $x^2+y^2-12x+24=0$

(b) $x^2+y^2+12x+24=0$

(c) $x^2+y^2+24x-12=0$

(d) $x^2+y^2-24x-12=0$

[IIT-JEE-2010]

21. The line 2 x + y = 1 is tangent to the hyperbola $\frac{x^2}{a^2}-\frac{y^2}{b^2}=1$. If this line passes through the point of intersection of the nearest directrix and the x-axis, then the eccentricity of the hyperbola is

[IIT-JEE-2010]

22. Let the eccentricity of the hyperbola $\frac{x^2}{a^2}-\frac{y^2}{b^2}=1$ be reciprocal to that of the ellipse $x^2+4y^2=4$. If the hyperbola passes through a focus of the ellipse, then

(a) the hyperbola is $\frac{x^2}{3}-\frac{y^2}{2}=1$

(b) a focus of hyperbola is $(2, 0)$

(c) eccentricity of hyperbola is $\frac{2}{\sqrt{3}}$

(d) the hyperbola is $x^2-3y^2=3$.

[IIT-JEE-2011]

23. Tangents are drawn to the hyperbola are $\frac{x^2}{9}-\frac{y^2}{4}=1$, parallel to the straight line 2x -y = 1. The points of contact of the tangents on the hyperbola are

(a) $\left(\frac{9}{2\sqrt{2}}, \frac{1}{\sqrt{2}}\right)$

(b) $\left(-\frac{9}{2\sqrt{2}}, -\frac{1}{\sqrt{2}}\right)$

(c) $\left(3\sqrt{3}, -2\sqrt{2}\right)$

(d) $\left(-3\sqrt{3}, 2\sqrt{2}\right)$

[IIT-JEE-2012]

ANSWER

1. (d)
2. (c)
4. (c)
6. $\frac{x^2}{9}-\frac{y^2}{4}=\left(\frac{x^2+y^2}{9}\right)^2$
7. $16x^2+10xy+y^2=2$
8. (a, b, c, d) 9. (d) 10.
12. (b)
13. (a)
14. $4\left(x^2+y^2\right)^2=36x^2-81y^2$
15. (a, c)
16. (a)
17. (b)
18. (a, c)
19. (A) $\rightarrow$(P) ; (B) $\rightarrow$(S, T) ; (C) $\rightarrow$ (R) ; (D) $\rightarrow$ (Q, S)
20. 1.(a) 2.(b)
21. 2
22. (b, d)
23. (a, b)

SELF ASSESSMENT TEST

Time : 3 Hrs. **Ch: The Hyperbola** **M.M. : 100**

Give answers the following questions :

1. If the normal to the rectangular hyperbola $xy=c^2$ at the point 't' meets the curve again at t_1, then the value of t^3t_1 is

(a) 1 (b) -1
(c) 0 (d) None

2. With one focus of the hyperbola $\frac{x^2}{9}-\frac{y^2}{16}=1$ as the centre, a circle is drawn which is tangent to the hyperbola with no part of the circle being outside the hyperbola. The radius of the circle is

(a) <2 (b) 2 (c) 11/3 (d) None

3. AB is a double ordinate of the hyperbola $\frac{x^2}{a^2}-\frac{y^2}{b^2}=1$ such that ΔAOB (where 'O' is the origin) is an equilateral

triangle, then the eccentricity of the hyperbola satisfies

(a) $e>\sqrt{3}$ (b) $1<e<\frac{2}{\sqrt{3}}$

(c) $e=\frac{2}{\sqrt{3}}$ (d) $e>\frac{2}{\sqrt{3}}$

4. If the product of the perpendicular distances from any point on the hyperbola $\frac{x^2}{a^2}-\frac{y^2}{b^2}=1$ of eccentricity $e=\sqrt{3}$ from its asymptotes is equal to 6, then the length of the transverse axis of the hyperbola is

(a) 3 (b) 6 (c) 8 (d) 12

5. If $x+iy=\sqrt{\phi+i\psi}$ where $i=\sqrt{-1}$ and f and ? are non zero real parameters, then f = constant and ? = constant, represents two systems of rectangular hyperbola which intersect at an angle of

(a) π/6 (b) π/3 (c) π/4 (d) π/2

6. The tangent to the hyperbola $xy=c^2$ at the point P intersect the x-axis at T and the y-axis at T'. The normal to the hyperbola at P intersects the x-axis at N and the y-axis at N'. The area of the triangles PNT and PN'T' are Δ and Δ' respectively, then $\frac{1}{\Delta}+\frac{1}{\Delta'}$ is

7. The ellipse $4x^2+9y^2=36$ and the hyperbola $4x^2-y^2=4$ have the same foci and they intersect at right angles, then the equation of the circle through the points of intersection of two conics is

(a) $x^2+y^2=5$

(b) $\sqrt{5}(x^2+y^2)-3x-4y=0$

(c) $\sqrt{5}(x^2+y^2)+3x+4y=0$

(d) $x^2+y^2=25$

8. At the point of intersection of the rectangular hyperbola $xy=c^2$ and the parabola $y^2=4ax$ tangents to the rectangular hyperbola and the parabola make an angle θ and ϕ respectively with the axis of X, then

(a) $\theta=\tan^{-1}(-2\tan\phi)$ (b) $\phi=\tan^{-1}(-2\tan\theta)$

(c) $\theta=\frac{1}{2}\tan^{-1}(-\tan\phi)$ (d) $\phi=\frac{1}{2}\tan^{-1}(-\tan\theta)$

9. Area of the quadrilateral formed with the foci of the hyperbola $\frac{x^2}{a^2}-\frac{y^2}{b^2}=1$ and $\frac{x^2}{a^2}-\frac{y^2}{b^2}=-1$ is

(a) $4(a^2+b^2)$ (b) $2(a^2+b^2)$

(c) (a^2+b^2) (d) $\frac{1}{2}(a^2+b^2)$

COMPREHENSION

The graph of the conic $x^2-(y-1)^2=1$ has one tangent line with positive slope that passes through the origin, the point of tangency being (a, b) . Then

10. The value of $\sin^{-1}\left(\frac{a}{b}\right)$ is

(a) 5π/12 (b) π/6 (c) π/3 (d) π/4

11. Length of the latus rectum of the conic is

(a) 1 (b) $\sqrt{2}$ (c) 2 (d) None.

12. Eccentricity of the conic is

(a) 4/3 (b) $\sqrt{3}$ (c) 2 (d) None.

(a) equal to 1 (b) depends on t

(c) depends on c (d) equal to 2.

ANSWER

1.(b)	2.(b)	3.(d)	4.(b)	5.(d)	6.(c)	7.(a)	8.(a)	9.(b)	10.(d)
12.(c)	12(d)								

❑❑❑